Essays on Deleuze

D1614729

Essays on Deleuze

Daniel W. Smith

EDINBURGH
University Press

© Daniel W. Smith, 2012

Edinburgh University Press Ltd
22 George Square, Edinburgh EH8 9LF

www.euppublishing.com

Reprinted 2013

Typeset in 10/12 Goudy Old Style
by Servis Filmsetting Ltd, Stockport, Cheshire, and
printed and bound in Great Britain by
CPI Group (UK) Ltd, Croydon CR0 4YY

A CIP record for this book is available from the British Library

ISBN 978 0 7486 4333 2 (hardback)
ISBN 978 0 7486 4332 5 (paperback)
ISBN 978 0 7486 4334 9 (webready PDF)
ISBN 978 0 7486 5537 3 (epub)
ISBN 978 0 7486 5536 6 (Amazon ebook)

Contents

III. Five Deleuzian Concepts

IV. Deleuze and Contemporary Philosophy

Acknowledgments

I would like to thank the publishers for permission to reprint material from the following articles and chapters:

"Deleuze and the Overturning of Platonism: The Concept of the Simulacrum," in *Continental Philosophy Review*, Vol. 38, Nos. 1–2 (Apr 2005), 89–123. Reprinted with permission of the editors.

"The Doctrine of Univocity: Deleuze's Ontology of Immanence," in *Deleuze and Religion*, ed. Mary Bryden (London: Routledge, 2001), 167–83. Reproduced with the permission of the Taylor & Francis Group.

"G. W. F. Leibniz," in *Deleuze's Philosophical Lineage*, ed. Graham Jones and Jon Roffe (Edinburgh: Edinburgh University Press, 2009), 44–66. Reproduced with the permission of Edinburgh University Press.

"Deleuze, Hegel, and the Post-Kantian Tradition," in *Philosophy Today* (Supplement, 2001), 126–38. Reprinted with the permission of the editors.

"Logic and Existence: Deleuze on the 'Conditions of the Real,'" in *Chiasmi International: Trilingual Studies Concerning the Thought of Merleau-Ponty*, Vol. 13 (2011), 361–77. Reprinted with permission.

"Deleuze's Theory of Sensation: Overcoming the Kantian Duality," in *Deleuze: A Critical Reader*, ed. Paul Patton (New York: Basil Blackwell, 1996), 29–56. By kind permission of Basil Blackwell.

"Deleuze, Kant, and the Theory of Immanent Ideas," in *Deleuze and Philosophy*, ed. Constantin V. Boundas (Edinburgh: Edinburgh University Press, 2006), 43–61. With the permission of Edinburgh University Press.

"The Place of Ethics in Deleuze's Philosophy: Three Questions of Immanence," in *Deleuze and Guattari: New Mappings in Politics and Philosophy*, ed. Eleanor Kaufman and Kevin Heller (Minneapolis: University of Minnesota Press, 1998), 251–69. Reproduced with the permission of the University of Minnesota Press.

"Flow, Code, and Stock: A Note on Deleuze's Political Philosophy," in *Deleuze Studies*, Vol. 5, supplement, *Deleuzian Futures* (Dec 2011), 36–55. Reprinted with the kind permission of Edinburgh University Press.

"Deleuze and the Question of Desire: Toward an Immanent Theory of Ethics," in *Parrhesia: A Journal of Critical Philosophy*, No. 2 (2007), 66–78. Reprinted with permission.

"'A Life of Pure Immanence': Deleuze's 'Critique et clinique' Project," translators' introduction to Gilles Deleuze, *Essays Critical and Clinical*, trans. Daniel W. Smith and Michael A. Greco (Minneapolis: University of Minnesota Press, 1997), xi–liii. Reproduced with the kind permission of the University of Minnesota Press.

"Deleuze on Bacon: Three Conceptual Trajectories in *The Logic of Sensation*," translator's preface to Gilles Deleuze, *Francis Bacon: The Logic of Sensation*, trans. Daniel W. Smith (Minneapolis: University of Minnesota Press, 2003), vii–xxxiii. Reproduced with the permission of the University of Minnesota Press.

"The Conditions of the New," in *Deleuze Studies*, Vol. 1. No. 1 (Jun 2007), 1–21. Reprinted with the permission of Edinburgh University Press.

"Deleuze and Derrida, Immanence and Transcendence: Two Directions in Recent French Thought," in *Between Deleuze and Derrida*, ed. John Protevi and Paul Patton (New York: Routledge, 2003), 46–66. With the permission of the Taylor & Francis Group.

"Mathematics and the Theory of Multiplicities: Deleuze and Badiou Revisited," in *Southern Journal of Philosophy*, Vol. 41, No. 3 (Fall 2003), 411–49. Reprinted with permission.

"The Inverse Side of the Structure: Žižek on Deleuze on Lacan," in *Criticism: A Quarterly for Literature and the Arts*, Vol. 46, No. 4 (Fall 2004), 635–50. Reprinted with permission.

"Klossowski's Reading of Nietzsche: Impulses, Phantasms, Simulacra, Stereotypes," in *Diacritics*, Vol. 35, No. 1 (2007), 8–21. Reprinted with permission.

"Deleuze and the Liberal Tradition: Normativity, Freedom, and Judgment," in *Economy and Society*, Vol. 32, No. 2 (May 2003), 299–324. With the kind permission of the Taylor & Francis Group.

Research for this book was undertaken with the financial support of the Center for Humanistic Studies at Purdue University, a Visiting Fellowship from the Leverhulme Trust at the Centre for Research in Modern European Philosophy at Middlesex University, a Vice-Chancellor's Postdoctoral Fellowship at the University of New South Wales, the Franke Institute for the Humanities at the University of Chicago, and a Chateaubriand Fellowship from the Embassy of France in the United States. The book was completed while I was a Visiting Professor at the American University of Beirut, and I am grateful to my colleagues in the Department of Philosophy for their hospitality and encouragement.

I would like to give my heartfelt thanks to Carol MacDonald at Edinburgh University Press, who suggested I gather together these essays and showed almost infinite patience and support during the preparation of the manuscript.

Abbreviations

References to the works below are given in the text using the following abbreviations, followed by the page number(s). I have occasionally introduced slight modifications in the cited translations.

The seminars Deleuze gave at the Université de Paris VIII–Vincennes à St. Denis are in the process of being transcribed and made available online by Richard Pinhas (at *Web Deleuze*, webdeleuze.com) and Marielle Burkhalter (at *La Voix de Gilles Deleuze*, www2.univ-paris8.fr/Deleuze), and are referred to in the text by their date, e.g., 15 Apr 1980.

ABC   *L'Abécédaire de Gilles Deleuze, avec Claire Parnet*, Paris: DVD Editions Montparnasse (1996, 2004). An English presentation of these interviews, by Charles Stivale, can be found at www.langlab.wayne.edu/CStivale/ d-g. References are by letter, not page number.

AO   Gilles Deleuze and Félix Guattari, *Anti-Oedipus*, trans. Robert Hurley, Mark Seem, and Helen R. Lane (New York: Viking, 1977).

B   Gilles Deleuze, *Bergsonism*, trans. Hugh Tomlinson and Barbara Habberjam (New York: Zone, 1988).

D   Gilles Deleuze and Claire Parnet, *Dialogues*, trans. Hugh Tomlinson and Barbara Habberjam (New York: Columbia University Press, 1987).

DI   Gilles Deleuze, *Desert Islands and Other Texts*, ed. Sylvère Lotinger, trans. Michael Taormina (New York: Semiotext(e), 2004).

DP   Paul Patton, *Deleuze and the Political* (London and New York, Routledge, 2000).

DR   Gilles Deleuze, *Difference and Repetition*, trans. Paul Patton (New York: Columbia University Press, 1984).

ECC   Gilles Deleuze, *Essays Critical and Clinical*, trans. Daniel W. Smith and Michael A. Greco (Minneapolis: University of Minnesota Press, 1997).

EPS   Gilles Deleuze, *Expressionism in Philosophy: Spinoza*, trans. Martin Joughin (New York: Zone, 1990).

ES Gilles Deleuze, *Empiricism and Subjectivity: An Essay on Hume's Theory of Human Nature*, trans. Constantin V. Boundas (New York: Columbia University Press, 1991).

F Gilles Deleuze, *Foucault*, trans. Seán Hand (Minneapolis: University of Minnesota Press, 1988).

FB Gilles Deleuze, *Francis Bacon: The Logic of Sensation*, trans. Daniel W. Smith (Minneapolis: University of Minnesota Press, 2003).

FLB Gilles Deleuze, *The Fold: Leibniz and the Baroque*, trans. Tom Conley (Minneapolis: University of Minnesota Press, 1993).

K Gilles Deleuze and Félix Guattari, *Kafka: Toward a Minor Literature*, trans. Dana Polan (Minneapolis: University of Minnesota Press, 1986).

KCP Gilles Deleuze, *Kant's Critical Philosophy: The Doctrine of the Faculties*, trans. Hugh Tomlinson and Barbara Habberjam (Minneapolis: University of Minnesota, 1984).

LS Gilles Deleuze, *The Logic of Sense*, trans. Mark Lester, with Charles Stivale, ed. Constantin V. Boundas (New York: Columbia University Press, 1990).

M Gilles Deleuze, *Masochism: Coldness and Cruelty*, trans. Jean McNeil (New York: Zone, 1989).

MI Gilles Deleuze, *The Movement-Image*, trans. Hugh Tomlinson and Barbara Habberjam (Minneapolis: University of Minnesota Press, 1986).

N Gilles Deleuze, *Negotiations, 1972–1990*, trans. Martin Joughin (New York: Colombia University Press, 1995).

NP Gilles Deleuze, *Nietzsche and Philosophy*, trans. Hugh Tomlinson (New York: Columbia University Press, 1983).

NVC Pierre Klossowski, *Nietzsche and the Vicious Circle*, trans. Daniel W. Smith (Chicago: University of Chicago Press, 1997).

OB Slavoj Žižek, *Organs Without Bodies: Deleuze and Consequences* (London: Routledge, 2003).

PI Gilles Deleuze, *Pure Immanence: Essays on A Life*, trans. Anne Boyman (New York: Zone, 2001).

PS Gilles Deleuze, *Proust and Signs: The Complete Text*, trans. Richard Howard (Minneapolis: University of Minnesota Press, 2000).

PV Gilles Deleuze, *Périclès et Verdi* (Paris: Minuit, 1988).

RP "Reversing Platonism (Simulacra)," trans. Heath Massey, published as an appendix to Leonard Lawlor, *Thinking Through French Philosophy: The Being of the Question* (Bloomington and Indianapolis: Indiana University Press, 2003), 163–77.

SPP Gilles Deleuze, *Spinoza: Practical Philosophy*, trans. Robert Hurley (San Francisco: City Lights, 1988).

TI Gilles Deleuze, *The Time-Image*, trans. Hugh Tomlinson and Robert Goleta (Minneapolis: University of Minnesota Press, 1989).

TP Gilles Deleuze and Félix Guattari, *A Thousand Plateaus*, trans. Brian Massumi (Minneapolis: University of Minnesota Press, 1987).

TRM Gilles Deleuze, *Two Regimes of Madness: Texts and Interviews 1975–1995*, trans. Ames Hodges and Mike Taormina (New York: Semiotext(e), 2006).

WP   Gilles Deleuze and Félix Guattari, *What is Philosophy?*, trans. Hugh Tomlinson and Graham Burchell (New York: Columbia University Press, 1994).

Preface

This volume brings together twenty essays on the work of the French philosopher Gilles Deleuze (1925–1995) that I have written over the past fifteen years. The first (Essay 6) was published in 1996, while the most recent (Essay 8) is appearing for the first time in this book. The original pieces were written as journal articles, book prefaces, and lectures, and although I have introduced minor revisions throughout—and in one case (Essay 2) restored an omitted section—the essays have been reproduced here largely in their original form. As a result, there remains a certain overlap among the essays, which occasionally return to the same themes from different points of view, while pursuing different trajectories. The essays have been organized into four sections, each of which examines a particular aspect of Deleuze's thought.

1. *Deleuze and the History of Philosophy*. Deleuze began his career with a series of books on various figures in the history of philosophy—Hume, Nietzsche, Kant, Bergson, and Spinoza—and the first set of essays explores three broad trajectories in Deleuze's approach to the history of philosophy. The first essay presents Deleuze's reading of Plato in light of Nietzsche's call for the "overturning" of Platonism, while the second essay uses Duns Scotus's concept of univocity to explore Spinoza's overturning of the medieval Aristotelian tradition. The final three essays constitute a trilogy that examines Deleuze's relationship to the pre- and post-Kantian traditions. Essay 3 provides a Deleuzian reading of Leibniz's philosophy, and Essay 4 discusses the frequently laid charge that Deleuze is anti-Hegelian. The fifth essay recapitulates these readings of Leibniz and Hegel by placing them in the context of the problem of the relation between logic and existence, and explores the reasons why Deleuze turned to the development of a philosophy of *difference*. Taken together, these essays show Deleuze's deep indebtedness to these traditions, as well as the manner in which he transformed them in the pursuit of his own philosophical project.

2. *Deleuze's Philosophical System*. Deleuze once remarked that he conceived of philosophy as a *system*, albeit a system that was open and "heterogenetic." The essays collected in this section attempt to explicate the broad outlines of Deleuze's philosophical system by taking as their initial point of reference one of the great

systems in the history of philosophy, namely, Kant's critical philosophy. In particular, the essays explore five philosophical domains derived from the architectonic structure of Kant's philosophy: *aesthetics* (theory of sensation), *dialectics* (theory of the Idea), *analytics* (theory of the concept), *ethics* (theory of affectivity), and *politics* (socio-political theory). Each essay, to a greater or lesser degree, shows how Deleuze takes Kant's characterization of these domains and reconceives them in a new manner, inserting them into a very different systematic framework. The use of these Kantian rubrics is primarily a heuristic device designed to exemplify the specificity of Deleuze's conception of a philosophical system, which, he says, "must not only be in perpetual heterogeneity, it must be a *heterogenesis*"—that is, it must have as its aim the genesis of the heterogeneous, the production of difference, the creation of the *new*.*

3. *Five Deleuzian Concepts*. Similarly, Deleuze famously defined philosophy as the creation of concepts, and this section moves from the broad outlines of Deleuze's philosophical system to a consideration of five specific Deleuzian concepts. The essays on the "New" and the "Open" deal primarily with issues in Deleuze's metaphysics and ontology, while the essay on "Desire" examines the role this concept plays in Deleuze's ethics of immanence. Many of Deleuze's writings were devoted to philosophical analyses of the arts, and the essays on "Life" and "Sensation" deal with, respectively, Deleuze's analyses of literature in *Essays Critical and Clinical* and the "logic of sensation" presented in his work on the painter Francis Bacon.

4. *Deleuze and Contemporary Philosophy*. The last section, finally, is devoted to analyzing the position that Deleuze occupies within contemporary philosophy, and the implications that his thought has for future philosophy. The first three essays contrast Deleuze with the work of three of his influential contemporaries with regard to a specific topic of debate: Jacques Derrida (on the relation of immanence and transcendence), Alain Badiou (on the nature of multiplicities), and Jacques Lacan (on the concept of structure). The fourth essay presents a Deleuzian reading of the work of Pierre Klossowski, an often-overlooked figure who exerted a strong influence on Deleuze. The final essay examines Paul Patton's important work on the ways in which Deleuze's thought might serve to rejuvenate the liberal tradition in political philosophy.

---

* Gilles Deleuze, "Letter Preface," in Jean-Clet Martin, *Variations: The Philosophy of Gilles Deleuze*, trans. Constantin V. Boundas and Susan Dyrkton (Edinburgh: Edinburgh University Press, 2010), 8: "I believe in philosophy as system. For me, the system must not only be in perpetual heterogeneity, it must be a *heterogenesis*—something which, it seems to me, has never been attempted."

PART I

Deleuze and the History of Philosophy

Platonism

The Concept of the Simulacrum: Deleuze and the Overturning of Platonism

The concept of the simulacrum, along with its variants (simulation, similitude, simultaneity, dissimulation), has a complex history within twentieth-century French thought. The notion was developed primarily in the work of three thinkers—Pierre Klossowski, Gilles Deleuze, and Jean Baudrillard—although each of them conceived of the notion in different yet original ways, which must be carefully distinguished from each other. Klossowski, who first formulated the concept in his extraordinary series of theologico-erotic writings, retrieved the term from the criticisms of the Church fathers against the debauched representations of the gods on the Roman stage (*simulacrum* is the Latin term for "statue" or "idol," and translates the Greek *phantasma*).[1] Deleuze, while acknowledging his debt to Klossowski, produced his own concept of the simulacrum in *Difference and Repetition*, using the term to describe differential systems in which "the different is related to the different *through* difference itself" (DR 299). Baudrillard, finally, took up the concept of the simulacra to designate the increasingly "hyperreal" status of certain aspects of contemporary culture.[2] It would thus be possible to write a philosophical history of the notion of the simulacrum, tracing out the intrinsic permutations and modifications of the concept. In such a history, as Deleuze writes, "it's not a matter of bringing all sorts of things under a single concept, but rather of relating each concept to the variables that explain its mutations" (N 31). That history, however, still remains to be written. What follows is a single sequence of that history, one that focuses on Deleuze's work, and attempts to specify the components of Deleuze's own concept of the simulacrum. As such, it can be conceived as a contribution to a broader reconsideration of the role that the notion of the simulacrum has played in contemporary thought.

THE REVERSAL OF PLATONISM

Deleuze developed his concept of the simulacrum primarily in *Difference and Repetition* (1968) and *Logic of Sense* (1969).[3] The problem of the simulacrum arises in the context of Deleuze's reading of Plato, or more precisely, in the context of his reading of Nietzsche's reading of Platonism. Nietzsche had defined the task of his philosophy, and indeed the philosophy of the future, as the reversal of Platonism. In an early sketch for his first treatise (1870–1), he wrote: "My philosophy is an *inverted Platonism*: the farther removed from true being, the purer, the finer, the better it is. Living in semblance as goal."[4] Deleuze accepts this gauntlet that Nietzsche throws down to future philosophy. But what exactly does it mean to "invert Platonism"? This is the question that concerns Deleuze, and the problem is more complex than it might initially seem. Could not every philosophy since Aristotle be characterized as an attempt to reverse Platonism (and not simply a footnote to Plato, as Whitehead once suggested)?[5] Plato, it is said, opposed essence to appearance, the original to the image, the sun of truth to the shadows of the cave, and to overturn Platonism would initially seem to imply a reversal of this standard relation: what languishes below in Platonism must be put on top; the super-sensuous must be placed in the service of the sensuous. But such an interpretation, as Heidegger showed, only leads to the quagmire of positivism, an appeal to the *positum* rather than the *eidos*.[6] More profoundly, the phrase would seem to mean the abolition of *both* the world of essence *and* the world of appearance. Yet even this project would not be the one announced by Nietzsche; Deleuze notes that "the double objection to essences and appearance goes back to Hegel, and further still, to Kant" (LS 253).

To discover "How the 'True World' Finally Became a Fable,"[7] Deleuze argues, one must go back even further, to Plato himself, and attempt to locate in precise terms the motivation that led Plato to distinguish between essence and appearance in the first place. In Deleuze's interpretation, Plato's singularity lies in a delicate operation of sorting or selection that *precedes* the discovery of the Idea, and that turns to the world of essences only as a criterion for its selective procedures. The motivation of the theory of Ideas lies initially in the direction of a will to select, to sort out, to *faire la différence* (literally, "to make the difference") between true and false images. To accomplish this task, Plato utilizes a method that will master all the power of the dialectic and fuse it with the power of myth: the method of division. It is in the functioning of this method that Deleuze uncovers not only the sense of Nietzsche's inverted Platonism, but also what was the decisive problem for Platonism itself—namely, the problem of simulacra.

THE METHOD OF DIVISION AS A DIALECTIC OF RIVALRY

"The creation of a concept," Deleuze writes, "always occurs as the function of a problem" (ABC H). The problem that concerned Plato was the problem of the Athenian democracy—or more specifically, the agonistic problem of *rivalry*. This can be clearly seen in the *modus operandi* of two of Plato's great dialogues on division, the *Phaedrus* and the *Statesman*, each of which attempts to isolate, step by step, the true statesman or the true lover from the claims of numerous rivals. In the *Statesman*, for example, Plato proposes a preliminary definition of the statesman as "the shepherd of men," the one who knows the pastoral care of men, who takes care of humans. But in the course of the dialogue, numerous rivals—including merchants, farmers, and bakers, as well as gymnasts and the entire medical profession—come forward to say, "*I* am the shepherd of men!" In the *Phaedrus*, similarly, an attempt is made to define madness, or more precisely, to distinguish well-founded madness, or true love, from its false counterparts. Here again, all sorts of rivals—lovers, poets, priests, soothsayers, philosophers—rush forward to claim, "*I* am the possessed! *I* am the lover!" In both cases, the task of the dialogue is to find a means to distinguish between the true claimant from its false rivals. "The one problem which recurs throughout Plato's philosophy," writes Deleuze, "is the problem of measuring rivals and selecting claimants" (DR 60).

Why did these relations of rivalry become "problematized" for Plato? Jean-Pierre Vernant and Marcel Detienne, in their work on the origins of Greek thought, have shown that such rivalries constituted an essential characteristic of the Athenian city. The path from myth to reason was not some sort of inexplicable "miracle" or "discovery of the mind," they argue, but was conditioned historically by the social structure of the Greek *polis*, which "laïcized" the mythic forms of thought characteristic of the neighboring empires by bringing them into the agonistic and public space of the *agora*.[8] In Deleuze's terminology, imperial states and the Greek cities were types of social formations that "deterritorialized" their surrounding rural territories, but they did so according to two different models. The archaic States "overcoded" the rural territories by relating them to a superior *arithmetic* unity (the despot), by subordinating them to a *transcendent* mythic order that was imposed upon them from above. The Greek cities, by contrast, adapted the surrounding territories to a *geometric* extension in which the city itself became a relay-point in an *immanent* network of commercial and maritime circuits. These circuits formed a kind of international market on the border of the eastern empires, organized into a multiplicity of independent societies in which artisans and merchants found a freedom and mobility that the imperial states denied them.[9]

This geometric organization was, in turn, reflected in the internal civic space of the cities. Whereas the imperial *spatium* of the state was centered on the royal palace or temple, which marked the transcendent sovereignty of the despot and his god, the political *extensio* of the Greek city was modeled on a new type of geometric space (*isonomia*) that organized the *polis* around a common and public center (the *agora*), in relation to which all the points occupied by the "citizens" appeared equal and symmetrical.[10] What the Greek cities invented, in other words, was the *agon* as a community of free men or citizens, who entered into agonistic relations of rivalry with other free men, exercising power and exerting claims over each other in a kind of generalized athleticism. In the Greek city, for example, a magistracy is an object of a claim, a function for which someone can pose a candidacy, whereas in an imperial State such functionaries were named by the emperor. This new and determinable type of human relation (agonistic) permeated the entire Greek assemblage; agonistic relations were promoted between cities (in war and the games), within cities (in the political Assembly and the legal magistratures), in family and individual relations (erotics, economics, dietetics, gymnastics), and even in the relation with oneself (for how could one claim to govern others if one could not govern oneself?).[11] What made philosophy possible, what constituted its historical condition of possibility, in Deleuze's view, was precisely this *milieu of immanence* that was opposed to the imperial and transcendent sovereignty of the State, and implied no pre-given interest, since it, on the contrary, presupposed rival interests.[12]

Finally, these agonistic relations of rivalry, and the social conditions that produced them, problematized the image of the thinker in a new way. Whereas imperial empires or states had their wise men or priests, possessors of wisdom, the Greeks replaced them with the philosopher, *philo-sophos*, the *friend* or lover of wisdom, one who searches for wisdom but does not possess it—and who is therefore able, as Nietzsche said, to make use of wisdom as a mask, and to make it serve new and sometimes even dangerous ends.[13] For Deleuze, this new definition of the thinker is of decisive importance: with the Greeks, the friend becomes a presence *internal* to thought. The friend is no longer related simply to another person, but also to an Entity or Essence, an Idea, which constitutes the object of its desire (*Eros*). "I am the friend of Plato," says the philosopher, "but even more so, I am the friend of Wisdom, of the True, of the Concept." If the philosopher is the friend of wisdom rather than a wise man or sage, it is because wisdom is something to which he lays claim, but does not actually possess. In this manner, however, friendship was made to imply not only an amorous desire for wisdom, but also a jealous *distrust* of one's rival claimants. This is what makes philosophy Greek and connects it with the formation of cities; the Greeks formed societies of friends or equals, but at the same time promoted relations of rivalry between them. If each citizen lays claim to something, he necessarily encounters rivals, so that two friends inevitably become a claimant and his rival. The carpenter may claim the wood, as it were, but he clashes with the forester, the lumberjack, and the joiner, who say, in effect, "I am the friend of the wood!" These agonistic relations would also come to determine the realm of thought, in which numerous claimants came forward to say, "*I* am the friend of Wisdom! *I* am the true philosopher!" In the Platonic dialogues, this rivalry famously culminates in the clash between Socrates and the sophists, who "fight over the remains of the ancient sage."[14] The "friend," the "lover," the "claimant," and the "rival" constitute what Deleuze calls the *conceptual personae* of the Greek theater of thought, whereas the "wise man" and the "priest" were the personae of the State and religion, for whom the institution of sovereign power and the establishment of cosmic order were inseparable aspects of a transcendent drama, imposed from above by the despot or by a god superior to all others.[15] While it is true that the first philosophers may have been sages or wise men immigrating to Greece in flight from the empires, what they found in the Greek city was this immanent arena of the *agon* and rivalry, which alone provided the constituent milieu for philosophy.[16]

It is within this agonistic milieu that Deleuze contextualizes the procedures of division found in the *Phaedrus* and the *Statesman*. What Plato criticized in the Athenian democracy was the fact that anyone could lay claim to anything, and could carry the day by force of rhetoric. The Sophists, according to Plato, were claimants for something to which they had no right. In confronting such situations of rivalry—whether in the domain of love, politics, or thought itself—Plato confronted the question, How can one separate the true claimant from the false claimant? It is in response to this problem that Plato would create the *Idea* as a philosophic concept: the Idea is used as a criterion for sorting out these rivals and judging the well-foundedness of their claims, authenticating the legitimate claimants and rejecting the counterfeits, distinguishing the true from the false, the pure from the impure.[17] But in so doing, Deleuze argues, Plato wound up erecting a *new* type of transcendence, one that differs from the imperial or mythic transcendence of the States or empires (although Plato would assign to myth its own function). With the concept of the Idea, Plato invented a type of transcendence that was capable of being exercised and situated *within* the field of immanence itself. Immanence is necessary, but it must be immanent *to* something transcendent, to an ideality. "The poisoned gift of Platonism," Deleuze comments, "is to have introduced transcendence into philosophy, to have given transcendence a plausible philosophical meaning . . . Modern philosophy will continue to follow Plato in this regard, encountering a transcendence at the heart of immanence as such" (ECC 137).

From this point of view, Deleuze argues that Aristotle's later criticisms misconstrue the essential point of Plato's method. Aristotle interprets division as a means of dividing a genus into opposing species in order to subsume the thing being investigated under the appropriate species—hence the continuous process of specification in search for a definition of the angler's art. He correctly objects that division in Plato is a bad and illegitimate syllogism because it lacks a "reason"—the identity of a concept capable of serving as a middle term—which could, for example, lead us to conclude that angling belongs to the arts of acquisition, and to acquisition by capture, and so on.[18] But the goal of Plato's method of division is completely different. The method of division is not a dialectic of contradiction or contrariety (*antiphasis*), a determination of species, but rather a dialectic of rivals and suitors (*amphisbetesis*), a selection of claimants.[19] It does not consist of dividing genera into species, but of selecting a pure line from an impure and undifferentiated material; it attempts to distinguish the authentic and the inauthentic, the good and the bad, the pure and the impure, from within an indefinite mixture or multiplicity. It is a question of "making the difference," but this difference does not occur between species; it lies entirely within the depths of the immediate, where the selection is made *without mediation*. Plato himself likens division to the search for gold, a process which likewise entails several selections: the elimination of impurities, the elimination of other metals "of the same family," and so on. This is why the method of division can appear to be a capricious, incoherent procedure that jumps from one singularity to another, in contrast with the supposed identity of the concept. But, Deleuze asks, "is this not its strength from the viewpoint of the Idea"? With the method of division, "the labyrinth or chaos is untangled, but without a thread or the assistance of a thread" (DR 59).

THE PLATONIC IDEA AS A CRITERION OF SELECTION

How does the concept of the "Idea" carry out this selection among rival claimants? Plato's method, Deleuze argues, proceeds by means of a certain irony. For no sooner has division arrived at its actual task of selection than Plato suddenly intervenes with a *myth*: in the *Phaedrus*, the myth of the circulation of souls appears to interrupt the effort of division, as does the myth of archaic times in the *Statesman*. Such is the second trap of division, the second irony: the first is the sudden appearance of rival claimants, the second this sudden appearance of evasion or renunciation. The introduction of myth seems to confirm all the objections of Aristotle; division, lacking mediation, has no probative force, and must thus allow itself to be replaced by a myth which could furnish it with an equivalent of mediation in an imaginary or narrative manner. Once again, however, this Aristotelian objection misses the sense of Plato's project. For the myth, says Deleuze, interrupts nothing, but is, on the contrary, the integrating element of division itself. If it is true that myth and dialectic are two distinct forces in Platonism in general, it is division that surmounts this duality and integrates, internally, the power of dialectic with that of myth, making myth an element of the dialectic itself.

In the Platonic dialogues, myth functions primarily as a narrative of *foundation*. In accordance with archaic religious traditions, the myth constructs a model of circulation by which the different claimants can be judged; it establishes a foundation which is able to sort out differences, to measure the roles and pretensions of the various rivals, and finally to select the true claimants.[20] In the *Phaedrus*, for example, Plato describes the circulation of souls prior to their incarnation, and the memory they carry with them of the *Ideas* they were able to contemplate. It is this mythic contemplation, the nature and degree of this contemplation, and the type of situations required for its recollection, that provide Plato with his selective criterion and allow him to determine the value and order of different types of madness (i.e., that of the lover, the poet, the priest, the prophet, the philosopher, and so on). Well-founded madness, or true love, belongs to those souls that have seen much, and retain many dormant but revivable memories. True claimants are those that "participate" in contemplation and reminiscence, while sensual souls, forgetful and narrow of vision, are denounced as false rivals. Similarly, the *Statesman* invokes the image of a god ruling both mankind and the world in archaic times. The myth shows that, properly speaking, only this archaic god merits the definition of the statesman as "king-shepherd of men." But again, the myth furnishes an ontological measure by which different men in the City are shown to share unequally in the mythical model according to their degree of participation—from the political man, who is closest to the model of the archaic shepherd-god; to parents, servants, and auxiliaries; and, finally, to charlatans and counterfeits, who merely parody the true politician by means of deception and fraud.[21]

The Platonic conception of "participation" (*metachein*, lit. "to have after") must be understood in terms of the role of this foundation: an elective participation is the response to the problem of a method of selection. "To participate" means to have a part of, to have after, to have secondhand. What possesses something firsthand is precisely the foundation itself, the Idea—only Justice is just, only Courage is courageous. Such statements are not simply analytic propositions but designations of the Idea as the foundation that possesses a given quality firsthand; only the Idea is "the thing itself," only the Idea is "self-identical" (the *auto kath' hauto*). "It is what objectively possesses a pure quality, or *what is nothing other than what it is*" (WP 29–30). Empirically speaking, a mother is not only a mother, but also a daughter, a lover, perhaps a wife; but what Plato would call the Idea of a mother is a thing that would only be what it is, a mother that would be nothing but a mother (the notion of the Virgin Mary could be said to be the Christian approximation of the Idea of a pure mother).[22] Plato's innovation is to have created a veritable concept of the Idea of something pure, a pure quality. The Idea, as foundation, then allows its possession to be shared, giving it to the claimant (the secondhand possessor), but only in so far as the claimant has been able to pass the test of the foundation. In Plato, says Deleuze, things (as opposed to Ideas) are always something *other* than what they are; at best, they are only secondhand possessors, mere claimants or "pretenders" to the Idea itself. They can only lay *claim* to the quality, and can do so only to the degree that they *participate* in the pure Idea. Such is the doctrine of judgment. The famous Neo-Platonic triad follows from this: the unparticipated, the participated, and the participant. One could also say: the father (the foundation), the daughter (the object of the claim), and the suitor (the claimant). The triad produces a series of participations in length, a hierarchy (the "chain of being") that distinguishes different degrees and orders of participation depending on the distance from or proximity to the foundational principle.[23]

What is the mechanism that allows the Idea to judge this degree of elective participation? If the foundation as essence is defined by the original and superior identity or *sameness* of the Idea, the claimant will be well founded only to the degree that it *resembles* or imitates the foundation. This resemblance is not merely an external correspondence, as the resemblance of one thing with another, but an *internal* and spiritual (or "noetic") resemblance of the thing to the Idea. The claimant conforms to the object of the claim only in so far as it is modeled internally on the Idea, which comprehends the relations and proportions that constitute essence. The act of founding endows the claimant with this internal resemblance and, on this condition, makes it legitimately participate in the quality, the object of the claim. The ordering of claimants or differences (classification) thus takes place within the comparative play of two similitudes: the exemplary similitude of an original identity, and the imitative or "mimetic" similitude of a more or less similar copy. This in itself marks a philosophic decision of the greatest importance to Deleuze: Platonism allows differences to be *thought* only by subordinating them to the principle of the Same and the condition of Resemblance (DR 127). The concept of the Idea, in Deleuze's analysis, thus consists of three components:

1. the differential quality that is to be possessed or participated in (e.g., being just)
2. the pre-existent foundation or Idea that possesses it firsthand, as unparticipatable (e.g., justice itself)
3. the rivals that lay claim to the quality (e.g., to be a just man) but can only possess it at a second, third, or fourth remove . . . or not at all (the simulacrum) (WP 30).

For Plato, then, "pretension" is not one phenomenon among others, but the nature of every phenomenon. The claimant [*prétendant*] appeals to the foundation, and it is a claim [*prétention*] that must be founded (e.g., the claim to be just, courageous, or pious; to be the true shepherd, lover, or philosopher), that must participate, to a greater or less degree, in the object of pretension, or else be denounced as without foundation. If Platonism is a response to the agonistic relations of power in the Greek world, the foundation is the operation of the *logos*; it is a test that sorts out and measures the differences among these pretensions or claimants, determining which claimants truly participate in the object of the claim.

THE COUNTER-METHOD OF THE SOPHIST: THE SIMULACRUM

An obvious implication follows from this analysis: does there not lie, at the limit of participation, the state of an *unfounded* pretension? The "truest" claimant, the authentic and well-founded claimant, is the one closest to the foundation, the secondhand possessor. But is there not, then, also a third- and fourth-hand possessor, continuing down to the nth degree of debasement, to the one who possesses no more than a mirage or simulacrum of the foundation, and is itself a mirage and a simulacrum, denounced by the selection as a counterfeit?[24] If the just claimant has its rivals, does it not also have its counterfeits and simulacra? This simulacral being, according to Plato, is in fact none other than the Sophist, a Protean being who intrudes and insinuates himself everywhere, contradicting himself and making unfounded claims on everything.

Thus construed, Deleuze considers the conclusion of the *Sophist* to be one of the most extraordinary adventures of Platonism. The third of the great dialogues on division, the *Sophist*, unlike either the *Phaedrus* or the *Statesman*, presents no myth of foundation. Rather, it utilizes the method of division in a paradoxical fashion, a "counter-utilization" that attempts to isolate, not the true claimant, but the false one, the sophist himself. From this point of view, Deleuze distinguishes between two spatial dimensions in Plato's thought. The dialogues of the *Phaedrus* and the *Statesman* move upward toward the "true lover" or the "true statesman," which are legitimated by their resemblance to the pure model and measured by their approximation to it. Platonic *irony* is, in this sense, a technique of *ascent*, a movement toward the principle on high, the ascetic ideal.[25] The *Sophist*, by contrast, follows a descending movement of *humor*, a technique of *descent* that moves downward toward the vanity of the false copy, the self-contradicting sophist. Here, the method of division can make no appeal to a foundational myth or model, for it is no longer a matter of discerning the true sophist from the false claimant, since *the true sophist is himself the false claimant*.

This paradoxical usage of the method of division leads the dialogue to a remarkable conclusion. "By dint of inquiring in the direction of the simulacrum," writes Deleuze, "Plato discovers, in the flash of an instant as he leans over its abyss, that the simulacrum is not simply a false copy, but that it calls into question the very notion of the copy . . . and of the model" (LS 294). In the final definition of the Sophist, Plato leads his readers to the point where they are no longer able to distinguish the Sophist from Socrates himself: "The dissembling or ironical imitator . . . who in private and in short speeches compels the person who is conversing with him to contradict himself."[26] The sophist appears in Deleuze as a particular "type" of thinker, an "antipathetic" persona in the Platonic theater who haunts Socrates at every step as his double. Plato wanted to reduce the sophist to a being of contra-diction: that is, the lowest power and last degree of participation, a supposed state of chaos. But is not the sophist rather the being that raises all things to their simu-lacral state, and maintains them in that state? Platonism in this manner "confronts sophism as its enemy, but also as its limit and its double; because he lays claim to anything and everything, there is the great risk that the sophist will scramble the selection and pervert the judgment" (ECC 136). This is the third moment of irony in Plato, irony pushed to its limit, to the point of *humor*, and it gives us another indication of what the overturning of Platonism entails for Deleuze. "Was it not necessary that irony be pushed to this point?" he asks, "and that Plato be the first to indicate this direction for the overthrow of Platonism?" (LS 295).

The essential Platonic distinction is thus more profound than the speculative distinction between model and copy, original and image, essence and appear-ance. The deeper, practical distinction moves between two kinds of claimants or "images," or what Plato calls *eidolon*.[27]

1. "Copies" (*eikones*) are well-grounded claimants, authorized by their internal resemblance to the ideal model, authenticated by their close participation in the foundation.
2. "Simulacra" (*phantasmata*) are like false claimants, built on a dissimilarity and implying an essential perversion or deviation from the Idea.

"It is in this sense that Plato divides the domain of *image-idols* in two: on the one hand the *iconic copies*, on the other the *phantastic simulacra*."[28] The great manifest duality between Idea and image is there only to guarantee the latent distinction between these two types of images, to provide a concrete criterion of selection. Plato does not create the concept of the model or "Idea" in order to oppose it to the world of images, but rather to select the true images, the icons, and to eliminate the false ones, the simulacra. In this sense, says Deleuze, Platonism is the *Odyssey* of phi-losophy; as Foucault comments, "with the abrupt appearance of Ulysses, the eternal husband, the false suitors disappear. *Exeunt* simulacra."[29]

In Deleuze's reading, then, Platonism is defined by this will to track and hunt down phantasms and simulacra in every domain, to identify the sophist himself, the diabolical insinuator (Dionysus). Its goal is "iconology," the triumph of icons over simulacra, which are denounced and eliminated as false claimants. Its method is the selection of difference (*amphisbetesis*) by the institution of a mythic circle, the establishment of a foundation, and the creation of the concept of the Idea. Its motivation is above all a *moral* motivation, for what is condemned in the simulacra is the malice by which it challenges the very notion of the model and the copy, thereby turning us away from the Idea of the Good (hence Plato's condemna-tion of certain poets along with the sophists). Put in naturalistic terms, the aim of Platonism is to deprive nature of the being that is immanent to it, to reduce nature to a pure appearance, and to judge it in relation to a moral Idea that transcends it, "a transcendent Idea capable of imposing its likeness upon a rebellious matter."[30] Finally, Platonism inaugurates a domain that philosophy would come to recognize as its own, which Deleuze terms "representation." Although the term "representation" will take on various avatars in the history of philosophy, Platonism ascribes to it a precise meaning: every well-founded pretension in this world is necessarily a re-presentation, since even the first in the order of pretensions is already second in itself, in its subordination to the foundation. The Idea is invoked in the world only as a function of what is not "representable" in things themselves.[31]

THE CONCEPT OF THE SIMULACRUM

With this "portrait" of Platonism in hand, we are in a position to understand what Nietzsche's "inverted Platonism" means for Deleuze. It does not simply imply the denial of the primacy of the original over the copy, of the model over the image (the "twilight of the idols"). For what is the difference between a copy and a simulacrum? Plato saw in the simulacrum a "becoming-unlimited" pointing to a subversive element that perpetually eludes the order that Ideas impose and things receive.[32] But in subordinating the simulacrum to the copy, and hence to the Idea, Plato defines it in purely negative terms; it is the copy of a copy, an endlessly degraded copy, an infinitely slackened icon. To truly invert Platonism means that the difference between copy and simulacrum must be seen, not merely as a difference of degree but as a *difference in nature*. The inversion of Platonism, in other words, implies an *affirmation* of the being of simulacra as such. The simulacrum must then be given its own concept and be defined in affirmative terms. In creating such a concept, Deleuze is following a maxim that lies at the core of his philosophical methodology: "What is the best way of following the great philosophers, to repeat what they have said, or *to do what they have done*, that is, to create concepts for problems that are necessarily changing?" (WP 28). The Deleuzian concept of the simulacrum can be defined in terms of three characteristics, which stand in contradistinction to the three components of the Platonic Idea summarized above.

1. First, Deleuze claims that, whereas "the copy is an image endowed with resemblance, the simulacrum is an image *without* resemblance" (LS 257). How are we to understand this rather strange formula? Deleuze suggests that the early Christian catechisms, influenced by the Neo-Platonism of the Church fathers, have familiarized us somewhat with the notion of an image that has lost its resemblance: God created man in His own image and to resemble Him (*imago Dei*), but through sin, man has lost the resemblance while retaining the image. We have lost a moral existence and entered into an aesthetic one (Kierkegaard); we have become simulacra. The catechism stresses the fact that the simulacrum is a demonic image; it remains an image, but, in contrast to the icon, its resemblance has been *externalized*. It is no longer a "resemblance," but a mere "semblance."[33] If the "noetic" resemblance of an icon is like the engendered resemblance of a son to his father, stemming from the son's internal participation in the father's filial line, the semblance of the simulacra, on the contrary, is like the ruse and trickery of an imposter; though his appearance may reflect the father's, the relation is purely external and coincidental, and his claim to inheritance a subversion that acts "against the father," without passing through the Idea.[34] The simulacrum still simulates the *effects* of identity and resem-

blance, but these are now completely external effects (like optical effects), divorced from any internal principle, and produced by completely different means than those at work in the copy.[35]

Deleuze's theological references here are not fortuitous, for there was a whole range of Christian experience that was familiar with the danger of the simulacrum. In *On Christian Doctrine*, for instance, Augustine developed a Platonic semiotic aimed at "making the difference" between true signs and false signs, or rather between two modes of interpretation of the same sign. He located his criterion of selection, not in an Idea, but in God himself, the only "thing" that can (and must) be enjoyed in itself. What he called *caritas* is the interpretation of signs as "iconic copies" that propel the restless movement of the soul toward the enjoyment of God (for his own sake, as the firsthand possessor) and the enjoyment of one's self and one's neighbor (for the sake of God, as secondhand possessors). *Cupiditas*, on the contrary, is the interpretation of signs for their own sake, the enjoyment of "one's self, one's neighbor, or any corporeal thing" for the sake of something other than God. Augustine was explicit about the aim of his theology: "the destruction of the reign of cupidity" (simulacra).[36] Augustine's polemic against Varro in the *City of God* would recapitulate many aspects of Plato's polemic against the Sophists.[37]

If simulacra later became the object of demonology in Christian thought, it is because the simulacrum is not the "opposite" of the icon, the demonic is not the opposite of the divine, Satan is not the Other, the pole farthest from God, the absolute antithesis, but something much more bewildering and vertiginous: *the Same*, the perfect double, the exact semblance, the doppelgänger, the angel of light whose deception is so complete that it is impossible to tell the imposter (Satan, Lucifer) apart from the "reality" (God, Christ), just as Plato reaches the point where Socrates and the Sophist are rendered indiscernible. This is the point where we can no longer speak of "deception" or even "simulation," but rather the positive and affirmative "power of the false" (*pseudos*). The Temptation and the Inquisition are not episodes in the great antagonism of Good versus Evil, but variants on the complex insinuation of the Same. How does one distinguish a revelation of God from a deception of the devil, or a deception sent by God to tempt men of little faith from a revelation sent by the devil to simulate God's test (God so closely resembling Satan who imitates God so well . . .)? The demonic simulacrum thus stands in stark contrast to the theological "symbol" (as defined, for instance, by Paul Tillich or Mircea Eliade), which is always iconic, the analogical manifestation of a transcendent instance. It is this experience of the simulacrum that Klossowski has revived and explored throughout his work. Foucault suggests that the concern over simulacra continued through the Baroque period, and did not finally fall into silence until Descartes's great simulacrum: the Evil Genius of the first *Meditation*, God's "marvelous twin," who simulates God and can mime all his powers, decreeing eternal truths and acting as if 2 plus 2 equals 5, but who is expelled from any possible existence because of his malignancy.[38] If Plato maligns the simulacrum, it is not because it elevates the false over the true, the evil over the good; more precisely, the simulacrum is "beyond good and evil" because it renders them *indiscernible* and internalizes the difference between them, thereby scrambling the selection and perverting the judgment.

2. Second, if the simulacrum is an image without resemblance, it is because the Idea itself no longer has the identity of a self-same model, but rather is now constituted by *difference-in-itself*. If the copy is submerged in dissimilitude, it is because the model is plunged into difference, so that it is no longer possible to say which is the model and which is the copy. If identity and resemblance persist, it is because they are now simply the *external* effects of the internal differential machinery of the simulacrum. Plato himself specifies how the simulacrum obtains this non-productive external effect of resemblance:

> the simulacrum implies huge dimensions, depths, and distances that the observer cannot master. It is precisely because he cannot master them that he experiences an impression of resemblance . . . Resemblance is always on the exterior, and difference—small or large—occupies the center of the system. (LS 258, RP 171)

The simulacrum differs in nature from the copy because it has internalized the differential nature of the Idea, and is thus constructed on a fundamental *disparity*—a "'disparateness' within an original depth" (DR 51). The simulacrum, in other words, is constructed on an *internal difference*, an internal disparity, which is not derived from any prior identity; it has "the disparate" [*le dispars*] as a unit of measurement and communication. "Placing disparates in communication, resonance, forced movement, would thus be the characteristics of the simulacrum" (RP 170–1).

Deleuze here makes an oft-overlooked distinction between the concept of the Identical and the concept of the Same. In Platonism, "the model can be defined only by a positing of identity as the essence of the Same (*auto kath' hauto*), as the essence of Ideas, and the copy by an affection of internal resemblance, the quality of the similar" (DR 265). In an inverted Platonism, however, this link between the Same and the identical is severed. When the Same passes to the side of things rather than Ideas, and indicates the indiscernibilty of things and their simulacra (Socrates is indiscernible from the Sophists, God from Satan), it is the identity of things that suffers a corresponding loss.

> The distinction between the same and the identical bears fruit only if one subjects the Same [the Idea] to a conversion which relates it to the different, while at the same time the things and beings that are distinguished in the different [copies] suffer a corresponding radical destruction of their *identity*. Only on this condition is difference thought in itself, neither represented nor mediated.[39]

When Deleuze writes that "modernity is defined by the power of the simulacrum" (LS 265), he seems to be implying that each era must create its own anti-Platonism, and that his own "simulacral" version is informed, at least in part, by the structures and techniques of modernist literature. On this score, certain twentieth-century modernist writers, including James Joyce, Alain Robbe-Grillet, Raymond Roussel, Pierre Klossowski, and Witold Gombrowicz—whose work has nothing to do with

Platonism or its reversal—have none the less made the "internal difference" constitutive of the work of art evident in their literary techniques, and Deleuze frequently
appeals to their writings as examples. In Roussel's novels, for example, a single
narrative is made to tell two different stories *simultaneously*. The procedure of *La
Doublure* rests on the double meaning of a homonym (the title can mean either
"The Understudy" or "The Lining"), which opens up a space in the heart of the
work that allows objects to take on a double meaning, each participating in two
stories at the same time; *Impressions of Africa* complicates this procedure, starting
with a quasi-homonym (*billard* / *pillard*), but hiding the second story within the
first.[40] Similarly, Joyce's *Finnegans Wake* can be said to have pushed such techniques
of internal disparity to their limit, invoking a letter that makes all the divergent
series or stories of the "chaosmos" communicate at once in a transversal dimension.
Yet Deleuze insists that all the arts, such as painting and sculpture—and even pre-
modernist arts—have their own techniques of internal difference, even if modern
literature comes to be a privileged example.[41] Indeed, in an inverted Platonism, *all*
things are simulacra; and as simulacra, they are defined by an internal disparity:
"Things are simulacra themselves, simulacra are the superior forms, and the difficulty facing everything is to become its own simulacrum . . . The important thing,
for the in-itself, is that the difference, whether small or large, be internal" (DR 67,
121).

3. The third characteristic of the simulacrum, finally, concerns the *mode* under
which this disparity or difference is apprehended, which Deleuze defines as a *problematic* mode. In the famous passage of the *Republic* where he expels the artist from
the City, Plato appeals to the user–producer–imitator triad in order to preserve an
"iconic" sense of imitation (imitation as *mimesis* rather than *apate* or "deception").[42]
The user is at the top of the Platonic hierarchy because he makes use of true *knowledge*, which is the knowledge of the model or Idea. Copies then produced by the
craftsman (*demiourgos*) are iconic to the degree that they reproduce the model internally; though the craftsman cannot be said to operate by true knowledge of the Idea,
he is none the less guided by a correct judgment or *right opinion* of the user's knowledge, and by the relations and proportions that constitute essence. Right opinion,
in other words, apprehends the external resemblance between the copy and the Idea
only to the degree that it is guaranteed by their internal (noetic) similarity.

What, then, is left for the false resemblance and internal dissemblance of the
simulacrum? Imitation takes on a pejorative sense in Plato only when it is applied to
the simulacrum, which does not reproduce the *eidos* but merely produces the *effect*
of resemblance in an external and unproductive way, obtained neither through true
knowledge (the user) nor through right opinion (the craftsman), but by trick, ruse,
or subversion, an art of *encounter* that lies outside of knowledge and opinion (the
artist or poet).[43] The simulacrum can only appear under the mode of a *problem*, as a
question, as that which forces one to think, what Plato calls a "provocative" ("Is it
true or false, good or evil?").[44] The *Republic* does not attack art or poetry as such; it
attempts to eliminate art that is simulacral or phantastic, and not iconic or mimetic.
Perhaps the genius of the Pop Art of the twentieth century lay precisely in its ability
to push the multiplication of images to the point where the mimetic copy changes

its nature and is reversed into the simulacrum (which is the originary model for Warhol's series of Campbell soup cans?).[45]

The "problematic" nature of simulacra points to the fact that there is something that contests *both* the notion of copy *and* that of model, and undermines the very distinction between the two. "By simulacrum we should not understand a simple imitation but rather the act by which the very idea of a model or privileged position is challenged and overturned" (DR 69). With the simulacrum, the order of participation is rendered impossible, since there is no longer any possible hierarchy, no second, no third. There is no privileged point of view, nor is there an object common to all points of view. Sameness and resemblance persist, but only as effects of the differential machinery of the simulacrum (will to power); the simulacrum simulates the father, the fiancée, and the claimant all at once in a superimposition of masks, for behind every mask there is not a true face, but another mask, and another mask behind that. As Nietzsche mused, in response to Plato's allegory of the cave: "Behind every cave, is there not, must there not be, another deeper cave—a more comprehensive, stranger, richer world beyond the surface, an abysmally deep ground behind every ground, under every attempt to furnish 'grounds'?"[46] "The only illusion," Deleuze comments, "is that of unmasking something or someone"—the illusion of presuming a face behind the mask, an originary model behind the copy, a true world beyond the apparent world (DR 106). As a simulacrum, the false claimant can no longer be said to be false in relation to a supposedly true model. Rather, the "power of the false" (*pseudos*) now takes on a positivity of its own; it assumes its own concept, and is raised to a higher power (NP 96). The *false* must be distinguished from the *power of the false*; the false takes on a "power" of its own when it is freed from the form of truth—that is, when the false is no longer presented as being true (that is, as an "error").[47] The true world is no longer opposed to the false world of simulacra; rather, "truth" now becomes an affirmation of the simulacrum itself, falsity (art) affirmed and raised to a higher power.[48]

PURE DIFFERENCE AS AN IMMANENT IDEA

These characterizations of the simulacrum lead us to a new consideration of the status of an inverted Platonism. Deleuze's project of overturning Platonism must not be taken as a rejection of Platonism—on the contrary. "That the overturning [of Platonism] should conserve many Platonic characteristics," writes Deleuze, "is not only inevitable but *desirable*" (DR 59). The simulacrum may be the focus of Deleuze's analysis of Platonism, but it is not the final word. The simulacrum scrambles the criteria of selection established by Plato and gives both difference and falsity a concept of their own. Far from refusing Platonism in its entirety, however, Deleuze's inverted Platonism retrieves almost every aspect of the Platonic project, but now reconceived from the viewpoint of the simulacrum itself. The simulacrum thus plays a double role in Deleuze's reading of Platonism: it shows how Plato failed in his attempt to "make the difference," but at the same time it opens up a path toward a retrieval of the Platonic project on a new basis. In this sense, Deleuze's inverted Platonism can at the same time be seen as a rejuvenated Platonism and even a completed Platonism.

What is the nature of this rejuvenated Platonism? Plato's error was to have remained "attached to that old Wisdom, ready to unfold its transcendence again" (WP 148). Deleuze refuses Platonism's appeal to transcendence: "Every reaction against Platonism is a restoration of immanence in its full extension and in its purity, which forbids the return of any transcendence" (ECC 137). A purely immanent theory of Ideas must thus begin with the simulacrum: there is a *being* of simulacra, which Plato attempted to deny. If the resemblance of the iconic copy is built upon the model of the identity of an ideal sameness, the disparity of the simulacrum is based upon another model, a model of *difference*, from which the dissimilitude or "internalized difference" of the simulacrum derives its power. "Simulacra are those systems in which the different relates to the different *by means of* difference itself. What is essential is that we find in these systems no prior identity, no internal resemblance: it is all a matter of difference" (DR 299). Indeed, was it not the differential nature of simulacra that motivated Plato to exorcise them in the first place? "On the basis of a first impression (difference is evil), [Plato] proposed to 'save' difference by representing it" (DR 29). An inverted Platonism, in return, implies the affirmation of difference itself as a "sub-representative" principle that accounts for the constitutive disparity of the simulacrum itself. "The cruelty [of the simulacrum], which at the outset seemed to us monstrous, demanding expiation, and could be alleviated only by representative mediation, now seems to us to constitute *the pure concept or Idea of difference*" (DR 67). In other words, simulacra require a new conception of Ideas: Ideas that are *immanent* to simulacra (rather than transcendent) and based on a concept of pure *difference* (rather than identity). *Immanence* and *internal difference* are thus the two touchstones of Deleuze's rejuvenated Platonism in *Difference and Repetition*.

Where does Deleuze find resources for developing his immanent dialectic? Deleuze notes that difference and the dissimilar (becoming) occasionally appear, in several important texts of Plato himself, not only as an inevitable characteristic of created copies, as a defect that affects images, a counterpart to their resemblance (they must differ in order to resemble), but as *a possible model that rivals the good model of the Same*, a Platonic equivalent to Descartes's evil demon.[49] An echo of this tension resonates in the dialogues when Socrates asks, ironically: Is there an Idea of *everything*, even of mud, hair, filth and excrement—or is there rather something that always and stubbornly escapes the Idea?[50] Plato raises these possibilities only to conjure them away, but they bear witness to the persistent though subterranean activity of a Dionysian world in the heart of Platonism itself, and to the possibility of its own domain.[51] But it was primarily Kant who inaugurated a purely *immanent* interpretation of Ideas, and exposed the illusion of assigning to Ideas a transcendent object. In the "Transcendental Dialectic" of the *Critique of Pure Reason*, Kant identified three primary transcendent Ideas, which he identified as the terminal points of traditional metaphysics: the Self, the World, and God. Such Ideas can have a positive use, Kant argued, when they are merely employed in a regulative manner, as horizons or focal points outside of experience that guide the systematization of our knowledge (the legitimate *immanent* employment of Ideas). But when we grant Ideas a constitutive employment, and claim that they refer to corresponding objects, we fall into an *illusion* of reason (the illegitimate *transcendent* employment of Ideas).

Yet even Kant was unable to push the immanent conception of Ideas to its limit. In the *Critique of Practical Reason*, Kant was willing to resurrect the transcendent Ideas and give them a practical determination as the postulates of the moral law. Deleuze's own project follows an initiative inaugurated by Salomon Maimon, who was the first post-Kantian to insist that Kant's own philosophy of immanence could only be completed through a return to the work of Hume, Spinoza, and Leibniz. For Deleuze, Ideas are immanent within experience because their real objects are *problematic* structures: that is, multiplicities constituted by converging and diverging series of singularities-events. In Kant, it is only the transcendent form of the Self that guarantees the connection of a series (the categorical "and . . . and"); the transcendent form of the World that guarantees the convergence of continuous causal series that can be extended (the hypothetical "if . . . then"); and the transcendent form of God that guarantees disjunction in its exclusive or limitative use (the disjunctive "either . . . or"). Freed from these appeals to transcendence, Deleuze argues, Ideas finally take on a purely immanent status, and the Self, the World, and God share a common death.

> The divergence of the affirmed series forms a "chaosmos" and no longer a World; the aleatory point which traverses them forms a counter-self, and no longer a self; disjunction posited as a synthesis exchanges its theological principle of diabolic principle . . . The Grand Canyon of the world, the 'crack' of the self, and the dismembering of God. (LS 176)

In *Difference and Repetition*, Deleuze will develop a set of formal criteria for Ideas in this purely immanent sense: difference, repetition, singularity, problematic, multiplicity, event, virtuality, series, convergence and divergence, zones of indiscernibility, and so on. *Difference and Repetition*, in this sense, presents a new conception of the *dialectic*. Platonism is dominated by the idea of establishing a criterion of selection between the thing itself and its simulacra: "Plato gave the establishment of difference as the supreme goal of the dialectic" (DR 67). But difference here remains an *external* difference between the authentic and the inauthentic; Platonism is able to "make the difference" only by erecting a model of the *Same* that assesses differences by their degree of resemblance to a transcendent Idea. In Deleuze's inverted Platonism, however, the distribution of these concepts is changed. If the difference between the thing and its simulacra is rendered indiscernible, then difference becomes *internal* to the thing itself (at the same time that its resemblance is externalized). Difference no longer lies between things and simulacra, since they are the *Same*; rather, difference is internal to things (things are themselves simulacra). What is required is thus a pure Idea of difference, an Idea that is *immanent* in things themselves. The immanent Idea is no longer a pure quality, as in Plato, but rather "the reason behind qualities" (DR 57). Deleuze describes his project in explicitly differential terms:

Every object, every thing, must see its own identity swallowed up in difference, each being no more than a difference between differences. Difference
must be shown *differing* . . . The object must therefore be in no way identical,
but torn asunder in a difference in which the identity of the object as seen by
a seeing subject vanishes. Difference must become the element, the ultimate
unity; it must therefore refer to other differences which never identify it but
rather differentiate it. (DR 56)

It is this immanent theory of Ideas that constitutes what Deleuze will call a "transcendental empiricism." Identity and resemblance still persist, but they are now
merely effects produced by the differential Idea. Difference

produces an image of identity as though this were the *end* of the different. It
produces an image of resemblance as the external *effect* of "the disparate" . . .
However, these are precisely a simulated identity and resemblance . . . It is
always differences that resemble one another, which are analogous, opposed
or identical: difference is behind everything, *but behind difference there is
nothing.* (DR 301, 57)

FIGURES OF AN INVERTED PLATONISM

Once the theory of Ideas is reconceived as both immanent and differential, the
Platonic dialectic can be taken up anew: "*each moment of difference must then find
its true figure*: selection, repetition, ungrounding, the question–problem complex"
(DR 68). Our final task is to analyze the function these four figures play in Deleuze's
inverted Platonism, and the link they have to Deleuze's theory of immanent Ideas.

   1. *The question–problem complex.* First, Deleuze pursues his inverted Platonism
by carrying out his critique at the level of what he calls the "question–problem
complex" (DR 66). In archaic myth, there is always a task to be performed, a riddle
to be solved; the oracle is questioned, but the oracle's response is itself a problem.
In Plato, this question–problem complex reappears in a new form: the appeal to the
Idea as a criterion of selection appears in the dialogues as the response to a particular
form of question. "The idea, the discovery of the Idea, is not separable from a certain
type of question. The Idea is first of all an 'objectity' [*objectité*] that corresponds, as
such, to a way of posing questions."[52] In Plato, this questioning appears primarily
in the form, What is . . .? [*ti estin?*].[53] Plato wanted to oppose this major form of the
question to all other forms—such as Who? Which one? How many? How? Where?
When? In which case? From what point of view?—which are criticized as being
minor and vulgar questions of opinion that express confused ways of thinking.

   When Socrates, for instance, asks "What is beauty?", his interlocutors almost
always seem to answer by citing "the one that is beautiful." Socrates triumphs; one
cannot reply to the question "What is beauty?" by citing *examples* of the beautiful,
by noting *who* is beautiful ("a young virgin"), just as one cannot answer the question "What is justice?" by pointing to *where* or *when* there is justice, and one cannot
reach the essence of the dyad by explaining *how* "two" is obtained, and so on. To

the question "What is beauty?" one must not point to beautiful things, which are only beautiful accidentally and according to becoming, but to Beauty itself, which is nothing but beautiful, that which is beautiful in its being and essence. Socrates ridicules those who are content to give examples rather than attain essences. The question "What is . . .?" thus presupposes a particular way of thinking that points one in the direction of essence; it is for Socrates *the* question of essence, the *only* question capable of discovering the Idea.[54]

One of Deleuze's most constant themes is that the critique of philosophers must take place at this level of questions or problems.

> A philosophic theory [he wrote in his first book] is a developed question, and nothing other. By itself, in itself, it consists not in resolving a problem, but in developing *to its limit* the necessary implications of a formulated question. It shows us what things are, what they would have to be, supposing that the question is a good and rigorous one. To place in question means to subordinate, to submit things to the question in such a way that, in this constrained and forced submission, they reveal an essence, a nature. To criticize the question means to show under what conditions it is possible and well-posed, that is, how things would not be what they are if the question were not posed in that way. Which is to say that these two operations are one and the same; or if you prefer, there is no critique of solutions, but only a critique of problems. (ES 119)

Thus the reversal of Platonism necessarily implies a critique of the question "What is . . .?"; for while it is certainly a blunder to cite an example of something beautiful when asked "What is beauty?", it is less certain that the question "What is . . .?" is a legitimate and well-formulated question, *even and above all for discovering essence*.

Already in Plato himself, the Socratic method only animates the early "aporetic" dialogues, precisely because the question "What is . . .?" prejudges the Idea as a simple and abstract essence, which is then obliged to comprehend the non-essential, and to comprehend it *in its essence*, which leads these dialogues into inextricable aporias. This is perhaps because the primary purpose of these early elenchic dialogues is preparative—their aim is to silence empirical responses in order to open up the region of the Idea *in general*, while leaving it to others to determine it *as* an Idea or as a problem. When Socratic irony is no longer taken *à la lettre*, when the dialectic is no longer confused with its propaedeutic, it becomes something serious and positive, and assumes other forms of questioning: Which one? in the *Statesman* and the *Phaedrus*, as we have seen; How many? in the *Philebus*; Where? and When? in the *Sophist*; In what sense? in the *Parmenides*. The "minor" questions of the sophists, Deleuze argues, were the result of a worked-out method, a whole sophistic art that was opposed to the Platonic dialectic and implied *an empirical and pluralistic conception of essence*, no longer as a foundation, but as an event or a multiplicity. "No doubt, if one insists, the word 'essence' might be preserved, but only on condition of saying that the essence is precisely accident, the event . . . The events and singularities of the Idea do not allow any positing of an essence as 'what the thing is'" (DR

191). Even in the Platonic texts, such a conception of the Idea was prefigured by the sophist Hippias, "he who refuses essences and yet is not content with examples" (NP 76). The fact is that the question "What is . . .?" poses the problem of essence in a blind and confused manner. Nietzsche wanted to replace the question "What is . . .?" with "Who is . . .?"; rather than posing the question, "What is truth?" he asks, "*Who* is in search of truth? What do those who ask 'What is truth?' really want? What type of will is being expressed in them?"[55] Similarly, when we ask "What is beauty?" we are asking, "From what viewpoint do things appear beautiful?"—and with something that does not appear beautiful to us, from what viewpoint would it become so? Where and When? (NP 75–9). If the sophists must be reproached, it is not for having utilized inferior forms of questioning, but for their inability to have determined the conditions within which they take on their transcendental meaning and their ideal sense, beyond empirical examples (DI 95).

Deleuze suggests that if one considers the history of philosophy, one will, in fact, search in vain for a philosopher who was satisfied with the question "What is . . .?" Aristotle's questions "*ti to on?*" and "*tis a ousia?*" do not signify "What is being?" or "What is substance?" but rather "*Which* [things] are beings?" ["*Qui, l'étant?*"] (DR 244n). Kant asked, "What is an object?" but only within the framework of a more profound question, "*How* is this possible?" When Leibniz was content to ask, "What is . . .?" he only obtained definitions that he himself considered nominal; when he attained real definitions, it was because of questions like "How?", "From what point of view?", "In which case?" Even Heidegger, when he formulated the question of Being, insisted that we can only gain access to Being by asking, not "What is Being?", but rather "*Who* is it?" (*Dasein*).[56] If Hegel took the question "What is?" seriously, it was because of his theological prejudices, since "the answer to 'What is X?' is always God as the locus of the combinatory of abstract possibilities" (DR 188). Deleuze's pluralist art does not necessarily deny essence, but it makes it depend in all cases upon the spatio-temporal and material coordinates of a problematic Idea that is purely *immanent* to experience, and that can *only* be determined by questions such as Who?, How?, Where and When?, How many?, From what viewpoint?, and so on. These "minor" questions are those of the accident, the inessential, of multiplicity, of difference—in short, of the event (problematics as opposed to theorematics).[57]

2. *Repetition*. Second, in an inverted Platonism, the notion of *repetition* can be said to assume an autonomous power along with that of *difference* (hence the title of Deleuze's magnum opus). Platonism relies on what Deleuze calls a "naked" model of repetition (representation): the copy repeats the identity of the ideal model as the first term in a hierarchical series (just as, in archaic religion, ritual is said to repeat myth). Naked repetition thus presupposes a mechanical or brute repetition of the Same: it is founded on an ultimate or originary instance or first time (A), which is then repeated a second, third, and fourth time (A^1, A^2, A^3, and so on.). In cases of psychic repetition, this originary term is subject to disguises and displacements, which are secondary yet necessary. In Freud, for instance, our adult loves "repeat" our childhood love for the mother, but our original maternal love is repressed and disguised in these subsequent loves by various mechanisms of condensation (metonymy) and displacement (metaphor). I repeat because I repress (amnesia),

and the task of therapy, through transference, is to recover this hidden origin (not to eliminate repetition, but to verify the authentic repetitions). In Plato, the form of time is introduced into thought under the category of reminiscence (*anamnesis*). The ultimate term or model is the Idea, but since Plato is unable to assign an empirical moment in the past when the Idea was present, he invokes an originary moment: the Idea has been seen, but in another life, in a mythical present (e.g., the circulation of souls in the *Phaedrus*). If to learn is to recollect, it is because the real movement of learning implies a distinction in the soul between a "before" and an "after"; there is a first time, in which we forget what we knew, and a second time, in which we recover what we have forgotten.[58] In either case, bare repetition refers back to a former present, whether empirical or mythical, which has a prior identity and provides the "thing" to be repeated. It is this originary identity, now lost or forgotten, that conditions the entire process of repetition, and in this sense remains independent of it.

But the question Deleuze poses is the following: are the disguises and variations, the masks and costumes, something added secondarily "over and above" the original term, or are they, on the contrary, "the internal genetic elements of repetition itself, its integral and constituent parts"? (DR 17). In this case, we would no longer have a "naked" repetition of the Same but a "clothed" repetition of the Different. It is in Proust's work that Deleuze finds a model for this clothed repetition, which he analyzes in detail in *Proust and Signs*. In Proust's novel *In Search of Lost Time*, the hero's various loves (for Gilberte, Mme. de Guermantes, Albertine) indeed form a series in which each successive love adds its minor differences and contrasting relations to the preceding loves. (Indeed, each particular love itself assumes a serial form— beginning, course, termination—in which the hero first explicates the hidden world enveloped in his lover, and then retraces his steps in forgetting her.) But in Proust, the series of loves does not refer back to the hero's mother; the childhood love for his mother is *already* a repetition of other adult loves (Proust's hero replays with his mother Swann's passion for Odette), and the mother's love in turn refers to repetitions he has not himself experienced. In other words, *there is no first term* in what is repeated that can be isolated from the series. My parents are not the ultimate terms of my individual subjectivity, but rather the middle terms of a much larger inter- subjectivity. At the limit, the series of all our loves transcends our experience, and links up with repetitions that are not our own, thereby acceding to a transubjective reality. The personal series of our loves thus refers both to a more vast transpersonal series and to more restricted series constituted by each love in particular.[59]

What, then, is being repeated throughout these series? What is the "content" that is being affected or modified within these series? In clothed repetition, what is repeated is not a prior identity or originary sameness, but rather a virtual object or event (an "object = x") which, in Lacan's terminology, is always displaced in relation to itself and has no fixed identity. The repeated object is *a difference that differentiates itself in being repeated*.[60] There is indeed, one might say, an "essence" that governs the series of our loves, but this essence, Deleuze insists, "is always differ- ence," and this difference differs from itself every time it is repeated.[61] It is a virtual- ity that is differenciated every time it is actualized. The variations, in other words, do not come from without, but express differential mechanisms which belong to the essence and origin of what is repeated. There is not an originary "thing" (model) which could eventually be uncovered behind the disguises, displacements, and illusions of repetition (copies); rather, *disguise and displacement are the essence of repetition itself*, which is in itself an original and positive principle.

> Repetition is constituted only with and through the *disguises* which affect the terms and relations of the real series, but it is so because it depends upon the virtual object as an immanent instance which operated above all by *displacement* . . . What is displaced and disguised in the series cannot and must not be identified, but exists and acts as the differenciator of difference. (DR 105, 300)

The clothed repetition of an inverted Platonism must thus be distinguished from the naked repetitions (re-presentation) of Platonism itself.

> *Re*-petition opposes *re*-presentation: the prefix changes meaning, since in the latter case difference is said only in relation to the identical, while in the former it is the univocal which is said of the different . . . When the identity of things dissolves, being escapes to attain univocity [Being = difference], and begins to revolve around the different. (DR 67)

Temporally, the differential object = x refers neither to an empirical moment nor to a mythical moment, but belongs essentially to the past, and as such is unrememberable in itself; what is repeated can never be represented in the present, but it always disguised in the roles and masks it produces. Clothed repetition, in other words, does not refer to something underneath the masks, but rather is formed from one mask to the other, in a movement of perpetual differentiation.

   3. *Ungrounding*. Third, these two immanent principles of difference and repetition can be said to come together in the notion of an "ungrounding," a *sans-fond*. Plato saw chaos as a contradictory state that must be subject to an order or a law from the outside; the Demiurge subjugates a rebellious matter, imposing on it the effect of the Same. He thus reduced the Sophist to contradiction, to that supposed state of chaos, the lowest power and last degree of participation. In reality, however, the Sophist is not the being (or non-being) of contradiction, nor the being of the negative; rather, the Sophist is the one who raises everything to the level of simulacra—that is, to the level of difference—and who maintains and affirms them in that state. Far from being a new foundation, the simulacrum allows no installation of a foundation-ground; rather, it swallows up all foundations; it assures a universal collapse, an "un-founding" [*effondement*], but as a positive event, a "gay science." The Platonic project of opposing the cosmos to chaos finds itself replaced by the immanent identity of chaos and cosmos, the "chaosmos." There is no longer a thread to lead us out of Plato's cave, to inaugurate our ascent toward the transcendent Idea, but only, as Nietzsche saw, a deeper cave behind every cave, an abyss beneath every foundation.

> By "ungrounding" [Deleuze writes], we should understand the freedom of the non-mediated ground, the discovery of a ground behind every other ground, the relation between the groundless and the ungrounded, the immediate reflection of the formless and the superior form which constitutes the eternal return. (DR 67)

Deleuze thus links the immanent identity of cosmos and chaos with Nietzsche's concept of the eternal return—the third form of repetition, beyond both naked and clothed repetition. The eternal return "is not an external order imposed upon the chaos of the world; on the contrary, the eternal return is the internal identity of the world and of chaos, the Chaosmos" (DR 299). If Plato reduced the simulacrum to the lowest power and last degree of participation, the eternal return raises the simulacrum to the highest power, the "nth" power. The "nth" power does not pass through varying degrees of participation (second, third . . .), but rather is immediately affirmed of chaos itself in order to constitute the highest power. Difference itself is a plastic and nomadic principle that operates beyond or beneath forms themselves; it is a principle that is "contemporaneous with the process of individuation, no less capable of dissolving and destroying individuals than of constituting them" (DR 38). The eternal return is the form of repetition that affirms difference itself, and raises it to the highest power.

> Repetition in the eternal return appears as the peculiar power of difference, and the displacement and disguise of that which repeats only reproduce the divergence and the decentering of the difference in a single movement of *diaphora* or transport. The eternal return affirms difference, it affirms dissemblance and disparateness, chance, multiplicity, and becoming. (DR 300)

4. *Selection*. Finally, the project of selection takes on a new form as well. The Platonic dialectic is dominated by the idea of establishing a criterion of selection between the thing itself and its simulacra.

> The question [Deleuze writes] is whether such a reaction [against Platonism] abandons the project of a selection among rivals, or on the contrary, as Spinoza and Nietzsche believed, draws up *completely different methods of selection*. Such methods would no longer concerns claims as acts of transcendence, but the manner in which an existing being is filled with immanence . . . Selection no longer concerns the claim, but power. (ECC, 137)

This is what distinguishes the *moral* vision of the world (Plato, Kant) from an *ethical* vision of the world (Spinoza, Nietzsche). If morality consists in *judging* actions or beings by relating them to transcendent values, ethics *evaluates* what we do or think according to the immanent mode of existence it implies. What would these immanent methods entail? The selective difference can no longer be an external difference (between true and false claimants), but must depend on an internal difference (between active and reactive / passive power). The selection, in short, must be based on the purely immanent criterion of a thing's *power* or capacities: that is, by the manner in which it actively deploys its power by going to the limit of what it can do, or on the contrary, by the manner in which it is cut off from its capacity to act. An immanent *ethical* difference (good / bad) is in this way substituted for the transcendent *moral* opposition (Good / Evil). The "bad" is an exhausted and degenerating mode of existence that judges life from the perspective of its sickness, that devaluates life in the name of "higher" values (the True, the Good, the Beautiful). The "good" is an overflowing, ascending, and exceptional form of existence, a type of being that is able to transform itself depending on the forces it encounters, always increasing its power to live, always opening new possibilities of life.[62] This ethical difference is internal to the existing being, and requires no appeal to transcendent criteria. "Only the philosophies of pure immanence escape Platonism," writes Deleuze, "from the Stoics to Spinoza or Nietzsche."[63]

EXEUNT SIMULACRA

Deleuze summarizes these contrasts between the copy and the simulacrum—between Platonism and inverted Platonism—by inviting us to consider two formulas: "Only that which resembles differs" and "Only differences can resemble each other." The first is an exact definition of the world as an icon; it bids us to think of difference only in terms of similarity, or a previous identity, which become the conditions of difference (Plato). The second defines the world of simulacra; it posits the world itself as a phantasm or simulacrum, inviting us to think of similarity and even identity as the result of a fundamental disparity, products or effects of a primary difference, or a primary system of differences (Nietzsche).

> What we have to ask [writes Deleuze] is whether these two formulas are simply two ways of speaking that do not change much; or if they are applied to completely different systems; or if, being applied to the same systems (at the limit, to the system of the World), they signify two incompatible interpretations of unequal value, one of which is capable of changing everything.[64]

In the end, Deleuze's analysis of the simulacrum entails more than a reading of latonism; it also constitutes one of the fundamental problems of contemporary thought.

> Modern thought [Deleuze writes in the preface to *Difference and Repetition*] was born out of the failure of representation, as the loss of identities, and the discovery of all the forces that were acting under the representation of the identical. The modern world is one of simulacra ... All identities are only simulated, produced like an "optical effect" by a more profound play [*jeu*] which is that of difference and repetition. *We would like to think difference in itself, and the relation of the different with the different, independent of the forms of representation that lead it back to the Same.*[65]

Deleuze's entire philosophical project can be seen as an explication of this declaration of intent.

An assessment of Deleuze's theory of Ideas (which passes through a reappraisal of Kant as well as Plato) lies beyond the scope of this paper. It was initially through his reading of Plato that Deleuze was able to pose the problem that lies at the genesis of his theory of Ideas (the problem of simulacra), and to indicate the role that the overturning of Platonism plays in his thought. However, there is a coda to this story. After the publication of *Difference and Repetition* (1968), the concept of the simulacrum more or less disappears from Deleuze's work in favor of the concept of the *agencement* or "assemblage." "It seems to me that I have completely abandoned the notion of the simulacrum," Deleuze noted in 1993.[66] There seem to be two reasons for this evolution. On the one hand, the notion that things simulate a transcendent Idea has a meaning only in the context of Platonism. In Deleuze's own ontology, things no longer "simulate" anything, but rather "actualize" immanent Ideas that are themselves real, though virtual. Deleuze thus uses the notion of the simulacrum to pose the Nietzschean problem of "anti-Platonism" within Plato himself, but then drops the notion as he forges his own ontological terminology. Within Deleuze's own work, the concept of the simulacrum is ultimately replaced by the concept of the assemblage [*agencement*], and the process of simulation is more properly characterized as the process of actualization (or even more precisely, the complex process of "differen t/c iation"). On the other hand, Deleuze does not ascribe to Greek thought the importance that one finds in Nietzsche (for whom post-Greek thought was little more than the history of a long error)[67] or Heidegger (who tended to fetishize Greek and German language and thought). Nietzsche said that a truth never reveals itself immediately, at its birth, but only in its maturation. Similarly, Deleuze's philosophical heroes, so to speak, tend to be found, not at the origins of philosophical thought (Socrates, Plato), but in its maturation in the seventeenth century (Spinoza, Leibniz). After *Difference and Repetition* and *Logic of Sense*, Plato's work does not receive another sustained discussion in Deleuze's writings until *What is Philosophy?* In this sense, Deleuze's sketch of Nietzsche's anti-Platonism serves as a propaedeutic endeavor whose primary role is to outline the motivations of Deleuze's own philosophical project. Finally, one could say that, as the concept of the simulacrum disappeared from Deleuze's writings, it was taken up by other writers (such as Baudrillard) and taken in a different direction, with different coordinates and in response to different problematics. Concepts, in this sense, have their own autonomy and history that go beyond the diversity of their adherents.

Univocity

The Doctrine of Univocity: Deleuze's Ontology of Immanence

"If God does not exist, everything is permissible." Deleuze likes to invert this Dostoyevskian formula from *The Brothers Karamazov* because, he says, the opposite is in fact the case: it is *with* God that everything is permissible. This is obviously true morally, since the worst atrocities have always managed to find a divine justification, and belief in God has never been a guarantor of morality. But it is also true aesthetically and philosophically. Medieval art, for example, is filled with images of God, and it would be tempting to see this merely as an inevitable constraint of the era, imposed from without by the Church. Deleuze suggests a different hypothesis. In the hands of great painters like El Greco, Tintoretto, and Giotto, this constraint became the condition of a radical emancipation; in painting the divine, one could take literally the idea that God must not be represented, an idea that resulted in an extraordinary liberation of line, color, form, and movement. With God, painting found a freedom it would not have had otherwise—a properly pictorial atheism.[1]

The same was true in philosophy. Until the revolution of the eighteenth century, philosophers were constantly speaking of God, to the point where philosophy seemed completely compromised by theology and the demands of the Church. But in the hands of great philosophers such as Spinoza and Leibniz, this constraint became the condition of an equally extraordinary liberation. With God, philosophical concepts were freed from the traditional task that had been imposed on them—the representation of things—and were allowed to assume fantastic dimensions. With the concept of God, everything was permissible. Or almost everything, for thinkers (like Spinoza) who went too far with the concept, or went too fast, often did so at their own peril. Deleuze thus harbors neither the antagonism of the "secular" who find the concept of God outmoded, nor the angst or mourning of those for whom the loss of God was crisis-provoking, nor the faith of those who would like to retrieve the concept in a new form. He remains fascinated with theological concepts, and regards medieval theologians in particular as a magnificent breed of thinkers who were able to invent, in the name of God, remarkable systems of logic and physics. Indeed, at several points in his writings, he picks up on certain "heretical" paths of theological thought closed off by orthodoxy and seemingly abandoned, and sets them to work philosophically in a different context.

Deleuze's appropriation of the medieval concept of univocity is the most obvious and important example of this unorthodox use of the Christian theological tradition. The doctrine of the "univocity of Being" is an ontological theory developed in the thirteenth century by Duns Scotus, following Henry of Ghent, in his magnum opus entitled *Opus Oxoniense*, which Deleuze calls "the greatest book of pure ontology."[2] In the Middle Ages, univocity was a heterodox position, constantly at the borders of heresy, and had limited currency outside the Scotistic school.[3] (The English word "dunce" is derived from the term of approbation used to describe the followers of Duns Scotus.) Moreover, the concept has a rather curious status in Deleuze's own work. The term is not even mentioned before 1968, when univocity suddenly becomes an important theme in almost all of Deleuze's writings. It first appears in *Expressionism in Philosophy: Spinoza*, where it forms the "keystone" of Deleuze's interpretation of Spinoza (even more so than the title concept of "expression").[4] It then assumes an even more prominent role in *Difference and Repetition* and *Logic of Sense*, where Deleuze not only identifies an entire tradition of univocity in the history of philosophy, running from Duns Scotus (against Thomism) through Spinoza (against Cartesianism) to Nietzsche (against Hegelianism), but also presents his own ontology as a univocal ontology, thereby identifying himself as the most recent inheritor of that tradition. And then, equally abruptly, and without explanation, the concept disappears, almost without a trace; it is scarcely mentioned in any of Deleuze's subsequent works.

What is the role of univocity in Deleuze's thought? And why does the concept have such a short-lived but intense trajectory in Deleuze's writings, like a flashing meteor? Despite Deleuze's provocative claim, there is no "tradition" of univocity in the history of philosophy, apart from the one he himself creates; there is hardly a secondary literature on the concept outside of Scotistic studies. Deleuze was more accurate when he remarked, in a seminar, that univocity is "the strangest thought, the most difficult to think, *if it has ever been thought*."[5] In what follows, I will attempt to follow the life of this "strange" concept as it appears, matures, and then passes away, as it were, within the flow of Deleuze's thought, creating unexpected "traversals" between otherwise disconnected thinkers and problems. Were one to "dramatize" the movement of this concept, it could perhaps be staged in four separate acts.

THE MEDIEVAL BACKGROUND

Act I would take us back to the medieval articulations of the concept. For Duns Scotus, as for many Scholastic philosophers, the object of theology was God, while the object of philosophy, or rather of the metaphysics crowning it, was *Being* as Being. In developing his theory of univocity, Duns Scotus was injecting himself into a lively thirteenth-century debate concerning the nature of Being; Being is said of beings, *but in what sense?* The Scholastics used three precise terms to designate the various ways of resolving the problem: equivocity, univocity, and analogy. To say that Being is *equivocal* means that the term "Being" is said of beings in several senses, and that these senses have *no common measure*; "God is" does not have the same sense as "man is," for instance, because God does not have the same type of being as man. By contrast, to say that Being is *univocal*, as Duns Scotus affirmed, means that Being has only one sense, and is said *in one and the same sense* of everything of which it is said, whether it be God or human, animal or plant. Since these positions seemed to lead to scandalous conclusions (equivocity denied order in the cosmos, univocity implied pantheism), a third alternative was developed between these two extremes: Being is neither equivocal nor univocal but *analogical*. This became the position of Christian orthodoxy, as formulated by Thomas Aquinas; there is indeed a common measure to the forms of Being, but this measure is analogical, and not univocal.

Why did Deleuze revisit this seemingly obscure Scholastic debate? The answer seems clear: the three books Deleuze published in 1968 to 1969 (*Expressionism in Philosophy: Spinoza, Difference and Repetition, Logic of Sense*) mark, among other things, the culmination of Deleuze's confrontation with Heidegger. This confrontation had been present in Deleuze's work from the start, even if Heidegger's name receives only passing mention in the texts.[6] As always, Deleuze brings a *contemporary* problematic to bear on his work in the *history* of philosophy. Heidegger (who wrote his own thesis on Duns Scotus) famously inaugurated the modern renaissance of ontology by posing the question of the "ontological difference": What is the difference between Being and beings? Or more precisely, How is Being distributed among beings? During the Middle Ages, this ontological problem had been intertwined with a similar, though not identical, set of theological questions: What is the difference between God and his creatures? Or put logically, in terms of the "divine names" tradition: In what sense can we predicate of God the same terms (e.g., goodness) that we use of his creatures? The concept of univocity was situated at the nexus of this complex set of philosophical and theological questions.

According to Deleuze, however, although Heidegger revived the question of ontology and gave "renewed splendor to the univocity of Being," he did not effect the necessary conversion according to which "univocal Being belongs only to *difference*" (that is, the term "Being" has one and only one sense, which is "difference").[7] Heidegger, in other words, was unable—or perhaps unwilling—to push the problematic of ontological difference to its necessary conclusion. This is the project that Deleuze takes up as his own in *Difference and Repetition*. In this sense, univocity must be seen as one of the concepts Deleuze uses in order to state and resolve Heidegger's ontological problematic in his own manner. For Deleuze, the only pure and fully realized ontology *must* be a univocal ontology, and only a univocal ontology is capable of thinking difference-in-itself, or of providing difference with its own concept. As Foucault put it, in his well-known essay on Deleuze, the univocity of Being is "the principal condition which permits difference to escape the domination of identity."[8] But this link between univocity and difference might seem obscure. If Being is univocal, what constitutes the *difference* between beings? Why does a philosophy of difference require a univocal ontology?

THE THREE FIGURES OF UNIVOCITY IN SPINOZA

In the second act, Deleuze begins to respond to these questions by turning, not to Duns Scotus, who plays the role of a precursor, but rather to Spinoza, who, according to Deleuze, gave the concept of univocity its fullest expression. "Univocity," Deleuze claims, "is the keystone of Spinoza's entire philosophy"—even though the word does not appear even once in Spinoza's texts.[9] Deleuze, however, often employs this "topological" method in his historical monographs; when he interprets Bergson in terms of the concept of "difference" (as formulated by Heidegger), or Leibniz in terms of a theory of "singularities" (borrowed from Albert Lautman), or Spinoza in terms of "univocity" (imported from Duns Scotus), he is using a "foreign" concept, not explicitly formulated by the thinkers at hand, to bring out aspects of their thought that might otherwise remain obscure.

Deleuze's affinity with Spinoza here is not incidental. Heidegger himself wrote notoriously little on Spinoza—a surprising omission, it would seem, since the *Ethics* is a work of pure ontology that poses the problem of ontological difference in terms of the difference between infinite substance (Being) and finite modes (beings). Deleuze's work on Spinoza, from this viewpoint, can be read as his means of working through the problematic of ontological difference in a new manner, just as *Difference and Repetition* could be read as a response to *Being and Time* (for Deleuze, Being is difference, and time is repetition). Where Heidegger returns to the Greeks (the origin), Deleuze turns to Spinoza (the middle). According to Deleuze, univocity assumes three figures in Spinoza's philosophy: the univocity of the attributes, the univocity of cause, and the univocity of modality. These are the three important scenes of the second act that show how Spinoza overturned the entire medieval theological tradition, at the price of his condemnation.

1. *The Univocity of the Attributes.* In the Middle Ages, as Heidegger says, ontology became an onto-theo-logy; the question of the Being of beings tended to be forgotten in favor of the thought of God as the supreme (ontic) being. The Christian concept of God was the inheritor of the Platonic "Good" and the Neo-Platonic "One," which were "above" or "beyond" Being (*hyperousios, epikeina tes ousias*): that is, transcendent to Being. Christian theology thus oscillated between a double requirement: *immanence* (the ontological requirement that the first principle be a *being*) and *transcendence* (the more powerful requirement that the transcendence of God be maintained, as the One *beyond* Being). The "divine names" tradition, in turn, was concerned with the manner in which the traditional divine attributes (e.g., goodness, love, wisdom, power, etc.) could be predicated of God: negatively or positively? As conditional affirmations, or negations marking the ablation of some privation? The Christian tradition identified two extreme (and heterodox) responses to this question: pure transcendence would imply the equivocity of terms, pure immanence their univocity. Between these two poles, orthodoxy developed a *via media* approach to the problem, centered in large part on the strategies of negation, eminence, and analogy. These five ways—equivocity, negation, eminence, analogy, univocity—entered into historically varying combinations in Christian thought, though two general approaches assumed the status of orthodoxy: a way of negation and a way of affirmation.

The way of negation, which came to be called "negative theology" (following Pseudo-Dionysus), admits that affirmations are able to designate God as cause, subject to rules of immanence, but insists that God as substance or essence can only be defined negatively, according to rules of transcendence. Meister Eckhart, for instance, prefers to say "God is not" rather than "God is," because "x is" is a statement that is said of beings, whereas God is eminently superior to Being, beyond Being.[10] This allows God to appear in his "supra-substantial" or "supra-essential" eminence, as far from all negation as from all affirmation. Negative theology can therefore be defined by its dynamics; one goes beyond affirmations (God is good) via negations (God is not good in the human sense of the term), and beyond both affirmations and negations to attain God's *eminence* (God is good with an "incomparable" or "ineffable" Goodness). By contrast, a theology with more positive ambitions, like that of Thomas Aquinas, relies on *analogy* to found new affirmative rules. Positive qualities can indeed belong to God substantially, but only in so far as they are treated "analogically," either in terms of an ordered relationship between two proportions—for instance, the divine goodness is to God as human goodness is to man (analogy of proportionality)—or by reference to a focal meaning or "prime analogate"—for instance, "Goodness," which God possesses eminently and creatures only derivatively (analogy of proportion). The way of affirmation must likewise be defined by a specific dynamic: it maintains the strength of the negative and the eminent, but comprehends them within analogy.[11]

The audacity of Spinoza's "heresy" was to have rejected both these orthodox approaches—the negative and the positive, the apophatic and kataphatic—and to have set against them the heterodox doctrine of the univocity of the divine attributes. For Spinoza, we know only two of God's infinite attributes (thought and extension), and these attributes are common forms predicable univocally of *both* God and his creatures. Though formally distinct, the attributes are ontologically univocal. To say that the attributes are univocal means, for example, that it is in the *same* form that bodies imply extension and that extension is an attribute of the divine substance (the position of immanence). If Spinoza radically rejects the notions of eminence, equivocity, and even analogy, it is because they imply that God possesses these perfections in a form *different* from that implied in his creatures, a "higher" form (the position of transcendence). Spinoza's genius lies in his having provided a profound explanation for his rejection of these orthodox positions: the problem they were attempting to solve, he says, was an altogether false one, for two reasons.

On the one hand, as Spinoza argues in the *Short Treatise*, theologians had tended to confuse God's *attributes* with his *propria* (properties). Following Aristotle, Spinoza defines a *proprium* as that which belongs to a thing, *but can never explain what it is*. The attributes that have traditionally been ascribed to God are not attributes, Spinoza explains, but mere *propria*. They reveal *nothing* of the divine essence. The *Short Treatise* distinguishes three types of *propria* of God: the first type are modalities of the divine essence that must be affirmed of *all* God's attributes (cause of itself, infinite, perfect, immutable, eternal, necessary . . .), or of a specific attribute (omniscience is affirmed of thought; omnipresence is affirmed of extension); the second type are those that qualify God in reference to his products or creations (cause of all things, predestination, providence); the third type, finally, do not even belong to God, but designate extrinsic determinations that merely indicate the way we imagine God, failing to comprehend his true nature (justice, charity, compassion). The basic error of theology is that it confuses God's essence with these *propria*, and this confusion pervades the entire language of eminences, negations, and analogies. When *propria* are given a substantial value that they do not have, the divine substance is given an inexpressible nature that it does not have either. And this error, in turn, has compromised the whole of philosophy. Even Descartes was content to define God as infinite perfection, though perfection and infinity are not attributes but merely modalities of the divine essence (*propria* of the first type).[12]

On the other hand, Spinoza offers a genetic account of this theological error in the *Tractatus Theologico-Politicus*. Why was the nature of God denatured in this way? Because, Spinoza explains, his predecessors lacked a proper *historico-critical method* for interpreting Scripture. They simply presumed that God had revealed his nature in Scripture. But in fact, the aim of Scripture is to give us models of life, to make us obey, and to ground our obedience through its warnings, commandments, and rules. "Revealed theology" concerns itself exclusively with *propria* of the third type, which appeal to our imaginations to make us serve a God of whose nature we remain ignorant. As for God's true attributes (thought and extension), they are made known through the light of Nature, not revelation. The nature of God is made manifest in the order of Nature, not in the teachings of the Bible. Spinoza likes to remind us that the prophets were men with vivid imaginations but weak understandings; Adam, Abraham, and Moses were not only ignorant of the true divine attributes, but also of most of the *propria* of the first and second type.[13] According to Harry Wolfson, the *Tractatus* overturned a long hermeneutical tradition that had been inaugurated centuries earlier by Philo; after Spinoza, Scripture could and would no longer be treated as a properly *philosophical* authority.[14]

The univocity of the attributes thus entails the absolute immanence of God and Nature, *Deus sive natura*, stripping God of any transcendence (it matters little whether this is understood as pantheism or atheism). What Deleuze finds in Spinoza, prior to Hume's and Kant's critiques of theology, or even Nietzsche's "death of God," is a quiet and confident philosophy of immanence. One can already sense Deleuze maneuvering between Scylla and Charybdis; univocity is as opposed to the negative eminence of the Neo-Platonists as to the positive analogies of the Thomists, each of which have their modern counterparts.

2. *The Univocity of Cause*. The second figure of univocity Deleuze finds in Spinoza is the univocity of cause; God is cause of all things *in the same sense* that he is cause of himself. Broadly speaking, medieval philosophy distinguished between three types of causes: a transitive cause, an emanative cause, and an immanent cause. A *transitive* cause is a cause that leaves itself in order to produce, and what it produces (its effect) is outside of itself. Christianity held to the idea of a real distinction between God and the world. If God created the world, and the world is exterior to God, then God must come out of himself in order to create the world; it therefore needed to see God as a purely transitive cause (creationism). An *emanative* cause,

by contrast, is a cause whose effect is exterior to it, but which none the less remains within itself in order to produce its effect. The sun, for example, remains within itself in order to produce, but what it produces (light) comes out of it. Such metaphors of luminosity are frequent in Plotinus and the Neo-Platonists, who pushed an emanative conception of cause to its furthest point. An *immanent* cause, finally, is a cause that not only remains within itself in order to produce, but one whose produced effect also remains within it. This is the conception of causality developed by Spinoza.

Here again, Christian theology adopted a syncretic solution: Is God a transitive cause, an emanative cause, or an immanent cause?[15] Orthodoxy insisted that God is a transitive cause, transcendent to the world (creation *ex nihilo*). How, then, does God create the world? He would have to have a model or idea of the world in his understanding, and he would create the world, in conformity with this model, through a free act of the divine will. But this would imply a fully immanent causality; the model or idea must remain in God's understanding, and God must remain in himself in order to contemplate it. To reconcile these two movements, one requires the idea of an emanative causality between the model of the world in God's understanding and the real world produced in conformity with this model. Medieval thinkers consequently had to combine the three types of causality in varying permutations. The idea of an immanent causality, Deleuze suggests, functioned as a kind of internal theoretical limit for philosophers and theologians up to the Renaissance (Nicholas of Cusa, Erigena, Petrarch, Bruno, Eckhart, the Rhine mystics)—a limit, however, that was always repulsed, out of a concern to avoid pantheism, through the doctrines of creation (by a transcendent being above his creatures) and emanation (from a transcendent One beyond Being). In a sense, the immanent cause was always present in philosophy, but Spinoza was the first thinker who was willing (and able) to take the concept of causality to its immanent limit, and to free it from all subordination to other processes of causality.

What are the consequences of an immanent causality? In an emanative causality, the One is the cause or "radical origin" of Being, but the cause (the One) remains beyond its effect (Being). The One does not come out of itself to produce Being, because if it came out of itself it would become Two. This is the sense of Plotinus' notion of the *gift*: Being is a gift or donation of the One, but the One necessarily remains beyond Being, it "is not." Ontologically, the universe is in this way rendered hierarchical; beings have more or less reality depending on their distance from or proximity to the One as the transcendent first principle (the "great chain of Being"). Morally, it allows Being to be judged because there is an authority higher than Being itself (the "system of judgment"). The One is thus inseparable from a negative theology or a method of analogy, which are required to maintain this eminence of the cause. We must not be led astray by the prefix "uni-" in the term "univocity"; a univocal ontology is by definition irreconcilable with a philosophy of the One, which necessarily entails an equivocal concept of Being.[16] Heidegger seems to have remained tied to a certain conception of eminence in his famous lecture on "Time and Being," where he developed the theme of the *es gibt*: that is, the "gift" (*Gabe*) of time and Being by the It.[17] Jacques Derrida, in his later works, has moved toward a philosophy of transcendence, influenced by Levinas and linked to the theme of a negative theology.[18]

Deleuze has followed a very different path. In Spinoza's immanent causality, not only does the cause remain in itself, but also its effect remains "immanate" within it, rather than emanating from it. The effect (mode) remains in its cause no less than the cause remains in itself (substance). Hence Deleuze's fondness for the "expressionistic" Renaissance notions of *complicare* and *explicare*, which he adopts for his own purposes in *Difference and Repetition*; all things are present to God (or Nature), who complicates them, and God is present to all things, which explicate and implicate him.

> Immanence of the image in the mirror, immanence of the tree in the seed— these two ideas are the basis for any expressionist philosophy. Even in Pseudo-Dionysus, the rigor of the hierarchies leaves open a virtual place for zones of equality, univocity, and anarchy. (TRM 262–3)

In Spinoza, similarly, *natura naturans* (substance and cause) and *natura naturata* (mode and effect) are interconnected through a mutual immanence; the cause remains in itself in order to produce, and the effect or product remains in the cause (SPP 92). In an immanent ontology, Being necessarily becomes univocal; not only is Being equal in itself, but it is also equally and immediately present in all beings, without mediation or intermediary. There is no distant cause or first cause, no final cause, no "chain of Being," no hierarchy, but rather a kind of anarchy of beings within Being (the One is no longer an *arche* or first principle). "The rock, the lily, the beast, the human equally sing the glory of God in a kind of crowned anarchy."[19] By extracting immanent causality from the other processes of causality, Spinoza flattened everything on to an absolutely infinite substance that possesses all attributes and comprehends all things as its modes; God is in the world, and the world is in God. (This, indeed, was the fatal accusation of every heresy: the accusation of immanence, the confusion of God with his creatures.) In Deleuze's language, Spinoza projected Being on to a fixed *plane of immanence*, within which all things move in a process of continuous variation, with no finality, no purpose, no pre-established harmony, but only "the necessary concatenation of the various effects of an immanent cause" (EPS 233).

3. *The Univocity of Modality (Necessity)*. Necessity is the third figure of univocity—the univocity of modality, after the univocity of the attributes and the univocity of cause.[20] The univocity of modality states that everything that is necessary, either through itself or through its cause. Far from negating the concept of freedom, the univocity of modality profoundly rejuvenates the concept of freedom by *separating it entirely from the concept of the will*, with regard both to substance and to modes (God and his creatures).

On the one hand (with regard to substance), those who ascribe an intellect (or an understanding) and a will to God's essence wrongly conceive of God according to anthropomorphic predicates that imagine God as a kind of prince or legislator (*propria* of the third type). Consider Leibniz's fantastic revision of the traditional notion of creation. God, he says, has an *infinite understanding*. The term "under-standing" must here be taken equivocally—it does not have a single sense—since God's infinite understanding is not the same as the finite understanding of humans (the analogy of Being). Before he creates the world, there an infinite set of "pos-sibilities" (possible worlds) in God's understanding, all of which have a certain weight depending on their degree of perfection. They all have a tendency to pass into existence, yet not all of them can do so, because they form incompatible (or incompossible) combinations. Only that set of possibles that has the greatest quan-tity of perfection will pass into existence, and it is precisely God's *will* that chooses the "best" of all possible worlds, in accordance with a calculus that chooses the most perfect combination (the Best).

Against Leibniz, Spinoza will hold that it is absurd to ascribe either an under-standing or a will to God's essence; these are the two great errors that distort both the notion of necessity and the notion of freedom.[21] For when God is conceived as having a will to choose (or to create *ex nihilo*), in the image of a prince or tyrant, or as having an understanding containing models or possibilities, in the image of a legislator, his supposed freedom is tied to physical contingency (will) or logical pos-sibility (intellect). As a result, we attribute *inconstancy* to God's power, since his will could have created something else, or else a certain *powerlessness*, since his power is limited by conceived models of possibility. If God could have produced a different order of Nature—that is, if he had conceived and willed something else concerning Nature, then both his intellect and will—that is to say, his essence or his nature—would have had to be different, and God would be other than what he is, which is absurd. Similarly, if we maintain that God does all things for the sake of the Good or the principle of the "Best," we place something outside of God, which does not depend on God, as a model to which he is subject or a goal toward which he aims, which is equally absurd.[22] In both cases, we grant existence to *abstractions*, such as Nothingness, in the case of creation *ex nihilo*; or the Good and the Best, in the case of legislative freedom.[23]

For Spinoza, God is free not because he wills in accordance with possibilities or models conceived in his understanding (from this viewpoint, the modal logic of possible worlds is simply theology for logicians). Rather, God is free because he nec-essarily acts and produces in accordance with his own nature (and not out of a capri-cious "freedom of the will") and because his understanding necessarily comprehends his own nature (and not because he conceives possibilities or models). If necessity is the only modality of all that is, it is because the only cause that can be called free is one *that exists through the necessity of its nature alone, and is determined by itself to act*. Thus God, who is constituted by an infinity of attributes, is the cause of all things in the same sense that he is the cause himself. And God is free because all his actions and productions (or creations) follow necessarily from his essence alone, without his conceiving possibilities or contingencies. Intellect and will are simply modes of the divine nature. The divine intellect (or infinite understanding) is simply a mode through which God comprehends nothing but his own essence and what follows from it; and his will is only a mode according to which all consequences follow from his essence or from that which he comprehends. As Deleuze puts it, "one is never free through one's will or through that on which it patterns itself [via the intellect], but through one's essence and through that which follows from it."[24]

On the other hand (with regard to modes), Spinoza once again gives a *genetic* account of the origin of the categories of possibility and contingency. If humans are born into "bondage" (the title of Part Four of the *Ethics*), it is because they are determined by causes outside themselves. By its very nature, human consciousness registers effects, but it knows nothing about their causes. The order of causes is an order of composition and decomposition of relations, which infinitely affects all of Nature. When my body "encounters" another body (or my mind encounters another mind), the two bodies sometimes enter into a composition that forms a more powerful whole (as when food nourishes me), while at other times one body decomposes the other, destroying the cohesion of its parts (as when poison makes me ill). But as conscious beings, we only ever apprehend the *effects* of these compositions and decomposition; we experience *joy* when a body encounters ours and enters into composition with it, and *sadness* when, on the contrary, a body threatens our own coherence. In other words, we only take in "what happens" to our body or mind, and our consciousness is simply the continual *awareness* of this passage from a lesser to a greater perfection (joy), or from a greater to a lesser (sadness). Consciousness thus has only an informational value, but the information it provides is necessarily confused and distorted; the human condition condemns us to have only *inadequate ideas*, effects separated from their real causes (knowledge of the first kind).

Consciousness is thus constituted by a triple illusion. Since it only takes in effects and is ignorant of causes, consciousness satisfies its ignorance by reversing the order of things, mistaking effects for causes (*the cosmological illusion of final causes or ends*). Moreover, it can believe *itself* to be a first cause, attributing to its will an imaginary power over the body—even though it does not even know what a body "can do" in terms of the causes that actually move it to act (*the psychological illusion of freedom*). Finally, in domains where it can no longer imagine itself to be a first cause or the organizer of ends, it imagines a provident God who himself operates by means of final causes (understanding) or free decrees (will), organizing everything in accordance with means–end relations in order to prepare for humans a world commensurate with his glory and his punishments (*the theological illusion*).[25] The categories of possibility and contingency are also illusions—but they are illusions that follow from the organization of the finite mode. For a mode's essence does not determine its existence; thus, if we consider the essence of a mode, its existence is neither posited nor excluded, and we apprehend the mode as contingent. And if we regard the extrinsic cases that make the mode exist, we still do not know if these causes will determine the mode, and we apprehend the mode as merely possible.[26] Contingency and possibility, in other words, are merely expressions of our ignorance. For Deleuze, Spinoza's critique has two culminating points: nothing is possible in nature (the essence of non-existing modes are not models or possibilities in a divine legislative intellect); and there is nothing contingent in Nature (existences are not produced through the action of a divine will which, like a prince, could have chosen different laws, or a different world) (SPP 94).

The entire effort of the *Ethics* is aimed at breaking the traditional link between freedom and the will (SPP 69). Freedom is a fundamental illusion of consciousness *in so far as* the latter is blind to causes, imagines possibilities and contingencies, and believes in the willful action of the mind over the body.[27] Yet *in so far as* a mode manages to form adequate ideas, these ideas are either common notions that express its internal agreement with other existing modes (knowledge of the second kind), or the idea of its own essence that necessarily agrees internally with the essence of God and all other essences (knowledge of the third kind).[28] Active affects follow necessarily from these adequate ideas, such that they are explained by the mode's own power. The existing mode is free when it comes into possession of its power: that is, when its *conatus* is determined by adequate ideas from which active affects follow—affects that are explained by its own essence. In other words, humans are not born free—they *become* free, or they free themselves. The univocity of necessity does not deny freedom; it denies that freedom is a property of the will.

> I say that a thing is free which exists and acts solely from the necessity of its own nature, and I say that a thing is constrained (*coactus*) which is determined by something else to exist and act in a fixed and determinate way . . . So you see that I place freedom, not in free decision, but in free necessity.[29]

For Spinoza, freedom is always linked to essence and what necessarily follows from it, not to will and what governs it.

These, then, are the three figures of univocity that Deleuze identifies in Spinoza: the univocity of the attributes (the attributes are said in one and the same sense of God and his creatures), the univocity of cause (God is cause of himself in the same sense that he is cause of all things), and the univocity of modality (God is necessary in the same sense that all things are necessary). Taken together, they effect what Deleuze calls a "pure" ontology: that is, *an ontology in which there is nothing beyond or outside or superior to Being.* But this is only the first half of the unfolding of the concept of univocity in Deleuze.

UNIVOCITY IN DELEUZE

"Have I been understood?— Univocity versus Analogy—": such is the Nietzschean gauntlet Deleuze throws down in *Difference and Repetition*, the third and most important act in the story of univocity. *Difference and Repetition* links the project of a pure ontology, as developed by Spinoza, with the problematic of difference, as formulated by Heidegger, and in the process goes beyond both Spinoza and Heidegger. The conversion Deleuze effects from identity to difference is as important as Spinoza's move from transcendence to immanence. According to Klossowski's thesis, the concept of God has always functioned as a guarantor of the principle of identity.[30] Even in Spinoza, modes are modifications *of* substance, and the concept of substance (or God) can still be said to maintain the rights of identity over difference. Deleuze's philosophy of difference must thus be seen as a kind of Spinozism *minus* substance, a purely modal or differential universe (in which the modality of necessity is replaced by the modality of 'virtuality' as the condition of the new, or the production of difference).[31] *Difference and Repetition* is an experiment in metaphysics whose aim is to provide a (transcendental) description of the world from the viewpoint of a principle of difference rather than the principle of identity. "In accordance with Heidegger's ontological intuition," Deleuze writes, "difference must be articulation and connection in itself; *it must relate the different to the different without any mediation whatsoever* by the identical, the similar, the analogous or the opposed" (DR 117). Despite his indebtedness to Heidegger, however, Deleuze never subscribed to the theme of the "overcoming of metaphysics." He describes himself as a "pure metaphysician,"[32] a classical philosopher who sees his philosophy as a system, albeit an open and "heterogenetic" system.[33] Though obviously indebted to such metaphysical thinkers as Spinoza, Leibniz, and Bergson, Deleuze appropriates their respective systems of thought only by pushing them to their "differential" limit, purging them of the three great terminal points of traditional metaphysics (God, World, Self). Deleuze's historical monographs, in this sense, are preliminary sketches for the great canvas of *Difference and Repetition*.

Aristotle appears as an important *dramatis persona* in *Difference and Repetition*, and for good reason. Aristotle held a famous thesis concerning difference: *different things differentiate themselves only through what they have in common.* This subordination of difference to identity can be seen in the schematization of Aristotle's ontology known as Porphyry's tree (Figure 2.1). In the middle regions of the tree, specific difference allows a genus or concept to remain the same in itself (identity) while becoming other in the opposing predicates (specific differences) that divide it. This process of specification in turn reaches a limit at either end of the table. At the lower end, a plurality of different individuals can be placed under a single concept only on the condition that a sensible resemblance between the individuals can be perceived. At the upper end, the differences between the highest genera or "categories" can be related to the concept of Being only through an operation that would come to be known as analogy. Aristotle thus subordinates difference to four interrelated principles: identity in the concept and the opposition of predicates (specific difference), resemblance in perception (individual difference), and the analogy of judgment (generic difference). Readers will recognize this quadripartite structure of "representation" as one of the recurring motifs of *Difference and Repetition*.

Deleuze contrasts the "univocity of Being" point by point with Aristotle's theory of the "analogy of Being," which dominated medieval philosophy prior to Spinoza. Is Being distributed among beings univocally or analogically? This question concerns a very specific problem: the relation of Being to the "categories." Kant defined a category as a concept that can be said of *every* object of possible experience (causality is a category because every object has a cause and is itself cause of other things). Aristotle's formulation amounts to the same thing: the categories are the different senses in which Being is said of beings, *they are different senses of the word Being.*[34] In Heidegger's formulation, the categories are the fundamental "determinations of the Being of beings," the fundamental ontological predicates.[35] But what, then, is the relation of Being, as the most general concept, to the categories, as the highest genera? Aristotle recognized that Being cannot be a univocal genus in relation to

Porphyry's Tree

	Type of Difference:	Governing Principle:
Being ↓ Substance etc.	generic difference (the categories)*	ANALOGY of judgment
↙ ↘ Corporeal Incorporeal ↘	specific difference	IDENTITY in the concept
Body	subaltern genus	
↙ ↘ Animate Inanimate ↘	specific difference	
Living thing	subaltern genus	OPPOSITION of predicates
↙ ↘ Sensitive Insensitive ↘	specific difference	
Animal	subaltern genus	
↙ ↘ Rational Non-rational ↘	specific difference	
Human	infima species	
↙ ↙ ↘ ↘ Socrates Plato Adam Caesar etc.	individual difference	RESEMBLANCE in perception

* Aristotle's list of categories: substance, quantity, quality, relation, place, time, modality, state, action, passion.

Figure 2.1[36]

the categories, and this for a precise reason: because *differences* "*are.*" To predicate Being as an overarching genus would deny the being of difference; or rather, it would mean that the genus "Being" would have to be predicated twice: once to its species, and once to its own differentiae.[37] Generic difference must therefore be of *another nature* than specific difference; whereas a genus in relation to its species is univocal, Being in relation to the categories is necessarily equivocal. The categories, Aristotle concluded, must therefore be related to each other *analogically*. Every philosophy of the categories, from Aristotle through Kant and Hegel, implies an analogical ontology.

In Aristotle, the analogy of Being has two fundamental forms, both of which would be taken up theologically by later thinkers such as Aquinas. On the one hand, the concept of Being has no content in itself, but only a *distributive* content that is proportional to the formally different categories of which it is predicated (analogy of proportionality). The "proportionality" involved here need not be understood in a strict mathematical sense (a:b::c:d), since the categories do not need to have an equal relation to Being, but only an internal relation. On the other hand, Being therefore tends to form a *hierarchical* series, in so far as the category of substance assumes the role of the primary category or the first sense (*pros hen*) of Being: everything that "is" is a substance, and in turn everything that is a substance has a quality, a quantity, a place, and so on (analogy of proportion).[38] These two forms of analogy are what Deleuze terms, respectively, the distributive "common sense" and the hierarchical "good sense" (or first sense) of Being.[39]

What is wrong with Aristotle's analogical vision of the world? Put simply, it provides an inadequate solution to the Heideggerian problematic of ontological difference. On the one hand, *it cannot posit Being as a common genus* without destroying the very reason one posits it as such: that is, the possibility of *being* for specific differences. It can conceive the universality of Being only as a quasi-identity (analogy). On the other hand, it has to relate Being to particular beings, but *it cannot say what constitutes their individuality*; it retains in the particular (the individual) only what conforms to the general (the concept). An equivocal or analogical concept of Being, in other words, can only grasp that which is univocal in beings. A true universal is lacking, no less than a true singular: Being has only a distributive common sense, and the individual has no difference except a general and reflexive one in the concept.[40]

Deleuze's thesis in *Difference and Repetition* is that only univocity can provide us with a truly *collective* sense of Being (and not merely a distributive sense) by giving us a comprehension of the play of *individuating differences* within beings (and not mere generalities in a network of resemblances). But this brings us, precisely, to the fundamental problem of a univocal ontology. If Being is said in *one and the same sense* of everything that is, then what constitutes the difference between beings? There can be no categories (in the Aristotelian–Kantian sense) in a univocal ontology; if we distinguish beings by their substance, or their form, or their generic and specific differences, then we are back in the analogical vision of the world. Yet if we say that Being is univocal, that there is no categorical difference between the senses of the word "Being," then we seem to fall into the thought of infamy: the thought of the inessential, the formless, the non-specific, the non-generic, the non-categorical. Between God and man, plant and animal, there can be no difference of category, no difference of substance, no difference of form. This is why Deleuze insists that univocity is such a difficult concept to *think*: How can we say that there are differences between beings, and none the less that Being is said in one and the same sense of everything that is?

Not surprisingly, it was Spinoza who foresaw the only possible type of solution to this problem. At this point, the only difference conceivable is difference as a *degree of power* (a physics of intensive quantities). The power or intensity of a being is its relation to Being. Why is the idea of difference as a degree of power linked to that of the univocity of Being? Because beings that are distinguished solely by their degree of power realize *one and the same* univocal Being, except for the difference in their degree of power (or its withdrawal). Difference as a degree of power is *a non-*

categorical difference in that it preserves the univocal sense of Being.[41] Beings are no longer distinguished by a qualitative essence (analogy of Being) but by a quantifiable degree of power (univocity of Being). We no longer ask what the essence of a thing is (for instance, man as a "rational animal" or "featherless biped"), but rather what its affective capacities are, since the power of an existing individual is expressed in a certain capacity for being affected.

This move already marks an important practical conversion in philosophy, which Deleuze describes as a shift away from a *morality* to an *ethics*. For Deleuze, morality is fundamentally linked to the notion of essence and the analogical vision of the world. In Aristotle, man's essence is to be a rational animal. If he none the less acts in an irrational manner, it is because there are *accidents* that turn him away from his essential nature; man's essence is a *potentiality* that is not necessarily realized. Morality can therefore be defined as the effort to rejoin man's essence, to realize one's essence. In an ethics, by contrast, beings are related to Being, not at the level of essence, but at the level of existence. Ethics defines a man not by what he *is* in principle (his essence), but by what he *can do*, what he is *capable* of (his power). Since power is *always* effectuated—it is never a potentiality, but always in act—the question is no longer, What *must* you do in order to realize your essence? but rather, What are you *capable* of doing by virtue of your power? As Eric Alliez has put it, if analogy is theological (onto-theology), univocity is ethical (onto-ethology).[42] The political problem, in turn, concerns the effectuation of this power: What conditions allow one's power to be effectuated in the best fashion? Conversely, under what conditions can one actually desire to be separated from one's power? One can see clearly how these ontological questions form the basis for the ethico-political philosophy (and corresponding "existential" notions) developed in *Capitalism and Schizophrenia*.

We might note here that Deleuze and Emmanuel Levinas, with their respective philosophies of immanence and transcendence, represent two very different approaches to the question of ethics in contemporary thought. If the *other* is the fundamental problem of transcendence, *difference* is the fundamental problem of immanence. For Levinas, ethics *precedes* ontology because it introduces an element of transcendence (the wholly other) that is necessarily "otherwise" than Being. For Deleuze (and Spinoza), ethics *is* ontology because beings are immediately related to Being at the level of their existence (intensity or degree of power as the element of immanence). This is why Spinoza entitles his pure ontology an *Ethics* rather than an *Ontology*; his speculative propositions concerning univocity can only be judged practically at the level of the ethics they envelop or imply.

But these ethical concerns are derived directly from the univocal ontology developed in *Difference and Repetition*, and the solution it offers to the problem of the ontological difference. Being must be able to account not only for the external difference between beings, but also for the fact that beings themselves are multiplicities marked by an "internal difference"; and the ontological difference must refer not only to the non-categorical difference between Being and beings, but also to the internal difference of Being *from itself*. The ontological concepts developed in *Difference and Repetition* are all non-categorical notions that preserve the univocity of Being by comprehending this co-articulation of Being and difference within themselves: "difference in intensity, disparity in the phantasm, dissemblance in the form of time, the differential in thought: opposition, resemblance, identity, and even analogy are only effects produced by these presentations of difference."[43] This is the meaning of Deleuze's formula "monism = pluralism" (univocity of Being = equivocity of difference) (TP 20). It is true that if analogy denies Being the status of the common genus because (specific) differences "are," then conversely, univocal Being is indeed common only in so far as (individuating) differences "are not" and must not be. This is the second fundamental problem of a univocal ontology that Deleuze confronts and takes to its limit: the (non-)Being of difference is, in fact, the reality of the *virtual* or the *problematic*. Univocal being, in other words, always presents itself in a "problematic" form. If one consigns "difference" to the actual or the empirical, to individuals constituted in experience, one inevitably falls back into an analogical or equivocal ontology, and subordinates difference to the rights of identity and negation. A reading of Deleuze's ontology would have to focus on these two fundamental problems.

But why, finally, in the fourth and final act, does univocity disappear from Deleuze's writings? The reason, in the end, is not difficult to discern. Other concepts, like that of the "simulacrum," meet similar fates.[44] Deleuze used Klossowski's concept of the "simulacrum" to think through the problematic of anti-Platonism; outside that context, the concept no longer held any "interest" (since beings no longer "simulate" anything), and was replaced, as it were, by the concept of the *agence-ment* or "assemblage." The same is true for univocity. Univocity was an arrow first shot by Duns Scotus, and which Deleuze then picked up and aimed elsewhere, using it to interpret Spinoza's philosophy, critique orthodox theology, and think through Heidegger's problem of ontological difference through a confrontation with Aristotle. Once its (already considerable) work was done, Deleuze's moved on. In *A Thousand Plateaus*, for instance, the logic of *est* ("is") gives way to a conjunctive logic of *et* ("and"), which "overthrows ontology," and places relations "outside everything which could be determined as Being, One, or Whole"[45] This is not an appeal to transcendence, but rather a deepening of immanence, requiring, in later works, the invention of new concepts such as the "plane of immanence," the "outside," the "interstice," and so on.[46] What the drama of univocity exemplifies is the *dynamic* nature of Deleuze's thought, which must be defined and comprehended in terms of its *movement*.

Leibniz

Deleuze on Leibniz: Difference, Continuity, and the Calculus

Deleuze once characterized himself as a "classical" philosopher, a statement that was no doubt meant to signal his indebtedness to (and affinities with) the great philosophers of the classic period, notably Spinoza and Leibniz.[1] Spinoza provided Deleuze with a model for a purely immanent ontology, while Leibniz offered him a way of thinking through the problems of individuation and the theory of Ideas.[2] In both cases, however, Deleuze would take up and modify Spinoza's and Leibniz's thought in his own manner, such that it is impossible to say that Deleuze is a "Spinozist" or a "Leibnizian" without carefully delineating the use to which he puts each of these thinkers. Although Deleuze published a book-length study of Leibniz late in his career, entitled *The Fold: Leibniz and the Baroque* (1988), his more profound (and perhaps more important) engagement with Leibniz had already occurred in *Difference and Repetition* (1968) and *Logic of Sense* (1969).[3] In these earlier works, Deleuze approached Leibniz from a resolutely post-Kantian point of view, returning to Leibniz in his attempt to redefine the nature of the transcendental field. Following Salomon Maimon, Deleuze had argued that, in order for Kant's critical philosophy to achieve its own aims, a viewpoint of *internal genesis* needed to be substituted for Kant's principle of *external conditioning*.[4] "Doing this means returning to Leibniz," Deleuze would later explain, "but on bases other than Leibniz's. All the elements to create a genesis, as demanded by the post-Kantians, are virtually present in Leibniz" (20 May 1980). One of these other "bases" was the formulation of a pure principle of *difference*, which alone would be capable of freeing thought from "representation" (whether finite or infinite), and its concomitant subordination to the principle of identity. As Maimon had shown, whereas identity is the condition of possibility of thought in general, it is difference that constitutes the genetic condition of *real* thought. In what follows, then, I would like to show how Deleuze uses Leibniz to "deduce" the necessity of a principle of difference from the principle of identity, by making his way through the four fundamental principles of Leibniz's philosophy: identity, sufficient reason, indiscernibility, and the law of continuity. What emerges from Deleuze's reading of Leibniz is, as he himself puts it, "a Leibnizian transcendental philosophy that bears on the event rather than the phenomenon, and replaces the Kantian conditioning" (FLB 163).

THE PRINCIPLE OF IDENTITY

We begin with the simplest statement of the principle of identity. The classical formula of the identity principle is "A is A": "blue is blue," "a triangle is a triangle," "God is God." But such formulae, says Leibniz, "seem to do nothing but repeat the same thing without telling us anything."[5] They are certain but empty; they do not force us to think. A more popular formulation of the principle of identity would be: "A thing is what it is." This formula goes further than the formula "A is A" because it shows us the ontological region governed by the principle of identity: identity consists in manifesting the identity between the thing and what the thing *is*, what classical philosophy termed the "essence" of a thing. In Leibniz, every principle is a *ratio*, a "reason," and the principle of identity can be said to be the *ratio* or rule of essences, the *ratio essendi*. It corresponds to the question, "Why is there something rather than nothing?" If there were no identity (an identity conceived as the identity of the thing and what the thing *is*), then there would be nothing. But Leibniz also provides us with a more technical formulation of the principle of identity, derived from logic: "every analytic proposition is true." What is an analytic proposition? It is a proposition in which the subject and the predicate are identical. "A is A" is an analytical proposition: the predicate A is contained in the subject A, and therefore "A is A" is true. But to complete the detail of Leibniz's formula, we would have to distinguish between two types of identical propositions: an analytic proposition is true either by reciprocity or by inclusion. An example of a proposition of *reciprocity* is "a triangle has three angles." This is an identical proposition because the predicate ("three angles") is the same as the subject ("triangle") and reciprocates with the subject. The second case, a proposition of *inclusion*, is slightly more complex. In the proposition "a triangle has three sides" there is no identity between the subject and the predicate, yet there is a supposed logical necessity; one cannot conceptualize a single figure having three angles without this figure also having three sides. There is no reciprocity here, but there is a demonstrable inclusion or inherence of the predicate in the subject. One could say that analytic propositions of reciprocity are objects of *intuition*, whereas analytic propositions of inclusion are the objects of a *demonstration*. What Leibniz calls *analysis* is the operation that discovers a predicate in a notion taken as a subject. If I show that a given predicate is contained in a notion, then I have done an analysis. All this is basic logic; up to this point, the Leibniz's greatness as a thinker has not yet appeared.

THE PRINCIPLE OF SUFFICIENT REASON

Leibniz's originality, Deleuze suggests, first emerges with his second great principle, the principle of sufficient reason, which no longer refers to the domain of essences but the domain of existences: that is, the domain of things that actually exist. The corresponding *ratio* is no longer the *ratio essendi* but the *ratio existendi*, the reason for existing. The corresponding question is no longer, "Why something rather than nothing?" but rather, "Why this rather than that?" The popular expression of this principle would be: "everything has a reason." This is the great cry of rationalism, which Leibniz will attempt to push to its limit. Why does Leibniz need this second principle? Because existing things appear to be *outside* the principle of identity. The principle of identity concerns the identity of the thing and what the thing is, even if the thing itself does not exist; I know that unicorns do not exist, but I can still say what a unicorn is. So Leibniz needs a second principle to make us think existing beings. Yet how can a principle as seemingly vague as "everything has a reason" make us think existing beings?

Leibniz explains how in his philosophical formulation of the principle of sufficient reason, which reads: "all predication has a foundation in the nature of things."[6] What this means is that everything that is truly predicated of a thing is necessarily included or contained in the concept of the thing. What is said or predicated of a thing? First of all, its essence, and at this level there is no difference between the principle of identity and the principle of sufficient reason, which takes up and presumes everything acquired with the principle of identity. But what is said or predicated of a thing is not only the essence of the thing, but also the totality of the affections and events that happen to or are related to or belong to the thing. For example: Caesar crossed the Rubicon. Since this is a true proposition, Leibniz will say that the predicate "crossed the Rubicon" must be contained in the concept of Caesar (not in Caesar himself, but in the concept of Caesar). "Everything has a reason" means that everything that happens to something—all its "differences"— must be contained or *included* for all eternity in the individual notion of a thing.

> If we call an "event" what happens to a thing, whether it submits to it or undertakes it, we will say that sufficient reason is what comprehends the event as one of its predicates: the concept of the thing, or its notion. "Predicates or events," says Leibniz.[7]

How does Leibniz arrive at this remarkable claim? He does so, Deleuze suggests, following Couturat, by reconsidering *reciprocity*. The principle of identity gives us a model of truth that is certain and absolute—an analytical proposition is necessarily a true proposition—but it does not make us *think* anything. So Leibniz reverses the formulation of the principle of identity using the principle of reciprocity: *a true proposition is necessarily an analytic proposition.* The principle of sufficient reason is the reciprocal of the principle of identity, and it allows Leibniz to conquer a radically new domain, the domain of existing things.[8] By means of this reversal, the principle of identity forces us to *think* something. The formal formula of the principle of identity ("A is A") is true because the predicate *reciprocates* with the subject, and Leibniz therefore applies this principle of reciprocity to the principle of identity itself. In its first formulation, however, the reciprocal of "A is A" is simply "A is A," and in this sense, the *formal* formulation prevents the reversal of the identity principle. The principle of sufficient reason is produced only through a reversal of the *logical* formulation of the principle of identity, but this latter reversal is clearly of a different order; it does not go without saying. Justifying this reversal is the task Leibniz pursues as a philosopher, and it launches him into an infinite—and perhaps impossible—undertaking. The principle of sufficient reason says not only that the notion of a subject contains everything that happens to the subject—that is, everything that is truly predicated of the subject—but also that we should be able to *demonstrate* that this is the case.

Once Leibniz launches himself into the domain of the concept in this way, however, he cannot stop. At one point in the *Metaphysics*, Aristotle—who exerted a strong influence on Leibniz—proposes an exquisite formula: at a certain point in the analysis of concepts, it is necessary to *stop* (*anankstenai*).[9] This is because, for Aristotle, concepts are *general*, not individual. Classical logic distinguishes between the order of the concept, which refers to a generality, and the order of the individual, which refers to a singularity. By nature, a concept was seen to be something that comprehends a *plurality* of individuals; it went without saying that the individual as such was not comprehensible by concepts. Put differently, philosophers have always considered that *proper names* are not concepts. At a certain point, then, the process of conceptual specification must stop; one reaches the final species (*infima species*), which groups together a plurality of individuals. Leibniz, however, does not heed Aristotle's warning; he does not stop. Instead, he attempts to push the concept to the level of the individual itself; in Leibniz, "Adam" and "Caesar" are concepts, and not simply proper names. The cry of sufficient reason—"Everything *must* have a reason"—is the problem that will propel Leibniz into an almost hallucinatory conceptual creation. "Leibniz pushes the presuppositions of classical philosophy as far as he can, down the paths of genius and delirium" (20 May 1980). It is not much use to raise objections or to argue against Leibniz, says Deleuze; one first has to let oneself go, and follow Leibniz in his production of concepts. What, then, is the delirious chasm into which Leibniz plunges?

If everything I attribute with truth to a subject must be contained in the concept of the subject, then I am forced to include in the notion of the subject not only the thing I attribute to it with truth, but also *the totality of the world*. Why is this the case? By virtue of a principle that is very different from the principle of sufficient reason: namely, the principle of *causality*. The principle of sufficient reason ("everything has a reason") is not the same thing as the principle of causality ("everything has a cause"). "Everything has a cause" means that A is caused by B, B is caused by C, and so on—a series of causes and effects that stretches to infinity. "Everything has a reason," by contrast, means that one has to give a reason for causality itself: namely, that the relation A maintains with B must in some manner be included or comprised in the concept of A.[10] This is how the principle of sufficient reason goes beyond the principle of causality: the principle of causality states the *necessary cause* of a thing but not its *sufficient reason*. Sufficient reason expresses the relation of the thing with its own notion, whereas causality simply expresses the relations of the thing with something else. Sufficient reason can be stated in the following manner: for every thing, there is a concept that gives an account both of the thing and of its relations with other things, including its causes and its effects. Thus, once Leibniz says that the predicate "crossing the Rubicon" is included in the notion of

Caesar, he cannot stop; he is forced to include the totality of the world in Caesar's concept. This is because "crossing the Rubicon" has multiple causes and multiple effects, such as the establishment of the Roman Empire and the death of Jesus; it stretches to infinity backward and forward by the double play of causes and effects. We therefore cannot say that "crossing the Rubicon" is included in the notion of Caesar without saying that the causes and effects of this event are *also* included in the notion of Caesar. This is no longer the concept of inherence or inclusion, but the fantastic Leibnizian concept of *expression*: the notion of the subject expresses the totality of the world. Each of us, in our concept, expresses or contains the entirety of the world. This is the first hallucinatory Leibnizian concept that follows from the principle of sufficient reason.

A second concept follows immediately, since there is a danger lurking here for Leibniz: if each notion of the subject expresses the totality of the world, that could seem to indicate that there is only a single subject, and that individuals are mere appearances of this universal subject (a single substance à la Spinoza, or absolute Spirit à la Hegel). But Leibniz cannot follow such a path without repudiating himself, since his entire philosophy remains fixed on the individual, and the reconciliation of the concept with the individual. To avoid this danger, Leibniz creates another new concept: each individual notion comprehends or includes the totality of the world, he says, but from a certain *point of view*. This marks the beginning of "perspectivist" philosophy, which would be taken up by later philosophers such as Nietzsche (who none the less understood perspectivism in a very different manner than Leibniz). Point of view, however, is such a common notion that one easily risks trivializing Leibniz's conception of perspectivism. Leibniz does *not* say that everything is "relative" to the viewpoint of the subject; this is what Deleuze calls an "idiotic" or "banal" notion of perspectivism. It would imply that the subject is prior to the point of view, whereas in Leibniz it is precisely the opposite. In Leibniz, the point of view is not constituted by the subject; rather, the subject is constituted by the point of view. Points of view, in other words, are the sufficient reason of subjects. The individual notion is the point of view through which the individual expresses the totality of the world.

But here again, Leibniz cannot stop. For what is it, then, that determines this point of view? Each of us may express the totality of the world, Leibniz tells us, but we express most of the world in an obscure and confused manner, as if it were a mere clamor, a background noise, which we perceive in the form of *infinitely small perceptions*. These minute perceptions are like the "differentials" of consciousness (Maimon), which are not given as such to conscious perception (apperception). However, there is a small, reduced, finite portion of the world that I express clearly and distinctly, and this is precisely that portion of the world that affects my *body*. Leibniz in this manner provides a deduction of the necessity of the body as that which occupies the point of view. I do not express clearly and distinctly the crossing of the Rubicon, since that concerns Caesar's body; but there are other things that concern my body—such as my writing of this essay—which I do express clearly. This is how Leibniz defines a point of view: it is the portion or the region of the world expressed clearly by an individual in relation to the totality of the world, which it expresses obscurely in the form of minute perceptions. No two individual substances occupy the same point of view on the world because none has the same clear or distinct zone of expression on the world.

The problem posed by the principle of sufficient reason thus leads Leibniz to create an entire sequence of concepts: expression, point of view, minute perceptions, and so on. "In the majority of great philosophers," writes Deleuze, "the concepts they create are inseparable, and are taken in veritable sequences. If you do not understand the sequence of which a concept is a part, you cannot understand the concept" (26 Nov 1980). But the notion of point of view will lead Leibniz into a final set of problems. For the world, Leibniz continues, has no existence outside the points of view that express it. The world is the "expressed" thing common to all individual substances, but what is expressed (the world) has no existence apart from what expresses it (individuals). In other words, there is no world *in itself*. The difficulty Leibniz faces here is this: each of these individual notions must none the less express the *same* world. Why is this a problem? The principle of identity allows us to determine what is contradictory: that is, what is *impossible*. A square circle is a circle that is not a circle; it contravenes the principle of identity. But at the level of sufficient reason, things are more complicated; Caesar not crossing the Rubicon and Adam not sinning are neither contradictory nor impossible. Caesar could have not crossed the Rubicon, and Adam could have not sinned, whereas a circle cannot be square. The truths governed by the principle of sufficient reason are thus not of the same type as the truths governed by the principle of identity. But how, then, can Leibniz at the same time hold that everything Adam did is contained for all time in his individual concept, and that Adam the non-sinner was none the less possible? Leibniz's famous response to this problem is this: Adam the non-sinner was possible in itself, but it was *incompossible* with the rest of the actualized world. Leibniz here creates an entirely new logical relation of incompossibility, a concept that is unique to Leibniz's philosophy, and which is irreducible to impossibility or contradiction. At the level of existing things, it is not enough to say that a thing is possible in order to exist; it is also necessary to know with what it is compossible. The conclusion Leibniz draws from this notion is perhaps his most famous doctrine, one which was ridiculed by Voltaire in *Candide* and by the eighteenth century in general: among the infinity of incompossible worlds, God makes a calculation and chooses the "Best" of all possible worlds to pass into existence, a world governed by a harmony that is "pre-established" by God. But this rational optimism seems to imply an infinite cruelty, since the best world is not necessarily the world in which suffering is the least.

THE PRINCIPLE OF THE IDENTITY OF INDISCERNIBLES

This sets us on the path of the third principle, the identity of indiscernibles. The principle of sufficient reason says: for every thing, there is a concept that includes everything that will happen to the thing. The identity of indiscernibles says: for every concept, there is one and only one thing. The principle of the identity of indiscernibles is thus the reciprocal of the principle of sufficient reason. Unlike

Leibniz's first act of reciprocity, however, this reciprocation is absolutely necessary. (The move from the principle of identity to the principle of sufficient reason, by contrast, was Leibniz's *coup de force* as a philosopher; he could undertake it only because he created the philosophical means to do so.) Banally, this means that there are no two things that are absolutely identical; no two drops of water are identical, no two leaves of a tree are identical, no two people are identical. But more profoundly, it also means—and this is what interests Deleuze—that in the final analysis *every difference is a conceptual difference*. If you have two things, there must be two concepts; if not, there are not two things. In other words, if you assign a difference to two things, there is necessarily a difference in their concepts. The principle of indiscernibles consists in saying that we have *knowledge* only by means of concepts, and this can be said to correspond to a third reason, a third *ratio: ratio cognoscendi*, or reason as the reason of knowing.

This principle of indiscernibles has two important consequences. First, as we have seen, Leibniz is the first philosopher to say that concepts are proper names: that is, that concepts are *individual* notions. In classical logic concepts are *generalities* which, by their very nature, cannot comprehend the singularity of the individual. But can we not say that the concept "human," for instance, is a generality that applies to all individual humans, including both Caesar and Adam? Of course you can say that, Leibniz retorts, but only if you have *blocked* the analysis of the concept at a certain point, at a finite moment. But if you push the analysis, if you push the analysis of the concept to infinity, there will be a point where the concepts of Caesar and Adam are no longer the same. According to Leibniz, this is why a mother sheep can recognize its little lamb: it knows its concept, which is individual. This is also why Leibniz cannot have recourse to a universal mind, for he remains fixed on the individual as such. This is Leibniz's great originality, the formula of his perpetual refrain: substance is individual.

Second, in positing the principle of indiscernibles (every difference is conceptual), Leibniz is asking us to accept an enormous consequence. For there are other types of difference, apart from conceptual difference, that might allow us to distinguish between individual things. For example, numerical difference: I can fix the concept of water and then distinguish the drops numerically, disregarding their individuality—one drop, two drops, three drops. A second type of difference: spatio-temporal difference. I have the concept of water, but I can distinguish between different drops by their spatio-temporal location (not this drop here but that drop over there). A third type: differences of extension and movement. I can retain the concept of water and distinguish between drops by their extension and figure (shape and size), or by their movement (fast or slow). These are all non-conceptual differences because they allow us to distinguish between two things that none the less have the same concept. Once again, however, Leibniz plunges on; he calmly tells us, no, these differences are pure appearances, provisional means of expressing a difference of another nature, and this difference is always conceptual. If there are two drops of water, they do not have the same concept. Non-conceptual differences only serve to translate, in an imperfect manner, a deeper difference that is always conceptual.

It is here that we reach the crux of the matter in Deleuze's reading of Leibniz. Although no one went further than Leibniz in the exploration of sufficient reason, Leibniz none the less subordinated sufficient reason to the requirements of "representation." By reducing all differences to conceptual differences, Leibniz defined sufficient reason by the ability of differences to be represented or mediated in a *concept*.

> According to the principle of sufficient reason, there is always one concept per particular thing. According to the reciprocal principle of the identity of indiscernibles, there is one and only one thing per concept. Together, these principles expound a theory of difference as conceptual difference, or develop the account of representation as mediation.[11]

In Aristotle, what "blocks" the specification of the concept beyond the smallest species is the individual itself. The concept provides us with a *form* for which the individual constitutes the *matter*; in Kant, it will be the forms of space and time that block the concept. Leibniz is able to reconcile the concept and the individual only because he gives the identity of the concept an *infinite* comprehension; every individual substance, or monad, envelops the infinity of predicates that constitutes the state of the world. Where the extension of the concept = 1, the comprehension of the concept = ∞. It is one and the same thing to say that the concept goes to infinity (sufficient reason) and that the concept is individual (indiscernibility). In pushing the concept to the level of the individual, however, Leibniz simply rendered representation (or the concept) infinite, while still maintaining the subordination of difference to the principle of identity in the concept.

For Deleuze, this subordination of difference to identity is illegitimate and ungrounded. We have seen that, in Leibniz, the principle of sufficient reason is the reciprocal of the principle of identity, and that the principle of indiscernibles is in turn the reciprocal of the principle of sufficient reason. But would not the reciprocal of the reciprocal simply lead us back to the principle of identity (6 May 1980)? The fact that it does *not*, even in Leibniz, points to the irreducibility of the principle of difference to the principle of identity. Deleuze's thesis is that, behind or beneath the functioning of the identical concept, there lies the movement of difference and multiplicity within an *Idea*. "What blocks the concept," writes Deleuze in *Difference and Repetition*, "is always the excess of the Idea, which constitutes the superior positivity that arrests the concept or overturns the requirements of representation" (DR 289). *Difference and Repetition* in its entirety can be read as a search for the roots of sufficient reason, which is formulated in a theory of non-representational Ideas. But "the immediate, defined as the 'sub-representative,' is not attained by multiplying representations and points of view. On the contrary, each composing representation must be distorted, diverted, and torn from its centre"—in order to reveal, not the immediacy of the given, but rather the differential mechanisms of the Idea that themselves function as the genetic conditions of the given.[12] Deleuze understands the term "Idea" largely in its Kantian sense, except that Kantian Ideas are totalizing, unifying and transcendent, whereas Deleuzian Ideas are differential, genetic, and immanent. It is on the basis of his post-Kantian return to Leibniz that Deleuze will develop his revised theory of Ideas in *Difference and Repetition*.

THE LAW OF CONTINUITY

These considerations bring us to the law of continuity. What is the difference between truths of essence (principle of identity) and truths of existence (principles of sufficient reason and indiscernibility)? With truths of essence, says Leibniz, the analysis is *finite*, such that inclusion of the predicate in the subject can be demonstrated by a finite series of determinate operations (such that one can say, "Q.E.D.").[13] The analysis of truths of existence, by contrast, is necessarily *infinite*: the domain of existences is the domain of *infinite analysis*. Why is this the case? Because if the predicate "sinner" is contained in the concept of Adam, and if we then follow the causes back and track down the effects, the entire world must be contained in the notion of Adam. When I perform the analysis, I pass from Adam the sinner to Eve the temptress, and from Eve the temptress to the evil serpent, and from the evil serpent to the forbidden fruit, and so on. Moving forward, I show that there is a direct connection between Adam's sin and the Incarnation and Redemption by Christ. There are *series* that are going to begin to fit into each other across the differences of time and space. (This is the aim of Leibniz's *Theodicy*: to justify God's choice of *this* world, with all its interlocking series.) Such an analysis is *infinite* because it has to pass through the entire series of elements that constitute the world, which is actually infinite; and it is an *analysis* because it demonstrates the inclusion of the predicate "sinner" in the individual notion of Adam. "In the domain of existences, we cannot stop ourselves, because the series are prolongable and must be prolonged, because the inclusion is not localizable" (FLB 51). This is the Leibnizian move that matters to Deleuze: at the level of truths of existence, an infinite analysis that demonstrates the inclusion of the predicate (sinner) in the subject (Adam) does *not* proceed by the demonstration of an identity. What matters at the level of truths of existence is not the *identity* of the predicate and the subject, but rather, that one passes from one predicate to another, from the second to a third, from the third to a fourth, and so on. Put succinctly: *if truths of essence are governed by identity, truths of existence are governed by continuity.* What is a world? A world is defined by its continuity. What separates two incompossible worlds? The fact that there is a discontinuity between the two worlds. What defines the best of all possible worlds, the world that God will cause to pass into existence? The fact that it realizes *the maximum of continuity for a maximum of difference*.

Now the notion of *infinite analysis* is absolutely original with Leibniz; he invented it. It seems to go without saying, however, that we, as finite beings, are incapable of undertaking an infinite analysis. In order to situate ourselves in the domain of truths of existence, we have to wait for experience; we know through experience that Caesar crossed the Rubicon or that Adam sinned. An infinite analysis might be possible for God, whose divine understanding is without limits, but this is hardly a satisfactory response. While we may be happy for God, we might also ask ourselves why Leibniz went to such trouble to present this whole story about analytic truths and infinite analysis if it were only to say that such an analysis is inaccessible to us as finite beings. It is here, however, that we begin to approach the originality of Deleuze's interpretation of Leibniz. For Leibniz, says Deleuze, indeed attempted to provide us finite humans with an artifice that is capable of undertaking a well-founded approximation of what happens in God's understanding, and this artifice is precisely the technique of the infinitesimal calculus or differential analysis. As finite beings, we can none the less undertake an infinite analysis, thanks to the symbolism of the *calculus*. The calculus brings us into a complex domain, having to do not only with the relation of Leibniz to Newton, but also with the debates on the mathematical foundations of the calculus, which were not resolved until the development of the limit-concept by Cauchy and Weierstrass in the late nineteenth and early twentieth centuries.[14] I would here like to focus on two aspects of Leibniz's work on the metaphysics of the calculus that come to the fore in Deleuze's own reading of Leibniz: the differential relation and the theory of singularities. These are two theories that allow us to think the presence of the infinite within the finite.

THE DIFFERENTIAL RELATION

Let us turn first to the differential relation. What is at stake in an infinite analysis is not so much the fact that there is an actually existing set of infinite elements in the world. The problem lies elsewhere. For if there are two elements—for example, Adam the sinner and Eve the temptress—then there is still a *difference* between these two elements. What, then, does it mean to say that there is a continuity between the seduction of Eve and Adam's sin (and not simply an identity)? It means that the relation between the two elements is an infinitely small relation, or rather, that *the difference between the two is a difference that tends to disappear*. This is the definition of the continuum: continuity is defined as the act of a difference in so far as the difference tends to disappear—continuity is a *disappearing* or *vanishing difference*. Between sinner and Adam I will never be able to demonstrate a logical identity, but I will be able to demonstrate (and here the word demonstration obviously changes meaning) a continuity—that is, one or more vanishing differences.

What is a vanishing difference? In 1701, Leibniz wrote a three-page text entitled "Justification of the Infinitesimal Calculus by That of Ordinary Algebra," in which he tries to explain that, in a certain manner, the differential calculus was already functioning before it was discovered, even at the level of the most ordinary algebra.[15] Leibniz presents us with a simple geometrical figure (Figure 3.1). Two right triangles—ZEF and ZHI—meet at their apex, point Z. Since the two triangles ZEF and ZHI are similar, it follows that the ratio y/x is equal to $(Y - y)/X$. Now if the straight line EI increasingly approaches point F, always preserving the same angle at the variable point Z, the length of the straight lines x and y will obviously diminish steadily, yet the ratio of x to y will remain constant. What happens when the straight line EI passes through F itself? It is obvious that the points Z and E will fall directly on F, and that the straight lines x and y will vanish; they will become equal to zero. And yet, even though x and y are equal to zero, they still maintain an *algebraic* relation to each other, which is expressed in the relation of X to Y. In other

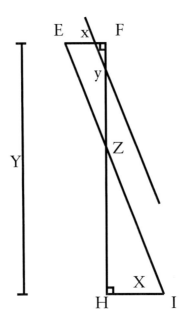

Figure 3.1

words, when the line EI passes through F, it is not the case that the triangle ZEF has "disappeared" in the common sense of that word. The triangle ZEF is still "there," but it is only there "virtually," since the relation x/y continues to exist even when the terms have vanished. Rather than saying the triangle ZEF has disappeared, Leibniz says, we should rather say that it has become unassignable even though it is perfectly determined, since in this case, although $x = 0$ and $y = 0$, the relation x/y is not equal to zero, since it is a perfectly determinable relation equal to X/Y. *Unassignable, yet perfectly determined*—this is what the term "vanishing difference" means; it is when the relation continues even when the terms of the relation have disappeared. The relation x/y continues when Z and E have disappeared. This is why the differential relation is such a great mathematical discovery; the miracle is that the differential relation dx/dy is not equal to zero, but rather has a perfectly expressible *finite* quantity, which is the differential derived from the relation of X to Y.

The differential relation is thus not only a relation that is *external* to its terms, but a relation that in a certain sense *constitutes* its terms. It provides Deleuze with a mathematical model for thinking "difference-in-itself" (the title of the second chapter of *Difference and Repetition*). The differential relation signifies nothing concrete in relation to what it is derived from—that is, in relation to x and y—but it signifies something else concrete—namely, a z—which is something *new*, and this is how it assures the passage to limits. Thus, to consider several famous examples, Leibniz can comprehend rest as an infinitely small movement, coincidence as an infinitely small distance, equality as the limit of inequalities, the circle as the limit of a polygon the sides of which increase to infinity. The "reason" of the law of continuity is thus the *ratio fiendi*, the reason of becoming. Things *become* through continuity: movement becomes rest; the polygon, by multiplying its sides, becomes a circle. This is the source of the popular formulation of the law of continuity in Leibniz: nature never makes leaps (there is no discontinuity in nature). What, then, is an infinite analysis? An infinite analysis fills the following condition: there is an infinite analysis, and a material for infinite analysis, when I find myself before a domain that is no longer directly ruled by identity, but a domain that is ruled by continuity and vanishing differences.

To understand what this theory of the differential relation means in concrete terms, consider the corresponding theory of perception that Leibniz develops in relation to it.[16] Leibniz had observed that we often perceive things of which we are not consciously aware. We recall a familiar scene and become aware of a detail we did not notice at the time; the background noise of a dripping faucet suddenly enters our consciousness at night. Leibniz therefore drew a distinction between conscious perceptions ("apperceptions," or molar perceptions) and unconscious perceptions ("minute" or molecular perceptions), and argued that our conscious perceptions must be related, not simply to recognizable objects in space and time, but rather to the minute and unconscious perceptions of which they are composed. I apprehend the noise of the sea or the murmur of a group of people, for instance, but not the sound of each wave or the voice of each person that compose them. These unconscious minute perceptions are related to conscious "molar" perceptions, not as parts to a whole, but as what is ordinary to what is noticeable or remarkable: a conscious perception is produced when at least two of these minute and "virtual" perceptions enter into a *differential relation* that determines a singularity: that is, a conscious perception. Consider the noise of the sea: at least two waves must be minutely perceived as nascent and "virtual" in order to enter into a differential relation capable of determining a third, which excels over the others and becomes conscious. Or consider the color green: yellow and blue can be perceived, but if the difference between them vanishes by approaching zero, then they enter into a differential relation (db/dy = G) that determines the color green; in turn, yellow or blue, each on its own account, may be determined by the differential relation of two colors we cannot detect (dy/dx = Y). The calculus thus functions in Leibniz as the psychic mechanism of perception, a kind of automatism that determines my finite zone of clarity on the world, my point of view. Every conscious perception constitutes a threshold, and the minute or virtual perceptions (infinitely small perceptions) constitute the obscure dust of the world, its background noise. They are not "parts" of conscious perception, but rather the "ideal genetic elements" of perception, or what Salomon Maimon called the "differentials of consciousness." The virtual multiplicity of genetic elements, and the system of connections or differential relations that are established between them, is what Deleuze terms the "Idea" of sensibility. It is the differential relations between these infinitely small perceptions that draw them into clarity, that "actualize" a clear perception (such as green) out of certain obscure, evanescent perceptions (such as yellow and blue). "The Idea of the world or the Idea of the sea are *systems of differential equations*, of which each monad only actualizes a partial solution."[17]

In Leibniz, then, the differential calculus refers to a domain that is both mathematical and psychological, a psycho-mathematical domain; there are differentials of consciousness just as there are differentials of a curve. Several important consequences follow from this. Space and time here cease to be pure *a priori* givens, as in Kant, but are determined *genetically* by the ensemble or nexus of these differential relations in the subject. Similarly, objects themselves cease to be empirical givens and become the product of these relations in conscious perception. Moreover, Descartes's principle of "clear and distinct" ideas is broken down into two irreducible values, which can never be reunited to constitute a "natural light": conscious perceptions are necessarily clear but confused (not distinct), while unconscious perceptions (Ideas) are distinct but necessarily obscure (not clear).[18] Indeed, Leibniz can be said to have developed one of the first theories of the unconscious, a theory that is very different from the one developed by Freud. The difference is that Freud conceived of the unconscious in a *conflictual* or *oppositional* relationship to consciousness, and not a *differential* relationship. In this sense, Freud was dependent on Kant, Hegel, and their successors, who explicitly oriented the unconscious in the direction of a conflict of will, and no longer a differential of perception. The theory of the unconscious proposed by Deleuze and Guattari in *Anti-Oedipus* is a differential and genetic unconscious, and thus thoroughly inspired by Leibniz.[19]

THE THEORY OF SINGULARITIES

There is a final problem that Deleuze points to in Leibniz's thought. On the surface, there would appear to be a contradiction between the principle of indiscernibles and the law of continuity. On the one hand, the principle of indiscernibles tells us that every difference is conceptual, that no two things have the same concept; to every thing there correspond determinate differences that are assignable in its concept. On the other hand, the principle of continuity tells us that things proceed via vanishing differences, infinitely small differences: that is, unassignable differences. Thus, Leibniz seems to be saying, at one and the same time, that every thing proceeds by an unassignable difference, and that every difference is assignable and must be assigned in the concept. The question is: Is it possible to reconcile the principle of indiscernibles with the law of continuity?

Deleuze's thesis is that the solution to this problem has to be posed in terms of the theory of *singularities*, which is an extension of the theory of differential equations. In logic, the notion of the "singular" has long been understood in relation to the "universal." In mathematics, however, the singular is related to a very different set of notions: the singular is distinguished from or opposed to the regular; the singular is what escapes the regularity of the rule. More importantly, mathematics distinguishes between singular points that are remarkable and those that are ordinary. Geometrical figures, for instance, can be classified by the types of singular points that determine them. A square has four singular points, its four corners, and an infinity of ordinary points that compose each side of the square (the calculus of *extrema*). Simple curves, such as the arc of circle, are determined by a single singularity, which is either a maximum or a minimum, or both at once (the calculus of *maxima* and *minima*).[20] The differential calculus deals with the more difficult case of complex curves. The singularities of a complex curve are the points in the neighborhood of which the differential relation changes sign (focal points, saddle points, knots, etc.); the curve increases, the curve decreases. These points of increase or decrease are the singular points of the curve; the ordinary points are what constitute the series between the two singularities. The theory of singularities provides Deleuze with his final, more technical definition of the law of continuity: the continuum is the prolongation of a singularity over an ordinary series of points until it reaches the neighborhood of the following singularity, at which point the differential relation changes sign, and either diverges from or converges with the next singularity. The continuum is thus inseparable from a theory or an activity of prolongation: there is a *composition* of the continuum because the continuum is a product.

In this way, the theory of singularities provides Deleuze with a model of individuation or determination: one can say of any determination in general (any "thing") that it is *a combination of the singular and the ordinary*: that is, it is a "multiplicity" constituted by its singular and ordinary points. Just as mathematical curves are determined by their points of inflection (extrema, minima and maxima, etc.), so physical states of affairs can be said to be determined by singularities that mark a change of phase (boiling points, points of condensation, fusion, coagulation, crystallization) and a person's psychology by their "sensitive" points (points where a person "breaks down" in anger or tears; states of joy, sickness and health, fatigue and vitality, hope and anxiety). But such singularities, Deleuze insists, can none the less be considered *apart from* their actualization in a physical state of affairs or a psychological person (see LS 52). Deleuze here reaches a domain that is distinct from, and logically prior to, the three domains that Kant would later denounce as transcendental illusions or Ideas: the Self, the World, and God. Each of these Ideas has a determinate place in Leibniz's philosophy: God is the Being who, faced with the infinity of possible worlds, chose to actualize this World, a world that exists only in its individual monads or Selves, which express the world from their own point of view. But what this Leibnizian schema presupposes, Deleuze argues, is the determination of a "transcendental field" that is prior to God, World, and Self, a field populated by singularities that are a-theological, a-cosmic, and pre-individual. It implies a transcendental logic of singularities that is irreducible to the formal logic of predication. Here, for example, are three singularities of the individual "Adam," expressed in an infinitive form: "to be the first man," "to live in a garden of pleasure," "to have a woman come out of one's rib." And then a fourth singularity: "to sin." We can prolong each of these four singular points over a series of ordinary points such that they all have common values in both directions; a continuity is established between them. But then add a fifth singularity: "to resist the temptation." The lines of prolongation between this fifth singularity and the first three are no longer convergent: that is, they do not pass through common values; there is a bifurcation in the series at this singularity, and a *discontinuity* is introduced. Adam the non-sinner is thus incompossible with this world, because it implies a singularity that *diverges* with this world.

The theory of singularities plays a double role in Deleuze's work on Leibniz. On the one hand, it allows Deleuze to solve the riddle posed by the relation between indiscernibility and continuity within Leibniz's own philosophy. The world "in itself" is indeed governed by the law of continuity, since continuity is nothing other than the composition of singularities in so far as they are prolonged over the series of ordinaries that depend on them. But the world does not exist "in itself"; it exists only in the individuals that express it. And the real definition of the individual is: *the accumulation or coincidence of a certain number of pre-individual singularities* that are extracted from the curve of the world, each of them being discontinuous and unique, and hence governed by the principle of indiscernibles. Individuation, in other words, "does not move from a genus to smaller and smaller species, in accordance with a rule of differenciation; it goes from singularity to singularity, in accordance with the rule of convergence or prolongation that links the individual to such and such a world" (FLB 64). On the other hand, Deleuze is not content simply to provide a reading of Leibniz. "These impersonal and pre-individual nomadic singularities," Deleuze writes, speaking in his own name, "are what constitute the *real* transcendental field" (LS 109). *Difference and Repetition* and *Logic of Sense* are Deleuze's attempt to define the nature of this transcendental field, freed from the limitations of Leibniz's theological presuppositions, and using his own conceptual vocabulary (multiplicity, singularity, virtuality, problematic, event, and so on). In Deleuze, the Ideas of God, World, and Self take on completely different demeanors than they do in Leibniz. *God* is no longer a Being who chooses the richest compossible world, but has now become a pure Process that makes *all* virtualities pass into existence, forming an infinite web of divergent and convergent series. The *World* is no longer a continuous curve defined by its pre-established harmony, but has become a chaotic universe in which divergent series trace endlessly bifurcating paths, giving rise to violent discords. And the *Self*, rather than being closed on the compossible world it expresses from within, is now torn open by the divergent series and incompossible ensembles that continually pull it outside itself (the monadic subject, as Deleuze puts it, becomes the nomadic subject).[21]

It is at this point that Deleuze's reading of Leibniz would end, and a reading of Deleuze's own philosophy would have to begin. Our aim here has been simply to follow Deleuze's deduction of a principle of difference, within Leibniz's own thought, from the simplest formulation of the principle of identity (A is A). An elaboration of Deleuze's own thought would have to move in the opposite direction, as it were, showing how Deleuze produces his own deduction of concepts starting from the principle of difference: the *differential relation* and its determinable elements, the resulting *singularities* that are extended in series (with their connective, convergent, and divergent syntheses), which thereby constitute a *multiplicity*, whose modal status is purely *virtual* (as opposed to constituting a set of "possibilities," as in Leibniz), and so on. It would not be an exaggeration to say that almost all of Deleuze's fundamental metaphysical concepts (difference, singularity, multiplicity, virtuality) are derived from this Leibnizian matrix. Classical reason, says Deleuze, collapsed under the blow of divergences, discordances, and incompossibilities, and Leibniz's philosophy was one of the last attempts to reconstitute a classical reason.

It did so by *multiplying its principles*, relegating divergences to so many possible worlds, making incompossibilities so many frontiers between worlds, and resolving the discords that appear in this world into the melodic lines of the pre-established harmony. But Leibniz's Baroque reconstitution could only be temporary. With the collapse of classical reason, the task of philosophy would be to think without principles, to start neither with the identity of God, nor the Self, nor the World, but rather a transcendental field of differences and singularities that conditions the construction of empirical selves and the actual world. This is the task that Deleuze adopts as his own: "We seek to determine an impersonal and pre-individual transcendental field that does not resemble the corresponding empirical fields" (LS 102). It is a thoroughly contemporary project, but one that allows Deleuze to reach back into the history of philosophy and make *use* of Leibniz's philosophy and Leibniz's concepts in the pursuit of his own philosophical aims.[22]

Hegel

Deleuze, Hegel, and the Post-Kantian Tradition

Deleuze has often been characterized as an "anti-dialectical" and hence "anti-Hegelian" thinker. Evidence for these characterizations is not difficult to amass. In his well-known "Letter to Michel Cressole" (reprinted in *Negotiations* as "Letter to a Harsh Critic"), Deleuze, while discussing his post-war student days in the 1940s and 1950s, says explicitly that, at the time, "what I detested most was Hegelianism and the dialectic" (N 6). *Nietzsche and Philosophy*, which Deleuze published in 1962, is an avowedly anti-Hegelian tract; its final chapter bears the ominous title, "Against the Dialectic" (NP 147–94). Even as late as 1968, Deleuze writes that the themes of his magnum opus, *Difference and Repetition*, were in part attributable, as he states in its preface, "to a generalized anti-Hegelianism" (DR ix). This theme is echoed by Vincent Descombes, in his influential book *Modern French Philosophy*, who characterizes the entire generation of philosophers to which Deleuze belongs—which includes Jacques Derrida, Michel Foucault, Jean-François Lyotard, and Michel Serres—by their reaction against Hegel, and in particular against Alexandre Kojève's reading of Hegel.[1] Foucault himself noted in his inaugural lecture at the Collège de France: "Whether through logic or epistemology, whether through Marx or Nietzsche, our entire epoch struggles to disengage itself from Hegel."[2]

These characterizations have been repeated so often in the secondary literature that they have assumed an almost canonical status. They are the lens through which Deleuze's thought is inevitably read and interpreted, to the point where they have become clichés (in Deleuze's sense of this term) that prejudge the nature of his thought and pre-program its interpretation and reception. Such characterizations, however, are at best partial and at worst inaccurate. Deleuze is not an anti-dialectical thinker as such; one of the explicit aims of *Difference and Repetition* is to propose a new conception of dialectics, based on a principle of difference (and affirmation) rather than a model of contradiction (and negation).[3] In this sense, Deleuze's early anti-Hegelianism is primarily polemical, and must be understood in the context of the revised theory of Ideas proposed in *Difference and Repetition*. In what follows, I would like to defend these claims, not by analyzing Deleuze's reading of Hegel as such, but rather by analyzing the context in which that reading should be understood. That context not only includes Deleuze's relation to the history of philosophy in general, but also and more particularly his relation to the post-Kantian tradition to which Hegel belongs. In his early work, when his anti-Hegelian polemics were strongest, Deleuze undertook a revisionary interpretation of the entire post-Kantian tradition—an interpretation in which the work of Salomon Maimon played a pivotal role. Deleuze's explicit critiques of Hegel, and his renewed concept of dialectics, should be understood in terms of the broader project Deleuze was pursuing in his work prior to the writing of *Difference and Repetition*.

DELEUZE AND THE HISTORY OF PHILOSOPHY

Deleuze's early polemical reaction against Hegel must be contextualized, both sociologically and personally, in terms of the academic institutional milieu in which Deleuze was trained as a philosopher. (This French milieu has been analyzed by Pierre Bourdieu in works such as *Homo Academicus* and *The State Nobility*).[4] When Deleuze was at the Sorbonne, doing philosophy meant doing the history of philosophy. In order to pass the *agrégation* examination in philosophy, which allowed one to teach in the French educational system, students were required to do close readings of classic texts in the history of philosophy. If they wanted to do "creative" work in this context, philosophy students necessarily had to do so in the context of interpretive readings of this type. François Châtelet, a fellow student at the Sorbonne, and later a colleague at Vincennes, recounts a story that illustrates the manner in which Deleuze, as a student, was able to negotiate the tension between the university's requirements and his own interpretive invention:

> I preserve the memory of a reading by Gilles Deleuze, who had to treat I don't know what classic theme of Nicholas Malebranche's doctrine before one of our most profound and most meticulous historians of philosophy, and had constructed his demonstration, solid and supported with peremptory references, around the sole principle of the irreducibility of Adam's rib. At the expression of this adopted principle, the master turned pale, and obviously had to keep himself from intervening. As the exposition unfolded, the indignation was changed into incredulity, and then, by the end, into admiring surprise. And he justly concluded by making us all return the next week with our own analysis of the same theme.[5]

It is not by chance, therefore, that the works of Deleuze and Jacques Derrida are frequently indexed on readings in the history of philosophy. (Both thinkers persistently return to the history of philosophy, even after "experiments" such as Derrida's *The Post Card* or Deleuze and Guattari's *A Thousand Plateaus*.)[6] Moreover, at the time, writing on certain figures often carried a certain political connotation; in seventeenth-century studies, for instance, Cartesians tended to be on the right, Spinozists on the left, and Leibnizians somewhere in the center.

There is also an idiosyncratic component to this question that is often overlooked. It has been suggested that thought proceeds by way of the conflict of generations, the young rebelling against their elders. This seems particularly true with philosophers, whose initiation into philosophy can often be traced to a kind of theoretico-amorous admiration that at some point crystallizes around a particular teacher—what Michèle Le Dœuff has termed the "theoretico-erotic transference" (and which Plato simply called "*eros*").[7] In the *Abécédaire*, Deleuze has traced his own initiation into philosophy, at age fourteen, to his curious encounter with a teacher named Pierre Halwachs, whom he met on the beaches at Deauville (ABC E). Later, it was certain faculty at the Sorbonne, such as Ferdinand Alquié and Jean Hyppolite, who would occupy this role. What allows the student to overcome this initial transference, or the disciple to break with the master, Le Dœuff suggests, is precisely an institutional framework, which provides a third term beyond the dynamics of a dual relationship. In some well-known passages, Deleuze has evoked the effect these institutional constraints and related personal affiliations had on his philosophical formation:

> I was taught by two professors, whom I liked and admired a lot: Alquié and Hyppolite . . . The former had long white hands and a stammer which might have been a legacy of his childhood, or there to hide a native accent, and which was harnessed to the service of Cartesian dualisms. The latter had a powerful face with unfinished features, and rhythmically beat out Hegelian triads with his fist, hanging his words on the beats. At the Liberation, we were still strangely stuck in the history of philosophy. We simply plunged into Hegel, Husserl and Heidegger; we threw ourselves like puppies into a scholasticism worse than that of the Middle Ages . . . After the Liberation, the history of philosophy tightened around us—without our realizing it—under the pretext of opening up a future of thought, which would also be the most ancient thought. The "Heidegger question" did not seem to me to be "Is he a bit of a Nazi?" (obviously, obviously) but "What was his role in this new injection of the history of philosophy?" . . . The history of philosophy has always been the agent of power in philosophy, and even in thought. It has played the role of a repressor: how can you think without having read Plato, Descartes, Kant, and Heidegger, and so-and-so's book about them? A formidable school of intimidation . . . So I began with the history of philosophy when it was still being prescribed. For my part, I could not see any way of extracting myself. I could not stand Descartes, the dualisms and the cogito, or Hegel, the triad and the operation of negation. (D 12–14)

One can discern in this passage several "reactions" on Deleuze's part. There is a reaction against Cartesian dualisms and Hegelian triads, which is as much a personal reaction against his teachers as a philosophical reaction. There is also a reaction against the institutionalization of the history of philosophy in the French university, and in particular the role Heidegger's thought played in it. Deleuze, for instance, never shared Heidegger's or Nietzsche's obsession with the Greeks; no doubt his avowed preference for the Stoics and Lucretius was at least in part a reaction against this Hellenophilia. Finally, there is a reaction against what he calls the "scholasticism" of "the three H's"—Hegel, Husserl, and Heidegger—which was prevalent after the Liberation. Many French philosophers, such as Levinas, Ricœur, Derrida, and Lyotard—began their careers with books on Husserl. Significantly, Deleuze never wrote directly on any of "the three H's," though he was obviously immersed in their work, and instead wrote his first book on Hume (*Empiricism and Subjectivity*, which was published in 1953), as if he wanted to add a fourth "H" of his own to the list.

In fact, Deleuze's decision to write on Hume as a student is an important part of the story of his anti-Hegelianism. English philosophy, led by Bertrand Russell, had already gone through its own reaction against Hegel (at least as represented by Bradley) a full half-century earlier than did the French, but for quite specific reasons. Drawing on the recent developments in logic stemming from the work of Frege and Peano, Russell developed the empiricist theme that relations are external to their terms, which became one of the standard criticisms laid against Hegel (for whom, like Leibniz, relations are internal to their terms). In France, this aspect of Anglo-American philosophy had been taken up by Jean Wahl, whom Deleuze would often cite, in his later writings, with regard to the priority Wahl gave to the conjunction "and" over the copula "is."[8] Throughout his career, Deleuze remained a great admirer of Russell, and was strongly antagonistic to the effects Wittgenstein's work had had on Anglo-American philosophy (ABC W). Writing on Hume, and declaring himself to be an empiricist in the British mold, in other words, was already a direct anti-Hegelian provocation.[9] For Hegel, empiricism itself was almost a non-philosophy, because it tried to grasp "this," "that," "here," and "now" in an immediate manner, whereas such indexicals are universals that can never grasp sensible experience in an unmediated way.[10] Deleuze dedicated his Hume book to his teacher, Jean Hyppolite—"a sincere and respectful homage," reads the dedication—and the provocation could hardly have been clearer: the twenty-six-year-old student respectfully presenting to his Hegelian teacher a thesis on the greatness of empiricism.

Indeed, Deleuze's analysis of Hume's empiricism can be read as an explicit challenge to Hegel's characterization of empiricism. The empiricist thesis, in its usual formulation, is that knowledge is derived from experience: that is, the intelligible is derived from the sensible. But Deleuze shows that, for almost every specific idea that Hume analyzes in the *Treatise on Human Nature* (causality, the world, the self, God), the search for a linear path that would reduce the idea to a corresponding impression leads almost immediately to an impasse. Instead, Hume attempts to unravel a more complex tissue of principles (the principles of human nature: association and passion) that habitually bind together separate impressions in order to produce ideas which are in fact inferences, and which affirm more than is really "given." In shifting the emphasis to associationism, Deleuze argues, Hume carried empiricism to a higher power; if ideas contain neither more nor less than sensible impressions, it is precisely because relations are exterior and heterogeneous to their terms. The essential distinction in Hume, in other words, is not between impressions *and* ideas, between the sensible and the intelligible, but rather between two sorts of impressions and ideas: impressions and ideas of terms, *and* impressions and ideas of relations.[11] In Hume, Deleuze argues, the empiricist world was deployed for the first time in its full extension—a conjunctive world of atoms and relations which would not find its complete development until Russell and modern logic. Through Hume, the early Deleuze seemed to have been linking himself to the anti-Hegelian polemics of the early Russell.

None the less, it could be argued that *Empiricism and Subjectivity* occupies a somewhat marginal position within Deleuze's corpus; Deleuze would eventually turn Hume's empiricism into what he would later come to call a "transcendental empiricism." This change was effected in the years between the publication of *Empiricism and Subjectivity* in 1953 and the appearance of *Nietzsche and Philosophy* in 1962, in which Deleuze's reaction against Hegel appears at its most intense. Deleuze has called this an "eight-year hole" in his life (1953 to 1961), during which he published very little.

> I know what I was doing, where and how I lived during those years [he would later say], but I know it almost abstractly, rather as if someone else were relating memories that I believe in but don't really have . . . That's what I find interesting in people's lives, the holes, the gaps, sometimes dramatic, but sometimes not dramatic at all. There are catalepsies, or a kind of sleepwalking through a number of years, in most lives. Maybe it's in th/ese holes that movement takes place. (N 138)

Externally, during these eight years, Deleuze married and had his first child, and moved through a series of temporary academic posts, from the *lycée* in Orleans to the Sorbonne and Centre National de la Recherche Scientifique in Paris. But a profound "intensive" movement of thought took place as well; Deleuze emerged pursuing a singular philosophical trajectory that would be worked out in a series of monographs on individual figures—Nietzsche (1962), Kant (1963), Proust (1964), Bergson (1966), and Masoch (1967)—that would culminate in *Difference and Repetition*.

DELEUZE'S METHODOLOGY: THE ROLE OF "BECOMING"

Deleuze's use of the history of philosophy, however, would ultimately have a significance that went beyond the reaction to these early institutional constraints. Deleuze clearly worked out his own "creative" philosophy in the context of his monographs on various figures in the history of philosophy, but the reason he did so, he would later explain, is that, in order to write and think, he needed to work with "intercessors" with whom he could enter into a kind of "becoming" (past philosophers were intercessors of this type, as was Guattari, in the present).[12] When reading Deleuze's monographs, as has often been noted, one has the distinct impression of entering a "zone" in which Deleuze's own project and that of the author at hand seem to become indiscernible. They constitute what Deleuze himself calls a "zone of indiscernibility"; on the one hand, there is a becoming-Deleuze of the thinker at hand, as it were; and on the other hand, there is a kind of becoming-Spinoza on

Deleuze's part, for instance, or a becoming-Leibniz, a becoming-Bergson, and so on. (This is what Bakhtin called a "free indirect style" of writing.)[13]

This by now familiar style, however, makes for some acute difficulties of interpretation: Where does Deleuze end and, say, Spinoza begin? Where does an explication become an interpretation, and an interpretation a creation (to use hermeneutical terms which Deleuze avoided)? These are not easy questions; such distinctions are, as Deleuze says, indiscernible. Put crudely: in all Deleuze's readings, one moves from a fairly straightforward "explication" of the thinker at hand, to a more specifically Deleuzian "interpretation," which often makes use of concepts incorporated from outside thinkers (for instance, Deleuze interprets Spinoza in terms of Duns Scotus's concept of "univocity," and Leibniz in terms of the mathematical theory of "singularities," although neither of these terms appears in Spinoza's or Leibniz's texts); and finally, one reaches a kind of "creative" point where Deleuze pushes the thought of the thinker at hand to its "differential" limit, purging it of the three great terminal points of metaphysics (God, World, Self), and thereby uncovering the immanent movement of difference in their thought. This is the point where Deleuze's own "system" would begin. Evaluating where these different points lie is one of the most challenging and difficult tasks in reading Deleuze—precisely because there are no clear-cut points where the transition is made.

Sometimes, however, interpreters have contented themselves with a quite different task: identifying Deleuze with (or distancing him from) certain philosophers in the history of philosophy, separating his "friends" from his "enemies." For instance, one could easily imagine drawing up the following four lists. The first would be a list of Deleuze's "canonical" philosophers, those to whom he devoted separate monographs: Hume, Nietzsche, Bergson, Spinoza, Leibniz. To this, one could then add a list of secondary names, philosophers Deleuze loves and refers to often, even though he never wrote a separate monograph on them: Lucretius, the Stoics, Duns Scotus, Maimon, Whitehead. Then there would be the list of Deleuze's ostensible enemies, which would include Plato, Kant, and Hegel. And finally, one could identify certain "hidden" thinkers that Deleuze confronts in a fundamental manner, but who are not frequently discussed directly—most notably Heidegger. With these lists in hand, one could begin to debate, for instance, about who Deleuze's "true" master is. Is it "really" Bergson, as Alain Badiou wants to claim?[14] Is it Nietzsche? Is it Spinoza? Deleuze's own comments in certain texts (such as the "Letter to Michel Cressole") tend to encourage this approach; he says he detested Hegelianism, sought a way to overturn Platonism, thought of his study of Kant as "a book on an enemy," and that his work tends toward "the great Spinoza-Nietzsche identity" (see N 125). But the distinction between Deleuze's friends and enemies, or the identification of Deleuze's "true" masters, is at best a preliminary exercise: necessary, perhaps, but certainly not sufficient. The fact is that Deleuze reads every philosopher in the history of philosophy—friend or enemy—in the same manner, following the same strategy, pushing each thinker, so to speak, to their differential limit. (Indeed, this is a point of affiliation with Hegel; Hegel pushes thought to its point of contradiction, Deleuze to the point of difference.) Deleuze indeed describes his Kant book as "a book on an enemy," but elsewhere he notes, more accurately, that Kant was one of the great philosophers of immanence, and Deleuze unhesitatingly places himself squarely in the Kantian heritage (even if Kant was unable to push the thought of immanence to its necessary conclusion: that is, to its differential conclusion).[15] Conversely, and for the exact same reason, Deleuze often departs from his "friends". He rejects Bergson's critique of intensity in *Time and Free Will*; his Leibnizianism is a Leibnizianism minus God; his Spinozism is a Spinozism minus substance; and Spinoza himself defined determination as negation—a position from which Deleuze broke strongly in his earliest work. But this does not mean that Deleuze is "anti-Spinoza" or "anti-Leibniz" or "anti-Bergson"—any more than he is simply "anti-Hegel." Such characterizations, while not entirely inaccurate, are far too simplistic; they miss the movement and "becoming" of Deleuze's thought, both in itself and in its complex relation to the history of philosophy.

THE POST-KANTIAN TRADITION: THE ROLE OF MAIMON

Why, then, did Deleuze not write directly on Hegel, the philosopher he says he detested, and push him to his differential limit? Jacques Derrida, in his early work, suggested one possible reason for avoiding a direct confrontation with Hegel: it is impossible to oppose Hegel, because opposition is the motor of the Hegelian system, and to oppose Hegel is to become part of the system. This, however, was not an issue for Deleuze, and his early work follows a quite different trajectory than Derrida's, despite certain points of convergence between their work. For instance, one does not find in Deleuze the kind of critique of "binary oppositions" that one finds in Derrida's early work. Nor does one find a concept of "closure" in Deleuze's writings: neither structural closure, since Deleuze from the start defined structures as open and differential (what he called structuralism is what was later termed "post-struc-turalism"),[16] nor the closure of metaphysics, since, far from seeing metaphysics as having exhausted its possibilities, Deleuze frequently dipped into the history of philosophy in order to retrieve, rejuvenate, and transform modes of thought that had been closed off (such as the tradition of univocity inaugurated by Duns Scotus—a trajectory that had been blocked by Christian orthodoxy). Though Derrida and Deleuze both participated in a shared anti-Hegelian reaction, they none the less posed their anti-Hegelian problems in different manners, which in turn led them to pursue quite different philosophical trajectories.

This brings us back, then, to the question of the specificity of Deleuze's anti-Hegelian trajectory. On this score, it would be hard to overemphasize the role played in Deleuze's thought by the eighteenth-century philosopher Salomon Maimon. Maimon is an obscure figure, largely forgotten in the English-speaking world. In France, however, he remains semi-canonical (Martial Guéroult wrote an important book on Maimon), and he exerted an enormous influence on Deleuze, who considered him "a great, great philosopher."[17] Maimon, a contemporary of Kant, was a Polish–Russian Jew who never attended a university, receiving his sole education from the Talmudic tradition while training to be a rabbi. He was exiled (Spinoza-like) from his community because of his unorthodox and radical views, and lived for several years as a wandering beggar, spending much of his time in taverns, and in constant poverty. He was crude, naive, and simple, sometimes embarrassingly outspoken, though he spoke an *ad hoc* mixture of Hebrew, Lithuanian, Yiddish, and Polish that few could understand. Somehow, he made his way to Berlin, and made contact with some of the intelligentsia there (including Mendelssohn, who, as a skilled linguist, was apparently one of the few people who could understand what Maimon was saying). In Berlin, he fell under the spell of Kant's critical philosophy, and wrote a manuscript on it entitled *Essay on Transcendental Philosophy*.[18] In April 1789, Marcus Herz, a old student and friend of Kant's, sent his former teacher a copy of Maimon's manuscript, recommending it to him and hoping it would receive Kant's blessing before publication. Kant, who was sixty-six, in failing health, and eager to finish the third Critique (which would not appear until a year later), was annoyed, and nearly returned the manuscript to Herz unopened. Six weeks later, however, Kant finally wrote back to Herz:

> But one glance at the work made me realize its excellence, and that not only had none of my critics understood me and the main questions as well as Mr. Maimon does, but also very few men possess so much acumen for such deep investigations as he.[19]

The letter continued with a lengthy reply to two sections of Maimon's manuscript. It was, to say the least, a remarkable turn of events.

But that is not the end of the story. Maimon's book was published, and read by another young philosopher, who was even more impressed than Kant.

> My respect for Maimon's talent is limitless [he wrote in a letter to Reinhold]. I firmly believe, and am ready to prove, that through Maimon's work the entire Kantian philosophy, as it is understood by everyone including yourself, is completely overturned . . . All this he has accomplished without anyone's noticing it and while people even condescend to him. I think that future generations will mock our century bitterly.[20]

This is from a letter by Fichte, who was dazzled by Maimon's book. Indeed, not only Fichte's philosophy, but the entire post-Kantian tradition—usually marked by the names Fichte, Schelling, and Hegel—can be said to have been generated by the critiques Maimon leveled against Kant in the midst of the fervor created by the critical philosophy. As Frederick Beiser says, in his superb study *The Fate of Reason*, to study Fichte, Schelling, or Hegel without having read Maimon is like studying Kant without having read Hume.[21] Deleuze, to be sure, was fully aware of Maimon's role in the post-Kantian tradition, and his strategy in approaching that tradition seems to have been as follows: rather than attacking Hegel directly, he instead went back to Maimon—that is, to the polemics that generated the post-Kantian tradition in the first place—and took them up anew, in his own manner, in order to formulate an alternate solution to those same problematics.

What was it, then, that Kant, Fichte, and Deleuze found so remarkable in Maimon's manuscript? For his part, Deleuze, at least, seems to have taken up three elements of Maimon's thought in his early work. First, within the context of the critical tradition, Maimon is the great philosopher of immanence.[22] Kant conceived of his transcendental philosophy as a purely immanent critique of reason, and in so far as Deleuze conceives of his own philosophy as the construction of a "plane of immanence," he aligns himself squarely within the critical tradition.[23] Maimon's greatness, however, was to have pushed the immanent claims of Kant's philosophy to their logical conclusion; almost all Maimon's critiques of Kant are aimed at eliminating the illegitimate vestiges of transcendence that still remain in Kant, given the presuppositions of a transcendental subject—with which Deleuze himself, of course, will break. (The "thing-in-itself," for instance, as Jacobi had already argued, is an illegitimate transcendent application of the category of causality.)

Second, from the viewpoint of immanence, Maimon's primary objection to Kant was that he had ignored the demands of a *genetic* method. This means two things. Kant assumes that there are *a priori* "facts" of reason (the "fact" of knowledge in the first Critique, and the "fact" of morality in the second Critique) and simply seeks the "condition of possibility" of these facts in the transcendental—a vicious circle that makes the condition (the possible) refer to the conditioned (the real) while reproducing its image. Maimon argues that Kant cannot simply assume these facts, but has to show that they can be deduced or *engendered* immanently from reason alone as the necessary modes of its manifestation. The critical philosophy cannot be content with a method of conditioning, but must be transformed into a method of genesis. An important consequence follows from this. Maimon argues that even if the categories, in Kant, are applicable to possible experience, they can never specify what objects they apply to in real experience. Causality may be a necessary concept for any possible experience, for example, but the concept itself gives us no means of distinguishing, within real experience, between what are necessary and universal connections and what are merely contingent constant conjunctions. Hume's skepticism remains unanswered, and Kant's famous duality between concept and intuition remains unbridgeable. Maimon was the first to say that this duality could only be overcome through the formulation of a principle of difference: whereas identity is the condition of possibility of thought in general, he argued, it is difference that constitutes the genetic condition of real thought.

These two exigencies laid down by Maimon—the search for the genetic elements of real thought (and not merely the conditions of possible thought), and the positing of a principle of difference as the fulfillment of this condition—reappear like a leitmotif in almost every one of Deleuze's books up through 1969, even if Maimon's name is not always explicitly mentioned. (Indeed, these are the two primary components of Deleuze's transcendental empiricism).[24] The post-Kantian philosophers, starting with Fichte, had themselves taken up Maimon's challenge, but in some fashion each of them still subordinated the principle of difference to the principle of identity. In Fichte, for example, identity is posited as the property of the thinking subject, with difference appearing only as an extrinsic limitation imposed from without (the non-self). Hegel, against Fichte, attempted to give a certain autonomy to the principle of difference by placing difference and identity in dialectical opposition; but even in Hegel, contradiction always resolves itself, and in resolving itself, it resolves difference by relating it to a ground. (This is the movement one finds in Hegel's *Logic*: identity, difference, differentiation, opposition, contradiction, ground.)[25] Deleuze returns to Maimon, it seems, in order to take up the option that was not pursued as such by post-Kantian philosophy (though its closest precursor is no doubt Schelling). In Deleuze, the principle of "difference-in-itself" is made to function as the genetic element of real experience; difference is the principle from which all other relations (identity, analogy, resemblance, opposition, contradiction, negation) are derived.[26]

Third, in pursuing these immanent aims, Maimon produced a revised transcendental philosophy of his own which he described as a *Koalitionssystem*, a "coalition system" that reached back to the pre-Kantians and incorporated elements of Hume, Spinoza, and Leibniz: a Kantian philosophy that begins with Humean skepticism and winds up with the rationalism of Leibniz and Spinoza.[27] In this sense, Maimon functions as a true precursor to Deleuze, who himself—not coincidentally—made use of Hume, Spinoza, and Leibniz in formulating his own coalition system. (Even in *The Fold*, a late work, several aspects of Deleuze's reading of Leibniz are explicitly derived from Maimon.)[28] But Deleuze does more than simply adopt Maimon's pre-Kantian trio. Perhaps more importantly, in his early work, Deleuze begins to trace out an alternate post-Kantian tradition that will ultimately link up Maimon with later philosophers such as Nietzsche and Bergson, thereby constructing, as it were, his own subterranean or "minor" post-Kantian tradition. For the post-Kantian tradition of Fichte, Schelling, and Hegel, in other words, Deleuze will substitute his own trio of Maimon, Nietzsche, and Bergson.

This is the reason that Deleuze's writings on Bergson and Nietzsche are infused with Maimonian themes, even if they are not always explicitly identified as such.[29] Consider, for example, the following text from *Nietzsche and Philosophy*.[30] Deleuze notes that it was the post-Kantians who "demanded a principle which was not merely conditioning in relation to objects, but which was also truly genetic and productive (a principle of internal difference or determination)." That is a statement of Maimon's critiques, though Maimon's name only appears in the footnote. "If Nietzsche belongs to the history of Kantianism," Deleuze continues, "it is because of the original way he deals with these post-Kantian [i.e., Maimonian] demands." How does Nietzsche satisfy these demands? On the one hand, Nietzsche, using his own "genealogical" method, was able to give a genetic account of knowledge and morality that was missing in Kant: not a critique of false knowledge or false morality, but a critique of true knowledge and true morality, and indeed of the value of truth itself.[31] On the other hand, the genealogical method itself led Nietzsche back to a principle of difference as the condition of the real: that is, the difference between active and reactive modes of existence that serve as the principle of all value. "Nietzsche," Deleuze concludes, "seems to have sought a radical transformation of Kantianism, a re-invention of the critique which Kant betrayed at the same time as he conceived it." The central theme of *Nietzsche and Philosophy* is that Nietzsche was the first philosopher to have truly managed to fulfill Maimon's post-Kantian demands. (The central chapter of the book is entitled, precisely, "Critique.") *Nietzsche and Philosophy*, in other words, wears its anti-Hegelianism on its sleeve, but its more profound theses are derived from Maimon and are aimed at a wholesale revision of the post-Kantian tradition. It is not difficult to trace out the same Maimonian influences in Deleuze's work on Bergson.[32]

HEGEL AND THE DIALECTIC

Maimon, in short, influenced the early Deleuze in at least these three areas: the adherence to the position of immanence; the posing of the problem of the genetic method and the principle of difference; and the construction of a coalition system integrating elements of Hume, Spinoza, and Leibniz. These themes provide an important context in which to place—and to assess—Deleuze's relation to Hegel and the post-Kantian tradition. Certain commentators have contended that the portrait of Hegel presented in *Nietzsche and Philosophy* is simplistic, and to a certain degree this is no doubt true.[33] But if Deleuze never wrote directly on Hegel, and if his characterizations of Hegel are largely made in passing, it is because these criticisms were relevant only in relation to Deleuze's larger project, which was primarily indexed on Kant, and not Hegel (transcendental empiricism). From this viewpoint, Deleuze's persistent criticism is that Hegel provides an inadequate solution to Maimon's primary post-Kantian problematic: the search for the conditions of real experience and not merely possible experience.

Put schematically, Deleuze's critiques are directed against several essential components of the Hegelian dialectic. First, Hegel's dialectic begins with concepts as generalities, "in this type of dialectical method, one begins with concepts that, like baggy clothes, are much too big: the One in general, the multiple in general, nonbeing in general ... In such cases, the real is recomposed with abstractions" and generalities (B 44). Second, in order to compensate for the generality of the concept, Hegel appeals to a method of contradiction. But "of what use is a dialectic that believes itself to be reunited with the real, when it compensates for the inadequacy of a concept that is too broad by invoking the opposite concept, which is no less broad and general?" (B 44). The analytic of concepts developed in *What is Philosophy?* should be assessed in light of this critique. Finally, the movement of contradiction is driven by means of the labor of the negative; in Hegel, the sign of difference is "not-X." The principle of identity "X is X" can be reformulated as "X is not not-X," which means that a thing includes in its being the non-being that it is not; the being of a thing is inseparable from the negation of the negation (is not ... not) (14 Mar 1978). Summarizing these critiques, Deleuze writes in *Difference and Repetition* that the "objection to Hegel is that he does not go beyond false movement—in other words, the abstract logical movement of 'mediation'" (DR 8).

However, these explicit criticisms of Hegel—against contradiction, against negation, against mediation—find their force and validity only in the alternate vision of "dialectics" that Deleuze himself provides. True to his conception of philosophy as the creation of concepts, *Difference and Repetition* (particularly in its fifth chapter, "Ideas and the Synthesis of Difference") attempts to develop a new concept of dialectics, which is more or less synonymous with the concept of "problematics": dialectics is the art of posing or constructing problems, expressed in the form of

Ideas (which Deleuze, like Kant, distinguishes from concepts). Indeed, according to Deleuze's biographer, François Dosse, *Difference and Repetition* was originally intended to be a thesis on "the Idea of the problem."[34] In this manner, Deleuze places himself squarely within the heritage of his so-called "enemies"—the great philosophers of dialectics: Plato and Aristotle, Kant, and Hegel—and develops his concept of dialectics through them, but also beyond them.

Aristotle, for instance, defined dialectics as the art of posing problems as the subject of a syllogism, while analytics gives us the means of resolving the problem by leading the syllogism to its necessary conclusion. But Aristotle was content to derive his problems from the propositions of common sense (for instance, "Is rational animal the definition of man or not?"), and to assess their legitimacy by considering "the opinions accepted by . . . the majority" in order to relate problems to general points of view, which thereby form the places (the *topoi*) that allow problems "to be established or refuted in discussion."[35] (In its most simplistic form, this is the kind of dialectics of opinion one finds on TV news shows, where the representatives of opposing viewpoints or propositions argue out their respective pro-and-con positions.) For Deleuze, this is a fundamental perversion of dialectics.

> Whenever the dialectic "forgets" its intimate relation with Ideas in the form of problems [he writes] it loses its true power and falls under the sway of the power of the negative, necessarily substituting for the ideal objectivity of the *problematic* a simple confrontation between opposing, contrary, or contradictory propositions. This long perversion begins with the dialectic itself [that is, with Plato], and attains its extreme form in Hegelianism. (DR 164)

Plato, for his part, recognized the profound link between Ideas and problems; but if he posited Ideas as transcendent essences, it was because he saw them as responses to a particular problem, or rather, a particular form of question: namely, the question "What is . . . ?" Kant's genius, in the "Transcendental Dialectic," was to assign a new status to Ideas: lacking any determinate object, he argued, Ideas are necessarily "problematic," which means that the true object of an Idea is the problem as such.[36] Kant, however, was still willing to preserve the transcendent status of Ideas as "foci" or "horizons" that transcend any possible experience, and it was on this point that Maimon proposed his fundamental inversion of Kant. Maimon insisted that Ideas are immanent to experience: that is, they are present in sensible nature and can be comprehended by the understanding. It is this immanent conception of dialectics that Deleuze attempts to push to its limit in *Difference and Repetition*. "Problems do not exist only in our heads," he writes, "but occur here and there in the production of an actual historical world" (DR 190). For this reason, a purely immanent dialectic must be derived from questions such as Who?, Where?, When?, How?, How much?, How many?, In which cases?—which are no longer questions of essence, but rather "those of the accident, of the event, of multiplicity—of difference" (DR 188).

This, then, is the context in which Deleuze's relation to Hegel should be understood. Deleuze is certainly not anti-dialectical, since he explicitly places himself in a long tradition of dialectical thought. At one level, he is not entirely anti-Hegelian, in so far as he is attempting to work out and respond to a similar set of post-Kantian problems; but at another level, he is anti-Hegelian in that he pursues these problems in a different manner than Hegel. In this sense, the Deleuze–Hegel relation needs to be assessed less in terms of Deleuze's explicit comments "against" Hegel than in terms of the alternate conception of dialectics he develops throughout his *œuvre*: a dialectic in which an affirmative conception of the "problematic" is substituted for the "labor of the negative," and a principle of difference is substituted for the movement of contradiction.

Pre- and Post-Kantianism

Logic and Existence: Deleuze on the Conditions of the Real

Here is a philosophical problem that lies at the core of Deleuze's interest in the rationalists, and particularly Leibniz.[1] By itself, thought has no means of distinguishing between the possible and the real. I can have a concept of 100 dollars in my mind, and while it may be important to me practically whether or not I actually have 100 dollars in my pocket, the existence of 100 dollars in reality changes nothing from the point of view of the concept: that is, from the viewpoint of pure thought. The position of the real is *outside the concept*; the existing thing is external to the concept. (This was Kant's argument against the ontological argument: *existence is not a predicate*; from the viewpoint of the concept, an existing God is no more perfect than a non-existing God.) Even though I know that unicorns do not exist, I can still form a concept or a representation of a unicorn, or define the essence of a unicorn.

For Deleuze, this is one of the fundamental problems of a theory of thought: How can thought leave this meager sphere of the possible in order to think the real: that is, to think existence itself, to think existing things. Pre-Kantians like Leibniz approached this problem in terms of the distinction between truths of *essence* ("A triangle has three sides") and truths of *existence* ("Caesar crossed the Rubicon"), while post-Kantians like Maimon approached the problem in terms of the distinction between the conditions of *possible* experience and the conditions of *real* experience. I would like to approach this logical problem from a semi-cinematic perspective. "Theoretically," Deleuze once mused, "Jean-Luc Godard would be capable of filming Kant's *Critique* or Spinoza's *Ethics*" (DI 141). In the 1990s, Godard did a multi-part film entitled *Histoire(s) du cinéma*; following Deleuze's suggestion, I am imagining Godard undertaking a similar project entitled *Histoire(s) de la philosophie*. I have no idea, of course, what Godard might have done in such a film, but none the less I am presenting the first part of this essay as a possible scenario for a single sequence of that multi-part film, which has as its title *Logic and Existence*, which I am borrowing from a well-known book by Jean Hyppolite.[2]

Here's the first shot: a radiant sphere hovering in the middle of nowhere. Nothing is written on it, but we know it is the sphere of logic. The film begins here for an obvious reason: if thought, on its own, is only capable of thinking the possible, it does so on the basis of what can be called *logical principles*. Classical logic famously identified three such principles. These are the principle of *identity* (which says that "A is A," or "A thing is what it is"), and then two smaller principles which seem to be specifications of the principle of identity: the principle of *non-contradiction* (which says that "A is not non-A," or "A thing is not what it is not") and the principle of the *excluded middle* (which says "either A or not-A," that is, between A or not-A, there is no middle term). Taken together, these three principles determine what is impossible—that is to say, what is *unthinkable* without contradiction: something that would not be what it is (which would contradict the principle of identity); something that would be what it is not (which would contradict the principle of non-contradiction); and something that would be both what it is and what it is not (which would contradict the principle of the excluded middle). This sphere of logic would seem to enclose us within the domain of the possible, or what classical philosophy called the domain of essences. But this opening shot sets up the problem with a visual image: *Is there any way in which these three classical principles can be used to exit the sphere of logic and penetrate existence itself?*

The response to this question will take us through three scenes, which correspond to three broad sequences in the history of philosophy, three attempts to resolve this problem using one of these logical principles. Scene one focuses on the pre-Kantians, the rationalists; its star is Leibniz, since it was he who attempted to extend the principle of *identity* to the whole of existence. Scene two focuses on the post-Kantians, primarily the German Idealists; its story culminates in Hegel, since it was he who attempted to extend the principle of *non-contradiction* to the whole of existence. Scene three, finally, looks at that loosely related group of thinkers that often tend to be called, precisely, "existentialists," since it is they who attempted to extend the principle of the *excluded middle* to existence. The screenplay reaches its climax with Deleuze: at the end, it briefly examines the reasons why Deleuze is at once fascinated with all three of these philosophical attempts to "think existence," but none the less thinks they fail, and why he ultimately charts out his own response to the problem. The ending, alas, is somewhat truncated, since the production went over budget, which meant that entire scenes wound up being consigned to the editing room floor.

LEIBNIZ AND THE PRINCIPLE OF IDENTITY

Scene one focuses on Leibniz, who would have been a perfect philosophical movie star, since he is a man of contradictions. He is somewhat reactionary, a defender of law and order, of the status quo, of "policing" in every sense of the term; he says malicious things about Spinoza; but at the same time he invents the calculus, and undertakes one of the most remarkable adventures of thought in the history of philosophy. The reason: Leibniz took the most basic principle of logic—the principle of identity—and attempted to make it penetrate existence in its entirety by formulating the *reciprocal* of the principle of identity: namely, the principle of sufficient reason. Scene one briefly shows how.[3]

The classical formulation of the principle of identity is "A is A." In this formula, the principle of identity is an absolutely certain thought, but it is none the less an empty thought. Are we truly *thinking* when we say "A is A"? It's not clear. The popular formulation of the principle of identity would be: "A thing is what it is."[4] Though this formula seems trite, it actually goes further than the formula "A is A" because it points to the domain of Being governed by the principle of identity—namely, the domain of *essences*: the principle of identity asserts the identity between a thing and what the thing *is* (its essence). But Leibniz's originality lies in the logical formulation he provides of the principle of identity: "every analytic proposition is true." It is this formula that lies at the basis of Leibniz's attempt to extend the principle of identity beyond the domain of essences and into the domain of existence. What is an analytic proposition? An analytic proposition is a proposition in which the subject and the predicate *reciprocate* with each other. The principle of identity is presented in the form of a reciprocal proposition: there is a subject, A; then the verb *is*; and then a predicate or attribute, A. The principle of identity states that, in the proposition "A is A," there is a reciprocity between the subject and the predicate, even though the distinction between subject and predicate remains. What Leibniz calls *analysis* is the operation that discovers a predicate in a notion taken as a subject.

But how can this new formula allow us to think existing beings? The principle of identity posits the identity of the thing and what the thing is, even if the thing itself does not exist; existing things thus appear to lie outside the principle of identity. In order to think existing beings, Leibniz will derive a new principle from the principle of identity, which he will call the principle of sufficient reason. The popular formulation of the principle of reason would be "everything has a reason." This is the fundamental battle cry of rationalism—everything *has to* have a reason, there *must* be a reason for everything that takes place—and the entire philosophical project of Leibniz, the greatest of the rationalists, is animated by his pursuit of the problem of sufficient reason. But how can the principle of sufficient reason allow us to think existing beings? This becomes clear in Leibniz's metaphysical formulation of sufficient reason: "all predication has a foundation in the nature of things" (FLB 42). What this means is that everything that is predicated of a thing must be included in the concept of the thing. What is said or predicated of a thing? If we say that what is predicated of a thing is its essence (what is *is*), then there is no difference between the principle of identity and the principle of sufficient reason. But what is said or predicated of a thing is not only the essence of the thing; it is also the totality of events that happen to the thing in its existence.[5] For example: Caesar crossed the Rubicon. Since this is a true proposition, Leibniz will insist not only that the predicate "crossed the Rubicon" must be contained in the Caesar's notion or concept, but moreover that we should be able to *demonstrate*, through an analysis, that this is the case.

This is an astonishing philosophical move, which would make for dramatic cinema, if thought itself could be filmed. The principle of identity provides us with a model of truth that is certain, yet it does not make us think anything, so Leibniz simply reverses the formulation of the principle of identity using the principle of reciprocity. The principle of identity says that an analytic proposition is necessarily a true proposition, whereas the principle of sufficient reason says that a true proposition is necessarily an analytic proposition. The principle of sufficient reason, in other words, is the reciprocal of the principle of identity, but this reversal was only made possible through Leibniz's logical reformulation of the principle of identity. It is through this reversal that Leibniz will attempt to use the principle of identity to conquer the domain of existence.

There are two things that might be said about Leibniz's principle of sufficient reason. The first is that it seems absolutely crazy; it is hard to see how anyone could take it seriously. Ian Hacking once wrote that "Leibniz's claim that in every true proposition the predicate is contained in the subject is the most absurd theory of truth that has ever been advanced."[6] It is easy to see why: Leibniz is claiming that, just as we can demonstrate that the predicate "three sides" is included in the subject *triangle*, we should be able to demonstrate that the predicate "crossing the Rubicon" is contained in the concept of *Caesar*. One can hardly imagine the conditions under which such a thing would be possible, unless we were God himself, with his infinite understanding. But the second point is this: Leibniz's posing of the problem of sufficient reason would mean nothing if he had not had the means to *create* the philosophical concepts that were necessary to explore the conditions of this problem (This is Deleuze's definition of philosophy: the creation of concepts in response to shifting problematics.) Here, we introduce a shot of Leibniz standing on a precipice, about to plunge into the labyrinth of the continuum, the maelstrom of the actual infinite. He is calm, tranquil, and confident, however, because for every problem posed by his search for sufficient reason he will create a concept adequate to it, even as he is falling into the abyss. Here are a few of those concepts—just enough to feel the power of Leibniz's thought.

First, if everything we attribute with truth to a subject is contained in the notion of the subject, then we must also include the *totality of the world* in the subject. Why? Because the principle of *sufficient reason* is not the same thing as the principle of *causality*. To say that "everything has a cause" means that A is caused by B, B is caused by C, and so on—a series of causes and effects extending infinitely in all directions. To say that "everything has a reason," however, means that we must give a *reason* for these causal relations; it means that the causal relation between A and B must itself be included in the notion of A. This is how the principle of sufficient reason provides the ground for the principle of causality: the principle of causality states the *necessary cause* of a thing but not its *sufficient reason*.[7] But opening up of this ground is precisely the abyss into which Leibniz is plunging. Once he says that the predicate "crossing the Rubicon" is included in the notion of Caesar, he cannot stop himself; he is forced to include the totality of the universe in Caesar's concept. The event "crossing the Rubicon" has multiple causes and effects that stretch to infinity, such as the establishment of the Roman Empire and the crucifixion of Jesus, and Leibniz cannot say that "crossing the Rubicon" is included in the notion of Caesar without saying that *all* the causes and effects of this event are *also* included in the notion of Caesar. This is the first hallucinatory concept Leibniz creates: the concept *expression*. Each of us, in our concept, expresses or contains the entirety of the universe.

But Leibniz immediately confronts another danger. If the concept of each subject expresses the totality of the world, would this not mean that there is only a single subject (like Spinoza's substance), and that individuals are merely the appearances or modifications of this universal subject? But Leibniz's philosophy is fixed on the individual, and he cannot admit such a claim without renouncing the principle of sufficient reason.[8] No problem, Leibniz responds. To avoid this danger, he will simply create another concept: each individual notion may indeed include the totality of the world, but it does so from a certain *point of view*. This marks the beginning of "perspectivist" philosophy, which Leibniz derives from the theory of conic sections.[9] Leibniz's claim is not that each individual expresses the totality of the world from its own point of view, as if everything were "relative" to the viewpoint of the subject, since in fact the exact opposite is the case: it is the subject that is constituted by the point of view. Point of view, in other words, is the sufficient reason of the subject; the individual notion is the point of view through which the individual expresses the totality of the world.[10]

But this propels Leibniz into a third problem: What determines this point of view? How does one distinguish between points of view? Once again, Leibniz plunges on: each of us expresses the totality of the world from a certain point of view, he tells us, but we necessarily express most of the world in an obscure and confused manner, as if it were a mere background noise. The totality of the world is really included in the individual notion, but primarily in the form of *infinitely small perceptions*—another concept. None the less, if there is finite neighborhood of the world that I express clearly and distinctly, it is precisely that neighborhood of the world affects my *body*; Leibniz here deduces the necessity of the body as that which occupies the point of view. I myself do not express clearly and distinctly the crossing of the Rubicon, for example, since that concerns Caesar's body. Each individual substance occupies a different point of view on the world because each of them has a different zone of clear and distinct expression on the world as a function of its body.

But Leibniz still cannot stop, for he now confronts a final danger: How do we know that each of these individuals is expressing the *same* world? This is a problem for the following reason. The principle of identity allows us to determine what is contradictory: that is, what is *impossible*. A square circle is a circle that is not a circle; it is impossible because it contravenes the principle of identity. But at the level of sufficient reason, Caesar not crossing the Rubicon or Adam not sinning in the Garden of Eden is neither contradictory nor impossible; Caesar could have not crossed the Rubicon, and Adam could have not sinned, whereas a circle cannot be square. The difficulty is: How can Leibniz hold that everything Adam did is contained for all time in his individual concept, and that Adam the non-sinner was none the less possible? This is where Leibniz invents perhaps his most notorious concept, which is in fact an entirely new logical relation: *incompossibility*. At the level of existing things, it is not enough to say that a thing is possible in order to exist; it is also necessary to know with what it is *compossible*. Adam the non-sinner was possible in itself, but it was *incompossible* with rest of the actualized world. Leibniz derived his most famous doctrine from the concept of imcompossibility; among the infinity of incompossible worlds God had in his mind at the moment of creation, God chose "Best" of all possible worlds to pass into existence, governed by a harmony that is pre-established by God. Thus, Leibniz says, when I want to demonstrate that the predicate "sinner" is contained in the concept of Adam—that is, when I perform an analysis of the concept "Adam"—I move backwards from Adam the sinner to Eve the temptress, and from Eve the temptress to the evil serpent, and from the evil serpent to the apple, and so on; moving forward, I show that there is *continuity* between Adam's sin and the Incarnation and Redemption by Christ. In other words, there are *series* that are going to begin to fit into each other across the differences of time and space, and the ultimate aim of Leibniz's great book *Theodicy* is to justify God's choice of *this* world as the "best" world, with all its interlocking series, and with all its suffering and cruelty.[11] Such an analysis is *infinite* because it has to pass through the entire series of elements that constitute the world, which is actually infinite; and it is an *analysis* because it demonstrates the sufficient reason for the inclusion of the predicate "sinner" in the individual notion of Adam.

It is here that we end scene one, for we seem to have reached a blockage. It seems to go without saying that we, as finite beings, are incapable of undertaking an infinite analysis; in order to situate ourselves in the domain of truths of existence, we have to wait for experience. Infinite analysis is possible for God, to be sure, but this is hardly a satisfactory answer. We may be happy for God (close-up of God, smiling), but then we would wonder why Leibniz went to such trouble to present this whole story about sufficient reason if it remains inaccessible to us as finite beings. This apparent blockage in Leibniz's thought will return at the end of our scenario, but what we have seen in scene one is the "delirious" creation of concepts one finds in Leibniz. Expression, point of view, minute perceptions, incompossibility: all these are concepts that are generated in Leibniz—created by him—as a result of his positing the problem of sufficient reason. This is why Deleuze says is it useless to pose objections to a philosopher; the more important thing, at least initially, is to extract the "problematic" generating their thought, and to follow it as far as one can.

HEGEL AND THE PRINCIPLE OF NON-CONTRADICTION

But now scene two intervenes. It begins with a tracking shot that moves past a number of philosophical figures: Descartes, Leibniz (again, briefly, in a flashback), then Kant and Fichte, and finally Hegel. Hegel is the culminating point of the second scene, which charts out the trajectory through which philosophy attempted to conquer existence, no longer through the principle of identity, as in Leibniz, but through the principle of contradiction.

Scene two begins with Descartes, who is another good philosophical movie star; suave, debonair, long hair, goatee, he sleeps until noon every day, and likes working in bed, which I personally admire. Christina, the Queen of Sweden, the story goes, forces him to get up early; this gives him pneumonia, and he dies. Prior to dying, however, Descartes had attempted to think existence in his own manner, and his undertaking would have even greater repercussions in philosophy than Leibniz's. In the *Meditations*, Descartes claimed that, in order to doubt, I must be thinking;

hence I am a thinking being. The question of doubt, it is true, does not bear on the existence of things, but rather on the *knowledge* I have of the existence of things. In so far as I doubt, there is a knowledge that I cannot doubt, which is the knowledge of myself as a thinking being. But in this manner, Descartes was the first thinker to introduce into philosophy a formula that would later be developed extensively in German philosophy: the "I = I" or the "Self = Self" (Ich = Ich). Now, although the "I = I" might appear to be simply a re-formulation of the principle of identity "A = A," in fact it has a completely different status. The identity A = A is the identity of the thing thought, and as such it is a *hypothetical* judgment. Its complete formulation would be: *if there is A, A is A; if A exists*, then A = A. But perhaps A does not exist, perhaps there is nothing. (This is why the principle of identity corresponds to the question, "Why is there something rather than nothing?") What Descartes showed was that the principle of identity is a purely *hypothetical* judgment; I can always doubt A, not only in its existence, but *even in its concept*. Thus, when Descartes says that there is one thing I cannot doubt, I = I, he did something radically new in philosophy: he discovered an identity that is no longer subject to this hypothetical condition; he discovered an *unconditioned* identity, or what came to be called a *thetic* or *categorical* judgment. This is the discovery of subjectivity: the position, or auto-position, of the subject, the I = I. Fichte would develop this thesis to its ultimate conclusion: one can only say "A is A" because A is *thought*, but what grounds the identity of what is thought is the reality of the thinking subject, the identity of the finite "I." Thus, the principle of identity, "A is A," founds its *ground* in the auto-position of the subject, the "I is I." In Descartes, the principle of identity left the sphere of logic and took a first baby step into the real, or into existence.

A brief flashback to Leibniz, for this is precisely where his philosophy intervened. For, although the I = I allowed Descartes to conquer a small island of existence, the Cartesian *cogito* is, as it were, enclosed in a citadel. Affirming something *other* than the thinking subject—such as the reality of something thought (mathematics) or the reality of something experienced (the sensible world)—will require an entire acrobatics, a series of complex reasonings on Descartes's part, all of which will appeal to the guarantee that God exists and is a truthful being. So, although Descartes had obtained his little island of existence—the *cogito*—what Leibniz sought to attain was the adequation of thought with existence in its *entirety*, the real in its *totality*. What Descartes did not see was that the I = I does not simply refer to the little island of the *cogito*, posited in the certitude of itself, but rather expresses or comprehends the *totality* of the world as the set of its own predicates. Such is the significance of the shift from Descartes's *cogito* to Leibniz's *monad*.

But now scene two jumps ahead to Kant, famous for the regularity of his daily walks, and the bizarre garters he made to hold up his socks. Kant and the post-Kantians would take up Leibniz's project, but in a new manner, taking it in a different direction. The reason: after Leibniz, no one could affirm that every true proposition is analytic. What had intervened was Kant's fundamental discovery of *synthetic* judgments. For Kant a judgment such as "The three angles of a triangle are equal to two right angles" is no longer an analytic judgment but a *synthetic* judgment, since its demonstration must pass through the concept of a square; the proposition is therefore a synthesis of two concepts. The results of discovery were profound. Although Descartes had located the ground of the principle of identity in the "I = I," what Kant discovered was that the "I = I" is a *synthetic* identity, and no longer simply an *analytic* identity.

It is here that perhaps the most famous episode in the attempt to reconcile logic and existence commences. The post-Kantian philosophers are precisely those philosophers who take Kant as their fantastic starting point, and who pursue the question: What is synthetic identity? What does the synthetic identity of the self consist of? The post-Kantian philosophers maintained that Kant had not adequately responded to the question he himself had posed. In order to give an account of synthetic identity, Kant had to invoke something *other*, something irreducible both to thought and to the Self: namely, sensibility, or the *a priori* forms of space and time. The post-Kantians, by contrast, wanted to ground synthetic identity in the Ego itself, and they therefore posited a new principle that was derived, no longer from the principle of identity, but from *the principle of non-contradiction*. For them, the Ego cannot posit itself as identical to itself except by opposing itself to a non-Ego, to that which is outside the Ego. As Fichte would show, synthetic identity can be expressed in the formula: "The I is not the not-I." Here again, this is another astonishing philosophical formula—almost like a chemical formula—that marked a prodigious discovery in philosophy. It means that the "I" can be posited as identical to itself only by being opposed to a not-I: that is, through a negation of the not-I (17 May 1983).

This line of thought would find its ultimate outcome in Hegel, who was the first philosopher to think that, when he said "things do not contradict themselves," he was saying something about things—that is, something about existence, and not merely about the possible. Not only was he saying something about things, but he was also saying something about how they are born and develop: they are born and develop by not contradicting each other. The Hegelian dialectic does not consist in denying the principle of non-contradiction, but rather in pushing it to its limit, and developing the principle of non-contradiction at the level of existence. If the principle of analytic identity is the empty principle of essences, with which one can only think what Hegel calls abstract essentiality, the principle of non-contradiction is the principle through which thought and the real are engendered and develop simultaneously—to the point where Hegel can say that "the real is the concept and the concept is the real."

THE EXISTENTIALISTS AND THE PRINCIPLE OF THE EXCLUDED MIDDLE

This brings us to a truncated scene three, whose stars are a race of thinkers who sought to reconcile thought and existence, no longer at the level of the principle of identity (whether analytic or synthetic), or even at the level of the principle of non-contradiction (as in Hegel), but rather at the level of the principle of the excluded middle (A or not-A, but not both). This is the thought of the "either . . . or," and no longer the thought of contradiction; it is the mode of the *alternative* and no longer the *negative*. If thought can join existence in the excluded middle, it is because it implies that *to think is to choose*, that the nature of my existence is determined by my choice. It is this means of conquering existence that came to be known, broadly, as "existentialism." It is a line of thought that has its own cast of characters: it begins with Pascal (a Catholic), would be continued in Kierkegaard (a product of the Reformation) and Sartre (an atheist), and is taken up in a modified form in Badiou (the militant activist). What was at stake in Pascal's wager, for instance, was not the existence or non-existence of a transcendent God, but rather the immanent modes of existence of those who must *choose* between his existence or non-existence. The result is a complex typology of different modes of existence: there are the *devout*, for whom there is no question of choosing; *skeptics*, who do not know how or are unable to choose; the creatures of *evil*, who are free to choose, but whose first choice places them in a situation where they can no longer repeat their choice, like Goethe's Mephistopheles; and finally, the men of *belief* or grace who, conscious of choice, make an "authentic" choice that is capable of being repeated in a steadfast spiritual determination.[12] Kierkegaard drew out the necessary consequences of this line of thinking: decision or choice covers as great an area as thought itself.

But this also means, secondly, that there are choices that I make only on the condition of saying, "I have no choice," like the woman who gives herself to a man on the condition of saying she is simply submitting to *his* choice, and not making a choice of her own—this is what Sartre called "bad faith." When Sartre wrote, after World War II, "We have never been more free than under the Occupation," he was speaking precisely of those shameful choices one makes on the condition of saying, "I had no choice!" In other words, in the end, we choose between choice and non-choice—the non-choice itself being itself a choice, since it is the *form* of choice that one appeals to when one believes that one has no choice. More recently, Alain Badiou has explicitly placed himself in the lineage of Pascal and Sartre when he locates the condition of the subject in its choice to maintain its fidelity to an event, thereby elevating the militant activist to the highest mode of existence (and no longer the person of belief or the "knight of faith"). In all these cases, one can see that there is a genuine displacement of the principle of the excluded middle: choice is no longer between two terms (A or not-A), but between two modes of existence; and ultimately, it is a choice between choice and non-choice. In this way, the principle of excluded middle—the last of our three logical principles—is now made to bear upon existence itself, but in a fundamentally new manner.

DELEUZE AND THE PRINCIPLE OF DIFFERENCE

We arrive now at the climax of the film, or perhaps its anticlimax. Unlike Leibniz or Descartes, Deleuze does not seem to lend himself to movie stardom. He read, he wrote, and he taught (when he was not ill), and outwardly, that sums up most of his life; the real drama took place in his thinking. So our final image is a shot of Deleuze sitting at a desk, writing—and we hold the shot for several minutes, to give a sense of the passing of time, à la Tarkovsky. Where does Deleuze fit into this story of *Logic and Existence* that we have just screened? In a sense, the answer is: nowhere. He writes about all three of these options, he is fascinated by them, and he is interested in the exact same problem: How can thought think existence? One of Deleuze's early lecture courses from 1956 has recently surfaced, and in it we can see Deleuze working through these same three traditions (in a different manner than I have done here), twelve years before he would finally publish his own "solution" to the problem, so to speak, in *Difference and Repetition* (1968).[13] For Deleuze, the fulfillment of this project of *Logic and Existence*, which animated much of modern philosophy, can only occur through the substitution of the principle of difference for the principle of identity (in all its variations: identity, contradiction, the excluded middle). The final scene can do little more than provide a sketch of the way in which Deleuze approaches the project of *Logic and Existence* in his own manner.

The story we have just examined—a particular sequence in the history of modern thought—can be said to oscillate between two poles: God and the Self, infinite substance and finite subject. Pre-Kantian thought found its principle in the analytic identity of the divine substance, while post-Kantian thought found its principle in the synthetic identity of the finite subject. For Deleuze, this supposed transformation no longer has any sense: God or Self, analytic identity or synthetic identity—it is one and the same thing, since the identity of the one finds its condition in the identity of the other. As Deleuze writes in *Difference and Repetition*, "the oneness and identity of the divine substance are in truth the only guarantee of a unique and identical self, and God is retained so long as the self is preserved" (DR 58). Nietzsche had already seen that the death of God becomes effective only with the death of the self, and both Foucault and Klossowski would develop this theme in their works.

As a result, the movement from the "A is A" to the "I is I" in post-Kantian philosophy—the move from God to the Self—did little more than to seal the form of what Deleuze calls "common sense," which is the *form* under which identity has been preserved in philosophical thought. Subjectively, it is the *same* self that perceives, knows, imagines, and remembers; it is the *same* self that breathes, sleeps, walks, and eats; and objectively, it is the *same* object that is seen, remembered, imagined, and conceived by this self; and as I move from one object to another, it is in the *same world* that I perceive, breathe, and walk in (LS 78). This is why Kant could present the "object = x" or the object in general as the objective correlate of the "I think" or the subjective unity of consciousness. Even Kierkegaard dreamed of a God and a self rediscovered in a theatre of faith. Taken together, these can be seen to constitute the two poles of what Deleuze calls the dogmatic image of thought: the *subjective* identity of the self and its faculties, and the *objective* identity of the thing (and of the world) to which these faculties refer. This seals the alliance between the *self*, the *world*, and *God* as the three great terminal points of metaphysics; difference—or the diverse—is related to the form of a subject's identity, the form of an object's or a world's permanence, with God being the supreme principle of identities.

More important than what happens before or after Kant, then, is what happens *within* Kant, in the first Critique, when he criticizes the Self, the World, and God as transcendent illusions, and thus invokes a mysterious coherence that excludes the coherence of the Self, the coherence of the world, and the coherence of God (as well as the coherence of language, which is capable of "denoting" everything else). If Deleuze can consider himself to be a "pure metaphysician," if he rejects the Heideggerian idea of "the end of metaphysics," it is because he believes it is possible to construct a metaphysics freed from the coordinates of the Self, the World, and God. "What is then revealed," he writes in *Difference and Repetition*, "is being, which is said of differences which are neither in substance nor in a subject" (DR 58). This is why Deleuze's metaphysics will focus on *impersonal individuations* that are no longer enclosed in a Self, and *pre-individual singularities* that are no longer enclosed in a God. This is the Dionysian world that Deleuze describes in *Difference and Repetition*, in which, as he puts it,

> the divergence of affirmed series forms a "chaosmos" and no longer a world; the aleatory point that traverses them forms a counter-self and no longer a self; and disjunction posited as a synthesis exchanges its theological principle for a diabolical principle . . . the Grand Canyon of the World, the "crack" of the self, and the dismembering of God.[14]

It is not that Deleuze denies subjects and objects have identities—it is simply that these identities are secondary; they are the effect of more profound relations of difference. As Deleuze says, just as there is no "pure" reason but only historically variable processes of "rationalization," so there is no universal or transcendental subject, but only diverse and historically variable forms of "subjectivation," and no object in general, but only variable forms of "objectivation," and so on. With this move, however, it becomes impossible for Deleuze to follow any of the paths we saw above, in our Godardian film, since they each utilize a variant of the principle of identity to think existence, whereas in Deleuze the identities of the Self, the World, and God have been dissolved.

But how, then, can one think the existence of a purely differential world? Clearly thought has to think difference directly, but Deleuze is fully aware of the paradox of such an enterprise; like Leibniz's project, it seems absurd. The image we began with—the sphere of logic—illustrated the problem that thought, on its own, can only think the possible, but it cannot think the real directly because the concept is blocked—and it is blocked precisely because the real is what is *different* from thought, *it is difference itself*. What is it that blocks the concept? For Aristotle, it was the accidents of *matter*; for Kant, it was the irreducibly *spatio-temporal* dimension of intuition—neither of which is conceptual. Deleuze himself states the problem clearly: "With the identical, we think with all our strength, but without producing the least thought: with the different, by contrast, do we not have the highest thought, but also that which cannot be thought?" (DR 226). This is the paradox that lies at the heart of Deleuze's project: difference is the highest thought, but also that which cannot be thought. This is why Deleuze's precursors adopted the strategy of utilizing the principles of thought itself—identity, non-contradiction, the excluded middle—and then attempted to think difference (or existence) *through* them. Deleuze in effect attempts the opposite strategy. For him, what blocks the concept is neither matter (Aristotle) nor sensibility (Kant). "*What* blocks the concept," he asks in *Difference and Repetition*, "if not the Idea? What remains outside the concept refers more profoundly to what is inside the Idea" (DR 220). The theory of Ideas takes us to the crux of the matter: what does it mean for Deleuze to say that difference can be grasped, not in a concept, but in an Idea? This is obviously a complex question, which the ending of our film presents in three interrelated images.

First, at the conclusion of the scene one, we saw that Leibniz's philosophy of sufficient reason was blocked, since it seemed that an infinite analysis of concepts could only be undertaken by God, with his infinite understanding, leaving us finite human beings mired in obscurity and confusion. But this is where Leibniz *overcame* his explicit intentions (in the Nietzschean sense of "self-overcoming"), since he wound up providing us finite humans with an artifice capable of undertaking a well-founded approximation of what happens in God's understanding, and this artifice is the technique of the infinitesimal calculus or differential analysis. We as humans can undertake an infinite analysis thanks to the symbolism of the *differential calculus*. In the calculus, the differential relation can be said to be a *pure relation*; it is a relation that persists even when its terms disappear, and it thus provides Deleuze with an example of what he calls the concept of *difference-in-itself*. Normally, we think of difference as a relation between two things that have a prior identity ("x is different from y"). With the notion of the differential relation, Deleuze takes the concept of difference to a properly transcendental level; the differential relation is not only *external* to its terms (Bertrand Russell's empiricist dictum), but it also *determines* its terms. In other words, difference here becomes *constitutive* of identity: that is, it becomes productive and genetic. This is what Deleuze means, in *Difference and Repetition*, when he says that relations such as identity, analogy, opposition, and resemblance are all secondary *effects* or results of prior relations of difference. Deleuze, in other words, approaches the problem of existence not through logic, which takes identity as its model, but through mathematics, which—in certain of its domains—developed a symbolism capable of thinking difference.[15] If Plato found in Euclidean geometry a model of static and unchanging essences, Deleuze finds in the calculus a model of pure change (and thus a transformation in the corresponding theory of Ideas). The calculus is a symbolism for the exploration of existence. It is not by chance that the "mathematicization" of Nature, which lies at the heart of the so-called scientific revolution, took place through the calculus; "laws of nature" are expressed in the form of differential equations (Nietzsche railed against speaking of laws of Nature, since the "law" is a social concept).[16] This is why, in the nineteenth century, philosophies of Nature—from Maimon to Novalis—often took the form of explorations in the metaphysics of the calculus, and Deleuze is certainly a heritor of this tradition, although he prefers to speak of a dialectic of the calculus, rather than a metaphysics.

Second, while it is true that the sensibility of the diverse is outside the concept (in Kant, intuitions are spatio-temporal; concepts are not), it is in Ideas that thought can think difference as the sufficient reason of the diverse. Deleuze will argue that *intensity* (intensive magnitude) is the sufficient reason of the sensible.

Intensity is never given in the diversity of experience, since it cancels itself out when it is explicated, but thought can none the less think it in the form of an Idea. The phenomenon of lightning, for instance, is the result of a difference of potential in a cloud, a difference in charge, but the condition under which the lightning appears is the resolution of this charge, the cancellation of the difference. Deleuze will therefore draw a sharp distinction between diversity and difference: "Diversity is given, but difference is that by which the given is given, that by which the given is given as diverse. Difference is not the phenomenon but the noumenon closest to the phenomenon" (DR 222). Difference, in other words, is the sufficient reason of the diverse, which is not given in a concept but in an Idea—and an Idea that can become actualized in various manners. This is Deleuze's response to Leibniz's problem of sufficient reason: there is an Idea of sensibility, just as there is an Idea of matter, and thought itself is capable of penetrating this Idea. Consider two further examples. The concept "mountain" might allow us to recognize Mt. Everest, but it says nothing about the fact that Everest is the ongoing actualization of a complex process, which includes the pressure of the India tectonic plate slamming into Asia, the folding of the earth's crust, the weathering and erosion of the Himalayan range, and so on. The concept "lion" might allow us to recognize an animal in front of us, but it says nothing about the lion's territories, the paths its takes, the times it hunts and rests. The latter are *spatio-temporal dynamisms* that cannot be derived from the concept, but are the actualization of a differential Idea. "There is nothing which does not lose its identity as this is constituted by concepts," Deleuze writes, "when the dynamic space and time of its actual constitution is discovered" (DR 218–19).

Third, and perhaps more importantly, what is the condition under which thought is capable of thinking difference as the sufficient reason of the sensible? Deleuze's response is that Ideas are always given to thought under the form of *problems*; if difference is that which cannot be thought, then thought is capable of thinking difference only under a *problematic* form—in other words, as something that provokes thought, which engenders thought, which problematizes thought (which is why, in the calculus, the differential exists in the problem, but must disappear in the solution). This is Deleuze's great theme against what he calls the dogmatic image of thought: thinking is not the result of a prior disposition, but the result of forces that act upon thought from the outside, of encounters that do violence to us, that force us to think, and what engenders thinking is always an encounter with a problem. *Who* is it that in fact searches for the truth? The best model is found, not in Plato's model of friends in dialogue, but Proust's model of the jealous lover, who finds himself living within a problem, and constrained, involuntarily, to explore its conditions. Such is the paradoxical status that Deleuze assigns to metaphysics: metaphysics can indeed tell us what the ultimate components of reality are, but these components turn out to be *problems*, of which we can have no "knowledge" *per se* (they are "obscure"), although they *provoke* us to think. *Being always presents itself to us under a problematic form.* This paradox is similar to the one expressed in the doctrine of univocity. Being has a single, univocal sense—but this single sense is *difference*: that is, a disguising and displaced difference that is "neither in substance nor subject," and is "no less capable of dissolving and destroying individuals than constituting them temporarily" (DR 38).

So we conclude with three "images"—difference-in-itself as a pure relation, intensity as the sufficient reason of sensibility, and the being of problems that provoke thought—which in fact can never be given in experience, but rather constitute the *conditions* of the real. And this, indeed, is the upshot of the scenario we have tried to present here under the rubric of *Logic and Existence*. The problem we began with was: How can thought think existence? How can thought get out of its concepts and logical principles and think the real? Our screenplay presented scenes from the three great trajectories in the history of modern philosophy that attempted to resolve this problem, drawing their inspiration from one of the three principles of classical logic: identity (culminating in Leibniz, the pre-Kantian), non-contradiction (culminating in Hegel, the post-Kantian), and the excluded middle (culminating in the existentialists). But when thought uses the principles of logic, in its attempt to penetrate existence, it remains in its own element (identity); it is thought imposing its own principles on existence. Our concluding images—which point to a sequel—show how Deleuze's contribution was to have inverted the procedure, so to speak. For Deleuze, thought must think something that is contrary to the principles of thought, it must think difference, it must think that which is absolutely different from thought but which none the less gives itself to thought, and wrests thought from its natural stupor. This is no longer thought attempting to think existence, but existence forcing itself on thought, forcing itself to be thought, albeit in the form of an intelligible problem or Idea. There is thus an intelligibility to Being, there are Ideas in sensibility itself, but they always present themselves under a problematic form, as a difference that forces itself to be thought. In this sense, one could say that Deleuze remains a rationalist, but it is a modified rationalism, a rejuvenated rationalism, a rationalism unbound—in short, perhaps, an empiricism.

Fin.

PART II

Deleuze's Philosophical System

Aesthetics

Deleuze's Theory of Sensation: Overcoming the Kantian Duality

Aesthetics since Kant has been haunted by a seemingly intractable dualism. On the one hand, aesthetics designates the theory of sensibility as the form of possible experience; on the other hand, it designates the theory of art as a reflection on real experience. The first is the objective element of sensation, which is conditioned by the *a priori* forms of space and time (the "Transcendental Aesthetic" of the *Critique of Pure Reason*); the second is the subjective element of sensation, which is expressed in the feeling of pleasure and pain (the "Critique of Aesthetic Judgment" in the *Critique of Judgment*). Deleuze argues that these two aspects of the theory of sensation (aesthetics) can be reunited only at the price of a radical recasting of the transcendental project as formulated by Kant, pushing it in the direction of what Schelling once called a "superior empiricism"; it is only when the conditions of experience in general become the genetic conditions of *real* experience that they can be reunited with the structures of works of art. In this case, the principles of sensation would at the same time constitute the principles of composition of the work of art, and conversely it would be the structure of the work of art that reveals these conditions.[1] In what follows, I would like to examine the means by which Deleuze attempts to overcome this duality in aesthetics, following this single thread through the network of his thought, even if in tracing this line we sacrifice a certain amount of detail in favor of a certain perspicuity. The first part analyzes Deleuze's theory of sensation; the second, his attempt to connect this theory with the structures of the work of art.

THE THEORY OF SENSATION: "THE BEING OF THE SENSIBLE"

1. *Beyond Recognition and Common Sense.* Deleuze frequently begins his discussions of aesthetics by referring to a passage in the *Republic* where Plato distinguishes between two types of sensations: those that leave the mind tranquil and inactive, and those that force it to think. The first are objects of *recognition* ("this is a finger"), for which sensation is a more or less adequate judge.

> In these cases [writes Plato], a man is not compelled to ask of thought the question, "What is a finger?" for the sight never intimates to the mind that a finger is other than a finger . . . There is nothing here which invites or excites intelligence.[2]

Deleuze defines recognition, in Kantian terms, as the harmonious exercise of our faculties on an object that is supposedly *identical* for each of these faculties: it is the *same object* that can be seen, remembered, imagined, conceived, and so on. To be sure, each faculty (sensibility, imagination, memory, understanding, reason) has its own particular given, and its own way of acting upon the given. We recognize an object, however, when one faculty locates its given as identical to that of another, or more precisely, when all the faculties together relate their given and relate themselves to a form of identity in the object. Recognition consequently finds its correlate in the ideal of *common sense*, which is defined by Kant, not as a special "sense" or a particular empirical faculty, but by the supposed identity of the subject that functions as the foundation of our faculties, as the principle that unites them in this harmonious accord. These are two poles of what Deleuze terms the "dogmatic" image of thought and which constitutes one of the main objects of his critique: the subjective identity of the self and its faculties (common sense), and the objective identity of the thing to which these faculties refer (recognition). Thus in Kant, the "object in general" or "object = x" is the objective correlate of the "I think" or the subjective unity of consciousness.[3]

But there also exists a second kind of sensation in the world, continues Plato, sensations that force us to think, that give rise to thought. These are what Deleuze will term "signs," for reasons we shall see below; they are no longer objects of recognition but objects of a fundamental encounter. More precisely, they are no longer even recognizable as objects, but rather refer to sensible qualities or relations that are caught up in an unlimited becoming, a perpetual movement of contraries. A finger is never anything but a finger, but a large finger can at the same time be said to be small in relation to a third, just as what is hard is never hard without also being soft, and so on. Recognition measures and limits these paradoxical qualities by relating them to an object, but in themselves, these "simultaneously opposed sensations," says Plato, perplex the soul and set it in motion; they force it to think because they demand "further inquiry." Rather than a voluntary and harmonious accord, the faculties here enter into an involuntary discord that lies at the base of Plato's model of education; sensibility compels the intelligence to distinguish the large and the small from the sensible appearances that confuse them, which in turn compels the memory to begin to remember the intelligible Forms.[4]

It is sensations of this second type, Deleuze argues, that constitute the basis for any possible aesthetic. Phenomenologists like Merleau-Ponty, Straus, and Maldiney had already gone a long way toward freeing aesthetics from the presupposition of recognition. They argued that sensation, or rather "sense experience" [*le sentir*], must be analyzed not only in so far as it relates sensible qualities to an identifiable object (the figurative moment), but in so far as each quality constitutes a field that stands on its own, even though it ceaselessly interferes with other qualifies (the "pathic" moment).[5] But they still remained tied to a form of common sense, setting up "natural perception" as a norm, and locating its conditions in a sensible form or Gestalt that organizes the perceptive field as a function of an "intentional consciousness" or "lived body" situated within the horizon of the world. If *Proust and Signs* occupies a critical place in Deleuze's œuvre, it is because À *la recherche du temps perdu*, in Deleuze's reading, presents itself as a vast experiment with sensations of this second type, but one freed from the presuppositions of *both* recognition and common sense. In Proust, these signs no longer simply indicate contrary sensible qualities, as in Plato, but instead testify to a much more complicated network of implicated orders of signs: the frivolous signs of society life, the deceptive signs of love, the sensuous signs of the material world, and the essential signs of art, which will come to transform the others. Proust's narrator will discover that, when he thought he was wasting his time, he had in fact already embarked on an intellectual apprenticeship to these signs, a search for their meaning, a revelation of their truth. In each of these orders, the search inevitably passes through two essential moments: an "objectivist temptation" that seeks for the meaning of the sign in the object emitting it (his lover, the madeleine), and a "subjective compensation" that seeks their meaning in a subjective association of ideas. But in each case, the hero discovers that the truth of signs "transcends the states of subjectivity no less than the properties of the object"; it is only in the work of art that their nature will be revealed and their truth made manifest.[6]

This distinction between the recognized object and the encountered sign, Deleuze argues, corresponds to a more general distinction between two images of thought. The "dogmatic" or rationalist image can be summarized in several interrelated postulates.

1. Thought as thought formally contains the truth (innateness of ideas, *a priori* nature of concepts); thinking is the voluntary and natural exercise of a faculty, and the thinker possesses a natural love for the truth, a *philia* (hence the image of the thinker as a *philo-sophos*, a friend or lover of wisdom).
2. We fall into error, we are diverted from the truth, by external forces that are foreign to thought and distract the mind from its vocation (the body, passions).
3. Therefore, all we need in order to think truthfully is a "method" that will ward off error and bring us back to the truthful nature of thought.[7]

It is against this more or less Greek image that Deleuze counterposes the empirical power of signs and the possibility of a thought "without image."

1. Thinking is never the product of a voluntary disposition, but rather the result of forces that act upon thought involuntarily from the outside; we search for truth, we begin to think, only when compelled to do so, when we undergo a violence that impels us to such a search, that wrests us from our natural stupor. What calls for thought, says Heidegger, is the perpetual fact that "we are not yet thinking."[8]
2. The negative of thought is not error—nor even superstition (Lucretius, Spinoza), illusion (Kant), or alienation (Hegel, Marx)—but more profound enemies that prevent the genesis of thought: convention, opinion, clichés, stupidity [*bêtise*].[9]

3. Finally, what leads us to truth is not "method" but "constraint" and "chance". No method can determine in advance what compels us to think; it is rather the fortuitousness of the encounter that guarantees the necessity of what it forces us to think.

Who is it that in fact searches for the truth? It is not the *friend*, says Proust, exercising a natural desire for truth in dialogue with others, but rather the *jealous lover*, under the pressure of his beloved's lies, and the anguish they inflict.[10] The jealous lover is forced to confront a problem, whose coordinates are discovered, not through Socrates' "What is . . .?" question, but by posing the types of minor questions that Plato rejected: What happened?, When?, Where?, How?, With whom? It is the problem that imposes the "claws of necessity" on the search for truth: not a "categorical imperative," as Kant would say, but a "problematic imperative," the imperative imposed by a problem. On this score, Deleuze once said that he considered himself to be a "pure metaphysician," and that he had little interest in the Heideggerian and Derridean themes of "overcoming" metaphysics. If the old metaphysics is a bad one, he says, then we simply need to construct a new metaphysics; in this sense, he says he considered himself one of the most naive philosophers of his generation (N 88). But this is perhaps a slightly feigned move on Deleuze's part. For if one asked of Deleuze the nature of his metaphysics, or the nature of ultimate reality, or the nature of Being itself, his response would be: Being is a *problem*. Being always presents itself to us under a problematic form, as a series of problematizations. Whence the two dense chapters at the heart of *Difference and Repetition*: Chapter 4 ("The Ideal Synthesis of Difference") analyzes the ideal and intelligible nature of the problems that constitute Being itself; Chapter 5 ("The Asymmetrical Synthesis of the Sensible") analyzes the way these problems are given us—under the sensible form of an intensity that does violence to thought. If Deleuze has always considered himself an empiricist, then, it is because, "on the path which leads to that which is to be thought, everything begins with sensibility."[11]

What, then, is a sign? In *Difference and Repetition*, Deleuze assigns two primary characteristics to the sign. The first is that the sign riots the soul, renders it perplexed, as if the encountered sign were the bearer of a problem. The second is that the sign is something that can *only* be felt or sensed [*ce qui ne peut être que senti*]; as Francis Bacon says, it acts directly on the nervous system, rather than passing through the detour of the brain.[12] It is this second characteristic that reveals most clearly the difference between the encountered sign and the recognized object: the latter can not only be felt, but can also be remembered, imagined, conceived, and so on, and thus assumes the accord of the faculties that Kant calls common sense. By taking the encountered sign as the primary element of sensation, Deleuze is pointing, *objectively, to a science of the sensible freed from the model of recognition and, subjectively, to a use of the faculties freed from the ideal of common sense*. Now Kant himself had already hinted at this latter possibility in the *Critique of Judgment* where, for the first and only time, he considered a faculty freed from the form of common sense: namely, the faculty of the imagination. Up to that point, Kant had been content to create as many common senses as there were natural interests of reasonable thought (knowledge, morality, reflection), common senses which differed according to the conditions of what was to be recognized (object of knowledge, moral value, aesthetic effect . . .). In the *Critique of Pure Reason*, for example, the faculties are made to enter into a harmonious accord in the speculative interest, in which the understanding legislates over and determines the function of the other faculties ("logical common sense"); in the *Critique of Practical Reason*, the faculties enter into a different accord under the legislation of reason in the practical interest ("moral common sense"); and even in the "Analytic of the Beautiful" of the *Critique of Judgment*, the reflective imagination is still said to be under the "aesthetic common sense."[13]

But the third Critique opened up the possibility of a new domain, a "disjunctive" theory of the faculties. In the "Analytic of the Sublime," the faculty of the imagination is forced to confront its own limit, its own maximum; faced with an immense object (the desert, a mountain, a pyramid) or a powerful object (a storm at sea, an erupting volcano), the imagination strives to comprehend these sensations in their totality, but is unable to do so. It reaches the limits of its power, and finds itself reduced to impotency. This failure gives rise to a pain, a cleavage in the subject between what can be imagined and what can be thought, between the imagination and reason. But what is it that pushes the imagination to this limit, what forces it to attempt to unite the immensity of the sensible world into a whole? Kant answers that it is nothing other than the faculty of reason itself; absolute immensity and power are Ideas of reason, Ideas that can be thought but cannot be known or imagined, and which are therefore accessible *only* to the faculty of reason. The sublime thus presents us with a *dissension*, a "discordant accord," between the demands of reason and the power of the imagination. But this painful admission also gives rise to a pleasure: in confronting its own limit, the imagination at the same time goes beyond this limit, albeit in a negative way, by representing to itself the inaccessibility of this rational Idea. It presents to itself the fact that the unpresentable exists, *and that it exists in sensible nature*.[14] From the empirical point of view, this limit is inaccessible and unimaginable; but from the transcendental point of view, it is that which can *only* be imagined, that which is accessible *only* to the imagination in its transcendental exercise.

The lesson of the "Analytic of the Sublime" is that it discovers this discordant accord as the condition of possibility for the harmonious accords of the faculties that Kant evoked in the first two critiques, an accord that is not derived from pre-existent external "facts" (the "fact" of knowledge, the "fact" of morality), but is engendered internally in the subject. It is this possibility of a disjunctive use of the faculties, glimpsed fleetingly by Kant with regard to the imagination, that Deleuze will extend to the entire critical project. Rather than having all the faculties harmoniously united in an act of recognition, each faculty is made to confront its own differential limit and is pushed to its involuntary and "transcendental" exercise, an exercise in which *something is communicated violently from one faculty to another, but does not form a common sense*. Such is the *use* of the faculties put forward by Proust: a sensibility that apprehends and receives signs; an intelligence, memory, and imagination that interpret them and explicate their meaning, each according to a certain type of sign; and a pure thought which discovers their essence as the sufficient reason of the sign and its meaning. What Deleuze calls a sign is therefore neither a recognizable object nor even a particular quality of an object, but constitutes the limit of the faculty of sensibility (and each faculty in its turn must confront its own limit). As Deleuze puts it, the sign is not a sensible being, nor even a purely qualitative being (*aisthēton*), but the being of the sensible (*aisthēteon*). From the empirical point of view, the sign, in and of itself, is unsensible, not in a contingent way, as if it were too small or too distant to be grasped by our senses, but in an essential way: namely, *from the point of view of recognition and common sense*, in which sensibility can only grasp what can also be grasped by the other faculties. But from the transcendental point of view, the sign is what can *only* be felt or sensed, that which is accessible *only* to the faculty of sensibility in its transcendental exercise. The sign, in short, points to a pure aesthetic lying at the limit of sensibility: an immanent Idea or differential field beyond the norms of common sense and recognition. What, then, is this Idea of sensibility? What are these forces of the "outside" that none the less give rise to thought?

2. *The Idea of Sensibility: Differential Relations and Differences in Intensity.* Already in 1790, Salomon Maimon, one of the first post-Kantians to return to Leibniz, had proposed an essential revision of Kant on precisely this point.[15] Leibniz argued that a conscious perception must be related, not to a recognizable object situated in space and time, but to the minute and unconscious perceptions of which it is composed. I apprehend the noise of the sea or the murmur of a group of people, for instance, but not the sound of each wave or the voice of each person that composes them. These unconscious "molecular" perceptions are related to conscious "molar" perceptions, not as parts to a whole, but as what is ordinary to what is noticeable or remarkable; a conscious perception is produced when at least two of these molecular perceptions enter into a *differential relation* that determines a singular point.[16] Consider, for example, the color green: yellow and blue can be perceived, but if their perception diminishes to the point where they become indiscernible, they enter into a differential relation ($db/dy = G$) that determines the color green; in turn, yellow or blue, each on its own account, may be determined by the differential relation of two colors we cannot detect ($dy/dx = Y$). Or consider the noise of the sea: at least two minutely perceived waves must enter into a relation capable of determining a third, which "excels" over the others and becomes conscious. These unconscious perceptions constitute the "ideal genetic elements" of perception, or what Maimon called the "differentials of consciousness." It is such a virtual multiplicity of genetic elements, and the system of connections or differential relations that are established between them, that Deleuze terms an "Idea": the relations are actualized in diverse spatio-temporal relationships, just as the elements are actualized in diverse perceptions and forms. A sign, in its first aspect, is thus an "effect" of these elements and relations in the Idea: a clear perception (green) is actualized when certain virtual elements (yellow and blue) enter into a differential relation as a function of our body, and draws these obscure perceptions into clarity.[17]

Deleuze suggests that Bergson, in *The Creative Mind*, had developed a somewhat parallel conception of the Idea, using the domain of color as an example. There are two ways of determining what colors have in common. *Either* one can extract from particular colors an abstract and general idea of color ("by removing from the red that which makes it red, from the blue what makes it blue, from the green what makes it green"); *or* one can make all these colors "pass through a convergent lens, bringing them to a single point," in which case a "pure white light" is obtained that "makes the differences between the shades stand out."[18] The first case defines a generic "concept" with a plurality of objects, in which the relation between concept and object is one of subsumption, and the state of difference remains exterior to the thing. The second case defines a differential Idea in the Deleuzian sense. The different colors are no longer objects *under* a concept, but constitute an order of mixture in coexistence and succession *within* the Idea. The relation between the Idea and a given color is not one of subsumption, but one of actualization and differentiation; and the state of difference between the concept and the object is *internalized* in the Idea itself. White light may be a universal, if you will, but it is a concrete universal, a *universal variation*, and not a genus or generality. The Idea of color is like white light, which "perplexes" within itself the genetic elements and relations of all the colors, just as the Idea of sound could be conceived of as white noise.[19]

This notion of the differential Idea finds its complement in the concept of *intensity*: these elements and relations are necessarily actualized in an intensive magnitude. Kant himself had defined the principle of intensity in the "Anticipations of Perception": we know *a priori* that the matter of sensations will have a degree of intensity and that this magnitude will change along a continuum starting from the point where intensity = 0.[20] But since he defined the *form* of sensibility as extended space, Kant limited the application of intensity to the *matter* of sensible intuitions that come to fill that space. But Maimon, like Hermann Cohen after him, argued that since space as a pure intuition is a continuum, it is the form of space itself that must be defined *a priori* as intensive quantity; there is therefore an internal and dynamic construction of space that necessarily *precedes* the representation of the whole as a form of exteriority (which implies that space is actualized in a *plurality of forms*).[21] In empirical experience, to be sure, we know only intensities or forms of energy that are already localized and distributed in extended space; intensity is inseparable from a process of extension that relates it to extended space and subordinates it to the qualities that fill space. But the corresponding tendency is no less true, since every extensity necessarily envelops or implicates within itself the intensity of which it is an effect. A "sign," in its second aspect, is an intensity produced by the asymmetry of the differential relations, whereas a "quality" appears when an intensity reaches a given order of magnitude and these relations are organized in consciousness.[22] Sensations thus present a double aspect: they necessarily refer to a virtual and implicated order of constitutive differences, but they tend to cancel out those differences in the extended order in which they are explicated. These intensive forces are never given in themselves; they cannot be grasped by the empirical senses, which only grasp intensity as already recovered or mediated by the quality that it creates. They can only be sensed from the point of view of the transcendental sensibility that apprehends it immediately in the encounter as the limit of sensibility itself. With the notion of intensity, Deleuze writes, "sensation ceases to be representative and becomes real." Hence the formula: "intensity is both the unsensible and that which can only be sensed" (DR 230). What Maimon derives from this Leibnizian argument is a transcendental method of genesis rather than one of simple conditioning; a clear sensation emerges from obscurity by a *genetic* process, as it were through a series of filters, a series of successive integrations or syntheses. In the *Critique of Pure Reason*, Kant reserved the power of synthesis for the active "I think," for the activity of the understanding, and conceived of the passive ego as a simple receptivity possessing no synthetic power. Because he considered the sensible to be a quality related to an object that sensibility intuited passively, he defined the transcendental form of space, as the condition of outer sense, by its geometric extension (pure intuition of objects or bodies). And if concepts in turn could be applied to intuitions, if a harmony was possible between the understanding and sensibility, it was only through the mysterious intermediary of the "schematism" of the imagination, which alone makes the spatio-temporal relations of intuition correspond to the logical relations of the concept. But the problem with the Kantian method of conditioning, as Maimon and Cohen were quick to point out, is that it leaves unexplained the purely *external* duality between the determinable (space as a pure given) and the determination (the concept as thought), invoking "hidden" harmonies between terms that remain external to one another.[23] What the post-Kantians argued (as did Freud) is that the passive ego is itself constituted by a prodigious domain of unconscious and passive syntheses that precede and condition the activity of the "I think." Beyond Kant's external method of conditioning, Maimon proposes an *internal* method of genesis in which the relation between the determinable and the determination is internalized in the Idea. Rather than perception presupposing an object capable of affecting us, and the conditions under which we would be capable of being affected, it is the reciprocal determination of differentials (dx/dy) that entails both the complete determination of the object as perception and the determinability of space-time as conditions: *space-time ceases to be a pure given in order to become the totality or nexus of differential relations in the subject, and the object ceases to be an empirical given in order to become the product of these relations in conscious perception.*

"Difference is not diversity," writes Deleuze, "diversity is given, but difference is that by which the given is given, by which the given is given as diverse" (DR 222). The error of the dogmatic image of thought is not to deny diversity, but to tend to comprehend it only in terms of generalities or genera. One of Deleuze's philosophic aims is to show that the singularity and individuality of the diverse can only be comprehended from the viewpoint of difference itself. The Idea of sensation is constituted by two interrelated principles of difference: the differential relations between genetic elements, and the differences in intensity that actualize these relations. They do not indicate some sort of metaphysical reality beyond the senses; as Ideas they are posited in order to account for sensibility, though they are not given in experience as such. Whereas in Kant, Ideas are unifying, totalizing, and transcendent, in Deleuze, they are differential, genetic, and immanent. It is the series of filters, for example, that accounts for what Nietzsche called the faculty of forgetting, or Bergson's claim that perception is necessarily eliminative and subtractive; subjectivity *is* (rather than simply *has*) an incomplete, prejudiced, and partial perception.[24] Conversely, the significance of sensory distortions, such as those achieved in pharmaco-dynamic experiences or physical experiences such as vertigo, is often to approach the intensive depth that is always implicated in the perception of extensity: a kind of "pedagogy of the senses," says Deleuze, that forms an integral part of transcendentalism.[25] Deleuze gives an account not only of "natural" perception, but also of experiences that are often classed as "pathological," to which he assigns a positivity of their own. Indeed, in his commentary on Leibniz, Deleuze goes so far as to write that "every perception is hallucinatory because *perception has no object*," since it refers exclusively to the psychical mechanism of differential relations among unconscious perceptions (FLB 93). This is why difference must be understood, not as an empirical fact or even as a scientific concept, but as a transcendental principle, as the sufficient reason of the sensible, as the being of the sensible.

Descartes had posited the "clear and distinct" as the highest principle of common sense, a principle that would be prolonged in various forms in the post-Kantian tradition extending through Fichte and Hegel: the finite mind finds its point of departure in a confused and obscure understanding of the world, and reason constitutes a universal progress towards the clear and distinct, "the light which renders thought possible in the common exercise of the faculties."[26] In the lesser-known figures of Maimon and Cohen, Deleuze finds a "minor" post-Kantian tradition leading indirectly to Bergson and Nietzsche: a clear idea is in itself confused, and is confused *in so far as it is clear*. The conscious perception of the noise of the sea, for example, is clear but confused, for our perception comprehends the whole confusedly, and only expresses clearly certain elements and relations depending on the threshold of consciousness determined by our body. Conversely, the components of the Idea are distinct but obscure: distinct, in so far as all the drops of water remain distinct as the genetic elements of perception, with their differential relations, the variations of these relations, and the singular points they determine; but obscure, in so far as they are not yet "distinguished" or actualized in a conscious perception. Every sensation, in short, is clear but confused, but is constantly plunged back into the distinct-obscurity from which it emerged. In Deleuze, *the principle of the clear and distinct is broken down into two irreducible values that can never be reunited to constitute a natural light.*

Deleuze's theory of sensibility, in sum, is opposed to Kant's on these three interrelated points: the element of sensation must be found in the sign and not the qualities of a recognizable object; the sign is the limit-object of the faculty of sensibility, beyond the postulates of recognition and common sense; the Idea of sensibility is constituted by differential relations and differences in intensity, which give a genetic account of thought and constitute the conditions of real, and not merely possible, experience, since the conditions are never larger than what they condition.

THE THEORY OF ART: "PURE BEINGS OF SENSATION"

1. *Philosophy and Art.* With this rather summary sketch of Deleuze's theory of sensation in hand, we are now in a position to determine its relation to the theory of art.

If Deleuze's many writings on art constitute an integral part of his philosophy, it is because works of art are themselves explorations of this transcendental realm of sensibility. The most general aim of art, according to Deleuze, is to produce a sensation, to create a "pure being of sensation," a sign (WP 167). The work of art is, as it were, a "machine" or "apparatus" that utilizes these passive syntheses of sensation to produce effects of its own. The genetic principles of sensation are thus at the same time the principles of composition of the work of art; and conversely, it is the structure of the work of art that reveals these conditions. Deleuze has consequently developed his "logic" of sensation through a creative interaction with the various arts. In *What is Philosophy?* Deleuze defines philosophy as a practice of concepts, a discipline that consists in the formation, invention, or creation of concepts. "One can very easily think without concepts," he writes, "but as soon as there is a concept, there is truly philosophy" (WP 32). Art is itself a creative enterprise of thought, but one whose object is to create sensible assemblages—or affects—rather than concepts. Great artists are also great thinkers, but they think in terms of *sensations* rather than concepts. Painters, for example, think in terms of lines and colors, musicians think in sounds, film-makers think in images, and so on. Neither discipline has any privilege over the other; to create a concept is neither more difficult nor more abstract than creating new visual or audible combinations; and conversely, it is no easier to read an image than it is to comprehend a concept.

As a philosopher, Deleuze's aim in his studies of the arts is to create the concepts that correspond to these sensible aggregates. *Francis Bacon: The Logic of Sensation* creates a series of philosophic concepts, each of which relates to a particular aspect of Bacon's paintings. The text is organized in a quasi-musical fashion, divided into seventeen sequences or series that develop local concepts as if they were melodic lines, which in turn are made to enter into increasingly complex contrapuntal relations, and which together form a kind of conceptual composition that parallels Bacon's sensible compositions. Similarly, Deleuze describes his two-volume *Cinema* as "a book of logic, a logic of the cinema" that sets out "to isolate certain cinematographic concepts," concepts that are proper to the cinema, but which can only be formed *philosophically* (N 47, MI ix). The same must be said for Deleuze's essays in music, literature, and the theater, notably those collected in *Essays Critical and Clinical.*

Modern art and modern philosophy converged on a similar problem: both renounced the domain of representation and instead took the *conditions* of representation as their object. Paul Klee's famous phrase echoes through Deleuze's writings on the arts like a kind of motif: *not to render the visible, but to render visible.*[27] Much of twentieth-century painting aimed, not at the reproduction of visible forms, but at the presentation of the non-visible forces that act behind or beneath these forms. It attempted to extract from these intensive forces "a block of sensation," to produce a material capable of "capturing" these forces in a sensation. When pious critics reproached Millet for painting peasants who were carrying an offertory like a sack of potatoes, Millet responded by saying that what matters in the painting is not *what* the peasant is carrying, but rather the exact weight common to the two objects; his aim was to render the force of that weight visible in the painting. In the paintings of Cézanne, who gave this notion of force its first full expression, mountains are made to exist uniquely through the geological forces of folding they harness, landscapes through their thermal and magnetic forces, apples through the forces of germination. Van Gogh even invented unknown forces, such as the extraordinary force of a sunflower (FB 49). Proust discovered that what the worlds of signs render visible is nothing other than the various invisible structures of time (passing time, wasted time, time regained).[28] Modern music has perhaps confronted this problem most directly, trying to develop a highly complex and elaborate material capable of making the non-sonorous forces of time audible, a material that could render duration sonorous, as in the rise of timbre in Stravinsky and Boulez, Edgar Varese's ionization of sound, or John Cage's experiments in noise such as the prepared piano.[29]

Properly speaking, there is no "theory of art" in Deleuze; "art" itself is a concept, but a purely nominal one, since there necessarily exist diverse problems whose solutions are found in heterogeneous arts. Hermann Broch wrote that "the sole *raison d'être* of a novel is to discover what only the novel can discover,"[30] and each of the arts, and each work of art, confronts its own particular problems, utilizing its own particular material and techniques, and attempting to capture intensive forces of very diverse types. To say that the aim of art is not to represent the world, but to present a sensation (which is itself a composition of forces, an intensive synthesis of differential relations), is to say that every sensation, every work of art is *singular*, and that the conditions of sensation are at the same time the conditions for the production of the *new*. For this reason, we will limit ourselves here to Deleuze's examination of the *œuvre* of a single artist in *Francis Bacon: The Logic of Sensation*.

2. *The "Figure."* One of the most important concepts in Deleuze's analysis of Bacon is what Deleuze calls, following Lyotard, the "figural," which stands opposed to figuration or representation. The danger of figuration or representation in painting is that it is both illustrative and narrative. It relates the image to an object that it supposedly illustrates, thereby subordinating the eye to the model of recognition and losing the immediacy of the sensation; and it relates the image to the other images in the painting, thereby tempting us to discover a narrative link between the images. As Bacon says, "The story that is already being told between one figure and another begins to cancel out the possibilities of what can be done with the paint on its own."[31] Figuration plays a similar role in painting as does recognition in philosophy. Painting has neither a story to tell nor an object to represent; the painting itself is a sensation, an encountered sign. But this is precisely what constitutes the difficulty of the artistic task: "It is a very, very close and difficult thing," says Bacon, "to know why some paint comes across *directly* onto the nervous system and other paint tells the story in a long diatribe through the brain."[32] We return to Deleuze's formula: the sensation produced by the painting is something that can only be felt or sensed.

How does one attain a sensation in painting? Bacon's attempt to "paint the scream" is an exemplary case in point. His aim is not to paint the visible horrors of the world before which one screams, he says, but rather the *intensive* forces that produce the scream, that convulse the body so as to create a screaming mouth; the violence of a horrible spectacle must be renounced in order to attain the violence of the sensation. Expressed as a dilemma, one might say: *either* he paints the horror (the "sensational") and does not paint the scream, because he represents a horrible spectacle and introduces a story; or he paints the scream directly (the "sensation") and does not paint the visible horror, because the scream is necessarily the capture of an invisible force. If Bacon, like Cézanne, was so severe with his own works, and either destroyed or renounced many of his paintings, including many of his screams, it was because they failed to attain the sensation, and fell back into the clichés of figuration and narration. Deleuze poses the problem in this way: "If force [intensity] is the condition of sensation, it is none the less not the force which is sensed, since the sensation 'gives' something completely different from the forces that condition it." So that the essential question of the artist becomes: "How will the sensation be able to turn in upon itself, extend or contract itself sufficiently, in order to capture, in what is given to us, forces that are not given, in order to make us sense these insensible forces, *and elevate itself to its own conditions?*" (FB 48). This, then, is the task faced by the artist: How can the material used by the artist (paint, words, stone) attain this level of forces? How can it become capable of "bearing" the sensation?

Deleuze suggests that there are two general routes through which modern painting escaped the clichés of figuration and attempted to attain the sensation directly: either by moving towards abstraction, or else by moving towards the figural. The first movement, towards abstraction, developed in several directions, but was perhaps marked by two extremes. At one pole, an *abstract art* like that of Mondrian or Kandinsky, though it rejected classical figuration, still retained an arsenal of abstract forms that tried to refine sensation, to dematerialize it, to reduce it to a purely optical code. It tended towards a plane of architectonic composition in which the painting became a kind of spiritual being, a radiant material that was primarily thought rather than felt, and called the spectator to a kind of "intellectual asceticism." At the other pole, abstract *expressionism*, like that of Jackson Pollock, went beyond representation not by painting abstract forms, but by dissolving all forms in a fluid and chaotic texture of lines and colors. It attempted to give matter its maximal extension, reversing its subordination to the eye, exhibiting forces by a purely manual line that no longer outlined or delimited anything, but was spread out over the entire surface.

Now in breaking with representation, both these poles of abstraction also broke with the ancient hylomorphic model, which conceived of the artistic task as the imposition of form upon matter; the abstractionists wanted to free up the *form* in an optical code, while the expressionists wanted to free up *matter* in a manual chaos. What the hylomorphic schema ignores in defining form and matter as two separate terms, as Gilbert Simondon showed, is the process of "continuous modulation" at work behind them.[33] Matter is never a simple or homogenous substance capable of receiving forms, but is made up of intensive and energetic *traits* that not only make that operation possible but continuously alter it (clay is more or less porous, wood is more or less resistant); and forms are never fixed molds, but are determined by the *singularities* of the material that impose implicit processes of deformation and transformation (iron melts at high temperatures; marble and wood split along their veins and fibers). This is the importance of Deleuze's notion of intensity: beyond prepared matter lies an energetic materiality in continuous variation, and beyond fixed forms lie qualitative processes of deformation and transformation in continuous development. What becomes essential in modern art, in other words, is no longer the matter–form relation, but the *material–force* relation. The artist takes a given energetic material composed of intensive traits and singularities, and synthesizes its disparate elements in such a way that it can harness or capture these intensities, what Paul Klee called "the forces of the cosmos."

This task is not without ambiguity, technical and otherwise. The synthesis of the disparate elements of a material requires a certain *degree of consistency*, without which it would be impossible to distinguish the elements that constitute the sensation. Klee, for example, said that in order to produce a complex sensation, in order to harness the forces of the cosmos and render them visible, one must proceed with a sober gesture that simplifies the material, selects it, limits it. All one needs is a pure and simple line, an inflexion, and he was infuriated when people complained about the "childishness" of his drawings.[34] If one multiplies the lines, if one elaborates too rich and complex a material, the claim is that one is opening oneself up to all events, to all irruptions of force, but in fact one can merely wind up producing nothing but a scribble that effaces all lines, a "sloppiness" that in fact effaces the sensation.

It was in order to avoid this danger, as well as the danger of formalism, that Bacon followed a second path, which finds its precursor in Cézanne, and for which Lyotard coined the term "figural." Whereas "figuration" refers to a form that is related to an object it is supposed to represent (recognition), the figure is the form that is connected to a sensation, and that conveys the violence of this sensation directly to the nervous system (the sign). In Bacon's paintings, it is the human body that plays this role of the Figure; it functions as the material support or framework that sustains a precise sensation. Bacon frequently begins by *isolating* the human body inside a contour, by putting it inside a circle, a cube, a parallelepiped; balancing it on a rail; placing it on an armchair or bed. The isolated Figure is then subjected to a series of *deformations* through a series of manual techniques: making random marks, throwing the paint at the canvas, scrubbing or brushing the painting. These techniques have a double effect: on the one hand, they undo the organic and extensive unity of the body, and instead reveal what Deleuze calls its *intensive* and *non-organic* reality; on the other hand, these marks also undo the optical organization of the painting itself, since this force is rendered in a precise sensation that does violence to the eye. The marks reveal the precise point of application of the intensive force contorting the body, a cramp or a spasm twisting the figure from within, making the body shudder or vibrate violently. Bacon's primary subject matter is the body deformed by a plurality of forces: the violent force of a hiccup, a scream, the need to vomit or defecate, of copulation, the flattening force of sleep. Despite those who find Bacon's paintings horrific, Bacon's figures are not tortured bodies, but ordinary bodies in ordinary situations of discomfort just as a person forced to sit for hours would inevitably assume contorted postures.

In Bacon, the Figure is the support for a precise sensation; without this support, the sensation would remain diffuse and ephemeral, lacking clarity and duration.

In many ways, Bacon's criticisms of expressionism had already been anticipated in Cézanne's criticisms of impressionism. Sensation is not in the "free" or disincarnate play of light and color; *it* is in the *body*, and not in the air, whether this body is the human body (Bacon) or the body of an apple (Cézanne). "Sensation is what is being painted," writes Deleuze, "what is painted on the canvas is the body, not in so far as it is represented as an object, but in so far as it is experienced as sustaining *this* sensation" (FB 32). This, then, is the *via media* followed by Bacon: without a material framework, the sensation remains chaotic, but on its own the framework remains abstract.

3. *The Asymmetrical Synthesis of the Sensible.* How does the Figure attain the "sensation" in Bacon's painting? We have seen that every sensation is intensive, that it implicates within itself a difference in quantity between unequal forces; it is thus necessarily *synthetic*, effecting a passive and asymmetrical synthesis between forces. "Every sensation is already an 'accumulated' or 'coagulated' sensation" (FB 33). A sensation cannot capture the "forces of the cosmos," in other words, unless the artist is capable of effecting such syntheses in the material. If we left the nature of these syntheses unexplored until now, it is because it is in the work of art that they are most clearly revealed. On this score, Deleuze has analyzed three fundamental types of asymmetrical syntheses of the forces that Bacon effects in his work.[35]

"Vibration," or the Connective Synthesis: the construction of a single series. The first type of synthesis is vibration, which characterizes a simple sensation. Even this simple type of sensation, however, is already composite, since it is defined by a difference in intensity that rises or falls, increases or decreases, an invisible pulsation that is more nervous than cerebral. Like every great painter, Bacon will attain this vibratory state primarily through a complex use of color. The Impressionists had already discovered the role of complementary colors in painting; if one is painting grass, there must not only be a green on the canvas, but also the complementary red, which will make the tone vibrate, and achieve a sunlit sensation that is produced by the "flash" between these two complementary colors. Cézanne, after having reproached Impressionists for submerging the object and depicting the atmosphere, refused to separate the tones according to the visual spectrum (the Newtonian conception of color) and instead mixed his complementary colors in critical proportions (in a manner closer to Goethe's theory of color than Newton's), thereby attempting to restore to the object a "Figure" through a progressive *modulation* of chromatic nuances.[36] Bacon will do much the same when he constitutes the flesh of his Figures through a flow of polychromatic colors, which are frequently dominated by blue and red, the colors of meat. "Each broken tone indicates the immediate exercise of a force upon the corresponding zone of the body or the head, it immediately renders a force visible" (FB 121). When Deleuze writes, in the preface to *Francis Bacon*, that the summit of the logic of sensation lies in the "coloring sensation," it is because, for the painter, everything is "rendered" through pure relations of color, *color is discovered as the differential relation upon which everything else depends.* Even a simple sensation is a relation between colors, a vibration. Jean-Luc Godard is one of the great colorists of the cinema, and his statement about *Weekend*—"It's not blood, it's *red*"—constitutes one of the great formulas of colorism.[37]

"Resonance," or the Conjunctive Synthesis: the convergence of (at least) two series. The second type of synthesis, more complex, is that of *resonance*. In this case, two simple Figures or sensations, rather than simply being isolated and deformed, confront each other, like two wrestlers, in a "hand-to-hand combat," and are thereby made to *resonate*. Bacon, for instance, frequently puts two bodies in a single painting, bodies that are copulating or sleeping entangled, in such a way that the bodies themselves are rendered indiscernible and made to resonate together in a single "matter of fact," in order to make something appear that is irreducible to the two: this sensation, this Figure. Deleuze argues that the great example of resonance in literature can be found in Proust's involuntary memory, in which two sensations (for instance, the present flavor of the madeleine and the past memory of Combray) are coupled together in order to make a pure Figure appear that internalizes the difference between the two sensations: Combray-in-itself. What is important in resonance is that (at least) two sensations are *coupled* together, and from them is extracted an ineffable "essence" (Proust) or "figure" (Bacon) that is irreducible to either of them: something new is produced.[38]

"Forced Movement," or the Disjunctive Synthesis: the affirmation of divergent series. Finally, there is the most complicated of these syntheses, what Deleuze calls a *forced movement*. This is no longer a coupling of sensations, but on the contrary their distention or deviation. In Bacon, this appears most clearly in the triptychs, in which the Figures, rather than being isolated or coupled, are set apart from each other in separate panels. How can the separated Figures of the triptychs be said to present a single "matter of fact"? It is because in them the separated Figures achieve such an extraordinary amplitude between them that the limits of sensation are broken; sensation is no longer dependent upon a Figure *per se*, but rather *the intensive rhythm of force itself becomes the Figure of the triptychs*. The Figures loosen their grip on each other, and are no longer united by anything but the *distance* that separates them, and the light, the air, or the void which inserts itself between them like a wedge. It is because of this amplitude that Deleuze assigns a privileged place to the triptychs in Bacon's work.[39]

Vibration, resonance, and forced movement are the concepts Deleuze creates to describe the three types of syntheses that Bacon utilizes to "paint the sensation." In general, these constitute the intensive conditions of sensation, the three "varieties" of compositions of sensation, the three modalities of a "being of sensation." To be sure, each of these syntheses coexists in Bacon's paintings, which are concrete assemblages of differences, mixed states. In the individual paintings, for example, the large fields of uniform color already effect a distancing function similar to that of the triptychs (disjunction), but are likewise themselves composed of subtle variations of intensity or saturation (connection); and vibrations in turn are already effects of resonance, since they couple together diverse levels of sensation (conjunction).[40] The important point is that the artist utilizes these intensive syntheses in order to produce "a pure being of sensation"; the work of art is a functional "machine" that *produces* effects of vibration, resonance, and forced movement. The question that must therefore be posed to a work of art is not "What does it mean?" (interpretation) but rather "How does it work?" (experimentation): "What are the connections, what are the disjunctions, the conjunctions, what use is made of the syntheses?" (AO 109).

The sensation itself, however, must not be confused with the material in which these syntheses are affected. Art is composition, but the technical composition of the material is not the same as the aesthetic composition of the sensation. It is true that in fact (*quid facti?*) the sensation lasts no longer than its support or materials (stone, canvas, chemical color, etc.). But in principle at least (*quid juris?*), the sensation is of a different order than the material, and exists in itself for as long as the material lasts. Oil painting, Deleuze suggests, provides a useful example of this distinction, since it can be approached in two manners. In a first case, the *sensation is realized in the material* and projected on to it; an outline is sketched on a white background, and color, light and shade are added afterwards. In a second case, which modern art has increasingly tended to adopt, it is the *material that passes into sensation*; rather than beginning with a sketch, the painter gradually "thickens" the background, adding color alongside color, piling up or folding the material in such a way that the architecture of the sensation emerges from the medium itself, and the material becomes indiscernible from the sensation. In either case, however, it is matter itself that becomes expressive, so that one can say of the sensation itself that it is metallic, crystalline, stony, coloring, and so on. The material constitutes the *de facto* condition of the sensation, and in so far as this condition is satisfied, even if only for a few seconds (as in Tinguely's self-destructing creations), it gives the compound of created sensations the power to exist and to be preserved in and of itself: a "monument."[41]

The work of art is thus a synthetic unity. But what is the nature of this unity, if the heterogeneous elements it synthesizes have no other relation to each other than sheer difference? The elements brought together by the work of art cannot be said to be fragments of a lost unity or shattered totality; nor can the parts be said to form or prefigure the unity of the work through the course of a logical or dialectical development or an organic evolution. Rather than functioning as their totalizing or unifying principle, the work of art can only be understood as the *effect* of the multiplicity of the disconnected parts. The work of art produces a unity, but this product is simply a new part that is added alongside the other parts. The artwork neither unifies nor totalizes these parts, but it has an effect on them because it establishes syntheses between elements that in themselves do not communicate, and that retain all their difference in their own dimensions. Art establishes "transversals" between the elements of multiplicities, but without ever reducing their difference to a form of identity or gathering up the multiplicity into a totality. The work of art, as a compound of sensations, is not a unification or totalization of differences, but rather *the production of a new difference*, and "style" in art always begins with the synthetic relations between heterogeneous differences.[42]

Deleuze's aesthetic theory is not a theory of reception, an analytic of the spectator's judgments of a work of art, but a theory of aesthetics written from the point of view of creation. Its guiding question is: What are the conditions for the production of the *new*? In light of this question, our aim has been to show how Deleuze's philosophy of "difference" overcomes the duality with which aesthetics has been encumbered since Kant. On the one hand, breaking with the model of recognition and common sense, and the image of thought from which they are derived, Deleuze locates the element of sensation, not in a recognizable object but in an encountered sign. The sign constipates the limit-object of sensibility, an intensive product of differential relations; it is intensity, and not the *a priori* forms of space and time, that constitutes the condition of real, and not merely possible, experience. On the other hand, these genetic principles of sensibility are at the same time the principles of composition of the work of art. The artist uses these intensive syntheses to produce a bloc of sensations, and in turn it is the work of art itself that reveals the nature of these syntheses. In this way, Deleuze's logic of sensation reunites the two dissociated halves of aesthetics: the theory of forms of experience (as "the being of the sensible") and the work of art as experimentation (as "a pure being of sensation"). "The work of art quits the domain of representation in order to become "experience," transcendental empiricism or the science of the sensible" (DR 56). If Deleuze's various writings on art are, as he says, "philosophy, nothing but philosophy," it is precisely because they constitute explorations of, and experimentations within, this transcendental domain of sensibility.

Dialectics

Deleuze, Kant, and the Theory of Immanent Ideas

One of Deleuze's primary aims in *Difference and Repetition* is to present a new theory of Ideas (dialectics) in which Ideas are conceived of as both immanent and differential. What I would like to examine in this essay is the relation between Deleuze's theory of Ideas and the theme of immanence, particularly with regard to the theory of Ideas found in Kant's three critiques.[1] In using the term "Idea," Deleuze is not referring to the common-sense use of the term, or the use to which empiricists like Hume or Locke put it, for whom the word "idea" refers primarily to mental representations. Rather, Deleuze is referring to the concept of the Idea that was first proposed by Plato, and then modified by Kant and Hegel. Plato, Kant, and Hegel are the three great figures in the history of the theory of Ideas, for whom Ideas are as much ontological as epistemological. Deleuze's name can now be added to that list, perhaps, since he has modified the theory of Ideas in a profound and essential manner.

I will focus on Deleuze's relation to Kant rather than Plato or Hegel, since Deleuze tends to index his own theory of Ideas primarily on Kant. There are two reasons for this. On the one hand, Deleuze's critique of Plato's theory of Ideas largely functions as a propaedeutic to his reading of Kant. For Deleuze, Plato created the concept of the Idea in order to provide a criterion to distinguish or "select" between things and their simulacra—for instance, between Socrates (the true philosopher) and the sophists (the simulacral counterfeits). Deleuze criticizes Plato for assigning Ideas a *transcendent* status, and he thus takes up Plato's project anew in order to rejuvenate it; Ideas, he argues, must be made *immanent*, and therefore *differential*. Yet this was already Kant's project; in the fascinating text at the opening of the Transcendental Dialectic, Kant criticizes Plato for assigning to Ideas a "transcendent object," while at the same time justifying his own appropriation of the Platonic concept of Ideas and giving them a new status.[2] On the other hand, if Plato functions as a precursor to Kant with regard to the theory of Ideas, Hegel functions as a rival successor. Despite his reputation, Deleuze is not "against the dialectic." Although this phrase appears as a chapter title in *Nietzsche and Philosophy*, being against the dialectic in this book more or less means being against Hegel's particular conception of the dialectic. The crucial chapter in *Nietzsche and Philosophy* is its central chapter, which is entitled, precisely, "Critique," indicating that the central focus of the book is Nietzsche's own position within the post-Kantian heritage. Following Kant, both Hegel and Deleuze attempted to create immanent conceptions of the dialectic; but for Hegel's use of contradiction and negation, Deleuze will substitute—as he puts it in his early writings—an appeal to difference and affirmation.[3] Deleuze is thus both close to and distant from Hegel: close, in that their projects are similar (developing a post-Kantian dialectic); but distant, in that they pursue this project in divergent manners.

Although Deleuze's early books are explicitly anti-Hegelian, the manifest anti-Hegelianism of Deleuze's early philosophical writings is sustained by a much deeper engagement with Kant. Following the work of Maimon, among others, the post-Kantians such as Fichte, Schelling, and Hegel developed Kant's thought in a direction that still found its ground in a principle of identity (Hegel's appeal to the principle of non-contradiction). The strategy of Deleuze's early work was to return to Kant himself, and take up again the problems that generated the post-Kantian tradition, but to develop solutions to those problems that were very different from the solutions that led to Hegel. In his attempt to develop a new theory of Ideas, and a new conception of dialectics, Deleuze would ultimately substitute for the "major" tradition of post-Kantian philosophy—Fichte, Schelling, Hegel—his own "minor" tradition comprised of Maimon, Nietzsche, and Bergson.

What one finds in Deleuze's philosophy is not a rejection of dialectics, but rather *a new concept of the dialectic* that breaks with previous conceptions. Aristotle defined dialectics as the art of posing problems as the subject of a syllogism, while analytics gives us the means of resolving the problem by leading the syllogism to its necessary conclusion. Dialectics in general thus concerns the nature of problems, and its concept changes with the notion of the *problematic* that is associated with it. (*Difference and Repetition* was originally intended to be a thesis on "the Idea of the problem.")[4] The Socratic and Platonic dialectics have their source in a particular type of problem or form of question: the "What is . . .?" question. Kant himself, in turn, would later define dialectical Ideas as "problems without solution."[5] But what was missed in these earlier characterizations of the dialectic, Deleuze argues, was the internal or immanent character of the problem as such, "the imperative internal element which decides in the first place its truth or falsity and measures its internal genetic power, that is, *the very object of the dialectic or combinatory, the "differential."*[6] In what follows, I would like to examine Deleuze's theory of Ideas (as immanent and differential), in a somewhat oblique manner, by comparing it to the theory of Ideas developed by Kant in his three critiques. From the viewpoint of the theory of Ideas, *Difference and Repetition* can be read as Deleuze's *Critique of Pure Reason*, just as *Anti-Oedipus* can be read as his *Critique of Practical Reason* (the theory of desire). If the theory of Ideas can be seen as the thread that unites Kant's critical project, Deleuze's own differential and immanent theory of Ideas (the plane of immanence) can similarly be seen as the "rhizome" that gathers together (but does not totalize) the diverse strands of Deleuze's own philosophical project.

IDEAS IN THE *CRITIQUE OF PURE REASON*

Let us begin with the *Critique of Pure Reason*. In the first critique, Kant distinguishes between three types of concepts: empirical concepts, a *priori* concepts or categories, and Ideas. Empirical concepts are concepts like "white" and "lily" that give us genuine knowledge. In a judgment of knowledge, such concepts are applied to a multiplicity (or manifold) of sensations; through the imagination I synthesize these perceptions, and in applying a concept to them, I can recognize the object before me ("So it's a white lily"). But Kant also identifies a second type of concept, which are a *priori* concepts or what Kant, following Aristotle, calls "categories." Categories are concepts that are applicable, not just to empirical objects such as tables and roses, but to all objects of possible experience. Neither the concept "white" nor the concept "flowers" is a category, since not every object is white, and not all white objects are lilies. But the concept of "cause" *is* a category, because I cannot conceive of an object that does not have a cause. If an angel were suddenly to appear and hover in the center of a room, our first question would be, "Where did that come from?" since it is part of our concept of *any* object whatsoever to have been caused by something else. Categories are thus a *priori* concepts that are applicable to every object of any possible experience. Indeed, Kant's notion of "possible experience" is derived from his notion of the category: it is the categories that define the domain of possible experience.

Finally, there is a third type of concept in the *Critique of Pure Reason*, which Kant calls "Ideas" (in a modified Platonic sense). An Idea is the concept of an object that goes beyond or transcends any possible experience. There are various kinds of transcendent concepts: for instance, anytime we speak of something "pure" or "absolute"—for example, the "pure gift" in Derrida, or "absolute zero" in physics, or even (in Kant's example) "pure earth, pure water, pure air"—we are outside the realm of possible experience, since experience presents us with impure mixtures and non-absolutes.[7] Although we can *think* such objects, we can never *know* them—since, for Kant, knowledge requires the application of a concept to intuitions, and we can never have an intuition of the objects of Ideas. Kant himself, however, famously focuses primarily on three transcendent Ideas, which constitute the three great terminal points of metaphysics: the soul, the world, and God. Each of these Ideas goes beyond any possible experience. There is no object that could correspond to such Ideas; we can never have a "possible experience" of them.

For example, the Idea of the world (as the totality of what is) has no intuition or perception that could correspond to it. We initially arrive at this Idea through an extension of the category of causality: that is, through the use of the hypothetical syllogism (if A, then B) —if A causes B, and B causes C, and C causes D, and so on. This series constitutes a kind of *problem* for us. We can continue working through this problem, continuing through the series indefinitely, until we finally reach the "Idea" of the totality of everything that is: the causal nexus of the world, or the Universe. Reason, in other words, can easily construct a concept of the world, but it can never have a perception or intuition of the world. Hence the famous Kantian distinction: we can *think* the world *as if* it were an object, but we can never *know* it. Strictly speaking, the world is not an object of our experience; what we actually know is the *problematic* of causality, a series of causal relations that we can extend indefinitely. *It is this problem, Kant says, that is the true object of the Idea of the world.* Hence, we are led into inevitable illusions when we ask questions about the world *as if* it were an object of experience. For instance: Did the world have a beginning in time, or is it eternal? Does it have boundaries in space, or does it go on forever? These are false questions because they are being asked about an object that does not exist as an object of possible experience. Whenever we think of the world as an object (rather than as the problematic of the series of conditions), we enter into the domain of a false problem, an illusion internal to reason itself. The same holds for our Ideas of the soul and God. In the "Transcendental Dialectic," the longest section of the *Critique of Pure Reason*, Kant analyzes the nature of the logical paradoxes or aporias that Reason is inevitably led into because of these illusions: the *paralogisms* of the soul, the *antinomies* of the world, the *ideal* of God. (One might note here that Jacques Derrida's later philosophy deals almost entirely with the aporetic status of transcendent Ideas such as the pure gift, unconditional forgiveness, the wholly other, and so on.)

This is why Kant was one of the first philosophers to formulate explicitly the difference between the ancient philosophical themes of transcendence and immanence: "We shall entitle the principles whose application is confined entirely within the limits of possible experience, *immanent*; and those, on the other hand, which profess to pass beyond these limits, *transcendent*."[8] But one must add immediately that "transcendent" and "transcendental" are not identical terms, and in fact are opposed to each other.[9] The aim of Kant's transcendental project is to discover criteria immanent to the understanding that are capable of distinguishing between two different uses of the syntheses of consciousness: legitimate immanent uses, and illegitimate transcendent uses (the transcendent Ideas). *Transcendental* philosophy is a philosophy of immanence, and implies a ruthless critique of *transcendence* (which is why Deleuze, at least on this score, does not hesitate to align himself with Kant's critical philosophy, despite their obvious differences). This is also why Kant can assign to Ideas a legitimate immanent use as well as an illegitimate transcendent use. The immanent use is regulative: Ideas constitute ideal *focal points* or *horizons* outside experience that posit the unity of our conceptual knowledge as a *problem*; they can therefore help regulate the systematization of our scientific knowledge in a purely immanent manner. The illegitimate transcendent use is constitutive: it falsely posits or constitutes an object that supposedly corresponds to the problem. At best, reason can simply postulate a harmony or (in Kant's terminology) an "analogy" between its Ideas and the material objects of experience; reason here is the faculty that says, "Everything happens *as if* . . ." (as if there were a world, or a soul, or a God . . .).

In *Difference and Repetition*, Deleuze identifies three components of Kant's concept of the Idea, which can be distinguished from the components of the Platonic Idea.[10]

1. First, ideas are *indeterminate* with regard to their object. Since their object lies outside of any possible experience, it can neither be given nor known, but only

represented as a problem. The real object of ideas, in other words, can only be comprehended in a *problematic* form, *as* a problem. (The concept of problematics is the only component of Kant's theory of Ideas that Deleuze will adopt without question.)

2. Second, Ideas are none the less *determinable* by analogy with the objects of experience (with regard to the content of phenomena), since concepts are capable of comprehending more and more differences on the basis of a properly infinite field of continuity.

3. Third, Ideas imply a regulative ideal of *infinite determination* in relation to the concepts of the understanding (or the form of phenomena), since my concepts are capable of comprehending more and more differences on the basis of a properly infinite field of continuity.

Now, in effect, this is the point where Chapter 4 of *Difference and Repetition* begins—the chapter entitled "Ideas and the Synthesis of Difference."[11] In an important passage, Deleuze defines an Idea as "an internal problematic objective unity of the undetermined, the determinable, and determination." But, he continues, "perhaps this does not appear sufficiently clearly in Kant." Why not? Because in Kant,

> two of the three moments [in the concept of the idea] remain as extrinsic characteristics: if Ideas are themselves undetermined [or problematic], they are determinable only in relation to objects of experience, and bear the ideal of determination only in relation to the concepts of the understanding. (DR 170)

Hence, he concludes, "the 'critical' point, the horizon or focal point at which difference *qua* difference serves to unite, has not yet been assigned" (DR 170). In other words, we have not yet reached a purely *immanent* conception of Ideas, since it is only a principle of difference that can determine, in a precise manner, the problematic nature of Ideas as such, thereby uniting the three aspects of the Idea (as undetermined, determinable, and reciprocally determined). What Deleuze derives from his reading of the theory of Ideas in the *Critique of Pure Reason* is essentially a program of his own: to develop a purely immanent theory of Ideas, pushing Kant's own trajectory to its immanent conclusions. Put simply, whereas Kantian ideas are unifying, totalizing, and conditioning (transcendent Ideas), for Deleuze they will become multiple, differential, and genetic (immanent Ideas). The question is: what leads Deleuze to develop his purely immanent theory of Ideas?

IDEAS IN THE *CRITIQUE OF JUDGMENT*

The answer to this question takes us to Kant's third critique, the *Critique of Judgment*, which in certain respects goes beyond the theory of Ideas developed in the first critique. I would simply like to make three points about Deleuze's relation to the third critique, each of which outlines an agenda that could no doubt be elaborated in more detail.

First, someone intervenes in our analysis before we even get to the third critique: namely, the Lithuanian-born philosopher Salomon Maimon (1753–1800). Though largely unknown in the English-speaking world, Maimon is a crucial figure in the history of post-Kantianism.[12] It was Maimon who posed the essential problems that animated the post-Kant heritage, and he is an important figure in Deleuze's own philosophical development. In 1790—a full year before the publication of the *Critique of Judgment*—Maimon published a book on Kant's thought entitled *Essay on Transcendental Philosophy*, whose importance Kant himself recognized ("None of my critics understand me and the main questions as well as Mr. Maimon does").[13] Maimon's primary objection was that Kant had ignored the demands of *a genetic method*, by which Maimon means two things. One the one hand, Kant simply assumes that there are *a priori* "facts" of reason (the "fact" of knowledge, or the "fact" of morality) and then seeks the "condition of possibility" of these facts in the transcendental. Against Kant, Maimon argues that it is illegitimate to assume these supposed "facts" of knowledge or morality; instead, one must show how they are *engendered* immanently from reason alone as the necessary modes of its manifestation. In short, a method of *genesis* has to replace the Kantian method of *conditioning*. On the other hand, Maimon says, such a genetic method requires the positing of a principle of difference in order to function: whereas identity is the condition of possibility of thought in general, it is *difference* that constitutes the genetic condition of real thought. These two exigencies laid down by Maimon—the search for the genetic elements of real experience (and not merely the conditions of possible experience), and the positing of a principle of difference as the fulfillment of this condition—reappear in almost every one of Deleuze's books up to *Difference and Repetition* (1968).

Second, Deleuze presumes that Kant, having read Maimon and declared him to be his most astute reader, effectively tried to respond to him in the *Critique of Judgment*. The *Critique of Judgment* is the only one of Kant's critiques to adopt a genetic viewpoint, and not merely the viewpoint of conditioning. This is why Deleuze finds the *Critique of Judgment* to be such an astounding book, "an unrestrained work of old age, which his successors have still not caught up with: all the mind's faculties overcome their limits, the very limits that Kant had so carefully laid down in the works of his prime" (WP 2). What plays the genetic role in the *Critique of Judgment*? Unsurprisingly, it is the Ideas of reason. The third critique famously begins with an analysis of aesthetic judgments of taste, in which the imagination as *free* enters into a spontaneous accord with the understanding as *indeterminate*—which is what Kant calls the "free play" of the faculties. In a judgment of knowledge ("This is a white lily"), the activity of the imagination (synthesizing and schematizing) is not free, since it is determined in conformity with concepts of the understanding. In an aesthetic judgment ("This white lily is beautiful"), by contrast, the imagination displays its freedom by no longer schematizing, but by reflecting on the *form* or composition of the object. Since it does not come into being under a determinate concept, this free play cannot be known intellectually, but can only be *felt* as a pleasure, which we presume can be communicated to others (aesthetic common sense). On the basis of this initial analysis, Kant puts forward the more profound argument that *every* determinate accord of the faculties—that is, every type of judgment—finds the ground of its possibility in the free and indeterminate accord of the faculties presented in "reflective" judgments (that is, in judgments made without a concept). This is the problem that animates the third critique: if this free accord of the faculties (or "powers" of the mind) grounds *every* act of judgment, from where does it come? Aesthetic judgment simply *posits* this free accord, but it does not explain how it is *engendered* in the subject. This is where the Ideas of reason intervene. If reflective judgments are made without a concept, *they always have an operative relationship to Ideas*, and the aim of the *Critique of Judgment* is to analyze the genetic role of four specific Ideas: the sublime, the symbol, genius, and the teleological Idea (purpose in Nature). The first three (aesthetic) moments are particularly illustrative for our purposes.[14]

In the first moment, Kant turns to the sublime as a model. In the feeling of the sublime, the imagination confronts something immense in nature, something infinite and formless, and it tries to comprehend this immensity in its totality—but it fails, and reaches the limit of its power. But what is it that constrains the imagination in this way? It is only in appearance, Kant tells us, that the sublime is related to sensible nature. In reality, it is nothing other than *reason*—an Idea of reason—that obliges us to try to unite the infinity of the sensible world into a whole or a totality. Whereas taste entails a relation between the imagination and the understanding, the sublime entails a relation between the imagination and reason. Reason can easily *think* immense magnitudes, but the imagination can scarcely retain seven or eight parts of a series at a time. Faced with something immense, reason says "Totalize!" and the imagination responds "I can't!" There is a discord between the faculties, a dissension, a pain. Yet at the same time, it gives rise to a pleasure. Just when the imagination thinks it has lost its freedom, through the violence of reason, it discovers its supersensible destination: that is, the fact that it can represent to itself the inaccessibility of a rational Idea—a kind of negative presentation of the Infinite that prepares us for the advent of the moral law. The important point, for Deleuze, is that the sublime is the object of a veritable *genesis*; it is generated by the conflict of these two faculties in the subject—the imagination and reason—and it is the Idea of reason that lies at the *genesis* of the feeling of the sublime.

The second moment—symbolization—goes even further, while utilizing the model furnished by the sublime. If I see a flower in front of me, I can make several different types of judgment about it: I can make a judgment of knowledge, using the concepts of the understanding ("This is a white lily"), or I can make a judgment of beauty, in the "free play" of the imagination and the understanding ("This white lily is beautiful"). But reason, looking over the shoulder of both the imagination and the understanding, can make a third type of judgment. It can "symbolize": that is, it can relate the concepts of color and flower, no longer to the white lily as such, but to something else—to an Idea, for instance, the Idea of pure innocence ("This white lily is a 'symbol' of innocence"). In this way we transfer "the reflection upon an object of intuition to quite a new concept, and one with which perhaps no intuition could ever directly correspond."[15] In symbolization, the *contents* or materials of nature (colors, sounds . . .), and not merely its *forms*, overwhelm the determinate concepts of the understanding; they "give food for thought," much more than is contained in the concept. The concepts of whiteness and lily are here enlarged beyond their usual use, and made to symbolize an Idea (innocence) that, though never given directly, is a reflexive analogue of the whiteness in the lily. In symbolization, in short, the Ideas of reason become the object of an indirect presentation in the free materials of nature.

Symbolization, in turn, provides the key to Kant's "deduction" of aesthetic judgments. It gives us a clue for explaining what the mere "analytic of the beautiful" could not explain—namely, *how* the imagination became free and the understanding became indeterminate in an aesthetic judgment. Although aesthetic pleasure is disinterested (it is not concerned with the existence of objects), Kant says that it can none the less be *united synthetically* with an interest of reason. This rational interest bears exclusively on the *aptitude* that nature possesses to produce beautiful forms that can be reflected in the imagination. This interest does not bear directly upon the beautiful form as such, but on the content used by nature to produce objects capable of being reflected formally. Nature, to be sure, produces both its contents and forms mechanistically, and in an aesthetic judgment, there is no *necessary* subjection of nature to our feeling of pleasure. None the less, reason itself has a "meta-aesthetic" interest in the *contingent* accord of the productions of nature with our aesthetic pleasure.

> It is of *interest* to reason that Ideas should have an objective reality ... that nature should at least indicate by a trace or sign that it encloses within itself a principle that allows us to admit a legitimate accord of its productions with our satisfaction.[16]

This is what appears in symbolization: when the free materials of nature contingently symbolize Ideas of reason, they allow the understanding to expand (its concepts are enlarged) and the imagination to become free (it no longer needs to schematize, under the legislation of the understanding, but becomes capable of reflecting form freely). The accord between imagination as free and the understanding as indeterminate is no longer merely assumed, but is shown to have been *engendered* by the interest of reason in the contingent accord of nature with our faculties. In Kant's deduction of aesthetic judgments, it is the Ideas of reason—and the interest of reason—that provide the principle of a transcendental genesis of the feeling of the beautiful.

The third moment, finally, complements the second: what symbolization does for the beautiful in nature, the principle of *genius* does for the beautiful in art. Genius is an innate disposition of a subject by means of which nature creates *another* nature (art) whose phenomena would be true events of the mind, which likewise "give food for thought" and force one to think. Kant defines genius as the faculty of aesthetic Ideas, but an aesthetic Idea is really the same thing as rational Idea: the former expresses what is inexpressible in the latter, turning a phenomenon of Nature (death, love . . .) into a spiritual event. Genius is thus close to symbolization (the genius extends the understanding and liberates the imagination), but instead of presenting the Idea indirectly in nature, the genius expresses it secondarily through the creation of a work of art. Kant's theory of genius thus sustains a tenuous equilibrium between a mature classicism and a nascent Romanticism (KCP 57): art is the incarnation of the Idea in the work of art, and the genius is the means by which nature gives to art a synthetic rule and a rich material. The move away from Romanticism in twentieth-century art would entail a break with both these Kantian themes: a de-consecration of the work of art (in favor, for instance, of Duchamp's ready-mades, temporary installations, happenings, improvisations) and a dis-investiture of the powers of the artist (in favor of a dispersal of the artistic act within everyday life).[17] Each of these three moments, however, exemplifies the Kantian theme that Ideas of reason can be presented in sensible nature. The sublime is a direct presentation of Ideas, which is produced by projection but remains negative, bearing upon the inaccessibility of the Idea; in symbolization, the presentation is positive but indirect, and is achieved by reflection; in genius or artistic symbolization, the presentation is positive but secondary, and is achieved through the creation of an "other" nature. (A fourth mode, analyzed in the second half of the *Critique of Judgment*, is teleological: a positive presentation of Ideas, primary and direct, which is produced in nature conceived as a system of ends.)

The first part of the *Critique of Judgment* thus presents us with three parallel geneses—from the sublime, the genesis of the reason–imagination accord; from the rational interest connected with the beautiful, the genesis of the imagination–understanding accord with regard to the beautiful in nature (symbolization); from genius, the genesis of the imagination–understanding accord with regard to the beautiful in art—all of which have their origin in the theory of Ideas. This is where Deleuze's reading of Kant differs sharply from Heidegger's: the secret of Kant's thought does not lie in the imagination, as Heidegger proposed, since the imagination always points beyond itself toward a theory of Ideas.[18] In the first two critiques, the faculties enter into harmonic relations under the regulation of a legislating faculty; but in the third critique, Kant shows that they are capable of entering into free and unregulated exercises, in which each faculty is pushed to its own limit, forming dissonant accords with each other, "a pathos that lets them evolve freely in order to form strange combinations as sources of time" (ECC 34). For Deleuze, it is in the theory of Ideas that the secrets of space, of temporality, of ethics, of sensibility, of thought, are to be found—even in Kant himself.

Third, Deleuze argues that, ultimately, Kant did not go far enough, even in the third critique (though Kant did go so far as to introduce the method of genesis). When Deleuze attempts to develop his own theory of Ideas in *Difference and Repetition*, he turns, not to Kant—who receives only a couple of pages of analysis at the beginning of the chapter on Ideas—but to Leibniz. In this, he takes his cue from Maimon himself, who argued that Kantianism could only be revised (into a "transcendental empiricism" rather than a "transcendental idealism") by means of a return to Hume, Leibniz, and Spinoza. In this sense, Maimon functions as a true precursor to Deleuze, who wrote monographs on all three of these thinkers. Deleuze himself is explicit on this point. "Doing this [that is, developing an immanent theory of Ideas] means returning to Leibniz," he remarked in one his seminars, "but on bases other than Leibniz's. All the elements to create a genesis, as demanded by the post-Kantians, are virtually present in Leibniz" (20 May 1980). This might seem somewhat surprising: Deleuze, the self-proclaimed empiricist, deriving his most important concepts from Leibniz, the arch-rationalist (and who himself never actually proposes a theory of Ideas, in this Kantian sense)? But it is not entirely difficult to see why Deleuze turns to Leibniz. There are two ways of overcoming the concept–intuition duality in Kant: either concepts are sensible things, as in Locke; or sensibility itself is intelligible, as in Leibniz (there are Ideas in sensibility itself). In effect, Deleuze takes this latter path.

Deleuze's readings of Leibniz, not only in *The Fold*, but even more so in *Difference and Repetition* and *The Logic of Sense*, are decidedly critical and post-Kantian appropriations of Leibniz. Many, if not most, of the fundamental criteria Deleuze uses to define immanent Ideas are derived from Leibniz, or from the subsequent history of the calculus: differential relations, singular points, ordinary points, fluxes or flows, the virtual, multiplicities or manifolds, and so on, which are themselves subject to a deduction in Deleuze's writings. The differential relation, for instance, is a relation that persists even when the terms of the relation have vanished. It is thus a "pure" relation; it is what Deleuze means by "difference-in-itself." Moreover, not only is the differential relation external to its terms, but it is also *constitutive* of its terms. The terms of the relation are completely undetermined (or virtual) until they enter into the differential relation; on their own, these elements remain purely determinable. Once such elements enter a differential relation, in turn, their reciprocal determination determines a singularity, a singular point. Every multiplicity (that is, every *thing*) is characterized by a combination of singular and ordinary points. In geometry, for instance, a square has four singular points—its corners—which are prolonged in an infinity of ordinary points that connect them. A cube, similarly, has eight singular points. The case of curves is more complicated: the differential relation determines a singular point in a curve, which continues over a series of ordinary points until it reaches another singularity, at which point the curve changes direction—it increases or decreases—and continues along another series of ordinary points, until it reaches another singularity, and so on.

For Deleuze, this is exactly how a life is composed or constructed—from singularity to singularity. The point where someone breaks down in tears or boils over in anger, for example, is a singular point in someone's psychic multiplicity, surrounded by a swarm of ordinary points—just as, in physics, the point where water boils (or freezes) is a singularity within that physical system. The question, What is singular and what is ordinary? is one of the fundamental questions posed by Deleuze's theory of multiplicities or Ideas. An acquaintance suddenly gets cross with me, and his unexpected anger may seem to mark a critical point, a phase transition, a singularity in his psychic being—but then someone leans over to me and whispers: "Don't worry, he does that all the time, it's completely ordinary." When water boils or freezes, it is a phase transition, a singularity, but at the same time, it is a completely ordinary event. One could say that these are the two poles of Deleuze's philosophy: "Everything is ordinary!" and "Everything is singular!"[19] Your reading of a book, in the here and now, is a singular moment; but at the same time it is a completely ordinary event. Yet Ideas are marked by a complex temporality: reading the book may be ordinary, yet in retrospect it may appear singular because, perhaps, it changes the way you think, or sparks an unrelated idea in you. We can never know such effects (or "actualizations") in advance, of course. In effect, Deleuze's theory of Ideas is an attempt to answer Plato's question: what *is* a thing, what is its essence? His answer, put briefly, is that every thing is a multiplicity, which unfolds and becomes within its own spatio-temporal coordinates (its own "internal metrics"), in perpetual relation with other multiplicities. Deleuze argues that Socrates' fundamental question "What is . . .?" set the theory of Ideas on the wrong track *from the start*, even though it was none the less this very question that opened up the domain of the Idea for philosophy. But the fundamental questions Deleuze links with Ideas are questions such as: How? Where? When? How many? From what viewpoint? and so on—which are no longer questions of essence, in the old sense, but questions of becoming, of the event, of temporality (although Deleuze himself does not hesitate to use the term "essence" in these contexts).[20]

In a technical sense, what Deleuze gets from Leibniz—following the lead of both Maimon and Kant's *Critique of Judgment*—is a purely immanent determination of Ideas (whereas in Kant, two of the three components of Ideas are defined extrinsically). First, the elements of an Idea are completely undetermined (or virtual); second, these elements are none the less determinable reciprocally in a differential relation (dx/dy); and third, to this reciprocal determination there corresponds the complete determination of a set of singularities (values of dx/dy), which defines a multiplicity (along with their prolongation in a series of ordinary points). It is these three coexistent moments—the undetermined, the determinable, and the determined—that give Ideas their genetic power.

IDEAS IN THE *CRITIQUE OF PRACTICAL REASON*

In order to get a better grasp of what it means to speak of the "genetic" power of Ideas, let me turn, finally, to Kant's second critique, the *Critique of Practical Reason*. One might easily—and correctly—surmise that Deleuze would have little sympathy for the second critique, with its appeals to transcendence (the moral law and the categorical imperative).[21] Yet the structure of the first chapters of *Anti-Oedipus* is indebted to—and indeed derived from—the second critique. Both *Anti-Oedipus* and the *Critique of Practical Reason* present themselves as theories of desire, and one of the aims of *Anti-Oedipus* is to present an immanent theory of desire, one that is derived from the immanent theory of Ideas developed in *Difference and Repetition*.

Kant posited three fundamental powers or faculties of the mind: the faculty of knowledge (first critique), the faculty of desire (second critique), and the feeling of pleasure and displeasure (third critique).[22] This distribution of the faculties was derived from the nature of our representations: every representation we have can be related to something other than itself—either to an *object* or to the *subject*. In the faculty of knowledge, a representation is related to an object from the viewpoint of its agreement or conformity with it (theory of reference or denotation). In the faculty of the feeling of pleasure and pain, the representation is related to the subject, in so far as the representation affects the subject by intensifying or weakening its vital force. In the faculty of desire, finally, the representation is likewise related to an object, but in this case it enters into a *causal* relationship with its object. Kant's definition of desire is extraordinary: desire is "a faculty which by means of its representations is the cause of the actuality of the objects of those representations."[23] This definition breaks with a long tradition in philosophy that defined desire in terms of *lack*: desire, says Kant, is a faculty that, given a representation in my mind, is capable of *producing the object that corresponds to it.*

We know why Kant defines the faculty of desire in causal or productive terms. The problem of freedom concerns the operation by which a free being can be said to be the cause of something: that is, in acting freely, the agent produces something that is not reducible to the causal determinisms of mechanism. "Practical reason," Kant writes, "is concerned not with objects in order to know them, but with its own capacity to make them real."[24] Of course, Kant is aware that real objects can be produced only by an external causality and external mechanisms; yet this knowledge does not prevent us from believing in the intrinsic power of *desire* to create its own object—if only in an unreal, hallucinatory, or delirious form. In what Kant calls the "pathological" productions of desire, what is produced by desire is merely a psychic reality. None the less, Kant brings about a Copernican Revolution in practical philosophy to which Deleuze is strongly indebted: desire is no longer defined in terms of *lack* (I desire something because I do not have it), but rather in terms of *production* (I produce the object because I desire it). The fundamental thesis of *Anti-Oedipus* is a stronger variant of Kant's claim: "If desire produces, its product is real. If desire is productive, it can be productive only in the real world and can produce only reality" (AO 26). How, then, does Deleuze work out this immanent conception of desire as productive of the real?

For Kant, the essential question of practical philosophy concerns the higher form of which each faculty is capable—a form that is no longer merely "pathological." A faculty has a higher form when it finds within itself the law of its own exercise, and thus functions autonomously. The higher form of desire, for Kant, is what he calls the "will."[25] *The will is the same thing as desire, but raised to its higher form*— that is, desire becomes will when it is determined by the representation of a pure form: namely, the moral law, which is the pure form of a universal legislation (the categorical imperative). Practical reason has to do with "a will that is a causality inasmuch as reason contains its determining ground."[26] Under such conditions we are acting freely. In Kant, however, the moral law requires the intervention of the three great transcendent Ideas as its postulates. "Freedom," as the fact of morality, implies the cosmological Idea of a supra-sensible world, independent of any sensible condition; in turn, the abyss that separates the noumenal Law and the phenomenal world requires the intermediary of an intelligible author of sensible Nature or a "moral cause of the world" (the theological Idea of a supreme being, or God)—an abyss that can only be bridged through the postulate of an infinite progress, which requires the psychological Idea of the immortality of the soul. This is the shortcoming of Kantian ethics: having denounced the transcendent Ideas of soul, world, and God in the first critique, Kant resurrects each of them, one by one, in the second critique, and gives them a practical determination.

Anti-Oedipus remains an incomprehensible book as long as one does not see its overall structure as an attempt, on Deleuze's part, to rewrite the *Critique of Practical Reason*. But what would a purely immanent theory of desire look like in the domain of practical reason? It would mean that one could no longer appeal to the moral law—and the transcendent Ideas that serve as its necessary postulates—but would instead have to synthesize desire with a conception of purely immanent Ideas? This is precisely what Deleuze does in the opening two chapters of *Anti-Oedipus*: the three syntheses by which he and Guattari define "desiring-machines" are in fact the same three Ideas that Kant defines as the postulates of practical reason (soul, world, and God), but now stripped entirely of their transcendent status, to the point where neither God, world, nor self subsists:

> The divergence of the affirmed series forms a 'chaosmos' and no longer a world; the aleatory point which traverses them forms a counter-self, and no longer a self; disjunction posed as a synthesis exchanges its theological principle of diabolic principle . . . The Grand Canyon of the world, the 'crack' of the self, and the dismembering of God. (LS 176)

In *Anti-Oedipus*, Deleuze gives a purely immanent characterization of the three syntheses—connection [world], disjunction [God], and conjunction [self]—and then shows how desire itself is constituted by tracing out series and trajectories following these syntheses within a given social assemblage. There are, of course, many other important themes in *Anti-Oedipus*—such as the problem of the relation between Marx and Freud (via Lacan), and the identity of political economy and libidinal economy; and behind Marx and Freud, ultimately, Deleuze's appeal to the immanent models of Nietzsche and Spinoza. But if *Difference and Repetition* can be read as Deleuze's *Critique of Pure Reason*, *Anti-Oedipus* can be read as his *Critique of Practical Reason*. What unites the two pairs of books, respectively, is the theory of Ideas—the thread that links together theoretical and practical philosophy. What separates them is the status of their respective theories of Ideas (dialectics), and the *use* to which the Ideas are put. Kant critiques the transcendent use of the Ideas in the *Critique of Pure Reason*, only to resurrect them in the *Critique of Practical Reason*, and to give them a practical determination. In *Difference and Repetition*, by contrast, Deleuze pushes the immanent ambitions of the *Critique of Pure Reason* to their conclusion, uniting (in an immanent principle of difference) the three aspects of the Idea sketched by Kant (the elements of the Ideas are at once undetermined, determinable, and reciprocally determined). In the practical philosophy developed in *Anti-Oedipus*, Deleuze proposes a theory of desire that, rather than seeking out the "higher" form of desire in the will, which has as its condition the synthesis of desire with its transcendent postulates (soul, world, God), instead seeks to explore the movement of desire, in a manner that is no less formal than Kant's, by tracing out the purely *immanent* syntheses of desire (connection, disjunction, conjunction). The new dialectic (theory of Ideas), whose formal components Deleuze develops in *Difference and Repetition*, could be said to receive its practical determination in *Anti-Oedipus*—with the difference that, in Deleuze, the determinations of the Ideas are practical *from the start* (hence the importance of such questions as How?, Where?, When?, How many?, From what viewpoint? and so on).

IMMANENT IDEAS AND LIVED EXPERIENCE

The preceding sections have attempted to explore the link between Kant's theory of Ideas—the thread of which can be traced through each of the three critiques—and Deleuze's revised theory of the Ideas, which is both dependent upon and critical of Kant. In this final section, I would like to present several concrete examples of the implications Deleuze's theory of immanent Ideas might have in the analysis of lived experience. At the very least, such examples serve to demonstrate that Deleuze's immanent theory of Ideas is not merely an exercise in speculation.

1. First, consider an everyday scenario such as the following. You wake up one morning, go to work, talk with some friends while sipping your coffee, sit outside in the sun during lunch, have dinner and a few drinks later in the evening, go home, feel slightly ill, and fall into bed early. What would be the Deleuzian portrait of a daily trajectory like this? If every "thing" is a multiplicity, my multiplicity necessarily changes dimensions, and enters a becoming, every time it is affected by another multiplicity: the heat of the sun, a conversation with a friend, the caffeine in my coffee. Each of these encounters introduces a variation in what Spinoza calls my "force of existing" (*vis existendi*) or "power of acting" (*potentia agendi*). I run into my friend Peter in the hall, but we have had a falling out, so I feel uneasy and uncertain around him, and my force of existing decreases; then I run into my friend Paul, who compliments me and buys me a drink, and my force of existing increases. In the park, the sun warms me, and expands my power; later I realize I am sunburned, and my power decreases. Drinking initially appears to increase my power, but the hangover the next morning seems to reduce it to zero. This is why Leibniz and Spinoza characterized us as "spiritual automatons": these events happen to us automatically, and are almost indifferent to our own subjectivity.[27] I have encounters and am affected by other multiplicities; at each moment these affections increase or decrease the intensity of my power, like a melody, a line of continuous variation or continuous becoming. Deleuze says he liked to imagine Spinoza strolling about, living his own existence, as a multiplicity, following this melodic line of continuous variation.

2. Second, now imagine yourself sitting in a classroom, listening to a lecture, though your mind is occasionally wandering off elsewhere. Leibniz had noted, famously, that we often perceive things that we are not consciously aware of, like a tap dripping at night. Leibniz therefore put forward the argument that our conscious perceptions are derived, not from the objects around us as such, but rather from the minute and unconscious perceptions of which they are composed, and which my conscious perception integrates. I can apprehend the noise of the sea or the murmur of a group of people, for instance, but not necessarily the sound of each wave or the voice of each person of which they are composed. A conscious perception is produced when at least two of these minute and virtual perceptions—two waves, or two voices—enter into a differential relation that determines a singularity, which

"excels" over the others, and becomes conscious, on the basis of my needs, or inter-ests, or the state of my body, Every conscious perception constitutes a constantly shifting threshold; the minute or virtual perceptions are like the obscure dust of the world, its background noise, what Maimon liked to call the "differentials of con-sciousness"; and the differential relation is the mechanism that extracts from these minute perceptions my own little zone of finite clarity on the world. This is what Deleuze means when he says there is an immanent and virtual Idea of sensibility that is not identical to my actual perceptions, and yet constitutes the real condition of sensibility itself.

3. Third, this is why Deleuze, following Spinoza, contests the Cartesian notion of the "clear and distinct." My conscious perception of the noise of the sea at the beach, for example, may be clear, but it is by nature confused, because the minute perceptions of which it is composed—the perceptions of each wave, or each drop of water—are not themselves clear, but remain obscure, since they have not been "distinguished" or actualized in a conscious perception. They can be apprehended only by thought, in an Idea—or at best, in fleeting states close to those of vertigo, or drowsiness, or dizzy spells. Deleuze suggests that philosophers should start from the obscure; a clear perception emerges from the obscure (or the virtual) by means of a genetic process (the differential mechanism). Yet at the same time, my clear perceptions are constantly plunging back into the obscure, into the virtual Idea of minute perceptions; by its very nature, perception is clear *and* obscure (*chiaroscuro*). For one can easily imagine the opposite case: since you are drowsy as you leave the classroom, you become dizzy, lose your balance going down the stairs, and begin to black out. What is happening? Your consciousness becomes disorganized and loos-ened, and is invaded by a flotilla of minute perceptions. You are not conscious of these minute perceptions, they do not stop being unconscious; rather, it is you who cease to be conscious. But you none the less experience these minute perceptions; there is, as it were, an unconscious lived experience of them. You do not represent them, nor do you perceive them, but they are there, swarming within you, like the obscure dust of the world. We all experience something similar to this whenever we listen to a lecture, drifting in and out of attention. To say that perception is by nature clear-obscure is to say that it is made and unmade at every moment, in all directions, constantly extracting the clear while constantly plunging hack into the obscure.

4. Fourth, and finally, one could say that what we call "freedom," the free act, makes use of the same mechanism. Suppose that I am at home hesitating between continuing to work and going out to have a drink with a friend. How do I decide? What constitutes my "free choice" in such a situation? There is no appeal to "deci-sion theory" in Deleuze; a decision theory would strip me of any supposed freedom, since the theory itself would provide the answer. Rather, just as my perceptions are conditioned by minute perceptions, so my decisions are conditioned by minute inclinations and motivations that remain unconscious, until they reach the thresh-old that constitutes my decision. "Staying home" or "going out" are not objects in a balance, but rather orientations or tendencies that are in constant flux, each of which integrates a host of minute perceptions and motives. My initial inclination to

go out not only integrates the sensation of drinking, but also the smell of the tavern, the camaraderie with friends, and so on. But at the same time, my soul also inclines toward staying at home, which integrates not only my writing and work, but my solitude, the silence of my environment. Then I incline again toward going out, but the inclination is not the same, because time has passed, and the affectivity is different. Even in a simple example such as this, making a decision is never a question of choosing between x (staying in) and y (going out), since both inclinations are multiplicities that include an unconscious multiplicity of auditory, gustative, olfactory, and visual perceptions—an entire "perceptio-inclinatory ensemble." When I deliberate, I am really oscillating between two complex perceptive and inclinatory poles—my home and the tavern—which "fold" my soul, Deleuze would say, in constantly variable directions. Arriving at a decision is a matter of "integrating" the minute inclinations in a distinguished or remarkable inclination. On which side will I fold my soul? With which minute inclinations and perceptions will I make a "decisive" fold? To say that we are free means that, in Leibniz's phrase, we are "inclined without being necessitated." During the day, in most of our actions—in all our habitual and machinal acts—we do not confront the question of freedom at all; such acts are done solely, one might say, to calm our disquietude. The question of freedom arises only when we posit the question of an act capable (or not) of "filling the amplitude of the soul at a given moment" (24 Feb 1987). A free act is an act that integrates the virtual perceptions and virtual inclinations into a remarkable inclination, which then becomes an inclination of the soul. Our decision is the result of the struggle between all these motives, conscious and unconscious—"a battling to and fro, a rising and falling of the scales."[28] Our calculation of consequences merely enters into this battlefield as one factor, one impulse, one element among others.

The aim of presenting these examples from lived experience is to show that, despite the abstract nature of his language, Deleuze is attempting to get at something concrete with his theory of immanent Ideas, and to show in what manner they can be said to constitute the conditions of *real* experience, and not merely possible experience. "This is what it's like on the plane of immanence," Deleuze writes, "multiplicities fill it, singularities connect with one another, processes or becomings unfold, intensities rise and fall" (N 146–7).

Analytics

On the Becoming of Concepts

What is Deleuze's concept of a concept?[1] In *What is Philosophy?*, Deleuze and Guattari famously define philosophy as an activity that consists in "forming, inventing, and fabricating concepts."[2] Deleuze seems to have held to this conception of philosophy as the creation of concepts from the very start of his career.[3] "The power of a philosophy," he wrote in one of his early books, "is measured by the concepts it creates, or whose meaning it rejuvenates—concepts that impose a new set of divisions on things and actions."[4] Even in high school, he recounts, when he was first introduced to philosophy, concepts struck him with the same force as literary characters, having their own temperament and vitality, and populating their own landscapes (ABC E). It was not until late in his life, however, in *What is Philosophy?* (1991), that Deleuze, working with Guattari, finally proposed his own "analytic of concepts," to borrow Kant's phrase, reaching the point where he could ask, "What have I been doing all my life?"[5] Deleuze compared the book, in passing, to Kant's *Critique of Judgment*, and the comparison is an apt one: both are works of old age, written at a time when thinkers often have little new to say, their "systems" already being well established.[6] Yet Kant's third critique is a book bristling with new concepts, pushing at the limits of Kant's carefully constructed architectonic, and setting the stage for Romanticism and what we now call, precisely, post-Kantian philosophy. In a similar manner, *What is Philosophy?*, far from being the self-reflective culmination of Deleuze's career, is much more his bequeathal to future philosophy, a handing-off of the baton; it too poses a plethora of new concepts and problems that are no doubt destined to be taken up by whatever a post-Deleuzian philosophy turns out to be. In what follows, I would to explore a constellation of problems that lies at the heart of *What is Philosophy?*: namely, the complex set of relations that Deleuze establishes between concepts, time, and truth.

THE BECOMING OF CONCEPTS

One of the most obvious features of Deleuze's analytic of concepts lies in the fact that, from a Deleuzian perspective, concepts do not have an *identity* but only a *becoming*. In his preface to the Italian translation of *Logic of Sense*, for example, Deleuze himself briefly charts out the becoming of one of his own concepts: the concept of intensity (TRM 65–6). In *Difference and Repetition* (1968), he notes, the concept of intensity is primarily related to the dimension of depth. In *Logic of Sense* (1969), the concept of intensity is retained, but it is now related primarily to the dimension of surface—same concept, but different components. In *Anti-Oedipus* (1972), the concept enters a third becoming that is related to neither depth nor surface: rising and falling intensities are now events that take place on a body without organs.[7] One might add a fourth becoming to Deleuze's list: in *What is Philosophy?* (1991), the concept of intensity is used to describe the status of the components of concepts, which are determined as intensive rather than extensive (which is one way in which Deleuze distinguishes himself from Frege, for whom concepts are extensional). In other words, the concept of intensity does not stay the same even within Deleuze's own corpus; it undergoes internal mutations.[8]

To this, one must add the fact that many of the concepts Deleuze utilizes have a long "becoming" in the history of philosophy, which he relies on and appropriates, and into which Deleuze's own work on the concept is inserted. The distinction between extensive and intensive quantities, for instance, dates back to medieval philosophy and Plotinus. Deleuze's concept of multiplicity—to take another example—was first formulated mathematically by Bernard Riemann, in his non-Euclidean geometry, who in turn linked it to Kant's concept of the manifold. Both Husserl and Bergson adopted Riemann's concept for their own philosophical purposes, and Deleuze first wrote about the concept with regard to Bergson's distinction between two types of multiplicity (continuous and discrete), which Deleuze developed in his own manner, and considered it one of the fundamental problems of contemporary thought.[9] On this score, one of the great texts in the history of philosophy is Kant's opening to the Transcendental Dialectic, where he explains why he is going to appropriate Plato's concept of Idea rather than coining his own term, since Plato was dealing with a problematic similar to the one Kant wants to deal with, although Plato, according to Kant, had "not sufficiently determined his concept."[10] Deleuze in turn undertakes another transformation when, in *Difference and Repetition*, he takes up Kant's theory of the Idea and modifies it in his own manner, claiming that Kant had not pushed to the limit the "immanent" ambitions of his own theory of Ideas.

Similarly, Deleuze seems to have initially intended *What is Philosophy?*, at least in part, to be a book on the concept of the "category," and thus a reworking of Kant's analytic of concepts.[11] In the Transcendental Analytic of *The Critique of Pure Reason*, Kant had famously drawn up his own list of categories, derived from his typology of judgments, which he attempted to deduce as the conditions of possible experience. In *Difference and Repetition*, Deleuze had explicitly distinguished his own fundamental concepts (problematic, virtuality, singularity, and so on) from Aristotelian or Kantian categories.[12] Yet both Whitehead and Peirce had drawn up very different tables of categories than Kant, and in the process they had *reinvented* or *recreated* the concept of a category. Deleuze seems to have come to see his own work in the same light:

> The conclusion to *A Thousand Plateaus* is, in my mind, a table of categories (but incomplete, insufficient). Not in the manner of Kant but in the manner of Whitehead. Category thus takes in a new meaning, a very special one. I would like to work on this point.[13]

For Deleuze, the *problem* that generated the concept of the category had changed. It was no longer a matter of determining the conditions of possible experience, but the conditions of *real* experience; and the conditions of the real were at the same time the conditions for the production of the *new*. Here again, the becoming of concepts within Deleuze's own work is a continuation of the becoming of concepts within the history of philosophy.

Even more tellingly, Deleuze says that even he and Guattari "never did understand the "body without organs' in quite the same way" (TRM 238), a revelation that is perhaps faint consolation to readers striving to comprehend *Capitalism and Schizophrenia*. Yet this is not a question of authorial intention. If one considers Deleuze and Guattari's jointly authored books as belonging fully to the trajectory of Deleuze writings, and equally fully to the trajectory of Guattari's writings, then one could take Deleuze's comment to imply that, even within a work like *Anti-Oedipus*, the concept of the "body without organs" has a different sense, a different becoming, depending on whether one reads it in the context of Deleuze's trajectory or Guattari's trajectory. In other words, even *within* a single work or project, Deleuze and Guattari's concepts do not have an identity that would be reducible to a simple definition. Indeed, Deleuze insists on this point: "Working together [with Guattari] was never a homogenization, but a proliferation, an accumulation of bifurcations" (TRM 238). Moreover, if Deleuze entered into a "becoming-Guattari" in his jointly authored works, one could say that he did the same thing in even his monographs, where he entered into a becoming-Spinoza, or a becoming-Leibniz (and Spinoza and Leibniz in turn were forced into a becoming-Deleuze), such that, even in his solo works, Deleuze's concepts never lose this status of becoming. As Deleuze said, "I am nearly incapable of speaking in my own name [*en mon nom*]" (TRM 65). In this sense, Deleuze's critique of the identity of the self or ego has as its exact parallel a critique of the identity of concepts. If "experimentation on ourselves is our only identity" (D 11), then the same is true of concepts: their only identity lies in experimentation—that is, in their intrinsic variability and mutations. For this reason, finally, a "becoming-Deleuze" similarly affects Deleuze's readers as well as those who attempt to write on his work. In Nelson Goodman's terminology, Deleuze's writings exemplify what they express: his texts are themselves problems, fields of vectors, multiplicities, or rhizomes whose singularities can be connected in a variety of ways, so that writing on Deleuze's texts is itself a becoming, a production of the new (not merely an "interpretation," as hermeneuticians might say).[14] One rarely finds "positions" in Deleuze's works ("Deleuze thinks that . . ."); rather, to read or write on Deleuze is to trace out trajectories whose directions are not given in advance of one's reading or writing. Even Deleuze's occasional appeals to various "-isms" ("vitalism," "transcendental empiricism") are less pledges of allegiance than oxymoronic provocations. In short, there is a becoming of concepts not only within

Deleuze's corpus, but also in each book and in each concept, which is extended to and draws from the history of philosophy, and is repeated in each act of reading.[15]

PHILOSOPHY AS CREATION

This, however, is what one would expect—both theoretically and practically—from a philosopher such as Deleuze. If Deleuze's philosophy is a philosophy of difference, then this differential status must be reflected in his own concepts, which cannot have an identity of their own without belying the entire nature of his project. But how, then, is one to understand this becoming of concepts? As an initial approach to this question, one could say that Deleuze's conception of philosophy as the creation of concepts has several interrelated consequences.

First, it defines philosophy in terms of an activity that has traditionally been aligned with art: namely, the activity of *creation*. For Deleuze, philosophers are as creative as artists, the difference being that what they create happens to be concepts rather than paintings, sculptures, films, or novels. In Deleuze's language, philosophers create *concepts*, whereas artists create sensible aggregates of *percepts* or *affects*, and scientists create *functions*. Deleuze's approach to the question "What is philosophy?" has the advantage of characterizing philosophy in terms of a well-defined occupation or a precise *activity*, rather than simply an *attitude*—for instance, knowing yourself, or wondering why there is something rather than nothing, or taking nothing to be self-evident. "To create concepts," Deleuze writes, "is, at the very least, to *do* something" (WP 7). Moreover, just as works of art bear the signature of the artist, so conceptual creations bear the signature of the philosopher who created them. In painting, we speak of Van Gogh's sunflowers or Jasper John's flags, just as in philosophy we speak of Descartes's *cogito*, or Leibniz's monads, or Nietzsche's will to power. In medicine, similarly, we speak of Alzheimer's disease and Parkinson's disease; in mathematics, of the Pythagorean theorem or the Hamiltonian number; and in science, of the Doppler effect or the Kelvin effect (LS 70). In all these cases, the proper name refers less to the person than to the work of art or to the concept itself—the proper name is here used to indicate *a non-personal mode of individuation*. In this sense, it would be possible to do a history of philosophy along the lines of an art history: that is, in terms of its great products or masterworks. "We dream sometimes of a history of philosophy that would list only the new concepts created by a great philosopher—his most essential and creative contribution" (ES ix). Indeed, Deleuze elsewhere muses that one could even quantify philosophy, attributing to each philosopher a kind of magic number corresponding to the number of concepts they created or transformed (a philosophical analogue, perhaps, to Erdős numbers in mathematics) (ABC H). From this point of view, Descartes's *cogito* and Plato's Idea would the philosophical parallels to Leonardo da Vinci's Mona Lisa or Michelangelo's Last Judgment—the great philosophical masterpieces, signed by their creators.

Second, Deleuze's definition of philosophy as the creation of concepts not only implies that philosophers are as creative as artists; more importantly, perhaps, it also implies that artists are as much thinkers as are philosophers—they simply think in terms of percepts and affects rather than concepts; painters think in terms of lines and colors, just as musicians think in sounds, writers think in words, filmmakers think in images, and so on. Jean-Luc Godard, for instance, once said that, in filmmaking, the decision to use a tracking shot rather than a panoramic shot was a profound activity of thought, since each type of shot produces a different type of space; panoramic shots are encompassing, giving us a global vision, as in projective geometry, whereas tracking shots construct a line, and link up local spaces and neighborhoods that in themselves can remain fragmentary and disconnected, more like Riemannian geometry (N 58). The idea that thought is necessarily propositional, or representational, or linguistic, or even conceptual is completely foreign to Deleuze.[16] "There are other ways of thinking and creating, other modes of ideation that, like scientific thought, do not have to pass through concepts" (WP 8). When sculptors mold a piece of clay, or painters apply colors or lines to a canvas, or filmmakers set up a shot, there is a process of thought involved; but that process of thought does not take place in a conceptual medium, nor even through the application of concepts to a sensible medium (Kant). Rather, it is a type of thinking that takes place directly in and through the sensible medium itself.

A third consequence follows from this. Neither of these activities—art or philosophy—has any priority over the other. Creating a concept is neither more difficult nor more abstract than creating new percepts or affects in art; conversely, it is no easier to comprehend an image, painting, or novel than it is to comprehend a concept. Philosophy, for Deleuze, can never be undertaken independently of art (or science, or politics, or medicine, and so on), and is constantly forming relations of mutual resonance and exchange with these other areas of thought. Philosophers can create concepts about art, just as artists and authors can create in conjunction with philosophical concepts—as, for instance, in so-called conceptual art. This is why Deleuze could constantly insist that, when he wrote on the arts, or on science, or on medicine, or on psychiatry, he did so *as a philosopher*, and that his writings in all these domains must be read as works of "philosophy, nothing but philosophy, in the traditional sense of the word."[17] In his studies of the arts, Deleuze's aim, as a philosopher, was to *create the concepts* that correspond to the sensible aggregates created by artists or authors. In his book *Francis Bacon: The Logic of Sensation*, Deleuze creates a series of philosophical concepts, each of which, he says, relates to a particular aspect of Bacon's paintings, but which also find a place in "a general logic of sensation."[18] In a similar manner, Deleuze insisted that his two-volume *Cinema* book can be read as "a book of logic, a logic of the cinema" that sets out "to isolate certain cinematographic concepts," concepts which are specific to the cinema, but which can only be formed philosophically (MI ix; N 47).

These three rubrics encapsulate, in summary form, Deleuze's characterization of the relationship between philosophy and art—or more generally, between philosophy and the act of creation: philosophers are as creative as artists (philosophers create concepts); artists and authors are as much thinkers as are philosophers (they simply think in a non-conceptual material or matter); and neither activity of creation has any priority whatsoever over the other. Some readers of *What is*

Philosophy? have none the less expressed surprise at Deleuze's somewhat curt alloca-
tion of separate tasks to philosophy (creating concepts), art (creating affects and
percepts), and science (creating functions). But Deleuze here is following the same
semi-Bergsonian procedure he adopted in his earlier works. In *Matter and Memory*,
Bergson attempted to analyze what he called *pure perception* and *pure memory*,
even though experience always presents us with mixtures of the two; the concepts
allow us to isolate tendencies that remain mixed in experience. Likewise, when
Deleuze distinguishes between active and reactive modes of existence in *Nietzsche
and Philosophy*, or different social formations ("primitive" societies, states, capitalism) in *Anti-Oedipus*, or different kinds of images in *Cinema*, he always presents
them as isolatable *types* that can be used to disentangle the mixtures presented in
experience.[19]

> To extract the concepts which correspond to a multiplicity is to trace the
> lines of which it is made up, to determine the nature of these lines, to see
> how they become entangled, connect, bifurcate . . . What we call a "map," or
> sometimes a "diagram," is a set of interacting lines. (D viii; N 33)

Deleuze utilizes the same approach in *What is Philosophy?* The significance of
the distinctions Deleuze establishes between philosophy, art, and science is primarily that they provide a point of reference from which to assess and explore
the resonances and exchanges—the becomings—that take place *between* these
three domains (as well as medicine, politics, psychiatry, and so on). Concepts,
for instance, are necessarily inseparable from affects and percepts; they make us
perceive things differently (percept) and they inspire new modes of feeling in us
(affect), thereby modifying, as Spinoza would say, our power of existing (13 Dec
1983). A concept that would be purely intelligible, and did not produce new affects
and percepts, would be an empty concept. Conversely, Deleuze was acutely aware
of "the dangers of citing scientific propositions outside their own sphere," which are
the dangers of "applying" scientific concepts in other domains, or else utilizing them
metaphorically and hence arbitrarily. "But perhaps these dangers can be averted,"
Deleuze concluded, "if we restrict ourselves to taking from scientific operators a
particular conceptualizable character which itself refers to non-scientific areas, and
converges with science without applying it or making it a metaphor."[20] In both
these instances, Deleuze is exploring the nature of the interrelations between separable domains; as always, Deleuze's analyses are primarily focused on difference—on
the in-between, the middle, the relational, the interstitial.

CONCEPT CREATION AND PHILOSOPHY: "VITAL" CONCEPTS AS SINGULARITIES

Deleuze seems to have intended his theory of concepts to apply specifically to *philosophical* concepts—the concepts created by philosophers—rather than to everyday
concepts of recognition, such as chairs or pearls. "As Michaux says, what suffices
for 'current ideas' does not suffice for 'vital ideas'—those that must be created"

(WP 207). An example of a "vital" concept—a concept that had to be created—is the concept of the "Baroque," the components of which Deleuze analyzes in *The Fold: Leibniz and the Baroque*.

> It is strange to deny the existence of the Baroque in the way one denies unicorns or pink elephants [Deleuze writes], for in these cases the concept is given, whereas in the case of the Baroque it is a question of knowing if one can invent a concept capable (or not) of giving it an existence. Irregular pearls exist, but the Baroque has no reason to exist without a concept that forms this very reason. (FLB 33)

In other words, vital concepts like the "Baroque" *create* their corresponding object, since the object does not pre-exist the formation of the concept. In being created, a concept posits itself and posits its object at one and the same time; the concept, in other words, is *self-referential* (WP 22). This is not true of the concepts of ordinary language, which are used to *denote* already-constituted objects or classes of objects (Russell). This is why Deleuze considered concepts to be multiplicities or manifolds: metric spaces are determined by coordinates external to the space, such as Cartesian coordinates, whereas non-metric spaces have internal metrics, which mark out their internal transformations, mutations, and passages (in Whitehead's sense of a "passage of Nature").[21]

But this seems to imply that philosophy is not the only milieu of concept creation. The puzzle that Heinrich Wölfflin addressed in his *Principles of Art History*, for instance, is the fact that all the works of art produced during the Baroque period look like . . . Baroque works of art. But the Baroque, as a style, does not exist apart from its concept, and what Wölfflin attempted to do in his art history "without names" (contra Vasari) was to isolate the components of the concepts of Classic art and Baroque art in the service of a broader history of modes of vision: the linear versus the painterly, plane versus recession, closed versus open form, clarity versus *chiaroscuro*, and multiplicity versus unity.[22] Though Deleuze breaks with aspects of Wölfflin's analyses—notably by insisting that the *fold* is a fundamental component of the concept of the Baroque—one can none the less see in Wölfflin's pioneering work a vast effort at concept creation.[23] A similar creation of concepts takes place in medicine. If conditions such as Parkinson's disease or Asperger's syndrome are named after doctors rather than patients, it is because the physicians were able to "isolate" the disease by constructing an original clinical concept for it. The components of the concept are the *symptoms*, the signs of the illness, and the concept becomes the name of a *syndrome*, which marks the meeting place of these symptoms, their point of coincidence or convergence (M 15–16).

> I would never have permitted myself to write on psychoanalysis and psychiatry [Deleuze once admitted], were I not dealing with a problem of symptomatology. Symptomatology is situated almost outside of medicine, at a neutral point, a zero point, where artists and philosophers and doctors and patients can encounter each other. (DI 134)

In this context, Arnold Davidson, in his work on the emergence of the concept of sexuality, has shown that, strictly speaking, there were no perverts or homosexuals prior to the nineteenth century—as opposed to, say, pederasts or sodomites—precisely because their concept had not yet been formulated.[24] Similarly, Ian Hacking has shown how, particularly in the human sciences, the creation of concepts such as multiple personality can have the effect of "making up people," creating phenomena, or making possible new modes of existence.[25] Concept creation, in short, does not seem to be the exclusive purview of philosophy. Although Deleuze occasionally speaks in this manner, he none the less writes, "as long as there is a time and place for creating concepts, the operation that undertakes this will always be called philosophy, or will be indistinguishable from philosophy *even if it is called something else*" (WP 9).

What is important about concept creation, in other words, is less its specific relation to philosophy than the fact that created concepts—"vital" concepts—in whatever domain they are created, must be understood as *singularities* (or rather, as sets of singularities, or multiplicities).

> There are two kinds of concepts [Deleuze notes], universals and singularities ... The first principle of philosophy is that universals explain nothing, but must themselves be explained ... Concepts are not universals, but sets of singularities that are extended into the neighborhood of other singularities. (N 156–7; WP 7)

But what does it mean to consider a concept as a set of singularities? Deleuze frequently appeals to a distinction Lévi-Strauss made between two types of propositions: only similar things can differ from each other, and only differences can resemble each other.[26] In the first, resemblance between things is primary; in the second, things themselves differ, and they differ first of all from themselves (internal difference). The first proposition posits resemblance as a condition of difference, and requires the postulation of an identical or universal concept (such as redness) for two things that differ from each other. According to the second proposition, resemblance or even identity is the effect of a primary difference or a system of differences. The concept of a *straight line* is a universal, because all straight lines resemble each other, and the concept can be defined axiomatically, as in Euclid. The concept of the *fold*, by contrast, is a singularity, because folds vary, and every fold is different; all folding proceeds by differentiation. No two things are folded in the same way—no two rocks, no two pieces of paper—nor is there a general rule saying that the same thing will always fold in the same way. In this sense, there are folds everywhere, but the fold is not a universal; rather, it is a "differentiator," a "differential." As Deleuze writes, "it is not at all a matter of bringing things together under one and the same concept [universals], but rather of relating each concept to the variables that determine its mutations [singularities]" (N 31). Or again, writing about his own conceptual creations: "What is interesting about concepts like *desire*, or *machine*, or *assemblage* is that they only have value in their variables and in the maximum of variables which they allow" (D 144). What is important about a vital or created concept is not its universality but its internal singularities—the singular points that it connects, the intensive components that it condenses, the becomings and mutations it enters into. This is why the concept of the fold is linked to Lévi-Strauss's second proposition: all folds differ, and this difference is primary; but they are, secondarily, made to resemble each other in the concept. The concept of the fold is a singularity—or more precisely, it is a multiplicity that marks the convergence of a set of singularities, which form the components of the concept—and the concept can only gain terrain by varying within itself, by bifurcating, by metamorphosing.

> One only has to comprehend mountains—and above all, to see and touch mountains—from the viewpoint of their foldings for them to lose their solidity, and for their millennia to once again become what they are: not permanences, but *time in the pure state*. (N 157)

With this claim that concepts are set of singularities (or multiplicities), we have reached the reason for the incessant "becoming" of Deleuze's concepts: the aim of Deleuze's analytic of concepts is to introduce *the pure form of time* into concepts, in the form of what he calls "continuous variation" or "pure variability." "The aim is not to rediscover the eternal or the universal, but to find the conditions under which something new is produced (creativeness)" (D vii).

FROM ORIGINARY TIME TO ORDINARY TIME

But what does it mean to introduce time into concepts? To answer this, we must take a short detour through Deleuze's philosophy of time. More specifically, we need to understand what Deleuze means when he refers to the *pure and empty form of time*—a phrase that recurs frequently throughout his writings.[27] According to Deleuze, the modern mutation in our conception of time occurred with Kant; in Kant's work, time assumed an independence and autonomy of its own for the first time. Before that, from antiquity through the seventeenth century, time had been subordinate to movement; time was the measure or "number" of movement. Since the plurality of movements implied a plurality of times, the ancients were led to ask the question: Is there something immobile, outside of movement—or at least a most perfect movement—around which all other movements could be measured, a great celestial schema, or what Leibniz would call a kind of "metaschematism"? Is there a movement of movements in relation to which all other movements can be coordinated? Since there were two major types of movement—the extensive movement of the cosmos, and the intensive movement of the soul—this question wound up being answered in two different ways. In the *Timaeus*, for instance, Plato sought to incorporate the movements of the cosmos into a vision of a "planetarium" comprised of eight globes, with the immobile earth at the center, surrounded by a sphere of "the fixed" (the stars) turning on its axis, with seven globes in between (the planets) turning in a reverse direction. These revolving globes start from an initial position, and eventually return to the same position: a great year or circuit of the "eternal return" which, by some calculations, was thought to last ten thousand years. It was precisely this movement of movements that provided a reference point by which all other movements were to be measured: an invariant, a permanence. Time, in this manner, was subordinated to eternity, to the non-temporal, to the non-tensed; in Plato's apt formula, time was "the moving image of eternity."[28] Similarly, Plotinus incorporated the intensive movement of the soul into the movement of the One, with its emanative processes of procession and conversion.[29] In both cases, the result was a hierarchization of movements depending on their proximity to or distance from the eternal: an *originary time* marked by privileged positions in the cosmos or privileged moments in the soul. The discovery of this invariant was the discovery of the true; the form of the true was that which was universal and necessary, *in all times and in all places*. This conception of time as the measure of movement remains ensconced in our common chronological "clock" time: days, months, and years measure terrestrial, lunar, and solar movements, while weeks and hours are primarily religious determinations of the soul (God rested on the seventh day); and our watches and clocks remain dependent on movement, whether that of a pendulum or a quartz crystal. Modernity no less than antiquity remains engaged in a vast effort to render both time and movement homogeneous and uniform (timetables, time zones, the global positioning system).

None the less, the Kantian revolution was prepared for by the fact that both these domains—the cosmos and the soul—were haunted by fundamental *aberrations* of movement, where a *derived time* increasingly tended to free itself from the posited originary time. The closer one came to the earth (the "sublunar"), the more the movements of the cosmos tended to become increasingly anomalous: the unpredictability of meteorological movements, the movement of everything that comes to be and passes away. (As Michel Serres notes, "scientists can predict the time of an eclipse, but they cannot predict whether they will be able to see it." It is not by chance that, in French and many Latin languages, the same word is used for time and weather—*le temps*—with its various cognates: *temperature, tempest, temperate, temperament, intemperate, temper*).[30] Does the sublunary world obey the metaschematism, with its proportional rules, or does it enjoy an independence from it, with its own anomalous movements and disharmonies? The Pythagorean discovery of irrational numbers had already pointed to a fundamental incommensurability between the speed and position of the various cosmic spheres. In short, the invariant provided by the "movement of movements" was threatened by *crises* when movement became increasingly aberrant. Similarly, the intensive movement of the soul became marked by a *fear* that its restless movements in derived time would take on an independence of their own, and would cease to be submitted to the originary time of the One or God (the Fall). The search for "universals" in philosophy is, in a sense, a remnant of this fear; the very term is derived from the Latin word *universus*, meaning "turned toward the One" (*uni-* "one" + *versus* "turned," the past participle of *vertere*).

However, these aberrant or derived movements—marked by meteorological, terrestrial, and spiritual contingencies—remained a downward tendency that still depended on the adventures of movement. They too posed a problem, a choice: either one could try to "save" the primacy of movement (saving the appearances), or one could not only accept but also *will* the liberation of time with regard to movement. There were two ways in which movement could be saved. The extensive harmony of the world could be saved by an appeal to the rhythms of *rural time*, with the seasons and harvests as privileged points of reference in the originary time of Nature. The intensive harmony of the soul could be saved by an appeal to *monastic time*, with its privileged moments of prayers and vespers; or more generally, by an appeal to an originary spiritual life of interiority (Luther). By contrast, the liberation of time would take place in the city, an "enemy" that was none the less engendered by both the rural communities and monasteries themselves. The time of the city is neither a rural life nor a spiritual life, but the time of everyday life; there is no longer either an originary time or a derived time, but only an *ordinary time*. The sources of this liberation of time were multiple, having roots in the Reformation as well as the development of capitalism. Max Weber, for instance, showed that the Reformation became conscious of this liberation of time by joining together the two ideas of a "profession"—the profession of faith and one's professional activity—so that mundane professions like that of a cobbler were deemed to be as dignified as any sacred calling. Unlike the monk, whose duty was to be otherworldly, denying the self and the world, the fulfillment of one's duty in worldly affairs became the highest form that the moral activity of individuals could take. There was only one time—everyday time—and it is in this time that we would now find our salvation.[31] Likewise, Marx showed that this vision of *temporal activity* ("What do you do with your time?"), which is no longer grounded in a cosmic rhythm or a spiritual harmony, would eventually find its new model in the "abstract" time of capitalism, which replaced the privileged moments of agricultural work with the any-instant-whatever [*l'instant quelconque*] of mechanized work. Time became money, the form under which money produces money (usury or credit), and money itself became "the course of time": the abstract time of capitalism became the concrete time of the city (7 Feb 1984). It was Heidegger who would ultimately produce a prodigious philosophical concept of the everyday and its relation to time, though he still maintained the old distinction between an originary (authentic) and a derived (inauthentic) time.

For Deleuze, the result of the liberation of time will be a fundamental change in the relationship of philosophy to the thought of everyday life (opinion). Through the seventeenth century, one could say that, philosophically, everyday life was suspended in order to accede to something that was not everyday: namely, a meditation on the eternal. The ordinary time of urban everydayness, by contrast, would no longer be related to the eternal, but to something very different: namely, *the production of the new*. Given the flow of average everydayness, I can either raise myself vertically toward the transcendent or the eternal, at least on Sundays (or Saturdays or Fridays), through understanding or faith; or I can remain at the horizontal flow of everydayness, in which temporality tends toward the new rather than the eternal. The production of the new will be the correlate of ordinary time in exactly the same way that the discovery of the true was the correlate of originary time with the ancients. The aim of philosophy will no longer be to *discover* pre-existent truths outside of time, but to *create* non-preexisting concepts within time.[32]

THE PURE AND EMPTY FORM OF TIME

If Kant was the first to give a philosophical expression to this new conception of time, it is because he freed time entirely from its subordination to movement, and rendered it independent and autonomous.[33] Kant drew the necessary consequences from the cosmological and psychological anomalies of movement: he liberated time from cosmology and psychology, as well as the eternal. In Kant, the Self, the World, and God are all shown to be transcendent illusions of reason that are derived from our new position in time. Time ceases to be the number of movement, and no longer depends on anything but itself; time no longer measures movement, but movement itself (whether originary or derived, anomalous or aberrant) now takes places within time. The reversal can be seen in the opening pages of the *Critique of Pure Reason*. Before Kant, time had largely been defined by succession, space by coexistence, and eternity by permanence.[34] In Kant, succession, simultaneity, and permanence are all shown to be *modes* or *relations* of time: succession is the rule of what is in different times; simultaneity is the rule of what is at the same time; and permanence is the rule of what is for all times. Put differently, succession (series) is the synthetic relation between the parts of time, simultaneity (set) is the synthetic relation between the contents of time, and what is permanent (duration) is something that endures in time by passing through successive states and possessing simultaneous states. In Kant, the self becomes a temporal entity that endures in time (permanence), that has intensive states (simultaneity), and that passes from one extensive state to another (succession). This is what Deleuze means, then, when he says that Kant reconceived time as a *pure and empty form*: time is an empty form that is no longer dependent on either extensive or intensive movement; instead, time has become the pure and immutable form of everything that moves and changes— not an eternal form, but precisely the form of what is *not* eternal (ECC 29). Yet time itself is neither succession, nor simultaneity, nor permanence, since time cannot be reduced to any of its modes, or to what takes place within time (its content). We cannot even say that the immutable form of time is permanent, since what is permanent—no less than what is successive or simultaneous—appears and is perceived in time, whereas the immutable form of time itself cannot be perceived. As the pure form of change, time itself is defined by its infinite variability, and the definition of *chaos* that Deleuze gives in *What is Philosophy?* is itself a description of the pure form of time: "Chaos is characterized less by the absence of determinations than by the infinite speed with which they take shape and vanish" (WP 42; cf. DR 28). In other words, within the manifold of time, chaos is defined by the lack of any synthesis or rhythm between these determinations, "which spring up only to disappear immediately, without consistency or reference, without consequence" (WP 118).

If there is any salvation within this pure and empty form of time—time rendered ordinary—it takes place, in Kant, through the activity of *synthesis*, which is a process brought to bear, not on time itself, but on the modes of time, in order to render both being and knowledge possible.[35] Under the aspect of succession, what appears in time is a multiplicity of parts, which must be synthesized by the subject in an *apprehension* that fixes them in an ever-variable present. Under the aspect of simultaneity, moreover, I must not only apprehend parts in order for knowledge to be possible, but I must also *reproduce* the past parts: that is, I must remember the preceding parts in time and synthesize or "contract" them with the present parts. Under the aspect of permanence, finally, I can synthesize the apprehended present and the previous reproduced presents with the permanence of something that endures in time, which is related to a concept in an act of *recognition* ("so it's a table"). Readers of *Difference and Repetition*—notably in the third chapter on repetition—will recognize the ways in which Deleuze modifies the Kantian analysis of synthesis in the direction of a concept of *passive syntheses*.[36] The first synthesis (present) is reformulated into the passive organic and corporeal syntheses (habit) that make any receptivity, in Kant's sense, possible. The second synthesis (past), following Bergson, posits the need for a concept of the "pure" past, without which the passing of time would be impossible. And the third synthesis (future), rather than appealing to *recognition*, instead is the condition for the production of the *new*. "The more we study the nature of time," Bergson would later write, "the more we shall comprehend that duration means invention, the creation of forms, the continual elaboration of the absolutely new."[37] The production of the new—including the activities of creation found in philosophy, science, and art—is the direct consequence of this liberation of time. Though the term rarely appears in the text, *What is Philosophy?* is a book on time, or more precisely, a study of the determinations of thought that take place within the pure form of time. What Hume called the association of ideas (resemblance, contiguity, causality) links together our ideas in time with a minimum of constant rules, thereby forming a realm of *opinion* that protects us from chaos. But philosophy, science, and art do more than this, and Deleuze describes their respective activities using his own (created) vocabulary. From the infinite *variability* of time, philosophers extract *variations* that converge as the components of a consistent concept; scientists extract *variables* that enter into determinable relations in a function; and artists extract *varieties* that enter into the composition of a being of sensation (WP 202).

A NEW ANALYTIC OF CONCEPTS

The new analytic of concepts presented in *What is Philosophy?* is an attempt to insert the form of time into philosophical concepts, assigning them a synthetic structure that is differential and temporal. While concepts have no identity, they must have a *consistency*, but this consistency must have as its necessary complement the internal *variability* of the concept.[38] Deleuze analyzes these two temporal aspects of concepts under the rubrics of exo-consistency and endo-consistency. For Deleuze, no concept is ever simple; not only does it link up with other concepts (exo-consistency), but each concept also has its own internal components (endo-consistency), which in turn can themselves be considered as concepts. Descartes's concept of the *cogito*, for instance, can be said to have three components: namely, thinking, doubting, and being: "I (who doubt) think, and therefore I am (a thinking being)." A concept is therefore always a multiplicity: it is composed of a finite number of distinct, hetero-geneous, and none the less inseparable components or variations; the concept itself is the point of coincidence, condensation, or accumulation of these component elements, which it renders consistent *in itself*; and this internal consistency in turn is defined by the zones of neighborhood [*voisinage*] or indiscernibility that it creates between these components. But like a hypertext, the concept of the *cogito* is an open-ended multiplicity that contains the potential for bridges that provide links or crossroads to other Cartesian concepts.[39] The idea of infinity is the bridge leading from the concept of *cogito* to the concept of God, a new concept that has three components forming the "proofs" for the existence of God. In turn, the third proof (ontological) assures the closure of the concept but also throws out a new bridge or branches off to a concept of extended being, in so far as the concept of God guaran-tees the objective truth value of our other clear and distinct ideas.

This exo-consistency of concepts extends to the history of philosophy as well. When Kant later criticized the Cartesian *cogito*, he did so in the name of a new problematic field: Descartes could not say under what form the "I think" is capable of determining the "I am," and this determinable form, Kant argued, is precisely the form of time. In this way, Kant introduced a new component into the Cartesian *cogito*. Yet to say that Kant "criticized" Descartes is simply to say that Kant con-structed a problem that could not be occupied or completed by the Cartesian *cogito*. Descartes created the concept of the cogito, but he expelled time from it as a form of *anteriority*, making it a simple mode of succession sustained by a continuous divine creation. If Kant introduced time as a new component of the *cogito*, he did so on the condition of *creating a new concept* of time: time now becomes a form of *interiority* with its own internal components (succession, but also simultaneity and permanence). Similarly, to ask if there are precursors to the *cogito*—for instance, in Augustine—is to ask:

> Are there concepts signed by previous philosophers that have similar or almost identical components, but from which one component is lacking, or to which others have been added, so that a cogito does not crystallize, since the components do not yet coincide in a self? (WP 26)

Concepts, in short, possess an *internal* history, a potential for transmutation into other concepts, which constitutes what Deleuze likes to call the "plane of imma-nence" of philosophy.

> Creating concepts is constructing some area in the plane, adding a new area to existing ones, exploring a new area, filling in what's missing. Concepts are composites, amalgams of lines, curves. If new concepts have to be brought in all the time, it's just because the plane of immanence has to be constructed area by area, constructed locally, going from one point to the next. (N 147)

It is precisely through this kind of analysis that one can account for the various kinds of conceptual becomings that one finds in Deleuze's own work, and the transformations he himself introduced into concepts drawn from the history of philosophy. "The history of philosophy," Deleuze writes, "means that we evaluate not only the historical novelty of the concepts created by the philosopher, but also the power of their becoming when they pass into one another" (WP 32).

A complete study of Deleuze's analytic of concepts would have to examine the way the form of time permeates the other aspects of Deleuze's analyses. Concepts, for instance, are never created willy-nilly, but always as the function of a *problem*, and the analytic of concepts developed in *What is Philosophy?* finds its necessary correlate in the dialectic of problems formulated in *Difference and Repetition*. Deleuze considered himself to be a "pure metaphysician," but his fundamental metaphysical position is that Being is a problem; Being always presents itself under a problematic form, as a series of problematizations that are themselves temporal.[40] One might say that Plato invents the concept of the Idea in response to the problem of rivalry in the Greek cities (Socrates contra the Sophists), Descartes creates the *cogito* in response to the problem of absolute subjective certainty, and Leibniz formulates a whole series of hallucinatory concepts—expression, perspective, compossibility, harmony—in response to the problem of sufficient reason: everything has a reason, everything *has to* have a reason. Philosophy is the creation of concepts, but the creation of concepts has as its condition the construction of a problem or problems, which are themselves temporal. To "problematize" a concept thus does not only mean that one places it in question; it means that one seeks to determine the nature of the problem to which it serves as a solution. While it is relatively easy to define the true and the false in relation to solutions whose problems are already stated, it is much more difficult to distinguish between well-posed and badly-posed problems, which is why philosophy has often taken the form of a critique of false problems (B 16–17). Kant criticized the concepts of the Soul, the World, and God for being derived from "problems without solution."[41] Bergson similarly argued that questions such as "Why is there something rather than nothing?" or "Why is there disorder rather than order?" or "Why is there this rather than that (when that was equally possible)?" are false problems derived from a confusion of the more with the less.[42] Wittgenstein even attempted to show that, through an analysis of language use, most philosophical problems could in fact be dissolved "like a lump of sugar in water."[43] Yet even more difficult than the critique of false or badly-formulated problems, as both Kierkegaard and Whitehead insisted, is the assessment of whether or not a problem is *important* or *interesting*.[44] Henri Poincaré said that, in mathematics, constructing a proof for an unimportant problem was worse than discovering a flaw in one's proof for a remarkable problem; the former will remain eternally trivial, while the latter can be corrected and may have already gained important terrain.[45] The truth of a solution, in other words, is less important than the truth or interest of the problem being dealt with (a problem always has the solution it "deserves"). The same is true in philosophy: one can read pages and pages that are not false, but are without interest or importance. It is true that the problem that animates a philosopher is not always clearly stated; to engage in the history of philosophy is to recover these problems, and thereby to discover what is innovative in the concepts being created. Mediocre histories of philosophy link up concepts as if they go without saying—as if they had not been created—without determining the problems to which they correspond. Similarly, mediocre philosophers are those who create no concepts and instead make use of ready-made notions; they remain in the realm of opinion, ignorant of the problems at issue. Problems in turn are expressed in the form of questions, and Deleuze's early writings are critical of the "What is . . .?" form of questioning, as a means of attaining essences, in favor of questions such as Who?, Which one?, How many?, How?, Where?, When?, In which case?, From what point of view? "For a long time, concepts had been used to determine what something is (its essence). We, on the contrary, are interested in the circumstances of a thing: in which cases, where and when, how, and so on? For us, a concept should express an event, and no longer an essence."[46] If one has neither a concept nor a problem, one is not doing philosophy; one must become an apprentice not only to the creation of concepts but also to the constitution of problems and questions.

Moreover, both problems and questions, in turn, presuppose pre-philosophical images of thought: that is, images of what it means to think that pre-exist any particular "method" of resolving a problem or creating a concept. Borrowing a term coined by Bakhtin, Deleuze suggests that every explicit method in philosophy envelops an implicit "chronotope" of thought: that is, a noetic landscape of space-time with its own geography, inhabited by what Deleuze would come to call a *conceptual persona*, a "somewhat mysterious" (WP 61) notion that appears in Deleuze's writings for the first time in *What is Philosophy?*[47] The temporal aspect of thought (the before and after) is the order of reasons that a thinker creates between concepts; the spatial aspect is its distribution of aims, means, and obstacles. But the conceptual character of philosophers—as opposed to their psycho-social or historical character—is an internal condition for the production of their concepts; it concerns "that which belongs by right to thought and only to thought," even if it remains inseparable from empirical, psychological, and social determinations (WP 69). To give a simple example: one could say that Plato, Descartes, and Kant all shared the same aim—the truth—but they inhabited the problem of truth through different conceptual characters. If Plato wanted to find the truth, for instance, if he wanted to find the intelligible essence behind appearances (the Idea), it is because he did not want to be deceived by the false claimants to truth that he found in the Athenian democracy (sophists, rhetoricians, orators, artists). This is the lived problem confronted by his thought: "I do not want to be deceived." But when Descartes sought the truth in the *Meditations*, he did so in relation to the different problem of subjective certitude: the senses deceive me, the scholastics deceive me, perhaps God is a malicious demon that deceives me, and in the end it is I who deceive myself and allow myself to be deceived. This is not the same way of posing the problem of truth; it is animated by a different conceptual character ("I do not want to deceive myself"), and it produces a different concept of truth. What is important to Descartes is that deception and error are themselves modes of thought, and thus the first certitude Descartes finds—the first truth—is the "I think": even when I am being deceived or am in error, I am still thinking. When Kant in turns says, "I want the truth," he again means something very different: "I do not want to deceive." This entails yet another manner of living the relation to truth. If Plato was marked by the Athenian democracy, Kant was a creature of the Reformation, and had discovered moral rigor. Kant thus subordinated knowledge (speculative reason) to morality (practical reason). Morality no longer depends on one's knowledge, as in the virtue of the sage or wise man; rather, knowledge is itself subject to a higher finality, the finality of a moral reason. "I do not want to deceive" indeed engenders Kant's search for the truth—the operation of knowledge—but it does so by strictly subordinating knowledge to a practical finality. If Kant does not want to deceive, it is because only beings that do not deceive are free, or can even claim to be free. In Kant, intelligible nature is no longer found in an essence, as in Plato, but in a community of moral beings, the kingdom of ends. In short, the concepts created by Plato, Descartes, and Kant fill a noetic space-time following a temporal order of reasons and a spatial order of aims, means and obstacles, but each of them refer to a prior image of thought inhabited by very different conceptual personae, which can be summarized in the cries, "I do not want to be deceived," "I do not want to deceive myself," and "I do not want to deceive." The differing methods of the three philosophers—dialectic, analytic, transcendental—are derived from these images, which preexist any explicit methodology.

THE POWER OF THE FALSE

Deleuze's analytic of concepts, in other words, introduces time not only into concepts, but also into the construction of problems and questions, as well as the transformation of images of thought and the conceptual characters that inhabit them. Indeed, one of the most significant implications of Deleuze's analyses is that the form of time places the concept of truth in crisis. Philosophers tend to speak of the true with a reverence once reserved for the divine, as if its value were unques-tioned.[48] Yet truth is itself a concept, with its own becoming. Nietzsche seems to have been correct when he said that he was the first see that the concept of truth poses a philosophical problem:

> Let us thus define our own task—the value of truth must for once be experi-mentally *called into question* . . . Suppose we want the truth: Why not rather untruth? Or uncertainty? Or ignorance? . . . Though it scarcely seems credible, it finally almost seems to us as if the problem had never even been put so far— as if we were the first to see it, fix our eyes on it, and *risk* it. For it does involve a risk, and perhaps there is none that is greater.[49]

Deleuze's thesis is that the concept of truth enters into crisis when it confronts the form of time; the *form of the true* gives way to the *power of the false*. Speaking in general terms, the true is not the same thing as the real; it is rather the distinc-tion between the real and the imaginary (or between essence and appearance). The false is not the imaginary; it is rather the confusion of the imaginary with the real (or of the apparent with the essential). What we call error is the act that con-sists of making this confusion; the false is effectuated in error, which confuses the imaginary and the real (DR 148). How, then, do we distinguish the false from the true? Only the true has a *form* (*eidos*); the false has no form, and error consists in giving the false the form of the true. Since Aristotle, the form of the true has had a precise sense: the universal and the necessary. The true is that which is universal and necessary, always and everywhere, in all times and in all places. This is not a universality of *fact* but a universality of *right*. In fact, it may be that people rarely think, and rarely think the true. But to say that only the true has a form is to insist that, in principle, if you think a triangle, you cannot deny that its three angles are necessarily equal to two right angles. Universality and necessity qualify the *judgments* that are made of the form of the true; since the false has no form, judgments made about it are by right deprived of all universality and necessity. Who, then, is the truthful person? In classical philosophy, what corresponds to the real in an idea is its power to *represent*, while what corresponds to the imaginary is the capacity of an idea (or image) to produce a *modification* of my body or soul. The former attains to essences, while the latter leaves one mired in appearances, and the anguish of the passions. The truthful person is thus someone who would allow their body and soul to be modified only by the form of the true. The activity through which this takes place can be called the *in-formation* of the soul by the true, which takes as its model the Eternal (the universal and the necessary).[50]

If time puts the concept of truth in crisis, it does so not at the level of its content ("truth changes with time"), but rather at the level of its form; the form of time takes the place of the (universal) form of the true. The false is thereby given a *power* of its own; if the false does not have a form, it none the less has a power. When does the false take on a power? When it is freed from the model of truth: that is, when *the false is no longer presented as being true*. What can disengage the concept of the false from the model of truth? The answer is: time. Just as Deleuze attempts to formulate a concept of difference-in-itself, freed from its subordination to the concept of identity, so he attempts to formulate a concept of the false-in-itself, freed from its subordination to the concept of truth (and error). But this in no way implies the banal conclusion that "everything is false," which would now be presented as a truth: as Nietzsche said, in one of his most profound phrases, in abolishing the true world we have also abolished the false world of appearances.[51] There is no longer either truth or appearance, and the false is no longer presented as being true; instead, the false assumes a power of its own. What, then, is the "power" of the false? If the form of the true is derived from the power of *judgment*, the power of the false is a power of metamorphosis: that is, a power of *creation*. Creative of what? At this point, there is no reason not to re-employ the word "truth." The power of the false is creative of truth—but this is, precisely, *a new concept of truth*: truth is no longer a timeless universal to be discovered, but a singularity to be created (in time). "Philosophy creates concepts, which are neither generalities nor even truths; they are rather of the order of the Singular, the Important, the New" (TRM 238).

When the form of time is put into the concept, the *falsifier* [*le faussaire*]—that is, the artist, the creator—takes the place of the truthful person. The falsifier is not a liar, since the liar is localizable (the liar "owns" his lies), whereas the falsifier is non-localizable; the power of the false exists only under the form of a *series* of powers. To ask "What is a falsifier?" is a badly-posed question, since the falsifier does not exist apart from an irreducible plurality or multiplicity; behind every falsifier there is only another falsifier (a mask behind every mask). The question becomes: where is one placed within the chain of falsifiers? As Nietzsche showed, the truthful person is himself nothing other than the first power of the false; Plato distinguished between the true world and the apparent world, but to do so he first had to *create* the concept of the Idea. If the power of the false is what Nietzsche called the will to power, one can distinguish two extremes or two powers within this will—namely, the will to *judge* and the will to *create*—and it is the latter that constitutes the higher power. On this score, Deleuze suggests that there have been three great presentations of the theme of the falsifier: in philosophy, the final book of Nietzsche's *Thus Spoke Zarathustra* (the chain of the "higher" men, each of which corresponds to a power of the false); in literature, Hermann Melville's final masterpiece, *The Confidence Man*; and in cinema, Orson Welles's last film, *F for Fake*.[52] The latter provides an instructive exploration of the difference between the painter Vermeer and Hans van Meegeren, the famous forger of Vermeer's works. How did van Meegeren pass off his forgeries as genuine Vermeers? Precisely because he made use of the criteria of experts, and the expert is someone who *judges*; the expert is able to recognize a true Vermeer by means of criteria he himself has established concerning Vermeer's style and periods. The forger then studies these criteria and uses them to produce the forgery, to the point where the expert will declare, "This is clearly a genuine Vermeer because it corresponds to all the criteria." The expert always has a forger within him, since they are both nourished off the same substance: the system of judgment (TI 146). What, then, is the difference between Vermeer and his forger? Both the artist and the forger belong to the chain of falsifiers, but Vermeer has a power of metamorphosis, whereas the forger and the expert scarcely know how to change; theirs is already an exhausted life that can do little more than judge the creations of others. The expert and the forger are united in their exaggerated taste for *form* (the form of the true), but the artist is able to take the power of the false to a higher degree that is realized, not in form, but in *transformation*. It is this same vision that animates Deleuze's conception of philosophy: philosophy is the enterprise of the creation of truth (the creation of concepts): that is, the will to power at its highest degree, which has as its necessary correlate the will "to have done with judgment" (ECC 126).

THE UNIVERSAL THOUGHT FLOW

There is a final topic to consider, which *What is Philosophy?* hints at but does not discuss in detail. If philosophy is the creation of concepts, what is the process that lies at the *real* genesis of concepts or the *real* origin of thinking? The question of how to "begin" has always been a delicate question in philosophy, and although Deleuze raises this question in *Difference and Repetition* (DR 129), we will approach the problem here by considering the following (somewhat obscure) passage from one of Deleuze's seminars on Leibniz:

What is given, at the limit, could be called a flow [*flux*]. It is flows that are given, and creation consists in cutting, organizing, and connecting flows, in such a manner that a creation is sketched out or made around certain singu-larities extracted from the flows . . . Imagine the universal thought flow as a kind of internal monologue, the internal monologue of everyone who thinks . . . The concept is a system of singularities extracted [*prélevé*] from a thought flow . . . One can also conceive of a continuous acoustic flow that traverses the world and that even encompasses silence (perhaps that is only an Idea, but it matters little if this Idea is justified). A musician is someone who extracts something from this flow. (15 Apr 1980)

Somewhat abruptly, and in a vaguely Spinozistic manner, Deleuze here posits the existence of what he calls the "universal thought flow," even if its status is simply that of a justifiable Idea: just as we may have an Idea of a continuous flow of matter in the universe, of which we ourselves are modifications, so we can conceive of a continuous flow of thought in the universe, of which we are likewise modifications. "I maintain," Spinoza similarly wrote, "that there is in Nature an infinite power of thinking."[53] The thoughts that come and go in our heads, of which we are neither the origin nor the author, are the products of this thought flow. Or more precisely, they are themselves the very movement of this universal flow of thought—a flow that is anonymous, impersonal, and indeterminate, like a continuous internal mon-ologue. Leibniz had already argued, against Descartes, that it is illegitimate to say "I think, therefore I am," not because "I am" does not follow from "I think," but rather because, from the activity of thought, I can never derive an "I." At best, Descartes can claim that "there is thinking" or that "thought has taken place."[54] Both Spinoza and Leibniz argued that there is an automatism to thought just as there is a mecha-nism of the body: we are all "spiritual automatons"—it is not *we* who think, but rather thought that takes place within us.[55] Nietzsche likewise observed that "a thought comes when 'it' wants, not when 'I' want,"[56] and in one of his notebooks he added:

A thought . . . comes up in me—where from? How? I simply don't know. It comes, independently of my will, usually surrounded and obscured by a mass of feelings, desires, aversions, and also other thoughts . . . One pulls it [the thought] out of this mass, cleans it off, sets it on its feet, and then sees how it stands and how it walks—all of this in an astonishing *presto* and yet without any sense of hurry. Just *who* does all this—I have no idea, and I am surely more a spectator than originator of this process.[57]

What, then, does it mean to say that a concept is a "system of singularities extracted [*prélevé*] from a thought flow"? To answer this question, we need to consider what we might call the "usual" status of the universal thought flow, and Deleuze has formulated a concept to describe it: *stupidity* [*bêtise*]. "Stupidity is a structure of thought as such" (NP 105). More to the point, to a certain degree, stupidity is the *basic* structure of the universal thought flow. The thoughts that pass through our mind every day are not falsehoods, nor are they errors or even a tissue of errors; every thought may be true, but they are none the less stupidities, inanities.

There is, no doubt, a certain provocation involved in Deleuze's use of this term (the French term *bêtise* is derived from *bête*, the word for a beast or an animal), since other philosophers have made a similar point by appealing to different concepts. Heidegger spoke of idle talk or idle chatter, and the fact that, most of the time, our thoughts are the thoughts of what "They" think (*Das Man*).[58] Plato spoke of the reign of the *doxa* or the realm of opinion, and he saw the task of philosophy as the attempt to break with the *doxa*, to extract oneself from opinion. But the point remains the same: the thoughts that pass through our heads, carried along by the universal thought flow, are stupid thoughts—thoughts that are determined, often, by the inanity of the culture that surrounds us. Is this not the aim of marketing and advertising: to modify the thought flow, to populate it with anonymous thoughts about making one's laundry brighter or one's teeth whiter? For Deleuze, the misadventure that constantly threatens thinking is not error or falsehood, but stupidity (clichés, ready-made ideas, conventions, opinions . . .). William James said that what prevents the creation of truth are the truths we think we already possess.[59] Moreover, at a deeper level, one might say that schizophrenia also reveals a possibility for thought, which is why Artaud plays such an important role in Deleuze's work.

> Artaud said that the problem (for him) was not to orient his thought, or to perfect the expression of what he thought, or to acquire application and method, or to perfect his poems, but simply *to manage to think something*. For him, this was the only conceivable "work." (DR 147)

In different ways, both the flow of stupidity and psychosis reveal the *internal* problem that thought itself constantly confronts: as Heidegger put it, "what is most thought-provoking in our thought-provoking time is the fact that *we are not yet thinking*."[60] On this score, Deleuze likes to cite a phrase of the French filmmaker Jean-Luc Godard: *pas une image juste, juste une image* ("not a just image, just an image"). Since we are constantly besieged by images that are nothing but clichés, the task of the filmmaker is not to create just or moral or uplifting images, but simply to create an image *tout court*—that is, to manage to create an image that is not a cliché. That in and of itself is enough: to create even a single image that is not a cliché. The same is true for the creation of concepts in the realm of thought: "to think is to create—there is no other creation—but to create is first of all *to engender 'thinking' within thought*" (DR 147).

Given the reign of stupidity in the realm of thought, and the reign of clichés in the realm of art (and even the reign of psychic clichés in our affective and perceptive life), what, then, is the process that constitutes a real act of creation? How is thinking engendered within the habitual clichés of the universal thought flow? We have already seen Deleuze's response: thinking is always engendered through the fortuitousness of an *encounter* with a problem (under the form of an intensity), which alone guarantees the necessity of what it forces us to think. Philosophy has long been content to assume a "dogmatic" image of thought which presupposes that thinking is a voluntary activity; that the thinker has a natural affinity for the truth; that we are led into error by what is foreign to thought (the body, the passions); and thus that what we need to think well is simply a method that will ward off error and bring us back to the truthful nature of thought (NP 103). But Deleuze is pointing to a generalized thought process that cannot be covered over with this reassuring dogmatic image. Thinking is never the result of a voluntary will, but rather the result of forces that act upon us from the outside: we search for "truth" and begin to think only when we are compelled to do so, when we undergo a violence that impels us to such a search and wrests us from our natural stupor. A lazy schoolboy who suddenly becomes "good at Latin" because he has fallen in love with a classmate is no less an instance of this than Leibniz's relentless pursuit of the problem of sufficient reason (PS 22), and there is no method that can determine in advance what compels us to think. The "conceptual persona" one finds in Deleuze is not the Platonic *friend*, voluntarily exercising a natural desire for the truth in dialogue with others about a "What is . . .?" question, but rather something akin to the *jealous lover*, involuntarily forced to confront a problem whose coordinates are derived precisely from the questions Plato rejected: What happened?, When?, Where?, Why?, With whom? Deleuze said that he himself frequently sought material in encounters outside of philosophy, although these occurred more often with films and paintings than with people (ABC C). But this is precisely why Deleuze, like Kant, distinguishes knowledge from thinking. *Knowledge* is only a result or an outcome—it is the establishment of a territory, a competence or specialization; but *thinking* is a process of learning or apprenticeship that is initiated by one's encounter with a problem, and necessarily stems from the depth of one's own ignorance (N 7).

> How else can one write but of those things which one doesn't know, or knows badly? [Deleuze asks in his preface to *Difference and Repetition*]. It is precisely there that we imagine having something to say. We write only at the frontiers of our knowledge, at the border which separates our knowledge from our ignorance and transforms the one into the other. Only in this manner are we resolved to write. To satisfy ignorance is to put off writing until tomorrow—or rather, to make it impossible.[61]

Yet the encounter with a problem would mean nothing if the universal thought flow were nothing but a flow of stupidity: that is, if it did not have its own singularities. Indeed, this is why the concept of "singularity" plays such an important role in Deleuze's philosophy. In mathematics, the singular is opposed to the regular; the singular is what escapes the regularity of the rule—it is the production of the new (the point where a curve changes direction). More importantly, some singularities are remarkable, while others are ordinary, and in this sense, one could say that there are two poles of Deleuze's philosophy: "Everything is remarkable!" and "Everything is ordinary!" (FLB 91; cf. TI 15). It is in terms of these two poles that we can understand the real genesis of concepts. In Deleuze's ontology, every moment, every event, every individual, every thought is singular. Being is difference: that is, it is the inexhaustible creation of difference, the constant production of new, the incessant genesis of the heterogeneous. Yet the ontological condition of difference is that, in being produced, singularities become regularized, made ordinary, "normalized" (in Foucault's sense). It is this reduction of the singular to the ordinary that Deleuze calls the apparatus of "capture" (TP 424): the inevitable processes of stratification, regularization, normalization—or perhaps what we might call "stupid-ization" in the realm of thought. The characterization of the "usual" status of the thought flow as having a structure of stupidity was thus a derivative characteriza-tion, for the thought flow is indeed constituted by remarkable singularities—but they are singularities that have been rendered ordinary and banal. As Nietzsche wrote, in a slightly different context, "fundamentally, all our actions are altogether incomparably personal, unique, and infinitely individual; there is no doubt of that. But as soon as we translate them into consciousness *they no longer seem to be*." This is why Deleuze insists that the distinction between the regular (what belongs to the rule) and the singular (what escapes the rule)—and even more so, between the remarkable and the ordinary—is much more important in philosophy than the dis-tinction between the true and the false.

If a concept is a "system of singularities extracted from a thought flow," this process of extraction has two necessarily correlative aspects—destruction (the destruction of the cliché) and creation (the creation of the new). Nowhere has Deleuze examined this two-fold process of thought in more detail than in his analy-sis of the act of painting in *Francis Bacon* (FB 71–90). Painters never simply work on the white surface of a canvas, Deleuze suggests, since the canvas is already filled, actually or virtually, with the images (clichés, perceptual schemata) that painters bring with them, so that the first task of the painter is not to cover the canvas, but *to empty it out*: to destroy the cliché. Bacon's technique was to make random marks, to throw the paint from various angles and at various speeds, or to scrub, sweep, or wipe the canvas—precisely in order to clear out locales or zones that would destroy the nascent cliché and make possible the creation of an image. It is as if a "catastrophe" or "chaos" overcame the canvas, which loosened the clichés of visual organization but at the same time outlined "possibilities of fact" for the emerging image being created—though with the perpetual possibility that one could botch the painting or fall back into the cliché.[62] And just as the painter must destroy the cliché in order to create an image, the philosopher can create only by first destroying the conventions of opinion. If there is a difference between painting and philosophy—as well as the other arts—it lies in the fact that in philosophy the battle against the cliché usually remains external to the work, even if it is internal to the author. Unlike the other arts, Deleuze suggests that painting tends to integrate the matrix of the catastrophe into itself; the work emerges from an optical catastrophe which remains present on the canvas. In rare cases of thinkers like Artaud, the collapse of ordinary linguistic coordinates can indeed belong fully to the work itself (TRM 184). But in all cases, whether in philosophy, science, or art, every creation—the engendering of thinking within thought—has as its inevitable condition the fight against clichés through the confrontation with a problem.

This, then, is the real process that lies at the genesis of every act of creation, and which unites the various aspects of Deleuze's analytic of concepts: if the singular is produced under conditions that constantly reduce it to the regular or the ordinary, then the task of creation amounts to a constant and ever-renewed struggle against the reign of clichés in order to extract singularities from the thought flow and make them function consistently as *variabilities* on a new plane of creation: the *variations* of a philosophic concept (the plane of immanence), the *variables* of a scientific function (the plane of reference), and the *varieties* of a work of art (the plane of composition).

Ethics

The Place of Ethics in Deleuze's Philosophy: Three Questions of Immanence

Michel Foucault, in his preface to the first volume of *Capitalism and Schizophrenia* (and revealingly, with apologies to its authors), wrote that "*Anti-Oedipus* is a book of ethics, the first book of ethics to be written in France in quite a long time" (AO xiii). Foucault's comment was clearly meant to be provocative. It is true that France does not have a strong tradition of "moral philosophy"; the concerns of the discipline, it has been suggested, were largely taken up in France by the various human sciences such as psychology and sociology.[1] Yet *Anti-Oedipus* was itself a work known primarily as a critique of psychoanalysis, and it bore little resemblance to what usually passes, in academic circles, for moral philosophy. For Foucault to insist that it was a book of ethics was tantamount to forcing his readers, at the very least, to regard the notion of "ethics" in a new manner. At the time Foucault wrote his preface, in 1977, he was himself, we now know, in the process of recasting the entire *History of Sexuality* project around precisely this reformulation of "the ethical question."[2] What was the basis of this reconceptualization of ethics that Foucault recognized in Deleuze's philosophy, and which he later explored, in his own manner, in his last works?

Deleuze nowhere explicitly attempts to put forward what could be called an "ethical theory" of his own. Yet he has always identified Spinoza and Nietzsche as his two primary philosophical precursors, and wrote important monographs on each of them.[3] These two thinkers, in Deleuze's work, constitute a kind of "minor" tradition of ethical thought. What they have in common is an attempt to rethink ethics (and philosophy as a whole) from a purely *immanent* point of view. In several interviews given after the publication of *Foucault* in 1986, Deleuze attempted to characterize this immanent conception of ethics by offering his own version of the distinction between "ethics" and "morality," which has often been drawn to distinguish modes of reflection that place greater emphasis, respectively, on the good or virtuous life (such as Aristotle or Stoicism) or on the moral law (such as Kantianism). He uses the term "morality" to define, in very general terms, any set of "constraining" rules, such as a moral code, that consists in judging actions and intentions by relating them to universal or transcendent values ("this is good, that is evil").[4] What he calls "ethics" is, on the contrary, a set of "facilitative" (*faculta-tive*) rules that evaluate what we do, say, and think according to the immanent mode of existence that it implies. One says or does this, thinks or feels that: *what mode of existence does it imply?* "We always have the beliefs, feelings, and thoughts we deserve," writes Deleuze, "given our way of being or our style of life."[5] The term "mode of existence" is not a psychological notion, but an ontological one. Spinoza and Nietzsche argued, each in their own way, that there are things one cannot do or think, or say or feel, except for the condition of being weak, base, or enslaved, unless one harbors a vengeance or *ressentiment* against life (Nietzsche), unless one remains the slave of passive affections (Spinoza); and there are other things one cannot do or think except on the condition of being strong, noble, or free, unless one affirms life or attains active affections. Deleuze calls this the method of "dramatization": actions and propositions are interpreted as so many sets of symptoms that express or "dramatize" the mode of existence of the speaker. "What is the mode of exist-ence of the person who utters a given proposition?" asks Nietzsche. "What mode of existence is *needed* in order to be able to utter it?"[6] Rather than *judging* actions and thoughts by appealing to transcendent or universal values, one *evaluates* them by determining the mode of existence that serves as their principle. A pluralistic method of explanation by immanent modes of existence is in this way made to replace the recourse to transcendent values; an immanent ethical difference (noble / base) is substituted for the transcendent moral opposition (Good / Evil).

This immanent conception of an "ethics without morality," however, has not fared well in the history of philosophy. Few philosophers have been more maligned and ridiculed than Spinoza and Nietzsche. They were condemned, by both their contemporaries and their successors, not only for being atheists, but also, even worse, for being "immoralists."[7] A potent danger was sensed to be lurking in the *Ethics* and the *Genealogy of Morals*: without transcendence, without universals, one will fall into the dark night of chaos, reduced to a pure "subjectivism" or "relativ-ism." A philosophy of immanence, it is argued, far from resolving the question of justification, seems to shift the problem on to an irresolvable terrain. It seems unable to put forth normative criteria by which certain modes of existence can be judged as acceptable and others condemned as reprehensible, and winds up espous-ing a kind of moral nihilism in which all "differences" are affirmed in their turn. Deleuze himself, in a late essay, states the problem in this way: "What disturbed us was that in renouncing judgment we had the impression of depriving ourselves of any means assessing the differences between existing beings, between modes of existence, as if everything were now of equal value" (ECC 134). Nietzsche, for instance, famously criticized morality for having been derived from a reactive or base mode of existence. But by what "right," according to what criteria, is a noble or active mode of existence "better" or "worth more" than a base one? Put succinctly: How can one evaluate modes of existence using criteria that are immanent to the mode itself without thereby abandoning any basis for comparative evaluation?

It is this problem that lies at the heart of an ethics of immanence, and Deleuze's response to it is a rigorous one. A mode of existence can be evaluated, apart from transcendental or universal values, by the purely immanent criteria of its *power* or capacity (*puissance*): that is, by the manner in which it actively deploys its power by going to the limit of what it can do (or on the contrary, by the manner in which it is cut off from its power to act and is reduced to powerlessness). Deleuze expresses this in various formulas throughout his work: modes of existence are evaluated "according to their tenor in 'possibilities,' in freedom, in creativity" (TRM 343–4); by "the manner in which the existing being (*existant*) is filled with (*s'emplit de*) immanence" (ECC 137); the ethical task entails "an amplification, an intensification, an elevation of power, an increase in dimensions, a gain in distinction" (FLB 73); "there are never any criteria other than the tenor of existence, the intensification of life" (WP 74). Modes of existence, in other words, must be evaluated according to the purely *intensive* criteria of their power and their capacity to affect and be affected. From afar, the meaning of this principle seems obscure, and has at times been subject to naive caricatures (for instance, that it simply valorizes "powerful" modes of existence, "superhuman" individuals who capriciously exert their power and will upon others). To explore the nature of Deleuze's immanent ethics, I would first like to analyze the complex relations it maintains with Kantianism; and then to examine, in summary fashion, some of the problems and positive tasks it poses, taking our cue primarily from Spinoza.

KANT AND IMMANENT ETHICS

Somewhat surprisingly, Deleuze presents this immanent conception of ethics not, as one might perhaps expect, as a rejection of Kantianism but, on the contrary, as its *fulfillment.* Kant's genius, in Deleuze's interpretation, was precisely to have conceived of a purely *immanent* critique of reason, a critique that did not seek, within reason, errors that come from an external cause (the body, the senses, the passions) but illusions that arise from within reason itself through the illegitimate (transcendent) use of the syntheses of consciousness. Yet the post-Kantian philosophers, from Salomon Maimon to Hermann Cohen, argued that Kant himself was unable to realize this project of immanent critique fully because he lacked a method that would allow reason to be critiqued internally without giving it the task of being its own judge. Kant's project was a critique of reason by reason itself; reason is both the judge and the judged, the tribunal and the accused. He therefore saw critique as a force that should be brought to bear on all claims to knowledge and morality—but not on knowledge and morality themselves, which were considered to be the "natural interests" of reason and thus were never placed in question. What Kant condemned was simply those illegitimate employments (illusions) through which reason, in its natural state, confuses those interests and allows these domains to impinge on one another.

> Thus total critique turns into a politics of compromise: even before the battle the spheres of influence have already been shared out. Three ideals are distinguished: What can I know? What should I do? What can I hope for? Limits are drawn to each one, misuses and trespasses are denounced, but the uncritical character of each ideal remains at the heart of Kantianism like the worm in

the fruit: true knowledge, true morality, and true religion. What Kant still calls—in his own terms—a fact: the fact of morality, the fact of knowledge.[8]

In his landmark book *Nietzsche and Philosophy*, Deleuze argues that it was Nietzsche who was finally able to fulfill the aims of the critical project precisely because he brought the critique to bear not merely on false claims to knowledge and morality but on truth itself: that is, on true morality and true knowledge. "We need a critique of moral values," writes Nietzsche in *The Genealogy of Morals*; "*the value of these values must first be called into question.*" And again: "The will to truth requires a critique—let us thus define our own task—the value of truth must for once be experimentally *called into question.*"[9] Nietzsche was not content to discover transcendental principles that would constitute the condition of possibility for the "facts" of reason (the "fact" of knowledge, the "fact" of morality); rather he was intent on discovering immanent principles that were truly genetic and productive, that would give an account of the *genesis* of knowledge and morality. What he called "genealogy" was a method that traced the origin of knowledge and morality to differential modes of existence that serve as their principle. As Deleuze writes,

> The problem of critique is that of the value of values [knowledge, morality], of the evaluation from which their value arises, thus the problem of their creation. Evaluation is defined as the differential element of corresponding values, an element which is both critical and creative. Evaluations, in essence, are not values but ways of being, modes of existence of those who judge and evaluate, serving as principles for the values on the basis of which they judge. (NP 1)

Deleuze's analysis of Kant's theory of the moral law is consequently worth examining in some detail here, since in effect it submits Kantianism itself to the critical reversal set in motion by Nietzsche. Deleuze suggests that, just as the *Critique of Pure Reason* effected a Copernican revolution by making the objects of knowledge revolve around the subject, so the *Critique of Practical Reason* effected an equally important revolution by making the Good revolve around the Law. He thereby inverted the relation that had prevailed since antiquity, and seemed in a position to invert what Nietzsche called "the ascetic ideal." But what actually takes place in the second Critique? In Plato, laws were a secondary or derived power, subordinate to the Good; if humans knew the Good, and how to conform to it, they would not need laws. From the point of view of *principles*, laws are only a "second resort," an imitation of the Good given to humans when the true politics is lacking. And from the point of view of *consequences*, the righteous person, in obeying the laws of his or her country, can none the less be said to be acting for the "Best," even though he or she retains the freedom to think of the Good and for the sake of the Good. Kant, in Deleuze's reading, effectively reversed this classical conception of the Law, as much from the point of view of the principles upon which the Law rests as the consequences it entails.[10]

    1. From the point of view of principles, laws are no longer seen to find their

foundation in a higher principle from which they would derive their authority. Instead, *the* Law is made into a first principle, a pure form of universality that has neither object nor content (since a content would imply a Good of which the Law would be the imitation . . .). It does not tell us what we must do; it does not present itself as a comparative or psychological universal ("Do unto others . . ."). Rather, it provides a subjective rule, a logical test, that we must obey no matter what our action: every action whose maxim can be *thought* without contradiction as universal, and whose motive has no other object than this maxim, will be a moral action or at least consistent with morality. Lying, for example, cannot be thought as a universal, because it at least implies people who believe the lie and who, in believing it, are not lying. In Kant, the Law becomes stripped of all content, its imperative being merely a categorical one. The Law does not tell us which *object* the will must pursue to be good but simply what *form* it must take to be moral. "It does not tell us what we must do, it simply tells us 'You must!', leaving us to deduce from it the Good, that is, the objects of this pure imperative" (ECC 32).

2. From the point of view of consequences, it is no longer possible to say that the righteous man obeys the Law for the sake of the Best. Since it is valid by virtue of its form alone and its content remains undetermined, the Law is not part of the domain of the understanding. The Law is not known and can never be known precisely because there is nothing in it to "know." We come across the Law only through its action, through a purely *practical* determination that is opposed to any speculative or theoretical proposition. The Law defines a realm of transgression where one breaks the Law *without ever knowing what it is*. It is this realm, Deleuze suggests, whose mechanisms were described with frightening detail by Kafka in *The Trial*: the Law acts and expresses itself through its sentence, and one can learn of this sentence only through its application in a punishment (K 44–45). Consequently, the person who tries to obey the moral imperative of the Law no longer becomes or even feels righteous; on the contrary, the Law makes one feel guilty, necessarily guilty, guilty *in advance*, and the more strict one's obedience, the greater one's guilt. Freud, in his analysis of the superego, uncovered the secret of this paradox of conscience: if duty presupposes a renunciation of our interests and desires, the moral Law will inevitably exert itself all the more strongly and rigorously, the deeper our renunciation. The Law thereby makes itself all the more severe to the degree that we observe it with exactitude.[11] And even guilt and punishment will not give us a final knowledge of our faults; the Law remains in a state of indeterminacy equaled only by the extreme specificity of the punishment. *It never acquits us*, no more of our virtues than of our faults.

Deleuze, in short, defines the Kantian moral Law in terms of two paradoxical poles: formal transcendence, from the point of view of principles; and *a priori* guilt, from the point of view of consequences. The modern critique of Kant's moral philosophy has tended to take as its point of departure these two poles. In his 1967 study entitled *Masochism*, for instance, in which this analysis of the Law first appeared, Deleuze argued that Sade and Masoch presented two "perverse" modes of existence that had as their aim the subversion of the moral Law: either by a new revolt that aims at a higher sovereign principle beyond the Law, an *ironic* principle that would no longer be the Good but rather the Idea of Evil or primary nature (Sade's institutional model of anarchy); or else by a *humorous* submission that eludes the imperative of the Law by turning punishment into a condition that makes possible the forbidden pleasure (Masoch's contractual model).[12] Deleuze's analyses in *Masochism*, in turn, can be read as a non-theistic version of Kierkegaard's analysis of the "suspension of the ethical": Job contests the Law in an ironic manner, "refusing all secondhand explanations, dismissing the general in order to attain the most singular as a principle, as a universal"; whereas Abraham submits to the Law humoristically, "but in this submission he recovers the singularity of the only son that the Law has commanded him to sacrifice" (DR 5–8). But these critiques, important as they are, only expose the paradoxes of the Kantian Law, its limits, pointing either to a "leap" beyond the Law into the religious or to a "transgression" of the Law through perversion.

Nietzsche's method of dramatization, by contrast, provides an immanent critique, not of the paradoxes but of the very principles of the moral Law. *Who* is it that says, "You must!"? It is the priest, and the categorical imperative expressed the purely formal aspect of the will to judge. Who is it that is always already guilty? It is the slave, laden with a responsibility-guilt of which he can never acquit himself. When Nietzsche laid out the three primary psychological categories of the slave in the *Genealogy of Morals*, he also marked out the evolution of the triumph of "morality," the genealogical origins of the moral Law: *ressentiment* ("It's your fault . . . ," moment of projective accusation and recrimination); the bad conscience ("It's my fault . . . ," moment of introjection; fault is internalized, turned back against oneself; one becomes guilty); and finally the ascetic ideal (moment of sublimation, triumph of reactive forces; life is "judged" in the name of values superior to life). At the same time, he also showed how the slave found its necessary correlate in the priest ("I want to judge, I must judge . . . "), who gives this guilt form, who exploits it to establish his power, who invents a new form of power as a power of judgment.[13] Morality, in this sense, constitutes what Deleuze calls a "system of judgment." Nietzsche famously identified the condition of judgment in "the consciousness of having a *debt* toward the divinity." It is the debtor–creditor relation, he argued, that lies at the origin of the ethico-moral realm; promises were given, commitments made to the future, and the "justice of the laws" existed to make one responsible for one's debts, "to create a memory for the future." The system of judgment appeared precisely when this debt was rendered *infinite* and therefore unpayable (Christianity); we were no longer indebted to another party but to the divine, to whom we have an infinite debt of which we can never acquit ourselves. "Debt becomes the relation of a debtor who will never finish paying to a creditor who will never finish using up interest on the debt" (NP 142).

For Deleuze, the moral Law in Kant is simply "*the juridical form assumed by the infinite debt*" (AO 215). Rather than submitting this system of judgment to a true critique, Kant erected "a fantastic subjective tribunal" that placed both the priest and the slave within the subject (ECC 126). It is *the same person* who now becomes both priest and believer, legislator and subject, judge and judged. In the name of practical reason, "reason" itself is made to represent our slavery and subjection as something superior that makes us reasonable beings. "The more you obey, the more you will become master, for you will only be obeying pure reason, in other words . . . yourself" (TP 376). Nowhere is this strategy made clearer than in the trajectory of the transcendent Ideas (Soul, World, God) in Kant's work. In the first Critique, Kant had denounced any transcendent use of the syntheses as illegitimate and illusory, relegating the Ideas to the "horizon" of the field immanent to the subject. But one by one, they are each resurrected in the second Critique and given a practical determination. "Freedom," as the "fact" of morality, implies *the cosmological Idea of a supra-sensible world*, independent of any sensible condition; in turn, the abyss that separates the noumenal Law and the phenomenal world requires the intermediary of an intelligible author of sensible Nature or a "moral cause of the world" (*the theological Idea of a supreme being*) and can only be bridged through the "postulate" of an infinite progress. Acquittal can only be hoped for, not in the here and now, but from the point of view of a progress that continues to infinity in an ever more exacting conformity to the Law. Since this path exceeds the limits of our life, it requires *the psychological Idea of the immortality of the soul* (the debtor must survive if the debt is to be infinite). This indefinite prolongation leads less to a paradise above than to a hell here below. It does not bestow immortality but condemns us to a "slow death," leaving us no other juridical alternatives than those proposed by Kafka: either an "apparent acquittal" or an "unlimited postponement." Or rather, Deleuze argues, it is not that judgment is deferred, put off until tomorrow, repressed to infinity; on the contrary, it is this very act of deferring, of carrying things to infinity, of making the debt infinite, that renders judgment possible. The condition of judgment is this relation between existence and infinity in the order of time, and "the one who maintains himself in this relation is given the power to judge and to be judged." The moral Law is thus a system of judgment that "condemns us to a servitude without end and annuls any liberatory process" (ECC 127–8).

The distinction between transcendence and immanence is not an absolute one, however, for even the illusions of transcendence can serve "to recharge the plane of immanence with immanence itself" (WP 73). The Christian tradition, for example, contains an important line of inspiration that can be traced from Pascal to Kierkegaard. What was at stake in Pascal's celebrated wager, as Deleuze interprets it, was not the existence or non-existence of a transcendent God but rather the immanent modes of existence of those who must choose between his existence or non-existence. A complex typology results: there are the *devout*, the guardians of order, for whom there is no question of choosing; the *skeptics*, who do not know how or are unable to choose; creatures of *evil*, whose initial choice places them in a situation where they can no longer repeat their choice, like Goethe's Mephistopheles; and finally, the person of *belief* or grace, the "knight of faith" who, conscious of choice, makes an "authentic" choice that is capable of being repeated in a steadfast spiritual determination.[14] Kierkegaard drew out the necessary consequences of this line of thought, showing that choice covers as great an area as thought itself. It is a question no longer of the existence of a transcendent God but of the immanent possibilities of those who "choose" to believe. None the less, Pascal's "gambler" (he who throws the dice) and Kierkegaard's "knight of faith" (he who makes the leap) remain men of faith; though the existence of God is not put into play in the wager, it is the perspective presupposed by it, the standpoint according to which one wins or loses. One still seeks to encounter a transcendence within the heart of immanence. This is why Deleuze argues that the comparisons often made between Nietzsche, on the one hand, and Kierkegaard and Pascal (or Lev Chestov and Charles Péguy), on the other, are only valid up to a certain point. As Nietzsche wrote, "'Without the Christian faith,' Pascal thought, 'you, no less than nature and history, will become for yourselves *un monstre et un chaos*': *This prophecy we have fulfilled*."[15]

THREE QUESTIONS OF IMMANENCE

For Deleuze, Nietzsche's "method of dramatization" entails both an inversion and a completion of Kant's critical project: it completes the project by finding a truly immanent principle of critique, but it also inverts Kant's philosophy by eliminating from it all vestiges of transcendence. Kant inaugurated the modern attempt to save transcendence by treating the plane of immanence as a field of consciousness; immanence was made immanent *to* a pure consciousness, a transcendental subject that actively synthesizes the field of experience. Much of Deleuze's career can therefore be seen as a profound critique not only of Kant's conception of the moral law, but equally of the Kantian subject that serves as its foundation. His first book, *Empiricism and Subjectivity* (1953), already informed by a rigorously post-Kantian viewpoint, argued that the essential question of Hume's empiricism was not "How is experience given to a subject?" but rather, "How is the subject constituted within the given?" (ES 87). In *Difference and Repetition* (1968) the Humean response—that the subject (human nature) is a derivative of the principles of association—was transformed into a "transcendental empiricism": the subject is no longer a transcendental instance that actively synthesizes experience, but is constituted *within* a plane of immanence by syntheses that are themselves passive.[16] But it will be Spinoza, even more than Nietzsche, who provides Deleuze with the resources to effect his "transmutation," grounding ethics in the notion of immanent "modes of existence" rather than through an appeal to a transcendental "subject." We can briefly sketch out the nature of an immanent ethics by posing three questions concerning modes of existence:

1. How is a mode of existence determined?
2. How are modes of existence to be evaluated?
3. What are the conditions for the creation of new modes of existence?

These questions are derived from the three moments of what Deleuze calls *the* ethical question in his analysis of Spinoza's *Ethics*, though we shall apply them here in a more general sense.[17] Together they serve to mark out, in a summary fashion, the problems and tasks posed by the "system of affects" that Deleuze would have replace the "system of judgment."

1. *How is a mode of existence determined?* Both Nietzsche and Spinoza take the *body* as their model for the analysis of modes of existence. "Essential: to start from the *body* and employ it as a guide."[18] In the *Ethics*, Spinoza defines the body

primarily in terms of two fundamental axes. On the one hand, a body is defined, extensively or kinetically, by a complex set of relations under which a multiplicity of parts is subsumed, which affect each other to infinity. On the other hand, a body is also defined, intensively or dynamically, by a certain degree of power: that is, by a certain capacity to affect or be affected by other bodies. On the first axis, I have knowledge of my body solely through its "affections" (*affectio*), which indicate the state of my body at a given moment in so far as it is submitted to the action of another body; sometimes, for instance, the two affected relations will combine to form a new composite relation (as when I ingest food), and sometimes one body will decompose the other, destroying the cohesion of one of its constituent parts (as when poison breaks down the blood). On the second axis, I have knowledge of my body through the "affects" (*affectus*) of which is capable: that is, through the manner in which my affections augment or diminish my power. I experience *joy* or pleasure when a body encounters mine and enters into composition with it, augmenting my power (food nourishes me); and *sadness* or pain when, on the contrary, another body threatens my coherence and diminishes my power (poison sickens me)—or at the limit, destroys me. Joy and sadness are passages, becomings, risings and fallings of my power, which pass from one state to another and are in constant variation.

It is this conception of the body that forms the basis for Spinoza's classification of modes of existence. A mode cannot be classified by the abstract notions of genus and species, as in Aristotelian biology (an arborescent schema of classification), but must rather be classified by its capacity to affect and to be affected: that is, by the affections of which it is "capable" (a rhizomatic schema).[19] When we define humans as "featherless bipeds" or "rational animals," for instance, we rely on *nominal* definitions that simply select out certain affects or traits at the expense of others. We arrive at a *real* definition of a mode of existence only when we define it in terms of its *power* or capacity to be affected—a capacity that is not a simply logical possibility but is necessarily actualized at every moment. For a given being, what is it affected by in the world? What leaves it unaffected? What does it react to positively or negatively? What are its nutrients and poisons? How can it take other beings into its world? What affects threaten its cohesion, diminishing it power, or even destroying it? *What can its body do?* We can know nothing about the power of a mode until we know what its affects are, how its body can (or cannot) enter into composition with the affects of other bodies.[20] In this manner, we can arrive at a classification of immanent "types" of modes of existence that are more or less general. (From this viewpoint, there are more differences between a racehorse and a workhorse, for instance, than between a workhorse and an ox: a workhorse does not have the same capacity to be affected as a racehorse, but rather has affects in common with the ox.) Whereas the theological doctrine of infinite debt determined the relation of the immortal soul with a system of judgments, Spinoza's ethics attempts to determine the finite relations of an existing body with the forces that affect it (ECC 128).

This, then, is the first feature of an immanent ethics: it replaces the notion of the transcendental subject with immanent modes of existence that are determined by their degrees of power and relations of affectivity. In his later works, Foucault suggested replacing the term "subject" with the term "subjectivation." Just as there is no "pure" Reason or rationality *par excellence*, he argued, but a plurality of heterogeneous *processes of rationalization* (of the kind analyzed by Alexandre Koyré, Gaston Bachelard, and Georges Canguilhem in the field of epistemology, Max Weber in sociology, and François Châtelet in philosophy), so there is no universal or transcendental Subject that could function as a basis for a universal ethics, but only variable and extraordinarily diverse *processes of subjectivation* (PV 14–17). The first positive ethical task would be to analyze the processes of subjectivation (passive syntheses) by which modes of existence are determined. It was this task that Foucault set for himself in the reformulated volumes of *The History of Sexuality* (in which sexuality forms only one aspect of these processes), where he analyzed the historical formations of subjectivation in the Greek, Roman, and Christian periods—modes of existence which could be said to have been summarily codified in the formulas, "Know yourself!" (Greek), "Master yourself!" (Roman), and "Deny yourself!" (Christian).[21]

This task is inevitably tied to the analysis of social formations, or what Deleuze terms an "assemblage" (*agencement*), and Foucault an "apparatus" (*dispositif*). Ethics is necessarily linked to political economy. But political philosophy is not necessarily tied to the political form of the State. Modern German philosophy, notably in Kant and Hegel, invented the fiction of a State that was universal in principle, defined as the rational organization of a community of free-thinking individuals submitted to the universality of a principle (the Law), in relation to which the particularity of States was merely an accident of fact, marking their imperfection or perversity.[22] The State and reason were in this way made to enter into a curious exchange: realized reason was identified with the *de jure* State, and the State was identified as the becoming of reason.[23]

But just as there is no universal subject, neither is there a universal State. The critique of the subject in Deleuze is necessarily linked to a critique of the State apparatus, and of modes of thought that wed the question of politics (and therefore ethics) to the destiny of the State. Since processes of subjectivation always take place within concrete social assemblages, one of the aims of the *Capitalism and Schizophrenia* project, as its title indicates, was to elaborate a general typology of various social assemblages and their corresponding processes of subjectivation. The theoretical core of the book is derived from the theory of synthesis put forward by Kant in the first critique (categorical, hypothetical, disjunctive), which Deleuze and Guattari reformulate into a theory of passive syntheses (connective, convergent, arithmetic, disjunctive).[24] The result is a typology of four basic types of social assemblages:

1. so-called "*primitive*" societies (and their modern equivalents), which effect syntheses of connection in segmented codes and territories, according to supple lines of filiation and alliance, and have specific mechanisms that ward off the formation of a centralized State
2. *State* apparatuses, which effect syntheses of convergence, forcing local codes to converge on a single center according to various mechanisms of capture or overcoding

3. nomadic *war machines*, which effect an arithmetic synthesis capable of occupying and distributing themselves over a smooth space, and are by nature external to the State; and finally

4. *capitalism*, which effects a disjunctive synthesis between labor and capital, and effectively decodes the codes and overcodings of previous formations.[25]

None of these formations exists in a pure form; each type simply seeks to mark out the consistency of a concept, and is valid only to the degree that it provides a critical tool for analyzing concrete assemblages and modes of existence, which are by definition mixed states requiring a "micro-analysis" of the syntheses and lines they actualize (N 86). The State is one social type among others, with its own history, its own complex relations with other social formations, and its own processes of capture, unification, and totalization. Modes of existence, as degrees of power, are determined by their affects: that is, by the lines of synthesis of the concrete social assemblage in which they exist. "The pursuits we call by various names," write Deleuze and Guattari, "schizoanalysis, micropolitics, pragmatism, diagrammatics, rhizomatics, cartography—have no other object than the study of these lines . . . to study their dangers, to mark their mixtures as well as their distinctions."[26]

2. *How is a mode of existence evaluated?* The first ethical question concerning the determination of modes leads directly into the second question: How does one evaluate modes of existence thus determined? This, one might say, is the ethical task properly speaking, and it is here that Deleuze (and Foucault) have come under criticism, even from sympathetic readers, for their apparent inability (or refusal) to put forward normative criteria of judgment, leading critics to caricature the political consequences of such a philosophy as everything from an "infantile leftism" to "neo-conservative."[27] What does it mean to evaluate modes of existence according to purely immanent criteria?

If modes of existence are defined as a degree of power (the capacity to affect and to be affected), then they can be evaluated in terms of the manner in which they come into possession of their power. From the viewpoint of an ethology of humans, Spinoza distinguishes between two types of affections: *passive* affections, which originate outside the individual and separate it from its power of acting; and *active* affections, which are explained by the nature of the affected individual and allow it to come into possession of its power. To the degree that a body's power of being affected is filled by passive affections, this power itself is presented as a *power of being acted upon*; conversely, to the degree that a body manages to fill (at least partially) its power of being affected by active affections, this capacity will be presented as a *power of acting*. For a given individual, its capacity to affect and be affected (its degree of power) remains constant and is constantly filled, under continuously variable conditions, by a series of affects and affections, while the power of acting and the power of being acted upon vary greatly, in inverse ratio to one another. But in fact this opposition between passive and active affections is purely abstract, for *only the power of acting is, strictly speaking, real, positive, and affirmative.* Our power of being acted on is simply a *limitation* on our power of acting, and merely expresses the degree to which we are separated from what we "can do."[28]

It is this distinction that allows Spinoza to introduce an "ethical difference" between various types of modes of existence. In Spinoza, an individual will be considered "bad" (or servile, or weak, or foolish) who remains cut off from its power of acting, who remains in a state of slavery or impotence; conversely, a mode of existence will be called "good" (or free, or rational, or strong) that exercises its capacity for being affected in such a way that its power of acting increases, to the point where it produces active affections and adequate ideas. For Deleuze, this is the point of convergence that unites Nietzsche and Spinoza. It is never a matter of judging degrees of power quantitatively; the smallest degree of power is equivalent to the largest degree once it is not separated from what it can do. It is rather a question of knowing whether a mode of existence, however small or great, can deploy its power, increasing its power of acting to the point where it goes to the limit of what it "can do" (DR 41). Modes are no longer "judged" in terms of their degree of proximity to or distance from an external principle, but are "evaluated" in terms of the manner by which they "occupy" their existence: the intensity of their power, their "tenor" of life.[29]

What an ethics of immanence will criticize, then, is not simply modes of thought derived from base modes of existence, but anything that *separates* a mode of existence from its power of acting. This is the second positive task of an immanent ethics. When Spinoza and Nietzsche criticize transcendence, their interest is not merely theoretical or speculative (to expose its fictional or illusory status), but rather practical and ethical; far from being our salvation, *transcendence expresses our slavery and impotence at its lowest point.*[30] This is why Foucault could interpret *Anti-Oedipus* as a book of ethics, in so far as it attempted to diagnose the contemporary mechanisms of "micro-fascism"—in psychoanalysis and elsewhere—that cause us to desire the very things that dominate and exploit us, and that cause us to fight *for* our servitude as stubbornly as though it were our salvation. At the same time, the book attempted to set forth the concrete historical conditions under which a mode of existence can come into possession of its power: in other words, how it can become *active*. This leads us to a third question.

3. *What are the conditions for the creation of new modes of existence?* How are modes of existence capable of being created actively rather than merely being determined passively? This question follows directly from the second, in so far as the *active* creation of new modes of existence can only occur on the condition that modes are capable of *affecting themselves*. This is the thread that unites the minor tradition of ethical thought that Deleuze draws upon: the Stoics, as Pierre Hadot has shown, thought of ethics as an *askesis*, an affect of the self upon itself, whose end was a self-transformation;[31] Spinoza, after defining a mode by its capacity for being affected, sought to define the means by which to render possible the attainment of active affections and adequate ideas; and Nietzsche discovered the artistic operation of the will to power as the invention of new "possibilities of life," a transvaluation of the value-positing element. This question of auto-affection is the object of some of Deleuze's most difficult and penetrating passages, such as those describing the need for common notions in creating active affections and attaining blessedness in Spinoza, or the final chapter of *Nietzsche and Philosophy*, where Deleuze charts out the transvaluation of negation into affirmation, reactive into active.[32]

The study of variations in these creative or productive processes of subjectivation is the third positive task posed by Deleuze's conception of ethics. Foucault, for his part, suggested in *The Use of Pleasure* that the relation of a mode to itself could be analyzed, historically, from the point of view of four aspects or rubrics:

1. *ethical substance* (ontology), which designates the material element of ourselves that is deemed to be relevant to our ethical conduct and open to transformation (feelings, intentions, desires);
2. *mode of subjection* (deontology), which designates the means by which one is incited to recognize what one considers to be one's "ethical" obligations (in relation to a divine law, a cosmological order, a rational rule, an aesthetic form;
3. *ethical work* (ascetics), which designates the "self-forming activity" that one exerts upon oneself (self-examination, meditation, confession, exercise, diet, the following of exemplary role models); and
4. *telos* (teleology), which designates the goal or mode of being toward which this ethical activity of auto-affection is directed.[33]

Here again, such a history of modes of auto-affection, which Foucault attempted to inaugurate, must be sharply distinguished from a history of moral codes, since it would map out the complex terrain and conditions in which new modes of existence appeared that were fundamentally irreducible to these codes.

Finally, for both Deleuze and Foucault, the aim of these typological and historical investigations is always borne upon the present: What is our present situation? What are our own modes of existence, our possibilities of life or processes of subjectivation (which are irreducible to our moral codes)? How and in what places are new modes of existence produced? It may be that the creators of new modes of existence are the "noble" (Nietzsche), or the "rational" (Spinoza), or the aestheticized existence of the "free man" (Foucault), or "minorities" (in the Deleuzian sense of this term).[34] One cannot know in advance, and these foci of creation change with different social assemblages. Deleuze has offered one such analysis of our present formation in an essay entitled, "Post-Script on Control Societies."[35] If Foucault spoke of societies of *discipline*, and their principal technique of enclosure (prisons, hospitals, schools, factories, barracks, families), Deleuze suggests that we are now entering into societies of *control*, which no longer operate by enclosure (hence the crisis facing each of these institutions) but, as Paul Virilio has shown, by processes of continuous control and instantaneous communication. Forms of resistance and delinquency have thereby changed accordingly: the strikes and "sabotage" of the nineteenth century have given way to piratings and the introduction of viruses of the late twentieth century. What may become increasingly important in the future, Deleuze suggests, are modes of existence that are able "to create vacuoles of non-communication, circuit breakers, so we can elude control" (N 175). But as Deleuze likes to insist, one can never predict in advance where these loci of experimentation will occur; one can only be attentive to the unknown that is knocking at the door.

The primary consequence of an immanent conception of ethics perhaps lies in its change of orientation away from the universal and toward the *singular*, and away from the historical toward the *actual*. One does not seek universals in order to judge, but singularities that are able of creating, of producing the new.

> When Foucault admires Kant for having posed the problem of philosophy, not in relation to the eternal but in relation to the Now, he means that the object of philosophy is not to contemplate the eternal, nor to reflect on history, but to diagnose our actual becomings. (WP 112)

History thinks in terms of the past, present, and future; but if history in this way surrounds and delimits us, it none the less does not tell us who we are, but from what we are in the process of differing ourselves. When Foucault wrote on disciplinary societies, or on Greek and Christian modes of subjectivation, for instance, he did so in order to find out in what ways we are *no longer* disciplinary, are *no longer* Greeks or Christians, and are becoming other. This difference between the present and the actual, for Deleuze, is much more important than the difference between the present and the past. The present is what we are, and for that reason, what we are already ceasing to be; the actual is not what we are, but rather what we are becoming, what we are in the process of becoming. History, in this sense of the term, is what separates us from ourselves, and what we have to traverse in order to think ourselves, whereas the actual is the formation of the new, the emergence of what Foucault called our "actuality."[36] To diagnose the becomings in each present that passes is the task that Nietzsche assigned to the philosopher as a physician, "the physician of civilization," or the inventor of new immanent modes of existence. To act against the past, and therefore on the present, in favor (one hopes) of a time to come: such, for Deleuze, is the task of the philosopher. This time to come is not the future of history, but the Now that is distinguished from every present; it is not an instant but a becoming, the "actual" or the "untimely," the conditions for the production of the new.

> This is perhaps the secret [concludes Deleuze], to make something exist, and not to judge. If it is so distasteful to judge, this is not because everything is of equal value, but on the contrary because everything that is of value can only create and distinguish itself by defying judgment. (ECC 135)

These three questions concerning the determination, evaluation, and creation of modes of existence serve to demarcate the problematics and tasks of a purely immanent ethics. In rejecting the idea of a transcendental subject, it seeks to define the immanent processes of subjectivation that determine variable modes of existence. In refusing all forms of transcendence, it evaluates the differences between these modes of existence on the basis of purely immanent criteria of power. Finally, in rejecting universals, it analyses the present in terms of the conditions it presents for the production of the singular: that is, for the creation of new modes of existence.

Politics

Flow, Code, and Stock: A Note on Deleuze's Political Philosophy

In *Anti-Oedipus*, the first volume of their *Capitalism and Schizophrenia* project, Deleuze and Guattari write that "the general theory of society is a generalized theory of flows" (AO 262).[1] The basic thesis of the book is that it is the business of every society to code these flows, and the "terrifying nightmare," of any society would be a flow that eludes its codes, that is, a *decoded* or *uncoded* flow (AO 139–40). While this terminology has become familiar to readers of Deleuze and Guattari, it is hardly a straightforward claim. To my knowledge, no other thinker has insisted that the notion of *flow* is the fundamental concept of political philosophy. In making this claim, Deleuze is clearly distancing himself from other approaches to social theory, which have instead been based, for instance, on a theory of the State (Plato) or the social contract (Hobbes) or the spirit of the laws (Montesquieu), or on the problems of "perpetual peace" (Kant) or legitimation (Durkheim, Habermas), and so on. The question I would like to address would thus serve as a necessary prolegomena to any consideration of Deleuze's political thought: Why did Deleuze insist that it was necessary to base his socio-political philosophy on a theory of flows?[2]

As a first approach to this question, Deleuze and Guattari explained, in an interview, that the concept of the flow was "a notion that we needed as an unqualified and undetermined notion [*notion quelconque*]": that is, as a purely *nominal* concept.[3] At this level, one can indeed conceive of extraordinarily varied types of concrete flows, and the ways they need to be controlled or coded. Most obviously, there is the flow of *water*, and the building of dams and dikes to control and channel the water (in the Western U.S. today, the question of the rights to a limited water supply is becoming increasingly acute). There are *economic* flows such as money and capital, along with the control of markets. There are *material* flows of raw matter and utilities such as oil and electricity, along with the control of the grid and the oil supply. There is the flow of *commodities*, along with their marketing and transport. There is the flow of *traffic*, along with the regulation of the highways and circulation (avoiding traffic jams), as well the mastery and control of speed.[4] There are *social* flows such as flows of populations, the flow of immigrants and foreigners over borders, along with the ability to control and monitor those borders (issuing passports, customs, and so on). There are flows of *sewage* and *refuse*, and the question of what to do with them. There are *somatic* flows such as urine, blood, sperm, sweat, faeces, milk, menstrual blood, and so on, with their various codings. (This is the example with which *Anti-Oedipus* opens: a breast emits a flow of milk, which is cut into by a baby's mouth, which becomes a flow of feces, cut off by the anus, and so on. Such is the lived experience of the infant, which has no sense of its organic body, but only of intensities such as hunger, or the need to defecate, and the flows and cutting of flows that satiate those needs.) One can even think of flows of *thought*, and the attempt to code and control the flow of thought via marketing, advertising, and the media (such as the flow of scientific knowledge, as well as a flow of stupidity and opinion).[5]

Now while all these examples indeed give us a sense of the problem Deleuze has isolated and placed at the center of his political philosophy—the problem of flows and their coding and control—it does not tell us where Deleuze got the concept from, nor why it lies at the basis of his social philosophy, nor how it functions philosophically in his work. For that, we need to turn to the domain of economics and Deleuze's analysis of capitalism, because it is here that Deleuze derives his real definition of what a flow is, and then extends it to domains outside of economics. Robert Heilbroner once wrote a popular survey of the great economic thinkers called *The Worldly Philosophers*, and it is a fitting title, since the great economists— the three greatest are Adam Smith, Karl Marx, and John Maynard Keynes—deal philosophically with the most practical of matters: money, and everything that goes with it.[6] While Deleuze only occasionally refers to Adam Smith, it is Deleuze's use of Marx and Keynes that I would like to focus on here.

DELEUZE, MARX, AND KEYNES

In a 1990 interview, Deleuze remarked: "I believe that Félix Guattari and myself have remained Marxists. This is because we do not believe in a political philosophy that would not be centered on the analysis of capitalism and its developments."[7] It is none the less true that, as Lyotard noted in a review he wrote of *Anti-Oedipus* immediately after its publication, *Capitalism and Schizophrenia* contains a critique of Marx that is implicit rather than explicit, since a surprisingly large number of classical Marxist concepts (alienation, ideology, the class struggle, work-value theory, the dialectic of contradiction) drop out of Deleuze and Guattari's analyses completely; they are neither analyzed nor criticized, but simply ignored.[8] Yet what Deleuze and Guattari retain of Marx's analyses is the definition of capitalism that lies at the heart of *Das Capital*, and it is in this sense that *Capitalism and Schizophrenia* can be said to present a Marxist theory of capitalism, but one that has been transformed and adapted to new conditions. The definition of capitalism that Marx gives in the first book of *Capital* is organized around the encounter of two elements of abstraction, or what Deleuze will call two decoded flows: the flow of *subjective labor* and the flow of *objective capital*. One the one hand, the flow of labor must no longer be determined or codified as slavery or serfdom, but must become naked and free *labor*, in the form of the worker having to sell his labor capacity; and on the other hand, wealth must no longer be determined as landed wealth or the money dealing of merchants, but must become pure, homogeneous, and independent *capital*, which is capable of buying this labor. Capitalism appears only when these two purely quantitative flows of unqualified capital and unqualified labor encounter each other and conjugate. I will leave to the side the complex historical analyses of *how* the conjugation of these two decoded flows of labor and capital took place, and *why* they first took place in Europe rather than elsewhere—this is, in part, the aim of Althusser and Balibar's influential book *Reading Capital.*[9] I would simply like to make two brief observations about how Deleuze interprets and uses this Marxist definition of capitalism.

1. *Political Economy and Libidinal Economy.* First, for Deleuze, the *philosophical* importance of the conjunction of labor and capital lies in their common movement away from *representation* to what Deleuze calls in several places "*the activity of production in general*" (AO 270, 302). Marx said that Luther's merit was to have determined the essence of religion, not on the side of the object (Does God exist or not?), but rather on the side of the subject, or what Kierkegaard called "interiority": faith as the source of religion. According to Marx, Adam Smith and Ricardo wound up doing something similar in political economy: they located the essence of wealth, not in its object (land or money), but rather in an abstract subjective essence, which is my *labor capacity*, or my capacity to produce. What faith is to religion, labor is to political economy: humans produce gods in the same way they produce automobiles. The same, moreover, was true of Freud: "His greatness lies in having determined the essence or nature of desire, no longer in relation to objects, aims, or even sources, but as an abstract subjective essence—libido or sexuality" (AO 270). This is why Deleuze can say that the discovery of labor (by Smith and Ricardo) and the discovery of the libido (by Freud) were really one and the same thing: political economy and libidinal economy are *one and the same economy*. "The discovery of *an activity of production in general and without distinction*, as it appears in capitalism, is the identical discovery of both political economy and psychoanalysis, beyond the determinate systems of representation" (AO 270, 302). Put differently, "desire is part of the infrastructure" (AO 104; cf. 63): our impulses and affects, and even our unconscious drives, what seems to be the most individual and personal part of ourselves (libidinal economy), are themselves immediately part of what Marx called the economic infrastructure: that is, the material base of every social formation (political economy). In other words, it is impossible to posit a mental reality to desire that is different from the material reality of social production ("there is no particular form of existence that can be labeled 'psychic reality,'" AO 27); nor can one claim, as Freud does, that the libido has to be "sublimated" (or desexualized or resolved) in order to invest the social field (AO 352); nor can one say that the relations between social production and desire are relations of "projection" and "introjection" (AO 28). This is one of the essential theses of *Anti-Oedipus*: libidinal economy and political economy are one and the same thing; they have an identical nature.

But Deleuze and Guattari immediately add a complementary thesis: although there is no *difference in nature* between the two economies, it is true that there is none the less a *distinction in regime* between them (AO 31). Technical machines, for instance, obviously work only if they are not out of order, which is what allowed Marx to posit a strict distinction, within political economy, between the means of production and the product: "Let us remember once again one of Marx's caveats: we cannot tell from the mere taste of wheat who grew it; the product gives us no hint as to the system and the relations of production" (AO 24). In libidinal economy, by contrast, the product is always implanting itself back into its production, such that "desiring-machines" function only on the condition that they are constantly breaking down (AO 31–2, 37, 151, 230)—whence the phenomena of manic depressions or bipolarity, psychoses, and, at the limit, schizophrenia. Much of the argument of *Anti-Oedipus* revolves around an assessment of the relations between these two economies, given their identical nature but differing regimes. The first two chapters develop a theory of the nature of the *syntheses* of the unconscious: desiring-machines *produce* by means of immanent syntheses (local and non-specific and connections, inclusive disjunctions, nomadic and polyvocal conjunctions), whereas social machines *represent* the former by means of transcendent syntheses (global and specific connections, exclusive disjunctions, segregative and biunivocal conjunctions). In both cases, "*the same syntheses are at issue*" (AO 116)—they have the same nature—but they are put to different uses. Desiring production and social production "are therefore the same machines, but not at all the same regime . . . or the same uses of syntheses" (AO 288). Social production *represents*, at a molar level, what is *produced*, by desiring production, at a molecular level. As a result, desiring production comes to be crushed by the requirements of representation, and comes to desire its own repression.

In the third chapter of *Anti-Oedipus*, Deleuze and Guattari in turn develop a tripartite typology of social formations ("primitives," States, capitalism). "In each case," they ask, "what is the relationship between social production and desiring-production, once it is said that they have identical natures and differing regimes?" (AO 262). "It could be," they will ultimately conclude, "that where the regimes are the closest, the identity in nature is on the contrary at its minimum [primitive and despotic formations]; and where the identity in nature appears to be at its maximum, the regimes differ to the highest degree [capitalism]" (AO 336). Social formations can therefore oscillate between two poles, depending on whether desiring-machines have a chance of causing their immanent connections to pass into the regime of the social machines (the active schizophrenic line of flight), or by contrast the social machines overcode desire through the transcendent syntheses of representation (the reactionary paranoiac investment). Yet as Deleuze and Guattari insist, "we cannot allow the difference in regime to make us forget the identity in nature . . . There are no desiring-machines that exist outside the social machines that they form on a large scale; and no social machines without the desiring-machines that inhabit them on a small scale" (AO 340). This idea that libidinal economy and political economy have differing regimes but none the less identical natures is one of the underlying threads that links together the entire socio-political analysis of *Anti-Oedipus*.[10]

Michel Foucault, in *The Order of Things*, had shown that a similar movement from representation to production had in fact occurred in numerous domains, to which Deleuze will often have recourse. In biology, for instance, we no longer define living beings by the external features or properties of an adult organism, but rather through genetics and embryology: that is, through the process by which the organism is produced. This is what marked the historical transformation from what was once called "natural history" (Aristotle) to the modern sciences of molecular biology (or genetics) and embryology; Deleuze's notion of social *coding* is in part derived from the idea of the genetic code. Likewise, in contemporary geology, Mount Everest is not seen as an "object," but rather as the result of an ongoing set of geological processes: the tectonic plate of India slamming into Asia, and the folding of the earth's crust to produce the Himalayan mountain range, as well as the forces of glaciation and erosion that are simultaneously wearing down the mountains. In *A Thousand Plateaus*, Deleuze will develop a concept of "stratification" derived from geology (the book contains a chapter called, precisely, "The Geology of Morals," TP 37–74). This, then, is the first philosophical point Deleuze derives from Marx (and, later, Foucault): the movement from representation to production.

2. *Universal History*. The second observation derives from the first: Marx held that, given this discovery of the activity of production in general, a *retrospective* reading of universal history was possible from the viewpoint of capitalism: that is, from the viewpoint of the two decoded flows of labor and capital (AO 140). Previous economies anticipate capitalism, but as something they warded off and avoided. Primitive economies, for instance, were based on codes, which operate at the level of representation, whereas capitalism is based on decoded flows, which operate at the level of production, and it was the "nightmare" of decoded flows that previous social formations were trying to avoid. But how does one go about doing a retrospective reading of universal history using the concept of flow? Marx himself did not have an explicit concept of flow; he defines neither labor nor capital in terms of flow. To understand Deleuze's concept of flow, we have to turn to the twentieth-century British economist, John Maynard Keynes. Deleuze isolates three contributions of Keynes's great book, *The General Theory of Employment, Interest, and Money*, which was published in 1936.[11] First, it presented the first modern theory of flows. "Stocks and flows are the two fundamental concepts of modern political economy, as formulated by Keynes," Deleuze comments. "The first great theory of flows can be found in Keynes' *The General Theory of Employment, Interest, and Money*" (14 Dec 1971). Second, it injected the problem of desire into the theory of money. "One of Keynes's contributions was the reintroduction of desire into the problem of money," Deleuze and Guattari write. "It is this that must be subjected to the requirements of Marxist analysis," notably with regard to finance and banking practices (AO 23). It is now a truism to say that psychology and economics are interrelated, and that stock markets are mirrors of the human psyche: "they can become depressed; they can even suffer complete breakdowns."[12] Third, Keynes proposed a new model of regulation and stimulus for the economy: in Deleuzian terms, Keynesianism was one of the laboratories for the production of axioms, during the New Deal and afterwards (TP 462). The issue of regulation is derived directly from the concept of flow: "the question is not that of freedom and constraint, nor of centralization or decentralization, but of the manner in which one masters the flows" (TP 462).

Keynes wrote *The General Theory* in the midst of the Great Depression, for which he was attempting to provide both a diagnostic and a cure. The theory of flows, and the injection of desire into economics, was part of Keynes's new diagnostic of the state of capitalism, which for Deleuze is an essential supplement to Marx's analyses. The push for regulation and government intervention, by contrast, was part of his cure; and today, the term "Keynesianism" has become largely synonymous with intervention in the economy (in 1971, Nixon uttered his famous phrase, "We're all Keynesians now"). But what interests Deleuze in Keynes's work is less interventionism *per se*, but rather the new analysis he gave of capitalism through the concepts of flows and stocks. In the wake of Keynes, flow and stock have now become two basic concepts in the analysis of dynamic systems in general.[13] So it is from an analysis of Keynes that we will be able to grasp the philosophical import of Deleuze's concept of flow.

FLOW, CODE, STOCK

As always, Deleuze extracts from Keynesian economics a number of concepts that he will use for his own philosophical purposes, all of which can be summarized in the concept of the *break-flow* (*coupure-flux*), or *schiz*.

1. *Flow*. From an economic point of view, a *flow* is the transmission (or exchange) of money—or more generally, of economic value—that moves from one pole to another: that is, there is an incoming and outgoing flow. The term "pole" here simply refers to the individuals or groups (firms, companies, corporations) that function as the *interceptors* of these incoming and outgoing flows (for instance, in one's bank account). "We are defining flows in political economy," Deleuze noted in a seminar, "its importance for contemporary economists confirms what I have been saying" (16 Nov 1971).

2. *Code*. Second, the correlative of the concept of a flow is that of a *code*, which is a form of inscription or recording that, in the capitalist formation, assumes the form of an *accounting system*; a transaction entered into the bank account of an individual or firm is the *recording* or *inscription* of this transmission of a flow (a change in assets or liabilities). A paycheck is an incoming flow; payment of a bill is an outgoing flow. Flow and code are reciprocally determined; it is impossible to grasp a flow other than by and through the operation that codes it. Strictly speaking, money is simply an inscription (only a small percentage of the monetary mass in the world exists as cash), which is why the development of the two-ledger accounting system was essential in the development of capitalism. It is important to note that, for Deleuze, a code is not something that is "applied" to a flow, as Kantian concepts are applied to intuitions; there is never a flow first and then a code that imposes itself upon it or is applied to it. What flows on the socius cannot appear as a flow except in correlation to a code; it is impossible to seize a flow other than by and through the operation that codes it. A flow is not recognizable as an economic flow, or a social flow, or a somatic flow, for instance, except by and through the code which encodes it. This is why Deleuze will say that a non-coded flow is an unnamable power; the nightmare of every society is the terror of a non-coded or decoded flow. My salary is

a coded flow, and I know its exact value; but the problem with the sub-prime mortgage derivatives that helped cause the 2009 recession was due to the fact, less that they had lost value, but that no one knew their value, or even know how to assess their value; they had become a decoded flow.

3. *Stock.* The third concept, after flow and code, is the concept of stock. If the flow is what moves from one pole to another, from one account to another, stock is what is related to one of these poles as its material or juridical possession: my bank account or the value of my investments—this is *my* portion of the flow, my *share* of the flow, "so it's mine."

We have here three elementary notions derived from economics—flow, code (or an accounting system), and stock—which are all interrelated and reciprocally determined: a monetary flow is in continuous variation; we only know the flow through its inscription or coding; and stock is the portion of the flow that is mine at a given moment. Readers of *Anti-Oedipus* will recognize that these three notions correspond to the three syntheses: flow is the connective synthesis of *production*; code is the disjunctive synthesis of *recording* or inscription; and stock is the conjunctive synthesis of *consumption*. The remainder of this paper will briefly discuss each of these terms in order to examine the complex interrelations Deleuze establishes between them.

THE CONCEPT OF FLOW

Let me return first to the concept of flow. Deleuze derives the concept of flow from Keynes and links it with Marx's conception of production. We have seen that Marx held that a retrospective reading of universal history was possible from the viewpoint of capitalism. Deleuze picks up on this idea, but interprets history as a progressive decoding of flows, and the history of money is one of the primary topics in Deleuze's retrospective reading.[14] Primitive economies functioned in terms of a code of barter: that is, in terms of a direct relation of exchange between objects. But the introduction of money as a "general equivalent" into these economies during colonialism was enough to destroy these codes (e.g., cargo cults). What money showed was that the objects being bartered in primitive economies were themselves simply qualified pieces of labor to which there corresponded a given quantum of value; they were qualified flows or forms of stock. In other words, primitive codes were *already* operating in conjunction with these flows, but they warded off these flows: primitive societies kept merchants and blacksmiths in subordinate positions, and cordoned off exchange and commerce, precisely because the "abstract or fictional quantity" of money was enough to break the primitive codes.

Deleuze holds to the thesis—following Édouard Will—that money was invented by the State, not as a means of encouraging commerce, but rather as a means of *controlling* commerce through taxation. The introduction of money meant that the State was able to insert itself into every transaction and siphon off a portion for itself in the form of a tax. This was the first step of decoding: the introduction of money as a pure flow, a pure abstraction, even if it initially remained tied to precious metals. But a second step of decoding followed: primitive societies operated with blocks of mobile and finite debts, but "money—the circulation of money—is the means for rendering the debt *infinite*" (AO 197). In other words, money initiates the duty of an interminable service to the State. One will *always* be indebted to the State; taxes are a debt that one can never finish paying off. Christianity, at least in its Pauline form, effectively "spiritualized" this concept of infinite debt: the wages of sin is death, a debt I can only pay off by eternal damnation; God, in his mercy, decides to pay off the infinite debt to himself by dying in our place; he redeems us, just as the Romans redeemed slaves by paying for them. In this sense, one could say that Christian theology is a spiritualized form of economics.

But in and of itself, the introduction of money, or monetary inscription, was not enough to form capitalism; money does not yet have a "body" of its own, and was simply inserted into the interstices of the pre-existing social bodies (the Earth, the Despot). Capitalism appears only when money ceases to be merely an abstraction that "formally unites . . . objects that are produced and even inscribed independently of it", and itself becomes a filiative capital, that is, when money begets money (AO 226–7). Capitalism, in other words, marks *a new threshold of decoding or deterritorialization.* What does this mean? In the capitalist formation, the two decoded flows of labor and capital are expressed by two forms of money, namely, payment and financing. The first has its roots in a simple circulation in which money is used as a means of payment: I receive my paycheck and pay my bills with it. Financemoney, however, is completely different. It constitutes what Deleuze calls call the capitalist form of infinite debt, a vast "dematerialization" or "demonitarization" of money (although the structures of finance have their own territoriality). Rather than transferring a pre-existing currency as a means of payment, finance capital is a flow that the banks create *ex nihilo* as a debt owing to themselves; it hollows out a negative money at one extreme (as a debt entered as a liability of the banks) while projecting a positive money at the other extreme (as a credit granted to the productive economy by the banks). It is this second form of money that constitutes the true "economic force" of capitalism, "the immense deterritorialized flow that constitutes the full body of capital" (AO 237). "Today we can depict an enormous, so-called stateless, monetary mass that circulates through foreign exchange and across borders, eluding control by the States, forming a multinational ecumenical organization, constituting a *de facto* supranational power untouched by governmental decisions."[15] This is the full body of capital into which the desire of each one of us is plugged.

Strictly speaking, there is no common measure between these two flows of money; money as a form of payment has an exchange value, but money as a structure of finance is a pure movement of creation and destruction. Whence the importance of *banks*: banks participate in both these flows, they are situated at the pivotal point between financing and payment. They function as exchangers or oscillators that convert the flows of financing—which is a mutant flow in constant variation—into segments of payment. Even though there is no common measure between these two flows, it is the banks that guarantee their "fictive homogeneity," which Deleuze calls a "profound dissimulation" (AO 229). In our time, States have become immanent to the capitalist system; and one of the primary functions of the State, as a regulator, is to ensure the convertibility between these two forms of money by guaranteeing credit, a uniform interest rate, the unity of capital markets, and so forth. This is why Deleuze insists that Marx's analysis of capital has to be supplemented by Keynes's analysis.

> It is unfortunate that Marxist economists too often dwell on considerations concerning the mode of production, and on the theory of money as the general equivalent as found in the first section of *Capital*, without attaching enough importance to banking practice, to financial operations, and to the specific circulation of credit money. (AO 230)

But it would be absurd to postulate a world super-government making the final decisions regarding this monetary mass, for there is no power that regulates the flow of capital itself, and neither the banks nor the State are even capable of predicting the growth in the money supply.

Now to say that libidinal economy and political economy are one and the same thing is tantamount to saying that

> the desire of the most disadvantaged creature will invest with all its strength, irrespective of any economic understanding or lack of it, the capitalist social field as a whole. Flows, who doesn't desire flows [capital], and relationships between flows, and breaks in flows? (AO 229)

This is why Deleuze can say that, in a sense, "it is the bank that controls the whole system and the investment of Desire" (AO 230):

> It is not by means of a metaphor that a banking or stock market transaction, a claim, a coupon, a credit, is able to arouse people who are not necessarily bankers . . . There are socioeconomic 'complexes' that are also veritable complexes of the unconscious, and they communicate a voluptuous wave from the top to the bottom of their hierarchy . . . For it is a matter of flows, stock, of breaks in and fluctuations of flows; desire is present wherever something flows and runs, carrying along with it interested subjects—but also drunken or slumbering subjects—toward lethal destinations. Hence the goal of schizoanalysis: to analyze the specific nature of the libidinal investments in the economic and political spheres, and thereby to show how, in the subject that desires, desire can be made to desire its own repression. (AO 105)

What, then, does Deleuze mean when he says that desire "is a matter of flows and stock" (AO 105), or that "every object presupposes the continuity of a flow" (AO 6)? Consider the fact that I first delivered this paper at a conference in Italy. The money I used to purchase my plane ticket came from my paycheck, which is derived from my university's endowment, a flow that is in turn linked to student's tuitions, investments in various corporations, perhaps illegal sweat shops. I subtracted from this flow to pay for my ticket, the coded price of which was fluctuating until I bought it, when it became my stock ("it's mine"). The flight was itself a material flow, as was the meal I ate on the plane (chicken salad, rice, chocolate cake), which was assembled at the airline's hub city from flows arriving from elsewhere: the red wine flowed from Napa Valley, the coffee from Central America. These flows are assembled in my meal; I break into these flows when I eat; it produces in me a wave of satisfaction (*voluptas*)—the portion or share of these flows that falls to me. Even thought is a flow: I receive the flow of opinion and received ideas, there is even an incoming flow from my reading of Deleuze's texts, and I cut into these flows, producing both breaks and captures, in order to produce this text. For Deleuze, persons are the *interceptors* of flows: I am the point of destination for numerous flows, which I intercept; and I am also the point of departure for the production of new flows, and it is precisely this synthesis and production of flows that Deleuze terms *desire*. Even our loves are interceptions of flows:

> Desire does not take as its object persons or things, but the entire surroundings that it traverses, the vibrations and flows of every sort to which it is joined, introducing therein breaks and captures . . . The persons to whom our loves are dedicated, including our parental persons, intervene only as points of connection, of disjunction, of conjunction of flows whose libidinal tenor of a properly unconscious investment they translate. (AO 292–3)

THE CONCEPT OF CODE

We have seen that flow and code are reciprocally determined: it is impossible to grasp a flow other than by and through the operation that codes it. Coding operates through a process of inscription or recording: in other words, by means of signs, whether these signs are numbers on a bank statement or marks inscribed directly on the body. These signs are non-signifying: that is, it does not matter what they "mean" or "symbolize" *per se*. What matters is how they function in the determination of a flow. The difficulties one encounters in comprehending Deleuze's concept of a code is that the very term brings to mind phrases like the "Morse code" or the "civil code," where everything is given in advance; you use the Morse code to send a message, or consult the civil code to see if an infraction has occurred. But the model that lies behind Deleuze's use of the term is primarily the biological notion of the *genetic code*: the concept of a code is "a common characteristic of human cultures and of living species," of social reproduction as much as biological reproduction (AO 289; cf. 248: "the general traits characterizing a code have been rediscovered today in what is called a genetic code"). There are at least three parallels we can point to between biological and social coding.

  1. *Inscription* (or Information). In both cases, the code is what allows for the transmission and reproduction of information, which is why Deleuze terms it a synthesis of inscription or recording. This information, however, is never pre-given, but is *produced* with each transmission. Already in *Difference and Repetition*, Deleuze had noted that the significance of sexed (rather than asexual) reproduction in biology lies in the fact that it entails "the incessant production of varied individual differences" (DR 249). In asexual reproduction, the parent simply reproduces itself,

whereas in sexual production the mixing of the genetic material of two parents produces a *new* individual, a mutation. The information contained in the genetic code
of the parents is indeed transmitted, but exact nature of the new individual is not
determined in advance; every coding is the production of the new.[16] The same is
true in social reproduction. Even in so-called "primitive" societies, kinship systems
are not structures that simply need to be applied, but practices that entail an entire
strategy or *praxis*; no one knows in advance who they are to marry. "Ethnologists are
constantly saying that kinship rules are neither applied nor applicable to real mar-
riages: not because these rules are ideal but rather because they determine critical
points where *the apparatus starts up again*" (AO 151).

2. *Molecular and Molar.* Second, we find in genetics the same distinction between
production (what goes on at the molecular level) and what we see *represented* in the
product (the molar organism). The code operates at a molecular level. For Deleuze,
this was one of Lacan's shortcomings: he discovered the code in what he called
"signifying chains" (functioning via metaphor and metonymy) in the domain of
the symbolic. But language, or the symbolic, is a molar organization, like the organism. The inverse side of the symbolic is what Deleuze at several points calls "the
real inorganization of desire." As Jacques Monod says, the genetic code is not a
structure, but a domain "where nothing but the play of blind combinations can be
discerned": the molecular domain of passive syntheses is a domain of "chance or *real
inorganization*" where everything is possible, and nothing is given in advance (AO
328, 289; cf. 39, 289, 309). Every coding, in other words, entails a constant decoding of what came before it: "The genetic code points to a genic decoding" (AO
328). This, then, is the primary sense of Deleuze's distinction between molecular
and the molar: social formations

> effect a unification, a totalization of the molecular forces through a statistical
> accumulation obeying the laws of large numbers. Thus unity can be the bio-
> logical unity or a species or the structural unity of a socius: an organism, social
> or living, is composed as a whole, as a global or complete object. (AO 342)

But desire necessarily functions at a molecular level.

3. *Surplus Value of Code.* Finally, the genetic code implies not only the dimension of *filiation* (*x* begets *y*), but also that of *alliance*. Deleuze often cites in this case
the relation of the wasp and the orchid: the wasp is an essential element in the
reproductive apparatus of the orchid because it transports its pollen. There is here
a "capture of code, a *surplus value of code*, a veritable becoming, a becoming-wasp of
the orchid and a becoming-orchid of the wasp" (TP 10). Rémy Chauvin speaks here
of "the *aparallel evolution* of two beings that have absolutely nothing to do with each
other."[17] Such transfers are in fact the basis for what we call genetic engineering,
and they have results analogous to those of "the abominable couplings dear to antiquity and the Middle Ages."[18] This is also why Deleuze can claim that evolutionary
schemas have abandoned the *arborescent* models of descent (the schema of a tree
and its branches) in favor of *rhizomatic* models, which operate in the heterogeneous
and jump from one already differentiated line to another. Such is the distinction

between filiation and alliance: genealogical trees (filiation) are scrambled by "trans-versal" communications between different lines (alliance). Whence the threat of viruses: "We evolve and die more from our polymorphous and rhizomatic flus than from hereditary diseases, or diseases that have their own line of descent" (TP 11).

Deleuze and Guattari make use of the same distinction in discussing social repro-duction, stressing the notion of alliance (marriage) over filiation: socially speaking, *debt* is the unit of alliance. But here too, they stress the need for a retrospective rereading of history. In so-called primitive societies, social reproduction passed through human reproduction (x begat y), whereas in capitalism social reproduc-tion passes through capital (money begets money) and human reproduction, and relations consequently become *privatized*. Relationships become primarily private matters. Moreover, if capitalism entails a movement from codes to what Deleuze calls an "axiomatic," it is primarily because codes deal with objects (already quali-fied flows) whereas capitalism operates in terms of the abstract quantities of capital and labor, which can only be subject to an axiomatic treatment. Finally, the term "decoding" can mean two things: either to decipher the secret of a code, or to undo a code. When Deleuze and Guattari use the term, they are referring to the latter. Yet for Deleuze and Guattari, an uncoded flow is a limit-concept or an Idea: that is to say, a *problematic*. It is not an ideal to be attained, but a problem that constantly demands resolution. The notion of "chaos" that one finds in ancient creation myths, as well as the retrieval of that notion in *What is Philosophy?*, are both harbingers of the apocalyptic state of purely decoded flows.

THE CONCEPT OF STOCK

A brief word, finally, on the concept of stock. Once again, we must note that stocks and flows are one and the same thing, but that they relate to fundamentally differ-ent units: stock is the attribution of value at a given point in time, whereas flow is what changes the value of stock over time (an inflow adds to stock, an outflow sub-tracts from the stock). Stock is any entity that accumulates or depletes in value over time, whereas a flow is the rate of a change in a stock. Stocks have a certain value at each moment in time, whereas a flow (incoming and outgoing) is what changes the values of a stock over time (appreciation and depreciation). In mathematical terms, the stock is the integral of the flow, while the derivative is the flow of changes in the stock. This is one of the fundamental principles of accounting: "only the study of flows allows one to realize the role of the incoming and outgoing movements involved in stock variations" (14 Dec 1971).

The stock–flow relation is what lies at the basis of what today is called "dynamic systems theory." Although I have drawn from the example of economics, the two notions can be applied to any dynamic system. The population of an animal species could be considered a stock; the inflow would be births, the outflow would be deaths, and these flows would vary the value of the stock (i.e., the population) over time. The guests in a hotel could be considered a stock; the inflow would be guests arriving, the outflow would be guests departing, and the stock would measure the guests at any given moment, whereas the flow variable would measure the guests over a period of time—say, a year. The water in a bathtub could be considered a stock; if a gallon of water drains out of the tub every minute, while at the same time a gallon of water is added from the faucet, the stock will remain the same, even though there is a constant flow. In short, a stock is the term for any entity that accumulates or depletes over time, while a flow is the rate of change in a stock; flows accumulate in stock. Identifying the flows and stocks in a given system is not always easy; a "deficit," for instance, is a flow (spending in excess of revenue), whereas a "debt" is an accumulated stock. Moreover, by their nature, one of the characteristics of stocks is that they interrupt or "decouple" flows.

Deleuze's socio-political theory is constructed on the basis of three interrelated concepts, which are derived from contemporary economic theory, and particularly Keynes: *flow*, which is the production of value; *code*, which is the inscription or recording of flows; and *stock*, which is the portion of the flow that belongs to me at a given moment in time, which I can spend and consume. To be sure, these are not the only concepts at work in *Anti-Oedipus*. Deleuze in turn links these three concepts with the three passive syntheses derived from Kant (connection, disjunction, conjunction) and the three types of production to which they correspond (the production of production, the production of inscription, the production of consumption). The three are summarized by Deleuze in the concept of the *schizz* or the *break-flow* (or more literally, the *flow-cut*, "*coupure-flux*"), which is the operation involved in every coding of flows.[19] The sole aim of these reflections has been to give a content to the unexpected claim that lies at the basis of the entire *Capitalism and Schizophrenia* project: namely, that in the contemporary situation an adequate socio-political theory must take the form of a theory of flows.

PART III

Five Deleuzian Concepts

Desire

Deleuze and the Question of Desire: Toward an Immanent Theory of Ethics

My title raises two questions—What is an immanent ethics? and What is the philosophical question of desire?—and my ultimate focus concerns the link between these two issues: What relation does an immanent ethics have to the question of desire?[1] Historically, the first question is primarily associated with the names of Spinoza and Nietzsche (and behind them, Leibniz), since it was they who posed the question of an immanent ethics in its most rigorous form. The second question is linked to names like Freud and Lacan (and behind them, Kant), since it was they who formulated the modern conceptualization of desire in its most acute form: that is, in terms of *unconscious* desire. It was in *Anti-Oedipus*, published in 1972, that Deleuze (along with Félix Guattari, his co-author) would attempt to formulate his own theory of desire—what he would call a purely *immanent* theory of desire. In his preface to *Anti-Oedipus*, Michel Foucault would claim, famously, that "*Anti-Oedipus* is a book of ethics, the first book of ethics to be written in France in quite a long time"—thereby making explicit the link between the theory of desire developed in *Anti-Oedipus* with the immanent theory of ethics Deleuze worked out in his monographs on Nietzsche and Spinoza (AO xiii).

My approach to these questions falls into three parts. In the first, I want to isolate two issues that lie at the heart of an immanent ethics. In the second part, I would like to examine in some detail two sets of texts from Nietzsche and Leibniz, which will flesh out some of the details of an immanent ethics. I will conclude with some all too brief comments on the nature of desire and a number of themes found in *Anti-Oedipus*.

ON THE NATURE OF AN IMMANENT ETHICS

Let me begin with my first question: What is an immanent ethics? Throughout his writings, Deleuze has often drawn a distinction between morality and ethics. He uses the term "morality" to describe any set of "constraining" rules, such as a moral code, that consists in judging actions and intentions by relating them to *transcendent* or universal values, while he uses the term "ethics" to describe any set of "facilitative" [*facultative*] rules that evaluates what we do according to the *immanent* mode of existence that it implies. According to Deleuze, this immanent approach to the question of ethics was developed most fully, in the history of philosophy, by Spinoza and Nietzsche, whom Deleuze has often identified as his own philosophical precursors.[2] Both Spinoza and Nietzsche argued, each in his own manner, that there are things one cannot do (or say, or feel, or think . . .) except on the condition of being weak, base, or enslaved, unless one harbors a vengeance or *ressentiment* against life (Nietzsche), unless one remains the slave of passive affections (Spinoza); and there are other things one cannot do except on the condition of being strong, noble, or free, unless one affirms life, unless one attains active affections (SPP 22–3; EPS 269). A pluralistic method of explanation by immanent modes of existence is in this way substituted for the recourse to transcendent values: the transcendent moral opposition (between Good and Evil) is replaced by an immanent ethical difference (between noble and base modes of existence, in Nietzsche; or between passive and active affections, in Spinoza). "*Beyond Good and Evil,*" wrote Nietzsche, "at least that does not mean 'Beyond Good and Bad.'"[3]

In Spinoza, for instance, an individual will be considered "bad" (or servile, or weak, or foolish) who remains cut off from its power of acting, who remains in a state of slavery with regard to its passions. Conversely, a mode of existence will be considered to be "good" (or free, or rational, or strong) that exercises its capacity for being affected in such a way that its power of acting increases, to the point where it produces active affections and adequate ideas. For Deleuze, this is the point of convergence that unites Nietzsche and Spinoza in their search for an immanent ethics: modes are no longer *judged* in terms of their degree of proximity to or distance from an external principle, but are *evaluated* in terms of the manner by which they "occupy" their existence—the intensity of their power, their "tenor" of life.[4] It is always a question of knowing whether a mode of existence—however great or small it may be—is capable of deploying its capacities, of increasing its power of acting to the point where it can be said to go to the limit of what it "can do" (DR 41). The fundamental question of ethics is not "What *must* I do?" (which is the question of *morality*) but rather "What *can* I do, what am I *capable* of doing (which is the proper question of an ethics *without* morality). Given my degree of power, what are my capabilities and capacities? How can I come into active possession of my power? How can I go to the limit of what I "can do"?

What an ethics of immanence will criticize, then, is anything that *separates* a mode of existence from its power of acting—and what separates us from our power of acting is, ultimately, the illusions of transcendence. (We should immediately point out that the illusions of transcendence go far beyond the transcendence of God; in the *Critique of Pure Reason*, Kant had already critiqued the concepts of the Self, the World, and God as the three great illusions of transcendence; and what he calls the "moral law" in the second critique is, by Kant's own admission, a transcendent law that is unknowable.) When Spinoza and Nietzsche criticize transcendence, their interest is not merely theoretical or speculative—exposing its fictional or illusory status—but rather practical and ethical.[5] This is no doubt the point that separates Deleuze most from the ethical thinking of Emmanuel Levinas—the great philosopher of transcendence, in so far as the Other is the paradigmatic concept of transcendence—as well as Jacques Derrida, who was much closer to Levinas than Deleuze on these matters. The ethical themes one finds in transcendent philosophies like those of Levinas and Derrida—an absolute responsibility for the Other that I can never assume, or an infinite call to justice that I can never satisfy—are, from the Deleuzian point of view of immanence, imperatives whose effect is to separate me from my capacity to act. From the viewpoint of immanence, in other words, *transcendence, far from being our salvation, represents our slavery and impotence reduced to its lowest point.*

But this is precisely why the question of desire is linked with the theme of an immanent ethics, and becomes a political question. For one of most difficult problems posed by an immanent ethics is the following: if transcendence represents my impotence (at the limit, my power reduced to zero), then under what conditions can I have actually been led to *desire* transcendence? What are the conditions that could have led, in Nietzsche's words, to "the inversion of the value-positing eye"— that is, to the whole history of nihilism that Nietzsche analyzes (and nihilism, for Nietzsche, is nothing other than the triumph of transcendence, the point where life itself is given a value of nil, *nihil*)? This is the fundamental political problem posed by an immanent ethics: How can people reach a point where they actually desire their servitude and slavery *as if it were their salvation*—for those in power have an obvious interest in separating us from our capacity to act? How can we *desire* to be separated from power, from out capacity to act?[6] As Deleuze writes, "the astonishing is not that some people steal or that others occasionally go out on strike, but rather that all those who are starving do not steal as a regular practice, and all those who are exploited are not continually out on strike" (AO 29). In other words, whereas other moral theories see transcendence as a necessary principle—the transcendence of the moral law in Kant, for instance, or the transcendence of the Other in Levinas—for Deleuze transcendence is the fundamental *problem* of ethics, what prevents ethics from taking place, so to speak.

This brief analysis has served to isolate two aspects of an immanent ethics: it focuses on the differences between modes of existence, in terms of their immanent capabilities or power (active versus reactive, in Nietzsche; active versus passive, in Spinoza), and it poses, as one of its fundamental problems, the urge toward transcendence that effectively "perverts" desire, to the point where we can actually desire our own "repression," a separation from our own capacities and powers.

NIETZSCHE AND LEIBNIZ: THE THEORY OF THE DRIVES

With these two aspects in mind, let me turn to the second part of my paper, which deals with the question of how Deleuze in fact characterizes modes of existence, with their powers and capacities. Put succinctly, one could say that Deleuze approaches modes of existence, ethically speaking, not in terms of their will, or their conscious decision-making power (as in Kant), nor in terms of their interests (as in Marx, for example), but rather in terms of their *drives*.[7] For Deleuze, conscious will (Kant) and preconscious interest (Marx) are both subsequent to our unconscious drives (desire), and it is at the level of the drives that we have to aim our ethical analysis. To explore this point, I would like to examine two sets of texts on the drives taken, not from Nietzsche and Spinoza, but rather from Nietzsche and Leibniz, since Leibniz was one of the first philosophers in the history of philosophy to have developed a theory of the unconscious.

The first set of texts comes from Nietzsche's early book entitled *Daybreak*, published in July 1881. Nietzsche first approaches the question of the drives by giving us an everyday scenario:

> Suppose we were in the market place one day [he writes], and we noticed someone laughing at us as we went by: this event will signify this or that to us according to whether this or that drive happens at that moment to be at its height in us—and it will be a quite different event according to the kind of person we are. One person will absorb it like a drop of rain, another will shake it from him like an insect, another will try to pick a quarrel, another will examine his clothing to see if there is anything about it that might give rise to laughter, another will be led to reflect on the nature of laughter as such, another will be glad to have involuntarily augmented the amount of cheerfulness and sunshine in the world—and in each case, a drive has gratified itself, whether it be the drive to annoyance, or to combativeness or to reflection or to benevolence. This drive seized the event as its prey. Why precisely this one? Because, thirsty and hungry, it was lying in wait.[8]

This is the source of Nietzsche's doctrine of *perspectivism* ("there are no facts, only interpretations"), but what is often overlooked is that, for Nietzsche, it is our *drives* that interpret the world, that are perspectival—and not our consciousness or perceptions. It is not so much that I have a different perspective on the world than you; it is rather that each of us has multiple perspectives on the world because of the multiplicity of our drives—drives that are often contradictory among themselves. "*Within ourselves*," Nietzsche writes, "we can be egoistic or altruistic, hard-hearted, magnanimous, just, lenient, insincere, can cause pain or give pleasure."[9] We all contain such a vast confusion of contradictory drives that we are, as Nietzsche liked to say, multiplicities, and not unities. Moreover, these drives are in a constant struggle or combat with each other; my drive to smoke and get my nicotine rush is in combat with (but also coexistent with) my drive to quit. This is where Nietzsche first developed his concept of the will to power—at the level of the drives. "Every drive is a kind of lust to rule," he writes, "each one has its perspective that it would like to compel all the other drives to accept as a norm."[10]

To be sure, we can combat the drives, fight against them—indeed, this is one of the most common themes in philosophy, the fight against the passions. In another passage from *Daybreak*, Nietzsche says that he can see only six fundamental methods we have at our disposal for combating the drives. For instance, if we want to fight our drive to smoke, we can avoid opportunities for its gratification (no longer hiding packs of cigarettes at home for when we run out), or we can implant regularity into the drive (having one cigarette every four hours so as at least to avoid smoking in between), or we can engender disgust with the drive, giving ourselves over to its wild and unrestrained gratification (say, smoking non-stop for a month) to the point where we become disgusted with it. And so on. But then Nietzsche asks: *Who* exactly is combating the drives in these various ways? His answer (given in a second aphorism taken from *Daybreak*) is this: The fact

> *that* one *desires* to combat the vehemence of a drive at all, however, does not stand within our own power; nor does the choice of any particular method; nor does the success or failure of this method. What is clearly the case is that in this entire procedure our intellect is only the blind instrument of *another* drive which is a *rival* of the drive whose vehemence is tormenting us . . . While "we" believe we are complaining about the vehemence of a drive, at bottom it is one drive *which is complaining about the other*; that is to say: for us to become aware that we are suffering from the *vehemence* [or *violence*] of a drive presupposes the existence of another equally vehement or even more vehement drive, and that a *struggle* is in prospect in which our intellect is going to have to take sides.[11]

What we call thinking, willing, and feeling are all "merely a relation of these drives to each other."[12]

Thus, what do I mean when I say "I am trying to stop smoking"—even though that same I is constantly going ahead and continuing to smoke? It simply means that my conscious intellect is taking sides and associating itself with a particular drive. It would make just as much sense to say, "Occasionally I feel this strange urge to stop smoking, but happily I have managed to combat that drive and pick up a cigarette whenever I want." Almost automatically, Nietzsche says, we take our *predominant* drive and for the moment turn it into the *whole* ego, placing all our weaker drives perspectivally *farther away*, as if those other drives were not *me* but rather an *it* (hence Freud's idea of the "id," the "it"—a concept he clearly derived from Nietzsche). When we talk about the "I," we are simply indicating which drive, at the moment, is sovereign and strongest; "the feeling of the I is always strongest where the preponderance [*Übergewicht*] is," flickering from drive to drive.[13] When we "will" something (to stop working and go to a tavern), there is a drive that *commands*, and a host of drives that *obey* (accompanied by "feelings of compulsion, force, pressure, resistance and motion"), but we identify our "I" with the drive that commands, and not the drives that obey (since the former is accompanied by a feeling of power and superiority).[14] But the drives themselves remain largely unknown to what we sometimes call the conscious intellect. As Nietzsche concludes,

> However far a man may go in self-knowledge, nothing however can be more incomplete than his image of the totality of *drives* which constitute his being. He can scarcely name the cruder ones: their number and strength, their ebb and flood, their play and counterplay among one another—and above all the laws of their *nutriment*—remain unknown to him.[15]

In other words, there is no struggle of reason against the drives; what we call "reason" is itself nothing more than a certain "system of relations between various passions," a certain ordering of the drives.[16]

Indeed, this is how Nietzsche explains the familiar sense we have that, as we grow up, we become more mature: that is, more *reasonable*. "Something that you formerly loved as a truth," he writes, "now strikes you as an error"; so you cast it off "and fancy that it represents a victory for your reason." But in fact, this is less a victory for your reason than a shift in the relations among your drives.

> Perhaps this error was as necessary for you then [Nietzsche continues], when you were a different person—and you are always a different person—as are all you present "truths" . . . What killed that opinion for you was your new life [that is, a different drive] and not your reason: *you no longer need it*, and now it collapses and unreason crawls out of it into the light like a worm. When we criticize something, this is no arbitrary and impersonal event; it is, at least very often, evidence of vital energies in us that are growing and shedding a skin. We negate and must negate because something in us wants to live and affirm—something that we perhaps do not know or see as yet.[17]

As Deleuze will put it, there is no "pure" Reason or rationality par excellence, but only a plurality of heterogeneous processes of rationalization, just as there is no universal or transcendental Subject that could function as a basis for a universal ethics, but only variable and extraordinarily diverse processes of subjectivation (PV 14–17).

This, however, is where the question of morality comes in for Nietzsche, for one of the primary functions of morality is to establish an "order of rank" among the drives or impulses: "Wherever we encounter a morality," Nietzsche writes, "we also encounter valuations and an order of rank of human impulses . . . Now one and now another human impulse and state held first place and was ennobled because it was esteemed so highly."[18] Consider any list of impulses—in our present morality, industriousness is ranked higher than sloth; obedience higher than defiance; chastity higher than promiscuity, and so on. One can easily imagine—and indeed find—other moralities that make a different selection of the drives, giving prominence, for instance, to impulses such as aggressiveness and ferocity (a warrior culture). When Nietzsche inquires into the *genealogy* of morality, he is inquiring into the *conditions* of any particular moral ranking of the impulses: why certain impulses are selected *for* and certain impulses are selected *against*. Behind this claim is the fundamental insight that there is no distinction between nature and artifice at the level of the drives. It is not as if we could simply remove the mechanisms of morality and allow the drives to exist in a "free" and "unbound" state; there is no such thing, except perhaps as an Idea. Kant liked to say that we can never get beyond our representations of the world; Nietzsche surmises that what we can never get beyond is the reality of the drives.[19] In fact and in principle, the drives and impulses are always *assembled* or *arranged*, from the start, in different ways, in different individuals, in different cultures, in different eras—which is why Nietzsche always insisted that there are a plurality of moralities (and what he found lacking in his time was an adequate *comparative* study of moralities).

In *On the Genealogy of Morality*, Nietzsche attempts to show that what we now call "morality" arises when one particular drive comes to the fore and dominates the selection and organization of all the others. He uses a French word to describe this drive—*ressentiment*—because the French verb *ressentir* means, not primarily "to resent," but rather "to feel the effects of, to suffer from." In a sense, morality is not unlike aesthetics: much aesthetic theory is written, not from the viewpoint of the artist who creates, but rather from the viewpoint of a spectator who is making judgments about works of art they did not create, and perhaps could not create. Similarly, morality has tended to be developed, not from the viewpoint of those who act, but rather from the viewpoint of those who feel the effects of the actions of others. Both are driven by a mania to judge; this is why philosophers are obsessed with analyzing "aesthetic judgments" and "moral judgments." The person whose fundamental drive is *ressentiment* is what Nietzsche calls a "reactive" type; they do not act, but rather re-act to the actions of others, and moreover, their reaction primarily takes the form of a feeling or sentiment (*ressentiment* as resentment) rather than an action.

This is the point Nietzsche makes in his famous parable about the lambs and birds of prey:

> That lambs dislike great birds of prey does not seem strange; only it gives no ground for reproaching these birds of prey for bearing off little lambs. And if the lambs say among themselves "these birds of prey are evil; and whoever is least like a bird of prey, but rather its opposite, lamb—would he not be good?" there is no reason to find fault with this institution of an ideal, except perhaps to say that birds of prey might view it a little ironically and say: "*we* don't dislike them at all, these good little lambs; we even love them: nothing is more tasty than a tender lamb."[20]

In this parable, the lambs are reactive types; not being able to act, or re-act, in the strict sense, their reaction can only take the form of a feeling or affect, which, in the moral realm, Nietzsche describes as an affect of resentment against those who act—I suffer, you who act are the cause of my suffering, it is your fault that I am suffering, and I therefore condemn your activity. Nietzsche's fundamental puzzle in the *Genealogy* is this: How did a morality derived from this fundamental drive of *ressentiment* come to dominate all others? How did reactive drives triumph over active drives?

Nietzsche attempts to give an answer in the first essay of the *Genealogy*: reactive forces triumph by positing the fiction that we are subjects endowed with free will. This is what Deleuze calls "the fiction of a force separated from what it can do," which is in part derived from the subject–predicate grammar of language. When we say "lightning flashes," for instance, we separate in language the lighting from the flash, as if the flash were an action or operation undertaken by a subject called lightning, as if the lightning were separate from the flash, and could perhaps have decided not to flash had it so chosen. But this is obviously a fiction: there is no lightning behind the flash, and the lightning and the flash are one and the same thing. Yet it is precisely this fiction that lies at the basis of morality: when we say "a subject acts," we are presuming that, behind every deed, there is a doer; behind every action or activity, there is an actor, and it is on the basis of this fiction that the moral judgments of good and evil enter into the world. When the lambs say, "birds of prey are evil," they are presuming that "the bird of prey is able to *not* manifest its force, that it can hold back from its effects and separate itself from what it can do" (NP 123), like the lightning that decides not to flash, and they can therefore condemn their action as evil, and hold the birds of prey "responsible" for it. At the same time, what is deemed to be "good" is the non-active position of the lambs. The lambs conclude: "Birds of prey are evil, because they 'choose' to perform the activity that is their own (carrying off little lambs), they do not hold back; whereas we lambs could carry off birds of prey if we wanted to, yet we choose not to, and therefore we are good." It is assumed here that one and the same force is effectively held back in the virtuous lamb and given free rein in the evil bird of prey. But one can easily see the sleight of hand at work here: the birds of prey are judged to be evil because they perform the activity that is their own, whereas the lambs judge themselves to be good because they do not perform the activity that they . . . do not have—as if their "reactive" position "were a voluntary achievement, willed, chosen, a deed, a meritorious act."[21]

In the remainder of the *Genealogy*, Nietzsche famously shows that, even though the positing of the subject is a fiction, it none the less has a real effect, like a contagion; activity is made ashamed of itself, and turns back against itself. "All instincts that do not discharge themselves outwardly *turn inward*," Nietzsche writes, which is "the origin of the bad conscience," and the concepts of guilt and sin.[22] The term "fault" no longer refers to others ("It's your fault") but to myself ("It's my fault"). What Nietzsche calls the "ascetic ideal," in its negative sense, marks the triumph of reactive forces; life is "judged" by transcendent values superior to life.

In *Anti-Oedipus*, Deleuze takes up this Nietzschean schema, *mutatis mutandis*. What he calls "desire" is nothing other than the state of the impulses and drives. "Drives," he writes, "are simply the desiring-machines themselves" (AO 35). Moreover, like Nietzsche, Deleuze insists that the drives never exist in an unbound state; nor are they ever merely individual. They are always assembled by social formations, and one of the aims of *Anti-Oedipus* is to construct a typology of such formations— "primitive" societies, States, capitalism, and, later, in *A Thousand Plateaus*, nomadic war machines—each of which organizes and assembles the drives and impulses in different ways. Behind this claim, there lies an attempt to resolve an old debate that concerned the relationship between Marx and Freud. Like Nietzsche, both Marx and Freud insisted, each in their own way, that our conscious thought is determined by forces and drives that go beyond consciousness, forces that are, as we say "unconscious" (though we have become far too accustomed to this word; it might be better to formulate a new one). Put crudely, in Marx, our thought is determined by our class ("class consciousness"); in Freud, it is determined by unconscious desires (stemming, usually, from familial conflicts). The nature of the relationship between these two unconsciousnesses—the "political economy" of Marx and the "libidinal economy" of Freud—was a problem that numerous thinkers tried to deal with in the twentieth century (Marcuse, Brown, Reich, and others). For a long time, the relation between the two was usually formulated in terms of the mechanisms of "introjection" and "projection". As an individual, I introject the interests of my class, my culture, my social milieu, which eventually come to determine my (false) consciousness; at the same time, the political economy was seen as a projection of the individual desires of the population that produced it. Deleuze and Guattari famously reject these mechanisms in *Anti-Oedipus*; they argue that political economy (Marx), on the one hand, and libidinal economy (Freud), on the other, are *one and the same economy*. "The only means of bypassing the sterile parallelism where we flounder between Freud and Marx," they write, is "by discovering . . . *how the affects or drives form part of the infrastructure itself*" (AO 63). This is an extraordinary claim: your very drives and impulses, even the unconscious ones, which seems to be what is most individual about you, are themselves economic—that is, they are already part of what Marx called the "infrastructure."

With these Nietzschean reflections in hand, I want to turn to my second text of an immanent ethics, which comes from Leibniz's *New Essays Concerning Human Understanding*.[23] Although the names of Nietzsche and Leibniz are not usually linked together by philosophers, the relation between the two thinkers is not an accidental one. In *The Gay Science*, Nietzsche praised Leibniz's critique of consciousness and his differential conception of the unconscious, the profundity of which he says, "has not been exhausted to this day."[24] In the *New Essays*, Leibniz asks: What would it mean to act "freely," given this theory of the drives? Leibniz asks us to consider a simple example. Suppose I am hesitating between staying at home and writing this paper, or going out to a tavern to have a drink with some friends. How do I go about making a decision between these two? The error, he suggests, would be to objectify these two options, as if "staying in" or "going out" were objects that could be weighed in a balance, and as if deliberation were an act of judgment in which the "I"—my self, my ego, my intellect—attempts to assess the direction toward which the balance is leaning, "all things being equal." But in fact these two options are not isolatable "objects" but rather two drives, or as Leibniz calls them, "motives" or "inclinations" of the soul. The strength of Leibniz's analysis in the *New Essays* is to show that drives or motives are not simple things, but rather complex "orientations" or "tendencies," each of which integrates within itself a host of "minute inclinations." My inclination to go to the tavern, for instance, includes not only the minute perception of the effect of the alcohol, or the taste and temperature of the drink, but also the clinking of glasses in the bar, the smoke in the air, the conversation with friends, the temporary lifting of one's solitude, and so on. The same is true of the inclination to stay at home and work, which includes the minute perceptions of the rustling of paper, the noise of my fingers tapping at the computer, the quality of the silence of the room when I stop tapping, the comfort (or frustration) that I find in my work. Both inclinations are formed within an unconscious complex of auditive, gustative, olfactory, and visual perceptions, an entire *perceptio-inclinatory ensemble*. Just as we have unconscious perceptions, we likewise are constituted by "insensible inclinations" or "disquietudes" of which we are not aware, but which pull us simultaneously in a multitude of directions.[25] Not only are all of us constituted by a multitude of unconscious drives; each drive is itself multiple, an infinite complex of minute perceptions and inclinations. It is these drives and motives that constitute the very tissue of the soul, constantly folding it in all directions. This is what Locke termed the "uneasiness" of the soul, its state of constant disquiet and disequilibrium, and Leibniz, its dark background, the *fuscum subnigrum*.

What, then, is the act of deliberation? At the moment when I am torn between staying home and going out for a drink, the tissue of my soul is in a state of disequilibrium—oscillating between two complex perceptive poles (the tavern and the study), each of which is itself swarming with an infinity of minute perceptions and inclinations. Here, the movement of the soul, as Leibniz says, more properly resembles a pendulum or "spring" rather than a balance—and often a rather wildly swinging pendulum at that.[26] The question of decision is: On which side will I "fold" my soul? With which minute inclinations and perceptions will I make a "decisive" fold? Arriving at a decision is a matter of "integrating" (to use a mathematical term) the minute perceptions and inclinations in a "distinguished" perception or a "remarkable" inclination.

The error of the usual schema of judgment is that, in objectifying my two options—staying home or going out—as if they were weights in a balance, it presumes that they remain the same in front of me, and that the deliberating self likewise remains the same, simply assessing the two options in terms of some sort of decision procedure (my interest, a calculus of probabilities, an assessment of potential consequences, and so on). But this falsifies the nature of deliberation: if neither the options nor the self ever change, how could I *ever* arrive at a decision? The truth of the matter is that, during the entire time the deliberation is going on, the self is constantly changing, and consequently is modifying the two feelings that are agitating it. What Leibniz (as well as Bergson, significantly) calls a "free" act will be an act that effectuates the amplitude of my soul at a certain moment, the moment the act is undertaken. It is an act that integrates the small perceptions and small inclinations into a remarkable inclination, which then becomes an inclination of the soul. But this integration requires time; there is a psychic integration and a psychic time of integration. Thus, at 10:15 p.m. I have a vague urge to go to the tavern. Why do I not go? Because at that moment, it remains in the state of a minute inclination, a small perception, a swarm. The motivation is there, but if I still remain at home working, I do not know the amplitude of my soul. Indeed, most of the time my actions do *not* correspond to the amplitude of my soul.

> There is no reason [says Deleuze] to subject all the actions we undertake to the criterion: Is it free or not? Freedom is only for certain acts. There are all sorts of acts that do not have to be confronted with the problems of freedom. They are done solely, one could say, to calm our disquietude: all our habitual

and machinal acts. We will speak of freedom only when we pose the question of an act capable or not of filling the amplitude of the soul at a given moment. (24 Nov 1987)

At 10:30 p.m., I finally say to myself, I'm going out for a drink. Is that because the drive to go out has won out over the drive to stay home working? Even that simplifies the operation, since what came into play may have been other motives that remain largely unknown to us, such as (these are examples given by Nietzsche in *Daybreak*): "the way we habitually expend our energy"; "or our indolence, which prefers to do what is easiest"; "or an excitation of our imagination brought about at the decisive moment by some immediate, very trivial event"; or "quite incalculable physical influences"; or "some emotion or other [that] happens quite by chance to leap forth."[27] As Bergson puts it, in terms very similar to Leibniz's,

> all the time that the deliberation is going on, the self is changing and is consequently modifying the [often unknown] feelings that agitate it. A dynamic series of states is thus formed which permeate and strengthen one another, and which will lead by a natural evolution to a free act . . . In reality there are not two tendencies, or even two directions, but a self which lives and develops by means of its very hesitations, until the free action drops from it like an over-ripe fruit.[28]

In Leibniz's terminology, to say that we are "free" means that we are "inclined without being necessitated." A free act is simply an act that expresses the whole of the soul at a given moment of duration—that is, an act that fills the amplitude of the soul at a given moment.

Parenthetically, one might contrast this theory of decision with the one proposed by Derrida in his well-known essay "Force of Law." Both Derrida and Deleuze insist that decision presupposes an Idea, almost in the Kantian sense. For Derrida, however, these Ideas—for instance, the Idea of justice, which would guide our juridical decisions—are, as he says, "infinitely transcendent," and hence the very condition of possibility of their effectuation is their impossibility. For Deleuze, such Ideas are purely immanent; the Idea is nothing other than the problematic multiplicity of these drives and minute inclinations, which constitutes the condition of any decision. In this sense, one might say that Deleuze "replaces the power of judgment with the force of decision" (ECC 49).

THE THEORY OF DESIRE

With these two analyses now in hand—Nietzsche's theory of the drives, as a way of approaching the nature of modes of existence; and Leibniz's theory of "freedom," in relation to his theory of minute inclinations—we can now turn to the question of desire, and the problem of how desire can desire its own repression. (What Deleuze means by the term "desire" is, of course, different from its usual usage: it refers to the state of our unconscious drives and inclinations.) There are a number of consequences that follow from these analyses.

First, there is a school of economics that sees human as rational agents who always act in such a way as to maximize their own interests (what is sometimes called "rational choice theory"). Deleuze's distinction between desire and interest seeks to put that claim in its proper context. Someone may have an interest, say, in becoming an academic, so he or she applies to the university, writes a thesis, attends conferences, and goes on the job market in hopes of securing an academic position. One may indeed have an interest in all that, which can be pursued in a highly rational manner. But that interest exists as a possibility only within the context of a particular social formation: if one can pursue that interest in a concerted way, it is first of all because one's desire—one's drives and impulses—is itself invested in the social formation that makes that interest possible. One's drives have been constructed and assembled in a way that allows one to have this particular interest. This is why Deleuze can say that desire as such is always positive. Normally, we tend to think of desire in terms of lack: if we desire something, it is because we lack it. But Deleuze reconfigures the concept of desire: what we desire, what we invest our desire in, is a social formation, and in this sense desire is always *positive*. Lack appears only at the level of interest, because the social formation (the infrastructure) in which we have already invested our *desire* has in turn produced that lack. The result of this analysis is that we can see why the proper *object* of a purely immanent ethics is not one's conscious will or one's conscious decisions, but neither is it my pre-conscious interests (class interest, in the Marxist sense). The true object of an immanent ethics is desire (the drives), and thus it entails, as both Spinoza and Nietzsche showed, an entire theory of *affectivity* at the basis of any theory of ethics.

The second consequence follows from the first. The primacy of the question of desire over both interest and will is the reason Deleuze says that the fundamental problem of political philosophy is one that was formulated most clearly by Spinoza: "Why do people fight for their servitude as stubbornly as though it were their salvation?" (AO 29). Why do we invest in a social system that constantly represses us, thwarts our interests, and introduces lack into our lives? Theoretically, the answer is straightforward: it is because our desires—that is, our drives and affects—are not our own. They are, if I can put it this way, part of the capitalist infrastructure; they are not simply our own individual mental or psychic realities ("There is no particular form of existence that can be labeled 'psychic reality'" [AO 30]). Nothing makes this more obvious that the effects of advertising and marketing, which are aimed at the direct manipulation of the drives and affects. I almost automatically reach for one brand of toothpaste rather than another, since I have a fervent *interest* in having fresh breath and cavity-free teeth—but this is because my desire is already invested in the social formation that creates that interest, and that creates the sense of lack I feel if my breath is not fresh or my teeth are not white.

Third, the difference between interest and desire could be said to parallel the difference between the rational and the irrational. Once interests have been defined within the confines of a society, what is "rational" is the way people pursue those interests and attempt to realize them—the interest for a job, or for cavity-free teeth.

But beneath that, one finds desire—investments of desire that are not to be confused with investments of interest, and on which interests depend for their determination and very distribution: "an enormous flow, all kinds of libidinal-unconscious flows that constitute the delirium of this society" (DI 263). As Deleuze will say,

> Reason is always a region carved out of the irrational—it is in no way sheltered from the irrational, but traversed by it and only defined by a certain kind of relationship among irrational factors. Underneath all reason lies delirium and drift. Everything about capitalism is rational, except capital . . . A stock market is a perfectly rational mechanism, you can understand it, learn how it works; capitalists know how to use it; and yet it is completely delirious, it is demented . . . It is just like theology: everything about it is quite rational—*if* you accept sin, the immaculate conception, and the incarnation, which are themselves irrational elements. (DI 262–3, translation modified)

Fourth, how does Deleuze conceptualize this movement of desire? Interestingly, *Anti-Oedipus* can be read as an explicit attempt to rework the fundamental theses of Kant's *Critique of Practical Reason*. Kant presents the second critique as a theory of desire, and he defines desire, somewhat surprisingly, in *causal* terms: desire is "a faculty which by means of its representations is the *cause* of the actuality of the objects of those representations." In its lower form, the products of desire are fantasies and superstitions; but in its higher form (the will), the products of desire are acts of *freedom* under the moral law—actions which are, however, irreducible to mechanistic causality. Deleuze takes up Kant's model of desire, but modifies it in two fundamental ways. First, if desire is productive or causal, then its product is itself *real* (and not illusory or noumenal); the entire socio-political field, Deleuze argues, must be seen as the historically determined product of desire. Second, to maintain this claim, Deleuze formulates an entirely new theory of "Ideas." In Kant, the postulates of practical reason are found in the transcendent Ideas of God, World, and the Soul, which are themselves derived from the types of judgment of relation (categorical, hypothetical, disjunctive). In response, Deleuze, in the first chapters of *Anti-Oedipus*, formulates a purely immanent theory of Ideas, in which desire is constituted by a set of constituting passive syntheses (connective, disjunctive, conjunctive).

Deleuze's theory of desire, however, is also developed partly in relation to Lacan, but by taking Lacan's thought in a direction that most Lacanians would never go, and indeed they would insist that one *cannot* go there. *Anti-Oedipus*, as its subtitle ("Capitalism and Schizophrenia") indicates, takes psychosis as its model for the unconscious. Lacan himself had said that the unconscious appears in its purest form in psychosis, but that in effect the unconscious remains inaccessible in psychotics, precisely because psychotics refuse symbolization. Thus, the dimension of the Real, in Lacan, can only appear as a kind of negative moment in Lacan, as a kind of "gap" or "rupture" in the field of immanence, thereby reintroducing an element of transcendence. Deleuze, in this respect, effectively inverts Lacan, and presents *Anti-Oedipus* in its entirety as a theory of the Real that is described in all its positivity—that is, as a sub-representative field defined by differential partial objects or intensities that enter into indirect syntheses; pure positive multiplicities where everything is possible (transverse connections, polyvocal conjunctions, included disjunctions); signs of desire that compose a signifying chain, but which are themselves non-signifying, and so on (AO 309). It is an analysis of *delirium*, showing that the delirium that threatens the heart of the self (*schizophrenia*) is one and the same thing as the delirium that exists at the heart of our society, and which appears most clearly in *capitalism*—a monetary mass that "exists" nowhere, is controlled by no one, and is literally delirious in its operations.

Finally, this is a way of suggesting that the concept of freedom—which plays such a decisive role in Kant's philosophy—also assumes a prominent place in Deleuze's own philosophy of desire, albeit in a new form: namely, as the question of the conditions for the production of the *new*. But as Deleuze frequently says, following thinkers like Salomon Maimon, what needed to happen in post-Kantian philosophy was a substitution of a viewpoint of *internal genesis* for the Kantian viewpoint of *external condition*. This is what one finds in Deleuze's post-Kantian (Nietzschean) reading of Leibniz: the idea that the "I think" of consciousness bathes in an unconscious, an unconscious of drives, motives, and inclinations, which contain the differentials of what appears in consciousness, and which would therefore perform the genesis of the conditioned as a function of the condition. In this sense, Deleuze's ethical philosophy might at first sight appear to be the opposite of Kant's ethical theory, with the latter's appeal to the transcendence of the Moral Law. Yet Kant himself insisted on a principle of immanence throughout his philosophy, even if he betrayed it in his books on practical philosophy. This is perhaps why, in Deleuze, the *content* of an immanent ethics is taken from Nietzsche and Spinoza, but its immanent *form* winds up being taken primarily from Kant. In this sense, one could say that Deleuze's work, with regard to practical and political philosophy, in the end is at once an *inversion* as well as a *completion* of Kant's critical philosophy.

Life

"A Life of Pure Immanence": Deleuze's "Critique et Clinique" Project

> The critical (in the literary sense) and the clinical (in the medical sense) may be destined to enter into a new relationship of mutual learning. (M 14)

Although *Essays Critical and Clinical* is the only book written by Deleuze that is devoted primarily to literature, literary references are present everywhere in his work, running almost parallel to the philosophical references. Deleuze first linked together the "critical" and the "clinical" in the study of Sacher-Masoch that he published in 1967.[1] The 1969 *Logic of Sense* is in part a reading of Lewis Carroll's work and includes supplementary material and chapters on Klossowski, Tournier, Zola, Fitzgerald, Lowry, and Artaud. Literary references occupy considerable portions of the two-volume *Capitalism and Schizophrenia*, which Deleuze wrote in the 1970s with Félix Guattari. He has written books on both Proust (1964) and Kafka (1975, with Guattari), as well as two long essays on Carmelo Bene (1979) and Samuel Beckett (1992). His 1977 *Dialogues* with Claire Parnet includes an important chapter entitled "On the Superiority of Anglo-American Literature." *Essays Critical and Clinical* includes eight newly revised articles that were originally published by Deleuze between 1970 and 1993, along with ten essays that appear here for the first time. Once again, names of philosophers (Plato, Spinoza, Kant, Nietzsche, Heidegger) appear side by side with names of literary figures (Melville, Whitman, D. H. Lawrence, T. E. Lawrence, Beckett, Artaud, Masoch, Jarry, Carroll). Although he first announced the idea for this book during a 1988 interview, it is clear that Deleuze had conceived of the "critique et clinique" project early on in his career and pursued it in various forms throughout his published work.[2]

What role do these literary analyses play in Deleuze's philosophical *œuvre*? In *What is Philosophy?* Deleuze and Guattari define philosophy as a practice of concepts, an activity that consists in the formation, invention, or creation of concepts, and indeed their work is marked throughout by an extraordinary conceptual inventiveness. But philosophy, Deleuze adds, necessarily enters into variable relations with other domains such as science, medicine, and art. Art, for instance, is an equally creative enterprise of thought, but one whose object is to create sensible aggregates rather than concepts. Great artists and authors, in other words, are also great think-ers, but they think in terms of percepts and affects rather than concepts; painters, one might say, think in the medium of lines and colors, just musicians think in sounds, filmmakers think in images, writers think in words, and so on. Neither activity has any privilege over the other. Creating a concept is neither more dif-ficult nor more abstract than creating new visual, sonorous, or verbal combinations; conversely, it is no easier to read an image, painting, or novel than it is to compre-hend a concept. Philosophy, Deleuze insists, cannot be undertaken independently of science and art; it always enters into relations of mutual resonance and exchange with these other domains, though for reasons that are always internal to philosophy itself.[3]

Deleuze therefore writes on the arts not as a critic but as a philosopher, and his books and essays on the various arts, and on various artists and authors, must be read, as he himself insists, as "works of philosophy, nothing but philosophy, in the traditional sense of the word."[4] The cinema, for instance, produces images that move, and that move in time, and it is these two aspects of film that Deleuze ana-lyzes in *The Movement-Image* and *The Time-Image*: "What exactly does the cinema show us about space and time that the other arts don't show?" (N 58). Deleuze thus describes his two-volume *Cinema* as "a book of logic, a logic of the cinema" that sets out "to isolate certain cinematographic concepts," concepts that are specific to the cinema . . . but that can only be formed philosophically (MI ix; N 47). *Francis Bacon: The Logic of Sensation* likewise creates a series of philosophical concepts, each of which relates to a particular aspect of Bacon's paintings, but also finds a place in "a general logic of sensation" (FB 3). *Essays Critical and Clinical* must be evaluated in the same manner: that is, in terms of the concepts Deleuze extracts from the literary works he examines and the links he establishes between philoso-phy, literature, and the other arts.[5] The book is not a mere collection of articles; though most of the essays are devoted to individual authors, the book develops a series of concepts like so many motifs that appear and reappear in different essays, which enter into increasingly complex contrapuntal relationships with each other, and which could likewise be said to find a place in a logic of literature—or rather, a logic of "Life." For if the *Cinema* volumes deal primarily with space and time, and *Francis Bacon* with the nature of sensation, Deleuze's writings on literature are pri-marily linked with the problematic of *Life*. "You have seen what is essential for me," he once wrote to a commentator; "this 'vitalism' or a conception of life as a non-organic power"; in a later interview, he added, "Everything I've written is vitalistic, at least I hope it is."[6]

The idea that literature has something to do with life is certainly not a novel one. In Deleuze's work, however, the notion of Life, as a philosophical concept, has a complex ontological and ethical status. In one of the last essays he published before his death in November 1995—a short, dense, abstract, yet strangely moving piece—Deleuze wrote of a scene from Charles Dickens's *Our Mutual Friend*. A rogue despised by everyone is brought in on the verge of death, and the people tending to him suddenly manifest a kind of respect and love for the slightest sign of life in the dying man.

No one has the least regard for the man [writes Dickens]. With them all, he has been an object of avoidance, suspicion, and aversion; but the spark of life within him is curiously separate from himself now, and they have a deep interest in it, probably because it is life, and they are living and must die.[7]

As the man revives, his saviors become colder, and he recovers all his crudeness and maliciousness. Yet "between his life and his death," comments Deleuze,

> there is a moment that is no longer anything but a life playing with death. The life of an individual has given way to an impersonal and yet singular life that disengages a pure event freed from the accidents of the inner and outer life, that is, from the subjectivity and objectivity of what happens. A *homo tantum* with whom everyone sympathizes, and who attains a kind of beatitude. This is a haecceity, which is no longer an individuation but a singularization: *a life of* pure *immanence*, neutral, beyond good and evil.

This non-organic vitality is made manifest most clearly, perhaps, in a newborn baby:

> Small infants all resemble each other and have hardly any individuality; but they have singularities—a smile, a gesture, a grimace—which are not subjective characteristics. Infants are traversed by an immanent life that is pure power, and even a beatitude, through their sufferings and weaknesses . . . With a young child, one already has an organic, personal relationship, but not with a baby, which concentrates in its smallness the same energy that shatters paving stones. With a baby, one has nothing but an affective, athletic, impersonal, vital relation. It is clear that the will to power appears in an infinitely more exact manner in a baby than in a man of war. (PI 30; ECC 133)

For Deleuze, Life is an impersonal and non-organic power that goes beyond any lived experience—an ontological concept of Life that draws on sources as diverse as Nietzsche (life as "will to power"), Bergson (the *élan vital*), and modern evolutionary biology (life as variation and selection). And if Life has a direct relation to literature, it is because writing itself is "a passage of Life that traverses both the livable and the lived" (ECC 1).

But the concept of Life also functions as an ethical principle in Deleuze's thought. Throughout his works, Deleuze has drawn a sharp distinction between morality and ethics. He uses the term "morality" to define, in general terms, any set of "constraining" rules, such as a moral code, that consists in judging actions and intentions by relating them to transcendent or universal values ("this is good, that is evil"). What he calls "ethics" is, on the contrary, a set of "facilitative" (*facultative*) rules that evaluates what we do, say, think, and feel according to the immanent mode of existence it implies. One says or does this, thinks or feels that: what mode of existence does it imply?[8] This is the link that Deleuze sees between Spinoza and Nietzsche, whom he has always identified as his philosophical precursors. Each of them argued, in his own manner, that there are things one cannot do or think except on the condition of being weak, base, or enslaved, unless one harbors a resentment against life (Nietzsche), unless one remains the slave of passive affections (Spinoza); and there are other things one cannot do or say except on the condition of being strong, noble, or free, unless one affirms life, unless one attains active affections. An immanent ethical difference (good / bad) is in this way substituted for the transcendent moral opposition (Good / Evil). "*Beyond Good and Evil*," wrote Nietzsche, "at least that does not mean 'Beyond Good and Bad.'"[9] The "Bad" or sickly life is an exhausted and degenerating mode of existence, one that judges life from the perspective of its sickness, that devaluates life in the name of "higher" values. The "Good" or healthy life, by contrast, is an overflowing and ascending form of existence, a mode of life that is able to transform itself depending on the forces it encounters, always increasing the power to live, always opening up new possibilities of life. For Deleuze, every literary work implies a way of living, a form of life, and must be evaluated not only critically but also clinically. "Style, in a great writer, is always a style of life as well, not at all something personal, but the invention of a possibility of life, a way of existing" (N 100).

Put differently, the question that links literature and life, in both its ontological and its ethical aspects, is the question of health. This does not mean that an author necessarily enjoys robust health; on the contrary, artists, like philosophers, often have frail health, a weak constitution, a fragile personal life (Spinoza's frailty, D. H. Lawrence's hemoptysis, Nietzsche's migraines, Deleuze's own respiratory ailments). This frailty, however, does not simply stem from their illnesses or neuroses, says Deleuze, but from having seen or felt something in life that is too great for them, something unbearable "that has put on them the quiet mark of death" (WP 172). But this something is also what Nietzsche called the "great health," the vitality that supports them through the illnesses of lived experience. This is why, for Deleuze, writing is never a personal matter; it is never simply a matter of our lived experiences. "You don't get very far in literature with the system 'I've seen a lot and been lots of places'" (N 134). Novels are not created with our dreams and fantasies, nor our sufferings and griefs, our opinions and ideas, our memories and travels, nor "with the interesting characters we have met or the interesting character who is inevitably oneself (who isn't interesting?)" (WP 170). It is true that the writer is "inspired" by lived experience; but even in writers like Thomas Wolfe or Henry Miller, who seem to do nothing but recount their own lives, "there's an attempt to make life something more than personal, to free life from what imprisons it."[10] Nor does Deleuze read works of literature primarily as texts, or treat writing in terms of its "textuality," though he by no means ignores the effect literature has on language. His approach to literature must thus be distinguished from Jacques Derrida's deconstructive approach.

> As for the method of deconstruction of texts [Deleuze once remarked], I see clearly what it is, I admire it a lot, but it has nothing to do with my own method. I do not present myself as a commentator on texts. For me, a text is merely a small cog in an extra-textual practice. It is not a question of commentating on the text by a method of deconstruction, or by a method of

textual practice, or by other methods; it is a question of seeing what use it has in the extra-textual practice that prolongs the text.[11]

For Deleuze, the question of literature is linked not to the question of its textuality, or even to its historicity, but to its "vitality": that is, its "tenor" of Life.

How, then, are we to conceive of this link between literature and life, between the critical and the clinical? Deleuze first raised this question in his 1967 book *Coldness and Cruelty* in the context of a concrete problem: Why were the names of two literary figures, Sade and Masoch, used as labels in the nineteenth century to denote two basic "perversions" in clinical psychiatry? This encounter between literature and medicine was made possible, Deleuze argues, by the peculiar nature of the symptomatological method. Medicine is made up of at least three different activities: symptomatology, or the study of signs; etiology, or the search for causes; and therapy, or the development and application of a treatment. While etiology and therapeutics are integral parts of medicine, symptomatology appeals to a kind of limit-point, pre-medical or sub-medical, that belongs as much to art as to medicine (DI 134). In symptomatology, illnesses are sometimes named after typical patients (Lou Gehrig's disease), but more often it is the doctor's name that is given to the disease (Parkinson's disease, Roger's disease, Alzheimer's disease, Creutzfeldt–Jakob disease). The principles behind this labeling process, Deleuze suggests, deserve careful analysis. The doctor certainly does not "invent" the disease, but rather is said to "isolate" it; he or she distinguishes cases that had hitherto been confused by dissociating symptoms that were previously grouped together and by juxtaposing them with others that were previously dissociated. In this way, the doctor constructs an original clinical concept for the disease: the components of the concept are the symptoms, the signs of the illness, and the concept becomes the name of a syndrome, which marks the meeting place of these symptoms, their point of coincidence or convergence. When a doctor gives his or her name to an illness, it constitutes an important advance in medicine, in so far as a proper name is linked to a given group of symptoms or signs. Moreover, if diseases are named after their symptoms rather than after their causes, it is because, even in medicine, a correct etiology depends first of all on a rigorous symptomatology: "Etiology, which is the scientific or experimental side of medicine, must be subordinated to symptomatology, which is its literary, artistic aspect."[12]

The fundamental idea behind Deleuze's "critique et clinique" project is that authors and artists, like doctors and clinicians, can themselves be seen as profound symptomatologists. Sadism and masochism are clearly not diseases on a par with Parkinson's disease or Alzheimer's disease. Yet if Krafft-Ebing, in 1869, was able to use Masoch's name to designate a fundamental perversion (much to Masoch's own consternation), it was not because Masoch "suffered" from it as a patient, but rather because his literary works isolated a particular way of existing and set forth a novel symptomatology of it, making the contract its primary sign. Freud made use of Sophocles in much the same way when he created the concept of the Oedipus complex.[13] "Authors, if they are great, are more like doctors than patients," writes Deleuze:

We mean that they are themselves astonishing diagnosticians or symptomatologists. There is always a great deal of art involved in the grouping of
symptoms, in the organization of a table [*tableau*] where a particular symptom
is dissociated from another, juxtaposed to a third, and forms the new figure
of a disorder or illness. Clinicians who are able to renew a symptomatological picture produce a work of art; conversely, artists are clinicians, not with
respect to their own case, nor even with respect to a case in general; rather,
they are clinicians of civilization . . . Symptomatology is always a question of
art. (LS 237; M 14)

It was Nietzsche who first put forward the idea that artists and philosophers are
physiologists, "physicians of culture," for whom phenomena are signs or symptoms
that reflect a certain state of forces.[14] Indeed, Deleuze strongly suggests that artists
and authors can go *further* in symptomatology than doctors and clinicians, precisely
"because the work of art gives them new means, perhaps also because they are less
concerned about causes" (DI 133).

   This point of view is very different from many psychoanalytic interpretations of
writers and artists, which tend to see authors, through their work, as possible or real
patients, even if they are accorded the benefit of "sublimation." Artists are treated
as clinical cases, as if they were ill, however sublimely, and the critic seeks a sign
of neurosis like a secret in their work, its hidden code. The work of art then seems
to be inscribed between two poles: a regressive pole, where the work hashes out
the unresolved conflicts of childhood, and a progressive pole, by which the work
invents paths leading to a new solution concerning the future of humanity, converting itself into a "cultural object." From both these points of view, there is no need to
"apply" psychoanalysis to the work of art, since the work itself is seen to constitute
a successful psychoanalysis, either as a resolution or a sublimation. This infantile
or "egoistic" conception of literature, this imposition of the "Oedipal form" on the
work of art, Deleuze suggests, has been an important factor in the reduction of literature to an object of consumption subject to the demands of the literary market.[15]

   Coldness and Cruelty provides one of the clearest examples of what might be
termed Deleuze's "symptomatological" approach to literature. At a conceptual
level, the book is an incisive critique of the clinical notion of "sadomasochism,"
which presumes that sadism and masochism are complementary forces that belong
to one and the same pathological entity. Psychiatrists were led to posit such a
"crude syndrome," Deleuze argues, partly because they relied on hasty etiological
assumptions (the reversals and transformations of the so-called sexual instinct),
and partly because they were "content with a symptomatology much less precise
and much more confused than that which is found in Masoch himself."[16] Because
the judgments of clinicians are often prejudiced, Deleuze adopts a literary approach
in *Coldness and Cruelty*, offering a differential diagnosis of sadism and masochism
based on the works from which their original definitions were derived. Three results
of Deleuze's analysis are important for our purposes. On the clinical side, Deleuze
shows that sadism and masochism are two incommensurable modes of existence
whose symptomatologies are completely different. Each chapter of *Coldness and*

Cruelty analyzes a particular aspect of the sadomasochistic "syndrome" (the nature of the fetish, the function of fantasy, the forms of desexualization and resexualization, the status of the father and mother, the role of the ego and superego, and so on), and in each case shows how it can be broken down into "symptoms" that are specific to the worlds of sadism and masochism. On the critical side, he shows that these clinical symptoms are inseparable from the literary styles and techniques of Sade and Masoch, both of whom, he argues, submit language to a "higher function": in Sade, an Idea of pure reason (absolute negation) is projected into the real, producing a speculative-demonstrative use of language that operates through quantitative repetition; in Masoch, by contrast, the real is suspended in a supra-sensual Ideal, producing a dialectical-imaginative use of language that operates through qualitative suspense. Finally, Deleuze shows how these new modes of existence and new uses of language were linked to political acts of resistance: in Sade's case, these acts were linked to the French revolution, which he thought would remain sterile unless it stopped making laws and set up institutions of perpetual motion (the sects of libertines); in Masoch's case, masochistic practices were linked to the place of minorities in the Austro-Hungarian empire, and to the role of women within these minorities.[17]

Deleuze initially saw *Coldness and Cruelty* as the first installment of a series of literary-clinical studies: "What I would like to study (this book would merely be a first example) is an articulable relationship between literature and clinical psychiatry."[18] The idea was not to apply psychiatric concepts to literature, but on the contrary to extract non-preexistent clinical concepts from the works themselves. As is often the fate with such proposals, Deleuze did not exactly realize the project in its envisioned form. Yet when Deleuze asked, ten years later, "Why is there not a 'Nietzscheism,' 'Proustism,' 'Kafkaism,' 'Spinozism' along the lines of a generalized clinic?," he implied that his monographs on each of these thinkers fell, to a greater or lesser degree, within the scope of the "critique et clinique" project (D 120). *Nietzsche and Philosophy*, for instance, shows how Nietzsche set out to diagnose a disease (nihilism) by isolating its symptoms (*ressentiment*, the bad conscience, the ascetic ideal), by tracing its etiology to a certain relation of active and reactive forces (the genealogical method), and by setting forth both a prognosis (nihilism defeated by itself) and a treatment (the revaluation of values). Deleuze thought that the most original contribution of his doctoral thesis, *Expressionism in Philosophy: Spinoza*, was its analysis of the composition of finite "modes" in Spinoza, which includes both a clinical diagnostic of their passive state (human bondage) and a treatment for their becoming-active (the "ethical" task) (EPS 11). In the first edition of *Proust and Signs* (1964), Deleuze interprets *In Search of Lost Time* as a symptomatology of various worlds of signs that mobilize the involuntary and the unconscious (the world of love, the social world, the material world, and the world of art, which comes to transform all the others).[19] Even in *Kafka: Toward a Minor Literature*, Deleuze and Guattari show how Kafka's work provided a symptomatological diagnosis of the "diabolical powers" of the future (capitalism, bureaucracy, fascism, Stalinism) that were knocking at the door. Certain essays collected in *Essays Critical and Clinical* could similarly be read as literary-clinical studies of specific writers. In all these works, what

Foucault called the "author function" has all but disappeared; the proper name does not refer to a particular person as an author but to a regime of signs or concepts, a determinate multiplicity or assemblage. Deleuze speaks of Nietzsche's philosophy or Proust's novel in much the same way one speaks of Alzheimer's disease in medicine, the Doppler effect or the Kelvin effect in science, the Hamiltonian number or the Mandelbrot set in mathematics: that is, as a non-personal mode of individuation. If we were to characterize the symptomatological method used by Deleuze, we could do so in terms of these two fundamental components: the function of the proper name, and the assemblage or multiplicity designated by the name.[20]

With the publication of *Anti-Oedipus* in 1972, however, the "critique et clinique" project took a new turn, or at least brought to the fore a tendency that would become ever more pronounced as Deleuze's own work progressed. *Anti-Oedipus* offers a now-famous critique of psychoanalysis that is primarily symptomatological: psychoanalysis, Deleuze and Guattari contend, fundamentally misunderstands signs and symptoms. Given the book's subtitle, *Capitalism and Schizophrenia*, one might expect Deleuze and Guattari to provide a symptomatological analysis of schizophrenia that would correct the errors and abuses of psychoanalysis. But in fact this is not quite the case. Schizophrenia is an acute phenomenon that poses numerous problems to the clinical method: not only is there no agreement as to the etiology of schizophrenia, but even its symptomatology remains uncertain. In early psychiatric accounts of schizophrenia (Kraepelin, Bleuler), the diagnostic criteria are given in purely negative terms: that is, in terms of the destruction the disorder engenders in the subject—dissociation, autism, detachment from reality. Psychoanalysis retains this negative viewpoint, in so far as it relates the syntheses of the unconscious to the father–mother–child triangle of the Oedipus complex (the ego): in neurosis, the ego obeys the requirements of reality and represses the drives of the id, whereas in psychosis the ego remains under the sway of the id, leading to a break with reality (AO 122). The problem with both psychiatry and psychoanalysis is that these negative symptoms are dispersed and scattered, and are difficult to totalize or unify in a coherent clinical entity, or even a localizable "mode of existence": "schizophrenia is a discordant syndrome, always in flight from itself."[21]

Anti-Oedipus therefore takes the "critique et clinique" project to a properly transcendental level. From the clinical viewpoint, one of its aims is to describe schizophrenia in its *positivity*, no longer as actualized in a mode of life but as the *process* of life itself. Deleuze and Guattari draw a sharp distinction between schizophrenia as a process and schizophrenia as a clinical entity (which results from an *interruption* of the process, as in the case of Nietzsche), although their use of the same term to describe both phenomena has led to numerous misunderstandings.[22] For what *Anti-Oedipus* terms "schizophrenia as a process" is nothing other than what *A Thousand Plateaus* terms "the process of Life" as a nonorganic and impersonal power.

> The problem of schizophrenization as a cure consists in this: how can schizophrenia be disengaged as *a power of humanity and of Nature* without a schizophrenic hereby being produced? A problem analogous to that of Burroughs

(How to incarnate the power of drugs without being an addict?) or Miller (How to get drunk on pure water?).[23]

From the critical side, Deleuze and Guattari once again appeal to the work of literary figures, especially a number of Anglo-American writers, whose work here assumes an importance it did not have in Deleuze's earlier work. "We have been criticized for over-quoting literary authors," they would later comment, "but is it our fault that Lawrence, Miller, Kerouac, Burroughs, Artaud, and Beckett know more about schizophrenia than psychiatrists and psychoanalysts?"[24] If literature here takes on a schizophrenic vocation, it is because the works of these writers no longer simply present the symptomatology of a mode of life, but rather attempt to trace the virtual power of non-organic Life itself.

How are we to conceive of this "schizophrenic vocation" of literature? In 1970 Deleuze wrote a new essay on Proust entitled "The Literary Machine," which was added to the second edition of *Proust and Signs*. Whereas the first edition of *Proust and Signs* considered the *Search* from the viewpoint of its interpretation of signs, "The Literary Machine" considers the work from the viewpoint of its creation, its *production* of signs.[25] Art, Deleuze argues, is essentially productive; the work of art is a machine for producing or generating certain effects, certain signs, by determinable procedures. Proust suggested that his readers use his book as an optical instrument, "a kind of magnifying glass" that would provide them with "the means of reading within themselves," in much the same way that Joyce described his works as machines for producing "epiphanies."[26] There is thus a "literary effect" produced by literature, much as we speak of an optical effect or an electromagnetic effect; and the "literary machine" is an apparatus capable of creating these effects, producing signs of different orders, and thus capable of functioning effectively. The question Deleuze here poses to the literary work is not "What does it mean?" (interpretation), but rather "How does it function?" (experimentation). "The modern work of art has no problem of meaning, it has only a problem of use."[27] But the claim that "meaning is use" requires a transcendental analysis:

> No one has been able to pose the problem of language except to the extent that linguists and logicians have eliminated meaning; and the *highest* power of language was discovered only when the work was viewed as a machine, producing certain effects, amenable to a certain use . . . The idea that meaning is nothing other than use becomes a principle only if we have at our disposal *immanent* criteria capable of determining legitimate uses, as opposed to illegitimate uses that would refer use to a supposed meaning and restore a kind of transcendence. Analysis termed transcendental is precisely the determination of these immanent criteria. (AO 109)

For Deleuze, these immanent criteria can be summarized in two principles.

First, the claim that meaning is use is valid only if one begins with elements that in themselves, apart from their use, are devoid of any signification. Modern literature has tended to pose this question in terms of the problem of a world in *fragments*, a world deprived of its unity, reduced to crumbs and chaos. We live in an age that no longer thinks in terms of a primordial Unity or Logos that we have lost (Platonism), or some future Totality that awaits us as the result of a dialectic or evolution (Hegelianism), or even a Subjectivity, whether universal or not, that could bestow a cohesion or unity upon the world (Kantianism). It is only when objective contents and subjective forms have collapsed and given way to a world of fragments, to a chaotic and multiple impersonal reality, that the work of art assumes its full meaning—"that is, exactly all the meanings one wants it to have according to its functioning; the essential point being that it functions, that the machine works."[28] The elements or parts of the literary machine, in short, must be recognized by their mutual independence, *pure singularities*, "a pure and dispersed anarchic multiplicity, without unity or totality, whose elements are welded and pasted together by the real distinction or the very absence of a link."[29] This is the principle of *difference*, which constitutes the first criterion: fragments or parts whose sole relationship is sheer difference, which are related to each other only in that each of them is different. "Dissociation" here ceases to be a negative trait of the schizophrenic and becomes a positive and productive principle of both Life and Literature.

Second, the problem of the work of art is to establish a system of communication among these parts or elements that are in themselves non-communicating. The literary work, Deleuze argues, must be seen as the unity of its parts, even though it does not unify them; the whole produced by the work is rather a "peripheral" totality that is added alongside its parts as a new singularity fabricated separately. Proust describes the *Search* as a literary apparatus that brings together heterogeneous elements and makes them function together; the work thus constitutes a whole, but this whole is itself a part that merely exists alongside the other parts, which it neither unifies nor totalizes. Yet it none the less has an effect on these parts, since it is able to create non-preexistent relations between elements that in themselves remain disconnected, and are left intact.[30] This is the empiricist principle that pervades Deleuze's philosophy, which constitutes the second criterion: *relations are always external to their terms*, and the Whole is never a principle, but rather an effect that is derived from these external relations, and that constantly varies with them. Russell demonstrated the insoluble contradictions set theory falls into when it treats the set of all sets as a Whole. This is not because the notion of the Whole is devoid of sense, but it is not a set and does not have parts; it is rather what prevents each set from closing in on itself, forcing it to extend itself into a larger set, to infinity. The Whole, in other words, is the Open, because it is its nature constantly to produce or create the new.

Deleuze thus describes his philosophy as a "logic of multiplicities," but he also insists that "the multiple *must be made*," that it is never given in itself (N 147; TP 6). This production of the multiple entails two tasks: obtain pure singularities, and establish relations or syntheses between them so as to produce a variable Whole that would be the "effect" of its disconnected parts. These are precisely the two paradoxical features of Life as a non-organic and impersonal power: it is a power of abstraction capable of extracting or producing singularities and placing them in continuous variation, and a power of creation capable of inventing ever-new relations and conjugations between these singularities. The former defines the vitality of life, the latter its power of innovation. Deleuze is here appealing, at least in part, to a model borrowed from biology, which defines Life (in the evolutionary sense) as a process consisting of the molecular production of variation and the *a posteriori* selection of these variants.[31] To be sure, Deleuze is aware of the dangers of invoking scientific propositions outside of their own domain: it is the danger of an arbitrary metaphor or a forced application. "But perhaps these dangers are averted," he writes in another context, "if we restrict ourselves to extracting from scientific operators a particular conceptualizable character which itself refers to non-scientific domains, and converges with science without applying it or making it a metaphor."[32] This is the "vitalism" to which Deleuze lays claim: not a mystical life force, but the abstract power of Life as a principle of creation.

From this point of view, the relation between the critical and the clinical becomes more complex. On the one hand, the term "critical" refers not only to criticism in the literary sense, but also to critique in the Kantian sense of the word. The philosophical question now concerns the determination of the genetic elements that condition the production of the literary work. (Deleuze, one should note, describes the "transcendental field" in a completely different manner than does Kant. Much like the genetic "code," it constitutes the conditions of real experience and not merely possible experience; and it is never larger than what it conditions, but is itself determined at the same time as it determines what it conditions.) On the other hand, the term "clinical" does not simply imply a diagnosis of a particular mode of existence, but concerns the criteria according to which one assesses the potentialities of "life" in a given work. It is no longer simply a question of ascertaining the symptomatology of a particular mode of life, but of attaining the genetic level of the double power of Life as a process.

Now in fulfilling these two vitalistic powers, modern literature can be said to have had five interrelated effects—effects that, as Deleuze suggests in his essay on Klossowski, are the inevitable consequences that follow from the death of God: *the destruction of the world, the dissolution of the subject, the dis-integration of the body, the "minorization" of politics, and the "stuttering" of language.*[33] Or rather, it would be more accurate to say that these are five themes of Deleuze's own philosophy that, in the context of his own work, enter into a certain resonance or affinity with the work of specific writers and artists. Deleuze has undertaken a formidable conceptual creation in each of these domains, and in what follows I would simply like to show, in a rather summary fashion, the role each of these themes plays in the context of Deleuze's "critique et clinique" project.

1. *The Destruction of the World* (Singularities and Events). Ontologically and logically, Deleuze locates the philosophical basis for modern literature in Leibniz. Leibniz conceives of the world as a "pure emission of singularities," and individuals (monads) are constituted by the convergence and actualization of a certain number of these singularities, which become its "primary predicates." Here, for instance, are four singularities of the life of Adam: to be the first man, to live in a garden of paradise, to have a woman emerge from one's rib, to sin. These singularities

cannot yet be defined as predicates, but constitute what Deleuze calls pure "events." Linguistically, they are like indeterminate infinitives that are not yet actualized in determinate modes, tenses, persons, and voices. The great originality of Deleuze's reading of Leibniz in both *The Fold* and *The Logic of Sense* lies in his insistence on the anteriority of this domain of singularities (the virtual) in relation to predicates (the actual).[34] "Being a sinner" is an analytic predicate of a constituted individual or subject, but the infinitive "to sin" is a virtual singularity-event in the neighborhood of which the monad "Adam" will be actualized. Such singularities constitute the genetic elements not only of an individual life, but also of the world in which they are actualized. For one can add to these four singularities a fifth one: to resist temptation. This singularity is not impossible in itself, but it is, as Leibniz put it, incompossible with the world in which Adam sinned. There is here a divergence or bifurcation in the series that passes through the first three singularities; the vectors that extend from this fifth singularity to the three others do not converge, they do not pass through common values, and this bifurcation marks a border between two incompossible worlds: Adam the non-sinner belongs to a possible world that is incompossible with our own. For Leibniz, the only thing that prevents these incompossible worlds from coexisting is the theological hypothesis of a God who calculates and chooses among them in a kind of divine game: from this infinity of possible worlds, God selects the "Best," the one richest with reality, which is defined by the set of convergent series that constitute it, and the set of monads that express it with varying degrees of clarity. Each monad, though it has neither door nor window, none the less expresses the same world in the infinite series of its predicates ("the pre-established harmony"), each of them being a different point of view on the single compossible world that God causes them to envelop ("perspectivism").

Literature acceded to its modernity, Deleuze suggests, not only when it turned to language as its condition, but when it freed the virtual from its actualizations and allowed it to assume a validity of its own. Deleuze often cites as an example Borges's famous story "The Garden of the Forking Paths," in which a purely virtual world is described in the labyrinthine book of a Chinese philosopher named Ts'ui Pen:

> In all fiction, when a man is faced with alternatives, he chooses one at the expense of others. In the almost unfathomable Ts'ui Pen, he chooses—simultaneously—all of them . . . Fang, let us say, has a secret. A stranger knocks at the door. Naturally there are various outcomes. Fang can kill the intruder, the intruder can kill Fang, both can be saved, both can die, etc. In Ts'ui Pen's work, all the possible solutions occur, each one being the point of departure for other bifurcations . . . You have come to my house, but in one of our possible pasts you are my enemy, in another, my friend.[35]

Leibniz had in fact given a similar presentation of the universe at the conclusion of the *Theodicy*—"an astonishing text," says Deleuze, "that we consider a source of all modern literature."[36] In Ts'ui Pen's labyrinth, however, God is no longer a Being who compares and chooses the richest compossible world, as in the *Theodicy*; he has now become a pure Process that passes through all these virtual possibilities, forming an infinite web of diverging and converging series. Divergences, bifurcations, and incompossibles now belong to *one and the same universe*, a chaotic universe in which divergent series trace endlessly bifurcating paths: a "chaosmos" and no longer a world.

Hindered as he was by theological exigencies, Leibniz could only hint at the principle of the "ideal play" that governs the relations among singularities considered in themselves. For the inherence of predicates in the expressive monad presupposes the compossibility of the expressed world, but both in turn presuppose the distribution of pure singularities that are a-cosmic and pre-individual, and are linked together in series according to rules of convergence and divergence. This liberation of the virtual implies a fundamentally new type of narration, whose conditions Deleuze outlines in a chapter of *The Time-Image* entitled "The Powers of the False."[37] Descriptions no longer describe a pre-existing actual reality; rather, as Robbe-Grillet says, they now stand for their objects, creating and erasing them at the same time. Time ceases to be chronological, and starts to posit the simultaneity of incompossible presents or the coexistence of not-necessarily-true pasts. Abstract space becomes disconnected, its parts now capable of being linked in an infinite number of ways through non-localizable relations (as in the Riemannian or topological spaces of modern mathematics). Concrete space is no longer either stable or unstable but metastable, presenting "a plurality of ways of being in the world" that are incompatible yet coexistent. Forces lose their centers of movement and fixed points of reference and are now merely related to other forces. "Perspectivism" no longer implies a plurality of viewpoints on the same world or object; each viewpoint now opens on to another world that itself contains yet others. The "harmony" of Leibniz's world gives way to an emancipation of dissonance and unresolved chords that are not brought back into a tonality, a "polyphony of polyphonies" (Boulez). Most importantly, perhaps, the formal logic of actual predicates is replaced by a properly "transcendental" logic of virtual singularities. It is under these virtual conditions (and only under these conditions) that Deleuze and Guattari speak of a "rhizome": that is, a multiplicity in which a singularity can be connected to any other in an infinite number of ways. Deleuze distinguishes, in general, between three types of syntheses among singularities: a connective synthesis (if . . . then), which bears upon the construction of a single series; a conjunctive synthesis (and . . . and), which is a method of constructing convergent series; and, most importantly, a paradoxical disjunctive synthesis (either . . . or), which affirms and distributes divergent series and turns disjunction into a positive and synthetic principle. (One of the essential questions posed by *The Logic of Sense* concerns the conditions in which disjunction can be a synthetic principle and not merely a procedure of exclusion.)[38] Narration, in short, can describe this virtual domain only by becoming fundamentally falsifying: neither true nor false in content—an undecidable alternative—but false in its form, what Nietzsche called the creative power of the false.[39]

Many of Deleuze's analyses of literature in *Difference and Repetition* and *The Logic of Sense* concern the various techniques by which such disjunctive syntheses have been put to use in language by various writers. *The Logic of Sense*, for instance, includes an analysis of the various types of "portmanteau words" created by Lewis

Carroll, which make language ramify and bifurcate in every direction: the contracting word, which forms a connective synthesis over a single series ("Your Royal Highness" is contracted into "y'reince"); the circulating word, which forms a conjunctive synthesis between two heterogeneous series (Snark = snake + shark; slithy = slimy + lithe, and so on); and the disjunctive word, which creates an infinite ramification of coexistent series (frumious = furious + fuming, in which the true disjunction is between" fuming-furious" and "furious-fuming," which in turn creates ramifications in other series).[40] Raymond Roussel produced his texts by making two divergent series resonate. In *La Doublure* this procedure rests on the double meaning of a homonym (the title can mean either "The Understudy" or "The Lining"); the space opened at the heart of the word is filled by a story and by objects that themselves take on a double meaning, each participating in two stories at the same time. *Impressions of Africa* complicates the procedure, starting with a quasi homonym, "billard/pillard," but hiding the second story within the first.[41] Gombrowicz's *Cosmos* is similarly structured around a series of hanged animals and a series of feminine mouths, which communicate with each other by means of strange interfering objects and esoteric words. Joyce's *Ulysses* implicates a story between two series, Ulysses / Bloom, employing a multitude of procedures that almost constitute an archaeology of the modes of narration: a prodigious use of esoteric and portmanteau words, a system of correspondences between numbers, a "questionnaire" method of questions / responses, the institution of trains of multiple thoughts. *Finnegans Wake* takes the technique to its limit, invoking a letter that makes all the divergent series constitutive of the "chaosmos" communicate in a transversal dimension.[42]Such a universe goes beyond any lived or livable experience; it exists only in thought and has no other result than the work of art. But it is also, writes Deleuze, "that by which thought and art are real, and disturb the reality, morality, and economy of the world" (LS 60).

2. *The Dissolution of the Subject* (Affects and Percepts). In such a chaotic and bifurcating world, the status of the individual changes as well: the monadology becomes a nomadology. Rather than being closed upon the compossible and convergent world they express from within (the monadic subject), beings are now torn open and kept open through the divergent series and incompossible ensembles that continually pull them outside themselves (the nomadic subject).

> Instead of a certain number of predicates being excluded by a thing by virtue of the identity of its concept, each "thing" is open to the infinity of singularities through which it passes, and at the same time it loses its center, that is to say, its identity as a concept and as a self. (LS 174)

An individual is a multiplicity, the actualization of a set of virtual singularities that function together, that enter into symbiosis, that attain a certain consistency. But there is a great difference between the singularities that define the virtual plane of immanence and the individuals that actualize them and transform them into something transcendent. A wound is actualized in a state of things or in the lived experience of an individual; but in itself it is a pure virtuality on the plane of immanence that sweeps one along in *a* life. "My wound existed before me," writes Joë Bousquet, a French poet shot in World War I. "I was born to embody it."[43] The question Deleuze poses with regard to the subject is "How can the individual transcend its form and its syntactical link with a world in order to attain the universal communication of events?" (LS 178). What he calls "schizophrenization" is a limit-process in which the identity of the individual is dissolved and passes entirely into the virtual chaosmos of included disjunctions. The schizophrenic quickly shifts from one singularity to another, never explaining events in the same manner, never invoking the same genealogy ("I, Antonin Artaud, am my son, my father, my mother, and myself"), never taking on the same identity (Nijinsky: "I am God. I was not God. I am a clown of God. I am Apis. I am an Egyptian. I am a Negro. I am a Chinaman. I am a Japanese . . .").[44] If Deleuze sees a fundamental link between Samuel Beckett's work and schizophrenia, it is because Beckett likewise situates his characters entirely in the domain of the virtual or the possible: rather than trying to *realize* a possibility, they remain within the domain of the possible and attempt to *exhaust* logically the whole of the possible, passing through all the series and permutations of its included disjunctions (the permutation of "sucking stones" in *Molloy*, the combinatorial of five biscuits in *Murphy*, the series of footwear in *Watt*). In the process, they exhaust themselves physiologically, losing their names, their memory, and their purpose in "a fantastic decomposition of the self."[45]

Even without attaining this limit, however, the self is not defined by its identity but by a process of "becoming." Deleuze and Guattari analyze this concept in a long and complex chapter of *A Thousand Plateaus* (TP 232–309). The notion of becoming does not simply refer to the fact that the self does not have a static being and is in constant flux. More precisely, it refers to an objective zone of indistinction or indiscernibility that always exists between any two multiplicities, a zone that immediately precedes their respective natural differentiation.[46] In a bifurcating world, a multiplicity is defined not by its center but by the limits and borders where it enters into relations with other multiplicities and changes nature, transforms itself, follows a line of flight. The self is a threshold, a door, a becoming between two multiplicities, as in Rimbaud's formula "I is another." One can enter a zone of becoming with anything, provided one discovers the literary or artistic means of doing so. Nowhere is this idea of becoming better exemplified than in Herman Melville's *Moby-Dick*, which Deleuze and Guattari consider to be "one of the greatest masterpieces of becoming" (TP 243). The relation between Captain Ahab and the white whale is neither an imitation or mimesis, nor a lived sympathy, nor even an imaginary identification. Rather, Ahab *becomes* Moby-Dick; he enters a zone of indiscernibility where he can no longer distinguish himself from Moby-Dick, to the point where he strikes himself in striking the whale. And just as Ahab is engaged in a becoming-whale, so the animal simultaneously becomes something other: an unbearable whiteness, a shimmering pure white wall. "To me, the white whale is that wall, shoved near to me. Sometimes I think there is naught beyond. But 'tis enough."[47] What is the reality of this becoming? It is obvious that Ahab does not "really" become a whale, any more than Moby-Dick "really" becomes something else. In a becoming, one term does not become another; rather, each term encounters the other, and the becoming is something between the two, outside the two. This "something" is what Deleuze calls a pure *affect* or *percept*, which is irreducible to the affections or perceptions of a subject. "Percepts are not perceptions, they are packets of sensations and relations that outlive those who experience them. Affects are not feelings [*sentiments*], they are becomings that go beyond those live through them (they become other)" (N 137). In *Moby-Dick*, both Ahab and the whale lose their texture as subjects in favor of "an infinitely proliferating patchwork" of affects and percepts that escape their form, like the pure whiteness of the wall, or "the furrows that twist from Ahab's brow to that of the Whale, or the 'horrible contortions' of the flapping lanyards that pass through the fixed rigging and can easily drag a sailor into the sea, a subject into death" (ECC 77). "We attain to the percept and the affect only as to autonomous and sufficient beings that no longer owe anything to those who experience or have experienced them" (WP 168).

What does it mean to speak of a pure affect as an "autonomous being"? In his chapters on "the affection-image" in *The Movement-Image*, Deleuze takes as one of his examples the climactic scene of G. B. Pabst's film *Pandora's Box*. Jack the Ripper, looking dreamily into Lulu's compassionate face in the light of a lamp, suddenly sees the gleam of a bread knife over her shoulder; his face, in close-up, gasps in terror, his pupils grow wider, "the fear becomes a paroxysm"; then his face relaxes again as he accepts his destiny, given the irresistible call of the weapon and the availability of Lulu as a victim. This scene, Deleuze suggests, can be grasped in two ways. On the one hand, it defines an "actual" state of affairs, localized in a certain place and time, with individualized characters (Lulu, Jack), objects with particular uses (the lamp, the knife), and a set of real connections between these objects and characters. On the other hand, it can also be said to define a set of qualities in a pure state, outside their spatio-temporal coordinates, with their own ideal singularities and virtual conjunctions: Lulu's compassionate look, the brightness of the light, the gleam of the blade, Jack's terror, resignation, and ultimate decisiveness.[48] These are what Deleuze call pure "possibles": that is, singular qualities or powers.

In Pabst's film, brightness, terror, decisiveness, and compassion are very different qualities and powers: the first is a quality of a sensation; the second is the quality of a feeling; the third, of an action; and the last, of a state. But these qualities are not themselves either sensations, feelings, actions, or states; rather they express the quality of a possible sensation or feeling. Brightness is not the same as a particular sensation, nor is decisiveness the same as a particular action; they are rather qualities that will be actualized under certain conditions in a particular sensation (the knife blade in the light of the lamp) or a particular action (the knife in Jack's hand). They correspond to what C. S. Peirce called "Firstness," the category of the Possible, which considers qualities in themselves as positive possibilities, without reference to anything else, independently of their actualization in a particular state of affairs. According to Deleuze, Peirce seems to have been influenced here by Maine de Biran, who had already spoken of pure affections, "unplaceable because they have no relation to a determinate space, present in the sole form of a 'there is . . . ' because they have no relation to a subject (the pains of a hemiplegic, the floating images of falling asleep, the visions of madness)." "Secondness," by contrast, is the category of the Real, in which these qualities have become "forces" that are related to each other (exertion–resistance, action–reaction, excitation–response, situation–behavior, individual–milieu) and are actualized indeterminate space-times, geographical or historical milieus, and individual people.[49]

Now, what Deleuze calls an affect is precisely the "complex entity" that, at each instant, secures the virtual conjunction of a set of such singular qualities or powers (the brightness, the terror, the compassion). Art does not actualize these virtual affects; rather, it gives them "a body, a life, a universe" (WP 177). The strength of Deleuze's discussion in *The Movement-Image* lies in its analysis of the way in which, in the cinema, such qualities or powers are obtained through the close-up; when we see the face of a fleeing coward in close-up, we see "cowardice" in person, freed from its actualization in a particular person. "The possibility of drawing near to the human face," writes Ingmar Bergman, "is the primary originality and distinctive quality of the cinema" (MI 99). Ordinarily, the face of a human subject plays a role that is at once individuating, socializing, and communicative; in the close-up, however, the face becomes an autonomous entity that tends to destroy this triple function: social roles are renounced, communication ceases, individuation is suspended. The organization of the face is undone in favor of its own material traits ("parts which are hard and tender, shadowy and illuminated, jagged and curved, dull and shiny, smooth and grainy"), which become the building material, the "*hyle*," of an affect, or even a system of affects (MI 103). Sometimes a face can be reflective, immutable and without becoming, fixed on a thought or object, expressing a pure Quality that marks a minimum of movement for a maximum of unity (Lulu's compassion); sometimes, by contrast, a face can be intensive, feeling a pure Power that passes through an entire series of qualities, each of them assuming a momentary independence, but then crossing a threshold that emerges on to a new quality (Jack the Ripper's series of ascending states of terror). Between these two poles, there can be numerous intermixings. But this is the way in which the face participates in the non-organic Life of things, pushing the face to its point of nudity and even inhumanity, as if every face enveloped an unknown and unexplored landscape. For Deleuze, the affective film *par excellence* is Carl Dreyer's *The Passion of Joan of Arc*, which is made up almost exclusively of short close-ups. Joan of Arc's trial is an event actualized in a historical situation, with individuated characters and roles (Joan, the bishop, the judges), with the affections of these characters (the bishop's anger, Joan's martyrdom). But the ambition of Dreyer's film is to extract the "Passion" from the trial: "All that will be preserved from the roles and situations will be what is needed for the affect to be extracted and to carry out its conjunctions—this 'power' of anger or of ruse, this 'quality' of victim or martyrdom" (MI 106). Bergman perhaps pushed the affection-image of the face to its extreme limit: in the superimposition of faces in *Persona*, the image absorbs two beings and dissolves them in a void, having as its sole affect a mute Fear, the fear of the face when confronted with its own "effacement" (MI 99–101).

Literature has its own means of extracting affects. "A great novelist," write Deleuze and Guattari, "is above all an artist who invents unknown or unrecognized affects and brings them to light as the becoming of his characters" (WP 174). It is not that they are proposing an aesthetic of pure qualities, for affects must always be considered from the standpoint of the becomings that seize hold of them. "Pure affects imply an enterprise of desubjectivation" (TP 270). The aim of literature, for Deleuze, is not the development of forms or the formation of subjects, but the displacement or catapulting of becomings into affects and percepts, which in turn are combined into "blocks of sensation" through their virtual conjunction. In Emily Brontë's *Wuthering Heights*, for example, Catherine and Heathcliff are caught up in a double becoming ("I *am* Heathcliff") that is deeper than love and higher than lived experience, a profound passion that traces a zone of indiscernibility between the two characters and creates a block of becoming that passes through an entire series of intensive affects.[50] In Kafka's *Metamorphosis*, Gregor Samsa is caught up, like Ahab, in a becoming-animal, but he finds himself Oedipalized by his family and goes to his death (K 39). In Chrétien de Troyes's novels, one finds catatonic knights seated on their steeds, leaning on their lances, awaiting chivalry and adventure. Like Beckett's characters, "the knight of the novel of courtly love spends his time forgetting his name, what he is doing, what people say to him, he doesn't know where he is going or to whom he is speaking"—an amnesiac, anataxic, a catatonic, a schizophrenic, a series of pure affects that constitutes the becoming of the knight (TP 174). It is at this level of the affect, as a genetic element, that life and literature converge on each other: "Life alone creates such zones where living beings whirl around, and only art can reach and penetrate them in its enterprise of co-creation" (WP 173).

What we have said of affects applies equally to *percepts*. Just as the affect goes beyond the affections of a character, so the percept goes beyond the character's perceptions of the landscape. A percept, says Deleuze, is "a perception in becoming," a potentialization that raises sight to the nth power and breaks with the human perception of determinate rnilieus (ECC 88). The character's relation to the landscape, writes François Zourabichvili, "is no longer that of an autonomous and preexistent inner life and an independent external reality supposed to reflect this life"; rather, the landscape "involves one in a becoming where the subject is no longer coextensive with itself."[51] In *Moby-Dick*, Captain Ahab has perceptions of the sea, but he has them only because he has entered into a relationship with Moby-Dick that makes him become-whale, and forms a compound of sensations that no longer has need of either Ahab or the whale: the Ocean as a pure percept. In *Seven Pillars of Wisdom*, T. E. Lawrence has perceptions of the Arabian desert, but he has entered into a becoming-Arab that populates the hallucinatory haze of the desert with the affects of shame and glory: the Desert as percept. In Virginia Woolf's *Mrs. Dalloway*, Mrs. Dalloway has perceptions of the town, but this is because she has passed into the town like "a knife through everything," to the point where she herself has become imperceptible; she is no longer a person, but a becoming ("She would not say of herself, I am this, I am that"): the Town as a percept.[52] What the percept makes visible are the invisible forces that populate the universe, that affect us and make us become; characters pass into the landscape and themselves become part of the compound of sensations. These percepts are what Woolf called "moments of

the world," and what Deleuze terms "haecceities," in which the mode of individuation of "a life" does not differ in nature from that of "a climate," "a wind," "a fog,"
or "an hour of a day." They are assemblages of non-subjectified affects and percepts
that enter into virtual conjunction. "The street enters into composition with the
horse, just as the dying rat enters into composition with the air, and the beast and
the full moon enter into composition with each other" (TP 262). The landscape
is no longer an external reality, but has become the very element of a "passage of
Life." As Deleuze and Guattari put it, "We are not *in* the world, we become *with* the
world" (WP 169).

How can such a "moment of the world" be made to exist by itself, to achieve an
autonomous status? In his chapter "The Perception-Image" in *The Movement-Image*,
Deleuze shows how Vertov's "kino-eye" attempted to attain, through cinematic
means, a perception as it was "before" humans, the pure vision of a non-human eye
(the camera) that would be in matter itself, making possible the construction of an
"any-space-whatever" released from its human coordinates. Similarly, in painting,
Cézanne spoke of the need always to paint at close range, no longer to see the wheat
field, to be too close to it, to lose oneself in the landscape, without landmarks, to
the point where one no longer sees forms or even matters, but only forces, densi-
ties, intensities: the forces of folding in a mountain, the forces of germination in an
apple, the thermal and magnetic forces of a landscape. This is what Cézanne called
the world before humanity, "dawn of ourselves," "iridescent chaos," "virginity of
the world": a collapse of visual coordinates in a universal variation or interaction.
Afterward, the earth can emerge, "stubborn geometry," "the measure of the world,"
"geological foundations"—though with the perpetual risk that the earth in turn may
once again disappear in a "catastrophe."[53] Paul Klee described the act of painting
in similar terms: "not to render the visible, but to render visible"—that is, to render
visible forces that are not visible in themselves. In music, Messiaen spoke of his
sonorous percepts as "melodic landscapes" populated by "rhythmic characters."[54]
In literature, Woolf's formula was "to saturate every atom": "to eliminate all waste,
deadness, superfluity," everything that adheres to our lived perceptions; but also to
saturate the percept, "to put everything into it," to include everything.[55] Whatever
the technical means involved, such percepts can only be constructed in art, since
they belong to an eye that we do not have. "In each case style is needed—the writer's syntax, the musician's modes and rhythms, the painter's lines and colors—to
raise lived perceptions to the percept and lived affections to the affect."[56]

Affects and percepts are thus the genetic and immanent elements constitutive
of a life. "The individuation of a life," write Deleuze and Guattari, "is not the same
as the individuation of the subject that leads it or serves as its support" (TP 261).
A "life" is constructed on *an immanent plane of consistency* that knows only relations between affects and percepts, and whose composition, through the creation
of blocks of sensations, takes place in the indefinite and virtual time of the pure
event (*Aeon*). A "subject" is constructed on *a transcendent plane of organization* that
already involves the development of forms, organs, and functions, and takes place
in a measured and actualized time (*Chronos*). It is true that the opposition between
these two types of planes is abstract, since one continually and unnoticeably passes

from one to the other; it is perhaps better to speak of two movements or tendencies, since there is no subject that is not caught up in a process of becoming, and affects and percepts presuppose at least a minimal subject from which they are extracted, or as an envelope that allows them to communicate.[57] In *A Thousand Plateaus*, Goethe and Kleist are presented as almost paradigmatic examples of these two tendencies in literature. Goethe, like Hegel, insisted that writing should aim at the regulated formation of a Subject, or the harmonious development of a Form; hence his emphasis on themes such as the sentimental education, the inner solidity of the characters, the harmony between forms, the continuity of their development, and so forth. In Kleist, by contrast, feelings are uprooted from the interiority of the subject and are projected outward into a milieu of pure exteriority: love and hate are pure affects (*Gemüt*) that pierce the body like weapons; they are instances of the becomings of the characters (Achilles' becoming-woman, Penthesilea's becoming-dog). There is no subject in Kleist, but only the affects and percepts of a life that combine into "blocks of becoming," blocks that may petrify in a catatonic freeze, and then suddenly accelerate to the extreme velocity of a flight of madness ("Catatonia is: 'This affect is too strong for me'; and a flash is: 'The power of this affect is sweeping me away'").[58] Proust, who is perhaps the most frequent point of reference in Deleuze's works, combines these two tendencies in an almost exemplary manner. In the course of "lost time," Proust progressively extracts affects and percepts from his characters and landscapes, so that the "plane of composition" of the *Recherche* emerges only gradually, as the work progresses, slowly sweeping everything along in its path, until it finally appears for itself in "time regained": the forces of pure time that have now become perceptible in themselves.[59] For Deleuze, it is only by passing through the "death of the subject" that one can achieve a true individuality and acquire a proper name.

> It's a strange business, speaking for yourself, in your own name, because it doesn't at all come with seeing yourself as an ego or a person or a subject. Individuals find a real name for themselves only through the harshest exercise in depersonalization, by opening themselves to the multiplicities everywhere within them, to the intensities running through them . . . Experimentation on ourself is our only identity. (N 6; D 11).

3. *The Dis-integration of the Body* (Intensities and Becomings). The dissolution of the logical identity of the subject has as its correlate the physical dis-integration of the organic body. Beneath the organic body, and as its condition, there lies what Artaud discovered and named: the *body without organs*, which is a purely intensive body. The body without organs is one of Deleuze's most notorious concepts; it appears for the first time in *The Logic of Sense*, is developed conceptually in *Anti-Oedipus*, and is the object of a programmatic chapter of *A Thousand Plateaus* entitled "How Do You Make Yourself a Body without Organs?" (TP 149–66). Deleuze finds its biological model in the egg, which is an intensive field, literally without organs, defined solely by axes and vectors, gradients and thresholds, displacements and migrations.[60] But here again, Deleuze appeals to embryology only in order to extract a philosophical

concept from it: the body without organs is the model of Life itself, a powerful non-organic and intensive vitality that traverses the organism; by contrast, the organism, with its forms and functions, is not life, but rather that which imprisons life. But for Deleuze, the body without organs is not something that exists "before" the organism; it is the intensive reality of the body, a milieu of intensity that is "beneath" or "adjacent to" the organism and continually in the process of constructing itself. It is what is "seen," for example, in the phenomenon known as internal or external "autoscopia": it is no longer *my* head, but I feel myself inside a head; or I do not see myself in the mirror, but I feel myself in the organism I see, and so on.

In *Anti-Oedipus*, Deleuze and Guattari make use of the concept of the body without organs to describe the experience of schizophrenics, for whom the body without organs is something that is primarily *felt* under the integrated organization of the organism, as if the organs were experienced as pure *intensities* capable of being linked together in an infinite number of ways. In *Naked Lunch*, Burroughs provides a vivid literary description of such a vital schizoid body:

> No organ is constant as regards either function or position . . . sex organs sprout everywhere . . . rectums open, defecate, and close . . . the entire organism changes color and consistency in split-second adjustments . . . The human body is scandalously inefficient. Instead of a mouth and an anus to get out of order why not have one all-purpose hole to eat *and* eliminate? We could seal up nose and mouth, fill in the stomach, make an air hole direct into the lungs where it should have been in the first place.[61]

In *Lenz*, George Büchner describes the stroll of a schizophrenic whose intensive organs enter into a becoming with all the elements of nature, to the point where the distinction between self and non-self, man and nature, inside and outside, no longer has any meaning.[62] D. H. Lawrence painted the picture of a similar body without organs in *Fantasia of the Unconscious*, with the sun and the moon as its two poles, and its various planes, sections, and plexuses.[63] But schizophrenics also experience states in which this anorganic functioning of the organs stops dead, as the intensities approach the limit where intensity equals zero. It is here that the body without organs becomes a model of Death, coextensive with Life. Authors of horror stories know this well, when they appeal to the terror not of the organic corpse, but of the catatonic schizophrenic; the organism remains, with its vacant gaze and rigid postures, but the vital intensity of the body is suspended, frozen, blocked. These two poles of the body without organs—the vital anorganic functioning of the organs and their frozen catatonic stasis, with all the variations of attraction and repulsion that exist between them—translate the entire anguish of the schizophrenic. For schizophrenics experience these naked intensities in a pure and almost unendurable state: beneath the hallucinations of the senses ("I see," "I hear") and the deliriums of thought ("I think"), there is something more profound, a feeling of intensity: that is, a *becoming* or a transition ("I feel"). A gradient is crossed, a threshold is surpassed or retreated from, a migration is brought about: "I feel that I am becoming woman," "I feel that I am becoming god," "I feel that I am becoming pure matter." When

Judge Schreber, in a famous case analyzed by Freud, says he is becoming a woman and can feel breasts on his naked torso, he is expressing a lived emotion that neither resembles nor represents breasts but rather designates a zone of pure intensity on his body without organs (AO 18–19).

Now, according to Deleuze and Guattari, what we call a "delirium" is the general matrix by which the intensities and becomings of the body without organs directly invest the socio-political field. One of the essential theses of *Anti-Oedipus* is that delirious formations are not reducible to the father–mother–child coordinates of the Oedipus complex. They are neither familial nor personal but world-historical; it's the Russians that worry the schizo, or the Chinese; his mouth is dry, someone buggered him in the subway, there are spermatozoa swimming everywhere; it's Franco's fault, or the Jews' . . . The great error of psychoanalysis was to have largely ignored the social, political, geographical, tribal, and, above all, *racial* content of delirium, or to have reduced it to the familial or personal. More importantly, for Deleuze, these delirious formations constitute "kernels of art," in so far as the artistic productions of the "mad" can themselves be seen as the construction of a body without organs with its own geopolitical and racial coordinates (AO 88–9). Artaud's "theater of cruelty" cannot be separated from his confrontation with the "races," and his confrontation with forces and religions of Mexico, all of which populate his body without organs. Rimbaud's "season in hell" cannot be separated from a becoming-Mongol or a becoming-Scandinavian, a vast "displacement of races and continents," the intensive feeling of being "a beast, a Negro, of an inferior race inferior for all eternity" ("I am from a distant race: my ancestors were Scandinavians; they used to pierce their sides and drink their own blood. I will make gashes on my entire body and tattoo it. I want to be as hideous as a Mongol . . . I dreamed of crusades, of unrecorded voyages of discovery, of republics with no history, of hushed-up religious wars, revolutions in customs, displacements of races and continents").[64] Zarathustra's "Grand Politics" cannot be separated from the life of the races that leads Nietzsche to say, "I'm not German, I'm Polish."[65] Delirium does not consist in identifying one's ego with various historical figures, but of identifying thresholds of intensity that are traversed on the body without organs with proper names. Nietzsche, for example, does not suddenly lose his reason and identify himself with strange personages; rather, his delirium passes through a series of intensive states that receive various proper names, some of which designate his allies, or manic rises in intensity (Prado, Lesseps, Chambige, "honest criminals"), others his enemies, or depressive falls in intensity (Caiaphas, Wilhelm Bismarck, the "antisemites")—a chaos of pure oscillations invested by "all the names of history," and not, as psychoanalysis would have it, by "the name of the father." Even when he is motionless, the schizophrenic undertakes vast voyages, but they are voyages in intensity; he crosses the desert of his body without organs, and along the way struggles against other races, destroys civilizations, becomes a woman, becomes God.

Deleuze and Guattari seem to go even further. If the body without organs is the model of Life, and delirium is the process by which its intensities directly invest history and geography, then every literary work—and not merely the productions of the mad—can be analyzed clinically as constituting a kind of delirium.

The question one must ask is, What are the regions of History and the Universe, what are the nations and races, that are invested by a given work of art? One can make a map of the rhizome it creates, a cartography of its body without organs. In *A Thousand Plateaus*, Deleuze and Guattari propose a brief cartographic sketch of American literature. In the East, there was a search for an American code and a recoding with Europe (Henry James, Eliot, Pound); in the South, an overcoding of the ruins of the slave system (Faulkner, Caldwell, O'Connor); in the North, a capitalist decoding (Dos Passos, Dreiser); but in the West, there was a profound line of flight, with its ever-receding limits, its shifting and displaced frontier, its Indians and cultures, its madness (Kerouac, Kesey, the Beats). It is from this clinical viewpoint that Deleuze writes of the superiority of Anglo-American literature.[66] D. H. Lawrence reproached French literature for being *critical* of life rather than *creative* of life, filled with a mania for judging and being judged. But Anglo-American writers know how to leave, to push the process further, to follow a line of flight, to enter into a becoming that escapes the *ressentiment* of persons and the dominance of established orders. Yet Deleuze and Guattari constantly point to the ambiguity of such lines of flight. For is it not the destiny of literature, American and otherwise, to fail to complete the process, such that the line of flight becomes blocked or reaches an impasse (Kerouac's sad end, Céline's fascist ravings), or even turns into a pure line of demolition (Woolf's suicide, Fitzgerald's crack-up, Nietzsche's and Hölderlin's madness)?[67] Kerouac took a revolutionary "flight" (*On the Road*) with the soberest of means, but later immersed himself in a dream of a Great America and went off in search of his Breton ancestors of a superior race. Céline, after his great experimentations, became the victim of a delirium that communicated more and more with fascism and the paranoia of his father. In *Anti-Oedipus*, Deleuze and Guattari suggest that a "universal clinical theory" of literature as delirium would have to situate works of art between two poles: a "paranoiac" pole, or literature as a disease, in which the intensities of the body without organs are invested in fascizing, moralizing, nationalist, and racist tendencies ("I am one of your kind, a superior race, an Aryan"); and a "schizophrenic" pole, or literature as the measure of health, which always pushes the process further, following the line of flight, invoking an impure and bastard race that resists everything that crushes and imprisons life ("I am a beast, a nigger . . . I am of an inferior race for all eternity").

4. *The "Minorization" of Politics* (Speech Acts and Fabulation). It is here that we confront Deleuze's conception of the political destiny of literature. Just as writers do not write with their egos, neither do they write "on behalf of" an already existing people or "address" themselves to a class or nation. When great artists such as Mallarmé, Rimbaud, Klee, Berg, or the Straubs evoke a people, what they find rather is that "the people are missing."[68] For Deleuze, this implies a new conception of the "revolutionary" potential of literature. The two great modern revolutions, the American and the Soviet, shared a belief in the finality of universal history in which "the people are already there," even if they exist in an oppressed or subjugated state, blind and unconscious, awaiting their actualization, their "becoming-conscious." America sought to create a revolution whose strength would lie in a universal

immigration, a melting pot in which émigrés from all countries would be fused in a unanimist community, just as Russia sought to make a revolution whose strength would lie in a universal proletarization, a communist society of comrades without property or family. Hence the belief that literature, or even the cinema (Eisenstein's *October*, Griffith's *Birth of a Nation*), could become an art of the masses, a supremely revolutionary or democratic art. But the failure of the two revolutions, heralded by numerous factors (the Civil War and the fragmentation of the American people; Stalinism and the liquidation of the Soviets, which replaced the unanimity of peoples with the tyrannical unity of a party, and the subsequent breakup of the Soviet empire), would come to compromise this unanimist belief. In the cinema, it was the rise of Hitler that sounded the final death knell. Benjamin, and then Syberberg, showed how, in Nazism, the cinema, as the art of automatic movement, did not coincide with the "masses become subjects" but with the masses subjected and reduced to psychological automatons: politics as "art," Hitler as filmmaker (Riefenstahl's *Triumph of the Will*). If art was to find a political task, Deleuze argues, it would have to be on a new basis: that is, on the basis of this very fragmentation and breakup—not that of addressing an already existing people, but of contributing to the invention of a people who are missing. Whitman had already noted that, in America, both the people and the writer confront a double problem: a collection of non-communicating fragments or immigrants, and a tissue of shifting relations between them that must constantly be created or acquired. But these conditions were perhaps clearer in the third world, hidden as they were in the West by the mechanisms of power and the systems of majority. For when a colonizer proclaims, "There has never been a people here," the people necessarily enter into the conditions of a becoming, they must *invent themselves* in new conditions of struggle, and the task of a political literature is to contribute to the invention of this unborn people who do not yet have a language.[69]

If the people are missing, says Deleuze, it is precisely because they exist in the condition of a *minority*. In *Capitalism and Schizophrenia*, Deleuze and Guattari offer an analysis of the present state of capitalism, not in terms of its contradictions and classes, but rather in terms of its "lines of flight" and its minorities.[70] The concept of the "minor" developed by Deleuze and Guattari is a complex one, having references that are musical, literary, and linguistic as well as juridical and political. In the political context, they argue, the difference between a majority and a minority is not a quantitative one. A majority is not defined by its large numbers, but by an ideal constant or standard measure by which it can be evaluated (for instance, white, Western, male, adult, reasonable, heterosexual, residing in cities, speaking a standard language . . .); any determination that deviates from this axiomatic model, by definition and regardless of number, will be considered minoritarian. "Man" constitutes a majority, for instance, even though men are less numerous than women or children; and minorities are frequently larger in number than the majority.[71] For Deleuze and Guattari, the true theoretical opposition is between those elements that enter into the class axiomatic of capitalism and those that elude or free themselves from this axiomatic (as "undecidable propositions" of the axiomatic, or non-denumerable multiplicities). It is true that minorities are "objectively" definable states—definable in terms of language, ethnicity, or sex, with their own territorialities. It is also true that minorities must necessarily struggle to become a majority—to be recognized, to have rights, to achieve an autonomous status, and so on (women's struggle for the vote, for abortion, for jobs; the struggle of the third world; the struggle of oppressed minorities in the East and West). But for Deleuze and Guattari, these struggles are also the index of another coexistent and almost subterranean combat. For the majority is in fact an abstract standard that constitutes the analytic fact of "Nobody"; everyone, under some aspect or another, is caught up in a becoming-minor. Moreover, in a certain manner, one could say that it is the majority that implies a state of domination, and not the reverse, since it entails a subjection to the model; and that it is the process of becoming-minoritarian, as a universal figure, that constitutes what is called "autonomy" (TP 291, 106). A minority by definition has no model; *it is itself a becoming or a process*, in constant variation, and the power of a minority is not measured by its ability to enter and make itself felt within the majority system. Minorities have the potential of promoting compositions (connections, convergences, divergences) that do not pass by way of the capitalist economy any more than they do the state formation. In their "Treatise on Nomadology—The War Machine," one of the most original and important texts in A *Thousand Plateaus*, Deleuze and Guattari attempt to describe the organizational conditions of social formations constructed along a line of flight, which are by nature variable and nomadic.[72] This is what they term the "minorization" of politics, in so far as minorities must be thought of as seeds or crystals of becoming whose value is to trigger uncontrollable movements within the mean or the majority.

If modern political literature and cinema can play a role in the constitution of minorities, it is because they are no longer undertaken on the basis of a "people" who are already there, awaiting their becoming-conscious and the possibility of revolution. Rather, they are constituted on a set of impossibilities in which the people are missing, in which the only consciousness is the consciousness of violence, fragmentation, the betrayal of every revolution, the shattered state of the emotions and drives: an impasse in every direction. For Deleuze, this is what constitutes the new object of a political literature or cinema: the *intolerable*—that is, a lived actuality that at the same time testifies to the impossibility of living in such conditions. And minority writers and filmmakers, faced with an illiterate public and rampant deculturation, confront the same set of impasses in their work. On the one hand, they cannot simply appeal to the collective fictions and archaic myths of their people, since, as in Rocha's film Black *God and White Devil*, it is often these same myths (of prophetism and banditism) that cause the colonized to turn against themselves—and to intensify—the capitalist violence they suffer from without (in this case, out of a need for idolization). Culturally, one could say that minorities are doubly colonized: by the stories, films, television programs, and advertisements that are imposed on them from without, but also by their own myths that have passed into the service of the colonizer from within. Yet on the other hand, neither can writers be content to produce individual utterances as invented stories or fictions, for by appealing to their own privileged experience ("I in my position as . . . "), they break with the condition of the colonized and necessarily pass over to the side of the colonizers—even if only aesthetically, through artistic influences. As Jean-Louis Comolli puts it, writers and filmmakers take as their object a double impossibility: "the impossibility of escaping from the group and the impossibility of being satisfied with it" (TI 219).

Between these two impossibilities, however, Deleuze points to a narrow path, one in which the artist takes real (and not fictional) characters and makes use of them as "intercessors," putting them in conditions in which they are caught in the "flagrant act" of "making up fictions," of "creating legends" or "story-telling" (Pierre Perrault, Glauber Rocha, Jean Rouch). In the midst of an intolerable and unlivable situation, a becoming passes *between* the "people" who are missing and the "I" of the author who is now absent, releasing a "pure speech act" that is neither an impersonal myth nor a personal fiction, but a *collective utterance*—an utterance that expresses the impossibility of living under domination, but thereby constitutes an act of resistance, and functions as the pre-figuration of the people who are missing. The author takes a step toward real characters, but these characters in turn take a step toward the author: a double becoming. Such collective utterances constitute what Pasolini termed *free indirect discourse*: that is, a newly created speech act that sets itself up as an autonomous form, a pure event that effectuates two acts of subjectivation simultaneously, as if the author could express himself only by becoming another through a real character, and the character in turn could act and speak only if his gestures and words were being reported by a third party.[73] When an author produces a statement in this way, it occurs necessarily as a function of a national, political, and social community—even if the objective conditions of this community are not yet given for the moment except in the literary enunciation. In literature, Deleuze frequently appeals to the texts of Kafka (in central Europe) and Melville (in America) that present literature as the collective utterance of a minor people who find their expression in and through the singularity of the writer, who in his very solitude is all the more in a position to express potential forces, and to be a true collective agent, a leaven or catalyst (as Klee says, "We can do no more").[74] Under these conditions, the speech act appears as a true *genetic element*, a virtuality that is capable of linking up, little by little, with other speech acts so as to constitute the free indirect discourse of a people or a minority, even if they as yet exist only as the potential of "diabolical powers to come or revolutionary forces to be constructed" (K 18).

In a different context, this is what Bergson termed "fabulation," which he saw as a visionary faculty that consists in creating gods and giants, "semi-personal powers or effective presences"; though it is first exercised in religion, Deleuze suggests that this is a faculty that is freely developed in art and literature, a mythmaking or fabulating function that brings *real* parties together to produce collective utterances or speech acts as the germ of a people to come. "We ought to take up Bergson's notion of fabulation," writes Deleuze, "and give it a political meaning."[75] Minority writers may find themselves surrounded by the ideology of a colonizer, the myths of the colonized, the discourse of intellectuals, and the information of the communications media that threatens to subsume them all; this is the material they have to work on. But "fabulation" is a function that extracts from them a pure speech act, a creative storytelling that is, as it were, the obverse side of the dominant myths and fictions, an act of resistance whose political impact is immediate and inescapable, and that creates a line of flight on which a minority discourse and a people can be constituted. "A minority never exists ready-made; it is only formed on lines of flight, which are also its way of advancing or attacking."[76] This fundamental affinity between the work of art and a people who are missing may never be entirely clear. There is no work of art that does not appeal to a people that does not yet exist. But artists, it is true, can only *invoke* a people; although their need for a people goes to the very heart of what they do, they cannot *create* a people, and an oppressed people cannot concern itself with art. Yet when a people creates itself, Deleuze suggests, through its own resources and sufferings, it does so in a way that links up with something in art, or rather that links up art with what it was lacking. Fabulation in this sense is a function common to both the people and art.

5. *The "Stuttering" of Language* (Syntax and Style). Finally, for Deleuze, the process of "becoming-minor" also describes the effect that literature has on language. Proust said that great literature opens up a kind of foreign language within the language in which it is written, as if the writer were writing as a foreigner or minority within his own language.[77] This foreign language is not another language, even a marginalized one, but rather the becoming-minor of language itself. Or as Deleuze puts it in his essay "He Stuttered," the writer introduces into language a stuttering, which is not simply a stuttering in speech, but a stuttering of the language itself (ECC 107–14). In this linguistic context, Deleuze and Guattari argue that the terms *major* and *minor* do not qualify two different languages, but rather two different treatments of language, two usages or functions of the same language, and link up in a direct manner with the political question of minorities.

This is not to deny the reality of the distinction between a major language and a minor language, between a language of power and a language of the people. Minorities and immigrants are often bilingual or multilingual, living in a "major" language that they often speak poorly, and with which they have difficult political relations; in some cases, they may no longer even know their own "minor" language or mother tongue. But this distinction requires a *genetic* account: under what conditions does a language assume power in a country, or even on a worldwide scale? Conversely, by what means can one ward off linguistic power? It is not enough to say that victors impose their language on the vanquished (though this is usually the case), for the mechanisms of linguistic power are more subtle and diffuse, passing through extensible and reversible functions, which are the object of active political struggles and even micro-struggles. Henri Gobard, in his book *L'Aliénation linguistique*, for which Deleuze wrote a short preface, has attempted to go beyond the simple major–minor duality by distinguishing four different types of language: *vernacular* (maternal or territorial languages of rural origin), *vehicular* (languages of commerce and diplomacy, which are primarily urban), *referential* (national or cultural languages that operate through a recollection or reconstruction of the past), and *mythic* (languages that refer to a spiritual, magical, or religious domain).[78] More precisely, these distinctions refer to different *functions* that can be assumed (or lost) by diverse languages in concrete situations, or by a single language over the course of time, each with its own mechanisms of power. For instance, Latin, as a language of power, was a vehicular language in Europe before becoming a referential or cultural language, and then a mythic one. When fundamentalists protest against having the Mass said in a vernacular language, they are trying to prevent Latin from being robbed of its mythic or religious functions; similarly, classicists bemoan the fact that Latin has been stripped of its referential or cultural function, since the educational forms of power it once exercised have been replaced by other forms. The present imperialism of American English, as a worldwide linguistic power, is due not only to its status as today's vehicular language, but also to the fact that it has managed to infiltrate various cultural, mythic, and even vernacular functions in other languages (hence the purist's denunciations of "Franglais," English contaminations of the contemporary French vernacular).

But these various mechanisms of power, by which one language acquires an imperialist power over others, are at the same time accompanied by a very different tendency. For the more a language acquires the characteristics of a major language, the more it tends to be affected by internal variations that transpose it into a "minor" language. English, because of its very hegemony, is constantly being worked on from within by the minorities of the world, who nibble away at that hegemony and create the possibility of new mythic functions, new cultural references, new vernacular languages with their own uses. British English is set in variation by Gaelic and Irish English; American English is set in variation by black English and various "ghetto languages," which cannot be defined simply as a sum of mistakes or infractions against "standard" English. Minor languages are not simply sublanguages (dialects or idiolects), but express the potential of the major language to enter into a becoming-minoritarian in all its dimensions and elements. Such movements, to be sure, have their own political ambiguities, since they can mix together revolutionary aspirations with reactionary and even fascistic tendencies (archaisms, neo-territorialities, regionalisms). Moreover, from a political viewpoint,

> it is difficult to see how the upholders of a minor language can operate if not by giving it (if only by writing in it) a constancy and homogeneity making it a locally major language capable of forcing official recognition (hence the political role of writers who assert the rights of a minor language). (TP 102)

The acquisition of power by a language and the becoming-minor of that language, in other words, are coexistent movements that are constantly passing and converting into each other in both directions. In this manner, Deleuze and Guattari, following Gobard, propose a kind of "geo-linguistics," a "micro-politics" of language (in Foucault's sense), in which the internal functions of language are inseparable from incessant movements of deterritorialization and reterritorialization.

What, then, does it mean to speak of a "minor literature"? Many of the writers that interest Deleuze are indeed those that find themselves in situations of bi- or multilingualism: Kafka, a Czech Jew writing in German; Beckett, an Irishman writing in French and English; Luca, a Romanian writing in French. It was Kafka who spoke most forcefully of the set of linguistic "impossibilities" that this situation imposed on him as a writer: the impossibility of *not* writing, "because national consciousness, uncertain or oppressed, necessarily exists by means of literature"; the impossibility of writing *other* than in the dominant language of German, because the Prague Jews had forgotten or repressed their native Czech vernacular, viewed Yiddish with disdain or suspicion, and could only dream of Hebrew as the mythic language of Zionism; the impossibility of writing *in* German, not only because of its standardized and vehicular status as a "paper language," but also because the "deterritorialized" elements introduced by Prague German into the Middle-High German of Vienna and Berlin threatened its cultural function ("a withered vocabulary, an incorrect use of prepositions, the abuse of the pronominal, the employment of malleable verbs," and so on).[79] For Deleuze, however, the situation described by Kafka is the situation faced by all writers, even those who are not bilingual. Creation, he says, necessarily takes place in such choked passages:

> We have to see creation as tracing a path between impossibilities ... A creator who is not grabbed around the throat by a set of impossibilities is not a creator. A creator is someone who creates their own impossibilities, and thereby creates the possible at the same time ... Without a set of impossibilities, you won't have a line of flight, the exit that is creation, the power of falsity that is truth. (N 133)

And Kafka's solution to this problem, his way out of the impasse, also has a validity that extends beyond his own situation. Rather than writing in Czech, Yiddish, or Hebrew, he chose to write in the German language of Prague, with all its poverty, and to push it even further in the direction of deterritorialization, "to the point of sobriety." Rather than writing in a minor language, he instead invented a minor *use* of the major language.

A minor literature, in other words, is not necessarily a literature written in a minor or marginalized language; for Deleuze, the term "minor" does not refer to specific literatures but rather to the revolutionary conditions for every literature, even (and especially) in the midst of a great or established literature: "Only the possibility of setting up a minor practice of a major language from within allows one to define popular literature, marginal literature, and so on" (K 18). As Deleuze and Guattari argue in a chapter of *A Thousand Plateaus* entitled "Postulates of Linguistics," the essential distinction is between two different treatments or uses of language, a major and a minor use. Language is by nature a heterogeneous and variable reality, but the variables of language can be treated in two different manners. Either one can carve out a homogeneous or standard system from a language by extracting a set of *constants* from the variables or by determining *constant relations* between them, thereby relegating pragmatics to external factors (Chomsky); or one can relate the variables of language to inherent lines of *continuous variation*, thereby making pragmatics the presupposition of all the other dimensions of language (Labov). The performative "I swear!," for example, is a very different statement depending on whether it is said by a son to his father, by a lover to his fiancée, or by a witness to a judge. But this variability can be interpreted in two different ways: either the statement can be said to remain constant in principle, its variations being produced by *de facto* and non-linguistic circumstances external to the linguistic system; or one could also say that each effectuation of the statement is an actualized variable of a virtual line of continuous variation immanent to the system, a line that remains continuous regardless of the discontinuous leaps made by the statement, and that uproots the statement from its status as a constant and produces its placing-in-variation. The first is the major treatment of language, in which the linguistic system appears in principle as a system in equilibrium, defined by its syntactical, semantic, or phonological constants; the second is the minor treatment, in which the system itself appears in perpetual disequilibrium or bifurcation, defined by pragmatic use of these constants in relation to a continuous internal variation. It may be that the *scientific* study of language, in order to guarantee the constancy of its object, requires the extraction of a systematic structure from language (though A *Thousand Plateaus* contains an interesting analysis of "minor sciences" that do not operate by means of this type of formalization) (TP 361–74). But Deleuze and Guattari suggest that this scientific model of language is inextricably linked with its political model, and the mechanisms by which a language becomes a language of power, a dominant or major language, homogenized, centralized, and standardized. When schoolteachers teach their students a rule of grammar, for example, they are not simply communicating a piece of information to them, but are transmitting an order or a command, since the ability to formulate grammatically correct sentences ("competence") is a prerequisite for any submission to social laws. "The scientific enterprise of extracting constants and constant relations," Deleuze and Guattari write, "is always coupled with the political enterprise of imposing them on speakers."[80] This is why the problem of becoming-minor is both a political and an artistic problem: "the problem of minorities, the problem of a minor literature, but also a problem for all of us: How to tear a minor literature away from its own language, allowing it to challenge the language and making it follow a sober revolutionary path?" (K 19).

For Deleuze, then, the "minor" use of language involves taking any linguistic variable—phonological, syntactical or grammatical, semantic—and placing it in variation, following the virtual line of continuous variation that subtends the entire language, and that is itself apertinent, asyntactic or agrammatical, and asemantic. It is through this minor use of language that literature brings about a decomposition or even destruction of the maternal language, but also the creation of a new minor language within the writer's own language. Many of the essays collected in *Essays Critical and Clinical* analyze the specific procedures utilized by various authors to make language "stutter" in its syntax or grammar: the schizophrenic procedures of Roussel, Brisset, and Wolfson, which constitute the very process of their psychoses; the poetic procedures of Jarry and Heidegger, who transform and transmute a living language by reactivating a dead language inside it; e. e. cummings's agrammaticalities ("he danced his did"), which stand at the limit of a series of ordinary grammatical variables; and the deviant syntax of Artaud's *cris-souffles* ("ratara ratara ratara / Atara tatararana / Otara otara katara"), which are pure intensities that mark a limit of language.[81] (In other contexts, Deleuze analyzes the phonetic stuttering of language in the theater, as in Robert Wilson's whispering without definite pitch, or Carmelo Bene's ascending and descending variations).[82] Such writers take the elements of language and submit them to a treatment of continuous variation, out of which they extract new linguistic possibilities; they invent a minor use of language, much as in music, where the minor mode is derived from dynamic combinations in perpetual disequilibrium. In a sense, this procedure of placing-in-variation is the most natural thing in the world; it is what we call a *style*. Style is a set of variations in language, a kind of modulation, and it is through style that language is pushed toward its own limit, and strains toward something that is no longer linguistic, but which language alone makes possible (such as the affects and percepts that have no existence apart from the words and syntax of the writer).[83]

> This is what style is [write Deleuze and Guattari], the moment when language is no longer defined by what it says, but by what causes it to move, to flow . . . For literature is like schizophrenia: a process and not a goal . . . a pure process that fulfills itself, and that never ceases to reach fulfillment as it proceeds—art as "experimentation."

Likewise, reading a text is never an act of interpretation, it "is never a scholarly exercise in search of what is signified, still less a highly textual exercise in search of a signifier"; it too is an act of experimentation, "a productive use of the literary machine . . . a schizoid exercise that extracts from the text its revolutionary force."[84]

Deleuze's "critique et clinique" project, in the end, can be characterized by three fundamental components:

1. the function of the proper name
2. the non-personal "multiplicity" or "assemblage" designated by the name; and
3. the active "lines of flight" of which these multiplicities are constituted.

The first two components define what we have called the symptomatological method. For Deleuze, writers are like clinicians or diagnosticians who isolate a particular "possibility of life," a certain way of being or mode of existence whose symptomatology is set forth in their work. In these conditions, the proper name refers not to the person of the author, but to the constellation of signs and symptoms that are grouped together in the work itself. The literary technique and style of the writer (the critical) is directly linked to the creation of a differential table of vital signs (the clinical), so that one can speak of a clinical "beckettism," "proustism," or "kafkaism" just as one speaks of a clinical "sadism" or "masochism." But the symptomatological method is only one aspect of Deleuze's project. The deeper philosophical question concerns the conditions that make possible this production of new modes of existence: that is, the ontological principle of Life as a non-organic and impersonal power. We have seen the two aspects of this active power of Life: on the one hand, it is a power of abstraction capable of producing elements that are in themselves asignifying, acosmic, asubjective, anorganic, agrammatical, and asyntactic (singularities and events, affects and percepts, intensities and becomings) and placing them in a state of continuous variation; on the other hand, it is a power of invention capable of creating ever-new relations between these differential or genetic elements (syntheses of singularities, blocks of becomings, continuums of intensities). These two ontological powers of Life—the production of variation and the selection and synthesis of variants—are for Deleuze the indispensable conditions of every creation.

Deleuze describes the artistic activity of the writer in the same terms. "The aim of writing," he says, "is to carry life to the state of a non-personal power" (D 50). The writer, like each of us, begins with the multiplicities that have invented him or her as a formed subject, in an actualized world, with an organic body, in a given political order, having learned a certain language. But at its highest point, writing, as an activity, follows the abstract movement of a line of flight that extracts or produces differential elements from these multiplicities of lived experience and makes them function as variables on an immanent "plane of composition." "This is what it's like on the plane of immanence: multiplicities fill it, singularities connect with one another, processes or becomings unfold, intensities rise and fall."[85] The task of the writer is to establish non-preexistent relations between these variables in order to make them function together in a singular and non-homogeneous whole, and thus to participate in the construction of "new possibilities of life": the invention of new compositions in language (style and syntax), the formation of new blocks of sensation (affects and percepts), the production of new modes of existence (intensities and becomings), the constitution of a people (speech acts and fabulation), the creation of a world (singularities and events). The negative terms we have used to describe the above rubrics (destruction, dissolution, disintegration, and so on) are therefore only partial characterizations, since they are merely the necessary propaedeutic to this positive activity of creation and invention. "To be present at the dawn of the world . . ."

It is this ontological and creative power of Life, finally, that functions as the ethical principle of Deleuze's philosophy. For what constitutes the health or activity of a mode of existence is precisely its capacity to construct such lines of flight, to affirm the power of life, to transform itself depending on the forces it encounters (the "ethical" vision of the world). A reactive or sickly mode of existence, by contrast, cut off from its power of action or transformation, can only judge life in terms of its exhaustion or from the viewpoint of the higher values it erects against Life (the "moral" vision of the world). "Critique et clinique," from start to finish, is as much an ethical project as it is an aesthetic one. In this regard, perhaps the most important piece included in *Essays Critical and Clinical*, in terms of Deleuze's own *œuvre*, is the programmatic essay entitled "To Have Done with Judgment."[86] For Deleuze, it is never a question of *judging* a work of art in terms of transcendent or universal criteria, but of *evaluating* it clinically in terms of its "vitality," its "tenor of Life": Does the work carry the process of Life to this state of an impersonal power? Or does it interrupt the process, stop its movement, and become blocked in the *ressentiment* of persons, the rigors of organic organization, the clichés of a standard language, the dominance of an established order, the world "as it is," the judgment of God? The renunciation of judgment does not deprive one of the means of distinguishing the "good" and the "bad." On the contrary, good and bad are both states of the becoming of Life, and can be evaluated by criteria that are strictly immanent to the mode of existence or the work of art itself.[87] Life does not function in Deleuze's philosophy as a transcendent principle of judgment but as an immanent process of production or creation; it is neither an origin nor a goal, neither an *arche* nor a *telos*, but a pure process that always operates in the middle, *au milieu*, and proceeds by means of experimentations and unforeseen becomings. Judgment, by contrast, operates with pre-existing criteria that can never apprehend the creation of the new, and what is of value can only come into existence by "defying judgment."

It is sometimes said that we must learn from life and not bury ourselves in books, and in a certain sense this is no doubt true. Yet we must also say that art and literature have no other object than Life, and that a "passage of Life" can only be seen or felt in a process of creation, which gives the non-organic and impersonal power of Life a consistency and autonomy of its own, and draws us into its own becoming.

> Art is never an end in itself [write Deleuze and Guattari]. It is only an instrument for tracing lines of lives, that is to say: all these real becomings that are not simply produced *in* art, all these active flights that do not consist in fleeing *into* art . . . but rather sweep it away with them toward the realms of the asignifying, the asubjective. (TP 187)

This is the point at which "critique" and "clinique" become one and the same thing, when life ceases to be personal and the work ceases to be merely literary or textual: a life of pure immanence.[88]

Sensation

Deleuze on Bacon: Three Conceptual Trajectories in "The Logic of Sensation"

*F*rancis *Bacon: The Logic of Sensation* is the record of Deleuze's confrontation with the work of the Irish-born British painter Francis Bacon (1909–92).[1] The book originally appeared in 1981, when Bacon and Deleuze were both at the height of their powers. Although already well known at the time, Bacon was hardly a canonical painter and was even suspect in certain circles for his figural leanings. When Deleuze's book appeared, it received a number of favorable reviews, but then was largely passed over in silence.[2] Today, however, *The Logic of Sensation* has come to be recognized as one of Deleuze's most significant texts in aesthetics. It was the first book Deleuze published after his decade-long collaboration with Félix Guattari on the two volumes of *Capitalism and Schizophrenia*. In the following years, Deleuze would publish a number of works on the arts, including the two-volume *Cinema* (1983, 1985), *The Fold: Leibniz and the Baroque* (1988), and the writings on literature collected in *Essays Critical and Clinical* (1993). *The Logic of Sensation* can thus be read not only as a philosophical study of Bacon's paintings but also as a crucial text within Deleuze's broader philosophy of art.[3]

Deleuze insisted that he wrote on the arts, not as a critic, but as a philosopher, and that his works on the various arts must therefore be read as works of "philosophy, nothing but philosophy, in the traditional sense of the word."[4] In *What is Philosophy?* (1991), Deleuze famously defines philosophy as an activity that consists in the creation of concepts. "One can very easily think without concepts, but as soon as there is a concept, there is truly philosophy" (N 32). Art itself is an equally creative activity, of course, but it is an activity whose object is to create sensible aggregates rather than concepts. As a philosopher, then, Deleuze's aim in his analyses of the arts is to create the concepts that correspond to these sensible aggregates. In *The Logic of Sensation*, Deleuze will invent an entire series of philosophical concepts that relate to particular aspects of Bacon's paintings, but which also find a place in what Deleuze will call "a general logic of sensation" (FLB 3). The text is organized in quasi-musical fashion, divided into seventeen sequences that develop concepts as if they were melodic lines, which in turn enter into increasingly complex contrapuntal relations that, taken together, form a kind of conceptual composition that parallels Bacon's sensible compositions. Readers who approach the book expecting a work of art criticism will be disappointed. There is little discussion of the socio-cultural milieu in which Bacon lived and worked; nor of his artistic influences or contemporaries, such as Lucian Freud or Frank Auerbach; nor of his personal life (his homosexuality, his lovers and friends, his drinking and gambling, his nights at the Colony Room Club), which played such an evident role in Bacon's work and in his choice of subjects. Even the secondary sources are sparse. Apart from two short texts by the French writers Michel Leiris and Marc Le Bot, the only secondary book Deleuze refers to is John Russell's 1971 now-classic study, *Francis Bacon*.[5] The links Deleuze establishes with Bacon's work are, as often as not, with writers (Conrad, Proust, Beckett, Kafka, Burroughs, Artaud) and musicians (Messiaen, Schumann, Berg) that figure prominently in Deleuze's other writings, but whom Bacon may or may not have been influenced by or even read / listened to. In this sense, *The Logic of Sensation* is a highly personal book, though it is hardly written in a personal style.

Deleuze wrote his study of Bacon at the suggestion of Harry Jancovici, the editor of the series in which the book first appeared, which was entitled *La Vue le texte*. The aim of the series was to explore the resonances between the visual arts and domains such as philosophy and literature, and it would come to include texts by the philosopher Jean-François Lyotard and the writer Michel Butor.[6] Deleuze never explains why he chose to write on Bacon in particular, and he scarcely mentioned Bacon in the seminars on painting he gave shortly after writing the book. Bacon, however, had a strong presence in Paris during the 1970s and 1980s. He maintained a studio near the Place des Vosges and was close friends with Michel Leiris, whose portrait he painted several times and who in turn wrote several important texts on Bacon.[7] It was the Grand Palais exhibition of 1971 in Paris that had cemented Bacon's international reputation, and the exhibition at the Galerie Claude Bernard in 1977 further solidified his position.[8] Deleuze undoubtedly encountered Bacon's work at some point at an exhibition in Paris—in a later interview, Deleuze says that he frequently went to art exhibitions and films on weekends, on the lookout for pre-cisely this kind of "encounter."[9] The book itself attests to the profound resonances Deleuze found between his own work and Bacon's paintings.

The relationship between the two men, however, was not personal. Deleuze and Bacon met only once, some time after the book was published. Deleuze had sent the original manuscript to Bacon, who was intrigued by the book and delighted with the attention. The two arranged to spend an evening together, and Deleuze arrived with what Bacon described as a little "court" of admirers. Michael Peppiatt, in his biography *Francis Bacon: Anatomy of an Enigma*, reports that, "although there was a perceptible sympathy and admiration between the two men, no friendship evolved."[10] Deleuze later recollected some of his impressions in an interview:

> You can sense in him a power and violence, but also a very great charm. After he is seated for an hour or so, he contorts himself in every direction, as if he were himself a Bacon painting . . . When I met Bacon, he said that he dreamed of painting a wave, but dared not believe such a venture could be successful. It is a lesson of the painter, a great painter who says to himself, "If only I could

manage to catch a little wave . . ." It's very Proustian; or Cézannian: "Ah! If only I could manage to paint a little apple!"[11]

According to Peppiatt, the two never met again.

Deleuze said that he wrote this book primarily with two things in front of him: reproductions of Bacon's paintings and the texts of David Sylvester's interviews with Bacon, which had been published in 1975 under the title *The Brutality of Fact*.[12] To some degree, this approach reflects the tension that exists between percepts and concepts: how does one talk in one medium (concepts) about the practices of another (percepts)? The dictum that one should heed what artists do, not what they say, is no less true for Bacon than for other artists. "I have often tried to talk about painting," he cautioned, "but writing or talking about it is only an approximation, as painting is its own language and is not translatable into words."[13] None the less, Bacon's interviews contain penetrating discussions of the practice of painting, and have been favorably compared with Delacroix's journals and da Vinci's notebooks. Deleuze himself insists that we do not listen closely enough to what painters have to say.

> The texts of painters operate much differently than their paintings . . . In general, when artists talk about what they do, they have extraordinary modesty, self-imposed rigor, and great strength. *They are the first to suggest the nature of the concepts and affects that are disengaged in their work*.[14]

Deleuze thus uses the interviews, not as definitive statements on Bacon's part, but rather as the starting point for his own conceptual inventions. Deleuze once wrote: "We sometimes dream of a history of philosophy that would list only the new concepts created by a great philosopher—his most essential and creative contribution" (TRM 55). *The Logic of Sensation* is best approached in exactly the same manner: as a book of philosophical concepts. The concepts Deleuze develops are sometimes drawn from everyday language, sometimes from specific scientific and art historical traditions, sometimes from Bacon's interviews, sometimes from Deleuze's own philosophical vocabulary. But the concepts themselves enter into multiple resonances and interactions, such that it is possible to trace numerous trajectories through the "rhizome" of the book. The remarks that follow attempt to isolate three such conceptual trajectories in *The Logic of Sensation*, which respectively concern Deleuze's formal analyses of Bacon's paintings, the general "logic of sensation" that underlies them, and the techniques through which painters can be said to participate in such a logic of sensation (the "coloring sensation").

The first trajectory concerns the concepts that Deleuze utilizes in his formal analyses of Bacon's work, which, he says, move "from the simplest to the most complex" aspects of Bacon's paintings. The question Deleuze poses to an artwork is not "What does it mean?" but rather "How does it function?" Deleuze thus treats Bacon's work as a multiplicity (although he does not use this term in the book) and attempts to isolate and identify the components of that multiplicity. Deleuze frequently returns to the three simplest aspects of Bacon's paintings—the Figure, the surrounding fields of color, and the outline or contour that separates the two—which taken together form a "highly precise system" that serves to isolate the Figure in Bacon's paintings (Chapter 1). But a first level of complexity immediately intervenes: the fields of color tend to curl around the contour and envelop the Figure, but at the same time the Figure itself tends to strain toward the fields, passing through wash-basins, umbrellas, and mirrors, subjected to the forces that contort it, that deform or contract it in a kind of "derisory athleticism," revealing the intensive "body without organs" beneath the extensive organic body (Chapter 3). In some cases, the Figure is dissipated entirely, leaving behind nothing but a sand dune or a jet of water—a pure Force that replaces the Figure (Chapter 5). A second level of complexity appears in the works in which Bacon paints coupled Figures that none the less resonate together in a single "matter of fact" (Chapter 9). A third level of complexity emerges in the triptychs, where this "matter of fact" includes not only the distances that separate the distinct panels but also the forced movement or *rhythms* that constitute the true Figure of the triptychs: the steady or "attendant" rhythm; an active, rising, or diastolic rhythm; and a passive, descending, or systolic rhythm (FB 60–70). Deleuze not only identifies these three fundamental rhythms found in Bacon's triptychs, but he also shows that even the simple paintings already function like triptychs, with their complex movements and combinatorial variability. A final level of complexity arises with regard to Bacon's handling of color (Chapter 10), and his construction of a properly "haptic" space, since it is primarily through the use of color (relations of tonality) that he brings about all these effects in his works (isolation, deformation, coupling, rhythm . . .). Deleuze's book is marked throughout by specific and detailed analyses of individual paintings, as well as assessments of their position within the movement of Bacon's *œuvre* as a whole.

The fundamental concept in all these analyses, however, is that of the *Figure*. Both modern art and modern philosophy can be said to have converged on a similar problem: both renounced the domain of representation and instead took the conditions of representation as their object. Deleuze suggests that twentieth-century art remained far ahead of philosophy in this regard, and that philosophers still have much to learn from painters. But he also suggests that there are two general routes through which modern painting escaped the clichés of representation and attempted to attain a "sensation" directly: either by moving toward *abstraction*, or by moving toward what Lyotard termed the *figural*. An abstract art like that of Mondrian or Kandinsky, though it rejected classical figuration, in effect reduced sensation to a purely *optical* code that addressed itself primarily to the eye. By contrast, abstract expressionism, like that of Pollock, went beyond representation, not by painting abstract forms, but by dissolving all forms in a fluid and chaotic texture of *manual* lines and colors (Chapter 14). Bacon in effect followed a "middle path" between these two extremes, the path of the Figure, which finds its precursor in Cézanne. Whereas "figuration" refers to a form that is related to an object it is supposed to represent, the "Figure" is the form that is connected to a sensation, and that conveys the violence of this sensation directly to the nervous system. In Bacon's paintings, it is primarily the human body that plays this role of the Figure;

it functions as the material support or framework that sustains a precise sensation. This is Bacon's solution to the problem he shares with Cézanne: how to extract the Figure from its figurative, narrative, and illustrational links? How to "paint the sensation" or "record the fact"?

This brings us to the second trajectory of concepts, which concerns the nature of the "logic of sensation" that constitutes the object of Deleuze's analyses in this book. The notion of "sensation" one finds in Deleuze is taken initially from the phenomenological tradition. Erwin Straus, in his classic book *The Primary World of the Senses* (1935), had established a fundamental distinction between perception and sensation.[15] Perception, he argued, is a secondary rational organization of a primary, non-rational dimension of sensation (or "sense experience," *le sentir*). Earlier in the century, Marius von Senden had recorded the experiences of congenitally blind people who were given sight after the operation to remove cataracts was developed. Initially such patients were afflicted by a painful chaos of forms and colors, a gaudy confusion of visual sensations within which they could distinguish neither shapes nor space. They would acquire a perception of the world only after an often-painful process of learning and apprenticeship, during which they developed the schemata and "Gestalten" capable of providing this pre-reflective sense experience with the coordinates familiar to ordinary perception.[16] Studies of infants have revealed in them a similar sensory world populated by pure intensities (of sound, light, hunger) in which the baby cannot yet distinguish between itself and its world.[17] "In sensory experience," writes Straus, "there unfolds both the becoming of the subject and the happenings of the world. I become only insofar as something happened, and something happens (for me) only insofar as I become . . . In sensing, both self and world unfold simultaneously for the sensing subject."[18]

This pre-rational world of sensation is not prior to the world of perception or representation, but strictly speaking is coextensive with it. It is precisely this world, the world of "lived experience," that phenomenologists have attempted to describe. Straus, for instance, proposed a related distinction between what he called geography and landscape. The geographical world, the world recorded on maps, is perceptual and conceptual; it is an abstract system of coordinates with an unspecified perspective. A landscape, by contrast, is sensory; it is a perspectival world, enclosed by a horizon that moves as our body moves. In a landscape, we do not so much move *in* space as space moves *with* us. Similarly, Maurice Merleau-Ponty, following Kurt Goldstein, distinguished between "touching" and "pointing": a patient who is able to scratch his nose at the point where a mosquito is biting him is unable, a moment later, to point to his nose with his finger. The former takes place within the "intentional" system of bodily space (sensation), whereas the latter requires an abstract coordination of points in external space (perception); in certain pathological cases the transition from the first to the second is blocked.[19] It is often difficult to separate sensation from perception, landscape from geography, since conceptual perception is such an integral part of our everyday experience of the world.

Yet for all his indebtedness to thinkers such as Straus, Merleau-Ponty, and Henri Maldiney, Deleuze is not a phenomenologist. Phenomenology is insufficient because it merely invokes the "lived body." But the lived body, says Deleuze, is still a "paltry thing in comparison with a more profound and almost unlivable Power," which is precisely the power of rhythm in its confrontation with chaos (FB 39). Sensation is itself constituted by the "vital power" of rhythm, and it is in rhythm that Deleuze locates the "logic of sensation" indicated in his subtitle, a logic that is neither cerebral nor rational. This linkage between sensation and rhythm can perhaps best be illustrated by means of a somewhat lengthy detour through Deleuze's reading of Kant's theory of perception, which forms a kind of complementary text to *The Logic of Sensation*.[20]

In the *Critique of Pure Reason*, Kant argues that perception requires a synthesis of what appears in space and time. In the first version of the transcendental deduction, Kant identifies three operations that make up a synthesis: apprehension, reproduction, and recognition. Since everything is a multiplicity and has a multiplicity of parts, perception begins when I synthesize these parts successively in an act of apprehension. I must also reproduce or "contract" the preceding parts when the following ones occur if a synthesis is to take place. These two aspects of spatiotemporal synthesis—the apprehension and reproduction of parts—are activities of the productive imagination and no longer sensibility.[21] But a third moment is required for a perceptual synthesis to be complete: this sensible complex of space and time must now be related to the form of an object (*recognition*). To be sure, one can imagine numerous sensations in which the diversity of space and time is *not* related to the object-form, such as hallucinations. It is rather *perception* as such that is constituted in such a manner that a sensible diversity is related to the form of an object. In other words, it is not so much that I perceive objects; it is rather my perception that presupposes the object-form as one of its conditions. Kant invented a famous formula for this object-form: the object = x. The object = x is a pure form of perception, just as space-time is the pure form of sensation. The object = x will receive a concrete determination (e.g., as a lion-object) only when it is related to the synthesized parts of a spatiotemporal diversity (a long mane, a loud roar, a heavy step . . .), such that I can say, "So it's a lion!" But the multiplicity of sensations that appear to us in the manifold of experience would never be referred to an object if we did not have at our disposal the empty form of the object = x, since there is nothing within sense experience itself that accounts for the operation by which I go beyond sensible diversity toward something I call an object. Where does this form come from? The object in general, Kant tells us, is the correlate of the "I think" or the unity of consciousness; it is the expression of the *cogito*, its formal objectivation. "Therefore the real (synthetic) formula of the cogito is: I think myself, and in thinking myself, I think the object in general to which I relate a represented diversity" (KCP 15–16). The predicates that are attributed to the object = x are what Kant calls the *categories* or the pure *a priori* concepts of the understanding; and the subsumption of a sensible diversity under a concept is what Kant calls an act of *judgment*.[22]

The *Critique of Pure Reason* thus presents us with an analysis of the edifice of perception: the apprehension of successive parts, the reproduction of preceding parts, recognition by means of the form of the object in general. Kant's analysis in effect moves from the form of space and time (the pure form of sensation) to a determined spatio-temporal form (apprehension and reproduction as syntheses of the imagination) to the form of the object = x (the pure form of perception). The philosophical adventure Deleuze explores in *The Logic of Sensation* begins at this point. While the post-Kantians such as Hegel took as their starting point Kant's theory of the "transcendental unity of apperception," Deleuze in effect moves in the opposite direction, breaking with the form of recognition that grounds that unity. There are neither categories (in Kant's sense) nor mediation (in Hegel's sense) in Deleuze, and one of his most insistent themes is "to have done with judgment" (Artaud). In *The Logic of Sensation*, Deleuze pushes to its limit a trajectory inaugurated in the *Critique of Judgment*, in which Kant explored the role of the imagination freed from the legislation of the understanding. Four elements of his analyses are particularly relevant to the themes of *The Logic of Sensation*.

1. *Aesthetic comprehension.* The first is the theme of "aesthetic comprehension" (measure). In the *Critique of Pure Reason*, Kant tells us that the act of synthesis begins with the apprehension of successive parts. In the *Critique of Judgment*, however, he in effect starts over and asks a question that went unformulated in the first critique: What counts as a part? To determine what constitutes a part, the imagination must have at its disposal a constant, or at least common, unit of measure. To be sure, the understanding could intervene and provide a mathematical evaluation of magnitudes in the fixed form of a *concept* of number (this object is "10 meters high" or "4 inches wide"). But the imagination does not have recourse to concepts, and in the nature of objects there is no such constant measure. The imagination can thus begin to carry out its syntheses only by choosing a *sensible* or qualitative unit of measure. Kant notes, almost in passing, that initially such a unit of measure is found primarily in the *human body*: "A tree judged by the height of man gives, at all events, a standard for a mountain."[23] In other words, I can use the height of a human being as the unit of measure to apprehend the parts of a tree ("this tree is as tall as ten men . . ."); in turn, I can then use the height of the tree to measure the mountain behind it ("that mountain is as high as twenty trees . . ."). Even at the level of simple perception, apprehension already implies something like a "lived evaluation" or "aesthetic comprehension" of a unit of measure, and "this primary (subjective, sensory, immediate, living) measure proceeds from the body."[24] This is the moment of phenomenology in Kant: aesthetic comprehension presupposes the situatedness of our bodies in the world, our "being-in-the-world." In the *Phenomenology of Perception* (1962), Merleau-Ponty analyzed in detail the manner in which our body provides us with such a "corporeal or postural schema" on the world.[25]

2. *Rhythm.* This leads to a second theme, that of *rhythm*. What Kant is saying in the *Critique of Judgment* (§26) is that even the most elementary act of the synthesis of perception presupposes a logical act (though Kant here gives the term logic a new meaning). Beneath the successive apprehension of parts, there is a kind of logical synthesis that requires a purely aesthetic comprehension of the unit of measure. "All estimation of the magnitude of objects of nature is in the last resort aesthetic (i.e., subjectively and not objectively determined)."[26] Because the measure is subjectively determined, it is subject to constant evaluation and re-evaluation, and is therefore

in *constant variation*. The unit of measure varies in each case depending on the thing to be perceived, just as the thing to be perceived depends on the chosen unit. I may evaluate a tree in relation to the human body, but at night I may evaluate the rising moon in terms of a coin held at close range. From the viewpoint of aesthetic comprehension, I am continually in the process of changing my unit of measure according to my perceptions. Following Maldiney, Deleuze describes this aesthetic comprehension of units of measure as the grasping of a *rhythm* (though Kant himself does not use this term), which takes place *without a concept*.[27] Aesthetic comprehension is the grasping of a rhythm with regard to both the thing to be measured and the unit of measure. Beneath both the measure and the units, there is rhythm. In this sense, concepts are *metrical*: they give one the beat, but beneath the concept there is the rhythm. "Rhythms are always heterogeneous, we plunge into them in a sort of exploration," an experimentation; even if you have a concept, "you do not yet have the rhythmicity of the things which are subordinated to it. A concept, at best, will give you the beat or the tempo" (28 Mar 1981, 4 Apr 1981). Beneath concepts, one always finds rhythmic blocks or complexes of space-time, spatio-temporal rhythms, ways of being in space and in time. The *foundation* of perceptual synthesis is aesthetic comprehension, but the *ground* on which this foundation rests is the evaluation of rhythm.

3. *Chaos*. But once we have reached this point, we cannot stop. In the *Critique of Judgment*, Kant finally becomes aware of an impending catastrophe: the ground (rhythm) upon which the foundation of the synthesis rests starts to tremble, as if in an earthquake. Kant presents a disconcerting scenario: I look at something, but my imagination wavers, I become dizzy, vertiginous. First catastrophe: I seek an appropriate unit of measure, but I cannot find one; or I choose one, but it is destroyed. I choose another, but it too proves to be inadequate, as if what I am seeing is incommensurable with any unit of measure. Second catastrophe: in my panic, I can perhaps see parts, completely heterogeneous parts, but when I come to the next one, my dizzy spell only becomes worse; I forget the preceding part; I am pushed into going ever further, losing more and more. Third catastrophe: What is striking my senses is unrecognizable; it is something that goes beyond any possibility of aesthetic comprehension. My entire structure of perception, in other words, is in the process of collapsing: I can no longer *apprehend* the successive parts; I cannot *reproduce* the preceding parts as the following ones arrive; and finally I can no longer *recognize* what the thing is. I can no longer qualify the object in general. Why does this happen? Because my aesthetic comprehension—that is, the evaluation of a rhythm that would serve as a foundation of measure—has become compromised, threatened. This is what Kant calls the experience of the *sublime*. The sublime takes place when the edifice of synthesis collapses: I no longer apprehend parts, I no longer reproduce parts, I no longer recognize anything. Instead of rhythm, I find myself drowned in a *chaos*.

What Kant discovers in the *Critique of Judgment* is that the synthesis of the imagination (apprehension, reproduction, recognition), which constitutes the edifice of knowledge, rests on a base of a different nature—namely, an aesthetic comprehension of both the thing to be measured and the unit of measure. Aesthetic comprehension is not part of the synthesis; it is the foundation on which the synthesis rests. But at the same time that Kant discovers this foundation, he also discovers the extraordinary variability of its ground (rhythm) and its fundamental fragility (chaos). Between the synthesis and its foundation, there is the constant risk that something will emerge from beneath the ground and break the synthesis. Why this fundamental fragility? According to Kant, it is because there are infinite phenomena in space and time (such as the immense ocean or the starry heavens) that risk overturning the aesthetic comprehension of the unit of measure. The imagination finds itself overturned, blocked before its own limit; it discovers its own impotence. We here reach the point that Deleuze calls the "bend" in sufficient reason: it is at one and the same time that we discover both the ground of the synthesis (rhythm) and its ungrounded nature (chaos). Fortunately, we are not caught up in the sublime all the time, which would be a terrible experience; normally we manage to hold on to our perception, and to relate spatio-temporal diversities to the object-form. The sublime, however, rests on a suppression of perception, an experience of the formless or the deformed. And yet: chaos itself can also be a germ of order or rhythm, and it is this rhythm–chaos couplet that lies at the heart of *The Logic of Sensation*.

When Deleuze was asked if the aim of *The Logic of Sensation* was to make readers see Bacon's paintings better, he conceded that it would necessarily have that effect if it succeeded.

> But [he continued] I believe that it has a higher aspiration, something everyone dreams of: to approach something that would be the common ground [*fond*] of words, lines, and colors, and even sounds. To write on painting, to write on music always implies this aspiration. (TRM 186)

This "common ground" is, precisely, rhythm:

> Rhythm appears as music when it invests the auditory level and as painting when it invests the visual level. This is a "logic of the senses," as Cézanne said, which is neither rational nor cerebral. What is ultimate is thus the relation between sensation and rhythm, which places in each sensation the levels and domains through which it passes. (FB 37)

In painting, it was Cézanne and Klee who best exemplified this complex relation between chaos and rhythm. Cézanne said that the painter must look beyond a landscape to its chaos; he spoke of the need to always paint at close range, to be so close to a wheat field that one loses oneself in the landscape, so that one no longer sees forms, or even matter, but only forces. Cézanne called this the "world before humanity," a complete collapse of visual coordinates in a universal variation or interaction, out of which, in the act of painting, the earth could emerge with its "stubborn geometry."[28] Similarly, Paul Klee, in his text *On Modern Art*, wrote of how rhythm emerges from chaos, and how the "grey point" jumps over itself and organizes a rhythm, "the grey point having the double function of being both chaos and at the same time a rhythm insofar as it dynamically jumps over itself."[29]

Translated into Kantian terms, both Cézanne and Klee mark the movement by which one moves from the synthesis of perception (apprehension, reproduction, recognition) to aesthetic comprehension (rhythm) to the catastrophe (chaos), and back again; the painter passes through a catastrophe (the diagram) and in the process produces a form of a completely different nature (the Figure).

4. *Force*. But there is a final moment to this Kantian trajectory. Kant himself presents us with a kind of consolation: at the very moment the imagination discovers its impotence, it makes us discover within ourselves a higher faculty that is stronger than the imagination: the faculty of Ideas, which is like a faculty of the infinite, of the supersensible. What is this faculty of Ideas? Kant famously identified two types of the sublime: the mathematical sublime and the dynamical sublime. For Deleuze, the latter is more profound than the former because the dynamical sublime finds its figure in the "unformed" or the "deformed" (the undoing of the object-form). The forces of Nature are unleashed: a flood, a fire, an avalanche, a hurricane at sea. What do I experience? The fact that I am nothing. It is all too much for me, too strong, too overwhelming, and I experience a kind of terror. As a mere human, I am nothing compared to Nature; faced with the unformed or deformed power of Nature, my own intensive power is reduced to close to zero. But at the same time, what is thereby awakened in me is a new power, a spiritual power, a faculty of Ideas that Kant identifies as the faculty of Reason, and by which humanity is revealed to be superior to Nature, pointing beyond Nature toward our spiritual destiny as moral beings (the noumenal as transcendent).[30]

But this is where Deleuze breaks with Kant and inverts the critical philosophy. For Deleuze, the faculty of ideas is no longer identified with Reason; rather, Deleuze posits Ideas within sensibility itself and defines them, not by their transcendence to Nature, but rather in terms of their immanence to experience itself (the noumenal as immanent). Ideas remain supra-sensible, but they now reveal the forces or intensities that lie behind sensations, and which draw us into non-human or inhuman *becomings*. In Deleuze, in other words, the power of Nature in the unformed or the deformed appears in the form of the *non-organic life of things*:

> The non-organic life of things, a frightful life, which is oblivious to the wisdom and limits of the organism . . . It is the vital as potent pre-organic germinality, common to the animate and the inanimate, to a matter which raises itself to the point of life, and to a life which spreads itself through all matter. (MI 50–5)

Bacon's primary subject matter is the "body without organs" that lies beneath the organism, the body in so far as it is deformed by a plurality of invisible forces: the violent force of a hiccup, of copulation, a scream, the need to vomit or defecate, the flattening force of sleep. In Cézanne, similarly, mountains are made to exist uniquely through the geological forces of folding they harness, landscapes through their thermal and magnetic forces, apples through their forces of germination. Van Gogh even harnessed as yet unknown forces, such as the extraordinary force of a sunflower. Klee's famous formula echoes through Deleuze's writings like a kind of leitmotif: *not to render the visible, but to render visible.* Sensations are given, but it is force that constitutes the condition of sensation. The artistic question then becomes: How to render sensible forces that are not themselves sensible? How to render the non-visible visible in painting, or the non-sonorous sonorous in music?

This leads us, finally, to the third line of concepts in Deleuze's book, which concerns the way in which painters—and Bacon in particular—produce this "logic of sensation." The aim of his book, Deleuze tells us, is not only to build a "general" logic of sensation, but to show how, in Bacon's work, its summit is found in the sensation of *color.* In arriving at this conclusion, Deleuze once again takes us through a kind of deduction of concepts. The first is the concept of the cliché. Clichés, Deleuze writes, are anonymous and floating images

> which circulate in the external world, but which also penetrate each of us and constitute our internal world, so that everyone possesses only psychic clichés by which we think and feel, are thought and felt, being ourselves one cliché among others in the world that surrounds us. (MI 208–9)

If Deleuze's philosophy is a *genetic* philosophy, the cliché is precisely what *prevents* the genesis of an image, just as opinion and convention prevent the genesis of thought. In this sense, one of the fundamental questions of Deleuze's philosophy is, What are the conditions for the production of the *new* (an image, a thought . . .)? Hence the essential role of the catastrophe: the condition for the genesis of the image (or the sensation) is at one and the same time the condition for the destruction of the cliché.

How, then, does the painter pass through the catastrophe and destroy the cliché? This is the role of what Deleuze calls the diagram or graph (Chapter 12), a term he derives from the semiotic theory of C. S. Peirce. Peirce had noted the important and often-overlooked role that diagrams play in mathematical thought. Although mathematics is often presented as a purely deductive or axiomatic science, theorematic reasoning usually involves the construction of diagrams and a kind of "ideal experimentation" with schemata consisting of points, lines, surfaces, and relations: "points are made and stretched . . . pins are stuck in maps . . . pages are covered in scribbles."[31] Mathematics, Peirce insisted, is as experimental as physics or chemistry, except that its experiments necessarily take on an ideal or "diagrammatic" form. In his semiological theory, Peirce had classified the diagram as a special case of the icon, "an icon of intelligible relations."[32] Although Deleuze admits his indebtedness to Peirce, he rejects the iconic status that Peirce assigned to the diagram, since it tends to conceive the diagram simply as a "copy" or graphic representation of intelligible relations or coordinates.[33] Deleuze, rather, prefers to assign to the diagram a much more strongly creative or genetic role: "the diagrammatic or abstract machine does not function to represent, even something real, but rather constructs a real that is yet to come, a new type of reality" (TP 142). As Deleuze explains in Chapter 13, the diagram acts as an analogical *modulator,* a conjunction of matter and. function.

Painters, Deleuze argues, have their own type of diagrammatism. What he terms a painterly diagram (an operative set of non-representational and non-signifying lines and colors) is the means by which painters, in their own way, pass through the experience of catastrophe. The painter's diagram undoes the optical organization of the synthesis of perception (clichés), but also functions as the "genetic" element of the pictorial order to come. Every painter, Deleuze suggests, will pass through this process in a different manner. "The diagram is indeed a chaos, a catastrophe," he writes, "but it is also a germ of order or rhythm" (FB 83). Using Wittgensteinian language, Deleuze says that the diagram constitutes a "possibility of fact," out of which the Fact itself will emerge. Plateau 11 of *A Thousand Plateaus* analyzes, in a more general manner, this complex emergence, out of chaos, of the elements of rhythm, with its territories and milieus (TP 310–50). The struggle against chaos in art, philosophy, and science is also one of the central themes of *What is Philosophy?*, notably in its final chapter, "From Chaos to the Brain."[34]

If the summit of Bacon's own logic of sensation is found in the "coloring sensation," it is because it is primarily (though not exclusively) through the use of color that Bacon effects his diagrammatic procedures. In this regard, Deleuze identifies two fundamental uses of color in the history of painting. The first, more traditionally, emphasizes relations of *value* between colors: that is, the contrast of shadow and light (*chiaroscuro*). It has as its correlate the construction of what Deleuze calls a *tactile-optical* space: that is, the representational space that was inaugurated by Greek art and refined in the Renaissance. Figuration is itself a consequence of this tactile-optical space. In such a space, bodies are not merely perceived optically but take on a sculptural or tactile quality (depth, contour, relief), producing the illusion of a three-dimensional space behind the frame. In Chapter 14, Deleuze shows how, in the history of art, this tactile- optical world would subsequently be broken and develop in two different directions: toward the exposition of a purely *optical* space, in which space is freed from its references to even a subordinate tactility (Byzantine art); and toward the imposition of a violent *manual* space, in which the hand begins to express itself in an independent way, producing a line that delineates nothing, and which the eye can barely follow (Gothic art). Deleuze's analyses of these developments draw heavily on the German art historical tradition of Aloïs Riegl, Heinrich Wölfflin, and Wilhelm Worringer, though without the last's appeal to a "will to art" (*Kunstwollen*).[35] These developments, in turn, would be recapitulated in their own way in modern art: abstraction would develop a purely optical code (Mondrian), whereas expressionism would move toward the extraction of a purely manual line (Pollock).

In Chapter 15, however, Deleuze will define Bacon's novelty in a twofold manner that breaks with these earlier conceptions of color and space. On the one hand, in his use of color, Bacon follows Cézanne and Van Gogh in replacing relations of value with relations of *tonality*: that is, with pure relations between the colors of the spectrum. Following Gilbert Simondon, Deleuze calls this a technique of *modulation* that relies on the relations between colors or the juxtaposition of tints. "The formula of the colorists is: if you push color to its pure internal relations (hot–cold, expansion–contraction), then you have everything" (FB 112). For the colorist, everything in painting—form and ground, light and shadow, bright and dark—is derived from pure relations of color. In this regard, Deleuze sees Bacon as one of the great colorists in the history of painting. Chapter 16 analyzes how the three formal elements of Bacon's paintings—the Figure, the contour, the structure—are all constructed by means of color: the internal variations of intensity in the structure, the "broken tones" of the Figures, the colored line of the contour. Thus, each element of Bacon's paintings converges in color, and it is modulation (the relation between colors) that explains the unity of the whole, the distribution of each element, and the way each of them acts upon the others. This is why Deleuze says that it is the "coloring sensation" that stands at the summit of Bacon's logic of sensation.

On the other hand, this use of color claims to bring out a peculiar kind of sense from sight: a *haptic* vision of color, as opposed to the optical vision of light. What Deleuze calls haptic vision is precisely this "sense" of colors. The *tactile-optical* space of representation presents a complex eye–hand relation: an ideal optical space that none the less maintains virtual referents to tactility (depth, contour, relief). From this, two types of subordination can occur: a subordination of the hand to the eye in *optical* space (Byzantine art), and a strict subordination of the eye to the hand in a *manual* space (Gothic art). But what Deleuze; following Riegl, terms *haptic* space (from the Greek verb *aptō*, to touch) is a space in which there is no longer a hand–eye subordination in either direction. It implies a type of seeing distinct from the optical, a close-up viewing in which "the sense of sight behaves just like the sense of touch."[36] Riegl argued that haptic space was the invention of Egyptian art and bas-relief, in which form and ground are experienced as being on the same plane, requiring a close vision. Deleuze in turn suggests that a new Egypt rises up in Bacon's work, this time composed uniquely of color and by color: the juxtaposition of pure tones arranged gradually on the flat surface produces a properly haptic space, and implies a properly haptic function of the eye (the planar character of the surface creates volumes only through the different colors that are arranged on it). In this regard, Deleuze will place Bacon in the great tradition of Turner, Monet, Cézanne, and Van Gogh—the great modern colorists who replaced relations of value with relations of tonality.

We have attempted to distinguish three conceptual trajectories in *The Logic of Sensation*, which respectively concern formal aspects of Bacon's paintings (isolation, deformation, coupling . . .), the non-rational logic of sensation (rhythm, chaos, force . . .), and the act of painting itself (clichés, the diagram, modulation . . .). Obviously, the three trajectories are interlinked; painting has its own manner of experimenting with the logic of sensation, and Bacon's path has a validity of its own that does not negate other paths such as abstraction or expressionism. In turn, each of these trajectories points beyond itself toward linkages with other arts such as music, cinema, and literature, such that *The Logic of Sensation* can itself be seen as an entry point into the conceptual proliferation of Deleuze's philosophy as a whole, and his other writings on the arts.

The New

The Conditions of the New

THE QUESTION OF THE NEW: CHANGE, CAUSALITY, EMERGENCE

What is the status of the *new* as a philosophical problem?[1] Deleuze frequently said that the question of the conditions for the production of *novelty* (Bergson) or *creativity* (Whitehead) was one of the fundamental questions of contemporary thought, entailing a profound shift in philosophy away from the eternal to the new, from the universal to the singular.[2] Most generally, Deleuze's response to this question was that the conditions of the new can be found only in a principle of *difference*, or more strongly, in a *metaphysics* of difference. The reason: if identity were the primary principle—that is, if identities are pre-given or presupposed, then there would in principle be no production of the new (no new differences).[3] Yet the status of the new is a highly complex problem. On the one hand, the "new" seems to be one of the most obvious phenomena in the world; every dawn brings forth a new day, and every day brings with it a wealth of the new—new experiences, new events, new encounters, new "news." If the new means "what did not exist before," then everything is new. On the other hand, one can say, with almost equal assurance, with the writer of Ecclesiastes (1:9–10), that there is nothing new under the sun; the dawn of today was just like the dawn of yesterday, and simply brings with it more of the same. The new seems to come in well-worn and predictable patterns and regularities. Talk of the new, in other words, immediately threatens to be pulled back into talk of the old. As the French saying puts it, *plus ça change, plus c'est la même chose* ("the more things change, the more they stay the same").

These complexities are due, in part, to the fact that the problem of the new is easily confused with a host of related but none the less distinguishable problems, including questions of transformation and change, causality and determinism, and the possibility of emergence (emergent qualities). One could, for instance, pose the question of the new in terms of the question of *change* or transformation; when artists create a painting or a piece of sculpture, they are simply rearranging matter that already exists in the world in a new way. Such a view of novelty would be merely combinatorial: melodies are made out of notes, paintings are made out of pigments, sculptures are hewn out of stone. This would be a simplified caricature of the hylomorphic schema: creation is the imposition of a new form (*morphe*) on a given material or matter (*hyle*), even if matter contains a certain potentiality for the form. Here, novelty is found on the side of the form, and matter is the passive receiver or receptacle of this newness. In this case, novelty would be little more than the rearrangement of matter in the universe into ever-new forms. The question of whether such novelty would eventually be exhausted would rest on a metaphysical question about the finitude or infinity of matter (and time) in the universe.

The question of novelty has also been linked to the question of *causality*: if everything has a cause, and if effects pre-exist in their causes, then only old things can come out of change. If there is nothing in the effect that was not already in the cause (or, to put it in logical terms, if there is nothing in the consequent that was not in the antecedent), then causal processes can give rise to objects that are new in number, but not new in kind—there can be *quantitative* or numerical novelty, as in mass-produced objects, but not *qualitative* novelty. Yet, as Mario Bunge has argued in his classic book *Causality and Modern Science*, this view, though consistent (and popular), is extreme, since it rests on a simplified and linear view of causality: effects can be (and usually are) determined by multiple causes (heat can be produced by friction, combustion, nuclear chain reactions, microwaves, and so on), and causes can have multiple effects (penicillin may cure my infection but kill someone allergic to it).[4] Causality, in other words, must be distinguished from the more general question of *determination*, since determination can be not only causal, but also statistical or probabilistic (determination of a result by the joint action of independent entities), structural or wholistic (determination of parts by the whole), teleological (determination by ends or goals), dialectical (determination by internal strife or synthesis of opposites), as well as dynamic or causal. Deleuze's proposal will be to see all such forms of determination as derivable from a metaphysical principle of difference: "Difference is the state in which one can speak of determination *as such*" (DR 28).

The question of the new, finally, must also be distinguished from the question of *emergence*, even though the two issues are closely related. Emergence is a phenomenon of widespread interest in contemporary science and philosophy. It is an issue that initially arose in a "physicalist" ontology, which holds that all existents are physical entities, and hence that all sciences, in principle, should be reducible to physics. The problem is that physicalism, at least in its radically reductionist versions, cannot take into account phenomena that have supra-physical (or emergent) properties that their physical components lack, such as the emergence of consciousness, or the emergence of new individuals, species, artifacts, institutions, and so on.[5] If radical novelty can be distinguished from emergence, however, it is because emergence implies the production of new quality at "higher levels" of complexity in a system, whereas the concept of the new in Deleuze—as well as Whitehead and Bergson—implies conditions in which novelty or creativity (difference) becomes a fundamental concept at the most basic ontological level.

The problem of the new must thus be distinguished from the problems of change, causality, or emergence, since in each of these cases the new (difference) appears, *mutatis mutandis*, as a secondary effect. If Deleuze, following Bergson and Whitehead, formulates an original conception of the new, it is because he repositions the new as a fundamental ontological concept: Being = Difference = the New. "The new, with its power of beginning and beginning again, remains forever new" (DR 136). As Bergson put it, "the more we study the nature of time, the more we shall comprehend that duration means invention, the creation of forms, the continual elaboration of the new."[6] None the less, the *new* remains primarily an operative concept in Deleuze's philosophy, which he tends to thematize explicitly under the rubric of *difference* (*Difference and Repetition*) or the *event* (*Logic of Sense*) or *time* (*The Time-Image*). When the theme of the new explicitly appears in Deleuze's writings, it is almost always tied to the question of the *conditions* of the new.

THREE TYPES OF CONDITIONS: THE LOGICALLY POSSIBLE, POSSIBLE EXPERIENCE, REAL EXPERIENCE

The properly Deleuzian question would therefore be: What are the ontological *conditions* under which something new can be produced? But this question, in turn, seems to entail a new conception of what constitutes a "condition," since, if the new were conditioned, this would seem to imply that it was *not* new, but already given in its conditions. To approach this problem, we can distinguish between three types of conditions with which philosophers have tended to concern themselves: the conditions that demarcate what is *logically* possible; the conditions that determine the limits of possible *experience* (Kant); and the conditions of *real* experience. For Deleuze, the problem of the new is coextensive with the attempt to determine the conditions of *real* experience (since the real *is* the new). What, then, does it mean to think the conditions of the real?

First, one could say that thought, *on its own*, is only capable of thinking the possible, and that it does so in the name of certain principles which one can call *logical principles*. Logical principles are principles that determine what is possible and what is not possible. Classical logic identified three such principles: the principle of *identity* (A is A, a thing is what it is), the principle of *non-contradiction* (A is not non-A, a thing is not what it is not), and the principle of the *excluded middle* (between A or not-A, there is no middle term). Taken together, these three principles determine what is impossible—that is to say, what is *unthinkable* without contradiction: something that would not be what it is, something that would be what it is not, and something that would be both what it is and what it is not. By means of these three principles, thought is able to think the world of what is possible (or what traditional philosophy called the world of "essences"). But this is why classical logic only goes so far: it leaves us within the domain of the possible.

Kant went a step further than this when he tried to demarcate, not simply the domain of the logically possible, but the domain of possible *experience*. This domain of possible experience is no longer the object of formal logic, but of what Kant called *transcendental* logic, and the transcendental conditions for demarcating possible experience are found in the *categories*. If logical principles demarcate the domain of the possible, transcendental categories demarcate the domain of possible experience. Causality is a category for Kant, for instance, since we cannot conceive of an object of our possible experience that has not been caused by something else. This transcendental logic allowed Kant to distinguish between what was immanent within and transcendent to this domain of experience. The object of empirical concepts is immanent to experience, and hence testable by hypothesis and experiment, whereas the object of *transcendent* concepts—or what Kant called, following Plato, *Ideas*—goes beyond any possible experience. The three great transcendent Ideas that Kant identified in the Transcendental Dialectic—the Soul, the World, and God—are *thinkable* (they are not logically inconsistent, given the principles of formal logic), but they are not *knowable*, since there could never be an object in experience that would correspond to them—they lie outside the domain of possible experience.

But the post-Kantian philosophers, starting with Salomon Maimon, attempted to push the Kantian transcendental project one step further: from the conditions of *possible* experience to the conditions of *real* experience. Kant had assumed that there are *a priori* "facts" of reason (knowledge, morality), and then sought the condition of possibility of these facts in the transcendental, thereby "tracing" the transcendental off the empirical and thinking the condition in the image of the conditioned. Maimon argued that it was illegitimate for Kant simply to *assume* these supposed facts; rather, in order truly to fulfill the ambitions of his critical project, Kant would have to show how they were *engendered* immanently from reason as the necessary modes of its manifestation. A method of *genesis*, in short, had to replace the simple method of *conditioning*. Moreover, to accomplish this task, the genetic method would require the positing of a principle of difference; identity may be the condition of possibility of thought in general, Maimon claimed, but it is difference that constitutes the genetic condition of the real. These two demands laid down by Maimon—the search for *the genetic elements of real experience* and the positing of a *principle of difference* as the fulfillment of this condition—could be said to be the two primary components of what Deleuze came to call his *transcendental empiricism*. "Without this [Maimonian] reversal," he once wrote, "the Copernican Revolution amounts to nothing" (DR 162).

Yet, as Martial Guéroult has shown, Maimon is a pivotal figure in post-Kantian thought precisely because he himself hesitated between two ways of solving the problem of genesis:

> Maimon oscillates between two solutions: first, to turn difference into a pure principle like identity . . . In a certain fashion this is the path Schelling will choose in the philosophy of Nature . . . This conception everywhere has the same consequences . . . : the suppression of the immanence in the knowing subject of the constitutive elements of knowledge; the finite subject Ego [*Moi*] is *posterior* to the realities of which it has knowledge . . . But another solution presents itself: identity being absolutely pure, and diversity always being a given (*a priori* and *a posteriori*), identity can be posited as the property of the thinking subject, and difference as an absence of identity resulting from the limitation of the subject.[7]

The latter will be the path followed by Fichte in his positing of the "I = I" as a thetic principle of identity. The former position, which we have summarized here, will be the path retrieved and pursued by Deleuze, in which the conditions of the real are united with the question of the new (difference).

THE CONDITIONS OF REAL EXPERIENCE: FIVE REQUIREMENTS

In speaking about conditions, then, we can trace out a trajectory from what constitutes the *logically possible* (determined by logical principles), what constitutes *possible experience* (determined by the categories), and the problem that Deleuze set for himself: what constitutes the genetic and differential conditions of *real experience*.[8] In so far as Deleuze's project constitutes a search for conditions—or, in pre-Kantian terms, a search for sufficient reason—Deleuze's philosophy can be said to be a transcendental philosophy. But as Deleuze says, with understatement, "the question of knowing how to determine the transcendental field is very complex" (LS 105), and takes us into a domain that is very different from what is often characterized as "transcendental arguments." Kant was the philosopher who discovered the prodigious domain of the transcendental. "He is the analogue of a great explorer," Deleuze writes, "not of another world, but of the upper and lower reaches of this one" (DR 135). However, Deleuze conceives of the transcendental in a very different manner than Kant. Throughout his work, he has laid out various requirements that must be met in determining the conditions of real experience, several of which are particularly relevant to our concerns, though they by no means exhaust the ways of approaching the problem.

First, as we have seen, for a condition to be a condition of real experience, and not merely possible experience, it must form "an intrinsic genesis, not an extrinsic conditioning" (DR 154). The genetic method means that the conditions of real experience must be able to account for novelty or the new, which means that the *future* must become the fundamental dimension of time.

Second, the condition cannot be in the image of the conditioned: that is, the structures of the transcendental field cannot simply be traced off the empirical. This was one of the fundamental critiques that the post-Kantians addressed to Kant; Kant had simply conceived of the transcendental in the image of the empirical. This was particularly clear in the deduction of first edition of the *Critique of Pure Reason*, where the transcendental structures (apprehension, reproduction, recognition) are traced from the empirical acts of a psychological consciousness. Although Kant suppressed this text in the second edition, the tracing method, with all its "psychologism," still persists, even if it is better hidden (DR 135). Deleuze, following Sartre, will strip the transcendental field of the presupposition of a transcendental subject or the form of consciousness; transcendental idealism becomes a transcendental empiricism (LS 105–6). But more importantly, the relation between the transcendental and the empirical is stripped of any resemblance: "the task of a philosophy that does not wish to fall into the traps of consciousness and the cogito is to purge the transcendental field of all resemblance" (LS 123). For Deleuze, the transcendental must be conceived of as a field in which "the different is related to the different *through* difference itself" (DR 299). When this field is actualized, it therefore differs from itself, such that every process of actualization is, by its very nature, the production of the new: that is, the production of a new difference. This is the task Deleuze sets for himself in the latter chapters of *Difference and Repetition*; the fourth chapter ("Ideas and the Synthesis of Difference") examines the completely differentiated nature of the transcendental field, while the fifth chapter ("Asymmetrical Synthesis of the Sensible") examines the manner in which this field is necessarily differenciated in its actualizations.

Third, to be a condition of real experience, the condition can be no broader than what it conditions—otherwise it would not be a condition of *real* experience, capable of accounting for the genesis of the real. It is for this reason that there can be no categories (at least in the Aristotelian or Kantian sense) in Deleuze's philosophy, since, as Deleuze puts it, the categories cast a net so wide that they let all the fish (the real) swim through it. But this requirement—that conditions not be broader than the conditioned—means that the conditions must be determined *along with* what they condition, and thus must change as the conditioned changes. In other words, the conditions themselves must be plastic and mobile, "no less capable of dissolving and destroying individuals than of constituting them temporarily."[9]

Fourth, in order to remain faithful to these exigencies, Deleuze continues, "we must have something unconditioned" that would be capable of "determining *both* the condition and the conditioned" (LS 123, 122), and which alone would be capable of ensuring a *real* genesis.[10] It is the nature of this unconditioned element that lies at the basis of Deleuze's dispute with the general movement of the post-Kantian tradition: is this unconditioned the "totality" (Kant, Hegel), which necessarily appeals to a principle of identity (the subject), or is it "differential" (which is Deleuze's position, modifying a position hinted at by Leibniz)? Indeed, Deleuze's appeal to the interrelated concepts of the foundation [*fondation*], the ground [*fond, fondement*], and the ungrounded [*sans-fond*] reflects his complex relation to the traditions of pre- and post-Kantianism. Both Spinoza and Leibniz, in their shared anti-Cartesian reaction, complained that Descartes had not gone far enough in his attempt to secure a foundation for knowledge; erecting a foundation is a futile enterprise if the ground itself is not firm and secure. Before laying the foundation, in other words, one must prepare the ground—that is, one must inquire into the *sufficient reason* of the foundation.[11] Deleuze describes *Difference and Repetition* in its entirety as an inquiry into sufficient reason, but with this additional caveat: in following the path of sufficient reason, Deleuze argues, one always reaches a "bend" or "twist" in sufficient reason, which "relates what it grounds to that which is truly groundless," the unconditioned (DR 154). It is like a catastrophe or earthquake that fundamentally alters the ground, and destroys the foundations that are set in it. All three of these aspects—foundation, ground, and the ungrounded—are essential to Deleuze's project.

Sufficient reason or the ground [he writes] is strangely bent: on the one hand, it leans towards what it grounds, towards the forms of representation; on the other hand, it turns and plunges into a groundlessness beyond the ground which resists all forms and cannot be represented. (DR 274–5)

In Deleuze's theory of repetition (temporal synthesis), for instance, the present plays the role of the foundation, the pure past is the ground, but the future the ungrounded or unconditioned: that is, the condition of the new.

Finally, the nature of the genesis that is at play here must therefore be understood as what Deleuze calls a *static* genesis (a genesis that takes place between the virtual and its actualization), and not a *dynamic* genesis (a historical or developmental genesis that takes place between actual terms, moving from one actual term to another).

These five themes recur in almost all of Deleuze's early writings as elaborations of the two post-Kantian demands that Deleuze appropriates from Maimon: the search for the genetic elements of real experience and the positing of a principle of difference as the fulfillment of this demand.

THE MODEL OF THE CALCULUS

However, it is one thing to lay out a general project like this; it is another thing to find a "method" (to use a term Deleuze disliked) capable of providing a way of *thinking* the conditions of the real that would fulfill these requirements. If logical principles determine the conditions of the possible, and the categories determine the conditions of possible experience, where can one go to search for the conditions of real experience (that is, the conditions for novelty itself)? Deleuze in fact appeals to several non-philosophical models in his work. One of them is artistic creation, and in a sense Deleuze's transcendental empiricism can be read, in large part, as a reworking of Kant's transcendental aesthetic.[12] Another model is molecular biology, which defines individuals in terms of a genetic structure that constitutes the real conditions of its external and visible properties, and thus constitutes a profound break with the traditional approach of "natural history" (DR 214–21). But the model I would like to focus on here is the mathematical model of the differential calculus. Many of the concepts that Deleuze develops in *Difference and Repetition* to define the conditions of the real—the differential relation, singularities, multiplicities or manifolds, the virtual, the problematic, and so on—are derived from the history of the calculus.

There are a number of reasons why Deleuze would turn to the model of calculus. Philosophy, of course, has always had a complex relationship with mathematics, but the particular *branch* of mathematics privileged by philosophers often says much about the nature of their philosophy. Since the late nineteenth and early twentieth centuries, for instance, philosophers have tended to focus on axiomatic set theory, since they were preoccupied with the question of the foundations of mathematics, with its twin programs of formalization and discretization. Plato, by contrast, famously appealed to Euclidean geometry as a model for Ideas because it defined forms or essences that were static, unchanging, and self-identical. Deleuze could be said to appeal to the calculus for the exact opposite reason: it is the calculus that provides him with a mathematical model of a principle of difference. The calculus is the primary mathematical tool we have at our disposal to explore the nature of reality, the nature of the real—the *conditions of the real*. When physicists want to examine the nature of a physical system, or engineers want to analyze the pressure on a weight-bearing load, they model the system using the symbolism of the calculus. What spawned the "scientific revolution" of the last three centuries was what Ian Stewart has called *the differential equation paradigm*: "the way to understand Nature is through differential equations."[13] Hermann Weyl wrote that "a law of nature is necessarily a differential equation" (FLB 47), and Bertrand Russell, perhaps even more strongly, claimed that "scientific laws can *only* be expressed in differential equations."[14] In this sense, one might say that the calculus is existentialism in mathematics, "a kind of union of mathematics and the existent."[15]

This is why Leibniz—who invented the calculus, along with Newton—remains an important figure for Deleuze. In the history of philosophy, Deleuze suggests, there were two great attempts to elucidate the conditions of the real, albeit in two different directions: Hegel (the infinitely large) and Leibniz (the infinitely small).[16] Deleuze's strategy, with regard to the history of philosophy, seems to have been to take up Maimon's critiques of Kant and to resolve them, not in the manner of the post-Kantians, such as Fichte and Hegel, but rather by following Maimon's own suggestions and returning to the pre-Kantian thought of Hume, Spinoza, and Leibniz. Of these three, it is Leibniz who plays a decisive role—at least with regard to the question of the real that concerns us here—since, in Deleuze's reading, he already had an implicit response to the two post-Kantian demands formulated by Maimon. "All the elements to create a genesis as demanded by the post-Kantians," Deleuze noted in one of his seminars, "are virtually present in Leibniz" (20 May 1980). The calculus, to be sure, takes us into a complex and heavily mined territory, with its own intricate history. Moreover, the calculus is not the only mathematical domain to which Deleuze appeals: group theory, topology, and non-Euclidean geometry, among others, also make frequent appearances throughout Deleuze's texts. It is not that Deleuze is setting out to develop a philosophy of mathematics, nor even to construct a metaphysics of the calculus. Deleuze appeals to the calculus primarily to develop a *philosophical* concept of difference, to propose a concept of difference-in-itself. "We tried to constitute a philosophical concept from the mathematical function of differentiation," Deleuze writes in the preface to *Difference and Repetition*. "We are well aware, unfortunately, that we have spoken about science in a manner which was not scientific" (DR xvi, xxi). Starting with the differential relation, we can follow, in a rather schematic manner, a "deduction" of the concepts that Deleuze extracts from the calculus for his philosophical purposes. This analysis would constitute a segment of a broader consideration of Deleuze's philosophy of difference.[17]

THE LOGIC OF RELATIONS

Let me turn first to the nature of the differential relation. To understand the importance of this concept for Deleuze—and the way in which this type of relation differs from logical relations, or even from real and imaginary relations in mathematics—we can perhaps make a brief foray into the philosophical problem of relations in general. The problem of relations has tortured philosophy since its inception, and since the Greeks, the question of relations has been linked to the problem of judgment. The simplest form of judgment is the judgment of *attribution*, A is B (e.g., the sky is blue), although it was recognized early on that every judgment of attribution is a kind of offense against the principle of identity (14 Dec 1982). It is easy to understand the relation of identity, A is A (the sky is the sky, a thing is identical to itself), but how is it possible to say that A is B? Philosophers explained it by saying that, in a judgment of attribution, A and B are not the same thing: a judgment of attribution attributes a *property* (blue) to a *subject* (sky), or an *attribute* to a *substance*, and thus could be said to lie at the origin of every metaphysics of substance. A more complicated form of judgment, however, is a judgment of *relation*, such as A is smaller than B (Peter is smaller than Paul). In a judgment of relation, we can no longer say that we are attributing a property to a subject, because if I say that "being smaller than" is a property of A, I would also have to say, at the same time, that "being taller than" is also a property of A, since there is also a C that is smaller than A ("Peter is smaller than Paul, but taller than Mary"). Plato had already pointed out that this would entail attributing contradictory properties to the same subject ("being smaller than," "being taller than"), which would seem to be an offense against the principle of non-contradiction, just as the judgment of attribution seems to be an offense against the principle of identity. (One could object by saying that the properties being predicated are not simply "smaller than" and "taller than," but rather "smaller than Paul" and "taller than Mary," but this does not solve the problem. Paul and Mary are themselves real beings, and while the *concept* of Peter may contain properties, it is not possible for the concept of Peter—a real being—to contain other real beings, and not simply properties.) A judgment of relation ("Peter is smaller than Paul"), in short, cannot be reduced to a judgment of attribution ("Peter has blue eyes"). When I say, "Peter is smaller than Paul," this relation is neither a property of Peter, nor a property of Paul; rather, it is something *between* the two. But what is this "between the two"? "The foundation [*fondement*] of the relation cannot be found in either of the terms that it unites: the mystery seems unfathomable" (1 Mar 1983). Where, then, is it to be found? Philosophy has offered at least three responses to this question.

First, Plato's ingenious response was to say that relations are pure Ideas that go beyond the sensible world: there is an Idea of the Small, and an Idea of the Large. When we say that "A is smaller than B, and greater than C," we are simply saying that A participates in the Idea of the Small in relation to term B, and that it participates in the Idea of the Large in relation to term C. But this simply restates the problem: relations are irreducible to the attributes or properties of a thing. Indeed, once one has discovered the world of relations, one might ask if, in the end, *every* judgment is not a judgment of relation—that is, if there are no properties at all, but *only* relations. Leibniz, second, took a quite different approach: he tried to show, at all costs, that *every* judgment of relation is reducible to a judgment of attribution, and he was willing to draw the necessary conclusion: every concept that designates a real being (Peter, Paul, Adam, Caesar) must contain the *totality* of all other concepts. Why? Because Peter is *related* to Paul, and more distantly to Caesar, and even more distantly to Adam, which amounts to saying that the concept of every real being necessarily expresses the totality of the world. Leibniz tried to save the judgment of attribution by claiming that relations are *internal* to their terms: if the concept of Peter contains all other terms, then all imaginable relations can be reduced to attributions—that is, to properties of the concept.[18] The greatness of Hume, finally, is to have come along and argued the exact opposite: namely, that relations are *external* to their terms. "For me," Deleuze said, "this proposition was like a clap of thunder in philosophy" (14 Dec 1982). Rather than invoking Ideas, or undertaking operations as complex as those of Leibniz, Hume's admonition is to accept exteriority. Prior to Hume, philosophers tended to support interiority; to comprehend something was to internalize it, whether in a concept or in one's head. Some sort of interiority was necessary. Hume arrives on the scene and says, "You are not seeing the world in which you live, which is a world of exteriority, an infinite patchwork of bits and pieces, irreducibly external to each other."[19] While properties are internal to the terms to which they are attributed, relations are exteriorities; one cannot give an account of relations by relating them to their terms. As Deleuze argued in his first book, on Hume, the fundamental thesis of empiricism is less that knowledge derives from sensible experience but, more profoundly, that relations are external to their terms (ES 98–9). Empiricism was thus faced with the formidable task of inventing a new logic, a logic of relations that breaks with the logic of attribution, which would begin with Hume's theory of probabilities and take on its definitive form in Bertrand Russell (PI 37–8). If the empiricists discovered the sensible world, what they discovered in it was an absolutely new formal logic of relations.

Deleuze will adopt Hume's empiricist stand on relations, but in developing his own transcendental empiricism, he will modify and develop it in several directions. One the one hand, he will link this analysis of relations with the concept of *becoming* (which does not assume its full importance as a concept in Deleuze's thought until A *Thousand Plateaus*).[20] If relations are external to their terms, and do not depend on them, then the relations cannot change without one (or both) of the terms changing. A resembles B, Peter resembles Paul: this relation is external to its terms, it is contained neither in the concept of Peter nor in the concept of Paul. If A ceases to resemble B, the relation has changed, but this means that the concept of A (or B) has changed as well. If properties belong to something solid, relations are far more fragile, and are inseparable from a perpetual becoming. Hitchcock's entire cinema, to give a non-philosophical example, was modeled on the evolution of relations (the innocent taken to be guilty) and a varied play of conjunctions (because ... although ... since ... if ... even if ...). In Mr. *and* Mrs. *Smith*, a minor comedy, Hitchcock asks, What happens to a couple who suddenly learn that their marriage was not legal, and thus that they have never been married (MI x, 202)? When a relation changes, what happens to its terms?

> One cannot think relation [Deleuze noted in a seminar] independent of a becoming that is at least virtual, whatever the relation might be. In my

opinion, the theorists of relation, however strong they might have been, have not seen this . . . A relation is not only external to its terms, but it is essentially transitive, in the sense of "transitory." (14 Dec 1982)

On the other hand, Deleuze will also push the thesis of the exteriority of relations to its radical limit. If relations are external to their terms and do not depend on them, if relation is the domain of becoming (if every relation envelops or implies change), then one might say that, at the limit, or at a deeper level, there are not even terms, but only packets of variable relations. What we call a term in itself is only a packet of relations. In this sense, one could say that Deleuze is in the process of dissolving the notion of substance into that of multiplicity. "In a multiplicity, what counts are not the terms or the elements, but what is 'between' them, the in-between, a set of relations that are inseparable from each other" (D viii). It is not unlike Virginia Woolf's dictum in literature: not to see things, but to see *between* things.[21] But what, then, does it mean to speak of a "pure relation": that is, a relation that is not only external to its terms, but a relation that persists even when its terms have disappeared?

THE DIFFERENTIAL RELATION

If Deleuze appeals to the model of the differential relation, then, it is because it offers an initial mathematical response to this question. The differential relation was discovered in the seventeenth century by Leibniz and Newton, and can be distinguished from *fractional relations*, which had been known since antiquity, and *algebraic relations*, which had only received a rigorous status in Descartes's work. Already in fractions, there appears a kind of independence of the relation from its terms. The fraction $\frac{2}{3}$, for example, is not a whole number, because there is no assignable number which, when multiplied by three, equals two. To be sure, we can decide, by convention, to treat fractions as numbers: that is, to subject them to the rules of addition, subtraction, and multiplication. Moreover, once we have the fractional symbolism at our disposal, we can treat numbers as if they were fractions: we can write 2 as $\frac{4}{2}$ or $\frac{6}{3}$. But in themselves, fractions are complexes of whole numbers, and as such, they provide a first approximation of a relation that is independent of its terms. None the less, this first approximation remains limited. In a fractional relation, the relation is still between two terms, and a *determinate* value must be assigned to the terms; that is, the terms must be given and specified (2 and 3). By contrast, in an algebraic relation, such as $x^2 + y^2 - R^2 = 0$, a determinate value no longer needs to be assigned to the terms; the terms of the relation are *variables*. It is as if the algebraic relation acquires a higher degree of independence than the fractional relations, since the terms of the relation no longer need to be specified as such. However, even though I need not assign a *determinate* value to the terms, the variable must none the less have a *determinable* value. The variables x and y can have various singular values, but they must none the less have a value. In an algebraic relation, in other words, the relation is indeed independent of any particular value of the terms, but it is still not independent of the determinable value of the variable.

The same is true in symbolic logic, in which the variable, though undetermined, must none the less sustain its identity throughout the arguments.

The differential relation constitutes the third step in this history of mathematical relations. In 1701, Leibniz wrote a short, three-page text entitled "Justification of the Infinitesimal Calculus" in which he illustrated the nature of the differential relation using an example from ordinary algebra.[22] In the differential relation dx/dy, dy in relation to y is equal to zero, and dx in relation to x is equal to zero—they are infinitely small quantities. Thus it is possible to write, as was done frequently in the seventeenth century, that $dx/dy = 0/0$. Yet the relation $0/0$ is not equal to zero; in the differential relation, *the relation subsists even when the terms disappear*. In this case, the terms between which the relation is established are neither determined, nor even determinable; the terms themselves have neither existence, nor value, nor signification (DI 176). The only thing that is determined is the reciprocal relation between the terms. The terms are reduced to vanishing terms, to vanishing quantities (or virtualities), yet the relation between these vanishing quantities is not equal to zero, but refers to a third term that has a *finite* value: $dx/dy = z$. Applied to a circle, for example, the differential relation dx/dy tells us something about a third thing, a trigonometric tangent. We can say that z is the limit of the differential relation, or that the differential relation tends toward a limit. When the terms of the relation disappear, the relation subsists because it tends toward a limit, z. When a relation is established between infinitely small terms, it is not annulled along with its terms, but tends toward a limit. This is the basis of the differential calculus as it was interpreted in the seventeenth century—an interpretation that was identical to the comprehension of an actual infinity. Weierstrass and Russell would eventually give the calculus a *static and ordinal* interpretation, which liberated the calculus from any reference to infinitesimals, and integrated it into a pure logic of relations.

This, then, is the importance Deleuze ascribes to the differential relation. It is a pure relation that provides an example of what Deleuze will call the concept of "difference-in-itself." Difference is a relation, and normally—that is to say, empirically, it is a relation between two things that have a prior identity ("x is different from y"). Relations require prior relata, and differences require prior identities. With the notion of the differential relation, however, Deleuze takes the notion of difference to a properly *transcendental* level: that is, to a domain where relations no longer depend on their terms. This is what distinguishes the model of the calculus from axiomatic set theory: the latter establishes relations between non-specified elements (axiom of extensionality), whereas in the former the elements are reciprocally determined by the relations themselves. Not only is the differential relation external to its terms, and not only does the relation persist even when its terms have disappeared, but one could also say that the relation determines its terms. Difference here becomes *constitutive* of identity—that is, it becomes productive and genetic, thus fulfilling Maimon's demand: a genetic philosophy finding its ground in a principle of difference.

SINGULARITIES AND MULTIPLICITIES

In a certain sense, one could say that this principle of difference is the starting point of Deleuze's philosophy, from which he will deduce a number of related concepts that constitute the conditions of real experience.[23] When a differential relation reciprocally determines two (or more) virtual elements, it produces what is called a *singularity*, a singular point. This is the first concept Deleuze deduces from the differential relation. In mathematics, the singular is not opposed to the university (as in logic), but rather to the ordinary or the regular; a singular point (or singularity) is distinguished from ordinary or regular points, particularly when speaking about points on a determinate figure. A square, for instance, has four singular points, its four corners or *extrema*, and an infinity of ordinary points that compose each side of the square (the calculus of extrema). Simple curves, like the arc of a circle, are determined by singularities that are no longer extrema, but maximum or minimum points (the calculus of maxima and minima). The singularities of complex curves are far more intricate: they constitute those points in the neighborhood of which the differential relation changes sign, and the curve bifurcates, and either increases or decreases (the differential calculus).

Such an assemblage of ordinary and singular points constitutes what Deleuze calls a *multiplicity*—a third concept. One could say of any *determination* in general—that is, of any individual—that it is a combination of the singular and the ordinary, of the remarkable and the regular. The singularities are precisely those points where something "happens" within the multiplicity (an event), or in relation to another multiplicity, causing it to change nature and produce something new. For instance, to take the example of a physical system, the water in my kettle is a multiplicity, and a singularity in the system occurs when the water boils or freezes, thereby changing the nature of the physical multiplicity (its phase space). Similarly, the point where a person breaks down in tears, or boils over in anger, is a singular point in their psychic multiplicity, surrounded by a swarm of ordinary points. Every determinate *thing* is a combination of the singular and the ordinary, a multiplicity that is constantly changing, in perpetual flux.

One can see that Deleuze is here breaking with a long tradition that defined things in terms of an essence or a substance—that is, in terms of an identity. Deleuze's philosophy of difference replaces the traditional concept of substance with the concept of multiplicity, and replaces the concept of essence with the concept of the event.[24] The nature of a thing cannot be determined simply by the Socratic question "What is . . .?" (the question of essence), but only through such questions such as How?, Where?, When?, How many?, From what viewpoint?, and so on (questions concerning events).[25] The question "What is singular and what is ordinary?" is one of the fundamental questions posed in Deleuze's ontology, since, in a general sense, one could say that "Everything is ordinary!" as much as one can say that "Everything is singular!" (FLB 91). A new-found friend might unexpectedly erupt in anger at me, and I might wonder what I could have done to provoke such a singularity in his psychic multiplicity; but then someone might lean over to me and say, "Don't worry, he does this all the time. It's nothing singular, it has nothing to do with you, it's the most *ordinary* thing in the world. We're all used to it." Assessing what is singular and what is ordinary in any given multiplicity is a complex task, which is why Nietzsche could characterize the philosopher as a kind of physician who assesses phenomena as if they were symptoms that reflected a deeper state of relations within the multiplicity at hand.

TWO EXAMPLES: LEIBNIZ AND SPINOZA

Curiously, although Leibniz was one of the great partisans of the thesis that relations are *internal* to their terms, his actual analyses—particularly in the *New Essays*—often tended to illustrate the opposite thesis. Like most great thinkers, he had one foot in the past (his theology) and one foot in the future (everything else). This is particularly true in Leibniz's theory of perception, which Deleuze often appeals to as an illustration of these notions. Leibniz had argued that the genesis of our conscious perceptions must be found in the minute and unconscious perceptions of which they are composed, and which my conscious perception "integrates." For instance, I can apprehend the noise of the surf at a beach, or the buzz of a group of people at a party, but not necessarily the sound of each wave or the voice of each person that they include. A conscious perception is produced when at least two of these minute and virtual perceptions—two waves or two voices—enter into a differential relation (dx/dy) that determines a singularity, which "excels" over the others and becomes conscious. Every conscious perception constitutes a constantly shifting threshold; the multiplicity of minute and virtual perceptions are like the obscure dust of the world, its background noise, what Maimon liked to call the "differentials of consciousness," and the differential relation is the psychic mechanism that extracts from this multiplicity my finite zone of clarity on the world. Leibniz thus divides the Cartesian appeal to the "clear and distinct" into two irreducible domains (DR 146, 213). My conscious perception of the noise of the sea, for example, is *clear but confused* (not distinct), since the minute perceptions of which it is composed remain indistinct. Conversely, the unconscious perceptions are themselves *distinct but obscure* (not clear): distinct, in so far as all the drops of water remain distinct as the genetic elements of perception, with their differential relations, the variations of these relations, and the singular points that they determine; but obscure, in so far as they are not yet "distinguished" or actualized in a conscious perception, and can only be apprehended by thought, or at best, in fleeting states close to those of drowsiness, or vertigo, or dizzy spells.

This is why Deleuze can say that the elements of a genetic philosophy demanded by Maimon were already present in Leibniz. Leibniz determines the conditions of real experience by starting with the obscure and the virtual (a multiplicity); a clear perception is actualized from the obscure by a genetic process (the differential mechanism). These minute perceptions do not indicate the presence of an infinite understanding in us—which was Kant's own criticism of Maimon (DR 192–3; FLB 89)—but rather the presence of an unconscious within finite thought—a differential unconscious that is quite different from the oppositional unconscious developed in Freud. As Deleuze writes,

Salomon Maimon—the first post-Kantian to return to Leibniz—drew all the consequences from this kind of psychic automatism of perception. Far from having perception presuppose an object capable of affecting us, and conditions under which we would be affectable [Kant], it is the reciprocal determination of differentials (dy/dx) that entails *both* the complete determination of the object as perception, and the determinability of space-time as a condition . . . The physical object and mathematical space both refer to a transcendental psychology (differential and genetic) of perception. Space-time ceases to be a pure given in order to become the totality or nexus of differential relations in the subject, and the object itself ceases to be an empirical given in order to become the product of these relations in conscious perception. (FLB 89)

This is what Deleuze means when he says that the conditions of real experience must be determined *at the same time* as what they are conditioning; space and time here are not the pre-given conditions of perception, but are themselves constituted in a plurality of spaces and times *along with* perception.

As a point of comparison, we might note that Deleuze also makes use of these same notions in a completely different seventeenth-century context: no longer Leibniz's theory of perception, but Spinoza's theory of individuation.[26] Spinoza held that an individual is composed of an infinity of parts, which he called "simple bodies." But what exactly counts as a simple body? Deleuze's thesis is that, in Spinoza, simple bodies are *actually infinite*. The actual infinite—which is one of the richest notions of the seventeenth century, at once metaphysical, mathematical, and physical—must be distinguished from both the finite and the indefinite. The formula of the *finite* says that, in any analysis, one reaches a term where the analysis ends—a term such as the "atom." The formula of the *indefinite* says that, no matter how far one pushes the analysis, whatever term one arrives at can always be divided or analyzed further, indefinitely, *ad infinitum*—there is never a final or ultimate term. The formula of the *actually infinite*, however, is neither finite nor indefinite. On the one hand, it says that there are indeed ultimate or final terms that can no longer be divided—thus it is against the indefinite; but on the other hand, it says that these ultimate terms go to infinity—thus they are not atoms but rather terms that are "infinitely small," or as Newton would say "vanishing terms." The notion of actual infinity thus implies a double battle against finitism and against the indefinite.

Three problems posed by this distinction are indicative for our purposes. First, since the terms of an actual infinity are smaller than any given quantity, they can never be treated one by one; that is, they cannot be treated numerically. It would be nonsensical to speak of an infinitely small term that can be considered singularly. Rather, infinitely small terms can only exist in infinite collections. Spinoza's simple bodies, in other words, are in fact *multiplicities*: the simplest of bodies exists as infinite sets of infinitely small terms, which means that they exist collectively and not distributively.[27] These types of multiplicities, however, have no parts: that is, they are *intensive*. Cantor's set theory, of course, would later rediscover the notion of actual infinity on a completely different basis, as *extensive*, and this raises an essential point for Deleuze. The theory of multiplicities, he argues, always entails two types of multiplicity (intensive and extensive, continuous and discrete, non-metric and metric, and so on), since what is important is precisely what takes place *between* the two: their constant transformations and becomings (WP 152). Second, even in Spinoza, these infinitely small terms have no interiority; they have strictly extrinsic relations of exteriority with each other. They form, in Spinoza's own language, a "modal" matter of pure exteriority. This points to a second feature of Deleuze's approach: although he constantly appeals to the "empiricist" dictum of the exteriority of relations, Deleuze winds up exploring this dictum most thoroughly in the "rationalist" thought of Spinoza and Leibniz (less because of their so-called rationalism, however, than because of their introduction of the problem of the infinite). Finally, Spinoza's claim that individuals are composed of an infinity of simple bodies, which are themselves infinite multiplicities, raises the question, How can we distinguish the simple bodies that belong to one individual from those that belong to another? Put differently, how can we distinguish one infinite collection from another infinite collection (as they cannot be distinguished by their parts, since infinite sets exceed any assignable number)? Here again, extensive and intensive multiplicities generated different responses: Cantor's theory of transfinite numbers implied an infinity of infinite extensive sets (aleph numbers), since the set of subsets of a given set is necessarily larger than the original set (WP 120); whereas in the seventeenth century, infinite multiplicities can be distinguished by their differential relation (of a greater or lesser power), since the infinitely small, or a vanishing quantity, cannot be defined independently of a differential relation (which Spinoza called a "relation of movement and rest"). But the question itself points to a third aspect of Deleuze's thought: the search for the conditions of real experience implies a turn away from the "constitutive finitude" of Kant's transcendental subject in favor of the question that preoccupied both Spinoza and Leibniz: Under what relation can the infinite belong to a finite individuality?

THE PROBLEMATIC, THE VIRTUAL, AND THE INTENSIVE

With these Leibnizian and Spinozistic examples in mind, we can return, in our deduction of Deleuzian concepts, to three final notions: the problematic, the virtual, and the intensive. The first two of these concepts correspond to the question: What is the status of the multiplicities constituted by these minute and unconscious perceptions? Deleuze will say that they are objects of Ideas, in a modified Kantian sense, because even though they are not *given* directly in phenomenal experience, they can none the less be *thought* as its conditions. They are, as it were, the noumenon closest to the phenomenon (DR 222). To move from conditions to the conditioned is to move from *a problem to its solution* or, what amounts to the same thing, from the *virtual to the actual*. It remains for us to examine the parallel structure of these two remaining concepts.

We sometimes think of philosophy as a search for solutions to perennial problems, and the terms "true" and "false" are used to qualify these solutions. But in fact the effort of the greatest philosophers was directed at the nature of the problems themselves, and the attempt to determine what a true problem was as opposed to a false one. In the "Transcendental Dialectic" of the first Critique, for instance, Kant tells us that the concept of the World (or the universe, the totality of what is) is an illusion, because it is generated from a false problem, derived from the category of causality. The problem of causality stems from the fact that an event A causes event B, B causes C, C causes D, and so on, and that this causal network stretches indefinitely in all directions. If we could grasp the totality of these series, we would have the World; but in fact, we *cannot* grasp this infinite totality. The true object of the Idea of the world is precisely this *problem*, this causal nexus. When, rather than grasping it as a problem, we instead think of it as an object (the World), and start posing questions about this object (Is it bounded or endless? Is it eternal or did it have a beginning?), we are in the domain of a transcendental illusion, prey to a false problem. This is why Kant said that an Idea—such as the Soul, the World, or God—is an objectively *problematic* structure; it is, as Kant said, "a problem to which there is no solution."[28]

Deleuze has something similar—though not identical—in mind when he says that the conditions of real experience have the *objective* structure of a problem. What does it mean to speak of a problem that has an objective existence—and is not simply a subjective obstacle to be overcome on the path to knowledge? The calculus once again provides a clue. Soon after its invention, it was the calculus that seemed to lend credence to the classical view of determinism, a clockwork universe without any novelty, in which the future was completely determined by the past. Differential equations had allowed mathematicians to predict, for instance, the next solar eclipse (Halley), the exact dates of the return of a comet (Lalande), or the fact that there was another body perturbing the orbit of the planet Neptune, which led to the discovery of Pluto (Le Verrier). The success in solving such astronomical problems led to extravagant claims like those of Laplace: eventually *every* future event will be explainable by the use of differential equations. Today, however, this belief in determinism, as supported by the calculus, has been undermined. The reason is simple: setting up differential equations is one thing, but solving them is quite another. Until the advent of computers, the equations that *could* be solved tended to be linear equations with convergent series, equations that "describe simple, idealized situations where causes are proportional to effects, and forces are proportional to responses."[29] Thus, early on in the history of the calculus, as Ian Stewart has written, "a process of self-selection set in, whereby equations that could not be solved were automatically of less interest than those that could."[30] The equations that could *not* be solved tended to be non-linear equations, which described fields whose infinite series diverge—and most differential equations have turned out to be non-linear equations. None the less, in the late 1800s, Henri Poincaré worked out a way to study such equations. Even though an exact solution was not attainable, Poincaré discovered that he could recognize the general patterns the solutions would have to take for the equations he was working with—such as centers, foci, saddle points, and nodes or knots. Today, through the use of computers, much more complicated solution patterns have been discovered, such as the well-known Lorenz attractor. Put simply, the solution to the equation will be found in one of the points in the attractor, but one cannot say in advance which point it will be, since the series defined by the equation diverge. This is why we cannot predict the weather more accurately—not because we ourselves lack knowledge of all the variables, but because the weather system itself is *objectively problematic*; at every moment in its actuality, it is objectively unassignable which trajectory of the attractor it will follow, since its problematic structure is constituted positively by an infinite set of *divergent series*, which is none the less entirely determined by the attractor itself.

But what, then, is the *modal* status of a problem separated from its solutions? This question brings us to the concept of the virtual, which has become one of Deleuze's most well-known concepts. The concept, however, has little to do with the popular notion of "virtual reality"; rather, it concerns the modal status of problematic Ideas. One might be tempted to assume that problems are the locus of *possibilities* waiting to be realized in their solutions. But Deleuze is strongly critical of the concept of possibility in this context, since it is unable to think the new; nor does it allows us to understand the mechanism of differenciation. The reason is that we tend to think of the possible as somehow "pre-existing" the real, like the infinite set of possible worlds that exist in God's understanding before the act of creation (Leibniz). The process of realization, Deleuze suggests, is then subject to two rules: a rule of resemblance and a rule of limitation. On the one hand, the real is supposed to *resemble* the possible that it realizes, which means that every thing is already given in the identity of the concept, and simply has existence or reality added to it when it is "realized." Moreover, the *means* by which the possible is realized in existence remains unclear; existence always occurs "as a brute eruption, a pure act or leap that always occurs behind our backs" (DR 211). On the other hand, since not every possible is realized, the process of realization involves a *limitation* or exclusion by which some possibilities are thwarted, while others "pass" into the real. With the concept of possibility, in short, *everything is already given*; everything has already been conceived, if only in the mind of God (the theological presuppositions of the modal logic of possible words are not difficult to discern).[31] Instead of grasping existence in its novelty, Deleuze writes, "the whole of existence is here related to a pre-formed element, from which everything is supposed to emerge by a simple 'realization'" (B 20; cf. 98).

In describing the modal status of problematic multiplicities, Deleuze proposes replacing the concept of the possible with the concept of the *virtual*, and substituting for the possible–real opposition the virtual–real complementarity. This is much more than a question of words or semantics. The virtual, as Deleuze formulates it, is not subject to a process of realization, but rather a process of *actualization*, and the rules of actualization are not resemblance and limitation, but rather *divergence* and *difference*—in other words, creation and novelty. "Problematic" and "virtuality," in this sense, are strictly correlative concepts in Deleuze's work. A problem is an objectively determined structure that can be thought apart from its (actual) solutions; it is a virtual multiplicity that is completely differentiated, with its differential relations, its reciprocally determined elements, its singularities, and its convergent and divergent series.[32] Yet the "essence" of a virtual multiplicity (or problem) is to actualize itself, to be actualized (or resolved); and in being actualized, it differs from itself, it necessarily becomes differenciated—that is, it produces difference, it is the production of the new.[33] The condition does not resemble the conditioned (any more than an egg resembles an adult), and the transcendental is not conceived in the image of the empirical. This is precisely how Deleuze fulfills the requirement that, in the conditions of the real, the different must relate to the different *through* difference itself (DR 299), which he summarizes in the complex notion of "differen *t/c* iation" (DR 246): a problem is completely differentiated (with a *t*)—that is, it is constituted by difference through and through (the differential relation, divergent series)—and in being actualized, it necessarily differenciates itself (with a *c*)—that is, it creates a new difference. "The entire Idea is caught up in the mathematical-biological system of differen *t/c* iation" (DR 220).

Thus, at every moment, my existence—like that of a weather system—is objectively *problematic*, which means that it has the structure of a problem, constituted by virtual elements and divergent series, and the exact trajectory that "I" will follow is not predictable in advance. In a moment from now, I will have actualized certain of those virtualities: I will have, say, spoken or gestured in a certain manner. In doing so, I will not have "realized a possibility" (in which the real resembles an already-conceptualized possibility), but will have "actualized a virtuality"—that is, I will have produced something new, a difference (the actual does not resemble the virtual in the way that the real resembles the possible). Moreover, when I actualize a virtuality, or resolve a problem, that does not mean that the problematic structure has disappeared. The next moment, so to speak, still has a problematic structure, but one that is now modified by the actualization that has just taken place. In other words, the actualization of the virtual also *produces* the virtual; the actual and the virtual are like the recto and verso of a single coin. This is what Deleuze means when he says that conditions and the conditioned are determined at one and the same time, and that conditions can never be larger than what they condition—thus fulfilling the Maimonian demands for the conditions of real experience. It is precisely for this reason that we can say, even speaking of ourselves, that every event is *new*, even though the new is never produced *ex nihilo* and always seems to fit into a pattern (this pattern is what we call, in psychic systems, our "character").

Finally, we can introduce a last form of difference into our deduction: intensity, or a difference of potential, which Deleuze analyzes in the fifth chapter of *Difference and Repetition* (DR 222–61). Why does Deleuze need to add this final concept of difference to his description of the transcendental field, or the conditions of the real? We have been speaking, out of convenience and habit, as if the actualization of the virtual produced a new *thing* (such as a perception), but of course this cannot be the case, since any differenciation of difference produces a new difference, which is, precisely, a *relation* and not a thing. Intensity, or difference in potential—to use the language of physics—is Deleuze's term for this new type of relation, which is derived from the comparison of powers expressed in any differential relation (y^2/x = P). "A state of affairs or 'derivative function' . . . does not actualize a virtual without taking from it a *potential* that is distributed in the system of coordinates" (WP 122; cf. DR 174–5). What, then, is this "difference of potential"? Deleuze uses various terms to describe it—intensity, disparity, the unequal-in-itself (and these are not all equivalent)—but perhaps the most telling phrase is that of "the dark precursor," which is a French term for the ominous signs that herald the onset of a storm. A bolt of lightning is a phenomenon that finds its condition in the buildup of an electrostatic charge in a cloud—that is, in the difference of potential between a negative and positive charge; the flash itself, when it occurs, is a "cancelling out" of this difference. This example provides a clue for understanding Deleuze's broader claim: namely, that intensity, or a difference of potential, is the condition of *everything* that appears. It is the reason of the sensible, the noumenon closest to the phenomenon (D 31). "Every phenomenon refers to an inequality by which it is conditioned . . . Every change refers to a difference which is its sufficient reason" (DR 222). And just as differentials must disappear in the solutions of a problem (DR 177–8), intensities necessarily cancel themselves out in the phenomena to which they give rise. Deleuze's analyses of the concept of intensity are among his most complex, but at one point he offers a highly concrete example of the notion, drawn from an everyday experience. At a party, I am hungry, so I go to a table a few feet away and grab an *hors d'œuvre*; a difference of potential is here opened up between my sensation of hunger and my perception of the food. My movement in space finds its sufficient reason in this difference of potential, and a kind of equalization of this difference in potential occurs when I pick up the *hors d'œuvre* and ingest the food. Yet this "cancelling out" of the difference does not mean it has disappeared, but that a *new* difference of potential has opened up: having satiated my hunger, I turn around and see a friend with whom I enter into conversation. It is precisely the *new* that links up virtual problems with their actualization in an intensity; the new "emerges like the act of solving such a problem, or—what amounts to the same thing—like the actualization of a potential and the establishing of communication between disparates" (DR 246).

With this we break off the deduction, somewhat arbitrarily, since our aim was not to explicate all of Deleuze's concepts, but to follow a rather specific trajectory through Deleuze's thinking about the problem of the new. First, there is the demarcation of the problem of the conditions of *real experience*, as opposed to what is logically possible or the conditions of possible experience. Second, there is the twofold demarcation of what it means to talk about conditions of real experience (or the new), derived from the work of Salomon Maimon: one must seek the *genetic* elements of real experience, and one must posit a principle of *difference* as the fulfillment of this demand. Finally, Deleuze finds in the model of the calculus various concepts of difference (the differential relation, singularities, multiplicities, and so on) that serve to demarcate a transcendental field that is both virtual and problematic, and which serves to define the conditions of real experience. For Deleuze, Being itself always presents itself under a problematic form, which means that it is constituted, in its actuality, by constantly *diverging* series: that is, by the production of the new. The resuscitation of a positive conception of divergent series, following the advent of non-Euclidean geometries and the new algebras, itself represents a kind of Copernican revolution in contemporary mathematics.[34] And Deleuze's philosophy of difference—in part derived from these mathematical advances—represents a Copernican revolution of its own in philosophy, in so far as it makes the problem of the new (difference) not simply a question to be addressed in a remote region of metaphysics, but rather the primary determination of Being itself.

The Open

The Idea of the Open: Bergson's Theses on Movement

Bergson put forward the thesis that "the open is the whole," and in this essay I would like to explore Bergson's idea of the open, as well as the manner in which Deleuze appropriated and made use of it in his own work.[1] The concept of the open, to be sure, is not unique to Bergson. Heidegger proposed his own concept of the open; there are poems by Rilke and Hölderlin on the open, which Heidegger picked up on and discussed; and Giorgio Agamben has recently written a book on the topic.[2] While I will not discuss these other writers, it is clear that the theme of the open is an important concern in contemporary philosophy. Despite the enormous differences between Heidegger and Bergson, they seem to have been in agreement in linking together three notions:

1. the whole, or totality
2. the open, or the idea of opening; and
3. time and temporality, or what Bergson calls duration.

It is the interrelation that Bergson establishes between these three notions that I would like to examine in what follows.

BERGSON'S METHOD OF INTUITION

Bergson called his methodological approach "intuition"—perhaps an ill-fated terminological choice, since what Bergson means by this term has little to do with its use in everyday language (as in the phrase "woman's intuition") or in mathematics. For Bergson, the world is a world of mixtures—what is given to us in experience are always mixtures or complexes of space-time (10 Nov 1981)—and Bergson utilizes the term "intuition" to describe the method through which one can comprehend the mixtures that are given to us in experience. The method has three aspects:

1. The task of philosophy is to *analyze* these mixtures.
2. To analyze is to seek out what is *pure* in any given mixture.
3. What is pure in a mixture are not elements but *tendencies*.[3]

For instance, the act of recognizing a friend in a hallway is a mixture that implies both perception (I see the person in front of me) and memory (I recognize them because I have a memory of their face). In *Matter and Memory*, Bergson therefore attempted to create concepts of *pure* perception and *pure* memory; since perception and memory are mixed in experience, we will have a confused conception of even a simple act of recognition if we are unable to separate out the isolatable "tendencies" of perception and memory. Deleuze and Guattari, in *Capitalism and Schizophrenia*, adopted this Bergsonian method when they isolated the concept of four "pure" social formations—primitive territorialities, States, capitalism, the war machine— even though in fact these types are only ever encountered in experience in concrete mixtures. It is only when we have isolated these pure concepts that we can begin to analyze the complexities of the mixtures found in any given social assemblage. In a similar manner, Deleuze will arrive at the Idea of the Open through an applica- tion of Bergson's method of intuition to the problem of movement. The question Bergson asks is: What is pure movement? What is movement as a pure tendency? At the beginning of *The Movement-Image* (MI 1–11), Deleuze summarizes Bergson's analyses of movement in terms of three theses, which I would like to use to structure the comments that follow:

1. Movement is distinct from the space covered.
2. The instant is an immobile section of movement.
3. Movement is a mobile section of duration (movement expresses a change in duration or the Whole, which is equivalent to the Open).

BERGSON'S FIRST THESIS: MOVEMENT IS DISTINCT FROM SPACE COVERED

Bergson's first thesis is that we have a tendency to confuse movement with the space traversed. Zeno's famous paradox of movement, for instance, depends on this confu- sion: Achilles will never catch up with the tortoise, or an arrow will never reach its target, because in order to reach its target, it first has to traverse half the space to the target, and then half of the remaining space, and then half of that remaining space, and so on to infinity. But Zeno, Bergson argues, confuses the *movement* of the arrow with the *space traversed* by the arrow. The space traversed is discrete or divisible, and divisible to infinity, whereas movement, as the act of traversing that space, is indivisible or continuous. In his first thesis, Bergson establishes a categorical opposi- tion between divisible space and indivisible movement: movement is not a divisible space, but an indivisible *duration*. Bergson then gives us a second presentation of his first thesis. If we begin with divisible space, as Zeno does, we can indeed reconsti- tute movement, but we can reconstitute it only as a succession: that is, as a succes- sion of *positions* in space or a succession of *moments* in time. In *Creative Evolution*, Bergson will call this the *cinematographic illusion*, the illusion through which cinema works; twenty-four *immobile* frames per second pass through the projector, but these immobile frames produce the illusion of movement taking place in a uniform time. Indeed, it is from these two notions—immobile frames or sections, and the form of succession to which we subject them—that we derive the idea of an abstract, homogeneous, equalizable, and uniform time. But this uniform conception of time misses the nature of movement for two obvious reasons. First, it tries to reconstitute movement out of something that is *not* movement: that is, out of immobile frames or instants. (Philosophers are doing nothing other when they utilize the symbolism of T^1, T^2, T^3, and so on, to analyze time.) Second, and more importantly, no matter how close the immobile instants are, there is always an interval between the two instances—and movement will always be happening in the interval, and not at the instant (no matter how small the interval may be). This is another way of saying that movement always takes place behind the back of the thinker. One can multiply the immobile cuts—the positions in space or the moments in time—but it is not by multiplying the immobile cuts that one can reconstitute movement.

An important consequence follows from this analysis: movement, which is always happening in the interval, can never be measured by an abstract and homogeneous time. Consider the walk of a human, the gait of a horse, the dash of a lion, the leaping of a gazelle, or the charge of a bull. These different movements cannot be said to unfold in a homogeneous time because they are irreducible to each other—there is no common measure between them. Each movement has its own duration, its own articulations, its own divisions and subdivisions (each of us has a style of walking that is recognizable to others). The Pythagoreans discovered that even the motions of the celestial spheres are incommensurable, just as there is no common unit that can measure the sides of the square and the diagonal of a square. Abstract time is composed of common units, but real movement is not. If Achilles overtakes the tortoise, it is because his own units of movement—Achilles' leaps and bounds—have no common measure with the small steps of the tortoise. A lion chases a gazelle: if the lion takes down the gazelle, it is because of its own running; if the gazelle escapes, it is because of its own leaps. There is no abstract time in which the chase unfolds, because there is always something *unforeseen*; we cannot say in advance who is going to win. The movement of the lion and the movement of the gazelle are two qualitatively different movements, two different durations; they are not composed of common units. One movement may interrupt the other, another movement might overtake it; it is with a leap that the lion will overtake the gazelle, and not with an abstract quantity displaceable in a homogeneous time. If we were to model these movements, they would take the form of non-linear equations—in other words, they would be *problems without solutions*. The idea toward which Bergson's first thesis is heading is the following: movement is fundamentally temporal, not spatial—that is, movement in space expresses, more profoundly, a multiplicity of different durations in time.

PARADOX AND THE SYSTEM OF JUDGMENT

What is the significance of Zeno's paradox, which claims that movement is impossible because the space traversed is infinitely divisible? From a scholarly viewpoint, Zeno's paradox is famous because it is an example of the method of exhaustion, an early version of the differential calculus, and it is clear that Zeno had a profound comprehension of the complexities and problems of Greek mathematics. At the same time, the paradox seems to flout the deliverances of experience. Zeno obviously knows that objects move, he knows that Achilles overtakes the tortoise and that the arrow reaches its target. Why, then, does he claim the opposite? The paradox seems to support the ancient image of the philosopher as someone with their head in the clouds (Thales); an archer could shoot an entire quiver of arrows into his target, and Zeno would be standing next to him with his paradox saying, "Look, I can prove to you that movement is impossible." The paradox seems fascinating and provocative, yet somehow ridiculous. Indeed, Socrates was famous for making a claim not dissimilar to Zeno's: evil does not exist, evil is nothing. This too seems to be a claim that flies in the face of common sense, but Socrates' argument is as instructive as Zeno's. Socrates asks his interlocutor, "You are an evil person? You want to kill?" The response: "Yes, I want to kill everyone." Socrates: "But why do you want to kill everyone?" Response: "No reason, just because I want to, it would give me pleasure!" Socrates: "But is pleasure a good or an evil for you?" Response: "Obviously giving myself pleasure is a good thing." And Socrates triumphs: "But now you are contradicting yourself. What you want is not to kill everyone; killing everyone is just a means. What you want is your pleasure: that is the true end of your actions. You are simply mistaken about the nature of the good." At which point, Socrates' interlocutors usually walk away, saying, "It's impossible to talk with you, Socrates . . . ." Socrates is trying to show that the evil person is mistaken: no one is voluntarily evil, since even the will of the killer is a will for the good. So find out what your good is: if it is killing, fine, but that is still a good, and you are not really seeking evil. Hence Socrates' refrain: Evil is nothing.

Socrates' point is that the evil person is someone who *judges badly*; they think they are pursuing evil when in fact they are pursuing the Good, their own good. The philosopher may have his head in the clouds, but he is none the less good because he claims to *judge well*. What philosophy invents, in other words, is a *system of judgment*. If a judgment takes the form of paradox, it is because, at its simplest level, paradox consists in saying: there is something which "is," yet which cannot be thought; x exists, and yet it is unthinkable. This is what links Zeno and Socrates: movement and evil are actually existing things, but the problem is how to *think* these existing things. What Zeno tries to show is not that movement "is not"; rather, he tries to show that movement as movement is unthinkable, that movement cannot be thought without contradiction. Similarly, at bottom, what Socrates wants to show is that evil as evil cannot be thought without contradiction. A paradox announces the unthinkability of something that exists.

Why does paradox give such intense pleasure to philosophers? The more one insists that what they are saying is ridiculous—movement cannot be thought, evil cannot be thought—the more the philosophers will retort: fine, as you like, but tell me how you deal with this paradox. At first sight, this would not seem to be a victory for thought; thought cannot think movement, it cannot think evil, it cannot think existence, it hardly seems to be able to think anything. What, then, can thought think? It turns out that thought can think thoughts such as "Only Justice is just" (Plato)—which amounts to saying that, if existence is unthinkable, what is thinkable is pure ideality, the Idea. The more philosophers are content to think ideality, the less they are content to think existing things. What are they in the process of doing? They are accomplishing the destiny of philosophy, which is to constitute a system of judgment: that is, a means of judging everything that is, everything that exists. This is Deleuze's version of a Nietzschean theme: life is judged in terms of values that are higher than life, and existence is judged in terms of idealities that are higher than existence. One of Deleuze's constant themes can be summarized in a phrase borrowed from Artaud, *to have done with judgment*: that is, to have done with the system of judgment. This is why Deleuze sets philosophers such as Spinoza and Nietzsche against Socrates. They say: evil may be nothing, but then *the good is nothing either*. But "beyond good and evil" does not mean beyond good and bad. On the contrary, it is only by ridding ourselves of the transcendent idealities of Good and Evil that we can begin to *think* the existing realities of the good and the bad. As Deleuze often repeats, he wants to explore the conditions of *real* experience and not merely possible experience. This is the lens—or at least one of the lenses—through which we should view Deleuze's interest in Bergson. If Zeno says movement is unthinkable, Bergson's retort is to ask: What are the conditions under which the reality of movement can become thinkable? Such is the upshot of Bergson's first thesis: movement is unthinkable as long as we confuse it with the space covered.

BERGSON'S SECOND THESIS ON MOVEMENT: THE INSTANT IS AN IMMOBILE SECTION OF MOVEMENT

We can now turn to Bergson's second thesis on movement. The first thesis says that it is an illusion to reconstitute movement from moments or instants. The second thesis, developed in *Creative Evolution*, says that there are in fact two types of illusion: that is, two ways of reconstituting movement from privileged instants—the ancient and the modern. A common way of characterizing this difference is to say that ancient science was qualitative whereas modern science is quantitative. But Bergson has his own way of assessing the difference: whereas the ancients related movement to *privileged moments*, modern science related movement to *any moment whatever*.[4] The shift from the ancient to the modern conception of movement was a fundamental revolution in thought.

For the ancients, movement had its natural articulations, as when we divide someone's life naturally into a period of childhood and a period of old age. Even though we know there is continuity in the temporality of someone's life, our perception and our language tend to isolate certain privileged moments or periods, "each presenting a kind of individuality."[5] The same holds for moving bodies, which, as Aristotle says, can be defined by their *downward* or *upward* movement, or their tendency to move toward a *center*. A pendulum, for instance, will eventually come to rest at a single point, and this culminating point or final term was set up as the essential moment of the movement of the pendulum, the *telos* toward which it was tending. From this viewpoint, Aristotle's Forms as well as Plato's Ideas "correspond to privileged or salient moments in the history of things."[6] Conceived in this way, movement expressed a "dialectic" of forms. Movement was the regulated transition from one Form or Idea to another, like the poses in a dance or the periods of a person's life. When water boils, for instance, it is not that the Form of the Cold becomes the Form of the Hot; rather, it is matter itself that passes from one form to the other, from the Form of the Cold to the Form of the Hot (10 Nov 1981). The operation through which a form is actualized or realized or "instantiated" in matter is what the Greeks called an "information"—just as a sculptor actualizes a human form in a block of marble by in-forming matter (10 Nov 1981). In themselves, the Forms are immobile—or, which amounts to the same thing, they are movements of pure thought—and it is matter that passes from one form to another. The movement of matter is physical, but the sequence of Forms is a purely logical or dialectical sequence.

The modern scientific revolution—its stroke of genius—consisted in relating movement, no longer to privileged instants, but to *any-instant-whatever*.[7] There is no longer any privilege of one instant over another instant or of one Form over another Form. In modern science, all moments are equal to each other, and equidistant from each other.[8] The great idea of Descartes's geometry is that a figure refers to a trajectory which is determinable at every instant of the trajectory—which means that Descartes no longer refers to a figure or Form, but to an *equation*. Movement is subject to an *analysis* rather than a *dialectic*. This is the revolution, in modern science, from transcendence to immanence: rather than reconstituting movement through transcendent instants that refer to Forms outside of movement, movement is reconstituted through the immanent elements of movement itself. In *Creative Evolution*, Bergson provides four examples of this transformation in modern science: modern astronomy (Kepler), which determined the relation between an orbit and the time needed to traverse it; modern physics (Galileo), which determined the relation between the space traversed by a falling body and the time it takes the body to fall; modern geometry (Descartes), which determined the equation of a flat curve—that is, the position of a point on a moving straight line at any moment in its course; and modern differential and integral calculus (Newton and Leibniz), which is based on the idea of sections or cuts that can be brought infinitely close together.[9] In modern science, the ancient dialectic of Forms is replaced by the mechanical succession of instants. "Modern science must be defined pre-eminently by its aspiration *to take time as an independent variable*," that is, by relating movement to any-instant-whatever."[10]

Now for Bergson, what remains common to these two approaches to movement—the ancient and the modern—is that they both recompose movement by means of something immobile, either through Forms that transcend movement and are actualized in matter, or through immobile cuts that are internal or immanent to movement (10 Nov 1981). In both cases, movement is sacrificed to the immobile, and duration is sacrificed to a uniform time. Put differently, one could say that for both ancient and modern science, *the Whole is given*: that is, the Whole is already given in advance.[11] For the ancients, eternity is given to us in the Forms or Ideas, and time is a degradation of the eternal. As Plato put it in the *Timaeus* (37d), "Time is the mobile image of eternity." Whence the idea of a circular time, which means that the *reason* for time lies outside of time in eternal Ideas, in the Forms. In modern science, the Whole is given in a different manner: not in the form of eternal Ideas outside of time, but in the form of time itself, in the sense that *the following instant repeats the preceding instant*. Movement is already finished, already given; it is not in process. The concept of "determinism," as exemplified by Laplace's demon—the presumption that the whole of the future and past can be determined from knowledge of the present—is itself derived from the idea that *the Whole is already given*. For both ancient and modern science, the Whole is givable in principle, even if we never attain it, given our finite understanding.

Now Bergson argues that modern science, by relating movement to any-instant-whatever and making time an independent variable, should have rendered possible a new metaphysics of time that broke with the old metaphysics of the eternal—that is, a new thought of time, a thought of duration. All that was needed was for science to renounce the idea that the Whole is given or even givable. Many modern thinkers, such as Kant, had said that the Whole is neither given nor givable, but they thereby thought that the Whole is a notion devoid of meaning, or at least a notion whose function is purely practical. But this is not Bergson's thesis. Bergson insists that the Whole is a perfectly consistent notion, on the condition that we understand that *the Whole is the Open*. At first sight, this might seem to be a strange hypothesis uniting two seemingly contradictory notions: the Idea of a fundamental openness, and the Idea of a Whole or a Totality, which would seem to imply something closed or finished. In saying that the Whole is the Open, Bergson is saying that the Whole is duration; it is creation. Bergson is establishing an equivalence between four terms: the Whole = the Open = duration = creation (or the new).

What both ancient science and modern science miss, according to Bergson, is that movement is always taking place in the interval: by reconstituting movement through immobile cuts, even modern science fails to grasp movement adequately. What is important is not the manner in which one instant succeeds another, but rather the manner in which movement continues from one instant to another. Movement is a phenomenon of *continuation*, and this continuation of movement from one instant to another is irreducible to any of the instants or to any succession of instants. What Bergson calls *duration* is precisely this continuation of movement from one instant to another. In movement, the preceding instant is continued in the following instant, but the following instant is not merely the repetition of the preceding instant. Rather, something new and unforeseen occurs in the following moment (the lion leaps on to the gazelle and kills it). The concept of duration thus implies a metaphysics that takes as its fundamental question: How can something new be produced?[12] It is this question that leads us to Bergson's third thesis.

BERGSON'S THIRD THESIS ON MOVEMENT: MOVEMENT IS A MOBILE SECTION OF DURATION

Bergson's first thesis said that *movement is distinct from the space covered* (space is divisible, but movement is not; it is a continuation). The second thesis said that *the instant is an immobile section of movement* (it is an illusion to reconstitute movement through immobile cuts, as in the cinema). Bergson's third thesis now says that *movement is a mobile section of duration*: that is, movement expresses a change in duration or in the Whole. What is duration? Duration is what changes, and what never ceases to change. But, then, what is change? This will be the substance of Bergson's third thesis: change is an affection of the whole. Movement is a relation between parts, but change is an affection of the Whole. More to the point: movement is merely an expression of duration—that is, any relation between parts expresses an affection of the whole. As Bergson will put it, every *translation* in space (movement as a relation between parts) expresses something more profound: that is, a *transformation* or a change in the Whole.[13] Beyond the mechanism of translation, in other words, we must imagine a mechanism of transformation (17 Nov 1981). I would like to explore this third thesis briefly by proposing two sub-theses, which will attempt to explicate Bergson's claim in terms of the concept of *difference of potential* and the concept of *relation*.

1. *First Sub-Thesis: Movement Implies a Difference of Potential (Difference in Intensity)*. Consider the following series of *real* movements. As the sun is setting, I leave my house in town and go for a walk in the country. This is a movement, a translation in space, but it is also an assignable transformation in the affection of the Whole: the whole of the town, the whole of the day, the whole of the country. While I am walking, a flock of birds takes off in flight in a migration—this too is a change in the whole, an expression of a climatic change. Later that evening, at a gathering, I am hungry, so I walk over to a table and eat an *hors-d'œuvre*: another transformation of the whole. To explain these transformations, Deleuze appeals to a concept derived from physics: a *difference of potential* (17 Nov 1981). At the gathering, a difference of potential is opened up between my sensation of hunger and the perception of the food, and my movement in space finds its sufficient reason in this difference of potential. A kind of equalization of this potential will take place when I absorb the food, at which point another difference of potential will be opened up in the whole: having satiated my hunger, I turn around a see a friend, and I walk over to him and start up a conversation. To move from one state of the whole to another state of the whole is to move from one difference of potential to another difference in potential—a system that is neither stable nor unstable but "metastable" (LS 103). Movements of translation thus never exist in a pure state, but always express deeper qualitative transformations in the whole; every movement of translation refers to a perturbation, a modification, a change in tension or energy, a passage from one difference to another. These differences of potential are never localizable, since what is localizable are the two terms between which the difference is established. Rather, the differences concern the whole—it is the whole that functions by means of differences that constitute the sufficient reason of every movement of translation. This is the theme that Deleuze develops in more detail in the fifth chapter of *Difference and Repetition*: "Every change refers to a difference which is its sufficient reason. Everything which happens and everything which appears is correlated with orders of differences: differences of level, temperature, pressure, tension potential, *difference of intensity*" (DR 222).

For this reason, the Whole, or wholes, must not be confused with sets; sets are closed systems, whereas the whole is the open. On this score, one can compare Bergson's examples of real movement (such as sugar melting in water) with the typical example of movement given in seventeenth-century physics: the movement of billiard balls.[14] If this example was so popular, it was because the seventeenth century was attempting to create a science of movement and the communication of movement. But when Bergson wants to make his point that translations in space express transformations of the whole, he purposely relies on different examples— that is, he considers examples of real movements, and not abstract movements grasped in artificial and isolated situations. Such is the difference between a set and a whole: a set is a collection of parts in a closed system, and everything that is closed is artificially closed, whereas the whole is duration and change—that is, the open (for Bergson, the whole can never be the set of all sets). It is true that the artificial division of a set or a closed system is not a pure illusion; it is well founded. A system can always be closed and isolated from duration; the organization of matter makes closed systems possible, and the deployment of space makes them necessary. Indeed, phenomena can only be studied scientifically by relating them to closed systems; it is only under these conditions that a system can be quantified, for what makes an equation possible is a system of coordinates (abscissa and ordinates). But this is the reason that science is incapable of grasping a movement of translation as the expression of a more profound transformation (a change in the whole). For no system can ever be entirely closed; as Deleuze writes, "the whole is not a closed set, but rather that by virtue of which any set is never absolutely closed, never completely sheltered, but that which keeps it open somewhere as if by the finest thread that attaches it to the rest of the universe" (MI 10).

Whole and part, in short, are two notions that do not exist on the same plane. Many thinkers have made the claim that the whole is something other than the sum of its parts, but Bergson's uniqueness lies in the justification he gives for this claim: parts are always in space, whereas the whole *is* time, it is *real* time. This is another way of saying that the whole is never given, since the whole is the open: it is constantly changing; it is duration; it is time itself. So two formulas that could be said to correspond to Bergson's first thesis now take on a more rigorous status: "immobile sections + abstract time" refers to closed sets whose parts are immobile cuts, and whose successive states are calculated in an abstract time; while "real movement + concrete duration" refers to the opening up of a whole that endures, and whose movements are so many mobile sections traversing the closed systems. For Bergson, the greatness of modern science was that it took time as an independent variable, and yet despite itself science remained grafted on to an ancient metaphysics. With the notion of duration, Bergson attempted to provide the metaphysics that corresponds to modern science, which is a metaphysics of real time rather than a metaphysics of the eternal.

Bergson's third thesis thus allows Deleuze to isolate three levels of real movement:

1. there are discrete objects in space
2. then there are the movements of these objects (translation), which are continuous from one moment to the next

3. but these movements find their sufficient reason as affections or transformations of the Whole, which is the Open (differences of potential).

All three of these levels coexist, and nothing would function if duration itself did not have the power of sometimes subdividing itself into sub-durations and rhythms (the leap of the gazelle, the dash of the lion), while at other times uniting and gathering together these rhythms and sub-durations into one and the same duration (the lion tackles the gazelle). Every movement is itself a mobile cut in the flux of duration, but duration (the whole) is a perpetual movement through which these flows of time are constantly being divided and gathered together (whence "the idea of a co-existence in duration of all degrees of expansion and contraction," DR 331 n14).

2. *Second Sub-Thesis: The Whole is Defined by Relations.* The second sub-thesis concerns the status of *relations*, and it is here that we approach Deleuze's own contribution to thinking the idea of the Open.[15] The problem of relations has haunted philosophy since its inception, and it is inextricably linked to the problem of judgment. The simplest form of judgment is the judgment of *attribution*: the sky is blue, A is B. But it is not difficult to see that every judgment of attribution is a kind of an offense against the principle of identity, A is A. While it is easy to comprehend "A is A" (a thing is identical to itself), how is it possible to say that "A is B"? Philosophy would ultimately explain this by saying that, in a judgment of attribution, A and B are not the same: the judgment attributes a *predicate* (blue) to a *subject* (sky), or a property or attribute to a substance. Every metaphysics of substance can be said to find its origin in the judgment of attribution.

But there is a second kind of judgment, more complex, which is the judgment of *relation*—for instance, A is smaller than B. Judgments of relation are very different from judgments of attribution, and opened up a different path for metaphysics. When we say "Peter is smaller than Paul," we are no longer attributing a property to a subject. If I say that "being smaller than" is a property of A, I would also have to say, at the same time, that "being taller than" is also a property of A, since there is also a C that is smaller than A ("Peter is smaller than Paul, but taller than Mary"). But Plato had already pointed out that this would entail attributing contradictory properties to the same subject ("being smaller than," "being taller than"), which would seem to be an offense against the principle of non-contradiction, just as the judgment of attribution seems to be an offence against the principle of identity. One might object by saying that the properties being predicated are not simply "smaller than" and "taller than," but rather "smaller than Paul" and "taller than Mary," but this does not solve the problem; Paul and Mary are themselves real beings, and while the concept of Peter may contain properties, but it is not possible for the concept of Peter to contain other real beings. So when I say, "Peter is taller than Paul," this relation is neither a property of Peter nor a property of Paul; rather, it is something *between* the two. But what is this "between the two"? To what does this "between" belong if it belongs to neither of the two terms? Philosophy has offered at least three responses to this question, which are exemplified in the positions of Plato, Leibniz, and Hume.

For Plato, relations do not depend on their terms because they are Ideas with a capital "I." For instance, there is an Idea of the Small and an Idea of the Large, and when we say that "A is smaller than B and greater than C," we are saying that A participates in the Idea of the Small in relation to term B and that it participates in the Idea of the Large in relation to term C. For Plato, relations are irreducible to attributes because they are pure Ideas that go beyond the sensible world. In a sense, Plato anticipates the path that Deleuze will take: once one has discovered the world of relations, one can ask if, in the end, *every* judgment is not a judgment of relation—that is, if there are not properties at all but *only* relations.

Leibniz took a quite different approach. He attempted to show that all judgments of relations were reducible to a judgment of attribution, and he was willing to draw the necessary conclusion: every concept that designates a real being (such as Peter, Paul, Adam, or Caesar), he realized, must contain the totality of all other concepts. Why? Because Peter is *related* to Paul, and more distantly, to Caesar, and even more distantly, to Adam—which amounts to saying that the concept of every being necessarily expresses the totality of the world. This means that, in Leibniz, relations are *internal* to their terms; and that if the concept of Peter contains all other terms, then all imaginable relations can be reduced to attributions, to properties of the concept.

The greatness of Hume, finally, was to have arrived on the scene and argued that relations are *external* to their terms. "For me," Deleuze would later comment, "this proposition was like a clap of thunder in philosophy" (14 Dec 1982). Hume's admonition is, "Accept exteriority." Rather than invoking Ideas, as Plato does, or undertaking operations as complex as those of Leibniz, Hume asks us to accept the world in which we live, which is a world of exteriorities. The fundamental thesis of empiricism is not that knowledge is derived from experience or that everything finds its origin in the sensible, but rather that relations are external to their terms. Properties may be internal to the terms to which they are attributed, but relations are exteriorities. Empiricism thus found itself faced with the task of creating a new logic—a logic of relations—which broke definitively with the logic of attribution. (This logic would begin with Hume's theory of probabilities, and take on a definitive form in Bertrand Russell.) Prior to Hume, one might say that philosophers would only support interiority; to comprehend something was to interiorize it—to interiorize it in a concept, interiorize it in a subject. Hume inaugurates a completely different theory of thought whose task is no longer to internalize but to reflect on a radical exteriority. Deleuze will ultimately derive two consequences from the principle of the exteriority of relations.

First, it is not possible to think relations without thinking of a *becoming*. When I say that "Peter resembles Paul," this resemblance is a relation that is not contained in the concept of either Peter or Paul, which means that *the relation cannot change without the concepts changing*; the resemblance can be accentuated or lost. Whereas properties are solid, relations are fragile; a relation is not only external to its terms, but it is essentially transitive, in the sense of "transitory." If it is so difficult to think relations, it is because relations imply or envelop change; relation is the domain of becoming. As Deleuze writes:

I believe that one cannot think relation independent of a becoming that is at least virtual, whatever the relation might be; and that, in my opinion, the theorists of relation, however strong they might have been, have not seen this. But I would like to insist on this point. (14 Dec 1982)

Second, once one starts down this path, one cannot stop. If there are relations between any two terms, and if the terms change when the relations change, then at the limit, perhaps there are no longer even terms but only packets of relations. What one calls a term (or a thing or a substance) is itself only a packet of relations: that is, a multiplicity or a manifold.

> Once you discover the world of relations, you can ask if *every* judgment is not a judgment of relation, that is, when you say "Peter has blue eyes," you can ask if that is not already a judgment of relation, and that there are not even properties but only relations. (14 Dec 1982)

Such is the mystery of relations: a relation is between two things, it unites them, but it cannot be reduced to either of them. For Deleuze, the greatness of Anglo-American philosophy is that it developed a metaphysics that consisted in seeing this "in-between" in itself and for itself. This where Deleuze's logic of relations links up with and extends Bergson's theses on movement: the whole is the open—that is, duration and change—but the domain of becoming itself implies a logic of pure relations.

PART IV

Deleuze and Contemporary Philosophy

Jacques Derrida

Deleuze and Derrida, Immanence and Transcendence: Two Directions in Recent French Thought

Giorgio Agamben, in a recent essay,[1] has identified two different trajectories in contemporary French philosophy, both of which pass through Heidegger: a trajectory of *transcendence*, which includes Levinas and Derrida, and goes back through Husserl to Kant; and a trajectory of *immanence*, which includes Foucault and Deleuze, and goes back through Nietzsche to Spinoza.[2] Deleuze and Levinas are no doubt the most obvious representatives of these two trajectories; Deleuze explicitly describes himself as a philosopher of immanence, while Levinas explicitly claims the mantle of transcendence (the "Other" being the paradigmatic concept of transcendence). But Derrida clearly belongs to the trajectory of transcendence as well, and Agamben's typology can thus provides us with a valuable grid for assessing the relation between Derrida and Deleuze, at least in a preliminary manner. Agamben does not himself develop his insight in detail, and perhaps for good reason. Immanence and transcendence are both highly overdetermined terms in the history of philosophy, and it is not immediately clear what it would mean to be a philosopher of either one. The very term "transcendence" has theological and spiritual overtones that tend to obscure the wider history and varied philosophical uses of the concept. Moreover, one might be tempted to question the use of such a "binary opposition" to characterize philosophers like Derrida and Deleuze, given their shared critique of the use of oppositional strategies in philosophy. But such a dismissal would be both hasty and superficial. Immanence and transcendence are relative terms, not opposites, which means that in each case one must ask: Immanent to what? Or transcendent to what? As such, immanence and transcendence can be helpful terms, not so much in determining the differing "positions" of Derrida and Deleuze, but rather as means of charting out their differing philosophical "trajectories," at least relative to each other. There are three traditional areas of philosophy, in particular, in which these terms have found a specific use—namely, the fields of subjectivity, ontology, and epistemology. Derrida and Deleuze have written on each of these topics, and although these fields certainly do not exhaust the themes of immanence and transcendence, they none the less provide points of reference from which we can evaluate the work of Derrida and Deleuze using

Agamben's typology. In what follows, then, I would like to consider each of these domains in turn, showing how, in each case, Derrida has explicitly aligned himself with a trajectory of transcendence, while Deleuze has consistently followed a trajectory of immanence. At best, this is a propaedeutic study, a kind of "vectorial" analysis that seeks to diagram, in a general manner, the divergent directions Derrida and Deleuze have followed in their philosophical careers, despite (or perhaps even because of) their initial interest in a number of shared problematics.

THE FIELD OF SUBJECTIVITY

The tradition of subjectivity provides us with a first and obvious model of transcendence. For any philosophy that begins with the subject or the mind—that is, much of post-Cartesian philosophy—the concept of immanence refers to the sphere of the subject, while transcendence refers to what lies outside the subject, such as the "external world" or the "Other." In this tradition, the term "transcendence" refers to that which transcends the field of consciousness immanent to the subject. On this score, one has only to think of the problems posed in Husserl's fifth *Cartesian Meditation*, the theme of "Being-with-Others" in Sartre, or Levinas's own philosophy of alterity. But one also finds, in the subjectivist tradition, a second, and perhaps more profound, problem of transcendence, which is what Sartre called, in his article of the same name, "The Transcendence of the Ego." In Kant, the ego or the "I think" accompanies all (or most of) my representations—it is precisely what makes them *mine*. Against Kant, Sartre pushed for a conception of an impersonal transcendental field that was without an ego, much like William James's notion of a "pure flux of consciousness."[3] In other words, when one says that the field of consciousness is immanent *to* a transcendental subject, one is already erecting the subject as an element of transcendence that goes beyond the flux of experience.[4] Already, then, we find two models of transcendence at work in the subjectivist tradition: the other (or the "world," in Heidegger) is what transcends the self, but the subject itself is already transcendent in relation to "experience" (passive syntheses). Consequently, one might say that there are two general means by which one can call into question the status of the transcendental subject (the well-known theme of the "death of the subject"): by appealing either to *the transcendence of the other* or to *the immanent flux of experience* itself. It would be simplistic to suggest that Derrida simply followed the first path and Deleuze the second, but the "elective affinities" of the two thinkers seems evident. Derrida and Deleuze, however, are both critical of the subjectivist tradition, and the more telling differences between them lie elsewhere.

THE FIELD OF ONTOLOGY

A second model for thinking about the immanence / transcendence distinction is related, not to the question of subjectivity (the field of consciousness), but rather to the question of ontology (the field of Being). Put simply, an immanent or pure ontology would be an ontology in which there is nothing "beyond" or "higher than" or "superior to" Being. By contrast, the fundamental ontological categories of transcendence would include the "God" of the Christian tradition, the "Good" in Plato, the "One" in Plotinus[5]—all of which are said to be "beyond" Being, "otherwise" than Being ("transcendent" to Being), and are thereby used to "judge" Being, or at least to account for Being.[6] On the question of Being, Derrida and Deleuze—like all contemporary thinkers—are clearly indebted to Heidegger, who inaugurated the renaissance of ontology in twentieth-century thought (which is why Heidegger rightly functions as the lynchpin in Agamben's classification). Yet it is equally clear that Deleuze and Derrida take Heidegger's ontological project in two very different directions: Deleuze attempts to develop an immanent ontology, while Derrida's deconstruction necessarily operates on the basis of a formal structure of transcendence.[7] On this score, we can make use of several rubrics to help map the divergent ontological trajectories of Derrida and Deleuze: their respective relation to metaphysics, their different concepts (or "quasi-concepts") of "difference," and their contrasting uses of the history of philosophy (using the "divine names" tradition as an example).

1. *The Status of Metaphysics*. Early in his career, Derrida took over, in his own manner, the Heideggerian task of "overcoming metaphysics," while Deleuze, for his part, would later say that "the death of metaphysics or the overcoming of philosophy" had never been an issue for him (WP 9). It would not be an exaggeration to say that it was their respective adoption and rejection of this Heideggerian problematic that initially set Derrida and Deleuze on their divergent trajectories of transcendence and immanence. In Derrida, metaphysics is determined by its structural "closure," and deconstruction is a means of disturbing this closure, creating an opening or an interruption. The notion of metaphysical closure itself depends on a movement of transcendence: that is, an "excess over the totality, without which no totality would appear."[8] Since one cannot transcend metaphysics as such—there is no "outside" to the metaphysical tradition—one can only destructure or deconstruct metaphysics from within. The project of "overcoming metaphysics," in other words, is an impossibility, but it is this very impossibility that conditions the possibility of deconstructing the philosophical tradition from within. Rather than trying to get outside metaphysics, one can submit "the regulated play of philosophemes" in the history of philosophy to a certain slippage or sliding that would allow them to be read as "symptoms of something that *could not be presented* in the history of philosophy."[9] Immanent within metaphysics, there lies a formal structure of transcendence that can never be made present as such, but that none the less functions as the condition (the "quasi-transcendental" condition) of metaphysics itself. Derrida thus situates his work, he says, at "the *limit* of philosophical discourse," at its margins, its borders or boundary lines.[10] The border he straddles is the border between the closed and immanent totality of metaphysics, with its exhausted concepts and philosophemes, and that which exceeds that totality: that is, a formal structure of transcendence that is, as it were, everywhere at work in metaphysics, though it can never be made present as such.

Derrida attempts to *think* this formal structure of transcendence through concepts

274 DELEUZE AND CONTEMPORARY PHILOSOPHY

such as *différance* (which is, then, at best a "quasi-concept," since the notion of a concept is itself metaphysical). If metaphysics is defined in terms of presence, then *différance* is that which marks "the disappearance of any originary presence,"[11] that which thereby exceeds or transcends metaphysics, and thereby, at the same time, constantly disrupts and "destabilizes" metaphysics. Commenting on Heidegger's notion of the "ontological difference," Derrida writes that

> there may be a difference still more unthought than the difference between Being and beings ... Beyond Being and beings, this difference, ceaselessly differing from and deferring (itself), would trace (itself) (by itself)—this *différance* would be the first or last trace if one still could speak, here, of origin and end.[12]

The long series of notions developed in Derrida's work—not only *différance* and the trace, but also text, writing, the hymen, the supplement, the pharmakon, the parergon, justice, messianicity, and so on—are all traces of this formal structure of transcendence, marked by their aporetic or antinomial status, their possibility conditioned by their impossibility, and so on. Deconstruction thus operates in *interval* between the closed totality of metaphysics and the formal transcendence of *différance* (or as he says in "Force of Law," the interval between the deconstructibility of law [*droit*] and the undeconstructibility of justice).[13]

Deleuze, by contrast, has a very different and non-Heideggerian relation to metaphysics. He described himself candidly as a "pure metaphysician" in the mold of Bergson and Whitehead. "I feel myself to be a pure metaphysician," he said in a late interview, "Bergson says that modern science hasn't found its metaphysics, the metaphysics it would need. It is this metaphysics that interests me."[14] He consequently saw himself as "the most naïve philosopher of our generation . . . the one who felt the least guilt about 'doing philosophy'" (N 88–9). If one is critical of traditional metaphysics, or metaphysical concepts such as identity or essence, he suggests, then the philosophical task is not to attempt to "overcome" metaphysics, but rather actively to construct *a different metaphysics*. This is why one does not find, in Deleuze, any general pronouncements concerning the "nature" of "Western metaphysics" (as "logocentric," or as a "metaphysics of presence"), since, as Derrida notes, the only position from which one could make such a pronouncement is a position of transcendence, which Deleuze rejects. Consequently, there is no concept of closure in Deleuze either (since closure likewise depends on transcendence). From the start, Deleuze defined structures as such—whether mathematical, philosophical, or otherwise—as fundamentally "open," and he saw metaphysics itself as an open structure, which is far from having exhausted its "possibilities." This not only means that the "creation of the new" is possible within metaphysics, but also that one can retrieve or repeat—to use Heidegger's term—avenues of thought in the history of metaphysics that were once opened, only to be quickly closed off again (for instance, the concept of univocity). Deleuze sees his work as being strictly *immanent* to metaphysics; creation and transformation is possible within metaphysics, and there are virtualities in past metaphysics that are capable of being reactivated, as it were, and inserted into new contexts, and new problematics. Metaphysics itself, in other words, is dynamic and in constant becoming.

2. *The Concept of Difference.* Put crudely, then, if Derrida sets out to undo metaphysics, Deleuze sets out simply to *do* metaphysics. The results can appear to be very similar—after Deleuze died, Derrida wrote, in a short memorial text, of the "near total affinity" he saw between Deleuze's work and his own—but in fact the context of their work is very different: a horizon of transcendence in Derrida (*overcoming* or going beyond metaphysics), and a function of immanence in Deleuze (*doing* metaphysics).[15] This difference may appear to be slight, but its very slightness acts like a butterfly effect that propels Derrida and Deleuze along two divergent trajectories that become increasingly remote from each other, to the point of perhaps being incompatible. Nowhere is this more evident than in Deleuze's own theory of difference. Deleuze and Derrida are both seen—rightly—as philosophers of difference. Derrida's essay "Différance" and Deleuze's book *Difference and Repetition* both appeared in 1968, and Heidegger's notion of the "ontological difference" between Being and beings was one of the primary impetuses (though not the only one) in their development of a theory of difference. But Derrida moves immediately in the direction of transcendence. What he was seeking, he tells us, is a difference "beyond Being and beings," and this is precisely how he characterizes *différance*: "a difference still more unthought than the [ontological] difference between Being and beings."[16] In *Difference and Repetition*, by contrast, Deleuze proposes an interpretation of the ontological difference that radicalizes it in the direction of immanence.

> In accordance with Heidegger's ontological intuition [he writes], difference must be articulation and connection in itself; it must relate different to different without any mediation whatsoever by the identical, the similar, the analogous or the opposed. There must be a differenciation of difference, an in-itself which is like a *differenciator* [a *Sich-unterscheidende*] by virtue of which difference is gathered all at once rather than represented on condition of a prior resemblance, identity, analogy, or opposition. (DR 117)

The project of *Difference and Repetition*, in other words, is to provide an immanent analysis of the ontological difference in which *the different is related to the different through difference itself*: Being must not only be able to account for the external difference between beings, but also the fact that beings themselves are marked by an "internal difference"; and the ontological difference must not only refer to the difference between Being and beings, but also the difference of Being from itself, "an alliance of Being and itself in difference" (DR 231). The concepts of difference that Deleuze develops in *Difference and Repetition*—"difference in intensity, disparity in the phantasm, dissemblance in the form of time, the differential in thought" (DR 145)—have a very different status than the notion of difference Derrida develops in his essay "Différance." For Derrida, *différance* is a relation that transcends ontology, that differs from ontology, that goes beyond or is more "originary" than the ontological difference between Being and beings. Deleuze's aim, by contrast, is to show that ontology itself is constituted immanently by a principle of difference (and is thus a "concept," in the Deleuzian sense of the term, and not merely a "quasi-concept"). Deleuze is not often thought of as a Heideggerian, but *Difference and Repetition* can be read as a direct response to *Being and Time* from the standpoint of immanence; for Deleuze, Being is difference, and time is repetition.

3. *The History of Philosophy*. Deleuze has himself provided a way of assessing the status of Derrida's quasi-concept of *différance*. In *What is Philosophy?*, Deleuze and Guattari present a rather summary typology of three general strategies by which transcendence has been introduced into philosophy. The first, and no doubt paradigmatic, type is the one found in Platonism and its variants: the field of immanence is a simple field of phenomena or appearances, which only possesses secondarily what is attributed first of all to the anterior unity of the Idea (or in later variants, to the "One beyond Being" in Plotinus, or to the transcendence of the Christian "God".[17] Modern philosophy effected a second type of transcendence: beginning with Descartes, and then with Kant, the *cogito* made it possible to treat the plane of immanence as a field of consciousness, which was attributed, as we have seen, no longer to the transcendence of the Idea, but rather to the transcendence of the Subject or the Ego. Finally, the third (and contemporary) form of transcendence—which is the one that concerns us—was introduced by phenomenology and its successors. When immanence becomes immanent to a transcendental subjectivity, it is from *within its own field* that the mark of transcendence must appear.

> Husserl conceived of immanence as the flux of lived experience within subjectivity [write Deleuze and Guattari], but since this lived experience, pure and even primordial, does not belong completely to the self that represents it to itself, it is in the regions of *non-belonging* that the horizon of something transcendent is reestablished. (WP 46)

Deleuze and Guattari do not name names here, but one can easily imagine examples. Levinas, for example, founds ethics on the infinite transcendence of the "Other" which challenges the status of the reflective subject and undoes the primacy of the Same.[18] In a different manner, Habermas attempts to ground ethics on the privileged transcendence of an intersubjective world populated by other selves, and regulated by a "communicative consensus." Whatever form it takes, in this contemporary moment of transcendence one no longer thinks of immanence as immanent *to* something (the Idea, the Subject), but on the contrary "one seeks to rediscover a transcendence *within* the heart of immanence itself, as a breach or interruption of its field" (WP 46). One seeks, in other words, a transcendence *within* immanence.

Derrida, in his own manner, clearly belongs to this contemporary (and post-phenomenological) tradition of transcendence. This is evidenced, moreover, in his many readings of texts in the history of philosophy, which attempt to uncover, within the immanent and manifest movement of traditional philosophical concepts and their "binary oppositions," a latent and transcendent movement of *différance* that is never present as such in the text but constantly serves to disrupt and destabilize it. This way of treating the history of philosophy raises a question that is intrinsically linked to the ontological theme of transcendence and immanence. What Heidegger bequeathed to contemporary philosophy was not only a rejuvenation of ontology, but also, concomitant with that, a certain treatment of the history of philosophy under the double theme of the "destruction" of the history of ontology as well as the "retrieval" or "repetition" of that history. Indeed, for the generation to which Deleuze and Derrida belonged, the philosophical training one received in the French university was oriented almost exclusively toward the history of philosophy. Deleuze and Derrida's contrasting relation to metaphysics is thus reflected in their contrasting relation to the history of philosophy. In this regard, we can consider, as a precise historical example, an aspect of the medieval philosophical tradition in which Heidegger took a strong interest—the theological tradition of the "divine names." Heidegger himself first formulated his ontological question in the context of these medieval debates, and in taking up these debates for their own account, Derrida and Deleuze have each moved in clearly differentiated directions: Derrida in the direction of "negative theology" (transcendence) and Deleuze in the direction of "univocity" (immanence).[19]

Heidegger wrote his doctoral thesis on Duns Scotus, who was engaged in a rather lively thirteenth-century debate concerning the nature of Being. Being is said of beings, *but in what sense?* The Scholastics used three precise terms to designate the various ways of resolving the problem: equivocity, univocity, and analogy. To say that Being is *equivocal* means that the term "Being" is said of beings in several senses, and that these senses have no common measure: "God is" does not have the same sense as "man is," for instance, because God does not have the same type of being as man. By contrast, to say that Being is *univocal*, as Duns Scotus affirmed, means that Being has only one sense, and is said in one and the same sense of everything of which it is said, whether it be God or man, animal or plant. Since these positions seemed to lead to scandalous conclusions—equivocity denied order in the cosmos, univocity implied pantheism—a third alternative was developed between these two extremes: Being is neither equivocal nor univocal but *analogical*, and there is indeed a common measure to the forms of Being, but this measure is analogical, and not univocal. This was the position of Aristotle, which Heidegger discusses in the opening pages of *Being and Time*: Being is said in several senses, and these senses are the categories, which are related to Being, and to each other, by means of analogy. Christianity famously transposed this ontological problem into a theological problem, which was concerned less with the relation of Being to being than the relation of God to his creatures (hence the Heideggerian thematic of "onto-theology"). Medieval theology had developed a syncretic solution to the immanence / transcendence problem: it insisted on the requirement of *immanence*—that is, the ontological requirement that the first principle (God) be a *being*; but it also insisted on the more powerful requirement of *transcendence*—that is, the requirement that the transcendence of God be maintained as the One *beyond* Being. What came to be known as the "divine names" tradition was situated at the nexus of these two requirements. The problem was: How can the traditional divine attributes—such as goodness, love, wisdom, power, and so on—which are finite and immanent, be predicated of God, who is infinite and transcendent? It was Thomas Aquinas who, following Aristotle, developed the Christian interpretation of analogy. Positive qualities can indeed belong to God substantially, but only in so far as they are treated "analogically": *either* in terms of an ordered relationship between two proportions (for example, the divine goodness is to God as human goodness is to man—the "analogy of proportionality"); *or* by reference to a focal meaning or "prime analogate" (for example, "Goodness," which God is said to possess eminently and creatures only derivatively—the "analogy of proportion").[20] In France, Neo-Thomists such as Étienne Gilson were the great defenders of analogy, which attempted to straddle the immanence / transcendence tension in theology.

It is not difficult to ascertain how Derrida and Deleuze position themselves rather definitively on either side of this orthodox divide. Derrida was, early on, seen to have a kind of "elective affinity" with what was known as "negative theology," which insisted that God in his absolute substance or essence can only be defined negatively, according to strict rules of transcendence. Meister Eckhart, for instance, preferred to say "God is not" rather than "God is," because "x is" is a statement that is said of beings like you and me, whereas God is eminently superior to Being, beyond Being.[21] This allows God to appear in his "supra-substantial" or "hyper-essential" eminence, as far from all negation as he is from any affirmation. In negative theology, one goes beyond affirmations (God is good) via negations (God is not good in the human sense of the term), and beyond both affirmations and negations to attain God's *eminence* (God is good with an "incomparable" or "ineffable" Goodness, a goodness that transcends all goodness, that is beyond goodness). Or, as Derrida says, what is "proper" to God is to have no properties as such, or to "be" "nothing." The logical formula of transcendence is to say that something "is" neither *x* nor *not-x*, because it is beyond them both.[22] Derrida, by his own admission, adopts this formula of transcendence in his analyses of *différance*. *Différance*, he says,

> "is" neither this nor that, neither sensible nor intelligible, neither positive nor negative, neither superior nor inferior, neither active nor passive, neither present nor absent, not even neutral, not even subject to a dialectic with a third moment, without any possible sublation (*Aufhebung*). Despite appearances, then, it [*différance*] is neither a concept nor even a name; it does *lend itself* to a series of names, but calls for another syntax, and exceeds even the order and the structure of predicative discourse. It "is" not and does not say what "is." It is written completely otherwise.[23]

It is true that Derrida is not "doing" a negative theology, in so far as the latter seems to reserve, "beyond all positive predication, beyond all negation, even beyond Being, some hyperessentiality, a being beyond Being" which would perhaps be given in some sort of "intuition or vision."[24] But although Derrida refuses to assign any *content* to this transcendence, what he retains from the tradition is its *formal* structure: *différance* is that which is never present as such, is absolutely other, discernible only through its trace, whose movement is infinitely deferred, infinitely differing from itself, definable, at best, in terms of what it is *not*. This is why Derrida can write: "I trust no text that is not in some way contaminated with negative theology, and even among those texts that apparently do not have, want, or believe they have any relation with theology in general."[25] There is no text of the metaphysical tradition that is not "contaminated" with this formal structure of transcendence, or this movement of *différance*.

When Deleuze, for his part, injects himself into the divine names tradition, he is equally critical of both analogy *and* negative theology, and explicitly aligns himself with the tradition of univocity (first formulated by Duns Scotus, and which Deleuze sees extended in Spinoza and Nietzsche). The reason is clear: the sole *raison d'être* of negative theology is to *preserve* transcendence (we have to negate all predicates or properties of God, because God transcends them all), whereas univocity is the position of immanence pushed to its most extreme point. As formulated by Duns Scotus, it says that the term "Being" is always used univocally; in other words, when I say that "God is" or "Man is" or "A cat is" or "A flea is," the word "is" is being used *in one and the same sense* in all these sentences. In other words, God does not have a different mode of being from other creatures—that is, a transcendent mode of being that could be accessed (or not) only through negation or analogy. The univocity of Being entails the radical denial of any ontological transcendence, and for this reason was a highly heterodox—and often heretical—position because it hinted at pantheism or even atheism. Deleuze suggests that the tradition of univocity was continued in Spinoza, for whom God and Nature are one and the same thing, and then in Nietzsche. In this sense, univocity can be read as the medieval ontological version of the "death of God." *Difference and Repetition* is, among other things, an attempt to follow through on the ontological—and not merely theological—implications of univocity. Tellingly, to my knowledge, Derrida never mentions the tradition of univocity in his writings. This example from the history of philosophy exemplifies the broad differences between the ontologies of Deleuze and Derrida: in Deleuze one finds an ontology that seeks to expunge from Being all remnants of transcendence, whereas in Derrida one finds an ontology that seeks to trace the eruptions and movements of transcendence *within* Being.

THE FIELD OF EPISTEMOLOGY

We turn now to the third context in which the immanence–transcendence distinction has played an historically important role, which is found in Kant and is oriented primarily toward epistemology. At one point, Kant describes the entire project of the first critique in terms of the immanence / transcendence distinction: "We shall entitle the principles whose application is confined entirely within the limits of possible experience, *immanent*, and those, on the other hand, which profess to pass beyond these limits, *transcendent*."[26] In a famous image, Kant portrays the domain of the understanding as a demarcated "territory" or island (immanence) surrounded by a vast ocean of metaphysical illusion (transcendence).[27] When I use a concept such as "table" or "chair" to synthesize my intuition or perceptions, I am operating immanently within the bounds of possible experience. But when I use a concept like the "soul" or the "world" or "God," I am going beyond the bounds of possible experience, transcending them. Following Plato, Kant will call these concepts that transcend experience "Ideas." The Idea of the world, for example, as the totality of what is, has no intuition or perception that could ever correspond to it. To use the famous Kantian distinction, we can *think* the World, but we can never *know* it; strictly speaking, it is not an object of our experience. Hence, we are led into inevitable *illusions* when we ask questions about the World *as if* it were an object of experience. For instance: Did it have a beginning in time, or is it eternal? Does it have boundaries in space, or does it go on forever? The same holds for our Ideas of the Soul and God: Soul, World, and God are all transcendent Ideas. In the "Transcendental Dialectic," the longest section of the *Critique of Pure Reason*, Kant analyzes the nature of the paradoxes or aporias that reason is led into because of these illusions: the paralogisms of the Soul, the antinomies of the World, the ideal of God. Kant called his project a *transcendental* philosophy because it sought *immanent* criteria that would allow us to distinguish between these legitimate and illegitimate uses of the syntheses of consciousness. In this sense, the "transcendental" is opposed to the "transcendent"; the aim of Kant's transcendental philosophy is the critique of transcendence, and hence the search for immanent criteria of critique—that is, immanent to reason itself. A transcendental critique is a purely immanent critique.

The Kantian formulation of the distinction between immanence and transcendence is useful to our purposes for two reasons. On the one hand, Kant defines his project in immanent terms as a critique of transcendence, and thus functions as a precursor to Deleuze. On the other hand, Kant none the less resurrects the transcendent Ideas, in the second critique, as the necessary postulates of *practical* reason, thereby assigning to Ideas an important regulative role, and in this respect functioning as a precursor to Derrida. Indeed, the notion of an "Idea" is an explicit touchstone for both Deleuze and Derrida. Deleuze devotes an entire chapter of his magnum opus *Difference and Repetition*, as one might expect, to developing a purely *immanent* theory of Idea (as a multiplicity). Derrida, for his part, repeatedly flags the fact that many of his notions—such as the gift, opening, democracy, etc.—have a status that is "analogous" to transcendent Ideas "in the Kantian sense."[28] For instance, in his analyses of the gift, Derrida says that a pure gift, a pure giving, is an impossibility, because when I say "Thank you," or even accept the gift, I start canceling the gift, since, in a movement of reappropriation, I am proposing a kind of equivalence between the giving and my gratitude. The transcendent logic of the pure gift is thereby incorporated into an immanent economy of exchange and debt. But this, says Kant, is the very nature of transcendent Ideas. Whenever we speak of something "pure" or "absolute" or "infinite," as Derrida often does (the "pure gift," "absolute responsibility," the "infinite other"), we are in the realm of transcendence, since we never encounter the pure or the absolute in our experience; it is never something that can be present to our experience. The Idea of a pure mother, for instance, would be the idea of a mother who would not be something other than a mother—not a daughter, not a lover, not a wife. We can *think* this Idea, but we do not encounter it in experience. (The Christian Idea of the "Virgin Mary," as the mother of God, might be said to approximate this Idea of a pure mother.) The same holds for the logic of the pure gift, of justice, of democracy, and so on. Indeed, in his book *Aporias*, Derrida explains that, when he was shopping around for a term to describe the formal status of his concepts—or rather his "quasi-concepts"—he initially thought of adopting the Kantian term "antinomy," but finally decided to use the Greek term "aporia" instead.[29] The reason is that he wanted to distance himself from Kant, since their respective problems, as he explains, are *analogous* but not identical (the difference, in part, lies in their *temporal* structure). The fundamental aporia or antinomy, for Derrida, is that the "condition of possibility" for, say, a "gift" or a "decision," is its very *impossibility*, which is why he describes his list of quasi-concepts as "so many aporetic places or dislocations."[30]

But if the notion of the "pure gift" is by definition a transcendent Idea, the immanent concept that corresponds to it is, precisely, *debt* (since any gift that is given is immediately incorporated into the cycle of exchange and indebtedness). This is in fact what one encounters in Deleuze's work: an immanent analysis of debt, and not a transcendent analysis of the pure gift. In this, Deleuze follows Nietzsche, whose own immanent critique of morality—the *Genealogy of Morals*—was grounded in an analysis of debt. It was in the debtor–creditor relation, Nietzsche writes, "that one person first encountered another person, that one person first *measured himself* against another."[31] In this regard, a certain compatibility exists between Derrida and Deleuze. Deleuze would no doubt agree that the condition of possibility for the "pure gift" is its impossibility, and that the gift itself has an "aporetic" status. But this simply points to the transcendence of the concept, and the need for an immanent analysis of gift-giving in so far as it is always enmeshed in the immanent relations of exchange and debt. Derrida and Deleuze each modify Kant's notion of "conditions of possibility" in formulas that sum up their philosophical projects. Derrida defines deconstruction as the experience of the possibility of the impossible—that is, the (impossible) possibility of the impossible "marks an absolute interruption in the regime of the possible."[32] Such is the formula of transcendence. Deleuze, for his part, defines his philosophy as a search, not for the conditions of possible experience, but rather the conditions of *real* experience. Such is the formula of immanence.

This distinction between the two different theories of Ideas one finds in Deleuze and Derrida is necessarily carried over into two different theories of desire. Plato had already linked Ideas to the theory of desire (Eros). In Kant, the *Critique of Practical Reason* is presented as an analysis of a "higher" faculty of desire that is determined by the representation of a pure form (an Idea)—namely, the pure form of a universal legislation, or the moral law. This same linkage is carried over in Deleuze and Derrida. For a certain period of time, Deleuze was characterized (at least in France) as a "philosopher of desire," in part because one of the aims of *Anti-Oedipus* (1972) had been to develop a purely *immanent* conception of desire. For our purposes, however, it is perhaps more useful to examine Deleuze's analyses of the contrasting *transcendent* conception of desire, since it anticipates, *mutatis mutandis*, the theory of desire one finds in Derrida. The transcendent theory of desire can be summarized in three distinct moments. First, if I desire something, it is because I lack that something. Whereas *need* is a relative lack that is satisfied as soon its object is attained, *desire* has traditionally been defined as an irremediable ontological lack which, by its very nature, is unrealizable—precisely because its object is transcendent, or absolutely other (the Good, the One, God, the Moral Law). From Plato and Augustine to Hegel and Freud, desire has been defined, ontologically, as a function of a field of transcendence, in relation to transcendence (as expressed in an Idea). Desire thus presents us with a "tragic" vision of humanity: as humans, we are incomplete and riddled with deficiencies, and ontological desire is the sign of our incompleteness, of our "lack of being." The "moral" of this vision, in turn, is that we need to *acquire* our being. In Plato, for instance, we need to make our desire coincide with the order of the Good, an order which desire itself furthers (*Symposium*). In St. Augustine, desire aims at God, an impossible desire (in this life) which accounts for the perpetual "restlessness" of the soul (*caritas* versus *cupiditas*). Hence, finally, the "dramatic" dimension of desire as expressed in the theme of the quest, the incessant search; the initial postulate of our lack of Being is pregnant with a series of intermediate postulates that lead to the ultimate postulate of a recovered Being.

But there is a second and third moment to this transcendent theory of desire. If desire aims at a transcendent object that is by nature unattainable, then what is it that comes to satisfy this desire? The answer: what satisfies this transcendent desire, and gives it a kind of immanence, is akin to what we call a state of *pleasure*. But this pleasure is, alas, a false immanence, a pseudo-immanence, a kind of delusion or illusion. Desire is calmed for a moment—but then begins again. In Freud, for instance, desire is experienced, energetically, as a disagreeable tension, a kind of "charge." To get out of this disagreeable state, a *discharge* is necessary, and this discharge is experienced as a pleasure. Humans will then have peace, their desire will be calmed—but only for a moment, for desire is reborn, and a new discharge becomes necessary. Pleasure, at this level, becomes the only immanent unit capable of measuring desire. The final moment: if desire is an "intentionality" that aims at what it lacks, and is measured in terms of a unit (pleasure as discharge) that is not its own, then we must say that these states of pleasure—such as orgasm or ecstasy, whether mystical or otherwise—only provide illusory or apparent satisfactions to desire; its "true" satisfaction is never present, but is perpetually delayed, indefinitely deferred. The irreducibility of desire to states of pleasure must be reaffirmed under another mode: it is the relation (as Lacan puts it) between an "impossible *jouissance*" and death. In other words, as long as desire is defined as a function of transcendence, as a desire for the other, then the condition of possibility for desire is its very impossibility (it can never fill its lack). In Deleuze's analyses, then, the transcendent theory of desire comprises three moments:

1. desire is the mark of our "lack" of being, since the object of desire is transcendent
2. one can only hope for illusory discharges of desire in acts of pleasure; and thus
3. desire is pursuing a *jouissance* that is ultimately impossible.[33]

In this manner, says Deleuze, the theory of desire is completely ensnared in a field of transcendence.

This is a quick summary of the analysis of desire presented in *Anti-Oedipus*, but it is not difficult to ascertain the degree to which Derrida participates in this tradition, and indeed pushes it to its limit. Not only does Derrida conceptualize a purely formal structure of transcendence under the guise of the "absolute other" or the *tout autre* (moreover, if the absolute other is irreducible to a concept, or a word, for example, it is because it transcends the orders of conceptualization, or language); he also undertakes a persistent exploration of the *experience* of this transcendence, which he often expresses, in terms almost identical to Deleuze's analysis of desire, as an "interminable experience," "the experience of the impossible," a "double bind." What does it mean to "live" the aporias of the gift or justice? Can one "experience" the impossible? Derrida replies: yes.

> If the gift is another name for the impossible, we still think it, we name it, we desire it. We intend it. And this even if or because or to the extent that we *never* encounter it, we never know it, we never verify it, we never experience it in its present existence or its phenomenon.[34]

What, then, is the nature of this "experience of the impossible"? Derrida replies: *a double bind*. The Idea of justice is *not* deconstructable, for Derrida, because it is an *infinitely transcendent* Idea that is unknowable; it provides no knowledge, and is independent of any determinable context.[35] This means, on the one hand, that we can only experience the Idea of justice *practically* as a *call*, as a call to justice, as an absolute demand for justice; but it also means, on the other hand, that the Idea of justice provides us no rule for determining when a decision is just or unjust. Hence the double bind of the aporetic experience: the condition of possibility for acting justly is grounded in the impossibility of ever knowing when or if an act is just. And as Derrida comments, "a double bind cannot be assumed; one can only endure it in a *passion*."[36] What, then, is the "passion" or "desire" specific to the experience of the impossible? It is a desire for the absolute other, and hence a desire that is *infinitely suspended*, whose fulfillment is *infinitely deferred*:

> Isn't it proper to desire to carry with it its own proper suspension, the death or the phantom of desire? To go toward the absolute other, isn't that the extreme tension of a desire that tries thereby to renounce its own proper momentum, its own movement of appropriation? . . . And since we do not determine ourselves *before* this desire, since no relation to self can be sure of preceding it, to wit, of preceding a relation to the other, . . . *all* reflection is caught in the genealogy of this genitive [i.e., "desire of . . ."].[37]

Thus, for Derrida, the possibility of *openness* or *invention* (e.g., the possibility of "an other justice," "an other politics," and so on)[38] is necessarily linked to the transcendent Idea of the *absolutely* other. The "disruptions" Derrida introduces into thought are the movements of this formal structure of transcendence. One can see clearly how Derrida's notion of desire, in relation to, for example, the "infinite Idea of justice," recapitulates the three moments of the transcendent theory of desire outlined by Deleuze:

1. the "call" to justice has as its object an "infinite" Idea that is unrealizable, and that transcends any determinable context;

2. what comes to fulfill the call to justice are "decisions" (e.g., by judges in a court of law), but these decisions as such cannot be determined to be just, so the call to justice is continually reborn; hence

3. the call to justice can never be fulfilled or satisfied, it is the experience of something that is fundamentally impossible.

Derrida seeks not only to disengage a formal structure of transcendence (*différance*), but to describe the desire or passion of that transcendence (defined as a double bind or experience of the impossible). For his part, Deleuze agrees with Derrida's analyses, and provides variations of his own, but they are always a prelude to eliminating transcendence and providing an *immanent* account of the same phenomenon: an immanent ontology (univocity), an immanent theory of Ideas (defined in terms of multiplicities and singularities), and an immanent theory of desire (defined as the prolongation or synthesis of singularities).

IMMANENCE, TRANSCENDENCE, AND ETHICS

No matter which formulation one considers, then, one finds Derrida and Deleuze following diverging philosophical trajectories, marked by these two vectors of transcendence and immanence. First, in the tradition of subjectivity, transcendence refers to what transcends the self (the other, the world)—or more profoundly, to the subject itself, as that which transcends the pure "flux of consciousness" or "flow of experience." One can critique the status of the subject by appealing to the transcendence of the Other, or by appealing to the conditions of the immanent flux of experience that the subject itself transcends (theory of intensity). Second, with regard to the question of ontology, transcendence refers to that which is "beyond" or "otherwise than" Being—or, in its more contemporary form, to relations to the other that "interrupt" Being, or erupt or intervene within Being. Whereas Deleuze defines both Being and beings immanently in terms of a genetic principle of difference, Derrida defines *différance* transcendently as "originary" difference that is beyond both Being and beings. Finally, from the viewpoint of a Kantian (or neo-Kantian) epistemology, transcendence refers to those Ideas of objects that lie outside the immanent realm of possible experience. Deleuze attempts to formulate an immanent theory of Ideas and desire, while Derrida attempts to define a purely formal structure of transcendence and the passion of the double bind that it entails. In each of these areas, Deleuze's and Derrida's projects move in very different directions, despite so many surface similarities and affinities.

But this leads to an obvious final question: How should one *assess* this difference? Can one say that the trajectory of transcendence or immanence is "better" than the other? This is a difficult question, perhaps reducible, in the end, to what one might call philosophical "taste." My own view is that the "philosophy of the future" (to use Nietzsche's phrase) needs to move in the direction of immanence, for at least two reasons. The most obvious reason is that the validity of a critique of transcendence above all stems from the theoretical interest to expose its fictional or illusory status—this has been a constant of philosophy from Hume through Kant to

Nietzsche, its "demystificatory" role. But the more important reason has to do with practical philosophy, with ethics and politics. Kant, Levinas, and Derrida, along with many others, while perhaps denying transcendence a constitutive status, are none the less willing to assign it a *practical* role (regulative, imperative, communicative, and so on). For Deleuze, this is equally illegitimate, but it seems to have been a source of genuine perplexity to Deleuze. There is a curious passage in *What is Philosophy?* where Deleuze and Guattari more or less ask: What *is* it with immanence? It should be the natural acquisition and milieu of philosophy, yet such is not always the case. Moreover, the arguments brought to bear against immanence are almost always *moral* arguments. Without transcendence, we are warned, we will fall into a darkness of chaos, reduced to a pure subjectivism or relativism, living in a world without hope, with no vision of an alternate future. Indeed, the two philosophers who pushed the trajectory of immanence the furthest—Spinoza and Nietzsche—were condemned by both their contemporaries and their successors, less for being atheists than for being immoralists. The danger that was sensed to be lurking in both the *Ethics* and the *Genealogy of Morals* was precisely the danger of immanence.

> Immanence can be said to be the burning touchstone of all philosophy [writes Deleuze] because it takes upon itself all the dangers that philosophy must confront, all the condemnations, persecutions, and repudiations that it undergoes. This at least persuades us that the problem of immanence is not abstract or merely theoretical. At first sight, it is not easy to see why immanence is so dangerous, but it is. It swallows up sages and gods. (WP 45)

From this practical point of view, Spinoza poses the most interesting test case of the position of immanence. Heidegger himself wrote notoriously little on Spinoza, which is a surprising omission, since Spinoza's *Ethics* is a work of pure ontology that explicitly poses the problem of the ontological difference in terms of the difference between the infinite substance (Being) and its finite modes (beings). Derrida too has written little on Spinoza. By contrast, Deleuze's reformulation of ontology in Spinozistic terms allows him not only to push the Heideggerian heritage in an immanent direction (rather than Derrida's transcendent direction), but also to understand that ontology in explicitly ethical terms. Like Spinoza, Deleuze defines beings immanently in terms of their intensity or "degree of power," a degree which is actualized at every moment in terms of the whole of one's "affections" (which are none the less in constant variation). The fundamental question of ethics is not "What *must* I do?" (the question of *morality*) but rather "What *can* I do?" Given my degree of power, what are my capabilities and capacities? How can I come into active possession of my power? How can I go to the limit of what I "can do"? The political question follows from this, since those in power have an obvious interest in separating us from our capacity to act. But this is what makes transcendence an eminently pragmatic and ethical issue. The ethical themes one finds in transcendent philosophies such as those of Levinas and Derrida—an absolute responsibility for the other that I can never assume, or an infinite call to justice that I can never satisfy—are, from the point of view of immanence, imperatives whose effect is to separate me from my capacity to act. From the viewpoint of immanence, in other words, *transcendence represents my slavery and impotence reduced to its lowest point*. This is why transcendence itself poses a precise and difficult ethical problem for a philosophy of immanence: If transcendence represents my impotence (power = o), then under what conditions can I have actually been led to *desire* transcendence? What are the conditions that could have led, in Nietzsche's words, to "the inversion of the value-positing eye"? How could I actually reach the point where I desire my slavery and subjection as if it were my salvation? (In a similar way, immanence poses a precise and difficult problem for a philosophy of transcendence: How can one bridge the interval that separates the transcendent from the immanent—for instance, the interval that separates the undeconstructability of justice from the deconstructability of the law?)

In short, the difference between the two philosophical trajectories of immanence and transcendence must be assessed and evaluated, not simply in the theoretical domain, but in the ethico-political domain. In part, this is because the speculative elimination of transcendence does not necessarily lead to its practical elimination, as one can see already in Kant. But more importantly, it is because it is at the ethical level that the difference between transcendence and immanence appears in its most acute and consequential form. On this score, it is perhaps the difference between Deleuze and Levinas that presents this contrast most starkly. For Levinas, ethics *precedes* ontology because it is derived from an element of transcendence (the Other) that is necessarily "otherwise" than Being (and hence privileges concepts like absolute responsibility and duty). For Deleuze, ethics *is* ontology because it is derived from the immanent relation of beings to Being at the level of their existence (and hence privileges concepts such as *puissance* [power or capacity] and affectivity). This is why Spinoza entitled his pure ontology an *Ethics* rather than an *Ontology*: his speculative propositions concerning the univocity of Being can only be judged practically at the level of the ethics they envelop or imply. Put summarily, for Levinas, ethics is derived from transcendence, while for Deleuze, transcendence is what prevents ethics. It seems to me that it is at this level—at the practical and not merely speculative level—that the relative merits of philosophies of immanence and transcendence need to be assessed and debated.

Alain Badiou

Mathematics and the Theory of Multiplicities: Deleuze and Badiou Revisited

Deleuze once wrote that "encounters between independent thinkers always occur in a blind zone," and this is certainly true of the encounter between Badiou and Deleuze.[1] In 1988, Badiou published his book *Being and Event*, which attempted to develop an "ontology of the multiple" derived from the mathematical model of axiomatic set theory.[2] Soon afterward, he tells us, he realized—no doubt correctly—that his primary philosophical rival in this regard was Deleuze, who similarly held that "philosophy is a theory of multiplicities,"[3] but whose own concept of multiplicities was derived from different mathematical sources and entailed a different conception of ontology itself. In 1997, Badiou published a study of Deleuze entitled *Deleuze: The Clamor of Being*, in which he confronted his rival directly and attempted to set forth their fundamental differences. The study, Badiou tells us in its introduction, was occasioned by an exchange of letters he had with Deleuze between 1992 and 1994, which focused directly on the concept of "multiplicity" and the specific problem of "an *immanent* conceptualization of the multiple."[4] On the opening page of the book, Badiou notes that "Deleuze's preferences were for differential calculus and Riemannian manifolds . . . [whereas] I preferred algebra and sets"[5]—leading the reader to expect, in what follows, a comparison of Deleuze's and Badiou's notions of multiplicity based in part, at least, on these differing mathematical sources.

Yet as one reads the remainder of *Deleuze: The Clamor of Being*, one quickly discovers that Badiou in fact adopted a quite different strategy in approaching Deleuze. Despite the announced intention, the book does not contain a single discussion of Deleuze's theory of multiplicities; it avoids the topic entirely. Instead, Badiou immediately displaces his focus to the claim that Deleuze is not a philosopher of multiplicity at all, but rather a philosopher of the "One." Nor does Badiou ever discuss the mathematical sources of Deleuze's theory of multiplicity. Instead, he puts forth a secondary claim that, in so far as Deleuze *does* have a theory of multiplicity, it is not derived from a mathematical model, as is Badiou's own, but rather from a model that Badiou terms variously as "organic," "natural," "animal," or "vitalistic."[6]

Critics have rightly ascertained the obvious aim of this double strategy of avoidance and displacement: since Badiou presents himself as an ontologist of the multiple, and claims that his ontology is purely mathematical, he wants to distance Deleuze as far as possible from both these concerns.[7] To get at what is interesting in the Badiou–Deleuze encounter, however, these all-too-obvious strategies need to be set aside, since the real terms of the confrontation clearly lie elsewhere. Badiou's general philosophical (or meta-ontological) position turns on the equation that "ontology = mathematics," since "mathematics alone thinks being."[8] The more precise equation, however, would be that "ontology = axiomatic set theory," since for Badiou it is only in axiomatic set theory that mathematics adequately "thinks" itself and constitutes a condition of philosophy.[9] Badiou's ontology thus follows a not uncommon reductionist strategy: physics is ultimately reducible to mathematics, and mathematics to axiomatic set theory. From a Deleuzian viewpoint, the fundamental limitation of Badiou's philosophy—but also its fundamental interest—lies in this identification of ontology with axiomatic set theory. Badiou's confrontation with Deleuze must consequently be staged directly on each of these fronts—axiomatics, set theory, and their corresponding ontology—since it is only here that their differences can be exposed in a direct and intrinsic manner.

From this viewpoint, two essential differences between Badiou and Deleuze immediately come to light. First, for Deleuze, the ontology of mathematics is *not* reducible to axiomatics, but must be understood much more broadly in terms of the complex tension between axiomatics and what he calls "problematics."[10] Deleuze assimilates axiomatics to "major" or "royal" science, which is linked to the social axiomatic of capitalism (and the State), and which constantly attempts to effect a reduction, or even repression, of the problematic pole of mathematics, itself wedded to a "minor" or "nomadic" conception of science. For this reason, second, the concept of multiplicity, even within mathematics itself, cannot simply be identified with the concept of a set; rather, mathematics is marked by a tension between extensive multiplicities or sets (the axiomatic pole) and virtual or differential multiplicities (the problematic pole), and the incessant translation of the latter into the former. Reformulated in this manner, the Badiou–Deleuze confrontation can be posed and explored in a way that is *internal* to both mathematics (axiomatics versus problematics) and the theory of multiplicities (extensive versus differential multiplicities).

These two criteria allow us to assess the differences between Badiou and Deleuze in a way that avoids the red herrings of the "One" and "vitalism." Although Badiou claims that "the Deleuzian didactic of multiplicities is, from start to finish, a polemic against sets,"[11] in fact Deleuze nowhere litigates against sets, and indeed argues that the translation (or reduction) of differential multiplicities to extensive sets is not only inevitable ontologically, but *necessary* scientifically.[12] What separates Badiou and Deleuze is rather the ontological status of events (in Badiou's sense). For Deleuze, mathematics is replete with events, to which he grants a full ontological status, even if their status is ungrounded and problematic; multiplicities in the Deleuzian sense are themselves constituted by events. In turn, axiomatics, by its very nature, necessarily selects against and eliminates events in its effort to introduce "rigor" into mathematics and to establish its foundations. It would be erroneous to characterize the problematic pole of mathematics as "merely" intuitive and operative, while "royal" axiomatics is conceptual and formalizable.

> The fact is [writes Deleuze], that the two kinds of science have *different modes of formalization* . . . What we have are two formally different conceptions of science, and ontologically, *a single field of interaction* in which royal science [e.g., axiomatics] continually appropriates the contents of vague or nomad science [problematics], while nomad science continually cuts the contents of royal science loose. (TP 362, 367)

The task Deleuze takes upon himself, then, is to formalize the distinction between problematic and axiomatic multiplicities in a purely intrinsic manner, and to mark the ontological and scientific transformations or conversions between the two.

Badiou, by contrast, in taking axiomatics as his ontological model, limits his ontology to the pole of mathematics that is constituted on the elimination of the events, and he therefore necessarily denies events any ontological status: "the event is forbidden, ontology rejects it."[13] As a consequence, he places himself in the paradoxical position of formulating a theory of the event on the basis of an axiomatic viewpoint that explicitly eliminates events. The event thus appears in Badiou's work under a double characterization. Negatively, so to speak, an event is undecidable or indiscernible from the ontological viewpoint of axiomatics; it is not presentable in the situation, but exists (if it can even be said to exist) on the "edge of the void" as a mark of the infinite excess of the inconsistent multiplicity over the consistent sets of the situation. Positively, then, it is only through a purely subjective "decision" that the hitherto indiscernible event can be affirmed, and made to intervene in the situation. Lacking any ontological status, the event in Badiou is instead linked to a rigorous conception of *subjectivity*, the subject being the sole instance capable of "naming" the event and maintaining a fidelity to it through the declaration of an axiom (such as "all men are equal," in politics; or "I love you," in love). In this sense, Badiou's philosophy of the event is, at its core, a philosophy of the "activist subject."

Deleuze and Badiou thus follow opposing trajectories in their interpretations of mathematics. For Deleuze, problematics and axiomatics (minor and major science) together constitute a single ontological field of interaction, with the latter perpetually effecting a repression—or more accurately, an arithmetic conversion—of the former. Badiou, by contrast, grants an ontological status to axiomatics alone, and in doing so, he explicitly adopts the ontological viewpoint of "major" science, along with its repudiation and condemnation of "minor" science. As a result, not only does Badiou insist that Deleuze's concept of a virtual multiplicity "remains inferior to the concept of the Multiple that can be found in the contemporary history of sets,"[14] but he goes so far as to claim "the virtual does not exist,"[15] in effect denying the "problematic" pole of mathematics in its entirety. Interestingly, this contrast between Badiou and Deleuze finds a precise expression in a famous poetic formula. Badiou at times places his entire project under the sign of Lautréamont's poetic paean to "severe mathematics," which Deleuze, for his part, cites critically:

In contrast to Lautréamont's song that rises up around the paranoiac–Oedipal–narcissistic pole [of mathematics]—"O *severe mathematics* . . . *Arithmetic! Algebra! Geometry! Imposing Trinity! Luminous triangle!*"—there is another song: O schizophrenic mathematics, uncontrollable and mad . . . .[16]

It is this *other* mathematics—problematics, as opposed to axiomatics as a "specifically scientific Oedipus"—that Deleuze attempts to uncover and formalize in his work. The obstacles to such a project, however, are evident. The theory of extensional multiplicities (Cantor's set theory) and its rigorous axiomatization (Zermelo-Fraenkel et al.) is one of the great achievements of modern mathematics, and in *Being and Event* Badiou was able to appropriate this work for his philosophical purposes. For Deleuze, the task was quite different, since he himself had to construct a hitherto non-existent (philosophical) formalization of differential or virtual multiplicities which are, by his own account, selected against by "royal" mathematics itself. In this regard, Deleuze's relation to the history of mathematics is similar to his relation to the history of philosophy: even in canonical figures there is something that "escapes" the official histories of mathematics. At one point, he even provides a list of "problematic" figures from the history of science and mathematics:

> Democritus, Menaechmus, Archimedes, Vauban, Desargues, Bernoulli, Monge, Carnot, Poncelet, Perronet, etc.: in each case a monograph would be necessary to take into account the special situation of these scientists whom State science used only after restraining or disciplining them, after repressing their social or political conceptions.[17]

Since Badiou has largely neglected Deleuze's writings on mathematics, in what follows I would first like to outline the nature of the general contrast Deleuze establishes between problematics and axiomatics, and then briefly identify the mathematical origins of Deleuze's notion of "multiplicities." With these resources in hand, we will then return to Badiou's specific critiques of Deleuze, partly to show their inherent limitations, but also to identify what I take to be the more relevant points of contrast between their respective philosophical positions.

PROBLEMATICS AND AXIOMATICS

Let me turn first to the problematic–axiomatic distinction. Although Deleuze formulates this distinction in his own manner, it in fact reflects a fairly familiar tension within the history of mathematics, which we must be content to illustrate hastily by means of three historical examples.

1. The first example comes from the Greeks. Proclus, in his *Commentary on the First Book of Euclid's Elements*, had already formulated a distinction, within Greek geometry, between problems and theorems.[18] Whereas theorems concern the demonstration, from axioms or postulates, of the inherent properties belonging to a figure, problems concern the construction of figures using a straightedge and compass.[19] In turn, theorematics and problematics each involve two different

conceptions of "deduction": in theorematics, a deduction moves from axioms to the theorems that are derived from it, whereas in problematics a deduction moves from the problem to the ideal accidents and *events* that condition the problem and form the cases that resolve it. "The event by itself," writes Deleuze, "is problematic and problematizing" (LS 54). For example, in the theory of conic sections (Apollonius), the ellipse, hyperbola, parabola, straight lines, and point are all "cases" of the projection of a circle on to secant planes in relation to the apex of a cone. Whereas in theorematics a figure is defined statically, in Platonic fashion, in terms of its essence and its derived properties, in problematics a figure is defined dynamically by its capacity to be affected—that is, by the ideal events that befall it: sectioning, cutting, projecting, folding, bending, stretching, reflecting, rotating. As a theorematic figure, a circle is an organic and fixed essence, but the morphological variations of the circle (figures that are "lens-shaped," "umbelliform," "indented," etc.) form problematic figures that are, in Husserl's words, "vague yet rigorous," "essentially and not accidentally inexact."[20] In Greece, problematics found its classical expression in Archimedean geometry (especially the Archimedes of "On the Method"), an "operative" geometry in which the line was defined less as an essence than as a continuous process of "alignment," the circle as a continuous process of "rounding," the square as the process of "quadrature," and so on.

   Proclus, however, had already pointed to (and defended) the relative triumph, in Greek geometry, of the theorematic over the problematic. The reason: to the Greeks, "problems concern only events and affects which show evidence of a *deterioration* or a projection of essences in the imagination," and theorematics thus could present itself as a necessary "rectification" of thought.[21] This rectification must be understood, in a literal sense, as a triumph of the rectilinear over the curvilinear.[22] The definition of the straight line as "the shortest distance between two points," for example, is understood dynamically in Archimedean geometry as a way of defining the length of a curve in pre-differential calculus, such that the straight line is seen as a "case" of the curve; in Euclidean geometry, by contrast, the essence of the line is understood statically, in terms that eliminate any reference to the curvilinear ("a line which lies evenly with the points on itself").[23] In the "minor" geometry of problematics, figures are inseparable from their inherent variations, affections, and events; the aim of "major" theorematics, by contrast, is "to uproot variables from their state of continuous variation in order to extract from them fixed points and constant relations" (TP 408–9), and thereby to set geometry on the "royal" road of theorematic deduction and proof. Badiou, for his part, explicitly aligns his ontology with the position of theorematics: "the pure multiple, the generic form of being, *never* welcomes the event in itself as its component."[24]

   2. By the seventeenth century, the tension between problems and theorems, which was internal to geometry, had shifted to a more general tension between geometry itself, on the one hand, and algebra and arithmetic on the other. Desargues's projective geometry, for instance, which was a qualitative and "minor" geometry centered on problems-events (as developed, most famously, in the *Draft Project of an Attempt to Treat the Events of the Encounters of a Cone and a Plane*, which Boyer aptly describes as "one of the most unsuccessful great books ever produced"),

was quickly opposed (and temporarily forgotten) in favor of the analytic geometry of Fermat and Descartes—a quantitative and "major" geometry that translated geometric relations into arithmetic relations that could be expressed in algebraic equations (Cartesian coordinates).[25] "Royal" science, in other words, now entailed an arithmetization of geometry itself. "There is a correlation," Deleuze writes, "between geometry and arithmetic, geometry and algebra which is constitutive of major science."[26] Descartes was dismayed when he heard that Desargues's *Draft Project* treated conic sections without the use of algebra, since to him "it did not seem possible to say anything about conics that could not more easily be expressed with algebra than without."[27] As a result, Desargues's methods were repudiated as dangerous and unsound, and his practices of perspective banned.

It would be two centuries before projective geometry was revived in the work of Monge, the inventor of descriptive geometry, and Poncelet, who formulated the "principle of continuity," which led to developments in *analysis situs* and topology. Topology (so-called "rubber-sheet geometry") concerns the property of geometric figures that remain invariant under transformations such as bending or stretching; under such transformations, figures that are theorematically distinct in Euclidean geometry, such as a triangle, a square, and a circle, are seen as one and the same "homeomorphic" figure, since they can be continuously transformed into one another. This entailed an extension of geometric "intuitions" far beyond the limits of empirical or sensible perception (à la Kant). "With Monge, and especially Poncelet," writes Deleuze, commenting on Léon Brunschvicg's work, "the limits of sensible, or even spatial, representation (striated space) are indeed surpassed, but less in the direction of a symbolic power of abstraction [i.e., theorematics] than toward a trans-spatial imagination, or a trans-intuition (continuity)."[28] In the twentieth century, computers have extended the reach of this "trans-intuition" even further, provoking renewed interest in qualitative geometry, and allowing mathematicians to "see" hitherto unimagined objects such as the Mandelbrot set and the Lorenz attractor, which have become the poster children of the new sciences of chaos and complexity. "Seeing, seeing what happens," continues Deleuze, "has always had an essential importance, greater than demonstrations, even in pure mathematics, which can be called visual, figural, independently of its applications: many mathematicians nowadays think that a computer is more precious than an axiomatic" (WP 128). But already in the early nineteenth century, there was a renewed attempt to turn projective geometry into a mere practical dependency on analysis, or so-called higher geometry (the debate between Poncelet and Cauchy).[29] The development of the theory of functions would eventually eliminate the appeal to the principle of continuity, substituting for the geometrical idea of smoothness of variation the arithmetic idea of "mapping" or a one-to-one correspondence of points (point-set topology).

3. This double movement of major science toward theorematization and arithmetization would reach its full flowering, finally, in the late nineteenth century, primarily in response to problems posed by the invention of the calculus. In its origins, the calculus was tied to problematics in a double sense. The first refers to the ontological problems that the calculus confronted: the differential calculus addressed the problematic of *tangents* (how to determine the tangent lines to a given curve), while

the integral calculus addressed the problematic of *quadrature* (how to determine the area within a given curve). The greatness of Leibniz and Newton was to have recognized the intimate connection between these two problems (the problem of finding areas is the inverse of determining tangents to curves), and to have developed a symbolism to link them together and resolve them. The calculus quickly became the primary mathematical engine of what we call the "scientific revolution." Yet for two centuries, the calculus, not unlike Archimedean geometry, itself maintained a problematic status in a second sense: it was allotted a para-scientific status, and labeled a "barbaric" or "Gothic" hypothesis, or at best a convenient convention or well-grounded fiction. In its early formulations, the calculus was shot through with dynamic notions such as infinitesimals, fluxions and fluents, thresholds, passages to the limit, continuous variation—all of which presumed a *geometrical* conception of the continuum: in other words, the idea of a process. For most mathematicians, these were considered to be "metaphysical" ideas that lay beyond the realm of mathematical definition. Berkeley famously ridiculed infinitesimals as "the ghosts of departed quantities"; D'Alembert famously responded by telling his students, *Allez en avant, et la foi vous viendra* ("Go forward, and faith will come to you").[30] The calculus would not have been invented without these notions, yet they remained problematic, lacking an adequate mathematical ground.

For a long period of time, the enormous success of the calculus in solving physical problems delayed research into its logical foundations. It was not until the end of the nineteenth century that the calculus would receive a "rigorous" foundation through the development of the "limit-concept." "Rigor" meant that the calculus had to be separated from its problematic origins in geometrical conceptions or "intuitions," and reconceptualized in purely arithmetic terms (the loaded term "intuition" here having little to do with "empirical" perception, but rather the "ideal" geometrical notion of continuous movement and space).[31] This "arithmetization of analysis," as Félix Klein called it,[32] was achieved by Karl Weierstrass, one of Husserl's teachers, in the wake of work done by Cauchy (leading Giulio Giorello to dub Weierstrass and his followers the "ghostbusters").[33] Analysis (the study of infinite processes) was concerned with *continuous* magnitudes, whereas arithmetic had as its domain the *discrete* set of numbers. The aim of Weierstrass's "discretization" program was to separate the calculus from the geometry of continuity and base it on the concept of number alone. Geometrical notions were thus reconceptualized in terms of sets of discrete points, which in turn were conceptualized in terms of number: points on a line as individual numbers, points on a plane as ordered pairs of numbers, points in n-dimensional space as n-tuples of numbers. As a result, the concept of the variable was given a static interpretation. Early interpreters had tended to appeal to the geometrical intuition of continuous motion when they said that a variable x "approaches" a limit (for instance, the circle defined as the limit of a polygon). Weierstrass's innovation was to reinterpret this variable x arithmetically as simply designating any one of a collection of numerical values (the theory of functions), thereby eliminating any dynamism or "continuous variation" from the notion of continuity, and any interpretation of the operation of differentiation as a process. Weierstrass, writes Deleuze, provided what he himself called a "static" interpretation of the differential and infinitesimal calculus, in which there is no longer any fluction toward a limit, no longer any idea of a threshold, but rather the idea of a system of choice, from the viewpoint of an ordinal interpretation.[34]

In Weierstrass's limit-concept, in short, the geometric idea of "approaching a limit" was arithmetized, and replaced by static constraints on discrete numbers alone (the episilon-delta method). Dedekind took this arithmetization a step further by rigorously defining the continuity of the real numbers in terms of a "cut": "it is the cut which constitutes . . . the idea cause of continuity or the pure element of quantitativity" (DR 172). Cantor's set theory, finally, gave a discrete interpretation of the notion of infinity itself, treating infinite sets like finite sets (the power set axiom)—or rather, treating all sets, whether finite or infinite, as mathematical objects (the axiom of infinity).[35]

Weierstrass, Dedekind, and Cantor thus form the great triumvirate of the program of discretization and the development of the "arithmetic" continuum (the redefinition of continuity as a function of sets over discrete numbers). In their wake, the basic concepts of the calculus—function, continuity, limit, convergence, infinity, and so on—were progressively "clarified" and "refined," and ultimately given a set theoretical foundation.[36] The assumptions of Weierstrass's discretization problem—that only arithmetic is rigorous, and that geometric notions are unsuitable for secure foundations—are now largely identified with the "orthodox" or "major" view of the history of mathematics as a progression toward ever more "well-founded" positions.[37] The program would pass through two further developments. The contradictions generated by set theory brought on a sense of a "crisis" in the foundations, which Hilbert's formalist (or formalization) program attempted to repair through *axiomatization*: that is, by attempting to show that set theory could be derived from a finite set of axioms, which were later codified by Zermelo-Fraenkel (given his theological leanings, even Cantor needed a dose of axiomatic rigor). Gödel and Cohen, finally, in their famous theorems, would eventually expose the internal limits of axiomatization (incompleteness, undecidability), demonstrating, in Badiou's language, that there is a variety of mathematical forms in "infinite excess" over our ability to formalize them consistently.

This historical sketch, though necessarily brief, none the less provides a basis from which we can pinpoint the differences between the respective projects of Badiou and Deleuze. In identifying ontology with axiomatic set theory, Badiou is adopting the position of "major" mathematics with its dual programs of "discretization" and "axiomatization." This contemporary orthodoxy has often been characterized as an "ontological reductionism." In this viewpoint, as Penelope Maddy describes it, "mathematical objects and structures are identified with or instantiated by set theorematic surrogates, and the classical theorems about them proved from the axioms of set theory."[38] Reuben Hersh gives it a more idiomatic and constructivist characterization:

Starting from the empty set, perform a few operations, like forming the set of all subsets. Before long you have a magnificent structure in which you can embed the real numbers, complex numbers, quaterions, Hilbert spaces, infinite-dimensional differentiable manifolds, and anything else you like.[39]

Badiou tells us that he made a similar appeal to Deleuze, insisting that "every figure of the type 'fold,' 'interval,' enlacement,' 'serration,' 'fractal,' or even 'chaos' has a corresponding schema in a certain family of sets . . . ."[40] Deleuze, for his part, fully recognizes this orthodox position: "Modern mathematics is regarded as based upon the theory of groups or set theory rather than on the differential calculus" (DR 180). None the less, he insists that the fundamental difference in kind between problematics and axiomatics remains, even in contemporary mathematics:

> Modern mathematics also leaves us in a state of antinomy, since the strict finite interpretation that it gives of the calculus nevertheless presupposes an axiom of infinity in the set theoretical foundation, even though this axiom finds no illustration in the calculus. What is still missing is the extra-propositional and sub-representative element expressed in the Idea by the differential, *precisely in the form of a problem.* (DR 178)

There are several reasons why Deleuze would refuse Badiou's identification of ontology with axiomatized set theory and maintain the ontological irreducibility of problematics. Most obviously, Badiou's ontology presumes the eventual reduction of physics (and the other sciences) to mathematics, which at present is itself no less a matter of faith than the eighteenth-century belief in the ghosts of infinitesimals. Freeman Dyson, to give one example among many, has strongly questioned this reductionistic presumption, predicting that "the notion of a final statement of the laws of physics [in a finite set of mathematical equations] will prove as illusory as the notion of a final decision process for all of mathematics."[41] More importantly, within mathematics itself, there are notions that remain outside the grasp of the discretization program—most notably the geometric continuum itself, the non-discrete "continuous continuum," which still maintains its problematic status. "According to this intuitive concept," mused Gödel, "summing up all the points, we still do not get the line; rather the points form some kind of scaffold on the line."[42] Or as Hermann Weyl put it,

> in spite of Dedekind, Cantor, and Weierstrass, the great task which has been facing us since the Pythagorean discovery of the irrationals remains today as unfinished as ever; that is, the *continuity* given to us immediately by intuition (in the flow of time and in motion) has yet to be grasped mathematically.[43]

(The term "continuum" is still used to denote both types of continuity—the continuous geometric continuum and the discrete arithmetic continuum—even though the two notions differ in kind.) In a seminar, Deleuze noted that "the idea that there is a quantitative becoming, the idea of the limit of this becoming, the idea that an infinity of small quantities tends toward the limit—all these were considered as absolutely impure notions, as non-axiomatic or non-axiomatizable" (29 Apr 1980). One of the aims of Deleuze's own theory of multiplicities is to assess the status of such notions *as* problematic.

A more recent example can help serve to illustrate the ongoing tension between problematics and axiomatics within contemporary mathematics. Even after Weierstrass's work, mathematicians using the calculus continued to obtain accurate results and make new discoveries by using infinitesimals in their reasoning, their mathematical conscience assuaged by the (often unchecked) supposition that infinitesimals could be replaced by Weierstrassian methods. Despite its supposed "elimination" as an impure and muddled metaphysical concept, the ghostly concept of infinitesimals continued to play a positive role in mathematics *as* a problematic concept, reliably producing correct solutions.

> Even now [wrote Abraham Robinson in 1966], there are many classical results in differential geometry which have never been established in any other way [than through the use of infinitesimals], the assumption being that somehow the rigorous but less intuitive ε, δ method would lead to the same result.[44]

In response to this situation, Robinson developed his *non-standard analysis*, which proposed an axiomatization of infinitesimals themselves, at last granting mathematicians the "right" to use them in proofs. Using the theory of formal languages, he added to the ordinary theory of numbers a new symbol (which we can call *i* for infinitesimal), and posited axioms saying that *i* was smaller than any finite number $1/n$ and yet not zero; he then showed that this enriched theory of numbers is consistent, assuming the consistency of the ordinary theory of numbers. The resulting mathematical model is described as "non-standard" in that it contains, in addition to the "standard" finite and transfinite numbers, non-standard numbers such as hyperreals and infinitesimals.[45] In the non-standard model, there is a cluster of infinitesimals around every real number *r*, which Robinson, in a nod to Leibniz, termed a "monad" (the monad is the "infinitesimal neighborhood" of *r*). Transfinites and infinitesimals are two types of infinite number, which characterize degrees of infinity in different fashions. In effect, this means that contemporary mathematics has "two distinct rigorous formulations of the calculus": that of Weierstrass and Cantor, who eliminated infinitesimals, and that of Robinson, who rehabilitated and legitimized them.[46] Both these endeavors, however, had their genesis in the imposition of the notion of infinitesimals *as* a problematic concept, which in turn gave rise to differing but related axiomatizations. Deleuze's claim is that the ontology of mathematics is poorly understood if it does not take into account the specificity and irreducibility of problematics.

With these examples in hand, we can make several summary points concerning the relation between the problematic and axiomatic poles of mathematics, or more broadly, the relation between minor and major science. First, according to Deleuze, mathematics is constantly producing notions that have an objectively problematic status; the role of axiomatics (or its precursors) is to codify and solidify these problematic notions, providing them with a theorematic ground or rigorous foundation. Axiomaticians, one might say, are the "law and order" types in mathematics: "Hilbert and de Broglie were as much politicians as scientists: they reestablished order" (TP 144). As Albert Lautman noted, "irrational numbers, the infinitely small, continuous functions without derivatives, the transcendence of e and of π, the transfinite had all been accepted by an incomprehensible necessity of fact before there was a deductive theory of them."[47] In this sense, axiomatics is a foundational but *secondary* enterprise in mathematics, dependent for its very existence on problematics. As Jean Dieudonné suggests,

> In periods of expansion, when new notions are introduced, it is often very difficult to exactly delimit the conditions of their deployment, and one must admit that one can only reasonably do so once one has acquired a rather long practice in these notions, which necessitates a more or less extended period of cultivation [*défrichement*], during which incertitude and controversy dominates. Once the heroic age of pioneers passes, the following generation can then codify their work, getting rid of the superfluous, solidifying the bases—in short, putting the house in order. At this moment, the axiomatic method reigns anew, until the next overturning [*bouleversement*] that brings a new idea.[48]

Nicholas Bourbaki puts the point even more strongly, noting that "the axiomatic method is nothing but the 'Taylor System'—the 'scientific management'—of mathematics."[49] Deleuze adopts a similar historical thesis, noting that the push toward axiomatics at the end of the nineteenth century arose at the same time that Taylorism arose in capitalism: axiomatics does for mathematics what Taylorism does for "work."[50]

Second, problematic concepts often (though not always) have their source in what Deleuze terms the "ambulatory" sciences, which includes sciences such as metallurgy, surveying, stonecutting, and perspective. (One need only think of the mathematical problems encountered by Archimedes in his work on military installations, Desargues on the techniques of perspective, Monge on the transportation of earth, and so on.) The nature of such domains, however, is that they do not allow science to assume an autonomous power. The reason, according to Deleuze, is that the ambulatory sciences

> subordinate all their operations to the sensible conditions of intuition and construction—*following* the flow of matter, *drawing and linking up* smooth space. Everything is situated in the objective zone of fluctuation that is coextensive with reality itself. However refined or rigorous, "approximate knowledge" is still dependent upon sensitive and sensible evaluations that pose more problems than they solve: problematics is still its only mode. (TP 373)

Such sciences are linked to notions—such as heterogeneity, dynamism, continuous variation, flows, etc.—that are "barred" or banned from the requirements of axiomatics, and consequently they tend to appear in history as that which was superseded or left behind. By contrast, what is proper to royal science, to its theorematic or axiomatic power, is "to isolate all operations from the conditions of intuition, making them true intrinsic concepts, or 'categories' . . . Without this categorical, apodictic apparatus, the differential operations would be constrained to follow the evolution of a phenomenon" (TP 373–4). In the ontological field of interaction between minor and major science, in other words,

> the ambulant sciences confine themselves to *inventing problems* whose solution is tied to a whole set of collective, nonscientific activities but whose *scientific solution* depends, on the contrary, on royal science and the way it has transformed the problem by introducing it into its theorematic apparatus and its organization of work. This is somewhat like intuition and intelligence in Bergson, where only intelligence has the scientific means to solve formally the problems posed by intuition. (TP 374)

Third, what is crucial in the interaction between the two poles is thus the processes of translation that take place between them—for instance, in Descartes and Fermat, an algebraic translation of the geometrical; in Weierstrass, a static translation of the dynamic; in Dedekind, a discrete translation of the continuous. The "richness and necessity of translations," writes Deleuze, "include as many opportunities for openings as risks of closure or stoppage" (TP 486). In general, Deleuze's work in mathematical "epistemology" tends to focus on the reduction of the problematic to the axiomatic, the intensive to the extensive, the continuous to the discrete, the non-metric to the metric, the non-denumerable to the denumerable, the rhizomatic to the arborescent, the smooth to the striated. Not all these reductions, to be sure, are equivalent, and Deleuze analyzes each on its own account. Deleuze himself highlights two of them. The first is "the complexity of the means by which one translates intensities into extensive quantities, or more generally, multiplicities of distance into systems of magnitudes that measure and striate them (the role of logarithms in this connection)"; the second, "the delicacy and complexity of the means by which Riemannian patches of smooth space receive a Euclidean conjunction (the role of the parallelism of vectors in striating the infinitesimal)" (TP 486). At times, Deleuze suggests, axiomatics can possess a deliberate will to halt problematics. "State science retains of nomad science only what it can appropriate; it turns the rest into a set of strictly limited formulas without any real scientific status, or else simply represses and bans it."[51] But despite its best efforts, axiomatics can never have done with problematics, which maintains its own ontological status and rigor.

> Minor science is continually enriching major science, communicating its intuitions to it, its way of proceeding, its itinerancy, its sense of and taste for matter, singularity, variation, intuitionist geometry and the numbering number . . . Major science has a perpetual need for the inspiration of the minor; but the minor would be nothing if it did not confront and conform to the highest scientific requirements. (TP 485–6)

In Deleuzian terms, one might say that while "progress" can be made at the level of theorematics and axiomatics, all "becoming" occurs at the level of problematics.

Fourth, this means that axiomatics, no less than problematics, is itself an inventive and creative activity. One might be tempted to follow Poincaré in identifying problematics as a "method of discovery" (Riemann) and axiomatics as a "method of demonstration" (Weierstrass).[52] But just as problematics has its own modes of formalization and deduction, so axiomatics has its own modes of intuition and discovery (axioms are not chosen arbitrarily, for instance, but in accordance with specific problems and intuitions).[53]

> In science an axiomatic is not at all a transcendent, autonomous, and decision-making power opposed to experimentation and intuition. On the one hand, it has its own gropings in the dark, experimentations, modes of intuition. Axioms being independent of each other, can they be added, and up to what point (a saturated system)? Can they be withdrawn (a "weakened" system)? On the other hand, it is of the nature of axiomatics to come up against so-called *undecidable propositions*, to confront *necessarily higher powers* that it cannot master. Finally, axiomatics does not constitute the cutting edge of science; it is much more a stopping point, a reordering that prevents decoded flows in physics and mathematics [= problematics] from escaping in all directions. The great axiomaticians are the men of State within science, who seal off the lines of flight that are so frequent in mathematics, who would impose a new *nexum*, if only a temporary one, and who lay down the official policies of science. They are the heirs of the theorematic conception of geometry. (TP 461)

For all these reasons, problematics is, by its very nature, "a kind of science, or treatment of science, that seems very difficult to classify, whose history is even difficult to follow."[54] None the less, according to Deleuze, the recognition of the irreducibility of problems and their genetic role has become "one of the most original characteristics of modern epistemology," as exemplified in the otherwise diverse work of thinkers such as Canguilhem, Bouligand, Vuillemin, and Lautman.[55] Beyond its significance in the interpretation of mathematics, problematics plays a significant role in Deleuze's theory of Ideas as well as his ontology ("Being" necessarily presents itself under a problematic form, and problems themselves are ontological). In all these domains, Deleuze's theory of problematics is extended in a theory of multiplicities, and it is to the nature of such multiplicities that we now turn.

DELEUZE'S THEORY OF MULTIPLICITIES

One of Badiou's most insistent claims is that Deleuze's theory of multiplicities is drawn from a "vitalist" paradigm, and not a mathematical one. The primary point I would like to establish in what follows is that, contra Badiou, Deleuze's theory is in fact drawn *exclusively* from mathematics—but from its problematic pole. Badiou at least admits that Deleuze's conception of multiplicities is derived in part from the differential calculus, but he concedes this point only to complain that Deleuze's "experimental construction of multiplicities is anachronistic because it is *pre-Cantorian*."[56] Cantor's set theory, however, represents the crowning moment of the tendency toward "discretization" in mathematics (the conception of sets as purely extensional), whereas Deleuze's project, as we have seen, is to formalize the conception of multiplicities that corresponds to the problematic pole of mathematics. In other words, problematics, no less than axiomatics, is the object of pure mathematics. Abel, Galois, Riemann, and Poincaré are among the great names in the history of problematics, just as Weierstrass, Dedekind, and Cantor are the great names in the discretization program, and Hilbert, Zermelo-Fraenkel, Gödel, and Cohen the great names in the movement toward formalization and axiomatization. Deleuze is fully aware of the apparent "anachronism" involved in delving into the pre-Weierstrassian theories of the calculus (Maimon, Bordas-Demoulin, Wronski, Lagrange, Carnot . . .). "A great deal of truly philosophical naiveté is needed to take the symbol dx seriously," he admits, while none the less maintaining that "there is a treasure buried in the old so-called barbaric or prescientific interpretations of the differential calculus, which must be separated from its infinitesimal matrix" (DR 170). The reason Deleuze focuses on role of the differential (dx), however, is twofold. On the one hand, in the calculus, the differential is by nature problematic; it constitutes "the internal character of the problem as such," which is precisely why it must *disappear* in the result or solution.[57] On the other hand, whereas Plato used geometry as a model for his conception of transcendent "Ideas" because he saw the latter as *unchanging* theorematic forms, Deleuze uses the calculus as a model for his conception of immanent Ideas because the differential provides him with a mathematical symbolism of the problematic form of *pure change* (Bergson had already spoken of the differential or "fluxion" as a mean of capturing, via mathematics, a vision of the *élan vital*).[58] Deleuze will thus make a strong distinction between "differential relations" and "axiomatic relations" (29 April 1980). Even in *Difference and Repetition*, however, the calculus is only one of several mathematical domains that Deleuze utilizes in formulating his theory of multiplicities: "We cannot suppose that differential calculus is the only mathematical expression of problems as such . . . More recently, other procedures have fulfilled this role better."[59] What is at issue, in other words, is neither the empirical or intuitive origin of mathematical problems (e.g., in the ambulatory sciences) nor the historical moment of their mathematical formalization (pre- or post-Cantorian). "While it is true that the [continuous] continuum must be related to Ideas and to their problematic use," Deleuze writes, "this is on condition that it no longer be defined by characteristics borrowed from sensible or even geometrical intuition" (DR 171). What Deleuze finds in pure mathematics is a rigorous conception of the constitution of problems as such, divorced not only from the conditions of intuition, but also from the conditions of their solvability. It is on the basis of this formalization that Deleuze, in turn, will be able to assign a precise status to mathematical notions such as continuous variation and becoming—which can only be comprehended under the mode of problematics. Space precludes a more detailed analysis of Deleuze's theory of multiplicities here; for our purposes, I would simply like to highlight three mathematical domains that have formalized the

theory of the problem, and which Deleuze utilizes in formulating his own conception of multiplicities as problematic.[60]

1. The first domain is the theory of *groups*, which initially arose from questions
concerning the solvability of certain *algebraic* (rather than differential) equations.
There are two kinds of solutions to algebraic equations: particular and general.
Whereas a *particular* solution is given by numerical values ($x^2 + 3x - 4 = 0$ has as its
solution $x = 1$), a *general* solution provides the global pattern of all particular solutions to an algebraic equation (the above equation, generalized as $x^2 + ax - b = 0$,
has the solution $x = \sqrt{a^2}/2 + b - a/2$). But such solutions, writes Deleuze, "whether
general or particular, find their sense only in the subjacent problem which inspires
them" (DR 162). By the sixteenth century, it had been proved (Tataglia-Cardan)
that *general* solvability was possible with squared, cubic, and quartic equations.
But equations raised to the fifth power and higher refused to yield to the previous
method (via radicals), and the puzzle of the "quintic" remained unresolved for more
than two centuries, until the work of Lagrange, Abel, and Galois in the nineteenth
century. In 1824, Abel proved the startling result that the quintic was in fact *unsolv-
able*, but the method he used was as important as the result. Abel recognized that
there was a pattern to the solutions of the first four cases, and that it was this pattern
that held the key to understanding the recalcitrance of the fifth. Abel showed that
the question of "solvability" had to be determined internally by the *intrinsic* conditions of the problem itself, which then progressively specifies its own "fields" of
solvability.

Building on Abel's work, Évariste Galois developed a way to approach the study
of this pattern, using the technique now known as *group theory*. Put simply, Galois
"showed that equations that can be solved by a formula must have groups of a particular type, and that the quintic had the wrong sort of group."[61] The "group" of an
equation captures the conditions of the problem; on the basis of certain substitu-
tions within the group, solutions can be shown to be indistinguishable in so far as
the validity of the equation is concerned.[62] In particular, Deleuze emphasizes the
fundamental procedure of *adjunction* in Galois:

> Starting from a basic "field" R, successive adjunctions to this field (R^1, R^2, R^3
> ...) allow a progressively more precise distinction of the roots of an equation,
> by the progressive limitation of possible substitutions. There is thus a succes-
> sion of "partial resolvants" or an embedding of "groups" which make the solu-
> tion follow from the very conditions of the problem. (DR 180)

In other words, the group of an equation does not tell us what we know about its
roots, but rather, as Georges Verriest remarks, "the objectivity of what we do *not*
know about them."[63] As Galois himself wrote, "in these two memoirs, and especially
in the second, one often finds the formula, *I don't know* . . . ."[64] This non-knowledge
is not a negative or an insufficiency, but rather a rule or something to be learned that
corresponds to an *objective* dimension of the problem. What Deleuze finds in Abel
and Galois, following the exemplary analyses of Jules Vuillemin in his *Philosophy of
Algebra*, is "a radical reversal of the problem–solution relation, a more considerable

revolution than the Copernican."[65] In a sense, one could say that "unsolvability" plays a role in problematics similar to that played by "undecidability" in axiomatics.

2. The second domain Deleuze utilizes is the calculus itself, and on this score Deleuze's analyses are based to a large extent on the interpretation proposed by Albert Lautman in his *Essay on the Notions of Structure and Existence in Mathematics*.[66] Lautman's work is based on the idea of a fundamental difference in kind between a problem and its solution, a distinction that is attested to by the existence of problems *without* solution. Leibniz, Deleuze notes, "had already shown that the calculus . . . expressed problems that could not hitherto be solved, or indeed, even posed" (DR 177). In turn Lautman establishes a link between the theory of differential equations and the theory of singularities, since it was the latter that provided the key to understanding the nature of *non-linear* differential equations, which could not be solved because their series diverged. As determined by the equation, singular points are distinguished from the ordinary points of a curve: the singularities mark the points where the curve changes direction (inflections, cusps, etc.), and thus can be used to distinguish between different *types* of curves. In the late 1800s, Henri Poincaré, using a simple non-linear equation, was able to identify four types of singular points that corresponded to the equation (foci, saddle points, knots, and centers) and to demonstrate the topological behavior of the solutions in the neighborhood of such points (the integral curves).[67] On the basis of Poincaré's work, Lautman was able to specify the nature of the difference in kind between problems and solutions. The conditions of the *problem* posed by the equation are determined by the existence and distribution of singular points in a differentiated topological field (a field of vectors), where each singularity is inseparable from a zone of objective indetermination (the ordinary points that surround it). In turn, the *solution* to the equation will only appear with the integral curves that are constituted the neighborhood of these singularities, which mark the beginnings of the differenciation (or actualization) of the problematic field. In this way, the ontological status of the problem as such is detached from its solutions; in itself, the problem is a multiplicity of singularities, a nested field of directional vectors which define the "virtual" trajectories of the curves in the solution, not all of which can be actualized. Non-linear equations can thus be used to model objectively problematic (or indeterminate) physical systems, such as the weather (Lorenz); the equations can define the virtual "attractors" of the system (the intrinsic singularities toward which the trajectories will tend in the long term), but they cannot say in advance which trajectory will be actualized (the equation cannot be solved), making accurate prediction impossible. A problem, in other words, has an objectively determined structure (virtuality), apart from its solutions (actuality).[68]

3. But "there is no revolution" in the problem–solution reversal, continues Deleuze,

> as long as we remain tied to Euclidean geometry: we must move to a geometry of sufficient reason, a Riemannian-type differential geometry which tends to give rise to discontinuity on the basis of continuity, or to ground solutions in the conditions of the problems. (DR 162)

This leads to Deleuze's third mathematical resource, the *differential geometry* of Gauss and Riemann. Gauss had realized that the utilization of the differential calculus allowed for the study of curves and surfaces in a purely intrinsic and "local" manner: that is, without any reference to a "global" embedding space (such as the Cartesian coordinates of analytic geometry).[69] Riemann's achievement, in turn, was to have used Gauss's differential geometry to launch a reconsideration of the entire approach to the study of space by analyzing the general problem of *n-dimensional* curved surfaces. He developed a non-Euclidean geometry (showing that Euclid's axioms were not self-evident truths) of a multi-dimensional, non-metric, and non-intuitable "any-space-whatever," which he termed a pure "multiplicity" or "manifold" [*Mannigfaltigkeit*]. He began by defining the distance between two points whose corresponding coordinates differ only by infinitesimal amounts, and defined the curvature of the multiplicity in terms of the *accumulation* of neighborhoods, which alone determine its connections.[70] For our purposes, the two important features of a Riemannian manifold are its variable number of dimensions (its *n*-dimensionality), and the absence of any supplementary dimension which would impose on it extrinsically defined coordinates or unity.[71] As Deleuze writes, a Riemannian multiplicity is

> an n-dimensional, continuous, defined multiplicity ... By *dimensions*, we mean the variables or coordinates upon which a phenomenon depends; by *continuity*, we mean the set of [differential] relations between changes in these variables—for example, a quadratic form of the differentials of the co-ordinates; by *definition*, we mean the elements reciprocally determined by these relations, elements which cannot change unless the multiplicity changes its order and its metric. (DR 182)

In his critique of Deleuze, Badiou suggests not only that a Riemannian manifold entails "a neutralization of difference" (whereas Riemannian space is defined differentially) and a "preliminary figure of the One" (whereas Riemannian space has no preliminary unity), but also that it finds the "subjacent ontology of its invention" in set theory (whereas its *invention* is tied to problematics and the use of infinitesimals). What Badiou's comments reflect, rather, is the inevitable effort of "major" science to translate an intrinsic manifold into the discrete terms of an extensive set (though, as Abraham Robinson noted, it is by no means clear that results obtained in differential geometry using infinitesimals are automatically obtainable using Weierstrassian methods).[72]

In *Difference and Repetition*, Deleuze draws upon all these resources to develop his general theory of problematic or differential multiplicities, whose formalizable conditions can be briefly summarized as follows.

1. The elements of the multiplicity are merely "determinable"; their nature is not determined in advance by either a defining property or an axiom (e.g., extensionality). Rather, they are pure virtualities that have neither identity, nor sensible form, nor conceptual signification, nor assignable function (principle of determinability).

2. They are none the less determined reciprocally as singularities in the differential relation, a "non-localizable ideal connection" that provides a purely intrinsic definition of the multiplicity as "problematic"; the differential relation is not only *external* to its terms, but *constitutive* of its terms (principle of reciprocal determination).

3. The values of these relations define the complete determination of the problem: that is, "the existence, the number, and the distribution of the determinant points that precisely provide its conditions" *as* a problem (principle of complete determination).[73]

These three aspects of sufficient reason, finally, find their unity in the temporal principle of progressive determination, through which, as we have seen in the work of Abel and Galois, the problem is resolved (adjunction, etc.) (DR 210). The strength of Deleuze's project, with regard to problematics, is that, in a certain sense, it parallels the movement toward "rigor" that was made in axiomatics; it presents a formalization of the theory of problems, freed from the conditions of geometric intuition and solvability, and existing only in pure thought (even though Deleuze presents his theory in a purely philosophical manner, and explicitly refuses to assign a scientific status to his conclusions).[74] In undertaking this project, he had few philosophical precursors (Lautman, Vuillemin), and the degree to which he succeeded in the effort no doubt remains an open question. Manuel De Landa, in a recent work, has proposed several refinements in Deleuze's formalization, drawn from contemporary science: certain types of singularities are now recognizable as "strange attractors"; the resolution of a problematic field (the movement from the virtual to the actual) can now be described in terms of a series of spatio-temporal "symmetry-breaking cascades," and so on.[75] But as De Landa insists, despite his own modifications to Deleuze's theory, Deleuze himself "should get the credit for having adequately *posed the problem*" of problematics.[76]

DELEUZE AND BADIOU

Equipped now with a more adequate understanding of Deleuze's conception of problematics, we can now return to Badiou's critique and see why neither of his two main theses concerning Deleuze articulates the real nature of their fundamental differences. Badiou's thesis that Deleuze is a philosopher of the One is the least persuasive, for several reasons. First, Badiou derives this thesis from Deleuze's concept of univocity, proposing the equation "univocity = the One." But already in Scotus, the doctrine of the "univocity of Being" was strictly incompatible with (and in part directed against) a Neo-Platonic "philosophy of the One." Moreover, Deleuze's explicit (and repeated) thesis in *Difference and Repetition* is that the only condition under which the term "Being" can be said in a single and univocal sense is if Being is said univocally of *difference as such* (i.e., "Being is univocal" = "Being is difference").[77] To argue, as Badiou does, that Deleuze's work operates "on the basis of an ontological precomprehension of Being as One" is in effect to argue that Deleuze *rejects* the doctrine of univocity.[78]

In other words, "Being is univocal" and "Being is One" are strictly incompatible theses, and Badiou's conflation of the two, as has been noted by several commentators, betrays a fundamental misunderstanding of the theory of univocity.[79] Second, while it is none the less true that Deleuze proposed a concept of the One compatible with univocity (e.g., the "One-All" of the plane of immanence as a secant plane cut out of chaos; see WP 35, 202–3), Badiou seems unable to articulate it in part because of the inconsistency of his own conception of the One, which is variously assimilated to the Neo-Platonic One, the Christian God, Spinoza's Substance, Leibniz's Continuity, Kant's unconditioned Whole, Nietzsche's Eternal Return, Bergson's *élan vital*, a generalized conception of Unity, and Deleuze's Virtual, to name a few.[80] The reason for this conceptual fluidity seems clear: since the task of modern philosophy, for Badiou, is "the renunciation of the One," and since for him only a set theoretical ontology is capable of fulfilling this task, the concept of the "One" effectively becomes little more than a marker in Badiou's writings for *any* non-set-theoretical ontology. But the fact that Augustine—to use a famous example—became a Christian (believer in God) by renouncing his Neo-Platonism (adherence to the One) is enough to show that these terms are not easily interchangeable, and that renouncing the One does not even entail a renunciation of God. Moreover, Kant had already showed that the idea of the "World" is a transcendent illusion. One can only speak of the "whole" of Being ("the totality of what is") from the viewpoint of transcendence; it is precisely the "immanence" of the concept of Being (univocity) that *prevents* any conception of Being as a totality. Third, and most important, the notion of the One does not articulate the difference between Badiou and Deleuze even on the question of "an immanent conception of the multiple." Extensive multiplicities (sets) and differential multiplicities (e.g., Riemannian manifolds) are *both* defined in a purely intrinsic or immanent manner, without any recourse to the One or the Whole or a Unity. The real *differend* must be located in the difference between axiomatics and problematics, major and minor science.

Badiou's thesis concerning Deleuze's "vitalism," by contrast, comes closer to articulating a real difference. (Badiou recognizes, to be sure, that Deleuze uses this biological term in a somewhat provocative manner, divorced from its traditional reference to a semi-mystical life-force.) Although Deleuze's formal theory of multiplicities is drawn from mathematical models, it is true that he appeals to numerous non-mathematical domains in describing the intensive processes of *individuation* through which multiplicities are actualized (biology, but also physics and geology). "Vitalism" enters the picture, in other words, at the level of individuation—hence the distinction, in *Difference and Repetition*, between the fourth chapter on "The Ideal Synthesis of Difference" (the theory of multiplicities, which appeals to mathematics) and the fifth chapter on "The Asymmetrical Synthesis of the Sensible" (the theory of individuation, which appeals to biology). But this distinction is neither exclusive nor disciplinary. Even in mathematics, the movement from a problem to its solutions constitutes a process of actualization; though formally distinct, there is no ontological separation between these two instances (the complex Deleuzian notion of "differen t/c ation"). As Deleuze explains,

> we tried to constitute a philosophical concept from the *mathematical* function of differentiation and the *biological* function of differenciation, in asking whether there was not a statable relation between these two concepts which could not appear at the level of their respective objects . . . Mathematics and biology appear here only in the guise of technical models which allow the exposition of the virtual [problematic multiplicities] and the process of actualization [biological individuation]. (DR xvi, 220–1)

Deleuze thus rejects Badiou's reduction of ontology to mathematics, and would no doubt have been sympathetic to Ernst Mayr's suggestion that biology might itself be seen as the highest science, capable of encompassing and synthesizing diverse developments in mathematics, physics, and chemistry.[81]

Badiou's resistance to this "vitalism" can be accounted for by his restricted conception of ontology. For Badiou, the term ontology refers uniquely to the discourse of "Being-as-being" (axiomatic set theory), which is indifferent to the question of existence. For Deleuze, by contrast, ontology encompasses Being, beings, *and* their ontological difference (using Heideggerian language), and the determinations of "Being-as-such" must therefore be immediately related to beings in their existence. This is why the calculus functions as a powerful test case in comparing Deleuze and Badiou. The calculus has been rightly described as the most powerful instrument ever invented for the mathematical exploration of the physical universe. In its initial formulations, however, as we have seen, the calculus mobilized notions that were unjustified from the viewpoint of classical algebra or arithmetic; it was a fiction, as Leibniz said, irreducible to mathematical reality. From these origins, however, one can trace the history of the calculus along two vectors, so to speak: toward the establishment of its foundations, or toward its use in an ever-deepening exploration of existence. The movement toward rigor in mathematics, by "royal" science, was motivated by the attempt to establish a foundation for the concepts of the calculus internal to mathematics. Badiou situates his work exclusively on this path, characterizing axiomatic set theory as "rational ontology itself."[82] Deleuze, by contrast, while stressing the foundational necessity of axiomatics, equally emphasizes the role of the calculus in the comprehension of existence.

> Differential calculus [he writes], is a kind of union of mathematics and the existent—specifically, it is the symbolic of the existent. It is because it is a well-founded fiction in relation to mathematical truth that it is consequently *a basic and real means of exploration of the reality of existence.*[83]

A law of nature, as Hermann Weyl says, is necessarily expressed as a differential equation, and it is the calculus that establishes this link between mathematics and existence (Einstein's general relativity, for instance, made use of the tensor calculus). While axiomatics established the foundations of the calculus *within* mathematics, it is in the calculus itself that one must seek out the relation of mathematics with *existence* (problematics). This is no doubt the fundamental difference between Badiou and Deleuze. Badiou eliminates existence entirely from his ontology (there is no "being" of matter, life, sensibility . . .). In Deleuze, however, existence is fully a dimension of ontology as such: "force" is a determination of the being of matter (Leibniz); "vitalism" is a determination of the being of living things (Bergson); "intensity" is a determination of the being of the sensible (Kant); and so on. It is this genetic and problematic aspect of mathematics that remains inaccessible to set theoretical axiomatics.[84]

Badiou's neglect of the "problematic" dimension of Deleuze's thought results in numerous infelicities in his reading of Deleuze. In *Deleuze: The Clamor of Being*, Badiou's approach is guided by the presumption that "the starting point required by Deleuze's method is always a concrete *case*."[85] But this is a false presumption: for Deleuze, the starting point is always the *problem*, and "cases" are themselves derived from problems. The fundamental question is to determine which problems are interesting and remarkable, or to determine what is interesting or remarkable within the problem as such (group theory). If one starts with the case, it is in order to determine the problem to which it corresponds ("the creation of a concept always occurs as the function of a problem") (ABC H). Paul Erdós famously assigned monetary values to mathematical problems, ranging from $10 to $3,000, depending not only on their degree of difficulty but also on their importance *as problems*, and he would pay out (often to graduate students) when the problem was solved.[86] Similarly, Poincaré used to say that proving an uninteresting problem was worse than discovering a flaw in one's proof for a remarkable problem: the latter can be corrected, but the former will remain eternally trivial.[87] The truth of a solution, in other words, is less important than the truth or "interest" of the problem being dealt with (a problem always has the solution it "deserves").

Nor can one say—as Badiou frequently does—that Deleuze simply falls back on the "concrete" with the aim of producing phenomenological descriptions of the "figural." Badiou goes so far as to claim that Deleuze's work "does not support the real rights of the abstract" and instead gives itself over to the "seductive scin-tillations of concrete analysis." At best, Badiou thinks Deleuze draws "powerful metaphors (and yes, I do mean metaphors)" from mathematics and produces little more than "a metaphorizing phenomenology of pure change."[88] Not only does this imply a simplified view of the "concrete" (as Deleuze notes, "the true opposite of the concrete is not the abstract, it's the *discrete* . . . Lived experience is an absolutely abstract thing"),[89] but also it entirely ignores Deleuze's development of a formal theory of problematics, and its complex mathematical sources. As Deleuze writes,

> we must not see mathematical metaphors in all these expressions such as "sin-gular and distinctive points" or "adjunct fields" . . . These are categories of the dialectical Idea, extensions of the differential calculus (*mathesis universalis*) . . . corresponding to the Idea in all its domains. (DR 190)

This avoidance, in turn, leads Badiou to make several misguided claims. In his book *Bergsonism*, for instance, Deleuze explicitly defines Bergsonian "intuition" as an elaborated method that consists in "the stating and creating of *problems*" (B 14). Badiou, to support his own theses, ignores this definition, and instead reinterprets

intuition as a method that thinks beings as "merely local intensities of the One."[90]
Similarly, Deleuze has suggested that

> the intuitionist school (Brouwer, Heyting, Griss, Bouligand) is of great impor-
> tance in mathematics, not because it asserted the irreducible rights of intui-
> tion, or even because it elaborated a very novel constructivism, but because it
> developed a conception of *problems*, and of a *calculus of problems* that intrinsi-
> cally rivals axiomatics and proceeds by other rules (notably with regard to the
> excluded middle).[91]

But when Badiou links Deleuze to "the constructivist, and indeed intuitionist
vision" of contemporary mathematics, he again ignores the link with problematics, and instead strangely construes the constructivist school as having pursued a
purely "descriptive" task that starts from the sensible intuition of "already complex
concretions."[92]

Badiou's emphasis on axiomatics also affects his readings of Deleuze's work in
the history of philosophy. Badiou, for instance, complains that "Deleuze neglects
the function of mathematics in Spinoza," for whom "mathematics alone thinks
being."[93] But this is not quite correct either: Deleuze explicitly criticizes Spinoza for
allowing his mathematics to assume a purely axiomatic form. "In Spinoza," Deleuze
writes, "*the use of the geometric method involves no 'problems' at all*" (DR 323 n21).
This is why, in his readings of Spinoza, Deleuze emphasizes the role of the scholia
(which are the only elements of the *Ethics* that fall outside the axiomatic deduc-
tions, and develop the theme of "affections") and the fifth book (which introduces
problematic hiatuses and contractions into the deductive exposition itself).[94] No
doubt it is this emphasis on the problematic aspects of the *Ethics* that rendered
Deleuze's Spinoza "unrecognizable" to Badiou, who focuses on the theorematic and
axiomatic apparatus.[95] Indeed, with regard to problematics, Deleuze suggests that
Descartes actually went further than Spinoza, and that Descartes the geometer went
further than Descartes the philosopher: the "Cartesian method" (the search for the
clear and distinct) is a method for solving problems, whereas the analytic procedure presented in Descartes's *Geometry* is focused on the constitution of problems
as such ("Cartesian coordinates" appear nowhere in the *Geometry*).[96] In all these
characterizations, one at times senses in Badiou the semi-patronizing attitude of the
"royal" scientist, who sees Deleuze's thought mired in problematics and its inferior
concepts, and lacking the robustness required for work in "severe mathematics" and
its "delicate axiomatics."

But perhaps the most striking omission in Badiou's work, especially given his
political interests, is his neglect of Deleuze's political philosophy, since the latter is
derived directly from these mathematical models. The central thesis of *Capitalism
and Schizophrenia* (whose very title reflects the axiomatics–problematics distinction)
is that capitalism itself functions on the basis of an axiomatic—not metaphorically,
but literally.[97] This is because capital as such is a problematic multiplicity: it can be
converted into *discrete* quantities in our paychecks and loose change, but in itself
the monetary mass is a *continuous* or intensive quantity that increases and decreases

without any agency controlling it. Like the continuum, capital is not masterable by an axiom; or rather, it constantly requires the creation of new axioms (it is "like a power of the continuum, tied to the axiomatic but exceeding it") (TP 466). In turn, capital produces other flows that follow these circuits of capital: flows of commodities, flows of population, flows of labor, flows of traffic, flows of knowledge, and so on—all of which have a necessarily "problematic" status from the viewpoint of the capitalist regime. The fundamental operation of the capitalist State, in Deleuze's reading, is to attempt to control these "deterritorialized" flows by axiomatizing them—but this axiomatization can never be complete, not only because of the inherent limits of any axiomatic, but also because new "problematics" are constantly in the process of being created . "The true axiomatic," Deleuze says, "is social and not scientific."[98] To take one well-known example: for Deleuze "minorities" are, in themselves, non-denumerable multiplicities; they can be brought into the capitalist axiomatic by being denumerated, counted, given their identity cards, made a part of the majority (which is a denumerable multiplicity—that is, a multiplicity of discrete numerical elements); but there is also a power to minorities that comes from *not* entering into the axiomatic, a power that does not reduce minorities to a mere "tear" or "rupture" in the axiomatic, but assigns to them an objective and determinable ontological positivity of their own *as* problematic.[99]

> The issue is not at all anarchy versus organization [writes Deleuze], nor even centralization versus decentralization, but a calculus or conception of *problems* of non-denumerable sets, against the *axiomatic* of denumerable sets. Such a calculus may have its own compositions, organizations, and even centralization; nevertheless, it proceeds not via the States or the axiomatic process but via a pure becoming of minorities.[100]

This brings us back again, finally, to the question of the *event*, which is where the Badiou–Deleuze *differend* appears in perhaps its starkest contrast. In effect, the respective ontologies of Deleuze and Badiou move in opposing directions: Deleuze's is a "bottom-up" ontology (from problematics to discretization-axiomatization), whereas Badiou's is a "top-down" ontology (elaborated exclusively from the viewpoint of axiomatics, denying the existence of problematics). From Deleuze's viewpoint, this denial of problematics constitutes the intractable limitation of Badiou's ontology, which consequently appears in two forms. On the one hand, for Badiou, Being is presented in purely *discrete* terms: what is "subtracted" from the "count-as-one" rule that constitutes consistent sets (knowledge) is an inconsistent or "generic" multiplicity, the pure discrete multiple of Being, which in itself remains indiscernible, unpresented, and unnamable as such (the void); an event—that which is not "Being-as-Being", if one occurs, intervenes "on the edge" of this void, and constitutes the condition of a truth-procedure. But this entire characterization revolves in the domain of the discrete; what is truly "unnamed" within it is the entire domain of problematics and its "repressed" notions, such as continuous variation. Such is the substance of the critique Deleuze addresses to Badiou in *What is Philosophy?* "The theory of multiplicities," he writes, "does not support the hypothesis of an 'any multiplicity whatever'": that is, a purely "generic" discrete multiplicity (WP 152). The discretization program found its point of "genesis" in problematics, and in any adequate mathematical ontology there must therefore be "at least two multiplicities, two types, from the outset"—namely, the continuous *and* the discrete, the non-metric *and* the metric, and so on. "This is not because dualism is better than unity," continues Deleuze, "but because the multiplicity is precisely what happens between the two": that is, in the movement of conversion that translates the continuous into the discrete, the non-metric into the metric, etc. It is precisely this movement of translation, and Deleuze's own formalization of problematic multiplicities, that we have attempted to sketch out above. On the other hand, for Badiou, the "truth" of Being is presented in a purely *axiomatic* form. As a result, the articulation or "thinking" of a inconsistent multiplicity—the operation of a "truth-procedure"—can only be *subjective*, since it is only by means of a purely subjective "decision" that an event can be affirmed, and the hitherto indistinguishable elements of the multiplicity can be named, thereby altering the "situation" through the declaration of an axiom. Badiou necessarily dissociates this process of subjectivation from ontology itself, since it is only the subject's "fidelity" to the event that allows the elements of the altered situation to achieve consistency. Hence the fundamental duality that Badiou posits between "Being" and "Event," and the separation of the articulation of Being from the path of the subject or truth. For Deleuze, by contrast, the genesis of truth (and the genesis of axiomatics itself) must always be found in *problematics*: Being necessarily presents itself under a problematic form, and problems and their ideal events always are ontological, not subjective. The generation of truth, in other words, is derived from the constitution of problems, and a problem always has the truth it "deserves" in so far as it is completely constituted *as* a problem. The greatness of the calculus in mathematics is that it provided a precise symbolism with which it could express problems that, before its invention, could not even have been posed. If Badiou is forced to define truth in purely subjective terms, it is because he wrongly limits his ontology to axiomatics, and denies himself the real ontological ground of truth in problematics.

The path followed by Badiou in *Being and Event*, then, is almost the exact inverse of that followed by Deleuze in *Difference and Repetition*, and the two paths exemplify Deleuze's own distinction between an immanent and a transcendent ontology. For Deleuze, a purely "immanent" ontology is one in which there is nothing "outside" Being or "other" than Being, and he therefore grants full ontological status to *both* problematics and axiomatics. Since Badiou limits his ontology to axiomatics, he is forced to reintroduce an element of transcendence in the form of the event, which is "supplemental" to ontology, "supernumerary": there can be no ontology of the event, since the event itself introduces a "rupture" into being, a "tear" in its fabric. In *What is Philosophy?*, this is exactly how Deleuze defines the "modern" way of saving transcendence: "it is now from *within* immanence that a breach is expected . . . something transcendent is reestablished on the horizon, in the regions of non-belonging," or as Badiou would say, from the "edge of the void" (WP 46-7). Whereas an immanent ontology "never has a supplementary dimension to that which transpires upon it," an ontology of transcendence "always has an additional dimension; it always implies a dimension supplementary to the dimensions of the given" (TP 266; SPP 128). In this sense, Badiou's is indeed an analogical and reflexive ontology that requires a mechanism of transcendence to "save" the event.[101] Though Badiou is determined to expel God and the One from his philosophy, he winds up reassigning to the event, as if through the back door, many of the transcendent characteristics formerly assigned to the divine. In Plotinus, it is the One which is "beyond" Being; in Badiou, it is the event which is "not being-as-being," that "interrupts" Being. In religious life, what is transformative is fidelity to God; in Badiou, it is fidelity to the event. In Christian theology, it is God who creates *ex nihilo*; in Badiou, it is the subject who proclaims the event and in a sense assumes those once divine powers (as Badiou declares triumphantly, "I conceptualize absolute beginnings!").[102] The primary aim of this paper has been to clarify, in a more adequate manner than Badiou did, the fundamental points of disagreement between the two philosophers. Deleuze, however, often insisted on the irreducibility of "taste" in philosophy, and if these analyses are correct, it would seem that Badiou's taste for discretization and axiomatization in mathematics concealed a deeper taste for a kind of transcendence-within-immanence, with its conceptualizations of total ruptures and absolute beginnings.

Jacques Lacan

The Inverse Side of the Structure: Žižek on Deleuze on Lacan

In an interview in 1995, shortly before his death, Deleuze was asked by his interviewer, Didier Éribon, about his relationship with Jacques Lacan. In response, Deleuze told the following story:

> Lacan noticed me when he devoted a session of his seminar to my book on Sacher-Masoch [1967]. I was told—although I never knew anything more than this—that he had devoted more than an hour to my book. And then he came to a conference at Lyon, where I was then teaching. He gave an absolutely unbelievable lecture . . . It was there that he uttered his famous formula, *"Psychoanalysis can do everything except make an idiot seem intelligible."* After the conference, he came to our place for dinner. And since he went to bed very late, he stayed a long time. I remember: it was after midnight and he absolutely had to have a special whisky. It was truly a nightmare, that night.
>
> My only great encounter with him was after the appearance of *Anti-Oedipus* [1972]. I'm sure he took it badly. He must have held it against us, Félix and me. But finally, a few months later, he summoned me—there's no other word for it. He wanted to see me. And so I went. He made me wait in his antechamber. It was filled with people, I didn't know if they were patients, admirers, journalists . . . He made me wait a long time—a little too long, all the same—and then he finally received me. He rolled out a list of all his disciples, and said that they were all worthless [*nuls*] (the only person he said nothing bad about was Jacques-Alain Miller). It made me smile, because I recalled Binswanger telling the story of a similar scene: Freud saying bad things about Jones, Abraham, etc. And Binswanger was shrewd enough to assume that Freud would say the same thing about him when he wasn't there. So Lacan was speaking, and everyone was condemned, except Miller. And then he said to me, "What I need is someone like you" [*C'est quelqu'un comme vous qu'il me faut.*].[1]

This is a revealing anecdote, for at least two reasons. First, one might say that the disciple Lacan wound up "getting" was not Gilles Deleuze but Slavoj Žižek, among others, which puts Žižek's encounter with Deleuze in *Organs Without Bodies* in a revealing retrospective light.[2] Second, and more importantly, Deleuze's personal encounter with Lacan took place *after* the publication of *Anti-Oedipus* in 1972. *Anti-Oedipus* presents, among other things, a famous critique (though not rejection) of psychoanalysis, which Deleuze and Guattari pursued, in part, by means of an engagement with Lacan's work. In this sense, one could say that Deleuze was indeed a Lacanian, but in the exact same manner that he was a Spinozist or a Leibnizian: he was neither a slavish follower nor a dogmatic reader of Lacan, but followed the internal trajectory of Lacan's thought to the point where he would push it to its "differential" limit (Deleuze's all-too-well-known image of philosophical "buggery," which makes thinkers produce their own "monstrous" children). Despite Deleuze's initial worries about Lacan's reaction to *Anti-Oedipus*, Lacan obviously did not dismiss the book. On the contrary, not only was his reading of the book the apparent basis of his "summons" to Deleuze, but also he even seems to have been influenced by *Anti-Oedipus* in his own thinking. Žižek himself suggests that Lacan's later work (after Seminar XI in 1964) is marked by an increased interest in the theory of the drives and anti-Oedipal themes (OB 102, 176). Given the complex status of the drives that one finds elaborated in *Anti-Oedipus* (for instance, the thesis that the "drives are part of the infrastructure itself," AO 63), one can assume that Lacan saw Deleuze neither as an antagonistic critic, nor even a potential bearer of orthodoxy (à la Miller), but rather a highly original fellow traveler.

This is what makes *Organs without Bodies* a bit of a disappointment, as well as a sharp departure from Lacan's own relationship to Deleuze. It is not so much that only about a quarter of Žižek's book (if that) is actually devoted to Deleuze, and the rest is Žižek doing his own thing. It is not even so much that he misreads Deleuze on this or that point; Deleuze wrote that "encounters between independent thinkers always occur in a blind zone," and this is no less true of the encounter between Žižek and Deleuze than the encounter between Badiou and Deleuze.[3] The disappointment is that, even though Žižek describes *Organs Without Bodies* as "a Lacanian book on Deleuze" (OB xi), he winds up saying nothing whatsoever about Deleuze's own work on Lacan. This, perhaps, is just a thwarted expectation; I had hoped to find in Žižek's book a kind of guide through the complexities of the Deleuze–Lacan encounter, yet nothing of the sort appears in the book. Instead, early on, Žižek quickly and curtly dismisses *Anti-Oedipus* as "arguably Deleuze's worst book" (OB 21), and immediately turns his attention elsewhere.

In this, *Organs Without Bodies* bears a strange resemblance to Alain Badiou's 1997 book *Deleuze: The Clamor of Being*. Badiou had seen Deleuze as his primary rival in developing an "ontology of the multiple," and he opens his book by expressly declaring that the source of his controversy with Deleuze was their differing philosophical conceptions of "multiplicities."[4] Yet as one reads on, one quickly discovers that the book does not contain a single discussion of Deleuze's theory of multiplicities; it ignores the topic entirely. Instead, Badiou is content simply to reiterate the dubious claim that Deleuze is *really* just a thinker of "the One"—almost like a politician avoiding reporters' questions by doggedly sticking to his talking points. Žižek admits that he relied "extensively" on Badiou's reading of Deleuze (OB 20n), and he rather slavishly adopts its theses and winds up reproducing a number of its errors regarding "univocity" and "vitalism" (Deleuze, Žižek dutifully repeats, is "the last great philosopher of the One," OB 121; cf. 28). But the resemblance to Badiou is stylistic as well as substantive, since one finds a similar strategy of avoidance and displacement in Žižek's book—a "Lacanian" book on Deleuze that does not contain a single discussion of Deleuze's reading of Lacan. Taking up Deleuze's own image, Žižek claims that he is engaging in a kind of "*Hegelian* [and, one might add, Lacanian] *buggery of Deleuze*" (OB 48). The ultimate aim of his book is to show us that Deleuze is "much closer to psychoanalysis and Hegel" (OB xi) than we might have expected—in other words, that Deleuze is *really* a kind of Žižekian *avant la lettre* (OB 69). As a result, Žižek's reading of Deleuze, at its most positive, is often little more than a transcription of Deleuze's concepts into Žižek's own Lacanian (and Hegelian) terminology. One does not grudge Žižek his project—he is certainly one of the most engaging and prolific thinkers alive today—but then one wonders why the detour through Deleuze was necessary at all, except as a kind of exercise in playful pop-Hegelian sublation.

None the less, there is a serious reading of Deleuze taking place in the midst of all the buggery. Žižek issues his perfunctory dismissal of *Anti-Oedipus* (1972) in order to elevate *Logic of Sense* (1969) to the status of Deleuze's pivotal work (no doubt, once again, in deference to the master, since Lacan discussed both *Coldness and Cruelty* and *Logic of Sense* in his seminar sessions). Deleuze himself summarized the fundamental question he was attempting to address in the *Logic of Sense* in the following manner:

> How can we maintain both that sense produces even the states of affairs in which it is embodied [sense as a principle of the *production* of beings], and that it is itself produced by these states of affairs or the actions and passions of bodies [sense as an impassive *effect* of material causes]?[5]

Žižek feigns a certain surprise that no one (before him) had perceived this tension (production versus effect) that lies at the heart of *Logic of Sense*, and he claims that it in fact holds the key to Deleuze's entire work (OB 21). The "conceptual edifice" of Deleuze's philosophy, Žižek argues, oscillates between these two "logics" of sense (or of the event), which are "fundamentally incompatible" (OB 20). "Is this opposition not that of materialism versus idealism? In Deleuze, this means: *The Logic of Sense* versus *Anti-Oedipus*" (OB 21). Put summarily, one finds two competing ontologies in Deleuze, one good, the other bad and naive: "sense as effect" is the good ontology, "sense as production" is the bad ontology. Sense as "effect" is good because it is Lacanian: the event is the irruption of the Real within the domain of causality (produced by a "quasi-cause," which Žižek revealingly identifies as *both* "the exact equivalent of Lacan's *objet petit a*" [OB 27] as well as Deleuze's "name for the Lacanian 'phallic signifier'" [OB 93]—thereby seeming to conflate the two poles of Lacan's theory of desire that Deleuze kept separate). "The basic premise of Deleuze's ontology [in *Logic of Sense*] is precisely that corporeal causality is *not* complete. In the emergence of the New, something occurs that *cannot* be described at the level of corporeal causes and effect" (OB 27). This something is the *event*: that is, "the point of non-sense sustaining the flow of sense . . . [which] fills in the gap of corporeal causality" (OB 28, 27). This gap entails a "positive notion of lack, a 'generative' absence" (OB 35), "an irreducible crack in the edifice of Being" (OB 41). This gap is the true domain of politics, since it marks out the difference between "the explosion of revolutionary Events" and the "'objective' material / socioeconomic processes taking place in reality" (OB 32). Hence the dualism that Badiou establishes between "being" and "event."

For this reason, the sole interpretive question that arises for Žižek is this: How and why did Deleuze move from the beautifully Lacanian *Logic of Sense* to the misguided and non-Lacanian *Anti-Oedipus*? The response to this question initially seems *ad hominem*: the culprit is the Félix Guattari virus that infected Deleuze's thought. Like many others (Derrida, Badiou), Žižek makes a rather easy distinction between the "good" Deleuze (the solo Deleuze) and the "bad" Deleuze (Deleuze with Guattari). Guattari's influence was partly political; the solo Deleuze, Žižek claims, was "a highly elitist author, indifferent to politics" (OB 20). Deleuze himself admitted that *Anti-Oedipus* had indeed marked a profound transformation in his work: "For my part, I made a sort of move into politics around May 68, as I came into contact with specific problems, through Guattari, through Foucault, through Elie Sambar. *Anti-Oedipus* was from beginning to end a book of political philosophy."[6] But behind the *ad hominem* musings there lies a more substantive claim: "The only serious philosophical question is what inherent impasse caused Deleuze to turn toward Guattari?" (OB 20). According to Žižek, the impasse was precisely the tension between the good ontology and the bad ontology: "Was Deleuze not pushed toward Guattari because Guattari represented an alibi, an easy escape from the deadlock of his previous position?" (OB 21). The easy escape was the abandoning of a good Lacanian ontology (event as effect) for a bad Guattarian ontology (event as production and becoming): "Deleuze deploys the One-Substance as the indifferent medium of multitude" (OB 33). Such, in short, is the upshot of the story that one finds in Žižek's brief engagement with Deleuze: a good Lacanian moment in *Logic of Sense* is immediately betrayed by *Anti-Oedipus* and the evil Félix Guattari. If Deleuze had stuck with the insights of *Logic of Sense*, he would have been able to enter into a becoming-Žižek, and not wandered off into the desert of Guattari.

But would it be possible to follow Lacan himself and read *Anti-Oedipus* as something other than Deleuze's worst book? How can we understand Lacan's own positive reaction to *Anti-Oedipus*? Is there perhaps a fidelity to Lacan's thought in *Anti-Oedipus* that is more profound than the rather easy appropriation found in *Logic of Sense*? Žižek is certainly correct to sense a shift in Deleuze's thought between *Logic of Sense* and *Anti-Oedipus*. "The surface–depth problem [of *Logic of Sense*] no longer concerns me," Deleuze remarked in 1973. "What interests me now are the relations between a full body, a body without organs, and flows that migrate" (DI 261). And Žižek is also correct to sense that this shift had something to do with Deleuze's association with Guattari. Deleuze later explained:

Oddly enough, it wasn't me who rescued Félix from psychoanalysis; he rescued me. In my study on Masoch [*Coldness and Cruelty*], and then in *Logic of Sense*, I thought I'd discovered things about the specious unity of sadism and masochism, or about events, that contradicted psychoanalysis but could be reconciled with it. Félix, on the other hand, had been and was still a psychoanalyst, a student of Lacan's, but like a "son" who already knew that reconciliation was impossible. *Anti-Oedipus* marks a break . . . . (N 144)

But what Žižek does not seem to realize (as Lacan obviously did) is that Deleuze's break with psychoanalysis was brought about by none other than Lacan himself. *Anti-Oedipus* is, among many other things, a reading of Lacan, and no doubt it would have had Lacan's name in the title had not so much else been going on in the book. Lacan is often presented as having effected a linguistic and structural reinterpretation of Freud. For Deleuze, however, this is not where Lacan's significance lies.

It's all very well to say to us: you understand nothing, Oedipus, it's not daddy-mommy, it's the symbolic, the law, the arrival of culture, it's the effect of the signifier, it's the finitude of the subject, it's the "lack-of-being" [*manqué-à-être*] which is life. (D 81)

Lacan's significance, rather, lies in the way in which he was able to push psychoanalysis to the point of its *auto-critique*, and it is precisely this Lacanian critique of psychoanalysis that Deleuze and Guattari take up and pursue in *Anti-Oedipus*.

There are problems that troubled Freud toward the end of his life: something is not right with psychoanalysis, something is stuck. Freud thought that it was becoming endless, the cure looked interminable, it was going nowhere. And Lacan was the first to indicate how far things had to be revamped. (DI 234)

Despite its reputation, *Anti-Oedipus* does not contain a single negative comment about Lacan, although it is occasionally critical of the direction his thought was taken in by certain of his disciples, and the orthodoxy that grew up around him.

This is all the more reason to regret the fact that Žižek, as a Lacanian, chose to overlook the Deleuze–Lacan encounter, and to dismiss *Anti-Oedipus* in a way that Lacan himself did not. Perhaps, someday, a reader with the competence to do so will analyze the outlines and the consequences of this encounter.[7] Lacking that competence, I can at least list a number of points that might be relevant to such an analysis, some of which Žižek has touched on, at least in passing, in his book.

1. *Immanence and Transcendence.* Deleuze has presented himself, famously, as a philosopher of immanence, and his critique of psychoanalysis takes place from the perspective of immanence. *What is Philosophy?* identifies three types of transcendence that have been constant temptations away from immanence: contemplation, or the transcendence of the Idea (Plato); reflection, or the transcendence of the Subject (Kant); and then a third type, which we might call the transcendence of the Breach or Rupture. "In this modern moment," Deleuze writes, "we are no longer

satisfied with thinking immanence as immanent to a transcendent; we want to think transcendence within the immanent, and it is from immanence that a breach is expected" (WP 47). In other words, it is from *within* immanence itself that one now seeks to locate "inconsistency" or the "void" (Badiou), or from which one seeks to find a "gap" or "rupture" within immanence, the "irruption" of the Real (Žižek). Whatever the terminology, Deleuze suggests, it is always the same model—"making us think that immanence is a prison from which the Transcendent will save us" (WP 47). Žižek candidly admits that this modern model of transcendence is his own model: "'Transcendence' is the illusory reflection of the fact that the immanence of phenomena is ruptured, broken, inconsistent" (OB 61). This new conception of transcendence, he notes, no longer refers either to a Beyond (God) or a Subject, but rather to "the gap within immanence" (OB 62). Immanence is what is given, what is actual; we therefore need to discover the breach, the rupture, the gap, the torsion or twist, that will save us from the actuality of the immanent (Being as multiple) through an irruption of the new (the Event, the transcendence within immanence). Žižek then asks the necessary question: "What if this gap in immanence is what Deleuze cannot accept?" (OB 61). And Žižek is indeed correct: Deleuze does *not* accept this modern appeal to transcendence in psychoanalytic thought.

> How many interpretations of Lacanianism [Deleuze asks] overtly or secretly pious, have in this manner invoked . . . a gap in the Symbolic? . . . Despite some fine books by certain disciples of Lacan, we wonder if Lacan's thought really goes in this direction. (AO 83, 53)

In other words, it is *out of fidelity to Lacan's thought* that Deleuze rejects the appeal to a gap in immanence.

2. *The Status of the Real.* How, then, does Deleuze break with this model? In certain respects, what is at stake in this question is the status of the Real, in the Lacanian sense, and Žižek recognizes this. "What matters to Deleuze is not virtual reality but *the reality of the virtual* (which, in Lacanian terms, is the Real)" (OB 3). In fact, Deleuze and Guattari explicitly characterize *Anti-Oedipus* as being, from start to finish, a theory of the Real.

> We were unable to posit any difference in nature, any border line, any limit at all between the Imaginary and the Symbolic . . . The true difference in nature is not between the Symbolic and the Imaginary, but between the Real machinic element, which constitutes desiring-production, and the structural whole of the Imaginary and the Symbolic, which merely forms a myth and its variants. (AO 83)

The aim of the book, they tell us, is "to renew, at the level of the Real, the tie between the analytic machine, desire, and production" (AO 53). In their language, the Real = desiring-production. The unconscious "is neither Imaginary nor Symbolic, it is the Real in itself, the 'impossible real' and its production . . . The machines of desire . . . constitute the Real in itself, beyond or beneath the Symbolic as well as the Imaginary" (AO 53). (Deleuze and Guattari will none the less insist that "the real is not impossible; on the contrary, within the Real everything is possible, everything becomes possible . . . It is only in the structure [the symbolic] that the fusion of desire with the impossible is performed, with lack defined as castration" [AO 27, 306]). What allows Deleuze to link the Real with the theory of desire in this manner (desire = production)?

3. *The Kantian Theory of Desire.* Anti-Oedipus can be said to find its primary model in the *Critique of Practical Reason*, since it was Kant who first defined the faculty of desire as a *productive* faculty ("a faculty which, by means of its representations, is the cause of the actuality of the objects of those representations").[8] We know why Kant defined desire in terms of production: the problem of freedom concerns the operation by which a free being can be the cause of something that is not reducible to the causal determinism of mechanism. Of course, Kant was aware that real objects could be produced only by an external causality and external mechanisms; in what he called "pathological" productions of desire, what is produced is merely a *psychic reality* (having a fantastic, hallucinatory, or delirious object) (AO 25). None the less, this was Kant's Copernican Revolution in practical philosophy; desire is no longer defined in terms of *lack* (I desire something because I do not have it), but rather in terms of *production* (I produce the object because I desire it). The fundamental thesis of Anti-Oedipus is a stronger variant of Kant's claim, Kant pushed to his necessary conclusion: "If desire produces, its product is real," and not merely a fantasy (AO 26). "There is no particular form of existence that can be labeled 'psychic reality'" (AO 27). Indeed, Deleuze states this conclusion in explicitly Lacanian terms: "The objective being of desire is the Real in and of itself" (the subject itself is a product of desire) (AO 27).

4. *Desire and Immanence.* But Deleuze is clearly not a Kantian in any straightforward sense. For Kant, the fundamental question concerns the *higher form* (non-pathological) of the faculty of desire: a faculty has a higher form when it finds *within itself* the law of its own exercise, and thus functions *autonomously*. The higher form of desire is what Kant calls the "will": desire becomes will when it is determined by the representation of a pure form (the moral law), which is the pure form of a universal legislation (the categorical imperative). In Kant, however, freedom, as the "fact" of morality, requires as its postulates the three great transcendent Ideas of the Soul, the World, and God. It is precisely the *transcendence* of the Moral Law that renders its object unknowable and elusive. Was this not what Lacan himself showed in his famous essay "Kant with Sade," to which Deleuze admits his indebtedness?[9] Anti-Oedipus can thus be said to have effected an immanent *inversion* of Kant (though it is no longer concerned with the synthesis of consciousness, but with the synthesis of the unconscious). In the first two chapters of Anti-Oedipus, Deleuze provides a purely immanent characterization of the three syntheses of the unconscious—*connection* (which forms a counter-Self, and no longer a Soul), *conjunction* (which forms a "chaosmos," and no longer a World), and *disjunction* (which exchanges it theological principle for a diabolical one)—and shows how desire (as the principle of production) constitutes the Real by tracing out series and trajectories following these syntheses within a given social assemblage. "The Real is the end product,

the result of the passive syntheses that engineer partial syntheses of desire as auto-production of the unconscious."[10]

5. *Lacan's Oscillation.* But, Deleuze asks, was not Lacan's own thought already moving in this immanent direction in 1972? In *Anti-Oedipus*, Deleuze and Guattari identified two poles in Lacan's theory of desire (which Žižek seems to conflate): "Lacan's admirable theory of desire appears to use to have two poles: one related to 'the object small *a*' as a desiring-machine, which defines desire in terms of a real production, thus going beyond any idea of need and any idea of fantasy; and the other related to the 'great Other' as a signifier, which reintroduces a certain notion of lack" (AO 27n). The innovation of *Anti-Oedipus* was that it attempted to follow the first path laid out by Lacan (an immanent concept of desire related to the *objet petit a*), despite the efforts of Lacan's "first disciples" (AO 83) to push his thought in the second "Oedipal" direction (desire related to the transcendence of the phallic signifier). Deleuze and Guattari admit that the oscillation between these two poles of desire was present within Lacan's own thought:

> We owe to Jacques Lacan the discovery of this fertile domain of a code of the unconscious, incorporating the entire chain—or several chains—of sense: a discovery thus totally transforming analysis . . . The chains are called "signi-fying chains" because they are made up of signs, *but these signs are not them-selves signifying* . . . If the first disciples were tempted to re-close the Oedipal [Symbolic] yoke, didn't they do so to the extent that Lacan seemed to main-tain a kind of projection of the signifying chains onto a despotic signifier? . . . The signs of desire, being non-signifying, become signifying in representation only in terms of a signifier of absence or lack. (AO 38, 83)

Following Lacan, *Anti-Oedipus* thus attempts to analyze the means by which the legitimate and immanent syntheses of desire (partial connections, inclusive disjunc-tions, polyvocal conjunctions—the Real production of desire, the *objet petit a*) are inverted and *converted* into illegitimate and transcendent syntheses (global connec-tions, exclusive disjunctions, biunivocal conjunctions—the Oedipal or Symbolic representation of desire via the "phallic signifier").

6. *Lacan's Anti-Oedipal Trajectory.* But once again, despite this oscillation, was it not Lacan himself who was pushing psychoanalysis away from Oedipus and the Symbolic? Žižek complains that "what Deleuze presents as 'Oedipus' is a rather ridic-ulous simplification, if not an outright falsification, of Lacan's position" (OB 80), pointing to the constant references to "au-delà de l'Œdipe" in the last decades of Lacan's teaching. But Deleuze and Guattari would agree with this latter characteri-zation—in their eyes, Lacan is himself the great anti-Oedipal thinker (they approv-ingly cite Lacan's 1970 claim that "I have never spoken of an Oedipus complex" [AO 53n]). Lacan, they write, "was not content to turn, like the analytic squirrel, inside the wheel of the Imaginary and the Symbolic" (AO 308). The Real is the internal limit to any process of symbolization, but it was not enough for Lacan to describe the Real, negatively, as a resistant kernel within the symbolic process upon whose internalized exclusion the symbolic is constituted (negation or exclusion as

constitutive). Rather, Lacan was pushing psychoanalysis to "the point of its self critique" (AO 310), where the Real would be able to appear in all its positivity: "the point where the structure, beyond the images that fill it [fantasies] and the Symbolic that conditions it within representation, reveals its reverse side as a positive *principle of nonconsistency* that dissolves it" (AO 311). Deleuze and Guattari thus present *Anti-Oedipus* as continuing a trajectory that was initiated by Lacan himself. "It was inopportune to tighten the nuts and bolts where Lacan had just loosened them . . . The object (small o) erupts at the heart of the structural equilibrium in the manner of an infernal machine, the desiring-machine" (AO 83).

7. *The Real and Schizophrenia.* Deleuze's term for the Real is "schizophrenia as a pure process" (which must be distinguished from the schizophrenic as a clinical entity), and it is with this concept that Deleuze takes Lacan's thought to its limit and conclusion. "It is this entire reverse side of the [symbolic] structure that Lacan discovers . . . schizophrenizing the analytic field, instead of oedipalizing the psychotic field" (AO 309). Following directions indicated by Lacan himself, *Anti-Oedipus* attempts to describe the Real in all its positivity: differential partial objects or intensities that enter into indirect syntheses; pure positive multiplicities where everything is possible (transverse connections, polyvocal conjunctions, included disjunctions); signs of desire that compose a signifying chain, but which are themselves non-signifying, and so on (AO 309). The domain of the Real is a "sub-representative field" (AO 300), but Deleuze does not hesitate to claim that "*we have the means to penetrate the sub-representational*" (DI 115). Conversely, if the Real is the sub-representative, then "illusion" (if one wants to retain this word) only appears afterwards, in the actual: it is only within the symbolic (representation) that desire appears negatively as lack, as castration. It is for this reason that Deleuze suggests that schizophrenia provides a better clue to the nature of the unconscious and the Real than neurosis: psychotics resist therapeutization because they have a libido that is too liquid or viscous, they resist entry into the symbolic (foreclosure), mistaking words for things. But "rather than being a resistance of the ego, this is the intense outcry of all of desiring-production" (AO 67). Some of Deleuze's most profound texts, such as "Louis Wolfson; or, The Procedure," are those that analyze the specifically schizophrenic uses of language, which push language to its limit and lay waste its significations, designations, and translations.[11] Deleuze suggests that the usual negative diagnostic criteria that have been proposed for schizophrenia—dissociation, detachment from reality, autism—are above all useful terms for *not listening* to schizophrenics. But in the end, this problem is not specific to schizophrenics: "we are *all* libidos that are too viscous and too fluid . . . [which] bears witness to the non-oedipal quality of the flows of desire" (AO 67; cf. 312).

8. *The Body Without Organs.* Hence, whereas *Logic of Sense* was content to remain at the surface of sense (like Lewis Carroll), *Anti-Oedipus* can be said to have plunged into the depth of bodies (Artaud); the logic of the passive syntheses (the Real) ultimately finds its model in the body—or more precisely, the "body without organs."[12] This well-known but complex Deleuzian notion has three fundamental components. Schizophrenics experience their organs in a non-organic manner: that is, as elements or singularities that are connected to other elements in the complex

functioning of a "machinic assemblage" (connective synthesis). But the break-down of these organ-machines reveals a second theme—that of the body without organs as such, a non-productive surface upon which the an-organic functioning of the organs is stopped dead in a kind of catatonic stupor (disjunctive synthesis). These two poles—the vital an-organic functioning of the organs and their frozen catatonic stasis, with all the variations of *attraction* and *repulsion* that exist between them—can be said to translate the entire anguish of the schizophrenic, which in turn points to a third theme, that of *intensive variations* (conjunctive synthesis). These poles are never separate from each other, but generate between them various forms in which sometimes repulsion dominates, and sometimes attraction: the paranoid form of schizophrenia (repulsion), and its miraculating or fantastic form (attraction). Schizophrenics tend to experience these oscillating intensities (manic rises in intensity, depressive falls in intensity . . .) in an almost pure state. Beneath the hallucinations of the senses ("I see," "I hear") and the deliriums of thought ("I think"), there is something more profound, a feeling of intensity: that is, a *becoming* or a transition ("I feel"). A gradient is crossed, a threshold is surpassed or retreated from, a migration is brought about: "I feel that I am becoming woman," "I feel that I am becoming god," "I feel that I am becoming pure matter . . . ." The innovation of *Anti-Oedipus* is to have penetrated into this sub-representative, schizophrenic domain of the body without organs, and made use of it as the model for the unconscious itself. The analysis of this unconscious entails a corresponding practice that Deleuze and Guattari will term "schizoanalysis."

9. *Psychoanalysis and Schizoanalysis*. What then is the difference between psychoanalysis and schizoanalysis? "Psychoanalysis settles on the imaginary [fantasy] and structural [symbolic] representatives of reterritorialization, while schizoanalysis follows the machinic indices of deterritorialization" (AO 316). One can only admire the enthusiasm with which Žižek analyzes the first movement, particularly in his section on the "phallus" (the "organ without a body" of the title) (see OB 87–95). The phallus, as the signifier of castration, is what effects a desexualization of the libido, and makes possible the "impossible" passage of the body (the drives) into symbolic thought, the passage from bodily depth to surface event (symbolic castration). Deleuze and Guattari could no doubt even agree with Žižek's claim that Oedipus is an "operator of deterritorialization" (83), in so far as every movement of deterritorialization (of the drives) is accompanied by a reterritorialization (on to the symbolic). "Schizophrenia as a process, deterritorialization as a process," they write, "is inseparable from the stases that interrupt it, aggravate it, or make it turn in circles, and reterritorialize it into neurosis, perversion, and psychosis" (the latter being the three main categories in Lacan's diagnostic schema) (AO 318). Oedipus and castration are indeed realities that psychoanalysis did not invent. But schizoanalysis, by contrast, moves in the exact opposite direction, and seeks to locate the indices of deterritorialization, within these reterritorializations, in a completely different manner than psychoanalysis: "not the gaping wound represented in castration [the gap in immanence], but the myriad little connections, disjunctions, and conjunctions" that constitute the real movement of the immanent process of desire (AO 314). Put crudely, psychoanalysis begins with the symbolic and seeks out the

"gaps" which mark the irruption of an "impossible" Real, whereas schizoanalysis starts with the Real as the immanent process of desire, and seeks to mark both the interruptions of this process (reterritorializations) and its continuations and trans-formations (becomings, intensities . . .).

10. *The Assembling of Desire.* The fundamental concept in Deleuze's theory of desire is thus the concept of the *assemblage [agencement]*. There exists a common but misguided critique of Deleuze and Guattari which claims that, in subtracting desire from lack, the law, and castration, they wind up invoking a state of nature, a desire that would be a natural and spontaneous reality that winds up being repressed by society.[13] But Deleuze and Guattari's argument is precisely the opposite: there is no desire other than assembled *[agencé]* desire. "Desire is never either a 'natural' or a 'spontaneous' determination . . . never a 'natural reality,'" writes Deleuze, but always results from "a highly developed, engineered setup *[montage]* rich in interac-tions," and it can neither be grasped nor conceived apart from a determinate social assemblage or apparatus.[14] Desire, as "desiring-production," is both productive and produced. Within any given assemblage of desire, there are, on the one hand, rigid lines of sedimentation and reterritorialization that tend to "normalize" desire, to "represent" or "symbolize" it; and then, on the other hand, there are supple lines of creativity and deterritorialization (lines of flight or escape) that allow the assem-blage to transform itself, or even to break down in favor of a future assemblage. These two types of vectors are immanent to any process of desire, to every "desiring-machine." What mechanisms of repression crush is not desire as a natural given, but precisely these cutting edges of assemblages of desire (the production of the new).[15] The question, at every moment, concerns the vector that desire is in the process of constructing or assembling (deterritorialization and reterritorialization, or—put in mathematical terms—continuity and discontinuity). But yet again, one must stress that it was Lacan himself who posed the question of desire in terms of these two poles or vectors: "In Lacan, the symbolic organization of the structure, with its exclusions that come from the function of the signifier, has as its reverse side the *real inorganization* of desire" (AO 328; cf. 39).

11. *Desexualization and Political Philosophy.* Finally, a brief comment about the relationship between Deleuze's political philosophy and his theory of desire. Freud held strongly to the hypothesis that the libido does not invest the socio-political field except on the condition that it be "desexualized" or "sublimated"—a hypoth-esis that Žižek takes up and defends ("Sexuality can universalize itself only by way of desexualization" [OB 91]). Deleuze and Guattari explicitly reject this Freudian principle. "Our entire hypothesis is, on the contrary, that the social field is invested by a sexual libido as such, and that this is in fact the fundamental activity of the libido" (21 Dec 1971). The concepts of sublimation and desexualization are linked to the implicit *familialism* of psychoanalysis. "At least in the beginning," the argu-ment goes, the unconscious is expressed in familial relations, and social relations only arise *afterward*. "'Symbolic castration' is a way for the subject to be thrown out of the family network, propelled into a wider social network" (OB 83). Against this familiar Freudian notion, Deleuze and Guattari not only argue that the libido *directly* invests social relations without any mediation (such as introjection / pro-

jection, desexualization / sublimation, or symbolization), but that this investment is there *from the start*, at the level of the drives. One of the most profound and far-reaching theses of Anti-Oedipus is that the libidinal economy of Freud and the political economy of Marx are *one and the same economy* ("affects or drives form part of the infrastructure itself" [AO 53]), even if they have different regimes. The concept of the assemblage is itself derived from this insight. It is not through a desexualizing extension that the libido invests socio-political relation; "on the contrary, it is through a restriction, a blockage, and a reduction that the libido is made to repress its flows in order to contain them in the narrow cells of the type 'couple,' 'family,' 'person,' 'objects'" (AO 293). In effect, this thesis is the basis of the political philosophy Deleuze begins to develop in Anti-Oedipus and continues in A Thousand Plateaus, although Žižek seems largely oblivious to it. Hence, it is hard to know what Žižek means when he characterizes Deleuze as "the ideologist of late capitalism" (184), since he says nothing of either Deleuze's analysis of capitalism or his critique of the concept of ideology.

These points, to be sure, hardly constitute a reading of Anti-Oedipus, one of Deleuze's most difficult and ambitious texts, and can do little more than point toward the direction of future work. But what is striking about Anti-Oedipus is the degree to which Deleuze and Guattari fully admit their indebtedness to Lacan, and describe their project as an attempt to take Lacan's profound thought to its differential and immanent conclusion. As Deleuze explained:

> Félix had talked to me about what he was already calling "desiring-machines": he had a whole theoretical and practical conception of the unconscious as a machine, of the schizophrenic unconscious. So I myself thought he had gone further than I had. But for all his unconscious machinery, he was still talking in terms of structures, signifiers, the phallus, and so on. That was hardly surprising, since he owed so much to Lacan (just as I did). But I felt it would all work even better if one found the right concepts, instead of using notions that didn't even come from Lacan's creative side, but from an orthodoxy built up around him. Lacan himself says, "I'm not getting much help." We thought we'd give him some schizophrenic help. And there's no question that we're all the more indebted to Lacan, once we've dropped notions like structure, the symbolic, or the signifier, which are thoroughly misguided [*mauvaises*], and *which Lacan himself has always managed to turn on their head in order to show their inverse side* (N 13–14)

In this sense, Deleuze can be seen as one of Lacan's most profound, but also most independent, disciples, inventing a whole new set of concepts to describe the inverse side of the symbolic structure (the real). He followed a completely different path than the other disciples, such as Jacques-Alain Miller, the keeper of orthodoxy; Alain Badiou, who gives an axiomatic treatment of the symbolic; or Žižek himself, the Lacanian reader of contemporary culture. The admiration Lacan and Deleuze had for each other's work was obviously deep and full of respect. Deleuze once wrote: "My ideal, when I write about an author, would be to write nothing that could cause him sadness" (D 119), and this was no doubt true of his treatment of Lacan in *Anti-Oedipus*. In return, Lacan once said of a book critical of his work, "I have never been so well read—with so much love," and one can almost imagine him making the same remark of *Anti-Oedipus*.[16] Perhaps one day, we will be provided with a more complete reading of the way in which Deleuze took up and developed Lacan's thought—and perhaps the way in which Lacan took up and develops Deleuze's insights in his later work. Žižek, unfortunately, is not that person. *Organs without Bodies: Deleuze and Consequences* is a fascinating romp through the Žižekian universe, full of penetrating insights and illuminating jokes, but as a reading of Deleuze it adds little to our understanding. The best place we have to go, still, for a Lacanian appreciation of Deleuze is not Žižek, but rather . . . Lacan himself.

Pierre Klossowski

Klossowski's Reading of Nietzsche: Impulses, Phantasms, Simulacra, Stereotypes

In his writings on Nietzsche, Pierre Klossowski makes use of various concepts—such as intensities, phantasms, simulacra and stereotypes, resemblance and dissemblance, gregariousness and singularity—that have no place in Nietzsche's own *œuvre*.[1] These concepts are Klossowski's own creations, his own contributions to thought. Although Klossowski consistently refused to characterize himself as a philosopher ("Je suis une 'maniaque,'" he once said. "Un point, c'est tout!"),[2] his work in its entirety was marked by an extraordinary conceptual creation. From this point of view, *Nietzsche and the Vicious Circle* can be read as a work in philosophy—at least in the idiosyncratic sense given to this term by Deleuze, who defined philosophy as the creation or invention of concepts (WP 2). No doubt, Klossowski remains an almost unclassifiable figure—philosopher, novelist, essayist, translator, artist—and attempting to analyze his work through the prism of philosophy may seem to be a reductive approach that belies the complexity of Klossowski's exceptional *œuvre*. Reading Klossowski as a conceptual innovator, however, at least has the advantage of allowing us to chart a consistent trajectory through Klossowski's difficult and often-labyrinthine text, without denying its other dimensions (affective, perceptive, literary, etc.). In what follows, then, I would like to examine three of Klossowski's most characteristic and important concepts—impulses and their intensities, phantasms, and simulacra and their stereotypes—as well as the precise interrelations he establishes among them. Taken together, these three concepts describe what Klossowski terms the tripartite economy of soul, which constitutes the implicit model through which he interprets Nietzsche's thought.

IMPULSES AS FLUCTUATING INTENSITIES

Klossowski describes his books on both Nietzsche and Sade as "essays devoted not to ideologies but to the *physiognomies* of problematic thinkers who differ greatly from each other."[3] This emphasis on the "physiognomy" of thinkers reflects Nietzsche's insistence on taking the *body* as a guide for philosophy rather than the *mind*, since the body is a more accessible phenomenon, less surrounded by myth and superstition.

"The body and physiology as the starting point," Nietzsche wrote. "Why? . . . The phenomenon of the body is the richer, clearer, more tangible phenomenon . . . Belief in the body is more fundamental than belief in the soul."[4] Klossowski himself, however, when writing of the intensive status of the impulses, frequently makes use of the term "soul" (*âme*), which is due in part, no doubt, to his interest in the theological literature of the mystics, such as Meister Eckhart and Theresa of Ávila. For the mystics, the depth of the soul is something irreducible and uncreated; it eludes the exercise of the created intellect, and can only be grasped negatively.[5] None the less, if one can find a similar apophaticism (or "negative theology") in Klossowski, it is related exclusively to the immanent and chaotic movements of the soul's intensive affects, and not to the transcendence of God. What is incommunicable in the soul (or body) are its "impulses"—their fluctuations of intensity, their rises and falls, their manic elations and depressive descents, which are in constant variation.

Nietzsche himself had recourse to a highly varied vocabulary to describe what Klossowski summarizes in the term "impulse": "drive" (*Triebe*), "desire" (*Begierden*), "instinct" (*Instinkte*), "power" (*Mächte*), "force" (*Kräfte*), "impulse" (*Reize, Impulse*), "passion" (*Leidenschaften*), "feeling" (*Gefühlen*), "affect" (*Affekte*), "pathos" (*Pathos*), and so on.[6] Klossowski frequently employs the musical term *tonalité* to describe these states of the soul's fluctuating intensities—their diverse tones, timbres, and changing amplitudes—which can take on various forms ("aggressiveness, tolerance, intimidation, anguish, the need for solitude, the forgetting of oneself") (NVC 6). At bottom, what these impulses express are what Klossowski calls "obstinate singularity" of the human soul, which is by nature non-communicable; they constitute what he calls "the unexchangeable depth" (*le fond inéchangeable*) or "the unintelligible depth" (*le fond inintelligible*) of the soul. What makes every individual a "singular case" or an "idiosyncrasy" is the unique constellation of impulses of which it is constituted. For Klossowski, the term "singular" is opposed not so much to the universal but to the gregarious, the species, what Nietzsche calls the "herd," which reduces the singularity of the individual to a common denominator, and expresses only what can be communicated. It is Nietzsche's theory of the impulses that lies at the origin of his doctrines of perspectivism ("there are no facts, only interpretations") and the will to power. It is our *impulses* or *drives* that interpret the world, that are perspectival—and not our "selves." All of us, as individuals, contain within ourselves such "a vast confusion of contradictory drives" that we are, as Nietzsche liked to say, multiplicities and not unities.[7] It is not that I have a different perspective on the world than you; it is rather that each of us has multiple perspectives on the world because of the multiplicity of our drives—drives that are often contradictory among themselves, and that are therefore in a constant struggle or combat with each other. "*Within ourselves*, we can be egoistic or altruistic, hard-hearted, magnanimous, just, lenient, insincere, can cause pain or give pleasure."[8] Moreover, each of our impulses is characterized by an internal will to power. "Every drive is a kind of lust to rule," Nietzsche writes, "each one has its perspective that it would like to compel all the other drives to accept as a norm."[9]

It is true that we can fight against the impulses, struggle against the dominance of the passions—this is one of the oldest themes in philosophy, from Platonism through Christianity. But Nietzsche asks: *Who* exactly undertakes such a struggle against the impulses?

> While "we" believe we are complaining about the vehemence of a drive [he answers], at bottom it is one drive *which is complaining about the other*; that is to say: for us to become aware that we are suffering from the *vehemence* of a drive presupposes the existence of another equally vehement or even more vehement drive, and that a *struggle* is in prospect in which our intellect is going to have to take sides.[10]

We tend to take our predominant drive and for the moment turn it into the whole of our ego, placing all our weaker drives perspectivally farther away, as if those other drives were not *me* but rather something else, something *other* inside me, a kind of "it," like the Freudian "id." When we talk about the "I," we are primarily indicating which drive, at the moment, is strongest and sovereign within us; my so-called "self-identity" is in fact a differential flickering from drive to drive. In other words, there is no struggle of reason against the drives; rather, what we call our "reason" is nothing more than a certain "system of relations between various passions" (WP 387), a certain ordering of the drives.[11] "Something that you formerly loved as a truth or probability," Nietzsche writes in *The Gay Science*, "now strikes you as an error; so you cast it off and fancy that it represents a victory for your reason." But it is less a victory for your reason, than a shift in the relations among your impulses, with their shifting intensities and tonalities.

> Perhaps this error was as necessary for you then, when you were a different person—you are always a different person—as are all you present 'truths' . . . What killed that opinion for you was your new life [that is, a new impulse] and not your reason: *you no longer need it*, and now it collapses and unreason crawls out of it into the light like a worm. When we criticize something, this is no arbitrary and impersonal event; it is, at least very often, evidence of vital energies in us that are growing and shedding a skin. We negate and must negate because something in us wants to live and affirm—something that we perhaps do not know or see as yet.[12]

This emphasis on fluctuating intensities of the body's impulses is one of the consequences of Nietzsche's declaration of the "death of God." One of Klossowski's most persistent themes is that the death of God implies the loss of both the identity of the Self and the coherence of the World. The Self, the World, and God are the three great terminal points of traditional metaphysics, which Kant had exposed as transcendent illusions in the *Critique of Pure Reason*.[13] In his essay on Klossowski, Deleuze emphasized the way in which Klossowski pushed Kant's thought toward a "new critique of reason":

> The order of God includes the following elements: the identity of God as the ultimate foundation, the identity of the world as the surrounding milieu, the

identity of the person as a well-founded agent, the identity of bodies as the base, and finally the identity of language as the power of *denoting* everything else. But this order of God is constructed against another order, and this order subsists in God, and consumes him from within . . . The order of the Antichrist is opposed point by point to the divine order. It is characterized by the death of God, the destruction of the world, the dissolution of the person, the disintegration of bodies, and a change in the function of language, which now expresses nothing but intensities. (LS 292, 294).

If God is dead, then all possible creation comes not from God but from chaos—that is, from the impulses—and the self is only the prolonged extremity of chaos. The death of god does not imply a rejection of religion, however, but rather its *revitalization*, a claim that Klossowski explored in his early essay "Nietzsche, Polytheism, and Parody."[14] *Thus Spoke Zarathustra* presents a fable explaining the transition from polytheism to monotheism (or what he elsewhere calls "monoto-theism"): when one of the gods declared himself to be the only god (the monotheistic god), the other gods (the gods of polytheism) laughed and slapped their knees and rocked in their chairs—until they laughed themselves to death![15] Polytheism died of laughter.[16] For Nietzsche, the creation of gods is one of the fundamental creative tasks of religion—just as for Deleuze the creation of concepts is one of the fundamental creative tasks of philosophy—and gods and demons are themselves the figures of the impulses and their fluctuating intensities. If polytheism is the expression of the multiplicity of the soul's impulses, its great *mise-en-scène*, monotheism implies the subordination of all the other impulses to the domination of a single, sovereign impulse, which Nietzsche, in the *Genealogy of Morals*, would identify as the impulse of *ressentiment*. The revaluation of values envisioned by Nietzsche necessarily implies the creation of new gods—that is to say, new affects. "How many new gods are still possible!" Nietzsche exclaims. "As for myself, in whom the religious, that is to say, god-forming instinct occasionally becomes active at impossible times—how differently, how variously the divine has revealed itself to me each time."[17] What Klossowski found in the religions of antiquity was a growling chaos of demons and goddesses expressing the fluctuation of the impulses; his great text, *Diana at Her Bath*, is explicitly presented as a kind of polytheistic inversion of Augustine's monotheistic *City of God*, pointing to a religion of the future.[18]

But the question Klossowski constantly poses about the impulses is: What criteria of value one can apply to the impulses if we can no longer appeal to a transcendent order (as in Plato), or a transcendental subjectivity (as in Kant), or the moments of an evolutionary dialectic (as in Hegel)? The criteria must become internal to the impulses themselves: Which impulses are healthy? Which are expressions of morbidity or sickness? Which are singular? Which express a will to gregariousness? Which are vigorous? Which are decadent?[19] If the impulses interpret, then the question is one of determining the "type" of interpretation offered by a given impulse or affect: active versus reactive, strong versus weak, healthy versus morbid, and so on.

In *Nietzsche and the Vicious Circle*, Klossowski stresses the fact that Nietzsche's own *valetudinary states* provided him with a kind of laboratory in which he

could study the life of the impulses. In his letters and notes, Nietzsche provides an almost constant evaluation of the implications of his migraines and
illnesses. "My nervous system is splendid in view of the immense work it has
to do; it is quite sensitive but very strong, a source of astonishment to me."[20] Or
again:

> My existence a *dreadful burden*: I would have rejected it long ago had I not
> been making the most instructive experiments in the intellectual and moral
> domain in just this condition of suffering and almost complete renuncia-
> tion—this joyous mood, avid for knowledge, raised me to heights where I tri-
> umphed over every torture and almost all despair.[21]

But exactly what experiments was Nietzsche conducting with his own impulses?
When Nietzsche experienced his migraines, Klossowski surmises, he not only found
it impossible to read or even write, but he also found it impossible to *think*. He
experienced his migraines as an aggression of his organism that suspended his own
thought, his own thinking. "Once he recovered his faculties, he tried to describe
this suspension of thought, to reflect on the functioning of the brain in relation
to the other organic functions—and he began to distrust his own brain" (NVC
23). Why this distrust? The issue concerns nothing other than our experience of
the *unity* of ourselves as subjects. What makes us experience the chaotic life of the
impulses as having a unity is the *phantasm* of what Klossowski calls, in French, the
suppôt. This word is derived from the Latin *suppositum*, "that which is placed under,"
and is closely linked to the terms *substantia* ("substance") or *subjectum* ("subject").
For Klossowski, the *suppôt* (or self) is itself a phantasm, a complex and fragile entity
that bestows a psychic and organic unity upon the moving chaos of the impulses.
It does this in part through the grammatical fiction of the "I," which interprets the
impulses in terms of a hierarchy of gregarious needs (both material and moral), and
dissimulates itself through a network of concepts (substance, cause, identity, self,
world, God) that reduces the combat of the impulses to silence.[22]

   "To understand Nietzsche," writes Klossowski, "it is important to see this *reversal*
brought about by the organism: *the most fragile organ it has developed* [namely, the
brain, the nervous system] comes to dominate the body, one might say, *because of*
its very fragility" (NVC 27). There is thus an intimate link, in Nietzsche's thought,
between the intellect or consciousness, on the one hand, and language and communication, on the other. Both the intellect and language are in the service of the
species, gregariousness, the herd—and not in the service of the singular case, the
individual. As Nietzsche writes in *The Gay Science*:

> It seems to me that the subtlety and strength of consciousness always were
> proportionate to a man's (or animal's) *capacity for communication* . . . Man,
> like every living being, thinks continually without knowing it; the thinking
> that rises to *consciousness* is only the smallest part of this—the most superfi-
> cial and worst part—for only this conscious thinking *takes the form of words,*
> *which is to say signs of communication* . . . My idea is that consciousness does

not really belong to man's individual existence but rather to his social or herd nature . . . Fundamentally, all our actions are altogether incomparably personal, unique, and infinitely individual; there is no doubt of that. But as soon as we translate them into consciousness *they no longer seem to be* . . . Whatever becomes conscious *becomes* by the same token shallow, thin, relatively stupid . . . All becoming conscious involves a great and thorough corruption, falsification, reduction to superficialities, and generalization . . . We "know" (or believe or imagine) just as much as may be *useful* in the interests of the human herd, the species.[23]

Even our "inner experience"—that which is seemingly most personal and most immediate to us—is subject to the same falsification: "'Inner experience' enters our consciousness only after it has found a language the individual understands . . . 'To understand' means merely: *to be able to express something new in the language of something old and familiar.*"[24] In Klossowski's terms, the function of language and the intellect is to convert the (unconscious) *intensity* into a (conscious) *intention*.

The task Nietzsche set himself, then, was an almost impossible task: to think without the ego, to think, not from the viewpoint of his conscious intellect, but rather from the complex viewpoint of the drives and impulses. "*Stop feeling oneself as this phantastic ego!*" Nietzsche admonished himself in one of his notebooks.

Learn gradually *to jettison the supposed individual*! Discover the errors of the ego! Realize that *egoism is an error*! But not to be understood as the opposite of altruism! That would be love of *other supposed* individuals! No! *Get beyond* "me" and "you"! *Experience cosmically*!

And again: "What is needed is *practice* in seeing with *other* eyes: practice in seeing apart from human relations, and thus seeing *objectively*!"[25]

PHANTASMS AS OBSESSIONAL IMAGES

This brings us to the second fundamental concept of Klossowski's: the *phantasm*. In Klossowski, the term refers to *an obsessional image* produced within us by the unconscious forces of our impulsive life; the phantasm is what makes each of us a singular case. "My true themes," writes Klossowski of himself, "are dictated by one or more obsessional (or "obsidianal") instincts that seek to express themselves."[26] Or as he says elsewhere, "I am only the *seismograph* of the life of the impulses."[27] The word "phantasm" is derived from the Greek *phantasia* (appearance, imagination), and was taken up in a more technical sense in psychoanalytic theory (theory of fantasy). For Klossowski, however, a phantasm is not, as in Freud, a substitution formation. As Lyotard explains, the phantasm "is not an unreality or de-reality, it is 'something' that grips the wild turbulence of the libido, something it invents as an incandescent object."[28]

Nietzsche himself tended to interpret the thought of the great philosophers in terms of their phantasms: that is, in terms of their dominant or sovereign impulses.

Philosophers simply express the movements of their own intensive states under the guidance of their dominant impulse (the will to knowledge).

> They claim it is a question of "the truth"—when at bottom it is only a question of themselves. Or rather: their most violent impulse is brought to light with all the impudence and innocence of a fundamental impulse: it makes itself sovereign . . . The philosopher is only a kind of occasion and chance through which the impulse is finally able to speak . . . What then did Spinoza or Kant do? Nothing but interpret their dominant impulse. But it was only the *communicable* part of their behavior that could be translated into their constructions. (NVC 4–5)

This is not dissimilar to Heidegger's claim that a philosopher thinks only one thought (in his case, the thought of "being"), or Bergson's claim that every philosopher has one intuition, and that the vastness of a philosopher's *œuvre* can be explained by the incommensurability between this intuition and the means they have at their disposal for expressing it.[29] In itself, the phantasm is incommunicable because it is unintelligible and unspeakable; but it is because it is unintelligible and incommunicable that it is also *obsessive*. Unintelligibility, incommunicability, and obsession are themselves the intensive components of Klossowski's concept of the phantasm.

Deleuze has provided a penetrating analysis of the nature of the phantasm in his book *Proust and Signs*—although he does not use the term "phantasm"—notably in the context of Proust's discussions of love (PS 26–38). Falling in love is an intensity, a high tonality of the soul, and our initial temptation is to seek for the meaning of that intensity, its explanation, in the object of our love, as if the beloved somehow held the secret to the intensity of our passion. But inevitably, the other person disappoints us on this score, and we then turn to ourselves to uncover the secret, thinking that perhaps the intensity was sparked by subjective associations we made within ourselves between the beloved and, perhaps, someone else (other lovers, our parents) or something else (a place, a moment). But this too fails. For what lies behind our loves—behind both the objectivist temptation and the subjectivist compensation—is precisely an incommunicable phantasm (which Proust himself called an "essence" rather than a phantasm). The fact is that our loves tend to repeat themselves; we fall in love with the same "type," we fall into the same patterns, we seem to make the same mistakes—our loves seem to form a series in which something is being repeated, but always with a slight difference. This "something" is nothing other than our phantasm, which we repeat obsessively, but which in itself remains incommunicable, and continues its secret work in us, despite all our attempts to decipher it. But as Deleuze notes, this amorous repetition is never a sterile or naked repetition of a prior identity; it is always a clothed or masked repetition of a difference, a repetition that is always productive of new differences.

> To repeat is to behave, but in relation to something unique or singular, which has nothing similar or equivalent . . . The mask is the true subject of

repetition. It is because repetition differs in nature from representation in that what is repeated cannot be represented, but must always be signified, masked by what signifies it, itself masking what it signifies. (DR 17–18)

What Klossowski calls a simulacrum, as we shall see, is a mask that, denouncing itself as such, traces the contours of what it dissimulates—namely, the phantasm as such. Proust himself says that it is only in *art* that such essences or phantasms are revealed (not in the object, not in the subject); it is only in art that the time we have lost in our loves can be regained and recovered.

Readers of Klossowski's fictions will be familiar with the phantasm that was the primary object of his own phantasmic obsession: the figure of Roberte, which he calls (in his postface to the trilogy, *The Laws of Hospitality*) the "unique sign" of his work.[30] Since the phantasm is by nature incommunicable, the subject who submits himself to its irresistible constraint can never have done with describing it. Klossowski's narrative work is thus traversed by a single repetition, carried along by one and the same movement. In effect, it is always the same scene that is repeated. The rape of Roberte in *Roberte ce soir*, the theatrical representations in *Le Souffleur*, the vision of the goddess in *Diana at her Bath*, the description of the statue of St. Therese in *The Baphomet*[31]—all articulate one and the same phantasm: the woman discovering the presence of her body under the gaze or the violence of a third party, who, whether an angel or a demon, communicates a guilty voluptuousness. Klossowski describes the entirety of his literary output in terms of his relation to this fundamental obsession: "I am under the dictation [*dictée*] of an image. It is the vision that demands that I say everything the vision gives to me."[32]

What, then, was Nietzsche's fundamental phantasm? Klossowski suggests that Nietzsche's most intense phantasm was the *eternal return*. (One should note, however, that the eternal return was not Nietzsche's only phantasm—Greece was a phantasm for the young Nietzsche, and Klossowski does not overlook the phantasms revealed in Nietzsche's own loves, such as Lou Salomé and Cosima Wagner.) But Nietzsche's phantasm was precisely *not* the eternal return as one of the explicit doctrines of Nietzsche's philosophy, nor even the eternal return as a thought. It was, rather, the eternal return as a *lived experience*, which was revealed to Nietzsche in Sils-Maria in August 1881, and experienced as an impulse, an intensity, a high tonality of the soul—and indeed as the *highest* possible intensity of the soul. It was with the revelation of the eternal return that Nietzsche's quest to find the highest, the most powerful affect, the healthiest and most vigorous impulse, the most *affirmative* affect, was fulfilled. "Thoughts," writes Nietzsche, "are the signs of a play and combat of affects; they always depend on their hidden roots."[33] On this score, Klossowski emphasizes the impression of strangeness felt by both Salomé and Franz Overbeck, his closest friend, when he revealed the eternal return to them—the disturbing tone of his hoarse voice, the spectacular character of the communication. Although Nietzsche would seek numerous forms of expression for the eternal return—ethical, scientific, or cosmological—none of them was capable of expressing the fundamental incommunicability of the phantasm itself. This is why

Klossowski says that the eternal return is not a doctrine, but rather the *simulacrum* of a doctrine.

SIMULACRA AND THEIR STEREOTYPES

This, then, brings us to the third term in Klossowski's vocabulary: the simulacrum.[34] A "simulacrum" is a willed reproduction of a phantasm (in a literary, pictorial, or plastic form) that simulates this invisible agitation of the soul. "The simulacrum, in its *imitative* sense, is the actualization of something in itself incommunicable and nonrepresentable: the *phantasm* in its obsessional constraint."[35] The term *simulacrum* comes from the Latin *simulare* (to copy, represent, feign), and during the late Roman Empire it referred to the statues of the gods that often lined the entrance to a city. More precisely, the simulacrum was an object that, although fabricated by humans, was the measure of the invisible power of the gods. According to Hermes Trismegistes, artists cannot animate the status of the gods by themselves; they have to invoke the souls of the gods, they have to seduce a demonic force, through imposture, in order to capture it and enclose it in an idol or image. *Simulacrum* is thus a sculptural term, which Klossowski applies, by extension, to pictorial, verbal, and written representations. Simulacra are verbal, plastic, or written transcriptions of phantasms, artifacts which *count as* (or are *equivalent to*, can be exchanged for) phantasms. In Klossowski, these demonic forces no longer refer to gods and goddesses, but to impulses and affects; more precisely, gods and goddesses are themselves simulacra of impulses and affects. In Klossowski, *mimesis* is not a servile imitation of the visible, but the simulation of the unrepresentable.[36]

For this reason, simulacra stand in a complex relationship to what Klossowski, in his later works, calls a "stereotype."[37] On the one hand, the invention of simulacra always presupposes a set of prior stereotypes—what Klossowski calls, in *Nietzsche and the Vicious Circle*, "the code of everyday signs"—which express the gregarious aspect of lived experience in a form already schematized by the habitual usages of feeling and thought (the herd). In this sense, the code of everyday signs necessarily inverts and falsifies the singularity of the soul's intensive movements by making them intelligible:

> How can one give an account of an irreducible depth of sensibility except by acts that betray it? It would seem that such an irreducible depth can never be reflected on or grasped save by acts perpetrated outside of thought—unreflected or ungraspable acts.[38]

Klossowski explains the movement that, through the phantasm, translates the movement of the impulses into the code of everyday signs:

> For the impulses to become a will at the level of consciousness, the latter must give the impulse an exciting state as an aim, and thus must elaborate the signification of what, for the impulse, is a phantasm: an anticipated excitation, and thus a possible excitation according to the schema determined by

previously experienced excitations ... A phantasm, or several phantasms, can be formed in accordance with the relations among impulsive forces ... In this manner, something new and unfamiliar is misinterpreted as something already known. (NVC 47)

On the other hand, Klossowski also speaks of a "science of stereotypes" in which the stereotype, by being "accentuated" to the point of excess, can itself bring about a critique of its own gregarious interpretation of the phantasm: "Practiced advisedly, the institutional stereotypes (of syntax) provoke the presence of what they circumscribe; their circumlocutions conceal the incongruity of the phantasm but at the same time trace the outline of its opaque physiognomy."[39] Klossowski's prose is itself an example of this science of stereotypes. By his own admission, his own works are written in a "'conventionally' classical syntax" that makes systematic use of the literary tenses and conjunctions of the French language, giving it a decidedly erudite, precious, and even "bourgeois" tone, but in an exaggerated manner that brings out its phantasmic structure. As Klossowski writes, "the simulacrum effectively simulates the constraint of the phantasm only by exaggerating the stereotypical schemes: to add to the stereotype and accentuate it is to bring out the obsession of which it constitutes the replica."[40] If Klossowski gave up writing after 1970, it is at least in part because, in attempting to express the incommunicable phantasm, he wound up preferring the eloquence of bodily gestures and images—what he calls "corporeal idioms"—to the medium of words and syntax. "There is but one universal authentic language: the exchange of bodies through the secret language of incorporeal signs."[41]

But whatever medium Klossowski uses, we can sense the vertiginous nature of this game between simulacra and stereotypes. If simulacra later became the object of demonology in Christian thought, it is because the simulacrum is not the "opposite" of the gregarious stereotype—just as the demonic is not the opposite of the divine, Satan is not the Other, the pole farthest from God, the absolute antithesis—but something much more bewildering: the Same, the perfect double, the exact semblance, the doppelgänger, the angel of light whose deception is so complete that it is impossible to tell the imposter (Satan, Lucifer) apart from the "reality" (God, Christ), just as Plato reaches the point, in the *Sophist*, where Socrates and the Sophist are rendered indiscernible. Klossowski's concern is not the problem of the Other, but the problem of the Same. The demonic simulacrum thus stands in stark contrast to the theological symbol, which is always iconic, the analogical manifestation of a transcendent instance.[42] Since incoherence is the law of the Klossowski's universe, he who dissimulates the most is he who most resembles his invisible model.

THE TRIPARTITE ECONOMY OF THE SOUL: THE EUPHORIA AT TURIN

What one finds in Klossowski, then, is a kind of threefold circuit in the economy of the soul:

1. first, there are impulses, with their rises and falls in intensity, their elations and depressions, which have no meaning or goal in themselves
2. second, these impulses give rise to phantasms, which constitute the incommunicable depth and singularity of the individual soul (the "ego" or the "I" is itself a phantasm that ascribes a unity to our impulsive life in the service of the species or the herd)
3. third, under the obsessive constraint of the phantasm, simulacra are produced, which are the reproduction or repetition of the phantasm (through the exaggeration of stereotypes).

Impulses, phantasms, simulacra-stereotypes: a threefold circuit. If Klossowski presents *Nietzsche and the Vicious Circle* as primarily an interpretation of Nietzsche's physiognomy, it is because it attempts to follow this threefold circuit as it is expressed in Nietzsche's thought:

1. Klossowski first attempts to describe the impulses or intensive powers that exercised their constraint on Nietzsche (notably those associated with his valetudinary states)
2. he then identifies the phantasms they produced in him, notably the phantasm of the Eternal Return, as the highest and most affirmative affect of the soul; and
3. finally, he presents an exposition of the various simulacra Nietzsche created to express them: namely, the concepts, doctrines, and figures of what we know as Nietzsche's "philosophy."

What is the aim or goal of this threefold circuit, its intention?

Nietzsche's unavowable project [writes Klossowski] is to act *without intention*: the impossible morality. Now the total economy of this intentionless universe creates intentional beings. The species "man" is a creation of this kind—*pure chance*—in which the intensity of forces is inverted into *intention*: the work of morality. The function of the simulacrum is *to lead human intention back to the intensity of forces*, which generate phantasms. (NVC 140)

But what exactly does this mean: "to lead human intention back to the intensity of forces"? On this question, perhaps the most important text in Klossowski's book on Nietzsche is the penultimate chapter entitled "The Euphoria of Turin," which examines Nietzsche's breakdown and madness through an analysis of the letters and notes Nietzsche wrote during the week of 31 December 1888 through 6 January 1889.

There are two obviously problematic readings of Nietzsche's madness: either madness is taken to be the logical and internal outcome of Nietzsche's philosophy, or else it was produced by an external cause (a syphilitic infection), having nothing whatsoever to do with the philosophy as such. Klossowski cuts a middle path between these two extremes. No one, he says, was more aware than Nietzsche of the tension between the *incoherence* of the impulses and the *coherence* of the subject [*suppôt*] that makes these impulses a property of the self. This is, at least in part, what Nietzsche meant by the famous phrase of *Ecce Homo*, "Dionysus versus the Crucified": Dionysus is the god of metamorphoses, of affirmation, who affirms the healthy and strong impulses in all their incoherence, whereas the Crucified is the god of the weak, of gregariousness, of the herd, the defender of the responsible self. This is why Klossowski emphasizes the importance of Nietzsche's migraines, for it was precisely when the lucidity of Nietzsche's brain was suspended that his self would be broken down into a kind of lucidity that was much more vast, yet more brief and fragile—a lucidity in which these mute forces and impulses of the body were awakened (NVC 31). By examining these alterations in his valetudinary states, Klossowski suggests, Nietzsche was searching for a new type of cohesion between his thought and the body as a *corporealizing* thought—that is, the body no longer as a property of the self, but as the fortuitous locus of impulses. Nietzsche, in other words, wanted to use his own lucidity to penetrate the shadows of the impulses. But how can one remain lucid if, in order to penetrate the shadows of the impulses, one must destroy the very locus of lucidity: namely, the self? For a long time, Nietzsche was content to observe this to-and-fro movement between the incoherence of the impulses (intensity) and the coherence of the self (intention).

What happened at Turin? It was the moment of apotheosis, where Nietzsche finally led "human intention back to the intensity of forces." "Nietzsche," writes Klossowski, "was never more lucid than during these final days in Turin. *What he was conscious of was the fact that he had ceased to be Nietzsche*, that he had been, as it were, emptied of his person" (NVC 235). Nietzsche did not suddenly lose his reason and begin to identify himself with strange personages; more precisely, Nietzsche the professor had had lost (or abrogated) his identity, and lucidly abandoned himself to the incoherence of the impulses, each of which now received a proper name of its own. The fact that he signed several of his letters as "The Crucified," that he chose the physiognomy of Christ to mask the loss of his own identity, shows the enormity of Nietzsche's ecstasy: Dionysus and the Crucified are no longer in opposition, but in a tenuous equilibrium. Nietzsche's delirium, in short, passed through a series of intensive states, in which his impulses each received various proper names, some of which designated his allies, or manic rises in intensity (Prado, Lesseps, Chambige, "honest criminals"), while others designated his enemies, or depressive falls in intensity (Caiaphas, Wilhelm Bismarck, the "antisemites")—a chaos of pure oscillations that was ultimately invested by "all the names of history" (and not, as certain psychoanalysts would have it, by "the name of the father").

The seeming lucidity of Nietzsche's madness was attested to, curiously, by two of Nietzsche's closest friends. On 21 January 1890, one year after the collapse in Turin, Peter Gast, Nietzsche's amanuensis, visited his friend at the asylum in Jena.

> He did not look very ill [Gast later wrote]. I almost had the impression that his mental disturbance consists of no more than a heightening of the humorous antics he used to put on for an intimate circle of friends. He recognized me immediately, embraced and kissed me, was highly delighted to see me, and gave me his hand repeatedly as if unable to believe I was really there.

But while going for long walks with Nietzsche every day, Gast could see that he did not want to be "cured": "it seemed—horrible though this is—as if Nietzsche were merely feigning madness, as if he were glad for it to have ended this way." These observations correspond with Franz Overbeck's feelings when he came to see Nietzsche a month later, in February 1890:

> I cannot escape the ghastly suspicion . . . that his madness is simulated. This impression can be explained only by the experiences I have had of Nietzsche's self-concealments, of his spiritual masks. But here too I have bowed to facts which overrule all personal thoughts and speculations.[43]

Although Klossowski does not cite these observations by Gast and Overbeck, he none the less poses the inevitable question: Where does Nietzsche's thought arrive at in this simulation of madness?

> Nietzsche's obsessive thought [Klossowski suggests] had always been that events, actions, apparent decisions, and indeed the entire world have a completely different aspect from those they have taken on, since the beginning of time, in the sphere of language. Now he saw the world beyond language: was it the sphere of *absolute muteness*, or on the contrary the sphere of *absolute language?* (NVC 251)

Klossowski necessarily leaves the question unanswered. Earlier in the book, he cites a note from the Spring of 1888 in which Nietzsche exhibited a certain guardedness about his own condition that obviously waned at the end of the year. It is entitled "The Most Dangerous Misunderstanding," and it concerns those who are taken to be sick or mad. Does their intoxication stem from an over-fullness of life, Nietzsche asks, or from a truly pathological degeneration of the brain? How can one discern the *rich* type from an *exhausted* type? This was Nietzsche's double fear as expressed in *Ecce Homo*: the fear of being taken for a prophet, but also the fear of being taken for a "buffoon for all eternity" (NVC 86). In short, how can one tell if the "high tonality" of the *Stimmung* of the eternal return is an expression of health and over-abundance, or an expression of exhaustion and sickness? This is a question derived from the paradoxical (or "antinomial") status of the doctrine of the eternal return. As a lived experience, Nietzsche initially experienced the eternal return, not as a thought, but as an impulse, a *Stimmung*, a "high tonality of the soul." As a *thought*, then, Klossowski insists that the eternal return can only ever be the *simulacrum* of a doctrine; it attempts to communicate a phantasm that is fundamentally incommunicable, and thus is a simulation (and hence a perversion) of that phantasm. Moreover, this paradox finds its concrete manifestation in the direct manipulation of the affects by our modern industrial (or capitalist) organization—for what is marketing or advertising except a willed and conscious manipulation of the affects *in the service of* gregarious needs and wants? The flows and metamorphoses of capital and commodities, with neither aim nor goal, are a concrete form of the most malicious caricature of Nietzsche's doctrine of the Eternal Return (NVC 171). Klossowski's book *Living Currency* (*La Monnaie vivante*) continues his reflection on the destiny of the impulses in industrial societies, and constitutes a kind of parody of political economy (in so far as the modern industrial and capitalistic order can itself be seen as a parody of the eternal return . . .).[44]

Each of these concepts—impulses and intensities, phantasms, simulacra and stereotypes—would require a more detailed analysis than we have been able to give them here. Taken together, however, they point to what I take to be the primary significance of Klossowski's work. With this circuit of impulse–phantasm–simulacrum, Klossowski has isolated a baroque and labyrinthine logic, with its complex operations of similitude, simultaneity, simulation, and dissimilation. It is something he uncovers, not only in Nietzsche's madness—which he neither condemns nor romanticizes—but also in the many other writers that have commanded his attention: the Marquis de Sade, and his perversions; Jonathan Swift, and his disproportionate vision of Gulliver, and so on. The Klossowskian economy thus follows a kind of circle: the impulses of the soul engender phantasms, from which are produced simulacra, which harden into stereotypes, but which in turn flow back to the originary vision, the originary pathos of the impulses. In this sense, there is no means to uncover the "truth" of this circuit. As Klossowski says, "if we demystify, it is only to mystify further . . . " (NVC 131).

Paul Patton

Deleuze and the Liberal Tradition: Normativity, Freedom, and Judgment

Paul Patton's *Deleuze and the Political* is without doubt one of the most significant books yet written on the work of Gilles Deleuze.[1] It is a short book, but its brevity belies its complexity. It approaches Deleuze's thought from a specific perspective—the question of the "political" (the book is part of Routledge's "Thinking the Political" series)—yet at the same time it provides a succinct and subtle assessment of Deleuze's philosophy as a whole.[2] The book contains concise overviews of such "idiosyncratic" (DP 1) Deleuzian concepts as "virtual multiplicities," "machinic assemblages," "becomings," and "deterritorializations," which will be invaluable to readers new to Deleuze's thought. At the specifically political level, it also contains the most extensive discussion yet of the abstract typology of social formations that constitutes the fundamental innovation of *Capitalism and Schizophrenia*, including Deleuze and Félix Guattari's important but ill-understood concept of "nomadic war machines." On both these fronts, Patton's analyses of Deleuze's concepts, though necessarily selective, are exemplary. Readers will find Patton to be a reliable and judicious guide through the labyrinth of Deleuze's novel concepts and political terminology.

Deleuze and the Political is a personal book as well. Patton is not only a well-known scholar of Deleuze but also a political thinker in his own right, having written widely on the history of modern political philosophy.[3] In reading the book, and particularly the chapter on power, one gets a clear sense of the figures who have influenced Patton's own political thought, which include Hobbes and Rawls as much as Nietzsche, Foucault, and Deleuze. Patton has also written on Aboriginal land rights in Australia, and published important analyses of the landmark 1992 Mabo case[4]; the final chapter of the book, which is one of its most original sections, attempts to examine and re-analyze the issues of colonization and native title from a specifically Deleuzian perspective. *Deleuze and the Political* can therefore be read not only as a commentary on Deleuze but also as a synthetic work of Patton's own, the result of years of research and reflection, bringing together these various interests into a coherent whole.

Of the many riches in *Deleuze and the Political*, I would like to focus here on a single aspect of the book: namely, Patton's analysis of Deleuze's relation to the "liberal" tradition of political philosophy. In my opinion, this is one of the most important contributions of Patton's study, if only because Deleuze's political thought has usually been read in the context of the Marxist tradition, and not the liberal tradition. While Patton does not ignore this Marxist heritage, Deleuze's relationship to Marxism is already well known and well documented. Deleuze explicitly characterized himself as a Marxist, insisting that "any political philosophy must turn on the analysis of capitalism and the ways it has developed" (N 171). But as Jean-François Lyotard observed long ago, *Capitalism and Schizophrenia* none the less contains an implicit critique of Marx, since a number of classical Marxist concepts—such as the super- and infrastructure, the workers' struggle, the proletariat, work-value theory—largely drop out of Deleuze and Guattari's analyses; they are neither analyzed nor criticized, but simply ignored.[5] Moreover, traditional Marxism taught that there was a limit beyond which the capitalist machine would break apart and finally collapse, and Marxist politics was built on the search for this limit: that is, for the revolutionary "conditions" that would make possible the appearance of a new type of social formation—first "crude communism" (the abolition of private property), then the positivity of a "fully developed humanism." Deleuze and Guattari likewise abandon this eschatological conception entirely, defining capitalism in terms of its lines of flight and its minorities rather than its contradictions and classes (capitalist versus proletariat) (N 171–2). This strategy in no way implies a rejection of Marxism, since Marx himself insisted that his own analyses of capitalism would necessarily have to be modified in light of changing conditions. Deleuze and Guattari are therefore able, without inconsistency, to situate themselves squarely in the Marxist tradition, while at the same time rejecting crucial Marxist concepts. The new concepts proposed in their analyses, they insist, are those required by the new problematics posed by the present state of capitalism. The result is a Marxist politics that functions with a new set of political concepts, such as lines of flight, difference, and becomings, all of which Patton analyzes in detail (DP 6–9).

In contrast to this critical affirmation of the Marxist tradition, however, Deleuze's relationship to the liberal tradition of political thought is much more tenuous, and often negative. Patton notes on his opening page that Deleuze's work "shows an almost complete lack of engagement with the central problems and normative commitments of Anglo-American political thought" (DP 1), largely ignoring the issues that most concern the liberal tradition, such as "the nature of justice, freedom, or democracy," or "normativity," or "procedural justification" (DP 1). If Deleuze was willing to ignore certain Marxist concepts, one might say that he was more or less willing to ignore the concepts of the liberal tradition *in toto*. This is where Patton intervenes. Could not the conceptual apparatus of the liberal tradition, he asks, be open to a similar transformation from a Deleuzian perspective, just as Deleuze himself transformed the Marxist tradition? Patton's book in this way injects itself as a forceful intervention in the current reception of Deleuze's thought: it stages a complex confrontation between Deleuze's political thought and the liberal tradition, in the context of which it attempts to demonstrate not only the contemporary relevance of Deleuze's concepts, but also the potential they have to transform *both* the Marxist and liberal traditions of political philosophy.[6] In proposing such a confrontation, Patton is staking out a new and rich territory in the study of Deleuze, and setting out a research agenda that will no doubt be taken up by others. Patton necessarily pursues this agenda somewhat obliquely in *Deleuze and the Political*, given the several aims of the book, and my aim in what follows is simply to highlight the way in which this particular trajectory unfolds in the course of Patton's analyses.

DELEUZE'S ANALYTIC OF CONCEPTS

In *What is Philosophy?* Deleuze and Guattari define philosophy, famously, as the *creation of concepts* (WP 5). Patton rightly makes this activity of concept creation the first explicit focus of his book, since it provides not only the viewpoint through which he presents Deleuze's thought, but also the basis upon which he undertakes his own revisionary project. "A guiding principle of this study," he writes, "is that Deleuze's contribution to political thought must be assessed in relation to his own concept and practice of philosophy" (DP 2). The first chapter ("Concept and Image of Thought: Deleuze's Conception of Philosophy") thus opens with an examination of the political concept of the "social contract," which Patton uses to illustrate the various aspects by which Deleuze and Guattari define a concept: its intensive *components*, which in turn constitute concepts in their own right (the state of nature, the restless desire for power, the artificial person that results from the contract); its internal *consistency* (the way these elements are linked together internally; the "endo-consistency" of the concept); its *plane of immanence* (the way the concept of the social contract links up externally with related concepts such as sovereignty, legitimation, justice; the "exo-consistency" of concepts). Surprisingly, Patton does not discuss the crucial Deleuzian notion of *conceptual personae*, which in the context of political philosophy might include the Leviathan, the Noble Savage, the Prince, and so on (WP 63). The *critique* of a concept can take place at any of these levels; one can add, subtract, or transform the components, or alter the relations between them. For instance, in Locke's version of the social contract, subjects are no longer determined by the desire for power, as in Hobbes, but rather by their ownership of property—a change in components—which in turn implies obligations toward oneself and others—a change in consistency. This is a good example of the transformative process through which concepts can be rejuvenated and renewed throughout history, and it lies at the basis of Patton's own project to reinterpret liberal concepts from a Deleuzian perspective. Finally, Patton emphasizes the fact that, in all these aspects, concepts always derive their necessity from historically determined *problematics* (DP 21). Whereas Hobbes's problematic was the constitution and legitimation of civil authority, for instance, John Rawls's problematic in *A Theory of Justice* concerns the principles of a just society, in the context of which Rawls himself would take up and transform the concept of the social contract yet again (DP 13).

This analysis, though scarcely three pages long, is a *tour de force*, and provides a far more accessible example of conceptual analysis than the one Deleuze and Guattari themselves provide in *What is Philosophy?* (via the somewhat obscure

Deleuzian concept of the *autrui*) (WP 16–19). It plays a double role in the context of Patton's study: it allows him to summarize Deleuze and Guattari's conception of concepts, while at the same time providing us with a capsule history of one of the founding concepts of the liberal tradition of political philosophy. It immediately leads us to the second explicit aim of the book—the one that concerns us—which is to show "the points of connection" between Deleuze's work and the Anglo-American tradition of political philosophy (DP 135). This, however, raises a preliminary but necessary question: *Why* did Deleuze himself largely ignore the political concepts of the liberal tradition such as the social contract? The reason for this evasion, Patton suggests, can be found in a fundamental shift in the status of the subject that is effectuated in Deleuze's philosophy. The general question posed by the theory of the social contract is: How can individuals enter into a mutually beneficial political alliance? In this sense, the social contract presupposes the prior existence of already-constituted individuals as political subjects. In Deleuze, by contrast, the subject itself becomes a secondary phenomenon, the product or the "effect" of more primary sets of flows or *processes* (what Foucault called "processes of subjectivation"). The political questions Deleuze asks are therefore always posed at the level of *pre-subjective* processes. For example: How is it that desire, as a process, can come to desire its own repression? How can a subjective (though abstract) process such as labor be "captured" by institutions or State apparatuses? The political philosophy developed in *Capitalism and Schizophrenia* attempts to analyze social formations primarily as physical systems defined in terms of their processes—or more precisely, in terms of a generalized theory of "flows" (*flux*): flows of matter, flows of population and commodities, flows of capital and labor, flows of traffic, flows of knowledge, flows of desire, and so on. Simplifying to the extreme, one could say that Deleuze is not a philosopher of the subject but a philosopher of pre-subjective processes or flows. This is the fundamental metaphysical shift in Deleuze's philosophy, and it is these processes that Deleuze's concepts attempt to describe.

The task Patton takes on, then, is to show if and how liberal political concepts can be retained and transformed in light of this metaphysical shift. In turn, the possibility of such a transformation, he suggests, must itself rest on Deleuze's own analytic of concepts, and on the "cognitive function" Deleuze assigns to them (26). On this score, Patton emphasizes the definition, provided in *What is Philosophy?*, that philosophical concepts "provide knowledge of pure events" (DP 26). But what is a "pure event"? Deleuze distinguishes between the actualization of an event in a state of affairs or in lived experience—that is, in *history*; and the pure event, which is irreducible to its actualizations, "the event in its *becoming*, in its specific consistency," which escapes history and is "utopic," both now-here and no-where (a play on Samuel Butler's utopian neologism *Erewhon*), and is expressed in a "self-positing concept" (DP 27). As an example of this distinction, Patton points to Kant's famous reflections on the French Revolution in *The Contest of the Faculties*, a text that has recently been taken up by thinkers as diverse as Foucault, Habermas, and Lyotard. Kant distinguished between "the concept of a revolution in favor of the universal rights of man as this was expressed in the 'enthusiasm' of Europeans for those ideals" (this is what marks their "becoming" in relation to the concept); and "the manner in which that concept and those ideals were actualized in the bloody events of 1789" (this is "history") (DP 27). Patton reformulates this Kantian distinction (between spectator and actor) into a Deleuzian one (between an event and a state of affairs), showing how political concepts such as "revolution" (considered as a kind of "territoriality") have a double structure. On the one hand, there is the concept in so far as it is actualized in or refers to a particular state of affairs (the actual events of 1789) where it effects movements of *relative* deterritorialization, movements that can be blocked or reterritorialized (the "betrayal" of the revolution, its inevitable disappointment); on the other hand, there is the concept in so far as it expresses a "pure event" that posits revolution as an *absolute* deterritorialization, a self-referential movement of pure immanence, a "pure reserve" that is never exhausted by its various actualizations (DP 97, 107, 136). Deleuze uses the term *utopia* to designate the "critical point" at which these two aspects of the concept are brought together: the point where the absolute deterritorialization expressed by the concept is connected with the present relative milieu.

> To say that revolution is itself a utopia of immanence [write Deleuze and Guattari] is to posit revolution as plane of immanence, infinite movement and absolute survey, but to the extent that these features connect up with what is real here and now in the struggle against capitalism, relaunching new struggles whenever the earlier one is betrayed. (WP 100)

It is this event-based theory of the concept that Patton puts to work in his revision of liberal political concepts. His method is to extract the "pure event" of a liberal concept in order to—at the same time—reinject it into the current situation, thereby effecting its transformation. "Remarkable or interesting concepts," Patton writes, "are those that can be taken up again and again in new circumstances, continuing to work their subversive way through history" (DP 133). This might appear to be a curious conception of the political, which is here defined in terms of one's relation to a concept or Idea rather than in terms of one's relation to a concrete state of affairs or a political situation. In Kant, for example, the "enthusiasm" of the Europeans, their becoming-revolutionary, is explicitly linked, not to the historical revolution as it unfolded before them in France, but rather to its *concept*: that is, to a "pure event," almost as if the revolution itself were something secondary. But as Hannah Arendt suggests in her *Lectures on Kant's Political Philosophy*, this is a definition of what political *philosophy* is:

> Robert Cumming recently wrote that "the subject matter of modern political philosophy . . . is not the polis or politics, but the relation between philosophy and politics." This remark actually applies to all political philosophy and, most of all, to its beginnings in Athens.[7]

Such seems to be the case with Deleuze: "The word 'utopia' designates *that conjunction of philosophy, or of the concept, with the present milieu*—political philosophy" (WP 100). Using Deleuze's own methodology, then, Patton's proposal is to treat certain liberal concepts (normativity, freedom, judgment) as "pure events" in this Deleuzian sense—utopian concepts that are irreducible to their various actualizations, whether in a state of affairs or a particular political theory, and hence are themselves capable of transformation in connection with changing historical problematics.

This methodological approach, however, raises a delicate problem that Patton does not discuss directly, although it is implicit in his entire project: the possibility of what one might call *exhausted* concepts. If certain concepts can be taken up again and transformed within philosophy (such as the social contract in Hobbes, Locke, and Rawls), it is because what the concept expresses (the "pure event") is irreducible to its actualizations.[8] But do some concepts, even as pure events, eventually become "exhausted"? Deleuze suggests that the concept of "truth" is itself so under- (or over-)determined in philosophy that the problematic to which it corresponds must always be carefully delineated (see DR 158–9). Elsewhere he and Guattari write, in a similar vein, that "reason is only a concept, and a very impoverished concept" at that (WP 1994). If Deleuze tended to ignore liberal concepts, or even certain Marxist concepts, was it because he deemed that such concepts had become exhausted, or were no longer relevant to contemporary problematics? Moreover, is this not why Deleuze defines philosophy as the creation of *new* concepts—new concepts that would constitute a response to changing conditions? Put simply, how does one assess the difference between the need to create a *new* concept in philosophy and the possibility of reactivating or transforming an *already-existing* concept?

One can raise this question already knowing, at least in principle, the inevitable response: there can be no pre-existent criteria to determine the direction a philosopher should take, which is why Deleuze constantly insists on the necessity of *experimentation*. But in practice, this is a difficult and complex question, which has given rise to some well-known and dramatic passages in the history of philosophy. In the *Critique of Pure Reason*, for instance, Kant takes care to explain carefully his appropriation of the Platonic concept of the "Idea," even as he introduces significant changes into the concept.[9] Likewise, in *A Theory of Justice*, Rawls is compelled to justify his own retention of the terminology of the social contract in the context of his theory of "justice as fairness,"[10] just as Heidegger takes care to explain his retention of the traditional concept of the "understanding" in *Being and Time* even as he dramatically reconfigures it as a fundamental *existential* of Dasein.[11] A similar drama is at work in Patton's book. Patton is not simply writing as a commentator, offering a generalized criticism of Deleuze's rejection of liberal political concepts. More subtly, he is writing as a philosopher, suggesting that Deleuze's philosophy can and should be re-evaluated in light of our contemporary historical situation and changing philosophical problematics. What light would the liberal concepts that Deleuze ignores shed on Deleuze's own political philosophy? Conversely, what kind of transformations could Deleuze's concepts introduce into the liberal tradition, given its current situation? In short, what kind of "becoming" would liberal and Deleuzian concepts enter into when they are brought into contact with each other? The fact is that one can never know in advance the course of the becoming of a given concept. As Deleuze writes, "it's not a matter of bringing all sorts of things under a single concept, but rather of relating each concept to the variables that explain its mutations" (N 31).

Deleuze's analytic of concepts, in short, can only be worked out experimentally, and in this case the experimentation is carried out on several "liberal" concepts that Patton, somewhat surreptitiously, imports into his analyses of Deleuze: normativity, freedom, and judgment (as well as a non-liberal concept, the social imaginary). This experimental confrontation is not heralded loudly, but is pursued quietly and patiently throughout the entire book. In the sections that follow, I would simply like to explore, in a provisional manner, how Patton transforms each of these concepts experimentally in the course of his analyses, in a way that points to a new understanding of the liberal tradition of political philosophy.

NORMATIVITY AS THE CONDITION OF THE NEW

The first liberal notion Patton makes use of in his reading of Deleuze is the concept of *normativity*. Though the term is not listed in the index, it appears frequently in the third section of the chapter on power (DP 9, 20, 49, 59, 87, 106, 135, 136, 144 n11). One of Patton's tasks in these two central chapters—on "Power" and "Desire"—is to argue that Deleuze's theory of desire can be brought together with the theory of power one finds in Foucault and Nietzsche, despite certain conceptual differences. The discussion of normativity that occurs in this context, however, touches a much more difficult question, one that lies at the heart of several recent debates in political philosophy. Critics such as Nancy Fraser and Jürgen Habermas, for instance, have argued that Michel Foucault's well-known theory of power is entirely "non-normative" (DP 59). Normativity is itself a somewhat overdetermined philosophical concept, one that corresponds to the question, "What is the source of the authority that moral considerations have over us?" It is usually contrasted with the descriptive, as "ought" is contrasted with "is." When Habermas and Fraser critique Foucault for failing to provide normative criteria for discriminating between different *ways* of exercising power, they are therefore accusing Foucault of failing to answer one of the central concerns of liberal political theory and the social contract tradition: namely, "When and in what ways is power, especially State power, justified?" (DP 59).

Patton attempts to respond to such criticisms from a Deleuzian perspective. "Unlike Foucault's analytic of power," he writes, Deleuze's approach to power is "*explicitly normative*" (DP 65, 49). This is a somewhat surprising claim, since Deleuze is often condemned along with Foucault for neglecting (or avoiding, or refusing . . .) questions of normativity. Indeed, one could imagine two possible Deleuzian responses to the criticisms of non-normativity. One might ask if normativity is a good or rigorous concept, and proceed to criticize the concept from a Deleuzian viewpoint. In this case, one could argue that Foucault and Deleuze do not address issues of normativity because their work entails a critique of the very notion of normativity. Patton, however, follows the opposite approach. He takes the problem of normativity seriously, and argues that despite appearances one can find an explicit normative criterion in Deleuze's work, which he identifies by name: "The overriding

346 DELEUZE AND CONTEMPORARY PHILOSOPHY

norm is that of deterritorialization" (DP 9). This is the third key thesis of *Deleuze and the Political*: "A central claim of the present study is that it is the concept of 'deterritorialization' which bears the weight of the utopian vocation which Deleuze and Guattari attribute to philosophy" (DP 9). In what sense, then, does Deleuze's notion of deterritorialization play the role of a normative concept?

If Deleuze's political philosophy effects a shift from subjects to processes, then the concept of normativity would have to be altered accordingly. According to Patton, this is exactly what occurs in Deleuze's work: it is the concept of deterritorialization that provides "a normative framework within which to describe and evaluate movements or processes" (DP 136). For Deleuze, to analyze a social formation is to unravel the variable lines and singular *processes* that constitute it as a multiplicity: their connections and disjunctions, their circuits and short-circuits, and above all their possible transformations. To introduce elements of transcendence into the analysis of such fields of immanence, says Deleuze, it is enough to introduce "universals" that would serve as constant coordinates for these processes, and effectively "stop their movement" (WP 47; N 85, 145–6). Deleuze constantly insists that universals are abstractions that explain nothing; they are rather what need to be explained. For instance, there is no such thing as a "pure reason" or a universal rationality, but rather a plurality of heterogeneous "processes of rationalization" of the kind analyzed by Alexandre Koyré, Gaston Bachelard, and Georges Canguilhem in the field of epistemology, Max Weber in sociology, and François Châtelet in philosophy. Likewise, there is no universal or transcendental Subject, which could function as the bearer of universal human rights, but only variable and historically diverse "processes of subjectivation," to use Foucault's term.[12] What one finds in any given socio-political assemblage is not a universal "Reason," but variable processes of rationalization; not universalizable "subjects," but variable processes of subjectivation; not the "whole," the "one," or "objects," but rather knots of totalization, foci of unification, and processes of objectification. Such processes operate within concrete multiplicities, and are relative to them, and thus need to be analyzed on their own account.

Deleuze would no doubt have followed the same approach in his analysis of normativity had he addressed the issue directly. Foucault himself spoke of the power of what he called the process of *normalization*, which creates us, as subjects, in terms of existing force relations and existing "norms." For Foucault, normalization is not merely an abstract principle of adjudication but an already actualized (and always actualized) power relation. Foucault's question then became: Is it possible to escape, or at least *resist*, this power of normalization? In Deleuze's terminology, the same question would be stated in the following terms: Within a given social assemblage or "territoriality," where can one find the "line of flight," or the movement of relative deterritorialization, by means of which one can escape from or transform the existing norm (or territoriality)? From this viewpoint, neither Foucault nor Deleuze avoids the issue of normativity; they simply analyze it in terms of an *immanent process*. The error of transcendence would be to posit normative criteria as abstract universals, even if these are defined in intersubjective or communicative terms. From the viewpoint of immanence, by contrast, it is the process itself that must

account for *both* the production of the norm and its possible destruction or altera-
tion. In a given assemblage, one will indeed find normative criteria that govern,
for instance, the application of the power of the State, but one will also find the
means for the critique and modification of those norms, their deterritorialization. A
truly "normative" principle must provide not only norms for condemning abuses of
power, but also a means for condemning norms that have themselves become abuses
of power (for instance, the norms that governed the treatment of women, slaves,
minorities, and so on). An immanent process, in other words, must at one and the
same time function as a principle of *critique* as well as a principle of *creation* (the
"genetic" method). "The conditions of a true critique and a true creation are one
and the same" (DR 139). The one cannot and "must" not exist without the other.

If deterritorialization functions as a norm for Patton, then, it is a somewhat paradoxical norm. Within any assemblage, what is normative is deterritorialization: that
is, the creation of "lines of flight" (Deleuze) or "resistance" (Foucault) that allow
one to break free from a given norm, or to transform the norm. What "must" always
remain normative is the ability to critique and transform existing norms: that is, to
create something *new* (the category of the new should be understood here in the
broad sense, including not only social change, but also artistic creation, conceptual
innovation, and so on.) One cannot have pre-existing norms or criteria for the
new; otherwise it would not be new, but already foreseen. This is the basis on which
Patton argues that Deleuze's conception of power is explicitly normative: "What a
given assemblage is capable of doing or becoming," he writes, "is determined by the
lines of flight or deterritorialization which it can sustain" (DP 106).[13]

Patton is therefore using the concept "normativity" in a quite different manner
than Fraser or Habermas. They would say that deterritorialization is not normative,
and cannot be, since it eludes any universal criteria and indeed allows for their
modification. Patton in effect responds by saying: for that very reason, it is deterritorialization that should be seen as a normative concept, even if that entails a new
concept of what normativity is. At one point in *Difference and Repetition*, Deleuze
writes that "one can conserve the word essence, if one wishes, but only on the
condition of saying that essence is precisely the accident or the event" (DR 191).
Patton seems to be saying something similar: one can conserve the word normativity, if one wishes, but only on the condition of saying that the normative is the new
or the deterritorialized. Patton's own trajectory is thus beginning to come into focus:
rather than simply dropping or ignoring the concept of normativity, he instead proposes to create a new concept of normativity by critiquing components of the old
one, and linking it up with a quite different set of related concepts. In this manner,
he is effecting a transformation of the liberal concept, while still attempting to
situate his own work fully within the liberal tradition.

THE CONCEPT OF "CRITICAL FREEDOM"

A second concept Patton incorporates into his analyses of Deleuze, and links to
the concept of normativity, is the concept of *freedom*, even though Deleuze himself
rarely uses this term in his writings (Guattari is said to have remarked that he

disliked words that, in French, end with an accent: *vérité, liberté, taraté taraté* . . .). Patton none the less entitles his fourth chapter "Desire, Becoming, and Freedom," and goes so far as to describe Deleuze's thought as an "ethics of freedom" (DP 83). In characterizing Deleuze's philosophy from the viewpoint of a concept that is foreign to Deleuze's own thought, Patton is in fact utilizing a strategy that is itself Deleuzian. In his books on Spinoza, for instance, Deleuze claims that the concept of univocity is "the keystone of Spinoza's entire philosophy" (SPP 63), even though the term "univocity" does not appear even once in Spinoza's texts. The effect of such a technique, however, is to produce what at one point Deleuze calls a "double becoming" (TI 221, 222): the introduction of a foreign concept can often serve as a prism or point of reference by which to evaluate the movement of thought of a given thinker, while at the same time the concept itself is transformed, and enters into its own becoming. (It none the less remains an interesting question to ask why Deleuze might have avoided concepts such as normativity and freedom, while freely adopting other highly charged philosophical concepts such as "idea" or "essence.")

How is the concept of freedom transformed when it is brought into contact with Deleuze's thought? What Patton finds in Deleuze's work is an activity of what he calls "critical freedom"—a term developed by James Tully in his book *Strange Multiplicity*—which he distinguishes from the notions of negative and positive freedom.[14] *Negative freedom*, as formulated by Isaiah Berlin in his canonical essay "Two Concepts of Freedom," is one of the concepts that lies at the heart of the modern liberal tradition.[15] It defines freedom negatively as "the absence of obstacles to possible choices and activities," an "area of non-interference" in which agents are allowed to pursue their desires and goals freely without having their choices limited by the intervention of others. By contrast, the concept of *positive freedom*, as championed by Charles Taylor, implies the stronger notion of "self-mastery" or "strong evaluation": that is, the idea of actively "exercising control over one's life" (DP 84) by evaluating and defining one's own desires and goals.[16] Berlin sees positive freedom as a threat to liberty because it implies that subjects will be constrained to act in prescribed manners; Taylor insists that our freedom of choice is always already partly limited and prescribed by our milieu, and that one evaluates and chooses only within the context of that milieu (culture, community, the state and its laws).

What both these notions of freedom share, however, is a conception of the subject as a determinate structure of interests, goals, and desires: the freedom of the subject lies in its ability to act in pursuit of these interests and goals. What they overlook, or underemphasize, Patton argues, is the fact that individuals often *distance* themselves from their initial (or inherited) preferences and *alter* them in fundamental ways (DP 84). This may happen at an individual level (a person altering or leaving a religious heritage) or in a social context where one is exposed to alternate ways of thinking and living (exposure to feminist or racial critiques, contact with other cultures or minorities within one's own culture). Such transformations presume a capacity to alter one's thought and actions, to "question in thought and challenge in practice one's inherited cultural ways" (DP 85), and it is this capacity that Tully terms "critical freedom." It is the freedom to critique, the freedom to be transformed, to be changed. It entails, as Foucault said, the ability to "think otherwise," or, as Deleuze might say, the capacity of the self to *affect* itself.[17] Patton's proposal here is to align Deleuze with Tully's contribution to liberal political thought, and to assign to critical freedom a "normative" status.

But how, then, does Patton position this notion of critical freedom within Deleuze's thought? Deleuze, in fact, is not completely silent with regard to the liberal tradition. In *A Thousand Plateaus*, Deleuze and Guattari attempt to show how, within the liberal tradition itself, the notion of the freedom of *subjects* is inevitably tied to an "image of thought" derived from the *State*. Social contract theory, in their analysis, operates between two poles, the subject and the legislator. As a subject I give up my freedom to the State in return for protection from others and from the state of nature (the State as an "agent of servitude"); in return for this servitude the State, as legislator, affords me the greatest possible scope of liberty (the State as the locus of negative freedom). In Kant's hands, however, this link between subject and legislator would be pushed to its limit in the notion of a subject that is subjected *only to itself* as a self-legislating rational being ("autonomy"): "The contract must be pushed to the extreme; in other words, it is no longer concluded between two people but between self and self, within the same person—*Ich* = *Ich*— as subjected and sovereign" (TP 460). In the Kantian formulation, freedom becomes defined as the *identity* of subject and legislator in the same person. "The more you obey [as subject], the more you will be master [as legislator], for you will only be obeying pure reason . . . in other words, *yourself*" (TP 376). What one finds here is a mysterious "nexum" between the subject, the State, and reason, which perhaps reached its apotheosis in certain forms of Hegelianism. Reason invents the fiction of a State that is universal by right, and elevates the State to a *de jure* rationality, such that realized reason is identified with the *de jure* State and the State is the becoming of reason itself (the particularity of States being a mere accident of fact); the State in turn provides thought itself with a model (the republic of free and rational minds, a *cogitatio universalis*) which is internalized in the self as both legislator and subject (under formal conditions that allows thought to conceptualize their identity) (TP 375–6, 556 n42).

Now if Deleuze's own philosophy breaks with this nexus, then any reformulation of the concept of freedom in Deleuzian terms would have to operate, not at the level of subjects or the State, but rather at the level of their genetic processes (subjectivation, stratification, rationalization). As Patton shows, this is indeed the case in one of the few texts in which Deleuze actually uses the term (DP 41–2). In *Difference and Repetition*, Deleuze writes that the "differential object" of sociability cannot be lived with actual societies, but "must be and can only be lived in the element of social upheaval (in other words, *freedom*, which is always hidden among the remains of the old order and the first fruits of a new)" (DR 193). Here, freedom is not equated with the liberty to move about and pursue one's interests within a given social formation or State; rather, it concerns the conditions of change for the social structure itself. (In *A Thousand Plateaus*, it is the war machine that will come to play this role, in contradistinction to the State.) Already in *Difference and Repetition*, then, Deleuze was giving the concept of freedom an altered set of components, making it correspond to one of the fundamental problems of his philosophy: namely, the conditions for the production of the new. (This is a different question from that of the conditions of *change*, since the new, in order to be truly new, can be neither foreseeable nor conceptualizable, nor even expected or hoped for.) Freedom, as a condition of the new, appears here as a limit-concept (or Idea) in a far more radical sense than one finds even in Kant.

When Patton parses this limit notion of freedom, he does so in terms of Deleuze's distinction between the *connection* and the *conjugation* of processes (DP 101–2). This distinction is a difficult and nuanced one in Deleuze's philosophy, but Patton argues that it functions as an immanent normative criterion for evaluating the modes of interaction between processes or flows. A *conjunction* of flows occurs when one flow blocks or constrains other flows, in such a manner that it brings the latter under the dominance of a single flow capable of "overcoding" them (hence Deleuze and Guattari's use of terminology such as "capture," "integration," "sedimentation," "stratification," and so on). By contrast, a *connection* occurs when two flows enter into relation in such a manner that something passes *between* them, and their interaction produces something *new* which introduces a real transformation in a given field. This third thing is what Deleuze terms a "becoming" (see TP 232–309), and Patton rightly characterizes Deleuze's philosophy of the new (or "ethics of freedom") as a politics of becoming. But he also stresses the complexities and uncertainties involved in such a politics.

> Whereas the normative status and the value of liberal freedom is straightforwardly positive, critical freedom is a much more ambivalent and risky affair: more ambivalent, since it involves leaving behind existing grounds of value, with the result that it is not always clear whether it is good or bad; risky, because there is no telling in advance where such processes of mutation and change might lead, whether at the level of individual or collective assemblages. (DP 87)

This is a succinct statement of Patton's revised concepts of normativity and critical freedom, and of the "exo-consistency" he is attempting to establish between them. Here again, one can get a clear sense of the conceptual apparatus Patton is in the process of creating, step by step, in the midst of his commentary on Deleuze.

THE THEORY OF JUDGMENT IN DELEUZE

The third foreign term Patton brings into his analyses, although only in passing, is the term *judgment*. At one point, he describes Nietzsche's thought as "a complex and nuanced system of judgment" (DP 63)—a phrase that brought me up short, since one of Deleuze's most persistent themes is the need "to have done with judgment" (a formula derived from Artaud, though Deleuze assigns it a much broader scope). Deleuze prefers the term "evaluation" to "judgment," and constantly criticizes what he, following Nietzsche, calls "the system of judgment" in philosophy. My initial reaction was that Patton's use of the word was simply infelicitous, but the more I read, the more it became clear that Patton's positive appeal to a theory of judgment was not incidental. Why is Deleuze "against" judgment? Judgment is the act of subsuming the particular under the general, and Deleuze's is clearly critical of the notion of the general or the universal. Universals explain nothing, Deleuze constantly says, but are themselves what need to be explained (D vii), and Patton likewise insists that there neither is nor can be any "transcendent point or uniform standard of judgment" (DP 64).

But, Patton asks, does this mean we must have done with the concept of judgment as such? Kant himself, for instance, in the *Critique of Judgment*, developed the rich notion of *reflective* judgments—judgments that start with the particular and look for the general, which is *not* given but merely has a "problematic" status.[18] Thinkers such as Jean-François Lyotard and Hannah Arendt have demonstrated the importance of the notion of reflective judgment for political philosophy. Deleuze's own distinction between the regular and the singular is germane here: the regular is that which is submitted to a general rule, which is regulated; but the singular is that which lies outside the rule. But is not this what we mean when we speak of "sound" judgment: the ability to act when there is no clear rule? This is a point that Arendt makes in her book *Eichmann in Jerusalem: A Report on the Banality of Evil*. What we expected, or at least hoped, of people in situations like that of Nazi Germany, she says, was

> that human beings be capable of telling right from wrong even when all they
> have to guide them is their own judgment, which, moreover, happens to be
> completely at odds with what they must regard as the unanimous opinion of
> all those around them . . . Those few who still were able to tell right from
> wrong *went really* only by their own judgments, and they did so freely [in an
> act of what Patton would call "critical freedom"]; there were no rules to be
> abided by, under which the particular cases with which they were confronted
> could be subsumed. They had to decide each instance as it arose, because no
> rules existed for the unprecedented.[19]

In his concluding chapter on native title entitled "Nomads, Capture, and Colonization," Patton seems to follow a trajectory similar to Arendt's. For Deleuze, the law is a kind of axiomatic system: laws or rights (such as human rights) are axioms from which certain theorems are deduced (e.g., torture is a violation of my rights). But undecidability is inherent in every axiomatic system: undecidable cases are what wind up in the courts, before a judge, who in the end must make a judgment in the absence of any rule (if there was a clear rule the case would not wind up in court). The decision, then, enters the body of law as a precedent, as a singularity. The law thus operates on two registers: legislators create laws and decide on axioms, rules; while the judiciary (common law) moves from case to case, from singularity to singularity; it is a prolongation of singularities. The landmark 1991 Mabo case of the Australian High Court, which first affirmed that native or Aboriginal title formed part of Australian common law, is such a singularity, and Patton analyzes the case in Deleuzian terms: it was not simply a deterritorialization of the State's legal mechanism of capture, but the creation of a kind of "zone of indiscernibility" between indigenous law and the common law (DP 128–9), a kind of "jurisprudential smooth space" (DP 31) which has had and will continue to have profound "prolongations." But Patton's analyses lead to the following question: Is the Mabo decision itself not the result of an act of *judgment*? Deleuze himself says that "it is jurisprudence which is truly creative of rights" (DP 3, 120); it is a potential space of metamorphosis. Why, then, does Deleuze want to have done with judgment? In jurisprudence, is it not an act of judgment that *creates* rights? Is not judgment operative at the level of both "court decisions" and "legislative enactments"? Is it not therefore possible to *retain* a concept of judgment (freed from the universal) when one speaks of the creation of rights in jurisprudence? Patton's analyses seem to point in this direction. Moreover, one can see how such a concept of judgment would link up with the other "liberal" concepts introduced by Patton: (a) deterritorialization is indeed "normative" because (b) it opens up a space of "critical freedom" within which (c) one can exercise a judgment, outside of pre-existing rules, that would be truly creative and productive of the new (for instance, new rights).

Patton's analyses of native title in Australia and of the creative role Deleuze assigns to jurisprudence is, in my opinion, one of the most original sections of *Deleuze and the Political* (DP 120–31), since it addresses the concept that perhaps lies at the heart of the liberal tradition: namely, the concept of *rights*. Yet again, this is a concept Deleuze rarely discusses, and when he does, he is critical of the very notion of human rights (or in French, *les droits de l'homme*, the universal "rights of man"). "The reverence people display toward human rights," Deleuze muses in the 1988–9 *Abécédaire* interview, "almost makes one want to defend horrible, terrible positions" (ABC G). Deleuze's critique, however, seems directed less against the concept of rights *per se* than against the *universal* status accorded to human rights, which turns it into a "pure abstraction," an "empty" concept, to the point where Deleuze can even speak of the "mystifications of human rights" (WP 225 n18). In Deleuze and Guattari's terminology, human rights are not universals but *axioms*, and they coexist within the capitalist market with other axioms—notably the axiom of the security of property, in the name of which supposedly democratic States will often simply ignore or suspend human rights. "What social democracy has not given the order to fire when the poor come out of their territory or ghetto?" (WP 107). Moreover, as Alain Badiou has remarked, axioms such as human rights do not concern individuals directly, in their concrete multiplicity, but only in so far as this multiplicity is reduced to a "one" that can be counted (the individual who votes, who is imprisoned, who contributes to Social Security, and so on).[20] In other words, "human rights say nothing about the immanent modes of existence of the people provided with rights" (WP 107).

In the *Abécédaire* interview, Deleuze points to the example of the then-unfolding situation in Armenia: Armenians living in an enclave in a Soviet Republic had been massacred by Turks; the survivors escaped into the Armenian republic, where they were almost immediately devastated by a tremendous earthquake. "It's like something out of the Marquis de Sade. These poor people have gone through the worst ordeals they could face, and they barely escape into shelter when nature starts it all up again" (ABC G). It is not sufficient, Deleuze continues, to insist that the

Turks had no right to massacre the Armenians, or that they violated the Armenians' rights. The abominations the Armenians suffered are not denials of abstract rights; they are *cases*, abominable cases, singular cases (even if such cases often resemble each other). In this case, what is at issue is a specific case of territorial organization: that is, an enclave in a Soviet Republic, surrounded by hostile Turks. How can the enclave be eliminated, or made livable? What can be done to enable the Armenians to extricate themselves from this situation, so they are no longer simply delivered into the hands of the Turks? The earthquake raised different questions concerning, for instance, the unsuitable construction of buildings. What is needed in each of these instances is not an application of universal rights, but rather the invention of jurisprudences so that, in each case, this or that will no longer be possible. Those are two quite different procedures. As Deleuze says, "there are no 'rights of man,' there is life, and there are rights of life. Only life proceeds case by case" (ABC G).

Deleuze is here simply following the trajectory laid out above: universal coordinates such as Rights explain nothing; what needs to be analyzed in a concrete assemblage are the *processes* by which rights are both created and critiqued. Hence the importance of jurisprudence: it provides Deleuze with a model for the creation of rights that are not universal, but are always linked to a given assemblage and the particularity of specific cases or singularities. In the *Abécédaire* interview, Deleuze also provides a more quotidian example. In the late 1970s, a taxi driver was successfully prosecuted in Paris for prohibiting passengers from smoking in his taxi. The pretext for the decision: a passenger in a taxi is like a tenant in an apartment. Tenants are allowed to smoke in their apartment under the right of use; taxis are like mobile apartments that passengers occupy as temporary tenants; therefore when someone takes a taxi they are considered to be a tenant and must be allowed to smoke. By the late 1980s, smoking was prohibited in every Parisian taxi, because taking a taxi was no longer equated with renting a private apartment, but was considered to be a public service, and it was legitimate to prohibit smoking in public areas. Such is the process of jurisprudence: it is not a question of universal rights; it is a question of a situation, and a situation that is evolving. "To act for freedom, to become a revolutionary," Deleuze says, "is to act on a plane of jurisprudence" (ABC G). This is the precise path Patton follows in his analyses of native title, and the implications of landmark decisions such as Mabo in Australia and Calder in Canada (DP 127–31). "We should not be too quick to discount the deterritorializing power of new rights," writes Patton, "Rights too are virtual singularities, the consequences of which are only actualized in specific court decisions, legislative enactments and the interactions between these" (DP 127).

And yet, despite his appeal to the process of jurisprudence, it remains noteworthy that Deleuze never offered a concomitant concept of judgment. Given his own theory of the concept, it would seemingly have been possible for Deleuze to retain the notion of judgment simply by altering the components of the concept, and Patton's analyses hint strongly at this possibility. Why, then, did Deleuze himself decline to take this path—a path that had been charted out by Arendt and Lyotard in their appeals to "reflective judgment"? This question perhaps takes us to the heart of the differences that separate Deleuze from his contemporaries. Jacques Derrida, for instance, once wrote that Lyotard "has launched a categorical challenge against our epoch . . . He is telling us: you have not had done with, you will *never* have done with judgment."[21] Intentional or not, it would not be difficult to read into this willful inversion of Artaud's phrase a direct challenge to Deleuze's thought as well. For his part, Derrida presented his own analysis (or deconstruction) of the theory of reflective judgment in his essay, "Force of Law: The 'Mystical Foundation of Authority.'"[22] The directions in which Deleuze and Derrida take their analysis of judgment are indicative of two general trajectories in contemporary French thought. In Kant, a reflective judgment is a judgment that is made in the absence of a rule—that is, without a determinate concept: the imagination becomes free at the same time that the understanding becomes indeterminate. But what is the condition that makes this "free play" of the faculties possible? It is possible, Kant says, only through the intervention of an *Idea* of reason. "Reflective judgment would not be able to trace its passages were it not inspired by the unity and systematicity that the suprasensible Ideas (of the Soul, the World, and God) 'project by analogy' into experience."[23] If determinate judgments operate under a rule or concept, reflective judgments rely on the directive role of Ideas and their "analogical" connections. One of the aims of the *Critique of Judgment* is to analyze the manner in which transcendent Ideas are presented in sensible nature through analogy (the sublime, symbolization, genius, and teleology).

But this is precisely the reason why Deleuze offers a strong critique of the "analogy of judgment" in *Difference and Repetition*. Since reflective judgments are grounded in Ideas (whereas determinate judgments are grounded in concepts), the difference between theories of reflective judgment can be evaluated in terms of the corresponding theory of Ideas. In Lyotard, for instance, Ideas are fundamentally "unpresentable." For Derrida, the judgments of the law operate on the basis of an infinite and transcendent "Idea of justice," in relation to which the condition of possibility for any decision or reflective judgment is its very impossibility. It is this element of transcendence, however, that Deleuze refuses; in the fourth chapter of *Difference and Repetition* ("Ideas and the Synthesis of Difference"), Deleuze attempts to develop a purely immanent and differential theory of Ideas (DR 168–221). It is this break with transcendence that allows Deleuze to effect a corresponding break with the doctrine of judgment. Immanent Ideas, in being actualized, are dramatized, but the agent of this dramatization is not judgment but rather *desire*. "Desire is productive," writes Patton, "in the sense that it produces real connections" (DP 70). Or as Deleuze and Guattari put it, simply: "Desire is the set of passive syntheses" (AO 26). In the realm of law or rights, Deleuze does not appeal to the transcendence of an infinite idea of justice; the movement of the immanent Idea is actualized in becomings and the production of affects—this is the process of desire itself. Immanent Ideas in Deleuze in a sense remain "regulative," but only in so far as they pose problems, they are "problematizing." Deleuzian Ideas map out directions and vectors of synthesis (connection, conjunction, disjunction) which are actualized, not by a conscious judgment, but through an unconscious process of desire (a "passive" synthesis). This is why Deleuze says the unconscious is not pre-given, but must itself be *constructed*: in the law, it is the process of desire that constructs the movement from case to case, the prolongation of singularities. This is also why Deleuze can say that the question of human rights "is not a question of justice, it is a question of jurisprudence"—that is, of desire (ABC G).

This is a good example of the "labor of the concept" one finds in Deleuze. It is a change in the concept of an "Idea" that allows Deleuze to "have done with judgment," and to replace the notion of a conscious reflective *judgment* (which is guided analogically by a transcendent Idea, in the Kantian sense) with an unconscious but productive process of *desire* (which effects the passive synthesis of an immanent Idea, in the Deleuzian sense). Kant himself presents the *Critique of Practical Reason* as an analysis of a "higher" faculty of desire that is determined by the representation of a pure form: namely, the pure form of a universal legislation (the moral law) (KCP 28–9). If a reflective judgment of beauty can be presented as a "symbol" of morality in the *Critique of Judgment*, it is because its object can be taken as the analogue of an Idea of reason (a white lily is the analogue of the Idea of innocence), and therefore can be said to "predispose" us to morality. Even in Kant, then, the function of the doctrine of reflective judgment is to point us in the direction of the "higher" faculty of desire, which is our ultimate destination as moral beings. Like Kant, Deleuze will insist on the fundamental role of desire in "practical" philosophy, but he will effect an inversion of Kant by synthesizing desire, not with a transcendent Idea of *universal* legislation, but with an immanent and differential Idea that operates through a prolongation of *singularities*. One of the aims of *Anti-Oedipus*, from this viewpoint, is to formulate criteria to distinguish between legitimate (immanent) and illegitimate (transcendent) syntheses of desire (AO 75), and in this sense, *Anti-Oedipus* can be read as Deleuze and Guattari's own version of the *Critique of Practical Reason*. The immanent relation Deleuze establishes between a differential Idea of jurisprudence and the process of desire can thus be contrasted with the aporetic relation Derrida establishes between an infinite Idea of justice and an impossible decision or judgment. For Deleuze, the Idea constitutes the condition of real experience, and not merely possible experience; for Derrida, the Idea constitutes the condition of possibility of justice only by constituting its impossibility at the same time. The differences between the two are profound. Patton's reflections seem to suggest that a concept of judgment might none the less be able to be reformulated in Deleuzian terms, but it would certainly have to take into account this conceptual movement of Deleuze's thought.

QUESTIONS OF THE IMAGINARY

There is a final non-Deleuzian term that Patton imports into his analyses of Deleuze, a notion that does not stem from the liberal tradition, but which can perhaps serve as a final example to demonstrate the scope of Patton's own project. This is the concept of the *social imaginary* (see DP 72, 79, 80, 81, 89, 119, 126). The notion of social imaginary has been utilized by various contemporary thinkers to refer to those imaginary constructions—such as political fables, collective illusions, legal fictions, metaphors, myths, and images—which, while often unconscious and unthought, are none the less constitutive of the embodied identity of individuals and collectivities.

Spinoza in particular emphasized the fundamental role of the imagination in social and political life. As Moira Gatens and Genevieve Lloyd have noted,

> Spinoza's account of the imagination is not a theory about a "faculty" but a theory about a permanent structure through which human beings are constituted as such . . . The strength of the social imaginary is that it constructs a logic of its own—a logic which cannot be shaken or undermined simply by demonstrating the falsity of its claims, its inherent contradictions or its aporias.[24]

Given Deleuze's indebtedness to Spinoza, one might expect to find in Deleuze's work a strongly developed theory of the imagination or the social imaginary. But in fact this is not the case. *Negotiations* includes an interview entitled "Doubts About the Imaginary," in which Deleuze asks the question: "Is 'the imaginary' a good concept?" and finds that it is "a rather indeterminate notion" (N 65–6).[25] Elsewhere, the reason Deleuze gives for having doubts about the concept is that the processes he analyzes throughout his work—becomings, de- and reterritorializations, flows, affects, and so on—belong to the domain of the *real* and not the imaginary (AO 30, 83, 304–7).

In several passages, however, Patton mounts a quiet challenge to Deleuze's doubts, intriguingly suggesting that these real processes none the less have an imaginary dimension. He (erroneously, in my view) equates Deleuze and Guattari's theory of the "socius" or the "body without organs" with a kind of social imaginary (DP 71–2; see 89: "the socius is the imaginary body of society as a whole"), and suggests that what Deleuze and Guattari define as "becomings," such as becoming-woman, can take place in relation to the images found in the social imaginary (DP 81). Patton does not develop these points in detail. Yet given his own emphasis on the role of concepts and the need for their consistency, his claims invite a number of interesting questions. How does Patton himself overcome Deleuze's "doubts about the imaginary"? How, within Deleuze's own work, do these "doubts about the imaginary" relate to Deleuze's own interest in the analysis of images (images of thought, the images of cinema, etc.)? How might Deleuze's thought relate to works such as Gatens and Lloyd's, *Collective Imaginings: Spinoza, Past and Present*, Michèle Le Dœuff's *The Philosophical Imaginary*, Benedict Anderson's *Imagined Communities*, and Cornelius Castoriadis's *The Imaginary Institution of Society*—all of which make use of the concept of the social imaginary in varying (and not necessarily commensurate) manners?[26] Most importantly, how could the concept of the social imaginary consistently connect with the revised liberal concepts Patton has introduced into his reading of Deleuze (normativity, critical freedom, judgment)?

These are large issues, and to my mind they remain genuinely open questions, prompted by Patton's admittedly passing appeal to the social imaginary. For my part, it seems there are at least three aspects of Deleuze's thought that might be relevant to an analysis of the social imaginary. Patton explicitly addresses the first aspect, which concerns the relation of images to embodiment (which admittedly constitutes a small part of the theory of the social imaginary). It has often been noted, for instance, that images of idealized bodies (in advertising and television, as well as less obvious imaginaries) can affect, even if unconsciously, my relation to my own body, to the point where I become willing to subject my body to the demands of the image (e.g., via dieting, bodybuilding, surgery, cosmetics, and so on). This can be seen as an instance of the more general problem of *desire*, which Deleuze and Guattari have identified as "*the* fundamental problem of political philosophy": "Why do people fight *for* their servitude as stubbornly as though it were their salvation?" (AO 29). In this case: Why would I voluntarily subject my body to an idealized image to which I can never conform, and whose real effect, in the end, is to produce in me the "sad" affects of inadequacy and resentment? Although this phenomenon is common, the mechanism by which it takes place is less so. How exactly does the social and public production of images affect the private production of my personal desires? Stated in broader terms: What is the relation between political economy (social production) and libidinal economy (production of desires)—in short, between Marx and Freud?

As Patton observes, this is a problem that is explicitly addressed in *Anti-Oedipus* (68–9). A common response is to say that I somehow "internalize" or "introject" the information and connotations contained in the images; and conversely, that the images themselves are nothing more than "projections" of the desires of those who consume them, to the point where the producers of the images can claim that they are simply "giving people what they want." But the entirety of *Anti-Oedipus* is directed against this thesis: "The Marx–Freud parallelism remains completely sterile and indifferent as long as it is expressed in terms that make them introjections or projections of each other without them ceasing to be utterly alien to each other" (AO 28–9). Deleuze and Guattari's claim is that the social production of images (or imaginaries) and the production of desire are *one and the same process*, and thus that there is no need to posit any mediating psychic operations such as introjection, projection, or sublimation to account for the power of images (or any aspect of social production). Patton analyzes this famous (and complex) thesis in his chapter on desire (esp. DP 68–70), which precludes any simple summary. But his analyses here link up with his earlier claims about the general orientation of Deleuze's philosophy: despite his doubts about the imaginary, Deleuze could no doubt acknowledge the existence of a social imaginary, but his primary concern would be with the underlying *processes* that account for both its production and its effects (in this case, image and embodiment). For Deleuze, as long as social production and desire are seen to be two different processes, the actual operation of social imaginaries would remain a mystery.

The second aspect concerns the question: *Why* is the imagination none the less not a prominent concept in Deleuze's philosophy? I would suggest that, in a sense, the imagination *does* play an important role in Deleuze's thought, but that it appears in a form that perhaps owes as much to Kant as it does Spinoza. In the schematism chapter of the *Critique of Pure Reason*, Kant makes a novel distinction between the *reproductive* imagination and what he calls the *productive* imagination.[27] The activity of the reproductive imagination is to reproduce a concept in images: a plate, the sun, or a wheel are images of a circle, just as a taut string or a figure drawn on a blackboard may be considered images of a line. But the activity of the productive imagination is quite different: here the imagination produces a "schema" that will allow me to construct something round or straight in experience that conforms to the concept. The schema is necessary, says Kant, because neither the concept nor the image tells me how to produce a circle or a line in intuition. The concept may allow me to *recognize* a straight line, but only a schema can tell me how it is possible to *construct* a straight line in experience. Kant thus argues that "the shortest path" should not be understood as a *predicate* of the concept "straight line," but rather as a *schema* for constructing a straight line ("follow the shortest path between two points . . ."). As a rule of production, a schema must therefore be seen as an aspect of lived experience, something that must be *lived* dynamically, as a dynamic process, albeit in conformity with a concept.

In *Difference and Repetition*, Deleuze reformulated Kant's theory of schemata into a complex theory of "spatio-temporal dynamisms" (manners of occupying space and time), to which Deleuze gave a much broader sphere of application.[28] In biology, for example, the concept of an animal can be determined by its genera and specific differences; but what *cannot* be derived from the concept is the way the animal inhabits space and time—its territory, the paths it follows, the times it takes these paths, the traces it leaves in its territory, the excitations to which it responds, the affects of which it is capable, and so on. This is why Deleuze exhibits such interest in the discipline of "ethology" (and frequently appeals to von Uexküll's ethological analysis of the tick), which attempts to classify animals in terms of their spatio-temporal dynamisms: that is, as blocs of space-time that are not only lived but also "embodied" (what can a body *do*?).[29] Similarly, ethnologists can be said to describe the spatio-temporal dynamisms of humans to the degree that they describe their manners and affects—dynamisms that will necessarily vary the generic concept "human."[30] Native Americans, for example, often died under colonialism because they could not survive the diseases such as influenza that were introduced by Europeans; they were not capable of the same affects. At a more abstract level, one of the aims of *Capitalism and Schizophrenia* was to develop a complex typology of such dynamisms that are actualized in concrete social formations, and enter into varying combinations and interactions; primitive societies, states, nomads, and capitalism all occupy space-time in different manners—forming territories (primitive), striating space (states), occupying a smooth space (nomads), deterritorializing and reterritorializing space (capitalism), etc. Deleuze explains, for instance, that war machines "have nothing to do with war but with a particular way of occupying, taking up, space-time, or *inventing new space-times*" (N 172; cf. 30). Moreover, the revolutionary potential he ascribes to war machines (or "metamorphosis machines," as Patton prefers to call them) is derived from their capacity to construct *new* spatio-temporal dynamisms. "People don't take enough account," Deleuze writes, pointing to one example among many, "of how the PLO [Palestine Liberation Organization] has had to *invent* a space-time in the Arab world" (N 172). If the imagination plays a role in Deleuze's political philosophy, in other words, it seems to appear primarily under this form of the productive imagination (production of spatio-temporal dynamisms), rather than that of the reproductive imagination (production of images), though the two roles of the imagination are obviously related. If this thesis is correct, then Deleuze's thought might open up a new way of thinking about the nature and functioning of social imaginaries as "spatio-temporal dynamisms."

The third aspect, finally, concerns the ways in which social imaginaries can be *transformed*. One (and only one) Deleuzian response to this question would address the political role of *art* (see DP 72–3). What we encounter in everyday life are images that have been reduced to the status of clichés—conventions and opinions that are in the service of forces other than themselves—and it is not difficult to produce works of art that merely reproduce such conventions (the "culture indus-try"). The political act of resistance against such ready-made images thus entails, in a sense, a struggle of image against image, and Deleuze repeatedly emphasizes the "battle against clichés" that artists must undergo *just to produce an image*—not a "just" image, as Godard says, but just an image, any image.

> To make an image from time to time: Can art, painting, and music have any other goal, even if the contents of the image are quite meager, quite mediocre? . . . It is extremely difficult to make a pure and unsullied image, one that is nothing but an image, by reaching the point where it emerges in all its singu-larity. (ECC 158)

At various points in his work, Deleuze discusses the political effect of such image-making or "fabulating," notably in his analyses of the status of third world politi-cal filmmaking in *The Time-Image* (TI 215–24), the role of the image in Samuel Beckett's work (ECC 152–74), and the battle against the cliché in Francis Bacon (FB 71–80). To be sure, the notion of the social imaginary encompasses far more than artistic or informational images, but the political function of art touches on the broad question of the enigmatic link between artistic creation and political change—both of which are instances of the Deleuzian problematic concerning the conditions for the production of the new.

There is much else to be said of Patton's book. Its strongest elements are certainly its readings of Deleuze's concepts and its overview of Deleuze's philosophical project, which will benefit all readers, beginning or advanced. But the more creative aspect of the book, as I see it, is this somewhat clandestine "Pattonian" project that is being worked out alongside the interpretation of Deleuze, of which we will no doubt see more in the future.[31] By forcing Deleuze's thought into a confrontation with the liberal tradition, Patton is able to show the way toward a transformation of such familiar concepts as normativity, freedom, and judgment. Moreover, Patton brings into his analyses other non-Deleuzian concepts—such as the "social imaginary"—which show that the scope of his own project goes beyond the Deleuze–liberalism confrontation. The next task, one might imagine, would be for Patton to show the consistency (endo- and exo-) of the conceptual apparatus he himself is in the process of developing. The outlines of such an apparatus, I have been suggesting, are already visible in *Deleuze and the Political*. Normativity is redefined in terms of the movement of processes of "deterritorialization"; these processes in turn consti-tute the condition for the exercise of "critical freedom": that is, the exercise of a judgment, outside of pre-existing rules, which would be productive of the new (the creation of rights, the creation and transformation of social imaginaries, the production of new space-times, etc.). *Deleuze and the Political*, then, does not simply present a reading of Deleuze, or even Deleuze's political philosophy. It is at the same time an elaboration of Patton's own project, one of whose aims is to challenge traditional liberal conceptions of politics. Patton accomplishes this not simply by "applying" Deleuze's thought to liberal concepts, but rather by forcing them into a becoming that itself produces something new, something irreducible to either Deleuze or liberalism, but which constitutes Patton's own singular contribution to contemporary political thought.

Notes

Essay 1: Plato
The Concept of the Simulacrum: Deleuze and the Overturning of Platonism

1. See, for instance, Pierre Klossowski, "Sacred and Mythical Origins of Certain Practices of the Women of Rome" [1968], in *Diana at her Bath* and *The Women of Rome*, trans. Sophie Hawkes (Boston: Eridanos, 1990), 132–8, as well as Jean-François Lyotard's commentaries (notably on the Augustine–Varro debate) in *Libidinal Economy* [1974], trans. Iain Hamilton Grant (Bloomington and Indianapolis: Indiana University Press, 1993), 66–76. In Klossowski, a *phantasm* is an obsessive but uncommunicable image produced within us by the unconscious forces of our impulsive life; a *simulacrum* is a reproduction of the phantasm that attempts to simulate (necessarily inadequately) this invisible agitation of the soul in a literary work, in a picture or a sculpture, or in a philosophical concept. Klossowski's concept of the simulacrum thus has very different components than those assigned to the concept by Deleuze.

2. See Jean Baudrillard, *Simulacra and Simulation*, trans. Sheila Faria Glaser (Ann Arbor: University of Michigan Press, 1994), esp. "The Precession of Simulacra," 1–42. For an analysis of Baudrillard's conception of simulacra, see Douglas Kellner, *Jean Baudrillard: From Marxism to Postmodernism and Beyond* (Stanford: Stanford University Press, 1989), 76–84.

3. *Logic of Sense* includes Deleuze's well-known article "Plato and the Simulacrum" as an appendix (LS 253–6). This article itself is a revised version of an earlier piece entitled "Renverser le platonisme," which first appeared in *Revue de métaphysique et de morale* 71/4 (Oct–Dec 1966), 426–38; an English translation by Heath Massey is included as an appendix to Leonard Lawlor, *Thinking Through French Philosophy: The Being of the Question* (Bloomington and Indianapolis: Indiana University Press, 2003), 163–77, under the title "Reversing Platonism (Simulacra)."

4. Nietzsche, *Grossoktavausgabe* (Leipzig, 1905 ff.), Vol. 9, 190, as cited in Martin Heidegger, *Nietzsche*, Vol. I: *The Will to Power as Art* (London: Routledge & Kegan Paul, 1981), 154.

5. Alfred North Whitehead, *Process and Reality*, ed. David Ray Griffin and Donald W. Sherburne (New York: Free Press, 1978), 29: "The safest general characterization of the European philosophical tradition is that it consists of a series of footnotes to Plato."

6. Heidegger, *Nietzsche*, Vol. I: *The Will to Power as Art*, 151–2. Heidegger analyzes Nietzsche's anti-Platonism in terms of the "raging discordance" between truth and art (see 151–220).

7. Friedrich Nietzsche, *Twilight of the Idols*, trans. Walter Kaufmann, in *The Portable Nietzsche* (New York: Viking, 1954), 485–6.

8. See, above all, Jean-Pierre Vernant, *The Origins of Greek Thought* (Ithaca, NY: Cornell University Press, 1982), and Marcel Detienne, *The Masters of Truth in Archaic Greece*, trans. Janet Lloyd (New York: Zone, 1999), esp. Chapter 5, "The Process of Secularization" (in French, *laïcisation*), both of whom link the advent of "rational" thought to the structure of the Greek *polis*, and explore the complex relations of philosophy to its precursors. Pierre Vidal-Naquet provides a helpful overview of the debates in "Greek Rationality and the City," in *The Black Hunter: Forms of Thought and Forms of Society in the Greek World*, trans. Andrew Szegedy-Maszak (Baltimore: Johns Hopkins University Press, 1986), 249–62.

9. WP 86–8. On the distinction between the State and the City as social formations, see TP 432–3.

10. On the spatial organization of the Greek *polis*, see Jean-Pierre Vernant, *Myth and Thought Among the Greeks* (London: Routledge & Kegan Paul, 1983), Part 3, esp. Chapter 8, "Space and Political Organization in Ancient Greece," 212–34. On relations of rivalry, see Jean-Pierre Vernant, "City-State Warfare," in *Myth and Society in Ancient Greece* (New York: Zone, 1990), esp. 29, 41–2.

11. This is the theme of Michel Foucault's *History of Sexuality*, Vol. 2: *The Use of Pleasure*, trans. Robert Hurley (New York: Vintage, 1985). Foucault argues that, within this agonistic field of power relations, the Greeks invented a new and specific form of power relation which he termed "subjectivation" (the relation of oneself to oneself), whose historical variations constituted the object of his research in last two volumes of *The History of Sexuality*, and of which sexuality or erotics constituted only a part.

12. We are here drawing on the political theory that Deleuze and Guattari develop in the two volumes of *Capitalism and Schizophrenia*, in which they sketch out a typology of different social formations ("primitive" societies, cities, states, capitalism, war machines) and the correlative "images of thought" they imply. See AO 139–271 and TP 351–473.

13. NP 5–6, 107. See also Alexandre Kojève, "Tyranny and Wisdom," in Leo Strauss, *On Tyranny* (New York: Free Press, 1963), 156. Nietzsche adds that, although the early philosophers could not help but adopt the mask of the wise man or priest, this strategy proved decisive for philosophy, since the philosopher increasingly came to adopt that mask as his own.

14. WP 9, translation modified. This concept of the "friend" is explored by Deleuze and Guattari in the introduction to *What is Philosophy?* (WP 2–6). See also N 162–3, F 100–3, and PV 16.

15. The important notion of "conceptual personae" is developed by Deleuze and Guattari in Chapter 3 of *What is Philosophy?* (WP 61–83). See also Vernant, *Origins*, 102–18.

16. Jean-Pierre Faye, *La Raison narrative* (Paris: Balland, 1990), 15–18: "It took a century for the word 'philosopher,' no doubt invented by Heraclitus of Ephesus, to find its correlate in the word 'philosophy,' no doubt invented by Plato the Athenian. The first philosophers were foreigners, but philosophy is Greek."

17. The word "claimant" translates the French *prétendant*, which can also mean "pretender," "suitor," or even "candidate." Its translation as "claimant" emphasizes the relation of the *prétendant* to its *prétention* ("claim"), but loses the connotations associated with the words "pretender" and "pretentious," which are also present in the French.

18. Aristotle, *Prior Analytics*, I, 31 and *Posterior Analytics*, II, 5 and 13. See Aristotle, *The Basic Works of Aristotle*, ed. Richard McKeon (New York: Random House, 1941), 92–3, 163–4, 175–9, as well as Deleuze's comments in LS 254 and DR 59–60.

19. Plato, *Statesman*, 303 d–e. On the distinction between *antiphasis* and *amphisbetesis*, see DR 60 and LS 293.

20. DR 61–2. On the relation between Platonism and archaic religion, see Mircea Eliade, *The Myth of the Eternal Return* (Princeton: Princeton University Press, 1954). Eliade characterizes archaic religion by the repetition of mythic archetypes and the symbolism of

the Center, and notes its explicit parallels with Platonism: "It could be said that this 'primitive' ontology has a Platonic structure; and in that case Plato could be regarded as the outstanding philosopher of 'primitive mentality,' that is, as the thinker who succeeded in giving philosophic currency to the modes of life and behavior of archaic humanity" (34). Deleuze is none the less critical of aspects of Eliade's approach to religion: "The idea that primitive societies are without history, dominated by archetypes and their repetition, is particularly weak and inadequate. It was not conceived by ethnologists, but by ideologues attached to a tragic Judeo-Christian consciousness that they wished to credit with the 'invention' of history" (AO 150, translation modified).

21. Deleuze and Guattari argue that philosophy is a discipline that consists in the creation of concepts, but Plato's concept of the Idea is an illuminating example of the complexity of this claim. Plato says that one must contemplate the Ideas, but *it was first of all necessary for him to create the concept of the Idea*. In this sense, writes Deleuze, Plato teaches the opposite of what he actually does:

> Plato creates the concept of the Ideas, but he needs to posit them as representing the uncreated that precedes them. He places time in the concept, but this time must be the Anterior. He constructs the concept, but as testifying to the preexistence of an objectity, under the form of a difference in time capable of measuring the distance or proximity of the possible constructor. This is because, in Platonic plane, truth is posited as presupposed, as already there. (WP 29)

22. See DR 85: "Beyond the lover and beyond the mother, coexistent with the one and contemporary with the other, lies the never-lived reality of the Virgin."

23. For Deleuze's interpretation of the Neo-Platonic heritage, see "Zones of Immanence," in TRM 261–4, and "Immanence and the Historical Components of Expression," in EPS 169–86.

24. In Augustine, for example, "absolute" dissimulation implies nothingness; thus the last of beings, if it is not nothingness, is at least an illusory simulacrum. See Étienne Gilson, *Introduction à l'étude de Saint-Augustin* (Paris: Vrin, 1929), 268.

25. On height, depth, and surface as orientations of thought, see LS, Series 18, "Of the Images of Philosophers," 127–33.

26. Plato, *Sophist*, 268b.

27. Plato, *Sophist*, 236c: "These then are two sorts of image-making [*eidolopoïke*]—the art of making likenesses [*eikones*], and phantastic or the art of making appearances [*phantasmata*]." See also *Sophist*, 264c–268d; and *Republic*, Book 10, 601d ff.

28. LS 296. Jean-Pierre Vernant has questioned the importance Deleuze ascribes to this distinction in "The Birth of Images," in *Mortals and Immortals: Collected Essays*, ed. Froma I. Zeitlin (Princeton: Princeton University Press, 1991), 164–85, esp. 169. But he none the less supports the thrust of Deleuze's reading when he says that the problem of the *Sophist* is "to articulate what an image is, not in its seeming but in its being, to speak not of the seeming of appearance but of *the essence of seeming, the being of semblance*" (182).

29. Michel Foucault, "Theatrum Philosophicum," in *Language, Counter-Memory, Practice* (Ithaca, NY: Cornell University Press, 1977), 167. Deleuze employs the Homeric image in LS 254.

30. DR 128. For a reading of Deleuze's work along naturalistic lines, see Alberto Gualandi, *Deleuze* (Paris: Les Belles Lettres, 1998). Gualandi argues that, for Deleuze, the task of a true philosophy of Nature would be "to eliminate any trace of transcendence, and at the same time, to give back to Nature its authentic depth, the Becoming and the virtualities that are inherent in it, the Being that is immanent to it" (36). For Nietzsche, this naturalistic project found its precursor in Heraclitus; for Deleuze, its great ancient representative was Lucretius, whose naturalism Deleuze analyzes in his article "Lucretius and the Simulacrum" (LS 266–79):

To distinguish in men what amounts to myth and what amounts to Nature, and in Nature itself, to distinguish what is truly infinite from what is not—such is the practical and speculative object of Naturalism. The first philosopher is a naturalist: he speaks about nature, rather than speaking about the gods. His condition is that his discourse shall not introduce into philosophy *new myths* that would deprive Nature of all its positivity. (LS 278)

The latter phrase is a reference to Plato.

31. On the use of the term "representation," see Michel Foucault, *The Order of Things* (New York: Vintage, 1973), which identifies a "classic" world of representation in the seventeenth century and outlines its limitations. Deleuze's characterization of Platonism bears certain affinities with this statement of Richard Rorty's: "Philosophy's central concern is to be a general theory of representation, a theory which will divide culture up into areas which will represent reality well, those which represent it less well, and those which do not represent it at all (despite their pretense to do so)." Richard Rorty, *Philosophy and the Mirror of Nature* (Princeton: Princeton University Press, 1979), 3.

32. *Philebus* 24d. On this theme, see Deleuze, LS, Series 1, "On Pure Becoming," 1–3.

33. Stanley Rosen has criticized Deleuze's reading of the *Sophist*, noting that "an image that does not resemble X cannot be an image of X." But Rosen here collapses Deleuze's distinction: an "image" can be either a *resemblance* (a true copy or icon that participates internally in the model) or a mere *semblance* (a false simulacrum or phantasy that feigns a merely external reflection). Though their usages overlap, these English terms none the less indicate the essential distinction between an icon and a simulacrum that Deleuze is attempting to establish. The *Oxford English Dictionary* (OED) defines resemblance as "the quality of being like or similar . . . A likeness, image, representation, or reproduction of some person or thing" (several of the historical examples in the OED refer, significantly, to the prelapsarian state of creation). Semblance, on the contrary, is defined as "the fact of appearing to view . . . An appearance or outward seeming *of* something which is not actually there or of which the reality is different from its appearance." Rosen's comment, it seems, would tend to collapse such terms as "image," "resemblance," "semblance," and even "mimesis" into mere synonymy. See Stanley Rosen, *Plato's Sophist: The Drama of Original and Image* (New Haven and London: Yale University Press, 1983), 172–3.

34. Jacques Derrida, in his essay "Plato's Pharmacy," in *Dissemination* (Chicago: University of Chicago Press, 1981), 61–171, locates a similar trinity at the heart of Platonism: the father of *logos*, *logos* itself, writing. Much of Derrida's early work focused on the Platonic conception of "writing" for precisely this reason: *writing is a simulacrum*, a false claimant in that it tries to capture the *logos* through violence and trickery without going through the father. In LS 297, Deleuze finds the same figure in the *Statesman*: the Good as the father of the law, the law itself, constitutions. Good constitutions are copies, but they become simulacra the moment they violate or usurp the law by evading the Good.

35. The simulacrum, in short, is a *differential system*, "a system where difference is related to difference *through* difference itself" (DR 277). It is precisely such systems that Deleuze analyzes in *Difference and Repetition*.

36. Augustine, *De Doctrina Christiana* (Indianapolis: Bobbs-Merrill, 1978), esp. 88–9.

37. Augustine, *Concerning the City of God Against the Pagans*, trans. Henry Bettenson (New York: Penguin, 1984), esp. Book VI. Klossowski's text *Diana at Her Bath* is explicitly presented as a kind of polytheistic inversion of Augustine's monotheistic *The City of God*; see his commentaries in *Diana at Her Bath and The Women of Rome*, 82–4, 131–8.

38. On all these themes, see Foucault's important essay on Klossowski, "The Prose of Acteon," trans. Robert Hurley, in Michel Foucault, *Essential Works of Foucault: 1954–1984*, Vol. 2:

Aesthetics, Method, and Epistemology, ed. James D. Faubion (New York: New Press, 1988), 123–35.

39. DR 66. See also DR 301: "The Same, forever decentered, effectively turns around difference only once difference, having assumed the whole of Being, applies only to simulacra which have assumed the whole of Being."

40. For a discussion of Roussel's work, see Michel Foucault, *Death and the Labyrinth: The World of Raymond Roussel* (Garden City, NY: Doubleday, 1986), esp. Chapter 2. For Deleuze's analyses, see DR 22, 121 and LS 39, 85. Roussel's language rests not simply on the combinatorial possibilities of language—the fact that language has fewer terms of designation than things to designate, but none the less can extract an immense wealth from this poverty—but more precisely on the possibility of saying two things with the same word, inscribing a maximum of difference within the repetition of the same word.

41. See DR 69, 55–6:

> It is not enough to multiply perspectives in order to establish perspectivism. To every perspective or point of view there must correspond an autonomous work with its own self-sufficient sense . . . Representation has only a single center, a unique and receding perspective, and consequently a false depth . . . Movement for its part implies a plurality of centers, a superposition of perspectives, a tangle of points of view, a coexistence of moments which essentially distort representation: paintings or sculptures are already such "distorters," forcing us to create movement.

42. Plato, *Republic,* X, 601d–608b. The notion of *mimesis* appears not to have been used in discussions of art prior to the fifth century. Until that time, the art of the poet had been regarded as one of "deception" (*apate*), and it is precisely this form of image-making that Plato aims to send into exile. See Vernant, "The Birth of Images," in *Mortals and Immortals,* 165, and note 2.

43. LS 265. On these points, see Martin Heidegger, *Nietzsche,* Vol. 1: *The Will to Power as Art,* 162–99.

44. Plato, *Republic,* VII, 523b ff.

45. For an analysis of Warhol's work in this context, see Paul Patton, "Anti-Platonism and Art," in *Gilles Deleuze and the Theater of Philosophy,* ed. Constantin V. Boundas and Dorothea Olkowski (New York: Routledge, 1994), 141–56.

46. Friedrich Nietzsche, *Beyond Good and Evil,* §289, in *Basic Writings of Nietzsche,* trans. Walter Kaufmann (New York: Modern Library, 1968), 414.

47. What disengages the false from the model of truth (as the universal and the necessary—what is true "at all times and in all places") is ultimately the form of time (see 12 Jun 1984). The phrase "power of the false" seems to be Deleuze's coinage, not Nietzsche's.

48. See NP 103:

> The activity of life is like a power of falsehood: duping, dissimulating, dazzling, and seducing. But, in order to be brought into effect, this power of the false must be selected, redoubled or repeated, and thus elevated to a higher power . . . It is *art* that invents the lies that elevate the false to this higher affirmative power, that turns the will to deceive into something that is affirmed in the power of the false. *Appearance,* for the artist, no longer signifies the negation of the real in this world, but this kind of selection, this correction, this redoubling, this affirmation. Then truth perhaps takes on a new signification. Truth is appearance. Truth signifies the effectuation of power, raising it to the highest power. In Nietzsche, "we the artists" = "we the seekers after knowledge or truth." (translation modified)

See also Nietzsche, *Twilight of the Idols,* "Reason in Philosophy," 6:

> For "appearance" in this case [the artist] means reality *once more*, only by way of selection, reinforcement, and correction. The tragic artist is no pessimist: he is precisely the one who says Yes to everything questionable, even to the terrible—he is *Dionysian*. (484)

49. See DR 319 n30. In the *Theaetetus*, for example, Socrates speaks of "two patterns eternally set before humanity, the one blessed and divine, the other godless and wretched" (176e). Similarly, the *Timaeus* (27d–28d) sets before the demiurge two possible models for the creation of the world, and before humanity two possible models for science ("Which of the patterns had the artificer in view when he created the world—the pattern of that which is unchangeable, or of that which is created?"). In TP 361–74, Deleuze analyses various "minor" sciences (Archimedean geometry, the physics of the atomists, the differential calculus, etc.) that were based on such a model of becoming, and replaced the hylomorphic model (the static relation of form–matter), which searches for laws by extracting constants, with a hydraulic model (the dynamic relation of material–forces), which placed the variables themselves in a state of continuous variation.

50. Plato, *Parmenides*, 130d.

51. See DR 127: "Insinuated throughout the Platonic cosmos, difference resists it yoke . . . It is as though there were a strange *double* which dogs Socrates' footsteps and haunts even Plato's style, inserting itself into the repetitions and variations of that style." On the effect that this "double" has on Plato's style, see DR 319 n29: "Plato's arguments are marked by stylistic reprisals and repetitions which testify to a meticulous attention to detail, as though there were an effort to 'correct' a theme in order to defend it against a neighboring, but dissimilar, theme that is 'insinuating' itself into the first."

52. See Deleuze's article "The Method of Dramatization," in DI 94–116, esp. 94–5. See also DR 64: "Being (what Plato calls the Idea) 'corresponds' to the essence of the problem or the question as such. It is as though there were an 'opening,' a 'gap,' an ontological 'fold' which relates being and the question to one another."

53. For an analysis of the role of the "What is . . .?" question in Plato, see Richard Robinson, *Plato's Earlier Dialectic*, 2nd edn. (Oxford: Clarendon, 1953), esp. Chapter 5, "Socratic Definition," 49–60.

54. Contemporary "antifoundationalism" implies, at the very least, the rejection of this Platonic form of questioning, of this search for a foundational essence.

> I cannot characterize my standpoint better [wrote Wittgenstein] than to say it is opposed to that which Socrates represents in the Platonic dialogues. For if asked what knowledge is (*Theatatus* 146a) I would list examples of knowledge, and add the words "and the like" . . . whereas when Socrates asks the question "What is knowledge?" he does not even regard it as a *preliminary* answer to enumerate cases of knowledge. (Ludwig Wittgenstein, manuscript 302, ¶14, as quoted in Garth Hallett, A *Commentary to Wittgenstein's "Philosophical Investigations"* (Ithaca, NY: Cornell University Press, 1977), 33–4.

In general, however, Deleuze was hesitant about Wittgenstein's work, which he thought had had a pernicious effect on Anglo-American philosophy; see ABC W.

55. Nietzsche, *The Will to Power*, §556, 301: "The question 'What is that?' is an imposition of meaning from some other viewpoint. 'Essence,' the 'essential nature,' is something perspectival and already presupposes a multiplicity. At the bottom of it there always lies 'What is that for *me*' (for us, for all that lives, etc.)."

56. See Martin Heidegger, *The Basic Problems of Phenomenology*, trans. Albert Hofstadter (Bloomington and Indianapolis: Indiana University Press, 1988), 119–20. On all these points, see DI 94–5, 105–7; DR 188; NP 75–8.

57. On the relation between such "minor" questions and problematics, see Gottfried Wilhelm

Leibniz, *New Essays on Human Understanding*, ed. and trans. Peter Remnant and Jonathan Bennett (Cambridge: Cambridge University Press, 1981), 368:

> It should be borne in mind that sometimes it is a matter of finding a truth or falsity of a given proposition, which is the same as answering the "whether" question, i.e., whether it is or isn't so; while sometimes the question to be answered is (other things being equal) more difficult—when it is asked, for instance "By whom and how," in which case something more has to be added. It is only questions like this, which leave part of the proposition blank, that the mathematicians call "problems."

58. See DR 16–19 (on Freud), and DR 87–8, 141–2 (on Plato).
59. On the theme of series in Proust, see PS 67–83. One of the essential critiques that Deleuze and Guattari level against psychoanalysis is that it reduces the unconscious to the familial coordinates of the primal scene or the Oedipal triangle ("daddy–mommy–me"). See, for instance, AO 97, 91:

> The father, mother, and the self are directly coupled to the elements of the political and historical situation: the soldier, the cop, the occupier, the collaborator, the radical, the resister, the boss, the boss's wife . . . The family is by nature eccentric, decentered . . . There is always an uncle from America; a brother who went bad; an aunt who took off with a military man . . . The father and mother exist only as fragments . . . inductors or stimuli of varying, vague import that trigger processes of an entirely different nature.

60. Jacques Lacan develops this theme most famously in his "Seminar on *The Purloined Letter*," trans. Jeffrey Mehlman, *Yale French Studies* 48 (1972), 55: "What is hidden is never but what is *missing from its place*, as the call slip puts it when speaking of a volume lost in the library. And even if the book be on an adjacent shelf or in the next slot, it would be hidden there, however visibly it may appear." See also LS 40–1, which cites a parallel text of Lewis Carroll's.
61. PS 75. Chapter 6 of this book ("Series and Group," 67–83) explores the mechanisms of difference and repetition exemplified in Proust's serial conception of love: difference as the law or essence of the series; the repetition of the terms as variation and displacement. In the conclusion of Part I ("The Image of Thought," 94–102), Deleuze analyzes the "anti-Greek" image of thought found in Proust, implicitly aligning it with Nietzsche's theme of an inverted Platonism.
62. See DR 54:

> Nietzsche reproaches all those selection procedures based upon the opposition or conflict with working to the advantage of the average forms and operating to the benefit of the "large number." Eternal return alone effects the true selection, because it eliminates the average forms and uncovers "the superior form of everything that is."

63. ECC 127. For a discussion of the criteria of selection in an immanent ethics, see Essay 4 in this volume.
64. DR 117; see also LS 261–2. The two formulas are derived from Claude Lévi-Strauss, *Totemism*, trans. Rodney Needham (Boston: Beacon, 1962), 77. Arthur Danto makes a similar point in *The Philosophical Disenfranchisement of Art* (New York: Columbia University Press, 1986), 171:

> The paradigm of a philosophical difference is between two worlds, one of which is sheer illusion, as the Indians believed this one is, and the other of which is real in the way we believe this very world is. Descartes' problem of distinguishing waking experience from dream experience is a limited variation of the same question . . . A world of sheer determinism might be imagined indistinguishable from one in which everything happens

by accident. A world in which God exists could never be told apart from one in which God didn't . . . Carnap would have said that such a choice is meaningless precisely because no observation(s) could be summoned to effect a discrimination . . . Whatever the case, it is plain that philosophical differences are external to the worlds they discriminate.

65. DR ix (translation modified). See also DR 301: "The history of the long error is the history of representation, the history of icons."

66. See Gilles Deleuze, "Lettre-préface," in Jean-Clet Martin, *Variations: The Philosophy of Gilles Deleuze*, trans. Constantin V. Boundas and Susan Dyrkton (Edinburgh: Edinburgh University Press, 2010), 8.

67. See LS 129: "Nietzsche takes little interest in what happened after Plato, maintaining that it was necessarily the continuation of a long decadence."

Essay 2: Univocity
The Doctrine of Univocity: Deleuze's Ontology of Immanence

1. See FB 11 and 25 Nov 1980.

2. DR 39 (35–42 contains Deleuze's "song" of univocity). See also LS 177–80.

3. Deleuze's interpretation of Duns Scotus relies primarily on Étienne Gilson's definitive *Jean Duns Scot: Introduction à ses positions fondamentales* (Paris: J. Vrin, 1952). In English, see Gilson's historical discussions in *History of Christian Philosophy in the Middle Ages* (London: Sheed & Ward, 1955), 454–71, and *Being and Some Philosophers* (Toronto: Pontifical Institute of Mediaeval Studies, 1952), 84–95.

4. Deleuze almost certainly developed the notion of univocity while researching his "secondary" thesis on Spinoza for the Doctorat d'État. François Dosse, however, notes that Deleuze had largely completed his thesis on Spinoza in the late 1950s, before the publication of *Nietzsche and Philosophy* in 1962, even though the thesis was not published until 1968. See his *Gilles Deleuze and Félix Guattari: Intersecting Lives*, trans. Deborah Glassman (New York: Columbia University Press, 2010), 118, 143.

5. 4 Jan 1974. This seminar includes Deleuze's discussion of the Scholastic approaches to the concept of Being.

6. Deleuze's 1956 essay, "Bergson's Conception of Difference," trans. Melissa McMahon, in John Mullarky, ed., *The New Bergson* (Manchester: Manchester University Press, 1999) is a reading of Bergson through the prism of Heidegger's problematic of ontological difference. See Constantin V. Boundas's analyses in "Deleuze-Bergsonian Ontology of the Virtual," in *Deleuze: A Critical Reader*, ed. Paul Patton (London: Basil Blackwell, 1996), 81–106, which makes the comparison. Miguel de Beistegui's *Truth and Genesis: Philosophy as Differential Ontology* (Bloomington and Indianapolis: Indiana University Press, 2004) is a superb analysis of the Heidegger–Deleuze relation.

7. DR 66. In the preface to *Difference and Repetition*, Deleuze cites "Heidegger's ever more pronounced orientation toward a philosophy of ontological Difference" (DR ix) as one of the factors that led him to write the book. The only direct confrontation, however, is the long footnote in Chapter 1 (DR 64–6), which concerns the notion of difference in Heidegger's thought. The note was apparently inserted at the insistence of Deleuze's thesis advisors, who no doubt recognized the subterranean battle lines being drawn in the book.

8. Michel Foucault, "Theatrum Philosophicum," in *Language, Counter-Memory, Practice: Selected Essays and Interviews*, ed. Donald F. Bouchard, trans. Donald F. Bouchard and Sherry Simon (Ithaca, NY: Cornell University Press, 1977), 172.

9. SPP 63. To my knowledge, Deleuze is the only commentator to have drawn this link between Duns Scotus and Spinoza on the question of univocity.

10. See Reiner Schürmann, *Meister Eckhart: Mystic and Philosopher* (Bloomington: Indiana University Press, 1978), 172–92. While recognizing Eckhart's affinities with immanence (see 176, 252 n56) and with an immanent causality (177), Schürmann none the less attempts to provide a qualified analogical interpretation of his teachings (179).

11. For Thomas Aquinas's formulations of analogy, see *Summa Theologica* 1.13.5. The way of affirmation found its greatest literary expression in Dante's *Divine Comedy*, and perhaps its most important modern proponent in Charles Williams. See, most notably, Charles Williams, *The Figure of Beatrice: A Study in Dante* (London: Faber & Faber, 1943).

12. See Spinoza, *Short Treatise*, in *The Collected Works of Spinoza*, ed. Edwin Curley (Princeton: Princeton University Press, 1985), 65–90, as well as Deleuze's commentary in SPP 104–5 and EPS 49–51, 55–61, 70–7.

13. See Spinoza, *Theological-Political Treatise*, trans. Samuel Shirley (Leiden: E. J. Brill, 1984), particularly Chapter 2.

14. See Harry Austryn Wolfson, *From Philo to Spinoza: Two Studies in Religious Philosophy* (New York: Behrman House, 1977).

15. On the distinction between these three types of causality, see 22 Mar 1983.

16. In his *Deleuze: The Clamor of Being*, trans. Louise Burchill (Minneapolis: University of Minnesota Press, 2000), Alain Badiou rightly notes the influence of Heidegger on Deleuze, but wrongly presents Deleuze's "univocal ontology" as if it were a Neo-Platonic "philosophy of the One." For instance, when Badiou writes that, in Deleuze, "the paradoxical or super-eminent One engenders, in an immanent manner, a procession of beings, whose univocal sense it distributes" (26), he is giving a description of an *emanative* ontology, not a univocal one. In general, like many medievals, Badiou combines transitive, emanative, and immanent elements in his treatment of univocity, thereby seeming to confirm Deleuze's adage, cited above, that univocity is "the strangest thought, the most difficult to think."

17. Martin Heidegger, *On Time and Being*, trans. Joan Stambaugh (New York: Harper & Row, 1972).

18. See in particular Jacques Derrida, *On the Name*, trans. Thomas Dutoit (Stanford: Stanford University Press, 1995). John D. Caputo has analyzed Derrida's theological appropriations in *The Prayers and Tears of Jacques Derrida* (Bloomington: Indiana University Press, 1997).

19. TRM 261. The term "crowned anarchy" is taken from what Deleuze considers to be Antonin Artaud's "masterpiece" (AO 211), his novelized biography of the third-century Roman emperor, *Heliogabalus, or The Crowned Anarchist*, trans. Alexis Lykiard (Clerkenwell: Solar, 2004).

20. Our analysis follows closely Deleuze's presentation of the univocity of modality in SPP, especially 93–4 (entry on the "Necessary") and 69–71 (entry on "Freedom").

21. Spinoza, *Ethics*, I, 17, scholia ("Neither intellect nor will pertain to God's nature") and I, 32, corollary 1 ("God does not produce any effect by freedom of the will").

22. For the first argument, see Spinoza, *Ethics*, I, 33, scholia 2: "If God had decreed, concerning Nature and its order, something other than what he did decree, that is, had willed and conceived something else concerning Nature, he would necessarily have had an intellect other than he now has, and a will other than he now has." For the second argument, see *Ethics*, I, appendix: "If God acts for the sake of an end, he necessarily wants something he lacks."

23. On the contrast that Spinoza establishes between abstractions and common notions, see SPP 44–8, 54–8.

24. SPP 70. Spinoza none the less distinguishes between the "idea of God" and his "infinite understanding" or infinite intellect; see SPP 80.

25. Deleuze discusses these illusions in SPP 20, 60. For the illusion of final causes, see *Ethics*, I, appendix ('all final causes are nothing but human fictions"); for the illusion of free will, see *Ethics*, V, preface ("the forces of the body cannot in any way be determined by those of the

mind"), as well as III, 2, scholia ("no one has yet determined what a body can do"); for the theological illusion, see *Ethics*, I, appendix ("they say that God has made all things for man, and man that he might worship God").

26. Spinoza, *Ethics*, IV, def. 3 and 4. See also I, 33, scholia: "A thing is called contingent only because of a defect in our knowledge."

27. Spinoza, *Ethics*, I, appendix; II, 35, scholia; V, preface. See also III, 2, scholia ("Men believe themselves free because they are conscious of their own actions, and ignorant of the causes by which they are determined") and I, 32 ("The will cannot be called a free cause").

28. The formation of adequate idea through the "common notions" is one of the primary foci of Deleuze's analysis of Spinoza. See EPS 255–88, and the summary provided in SPP 54–8.

29. Spinoza, Letter 58, to G. H. Schuller, in *Spinoza: Complete Works*, trans. Samuel Shirley (Indianapolis: Hackett, 2002), 908–9.

30. See Deleuze's essay on Klossowski in LS, where he contrasts the "order of God" with the "order of the Anti-Christ" (LS 292, 294).

31. See DR 40–1. Whitehead, in *Process and Reality*, ed. David Ray Griffin and Donald W. Sherburne (New York: Free Press, 1978), proposes a similar modification of Spinoza: "Spinoza bases his philosophy upon the monistic substance, of which the actual occasions are inferior modes. The philosophy of organism inverts this point of view" (81). Similarly, if Deleuze is Leibnizian, it is only by eliminating the idea of a God who chooses the "best" of all possible worlds, with its pre-established harmony; in Deleuze, incompossibilities and dissonances belong to one and the same world, the only world, our world.

32. See Deleuze's interview with Arnaud Villani in the latter's *La Guêpe et l'orchidée: Essai sur Gilles Deleuze* (Paris: Belin, 1999), 130: "I feel myself to be a pure metaphysician . . . Bergson says that modern science hasn't found its metaphysics, the metaphysics it would need. It is this metaphysics that interests me."

33. See Deleuze, "Letter Preface," in Jean-Clet Martin, *Variations: The Philosophy of Gilles Deleuze*, trans. Constantin V. Boundas and Susan Dyrkton (Edinburgh: Edinburgh University Press, 2010), 8: "I believe in philosophy as system. For me, the system must not only be in perpetual heterogeneity, it must be a *heterogenesis*—something which, it seems to me, has never been attempted."

34. See Aristotle, *Categories*, 4, 1b25 (list of the categories) and *Physics*, Book 1, Chapter 2, 185a21 ("'Is' is used in several senses") in *The Basic Works of Aristotle*, ed. Richard McKeon (New York: Random House, 1941), 8, 220.

35. Martin Heidegger, *Hegel's Phenomenology of Spirit*, trans. Parvis Emad and Kenneth Maly (Bloomington: Indiana University Press, 1988), 102; cf. 117.

36. This diagram of Porphyry's tree is adapted from E. M. Curley, *Spinoza's Metaphysics: An Essay in Interpretation* (Cambridge, MA: Harvard University Press, 1969), 29.

37. See Aristotle, *Metaphysics*, III, 3, 998b22–7, in *The Basic Works of Aristotle*, 723:

> It is not possible that either unity or being should be a single genus of things; for the differentiae of any genus must each of them both have being and be one, but it is not possible for the genus taken apart from its species (any more than for the species of the genus) to be predicated of its proper differentiae; so that *if unity or being is a genus, no differentia will either have being or be one.*

38. See Aristotle, *Metaphysics*, IV, 2, 1003a33–4, in *The Basic Works of Aristotle*, 732 (translation modified): "Being is said in several senses, but always with reference to a single term (*pros hen*)."

39. On the relation between "common sense" and "good sense," see DR 269 and LS 75–9.

40. For Deleuze's summary of his criticisms of Aristotle, see DR 269–70.

41. The interpretation of Spinoza's "degree of power" in terms of the concept of intensity is another Deleuzian innovation. In *Difference and Repetition*, however, the concept of

intensity is no longer linked to that of substance, as in Spinoza, but takes on an autonomous status, defined formally (following Kant) as a difference that divides into itself, an *individuating difference*, in relation to a limit where intensity = 0.

42. See Eric Alliez, *La Signature du monde* (Paris: Cerf, 1993), Chapter 3, "Onto-éthologiques," 67–104.

43. DR 145. One could conserve the notion of a "category" in a univocal ontology, as do Peirce and Whitehead (see DR 284–5), on the condition of defining categories in a new manner, as differential concepts or Ideas. In an interview in Arnaud Villani, *La Guêpe et l'orchidée* (Paris: Belin, 1999), Deleuze comments:

> The conclusion to *A Thousand Plateaus* is, in my mind, a table of categories (but incomplete, insufficient). Not in the manner of Kant [or Aristotle], but in the manner of Whitehead [or Peirce]. Category thus takes in a new meaning, a very special one. I would like to work on this point. (130)

François Dosse, in *Gilles Deleuze and Félix Guattari: Intersecting Lives*, trans. Deborah Glassman (New York: Columbia University Press, 2010) cites a 1981 letter in which Deleuze suggests to Guattari that the evolving theory of categories be a focus of their project: "Pierce and Whitehead make modern tables of categories: how has this idea of categories evolved?" (4). The analytic of concepts developed in *What is Philosophy?* can be read as the direct result of Deleuze's rethinking of the problem of the categories.

44. See Deleuze, "Lettre-préface," in Jean-Clet Martin, *Variations: The Philosophy of Gilles Deleuze*, trans. Constantin V. Boundas and Susan Dyrkton (Edinburgh: Edinburgh University Press, 2010), vii: "It seems to me that I have completely abandoned the notion of the simulacrum."

45. D57:

> The whole of grammar, the whole of the syllogism, is a way of maintaining the subordination of conjunctions to the verb to be, of making them gravitate around the verb to be. One must go further: one must make the encounter with relations penetrate and corrupt everything, undermine being, make it topple over. Substitute AND [ET] for IS [EST]. A *and* B. The And is not even a specific relation or conjunction, it is that which makes relations shoot outside their terms and outside the set of their terms, and outside everything which could be determined as Being, One, or Whole.

See also TP 25.

46. See, for instance, TI 180: "The whole undergoes a mutation, because it has ceased to be the One-Being, in order to become the constitutive 'and' of things, the constitutive between-two [*entre-deux*]."

Essay 3: Leibniz
Deleuze on Leibniz: Difference, Continuity, and the Calculus

1. See Deleuze's remark in his Letter-Preface to Jean-Clet Martin's *Variations: The Philosophy of Gilles Deleuze*, trans. Constantin V. Boundas and Susan Dyrkton (Edinburgh: Edinburgh University Press, 2010), vii: "I feel that I am a very classical philosopher. I believe in philosophy as a system."

2. See EPS 11:

> What I needed was both (1) the expressive character of particular individuals, and (2) an immanence of being. Leibniz, in a way, goes still further than Spinoza on the first point. But on the second, Spinoza stands alone. One finds it only in him. This is why I consider myself a Spinozist, rather than a Leibnizian, although I owe a lot to Leibniz.

3. Deleuze also devoted two series of sessions of his seminar at the University of Vincennes-St. Denis to Leibniz, first in 1980, and then again in 1987, when he was at work on *The Fold*. My discussion here follows closely the deduction presented in the 1980 seminars.

4. For a discussion of Deleuze's relation to Maimon and the post-Kantian tradition, see Graham Jones, *Difference and Determination: Prolegomena Concerning Deleuze's Early Metaphysic*, unpublished Ph.D. thesis, Monash University, 2002.

5. Gottfried Wilhelm Leibniz, *New Essays on Human Understanding*, trans. and ed. Jonathan Bennett and Peter Remnant (Cambridge: Cambridge University Press, 1981), 361.

6. See Gottfried Wilhelm Leibniz, *Philosophical Papers and Letters*, 2nd edn., ed. Leroy E. Loemker (Dordrecht: D. Reidel, 1969), 307: "It is certain that every true predication has some basis in the nature of things, and when a proposition is not an identity, that is to say, when the predicate is not expressly contained in the subject, it must be included in it virtually" (*Discourse on Metaphysics* 8).

7. FLB 41. See Leibniz, *Philosophical Papers and Letters*, 310: "Everything that happens to some person is already contained virtually in his nature or concept, just as the properties of the circle are contained in its definition" (*Discourse on Metaphysics* 13).

8. See Louis Couturat, "On Leibniz's Metaphysics," in Harry G. Frankfurt, ed., *Leibniz: A Collection of Critical Essays* (Garden City, NY: Anchor, 1972), 22: "The principle of identity states: every identity (analytic) proposition is true. The principle of reason affirms, on the contrary: every true proposition is an identity (analytic)."

9. See Aristotle, *Metaphysics*, Book 2, II, 994b, 22–5, in *The Basic Works of Aristotle*, 714: "How can we apprehend things that are infinite in this way . . . if we do not make a stop?"

10. See Benson Mates, *The Philosophy of Leibniz: Metaphysics and Language* (Oxford: Oxford University Press, 1986), 157: "To discover the reason for the truth of the essential proposition 'A is B' is to analyze the concept A far enough to reveal the concept B as contained in it." Deleuze, however, would disagree with Mates's statement that Leibniz "appears to use the terms 'reason' and 'cause' interchangeably" (158), despite the ambiguities of several Leibnizian texts.

11. DR 12. On the relation of difference and repetition in the classical theory of the concept, see DR 288: difference is always inscribed within the identity of the concept in general, and repetition is defined as a difference *without* a concept, that is, in terms of the numerically distinct exemplars or individuals that are subsumed under the generality of the concept (x^1, x^2, x^3, . . . x^n), and which block further conceptual specification.

12. DR 56. See also 222: "Difference is not diversity. Diversity is given, but difference is that by which the given is given as diverse."

13. However, Deleuze will argue, against Leibniz himself, that the analysis of essences must itself be infinite, since it is inseparable from the infinity of God. See FLB 42.

14. For an analysis of Deleuze's relation to the history of the calculus, see Essay 15.

15. Gottfried Wilhelm Leibniz, "Justification of the Infinitesimal Calculus by That of Ordinary Algebra," in *Philosophical Papers and Letters*, 545–6.

16. Deleuze analyzes this theory in an important chapter, entitled "Perception in the Folds," in FLB 85–99.

17. Alberto Gualandi, *Deleuze* (Paris: Les Belles Lettres, 1998), 49. Gualandi's book is one of the best short introductions to Deleuze's work, emphasizing Deleuze's philosophy of nature.

18. Kant had already objected that Maimon, by returning to Leibniz, thereby reintroduced the duality between a finite understanding (consciousness) and an infinite understanding (the divine), which the entire Kantian critique had attempted to eliminate. See Immanuel Kant, letter to Marcus Herz, 26 May 1789, in Arnulf Zweig, ed., *Immanuel Kant: Philosophical Correspondence, 1759–99* (Chicago: University of Chicago Press, 1967), 150–6. Against Kant, however, Deleuze argues that

the infinite here is only the presence of an *unconscious* in the finite understanding, a unthought in finite thought, a non-self in the finite self (whose presence Kant himself was forced to discover when he hollowed out the difference between a determining ego and a determinable ego). For Maimon as for Leibniz, the reciprocal determination of differentials does not refer to a divine understanding, but to minute perceptions as the representatives of the world in the finite self. (FLB, 118–19)

See also DR 192–3.

19. See DR 106–8 (as well as the whole of AO), which contain Deleuze's most explicit advocation of a differential unconscious (Leibniz, Fechner) over a conflictual unconscious (Freud).

20. See Leibniz's analysis of simple curves in *"Tentamen Anagogicum*: An Anagogical Essay in the Investigation of Causes," in Loemker, ed., *Philosophical Papers and Letters*, 477–85.

21. See LS 174:

Instead of a certain number of predicates being excluded by a thing by virtue of the identity of its concept, each 'thing' is open to the infinity of predicates through which it passes, and at the same time it loses its center, that is to say, its identity as a concept and as a self.

22. An early version of this paper appeared under the title "Difference, Continuity, and the Calculus," in Stephen Daniel, ed., *Current Continental Theory and Modern Philosophy* (Evanston, IL: Northwestern University Press, 2005), 127–47.

Essay 4: Hegel
Deleuze, Hegel, and the Post-Kantian Tradition

1. Vincent Descombes, *Modern French Philosophy*, trans. L. Scott Fox and J. M. Harding (Cambridge: Cambridge University Press, 1980), 12: "In 1945, all that was modern sprang from Hegel . . . In 1968, all that was modern was hostile to Hegel." Kojève's course on Hegel was given at the École Pratique des Hautes Études from 1933 to 1939, and was regularly attended by figures such as Raymond Aron, Georges Bataille, Alexandre Koyré, Pierre Klossowski, Jacques Lacan, Maurice Merleau-Ponty, and Eric Weil, among others. The text of the course was compiled by Raymond Queneau and published in 1947. An English translation appeared in 1969: Alexandre Kojève, *Introduction to the Reading of Hegel*, ed. Allan Bloom, trans. James H. Nichols, Jr. (New York: Basic, 1969).

2. Michel Foucault, "The Discourse on Language," in *The Archaeology of Knowledge*, trans. A. M. Sheridan Smith (New York: Pantheon, 1972), 235, as cited in Descombes, *Modern French Philosophy*, 12.

3. In *Difference and Repetition*, Deleuze links his concept of dialectics to the notion of the problematic: "Whenever the dialectic 'forgets' its intimate relation with Ideas in the form of problems . . . it loses its true power" (DR 164); "Problems are always dialectical: the dialectic has no other sense" (DR 179).

4. Pierre Bourdieu, *Homo Academicus*, trans. Peter Collier (Stanford: Stanford University Press, 1988); *The State Nobility: Elite Schools in the Field of Power*, trans. Lauretta C. Clough (Stanford: Stanford University Press, 1988).

5. François Châtelet, *Chronique des idées perdues* (Paris: Stock, 1977), 46. Michel Tournier provides a similar tribute in *The Wind Spirit: An Autobiography*, trans. Arthur Goldhammer (Boston: Beacon Ness, 1988), 127–8: as a student, Deleuze "possessed extraordinary powers of translation and rearrangement: all the tired philosophy of the curriculum passed through him and emerged unrecognizable but rejuvenated, with an air of freshness, undigestedness, and raw newness, utterly startling and discomfiting our weakness and laziness." See also 134–5 and 157.

6. Jacques Derrida, *The Post Card*, trans. Alan Bass (Chicago: University of Chicago Press, 1987).

7. See Michèle Le Dœuff, "Long Hair, Short Ideas," in *The Philosophical Imaginary*, trans. Colin Gordon (Stanford: Stanford University Press, 1989), 105–6. Deleuze himself makes a similar point in *Difference and Repetition*: "There is something amorous—but also something fatal—about all education"(DR 23).

8. See TP 526 n32: "Jean Wahl's works contain profound reflections on this sense of 'and,' on the way it challenges the primacy of the verb 'to be.'"

9. See D vii: "I have always felt that I am an empiricist, that is, a pluralist."

10. See G. W. F. Hegel, *Phenomenology of Spirit*, trans. A. V. Miller (Oxford: Oxford University Press, 1979), section on "Sense Certainty." See also Deleuze's comment in NP 4: "Hegel wanted to ridicule pluralism, identifying it with a naive consciousness which would be happy to say 'this, that, here, now'—like a child stuttering out its most humble needs."

11. William James had already spoken of impressions of relations; see his *Principles of Psychology* [1890] (New York: Dover, 1950), Vol. I, 245: "We ought to say a feeling of and, a feeling of if, a feeling of but and a feeling of by, quite as readily as we say a feeling of blue, a feeling of cold."

12. See N 122–4. The French term "Intercesseurs" in the title is translated as "Mediators."

13. Deleuze analyzes this notion in his cinema books, but it seems equally applicable to his own work. See MI 73: free indirect discourse "testifies to a system which is always heterogeneous, far from equilibrium."

14. Alain Badiou, *Deleuze: The Clamor of Being*, trans. Louise Burchill (Minneapolis: University of Minnesota Press, 2000), 39: "Deleuze is a marvelous reader of Bergson, who, in my opinion, is his real master, far more than Spinoza, or perhaps even Nietzsche."

15. See N 145:

> Setting out a plane of immanence, tracing out a field of immanence, is something all the authors I've worked on have done (even Kant—by denouncing the transcendent use of the syntheses, although he sticks to possible experience rather than real experimentation). (translation modified)

Moreover, the central chapter of *Nietzsche and Philosophy* is entitled "Critique"; beneath the explicit "anti-Hegelian" theme of the book there lies a profound engagement with Kant and the post-Kantian tradition in general, and of which Hegel is only a part (see NP 51–2 for Deleuze's comments on the relation between Nietzsche and post-Kantianism).

16. Deleuze's 1972 essay "How Do We Recognize Structuralism" (in DI 170–92) in effect defines structuralism by means of Deleuze's own "post-structuralist" terminology: difference, multiplicity, virtuality, and so on. Deleuze's radical critique of structuralism seems to have been what attracted Lacan to Deleuze's work prior to *Anti-Oedipus*: "You will see that he [Deleuze] says somewhere that the essence of structuralism, if this word has any meaning . . . is a blank, a lack in the signifying chain, and that which results from errant objects in the signifying chain" (Jacques Lacan, *Le Séminaire*, livre XVI: *D'un autre à l'autre* (1968–1969) (Paris: Seuil, 2006), 134, as cited in François Dosse, *Gilles Deleuze and Félix Guattari: Intersecting Lives*, trans. Deborah Glassman (New York: Columbia University Press, 2010), 188.

17. 14 Mar 1978. Martial Guéroult's book is *La Philosophie transcendentale de Salomon Maïmon* (Paris: Alcan, 1929). Guéroult's subsequent study, *L'Evolution et la structure de la Doctrine de la Science chez Fichte*, 2 vols. (Paris: Les Belles-Lettres, 1930), also contains an important discussion of Maimon, and Deleuze relies heavily on both books. Maimon recounted his extraordinary and tragic life in his autobiography, which is available in a truncated English translation: *Salomon Maimon: An Autobiography* [1888], trans. J. Clark Murray (Champaign-Urbana, University of Illinois Press, 2001).

18. Salomon Maimon, *Essay on Transcendental Philosophy* (1790), trans. Nick Midgley, Henry Somers-Hall, Alistair Welchman, and Merten Reglitz (London: Continuum, 2010).

19. Immanuel Kant, *Philosophical Correspondence*, ed. and trans. Arnulf Zweig (Chicago: University of Chicago Press, 1967), 151. Five years later, however, after leaving several letters from Maimon unanswered, Kant expressed a certain incomprehension of his project in a letter to Reinhold:

> For the past three years or so, age has affected my thinking . . . I feel an inexplicable difficulty when I try to project myself into other people's ideas, so that I seem unable to grasp anyone else's system and to form a mature judgment of it . . . This is the reason why I can turn out essays of my own, but, for example, as regards the "improvement" of the critical philosophy by Maimon . . . I have never really understood what he is after and must leave the reproof to others. (letter to K. L. Reinhold, 28 Mar 1794, 211–12)

The assessment, however, was not limited to Maimon: "I cannot even make Professor Reinhold's work clear to me" (letter to J. S. Beck, 1 Jul 1794, 217).

20. J. G. Fichte, *Briefwechsel*, III/2, 282, as cited in the Introduction to Immanuel Kant, *Philosophical Corrrespondence*, 28.

21. Frederick C. Beiser, *The Fate of Reason: German Philosophy From Kant to Fichte* (Cambridge, MA: Harvard University Press, 1987), 286. Beiser's study contains a chapter (285–323) analyzing the main themes of Maimon's thought. His articles "Introduction to Hegel and the Problem of Metaphysics," in *The Cambridge Companion to Hegel*, ed. Frederick C. Beiser (Cambridge: Cambridge University Press, 1993), 1–24, and "The Context and Problematic of post-Kantian Philosophy," in *A Companion to Continental Philosophy*, ed. Simon Critchley (Oxford: Blackwell, 1998), 21–34, discuss Maimon's influence on post-Kantian thought. In English, one can also consult: Samuel Atlas, *From Critical to Speculative Idealism: The Philosophy of Salomon Maimon* (The Hague: Martinus Nijhoff, 1964); Samuel H. Bergman, *The Philosophy of Salomon Maimon*, trans. Noah L. Jacobs (Jerusalem: Magnes, 1967); and Jan Bransen, *The Antinomy of Thought: Maimonian Skepticism and the Relation between Thoughts and Objects* (Dordrecht and Boston: Kluwer Academic, 1991).

22. Guéroult, *Fichte*, Vol. 1, 110: "For Maimon, the only untouchable aspect of the critical philosophy was the Copernican spirit of the method: nothing can be advanced that cannot be immediately justified from the viewpoint of the *immanent* consciousness in which alone the relation of the subject to the object must be determined."

23. On immanent critique in Kant, see NP 91; on Deleuze's relation to Kant, see N 145.

24. Deleuze, for instance, applies this Maimonian formula at various instances to the work of Schelling, Bergson, Nietzsche, Foucault, and even Pasolini.

> One must not raise oneself to conditions as to conditions of possible experience, but as to conditions of real experience: Schelling had already proposed this aim and defined his philosophy as a superior empiricism. The formula is valid for Bergsonism as well. (DI 36, translation modified)

> The Nietzsche and the Kantian conceptions of critique are opposed on five main points: 1. Genetic and plastic principles that give an account of the sense and value of beliefs, interpretations and evaluations rather than transcendental principles which are conditions for so-called facts. (NP 93)

> Foucault differs in certain fundamental respects from Kant: the conditions are those of real experience, and not of possible experience. (F 60; the final phrase of this sentence is inadvertently omitted from the English translation)

> If it is worth making a philosophical comparison, Pasolini might be called post-Kantian (the conditions of legitimacy are the conditions of reality itself) while Metz and his

followers remain Kantians (the falling back of principle upon fact). (TI 286 n8, translation modified)

25. See G. W. F. Hegel, *Science of Logic*, trans. A. V. Miller (London: George Allen & Unwin, 1969), Vol. 1, Book 2, Section 1, Chapters 2 and 3, 408–80.

26. Guéroult, in *Fichte*, Vol. l, 126–7, shows that in Maimon himself the relationship between difference and identity remains highly ambiguous, oscillating between all these positions; our discussion of Maimon here is necessarily simplified.

27. Maimon seems to have adopted the phrase "coalition system" from Kant himself, who used it in a pejorative sense in the *Critique of Practical Reason* (Book I, Chapter 1, Theorem II, Remark 1), in *Immanuel Kant: Practical Philosophy*, trans. Mary J. Gregor (Cambridge: Cambridge University Press, 1996), 158, where he accused his contemporaries of adopting "a *coalition system* of contradictory principles," rather than attempting to achieve consistency.

28. See FLB 89 (translation modified):

> Even more than Fichte, Salomon Maimon, the first post-Kantian to return to Leibniz, drew out all the consequences of such a psychic automatism of perception: far from perception presupposing an object capable of affecting us, and the conditions under which we would be affectable, the reciprocal determination of differentials (dy/dx) entails the complete determination of the object as perception, and the determinability of space-time as a condition. Beyond the Kantian method of conditioning, Maimon restores an internal subjective genesis.

29. Deleuze's comment on Nietzsche is equally applicable to himself: "The philosophical learning of an author is not assessed by number of quotations, but by the apologetic or polemical directions of his work itself" (NP 162).

30. NP 51–2. The footnote refers the reader to Guéroult's book on Maimon, as well as Jules Vuillemin's *L'Héritage kantien et la révolution copernicienne* (Paris: Presses Universitaires de France, 1954), which Deleuze cites frequently throughout his early writings.

31. For Nietzsche's problematization of knowledge and morality, see *On the Genealogy of Morals*, in *Basic Writings of Nietzsche*, ed. and trans. Walter Kaufmann (New York: Modern Library, 1968): "The will to truth requires a critique—let us thus define our own task—the value of truth must for once be experimentally *called into question*" (Essay III, §24, 589); "Let us articulate this *new demand*: We need a *critique* of moral values, *the value of these values must first be brought into question*" (Preface, §6, 456).

32. Maimonian themes punctuate Deleuze's 1966 *Bergsonism*. (1) On the genetic method, and the search for conditions of real (and not merely possible) experience, see B 23, 26–8, 96–8 (Bergson's critique of the category of the possible). (2) On the principle of difference, B 91–3, and Deleuze's early article, "Bergson's Conception of Difference," trans. Melissa McMahon, in *The New Bergson*, ed. John Mullarkey (Manchester: Manchester University Press, 2000), 32–51.

33. See, for instance, Daniel Breazeale's criticisms in "The Hegel–Nietzsche Problem," in *Nietzsche-Studien* 4 (1975), 146–64.

34. François Dosse, *Gilles Deleuze and Félix Guattari*, 119.

35. Aristotle, *Topics*, Book 1, 100a30–100b30, in *The Basic Works of Aristotle*, ed. Richard McKeon, trans. W. A. Pickard-Cambridge (New York: Random House, 1941), 188. See DR 160.

36. Immanuel Kant, *Critique of Pure Reason*, trans. Norman Kemp Smith (London: Macmillan, 1929): An Idea is "a problem to which there is no solution" (319, A328/B384); "if the universal is admitted as *problematic* only, and is a mere Idea, the particular is certain, but the universality of the rule of which it is a consequence is still a problem" (535, A646/B674). See Deleuze's analysis in DR 168–70.

Essay 5: Pre- and Post-Kantianism
Logic and Existence: Deleuze on the Conditions of the Real

1. This paper was originally presented at the conference "Deleuze and Rationalism," which took place on 16–17 March 2007 at the Centre for Research in Modern European Philosophy at Middlesex University, London.

2. Jean Hyppolite, *Logic and Existence* [1952], trans. Leonard Lawlor and Amit Sen (Albany: State University of New York Press, 1997). This book completes the project Hyppolite began with *Genesis and Structure of Hegel's "Phenomenology of Spirit,"* trans. Samuel Cherniak and John Heckman (Evanston, IL: Northwestern University Press, 1979), and examines the relation between the phenomenology and the logic. Deleuze wrote an important review of the book in 1954, "Jean Hyppolite's *Logic and Existence,"* which is included as appendix to the English translation (191–5).

3. The paragraphs that follow are a recapitulation, in part, of the reading of Leibniz proposed in Essay 3.

4. Gottfried Wilhelm Leibniz, *New Essays on Human Understanding*, ed. and trans. Peter Remnant and Jonathan Bennett (Cambridge: Cambridge University Press, 1981), 408.

5. See Wilfred Sellers, "Meditations Leibniziennes," in *Leibniz: Metaphysics and Philosophy of Science*, ed. R. S. Woolhouse (Oxford: Oxford University Press, 1981), 31. "If the nature of a substance is to account for its individuality, it must account for episodes [events], and not merely the capacities, powers, and dispositions—all, in principle, repeatable—which were traditionally connected with the natures of things."

6. Ian Hacking, "What Mathematics Has Done to Some and Only Some Philosophers," in *Proceedings of the British Academy* 103 (2000), 83–138: 105.

7. Leibniz, "On the Radical Origination of Things" [1697], in Leroy E. Loemker, ed., *Philosophical Papers and Letters* (Dordrecht, Holland: D. Reidel, 1956), 486: "However far you go back to earlier states, you will never find in those states a full reason why there should be any world rather than none, and why it should be as it is."

8. Leibniz wrote a short text entitled "Reflections on the Doctrine of a Single Universal Mind" [1702], in Loemker, ed., *Philosophical Papers and Letters*, 554–60, in which he shows that, although there is indeed a universal mind (God), it does not in any way prevent substances from being individual. See Deleuze's commentary in his seminar of 15 Apr 1980.

9. On Leibniz's derivation of the concept of point of view from the theory of conic sections, see Michel Serres, *Le Système de Leibniz et ses modèles mathématiques* (Paris: PUF, 1968), Part 3, "Le point fixe," 647–712.

10. See Leibniz, "Monadology" [1714], §57, in Loemker, ed., *Philosophical Papers and Letters*, 648:

> Just as the same city viewed from different sides appears to be different and to be, as it were, multiplied in perspectives, so the infinite multitude of simple substances, which seem to be so many different universes, are nevertheless only the perspective of a single universe according to the different points of view of each monad.

11. Gottfried Wilhelm Leibniz, *Theodicy: Essays on the Goodness of God, the Freedom of Man, and the Origin of Evil*, trans. E. M. Huggard, ed. Austin Farrer (La Salle, IL: Open Court, 1985).

12. Blaise Pascal, *Pensées*, trans. W. F. Trotter (New York: E. P. Dutton, 1958), §418. Deleuze analyzes this Christian tradition in his two-volume *Cinema*, where he draws a parallel between the philosophy of Pascal and Kierkegaard and the films of Bresson and Dreyer; see MI 114–16 and TI 176–9. Bresson perhaps even offers a fifth type of mode of existence in his great film *Au hasard, Balthazar*: the donkey who possesses the innocence of one who cannot choose, but who none the less suffers the effects of the choices or non-choices of

humans, which ultimately kill it—one of the most poignant scenes in the history of cinema (see MI 116).

13. *Qu'est-ce que fonder?* [What is Grounding?], cours hypokhâgne, at Lycée Louis le Grand, Paris, 1956–7, available at webdeleuze.com.

14. Although this quotation is from *Logic of Sense* (LS 176), it summarizes the essential themes of *Difference and Repetition*.

15. The limitation of so-called "analytic metaphysics" is its reliance on a logicist, formalist, and set theoretical metaphysics inherited from the nineteenth century. See, for instance, Ted Sider's stated assumption, in *Four-Dimensionalism* (Oxford: Oxford University Press, 2001), "that modern logic's quantificational apparatus mirrors the structure of reality" (xvi). As Whitehead pointed out, the notion of the *variable* is itself a derivative of the principle of identity. Alfred North Whitehead, *Modes of Thought* (New York: Free Press, 1938), 106: "The variable, though undetermined, sustains its identity throughout the arguments." See also Friedrich Nietzsche, *Will to Power*, trans. Walter Kaufmann and R. J. Hollingdale (New York: Random House, 1967), §512, 227: "Logic is bound to the condition: assume there are identical cases"; and §516, 279: "Supposing there were no self-identical 'A,' such as is presupposed by every proposition of logic (and of mathematics) . . . ."

16. Friedrich Nietzsche, *Writings from the Late Notebooks*, ed. Rüdiger Bittner, trans. Kate Sturge (Cambridge: Cambridge University Press, 2003), 36[18], 24: "I take good care not to talk about chemical '*laws*': that has a moral aftertaste . . . ." See also EPS 268:

> The less we understand the laws of nature, that is, the norms of life, the more we interpret them as orders and prohibitions—to the point where the philosopher must hesitate before using the word "law," so much does it retain a moral aftertaste: it would be better to speak of "eternal truths."

Essay 6: Aesthetics
Deleuze's Theory of Sensation: Overcoming the Kantian Duality

1. For Deleuze's formulations of the aesthetic problem, see DR 56–7, 68 and LS 260.

2. Plato, *Republic*, VII, 523b. Deleuze appeals to this text in DR 138–42, 236; NP 108, 210 n33); PS 100–1.

3. See Deleuze's analyses in KCP, esp. 15.

4. Plato, *Republic*, 524d; see also *Philebus*, 24d; *Parmenides* 154–5; and *Theaetetus*, 152–5. These paradoxes, known in antiquity as Megarian sorites ("How many grains constitutes a heap?"), are treated in formal logic as "vague predicates." See Pascal Engel, *The Norm of the True* (Toronto: University of Toronto Press, 1991), 199–215. Deleuze treats the theme of becoming in LS 1–3.

5. See Maurice Merleau-Ponty, *Phenomenology of Perception*, trans. Colin Smith (London: Routledge & Kegan Paul, 1967), 216–17; Erwin Straus, *The Primary World of the Senses: A Vindication of Sensory Experience*, trans. Jacob Needleman (New York: Free Press, 1963), 316–31; and Henri Maldiney, *Regard parole espace* (Lausanne: L'Age d'Homme, 1973), 134–8. For Deleuze's criticisms, see MI 57, FB 37–9, and DR 137.

6. PS 37–8. Plato, in Deleuze's reading, remains tied to the model of recognition in two ways: in defining the sign as a qualitative contrariety, Plato confused the being of the sensible with a simple sensible being [*aistheton*], and he related it to an already-existing Idea that merely shifted the operation of recognition to the process of reminiscence. For the critique of Plato, see DR 141–2; for Proust's break with Platonism, see PS 108–15.

7. The analysis of images of thought is one of the central objects of Deleuze's philosophy: see in general PS 94–102, NP 103–10, and DR 127–67. More specific analysis of these "noological" themes can be found in LS 127–33 (height, depth, and surface as coordinates

of thought) and TP 3–25 (the tree and the rhizome as images of thought), 374–80 (the State-form versus "nomad" thought), and 474–500 (the smooth and the striated).

8. Martin Heidegger, *What is Called Thinking*, trans. Fred D. Wieck and J. Glenn Gray (New York: Harper & Row, 1968), 28. Heidegger, however, still retains the theme of a desire or *philia*, substituting metaphors of the "gift" for those of violence, and adhering to the subjective presupposition of a pre-ontological understanding of Being. If Artaud plays an important role in Deleuze's thinking, it is because his case presents, in its clearest form, the fact that what thought is forced to think is its own impotence, its own incapacity to take on form on its own; Artaud's problem was not to orient his thought, but simply to manage to think *something*. Hence the determining importance of images of thought: can being mad belong to thought in principle, or is it simply a contingent feature of the brain that should be considered as a simple fact? See DR 146–7 (commentary on Artaud) and 321 n11 (criticisms of Heidegger).

9. Deleuze has analyzed each of these figures of negativity: on stupidity, see NP 105 ("stupidity is a structure of thought as such . . . it is not error or a tissue of errors . . . there are imbecile thoughts, imbecile discourses that are made up entirely of truths"); on convention, see PS 95 ("truths remain arbitrary and abstract so long as they are based on the goodwill of thinking. Only the conventional is explicit . . . Minds communicate to each other only the conventional"); on opinion, see WP 144–50 ("opinion is a thought closely molded on the form of recognition"); on clichés, particularly as they pose a problem for the artist, see MI 208–9 and FB 71–80.

10. According to Proust, jealousy is not a disease of love but its truth, its finality, and all love is "a dispute over evidence," "a delirium of signs" (PS 132, 138).

11. DR 144. See also EPS 149:

> One is always struck by the diverse inspirations of empiricists and rationalists. One group is surprised by what fails to surprise the others. If we listen to the rationalists, truth and freedom are, above all, rights; they wonder how we can lose our rights, fall into error or lose our freedom . . . From an empiricist viewpoint, everything is inverted: what is surprising is that men sometimes manage to understand truth, sometimes manage to understand one other, sometimes manage to free themselves from what fetters them.

12. Francis Bacon, *The Brutality of Fact: Interviews with David Sylvester* (London: Thames & Hudson, 1975), 18.

13. Kant presents this theory of common sense in the *Critique of Judgment*, trans. James Creed Meredith (Oxford: Oxford University Press, 1952), §18–22 (81–9), §40 (150–4).

14. See Kant, *Critique of Judgment*, §29, General Remark (127). Kant's "Analytic of the Sublime" lies at the centre of Jean-François Lyotard's conception of "postmodern" art, which he defines as that which *presents the unpresentable*. See his essay "Answering the Question: What is Postmodernism?," in *The Postmodern Condition: A Report on Knowledge*, trans. Geoff Bennington and Brian Massumi (Minneapolis: University of Minnesota Press, 1984), 71–82. There is a profound difference between Deleuze and Lyotard, despite numerous lines of convergence between their respective theories of art: Deleuze's theory is derived from an analysis of sensibility (intensity), whereas Lyotard's is derived from the faculty of the imagination (the sublime). Lyotard sometimes speaks of the "imagination or sensibility" in the same sentence (e.g., 80, 81), but without ever taking the further step of extracting the limit-element of sensibility, which is precisely not that of the imagination. The difference would seem to bear on the nature of the Ideas appealed to in each instance: transcendent in the case of the imagination, immanent in the case of sensibility. For Lyotard's analysis of the sublime, see his important commentaries in *Lessons on the Analytic of the Sublime*, trans. Elizabeth Rottenberg (Stanford: Stanford University Press, 1994).

15. Salomon Maimon, *Essay on Transcendental Philosophy* [1790], trans. Nick Midgley, Henry

Somers-Hall, Alistair Welchman, and Merten Reglitz (London: Continuum, 2010). For commentary, see above all Martial Guéroult, *La Philosophie transcendental de Salomon Maïmon* (Paris: Alcan, 1929), esp. 55ff and 76ff; Sylvain Zac, *Salomon Maïmon: Critique de Kant* (Paris: Cerf, 1988), esp. Chapter 6; and Frederick Beiser, *The Fate of Reason: German Philosophy From Kant to Fichte* (Cambridge, MA: Harvard University Press, 1987), 295–303.

16. *Note on the differential relation.* The nature of the differential relation can be made clear by comparing three types of relation distinguished in mathematics. A first type is established between elements that are themselves independent or autonomous, such as 3 + 2 or 2/3. The elements are real, and these relations themselves must be said to be *real*. A second type, e.g., $x^2 + y^2 - R^2 = 0$ (the algebraic equation for the circle), is established between terms whose value is unspecified, but which nevertheless must *in each case* have a determined value. Such relations can be called *imaginary*. But the third type of relation is established between elements that themselves *have no determined* value, but that nevertheless are determined reciprocally in the relation: thus $ydy + xdx = 0$ (the universal of the circumference or the corresponding function), or $dy/dx = -x/y$ (the expression of a curve and its trigonometric tangent). These are *differential* relations. The elements of these relations are undetermined, being neither real nor imaginary: dy is completely undetermined in relation to y, dx is completely undetermined in relation to x. Yet they are perfectly determinable in the differential relation; the terms themselves do not exist apart from the differential relation into which they enter and by which they are reciprocally determined. This differential relation, in turn, determines a singular point, and it is the set of these points that determines the topological space of a given multiplicity or manifold (a triangle, for example, has three singular points, while curves and figures are derived from more complex distributions). See Deleuze, "How Do We Recognize Structuralism?," in DI 170–92, FLB 88, and DR 172–5.

17. For Deleuze's interpretation of Leibniz's theory of perception, see FLB, Chapter 7, "Perception in the Folds," 85–99, from which the above examples are taken. For Leibniz's primary texts, see *Philosophical Papers and Letters*, ed. Leroy E. Loemker (Dordrecht: D. Reidel, 1969), esp. *Discourse on Metaphysics*, §33 (324–5); *Monadology*, §20–25 (645); and *Principles of Nature and Grace*, §13 (640), as well as *New Essays on Human Understanding*, ed. and trans. Peter Remnant and Jonathan Bennett (Cambridge: Cambridge University Press, 1981), Chapter 1.

18. Henri Bergson, *The Creative Mind*, trans. Mabelle L. Andison (Totowa, NJ: Littlefield, Adams, 1946), 225. Deleuze analyses this example in "Bergson's Conception of Difference," in DI 32–52, and draws out its consequences in LS 136:

> To have a color is not more general than to be green, because it is only this color, and this green which is this nuance, and is related in the individual subject. This rose is not red without having the redness of this rose.

Deleuze is closer to Goethe than Newton. Goethe's theory of color has similarly been retrieved in certain contemporary scientific theories. Redness is no longer perceived as a band-width of light but as a singularity within a chaotic universe, whose boundaries are not always easy to describe; see James Gleick, *Chaos: Making a New Science* (New York: Viking 1987), 164–6.

19. Likewise, one could speak of a white society or a white language, which contains in its virtuality all the phonemes and relations destined to be actualized in the diverse languages and in the remarkable parts of a *same* language; see DR 203–7. For a fuller analysis of musical form along these lines, see Jean-François Lyotard, "Several Silences," in *Driftworks*, ed. Roger McKeon (New York: Semiotext(e), 1984), 99–110.

20. Immanuel Kant, *Critique of Pure Reason*, trans. Norman Kemp Smith (London: Macmillan, 1929), 203–4, A169/B21:

> Every sensation has a degree, that is, an intensive magnitude which can always be diminished [to the point where the intensity = o] . . . Every color, as for instance red, has a degree which, however small it may be, is never the smallest; and so with heat, the moment of gravity, etc.

21. Hermann Cohen, *Kants Theorie der Erfahrung*, 2nd edn. (Berlin: Dümmler, 1885), 428:

> Space and time itself, the sensible conditions of the unity of consciousness, insofar as they represent *quanta* continua, are constituted as continua by the reality of intensive magnitude as the condition of thought. Intensive magnitude consequently appears immediately as the prior condition of the extensive . . . Such as the necessity that led to the finitely small, positing something that became a unity not in relation to One but in relation to Zero.

See Jules Vuillemin's commentaries in *L'Héritage kantien et la révolution copernicienne: Fichte, Cohen, Heidegger* (Paris: Presses Universitaires de France, 1954), 132–207.

22. See DR 20:

> By "sign" we mean what happens within such a [differential] system, what flashes across the intervals when a communication takes place between disparates. The sign is indeed an effect, but an effect with two aspects: in one of these it expresses, qua sign, the productive dissymmetry; in the other it tends to cancel it.

23. Kant, in the *Critique of Pure Reason*, admitted that this schematizing power of the imagination was "blind" (112, A78/B103), "an art concealed in the depths of the human soul," an activity "nature is hardly likely ever to allow us to discover" (183, A141/B180–1). It is for this reason that Heidegger took the imagination as the focal point of his reading of Kant, in *Kant and the Problem of Metaphysics*, trans. James S. Churchill (Bloomington: Indiana University Press, 1962), although Deleuze breaks with Heidegger's reading.

24. Nietzsche, *Genealogy of Morals*, in *Basic Writings of Nietzsche*, ed. and trans. Walter Kaufmann (New York: Modern Library, 1968), Essay II, §1, 493–4:

> What we experience and absorb enters our consciousness as little while we are digesting it . . . as does the thousandfold process involved in physical nourishment . . . so that it will be immediately obvious how there could be no happiness, no cheerfulness, no hope, no pride, no *present*, without forgetfulness.

Henri Bergson, *Matter and Memory*, trans. Nancy Margaret Paul and W. Scott Palmer (New York: Zone, 1988), 35–6: we never perceive objects *per se*, but rather objects minus those aspects that do not interest us as a function of our needs.

25. DR 237. In the chapter on "The Perception-Image" in *The Movement-Image*, Deleuze argues that, if the cinema goes beyond normal perception, it is in the sense that it reaches this genetic element *of all* possible perception: "In the 'kino-eye,' Vertov was aiming to attain or regain the system of universal variation in itself," to "reach 'another' perception, which is also the genetic element of all perception" (MI 80–6).

26. DR 213. Martial Guéroult discusses the role this notion played in post-Kantian philosophy in *L'Évolution et la structure de la Doctrine de la Science chez Fichte* (Paris: Les Belles Lettres, 1930), Vol. 1, 14–15: "Clear and distinct understanding was posited as the fruit of a continuous development whose point of departure was the confused understanding, the sole form under which the totality of the universe could be given originally in the finite mind."

27. Paul Klee, "Schopferische Konfession," in *Das Bildnerische Denken*, ed. Jürg Spiller (Basel: Schwabe, 1964), 76, as quoted in FB 48 and TP 342. See also Maldiney's commentary in *Parole regard espace*, 143–6. Lyotard's similar formula—"not to represent, but to present the unpresentable"—is discussed in "The Sublime and the Avant-Garde," in *The Inhuman: Reflections on Time* (Stanford: Stanford University Press, 1988), 89–107.

28. See PS 18: "Time seeks out bodies in order to become visible, seizing bodies wherever it encounters them so as to cast its magic lantern," modifying this feature of someone we knew long ago, elongating, blurring, or crushing that one. Deleuze distinguishes four structures of time in Proust: lost time is both "passing time" and "wasted time"; time regained is both a "time recovered" at the heart of time lost, and an "original time" that is affirmed in art.

29. For these examples, see TP 343 and FB 48.

30. Quoted in Milan Kundera, *The Art of the Novel*, trans. Linda Asher (New York: Grove, 1988), 5, 36.

31. Bacon, *The Brutality of Fact*, 23.

32. Ibid., 18.

33. See Gilbert Simondon, *L'Individu et sa genèse physico-biologique* (Paris: Presses Universitaires de France, 1964); Deleuze was strongly influenced by Simondon's text.

34. Paul Klee, *On Modern Art*, trans. Paul Findlay, intro. Herbert Reed (London: Faber, 1966), 53: "Had I wished to present man 'as he is,' then I should have had to use such a bewildering confusion of lines that pure elementary representation would have been out of the question. The result would have been vagueness beyond recognition."

35. The primary texts on these sensible syntheses in art are: FB 60–1, WP 167–8, and PS 148–60.

36. In Newton, for example, the "optical" grey is obtained through a combination of black and white, whereas in Goethe the "haptic" grey is obtained through a combination of green and red. See Goethe, *Color Theory*, ed. Rupprecht Matthaei (New York: Van Nostrand, 1971). On Cézanne's relation to the Impressionists with regard to color, see Maurice Merleau-Ponty, "Cézanne's Doubt," in *The Essential Writings*, ed. Alden L. Fischer (New York: Harcourt, Brace & World, 1969), 236.

37. MI 118. On these relations of color, see Deleuze's discussion in FB, Chapter 15, "Bacon's Trajectory," 109–15.

38. On the role of resonance in involuntary *memory*, see PS, Chapter 6, "The Secondary Role of Memory," 52–66 (Joyce's "epiphanies," Deleuze argues, can be analyzed in the same manner). On coupling in Bacon, see FB, Chapter 9, "Couples and Triptychs," 55–61.

39. On "forced movement" in Bacon, see FB, Chapter 10, "What is a Triptych?," 62–70. The question concerning the conditions under which disjunction can be a form of synthesis (and not an analytic procedure that excludes the predicates of a thing by virtue of the identity of its concept) is one of the decisive questions posed by a philosophy of difference, though it lies beyond the scope of this paper. For Deleuze's discussions of the problem, see "La synthèse disjonctive" (with Guattari), *in L'Arc* 43 (1970), 54–62 and LS 172–6, 294–7.

40. In WP 168, Deleuze suggests that, of all the arts, it is perhaps sculpture that presents these three syntheses in an almost pure state: first, there are the sensations of stone, marble, or metal, which vibrate according to strong and weak beats; second, there are the protuberances and cavities in the material, which establish powerful combats that interlock and resonate with each other; and finally, there is the set-up of the sculpture, with large empty spaces between groups, or even within a single group, in which one no longer knows if it is the light or air that *sculpts* or is sculpted.

41. On the relation of the sensation to the material, see WP, Chapter 7, esp. 191–7.

42. See AO 42: the work of art "is a whole *of* its constituent parts but does not totalize them; it is a unity *of* its particular parts but it does not unify them; rather, it is added to them as a new part fabricated separately." On Deleuze's use of the concept of transversality, originally formulated by Guattari, see PS 168 (and 188 n5).

Essay 7: Dialectics
Deleuze, Kant, and the Theory of Immanent Ideas

1. This paper was originally presented as a lecture entitled "Idea and Immanence in Deleuze" at the Collegium Phenomenologicum in Città di Castello, Italy, on 31 July 2003, directed by Leonard Lawlor, and benefited from the critical comments of the Collegium members.

2. See Immanuel Kant, *Critique of Pure Reason*, trans. Norman Kemp Smith (New York: Macmillan, 1929), 309, A312/B368: "Despite the great wealth of our languages, the thinker often finds himself at a loss for the expression which exactly fits his concept, and for want of which he is unable to be really intelligible to others or even to himself." One finds a similar passage in the preface to the *Critique of Practical Reason*, in Immanuel Kant, *Practical Philosophy*, trans. and ed. Mary J. Gregor (Cambridge: Cambridge University Press, 1996), Preface, 5:11, 145.

3. The themes of difference and affirmation—as well as the confrontation with Hegel—largely disappear from Deleuze's writings after the publication of *Difference and Repetition* in 1968.

4. See François Dosse, *Gilles Deleuze and Félix Guattari: Intersecting Lives*, trans. Deborah Glassman (New York: Columbia University Press, 2010), 119.

5. Kant, *Critique of Pure Reason*, 319, A328/B384: An Idea is "a problem to which there is no solution."

6. DR 161–2. In the calculus, it is the differential that defines the nature of problems, which is why it must disappear in the solution.

7. Kant, *Critique of Pure Reason*, 534, A645–6/B673–4:

   These concepts of reason are not derived from nature; on the contrary, we interrogate nature in accordance with these Ideas, and consider our knowledge defective as long as it is not adequate to them. By general admission, *pure earth, pure water, pure air*, etc., are not to be found. We require, however, the concepts of them (though, insofar as their complete purity is concerned, they have their origin solely in reason) in order properly to determine the share which each of these natural causes has in producing appearances.

8. Kant, *Critique of Pure Reason*, 298–9, A295–6/B352.

9. Kant, *Critique of Pure Reason*, 299, A296/B352: "*Transcendental* and *transcendent* are not interchangeable terms."

10. For the components of the Platonic Idea, see Essay 10, in this volume.

11. DR 168–221. The title in French is "Synthèse idéal de la différence," "The Ideal Synthesis of Difference."

12. See Frederick C. Beiser, *The Fate of Reason: German Philosophy from Kant to Fichte* (Cambridge, MA: Harvard University Press, 1987), 286: "To study Fichte, Schelling, or Hegel without having read Maimon's *Versuch* [*Essay on Transcendental Philosophy*] is like studying Kant without having read Hume's *Treatise*."

13. Immanuel Kant, *Philosophical Correspondence*, ed. and trans. Arnulf Zweig (Chicago: University of Chicago Press, 1967), 151.

14. The analyses that follow are summaries of Deleuze's detailed reading of the *Critique of Judgment*, which can be found in his article, "The Idea of Genesis in Kant's Aesthetics", trans. Daniel W. Smith, *Angelaki*, Vol. 5, No. 3 (Dec 2000), 39–70.

15. Immanuel Kant, *Critique of Judgment*, trans. James Creed Meredith (Oxford: Oxford University Press, 1952), §59, 223.

16. Kant, *Critique of Judgment*, §42, 159, translation modified.

17. Alain Badiou makes this point in *The Century*, trans. Alberto Toscano (Cambridge: Polity, 2007), 153–4, in the context of developing his own nascent theory of the Idea. See also his "The Idea of Communism," in *The Communist Hypothesis*, trans. David Macey and Steve Corcoran (London: Verso, 2010), 229–60.

18. Martin Heidegger, *Kant and the Problem of Metaphysics*, trans. James S. Churchill (Bloomington: Indiana University Press, 1962).

19. Gilles Deleuze, *The Fold: Leibniz and the Baroque*, trans. Tom Conley (Minneapolis: University of Minnesota Press, 1993), 61; Deleuze uses these two phrases to characterize Leibniz's philosophy as a whole.

20. See DR 191: "No doubt, if one insists, the word 'essence' might be preserved, but only on condition of saying that the essence is precisely the accident, the event."

21. Note how Kant inverts the relation between immanence and transcendence in the passage from the first to the second critique:

> It is incumbent to the *Critique of Practical Reason* as such to prevent empirically conditioned reason from presuming that it, alone and exclusively, furnishes the determining ground of the will [or desire]. If it is proved that there is pure reason, its use alone is immanent; the empirically conditioned use, which lay claim to absolute rule, is on the contrary transcendent and expressed itself in demands and commands that go quite beyond its sphere—precisely the opposite relation from what could be said of pure reason in its speculative use. (*Critique of Practical Reason*, Introduction, 5:16, 148–9.)

22. Kant, *Critique of Judgment*, Introduction, §3, 15–16: "The faculties of the soul are reducible to three, which do not admit of any further derivation from a common ground: the faculty of knowledge, the feeling of pleasure and displeasure, and the faculty of desire."

23. Kant, *Critique of Practical Reason*, Preface, 5:9n, 143–4.

24. Kant, *Critique of Practical Reason*, 5:89, 212.

25. Kant, *The Metaphysics of Morals*, in *Practical Philosophy*, 6:213, 374:

> The faculty of desire whose inner determining ground . . . lies within the subject's reason is called the will. The will is therefore the faculty of desire considered not so much in relation to action, but rather in relation to the *ground* determining choice to action.

26. Kant, *Critique of Practical Reason*, 5:89, 212.

27. See Spinoza, *Emendation of the Intellect*, in *The Collected Works of Spinoza*, ed. and trans. E. Curley, 2nd edn. (Princeton: Princeton University Press, 1985), §85, 37: "So far as I know they [the ancients] never conceived the soul (as we do here) as acting according to certain laws, like a spiritual automaton"); and Leibniz, "Clarification of the Difficulties Which Mr. Bayle has Found in the New System of the Union of Soul and Body," in Gottfried Wilhelm Leibniz, *Philosophical Papers and Letters*, ed. Leroy E. Loemker (Dordrecht: D. Reidel, 1969), 495: "The soul is a most exact spiritual automaton."

28. Friedrich Nietzsche, *Daybreak*, trans. R. J. Hollingdale (Cambridge: Cambridge University Press, 1982), §129, 129.

Essay 8: Analytics
On the Becoming of Concepts

1. An early version of this paper was presented at the workshop entitled "Between Deleuze and Simondon," 18–19 September 2009, Palazzo Pesaro-Papafave, Venice, Italy, which was the fourth workshop sponsored by the European Network in Contemporary French Philosophy. I am indebted to the founders and organizers of the network: Miguel de Beistegui, Arnold I. Davidson, Frédéric Worms, and Mauro Carbone.

2. WP 2, citing Nietzsche, *The Will to Power*, trans. Walter Kaufmann and R. J. Hollingdale (New York: Random House, 1967), §409, 220: Philosophers "must no longer accept concepts as a gift, nor merely purify and polish them, but must first *make* and *create* them, present them and make them convincing." Whitehead seems to have had a similar conception of philosophy: "Progress in truth . . . is mainly a progress in the framing of

concepts." Alfred North Whitehead, *Religion in the Making* (New York: Fordham, 1996), 131.

3. Guattari, who did not explicitly assume the mantle of a philosopher, seemed to have seen the activity of thought in a different vein, preferring the production of flows or diagrams over the creation of concepts (TRM 238). For analyses of Guattari's "diagrammaticism," see Gary Genosko, *Félix Guattari: An Aberrant Introduction* (London and New York: Continuum, 2002), and Jannell Watson, *Guattari's Diagrammatic Thought* (London: Continuum, 2009). The publication of Guattari's *The Anti-Oedipus Papers* (New York: Semiotext(e), 2006) opened an interesting window into Guattari's working methods. For a review, see Daniel W. Smith, "Inside Out: Guattari's *Anti-Oedipus Papers*," in *Radical Philosophy* 140 (Nov–Dec 2006), 35–9.

4. EPS 321. Although it was published in 1968, François Dosse notes that Deleuze had largely completed his secondary thesis on Spinoza (*Expressionism in Philosophy: Spinoza*) in the late 1950s, before the publication of *Nietzsche and Philosophy* in 1962. See François Dosse, *Gilles Deleuze and Félix Guattari: Intersecting Lives*, trans. Deborah Glassman (New York: Columbia University Press, 2010), 118, 143.

5. WP 1. For a different approach to Deleuze's analytic of concepts, oriented around the notion of the event, see Daniel W. Smith, "'Knowledge of Pure Events': A Note on Deleuze's Analytic of Concepts," in *Ereignis auf Französisch. Zum Erfahrungsbegriff der französischen Gegenwartsphilosophie: Temporalität, Freiheit, Sprache*, ed. Marc Rölli (Munich: Wilhelm Fink, 2003), 363–74.

6. WP 2. Deleuze considered the *Critique of Judgment* to be "one of the most important books in all of philosophy" (31 Mar 1981).

7. See also DI 261: "I've undergone a change. The surface–depth opposition no longer concerns me. What interests me now is the relationships between a full body, a body without organs, and flows that migrate."

8. The same is true of Deleuze's other concepts as well. The concept of affect, for example, first arises in Deleuze's work on Spinoza, where it designates the passage from one intensity to another in a finite mode, which is experienced as a joy or a sadness. In *A Thousand Plateaus* and *What is Philosophy?*, however, the affect is no longer "the passage from one lived state to another," but has assumed an autonomous status—along with percepts—as a becoming that takes place between two multiplicities. See WP 173: "The affect is not the passage from one lived state to another but man's nonhuman becoming."

9. What is important to Deleuze is not only the concept of multiplicity, nor even the *types* of multiplicities he analyses, but the relations and transformations between these types (WP 152): that is, the transformation from the continuous to the discrete, from the problematic to the axiomatic, the intensive to the extensive, the non-metric to the metric, the non-denumerable to the denumerable, the rhizomatic to the arborescent, the smooth to the striated, the molecular to the molar, and so on. When asked about the concept of "micro-physics" in the 1981 interview with Arnaud Villani, Deleuze responded:

> The distinction between macro and micro is very important, but it perhaps belongs more to Félix than to myself. For me, it is rather the distinction between two types of multiplicities. For me, that is the essential point: that one of these two types refers to micro-multiplicities is only a consequence. Even for the problem of thought, and even for the sciences, the notion of multiplicity, as introduced by Riemann, seems much more important than that of microphysics. (Arnaud Villani, *La Guêpe et l'orchidée* (Paris: Belin, 1999), 130)

10. Kant, *Critique of Pure Reason*, trans. Norman Kemp Smith, (London: Macmillan, 1929), "The Ideas in General," 309–14, A312–20/B368–77.

11. Deleuze first mentioned *What is Philosophy?* (1991) in the 1981 interview with Arnaud

Villani, in response to a question about the books he was hoping to write after completing *A Thousand Plateaus*: "I have just finished a book on Francis Bacon, and all I have left now are two projects: one on 'Thought and Cinema,' and another which would be a large book on 'What is Philosophy' (with the problem of the categories)." See Villani, *La Guêpe et l'orchidée*, 130.

12. See DR 284–5:

> We have continually proposed descriptive notions . . . None of this, however, amounts to a list of categories. It is pointless to claim that a list of categories can be open in principle: it can be in fact, but not in principle. For categories belong to the world of representation, where they constitute forms of distribution according to which Being is repartitioned among beings following the rules of sedentary proportionality. That is why philosophy has often been tempted to oppose notions of a quite different kind to categories, notions which are really open and which betray an empirical and pluralist sense of Ideas: 'existential' as against essential, percepts as against concepts, or indeed the list of empirico-ideal notions that we find in Whitehead, which makes *Process and Reality* one of the greatest books of modern philosophy.

13. Deleuze made this remark in his interview with Arnaud Villani. See Villani, *La Guêpe et l'orchidée*, 130. François Dosse, in *Gilles Deleuze and Félix Guattari*, cites a 1981 letter from Deleuze to Guattari which presented the problem of the categories as an integral part of their joint project: "Pierce and Whitehead make modern tables of categories: how has this idea of categories evolved?" (14).

14. For the distinction between expression and exemplification, see Nelson Goodman, *Languages of Art*, 2nd edn. (Indianapolis: Hackett, 1976).

15. Summarizing all these becomings, Deleuze comments: "There's nothing more unsettling than the continual movement of something that seems fixed" (N 157).

16. See Deleuze's article, "What is the Creative Act?" (TRM 312–24), which was originally presented as a lecture to the Fémis film school in Paris under the title, "Having an Idea in Cinema."

17. TRM 176, translation modified. See Gilles Deleuze, "8 ans après: Entretien 1980" (interview with Catherine Clément), in *L'Arc* 49 (rev. edn., 1980), special issue on Deleuze, 99.

18. For an analysis of the concepts Deleuze creates in his *Francis Bacon*, see Daniel W. Smith, "Deleuze on Bacon: Three Conceptual Trajectories in *The Logic of Sensation*," in FB vii–xxxiii.

19. For an analysis of the relation between Deleuze's treatment of concepts in *What is Philosophy?* and the treatments of social assemblages in *Capitalism and Schizophrenia*, see Craig Lundy, *History and Becoming in Deleuze's Philosophy of Creativity* (Edinburgh: Edinburgh University Press, 2012).

20. TI 129. In this essay, I have left to the side Deleuze and Guattari's treatment of science, which none the less seems to have gone through a certain evolution. In 1983, Deleuze noted in a seminar , simply, that "concepts can be of different types, they can be scientific, they can be philosophical" (13 Dec 1983). By May 1984, however, Deleuze was clearly seeking to distinguish science from philosophy, defining the former as a "system of operators"—although Deleuze immediately added that the notion of an *opérateur* could function as a definition of science only if one was capable of answering the question, "What are the differences between mathematical operators, physical operators, and chemical operators?" (29 May 1984). Deleuze would make use of the term *opérateur* in the 1985 *The Time-Image* as well (TI 129). In the same seminar, Deleuze defined art as the creative activity that consists in creating "characters" [*personages*], as if he had not yet clearly disengaged the notion of "conceptual personae," which, in *What is Philosophy?*, serves as a

condition for the philosophical creation of concepts. The definition of science in terms of *functions*, in *What is Philosophy?* (1991), thus seems to have been a rather late formulation, itself the result of a series of experimentations and becomings.

21. See Alfred North Whitehead, *The Concept of Nature* (Cambridge: Cambridge University Press, 1920), 54: "I am in full accord with Bergson, though he uses 'time' for the fundamental fact which I call the 'passage of nature.'"

22. Heinrich Wölfflin, *Principles of Art History: The Problem of the Development of Style in Later Art* (1915), trans. M. D. Hottinger, from the 7th German edition (1929) (New York: Dover, 1932). Wilhelm Worringer would later undertake a similar conceptual analysis of the concept of the Gothic, which Deleuze appeals to frequently. See Wilhelm Worringer, *Form in Gothic* (1911), ed. Herbert Read (London: G. P. Putnam's Sons, 1927), as well as *Abstraction and Empathy: A Contribution to the Psychology of Style* (1908), trans. Michael Bullock (Chicago: Elephant Paperbacks, 1997).

23. For a penetrating analysis of Wölfflin's work along these lines, see Arnold I. Davidson, "Styles of Reasoning: From the History of Art to the Epistemology of Science," in *The Emergence of Sexuality: Historical Epistemology and the Formation of Concepts* (Cambridge, MA: Harvard University Press, 2001), 125–141.

24. Arnold I. Davidson, "Closing Up the Corpses: Diseases of Sexuality and the Emergence of the Psychiatric Style of Reasoning" and "Sex and the Emergence of Sexuality," in *The Emergence of Sexuality*, 1–65. See also David Halperin's now-classic analysis, *One Hundred Years of Homosexuality: And Other Essays on Greek Love* (New York: Routledge, 1989).

25. See, in general, Ian Hacking, "Making Up People," in *Historical Ontology* (Cambridge, MA: Harvard University Press, 2002), 99–114; and "Biopower and the Avalanche of Printed Numbers," in *Humanities in Society* 5 (1982), 279–95. For Hacking's analysis of specific concepts and their corresponding modes of existence, see: (1) on *multiple personality*: "The Invention of Split Personalities," in *Human Nature and Natural Knowledge*, ed. Alan Donagan, Anthony N. Perovich, Jr., and Michael V. Wedlin (Dordrecht: Springer, 1986), 63–85; (2) on *child abuse*: "The Making and Molding of Child Abuse," in *Critical Inquiry* 17 (Winter 1991), 253–88; and (3) on *autism*:"What is Tom Saying to Maureen?," in *London Review of Books*, Vol. 28, No. 9 (May 2006), 3–7.

26. See N 156, LS 261–2, and DR 116. These texts are all referring to Claude Lévi-Strauss, *Totemism*, trans. Rodney Needham (Boston: Beacon, 1963), 77: "It is not the resemblance, but the differences, which resemble each other."

27. For a comprehensive analysis of Deleuze's concept of time, which we are merely summarizing here, see James Williams, *Gilles Deleuze's Philosophy of Time* (Edinburgh: Edinburgh University Press, 2011). Williams focuses primarily on *Difference and Repetition* and *Logic of Sense* rather than the analyses of time presented in the *Cinema* books (see 159–64), although the later works seem to expand on Deleuze's earlier discussions of time in crucial ways.

28. Plato, *Timaeus*, 37d. Aristotle's definition is similarly indexed on movement: "time is the number of motion in respect of before and after" (*Physics* 219b2).

29. Deleuze discusses the conceptions of time in Plato and Plotinus; see the series of seminars from 7 February 1984 to 27 March 1984. Descartes's modern solution to the same problem was to conserve something invariant "in" movement: namely, the quantity of movement, mv, the product of mass times velocity.

30. See Michel Serres, *The Birth of Physics*, trans. Jack Hawkes, ed. David Webb (Manchester: Clinamen, 2000), 67; and Michel Serres, *Atlas* (Paris: Julliard, 1994), 100.

31. See Max Weber, *The Protestant Ethic and the Spirit of Capitalism* [1905]; *and Other Writings* (London: Penguin, 2002), as well as 27 Mar 1984.

32. For Deleuze's elucidation of these themes, see 17 Apr 1984 and 4 May 1984. See also TRM

238: "Philosophy creates concepts, which are neither generalities nor even truths; they are rather of the order of the Singular, the Important, the New."

33. One of the themes of Deleuze's two-volume *Cinema* is that the cinema, in its much shorter history, none the less recapitulated this philosophical revolution in the movement–time relation. For a useful summary of this revolution in the concept of time, albeit from a slightly different perspective than Deleuze's, see John Dewey, "Time and Individuality" (1940), in *The Essential Dewey*, Vol. 1., *Pragmatism, Education, Democracy*, ed. Larry A. Hickman and Thomas M. Alexander (Bloomington and Indianapolis: Indiana University Press, 1998), 217–26.

34. See Gottfried Wilhelm Leibniz, *The Leibniz–Clarke Correspondence*, ed. H. G. Alexander (Manchester: Manchester University Press, 1956), 15:

> As for my own opinion, I have said more than once that I hold space to be something purely relative, as time is – that I hold it to be an order of coexistences, as time is an order of successions. For space denotes, in terms of possibility, an order of things that exist at the same time, considered as existing together, without entering into their particular manners of existing. And when many things are seen together, one consciously perceives this order of things among themselves.

35. Deleuze insists that it is important not to confuse the synthesis of time with time itself. Martin Heidegger, in *Kant and the Problem of Metaphysics*, trans. James S. Churchill (Bloomington: Indiana University Press, 1962), reintroduced an originary time because he wrongly consider the synthesis of time to be an originary time. See Deleuze's critique in 17 Apr 1984.

36. For the *active syntheses* of the transcendental ego found in Kant, Deleuze substitutes a theory of *passive synthesis*, derived in part from Husserl. Joe Hughes provides an insightful analysis of the concept of passive synthesis in *Deleuze and the Genesis of Representation* (London and New York: Continuum, 2008), esp. 8–19. See also Keith Faulkner, *Deleuze and the Three Syntheses of Time* (New York: Peter Lang, 2005).

37. Henri Bergson, *Creative Evolution*, trans. Arthur Mitchell (New York: Henry Holt, 1911), 13.

38. Bellour nicely summarizes the tension inherent in Deleuze's analytic when he asks: "How can the concept be both what suspends, arrests, consists, and what flees, opens all lines of flight?" See Raymond Bellour, "Thinking, Recounting: The Cinema of Gilles Deleuze," trans. Melissa McMahon, in *Discourse*, Vol. 20, No. 3 (Fall 1998), 56–75 (71).

39. Paul Patton makes the comparison between Deleuzian concepts and hypertext documents in his review of *What is Philosophy?* in the *Times Literary Supplement*, 23 Jun 1995, 10–12.

40. See Villani, *La Guêpe et l'orchidée*, 130:

> I feel myself to be Bergsonian, when Bergson says that modern science has not found its metaphysics, the metaphysics it needs. It is this metaphysics that interests me . . . It is in this manner, it seems to me, that philosophy can be considered as a science: determining the conditions of a problem.

Following Deleuze, Michel Foucault would later take up this concept of "problematization" in interpreting the course of his own work. See Michel Foucault, "Polemics, Politics, and Problematizations," in *The Foucault Reader*, ed. Paul Rabinow (New York: Pantheon, 1984), 381–90.

41. Immanuel Kant, *Critique of Pure Reason*, 319, A328/B384: "The absolute whole of appearances [the World] is only an Idea, since it remains a *problem* to which there is no solution."

42. B 17–18. See Bergson's classic article "The Possible and the Real," in Henri Bergson, *The Creative Mind*, trans. Mabelle L. Andison (Totowa, NJ: Littlefield, Adams, 1946), 91–106.

43. Ludwig Wittgenstein, *Philosophical Occasions, 1912–1951*, ed. James Klagge and Alfred Mordmann (Indianapolis: Hackett, 1993), 193. No doubt this was one reason Deleuze was not sympathetic to Wittgenstein: the dissolution of false problems has as its necessary correlate the construction of true problems.

44. Kierkegaard argued that the *interesting* is one of the fundamental categories of philosophy. See Søren Kierkegaard, *Fear and Trembling*, trans. Alastair Hannay (London: Penguin, 1985), 109: "The category I would like to examine a little more closely is that of the *interesting* . . . ."

45. See N 130: "Poincaré used to say that many mathematical theories are completely irrelevant, pointless. He didn't say they were wrong—that wouldn't have been so bad."

46. N 25. For the idea of a "philosophy of circumstances," see Michel Serres, *The Five Senses*, trans. Margaret Sankey and Peter Cowley (London: Continuum, 2008), esp. 282–88.

47. Mikhail M. Bakhtin, "Forms of Time and of Chronotope in the Novel," in *The Dialogical Imagination: Four Essays*, trans. Caryl Emerson and Michael Holquist, ed. Michael Holquist (Austin: University of Texas Press, 1981), 84–258.

48. Similarly, one could say that our culture has yet to develop a secularized relation to science; see Serres, *The Five Senses*, 334–5.

49. Friedrich Nietzsche, *Genealogy of Morals*, Essay III, §24, 153.

50. On the concept of information, in this sense, see Gilbert Simondon, *L'Individuation à la lumière des notions de forme et d'information* (Grenoble: Jérôme Millon, 2005).

51. Friedrich Nietzsche, *The Twilight of the Idols*, "How the 'True World' Finally Became a Fable," in *The Portable Nietzsche*, ed. and trans. Walter Kaufmann (New York: Viking, 1954), 486.

52. See TI 134, 145, as well as 8 Nov 1983 and 12 Jun 1984.

53. Spinoza, Letter 32, to Oldenburg, 20 Nov 1665, in *Spinoza: The Complete Works*, trans. Samuel Shirley (Indianapolis: Hackett, 2002), 849.

54. James made a similar point in his analysis of what he called "the stream of thought." See William James, *The Principles of Psychology* (1890), Vol. 1 (New York: Dover, 1950), 224–5:

> The first fact for us . . . is that thinking of some sort goes on . . . If we could say in English 'it thinks,' as we say 'it rains' or 'it blows,' we should be stating the fact most simply and with the minimum of assumption. As we cannot, we must simply say that *thought goes on*.

55. Spinoza, *The Emendation of the Intellect*, §85, in *The Collected Works of Spinoza*, ed. and trans. Edwin Curley (Princeton: Princeton University Press, 1985), 37: "So far as I know they [the ancients] never conceived the soul (as we do here) as acting according to certain laws, like a spiritual automaton." Leibniz, for his own reasons, appealed to the same image. See "Clarification of the Difficulties which Mr. Bayle has Found in the New System of the Union of Soul and Body," in Gottfried Wilhelm Leibniz, *Philosophical Papers and Letters*, 2nd edn., ed. Leroy E. Loemker (Dordrecht: D. Reidel, 1969), 495: "The soul is a most exact spiritual automaton."

56. Friedrich Nietzsche, *Beyond Good and Evil*, §17, in *Basic Writings of Nietzsche*, ed. and trans. Walter Kaufmann (New York: Modern Library, 1968), 214.

57. Friedrich Nietzsche, *Writings from the Late Notebooks*, ed. Rüdiger Bittner (Cambridge: Cambridge University Press, 2003), 34 (= Notebook 38[1] = KSA 11:38[1]). See also DR 118:

> It is not even clear that thought, in so far as it constitutes the dynamism peculiar to philosophical systems, may be related to a substantial, completed, and well-constituted subject, such as the Cartesian Cogito: thought is, rather, one of those terrible movements which can be sustained only under the conditions of a larval subject.

58. Martin Heidegger, *Being and Time*, trans. John Macquarrie and Edward Robinson (New York and San Francisco: Harper & Row, 1962), §§25–7, 35.

59. William James, *Pragmatism* [1907] (New York: Dover, 1995), 24.

60. Martin Heidegger, *What is Called Thinking*, trans. Fred D. Wieck and J. Glenn Gray (New York: Harper & Row, 1968), 64.

61. DR xxi. Deleuze and Guattari similarly suggest that *Anti-Oedipus* was written out of ignorance: "We would like to speak in the name of an absolute incompetence" (AO 380; cf. 232, 238, 334).

62. On the time (or temporal synthesis) proper to painting, see 31 Mar 1981.

Essay 9: Ethics
The Place of Ethics in Deleuze's Philosophy: Three Questions of Immanence

1. See Monique Canto-Sperber, "Pour la philosophie morale," in *Le Débat* 72 (Nov–Dec 1992), 40–51.

2. See the introduction to Michel Foucault, *The Use of Pleasure*, trans. Robert Hurley (New York: Vintage, 1985), 3–32, where Foucault explains the reformulation of the project.

3. See N 135: "Everything tended toward the great Spinoza-Nietzsche identity"

4. See Martin Heidegger, *Nietzsche*, Vol. 4: *Nihilism*, trans. Frank A. Capuzzi, ed. David Farrell Krell (San Francisco: Harper & Row, 1982), section 12, "Nietzsche's 'Moral' Interpretation of Metaphysics," 76–7: "By 'morality,' Nietzsche usually understands a system of evaluations in which a transcendent world is posited as an idealized standard of measure."

5. NP 1. For the distinction between "morality" and "ethics," see N 100, 113–14. "Règles facultatives" is a term Deleuze adopts from the sociolinguist William Labov to designate "functions of internal variation and no longer constants"; see F 147 n18.

6. On the notion of "dramatization," see NP 75–9.

7. At best, the Spinozistic and Nietzschean critiques were accepted as negative moments, exemplary instances of what must be fought against and rejected in the ethico-moral domain. See, for example, Alasdair MacIntyre, *After Virtue: A Study in Moral Theory*, 2nd edn. (Notre Dame, Indiana: University of Notre Dame Press, 1984), who, for his part, summarized the contemporary ethical options in the chapter entitled, "Aristotle or Nietzsche?": "The defensibility of the Nietzschean position turns *in the end* on the answer to the question: was it right in the first place to reject Aristotle?" (117).

8. NP 89–90. See Immanuel Kant, *Critique of Practical Reason*, in *Immanuel Kant: Practical Philosophy*, trans. Mary J. Gregor (Cambridge: Cambridge University Press, 1996), §7, Remark, 165: the consciousness of the moral law is "not an empirical fact, but the sole fact of pure reason, which, by it, proclaims itself as originally lawgiving."

9. Friedrich Nietzsche, *On the Genealogy of Morals*, in *Basic Writings of Nietzsche*, ed. and trans. Walter Kaufmann (New York: Modern Library, 1968). Preface, §6, 456; Essay 3, §24, 589.

10. The discussion that follows is a summary of Deleuze's analysis of the Moral Law in Chapter 7 of *Masochism: Coldness and Cruelty*, entitled "Humor, Irony, and the Law" (M 81–90).

11. Sigmund Freud, *Civilization and its Discontents*, trans. James Strachey (New York: W. W. Norton, 1961), 72–3.

12. M 86–90. "Perversion" plays an important role in Deleuze's writings as a specific type of mode of existence that retains a positivity of its own.

13. For Deleuze's analysis of the slave and the priest as modes of existence, see NP, Chapter 4, "From Ressentiment to the Bad Conscience," 111–45. Deleuze provides a useful summary of his interpretation in PI 17–41.

14. Deleuze's analysis of this tradition is found in his two-volume *Cinema*, where he draws a parallel between the philosophy of Pascal and Kierkegaard and the films of Bresson and Dreyer. See MI 114–16 and TI 176–9.

15. Friedrich Nietzsche, *Will to Power*, trans. Walter Kaufmann and R. J. Hollingdale (New York: Random House, 1967), §83, 51–2.

16. DR 86–7. The concept of "passive synthesis" is taken from Husserl; see Joe Hughes, *Deleuze and the Genesis of Representation* (London: Continuum, 2008), 10–19.

17. See EPS for Deleuze's three formulations of "the ethical question" in Spinoza:
    . 1. Of what affections are we capable? What is the extent of our power? (226)
    . 2. What must we do to be affected by a maximum of joyful passions? (273)
    . 3. How can we come to produce active affections? (246)

18. Nietzsche, *The Will to Power*, §532, 289; see also §489, 270.

19. On the distinction between "arborescent" and "rhizomatic" models of thought, see TP 3–25. For Spinoza's critique of the Aristotelian tradition, see SPP 44–8, and EPS 277–8.

20. See Spinoza, *Ethics*, Book 3, prop. 3, scholium, in *The Collected Works of Spinoza*, trans. Edwin Curley, 2nd edn. (Princeton: Princeton University Press, 1985), 495: "No one has yet determined what a body can do." This phrase is repeated like a leitmotif in several of Deleuze's books.

21. See the final volumes of Michel Foucault's *The History of Sexuality*: Vol. 2: *The Use of Pleasure*, trans. Robert Hurley (New York: Vintage, 1985), and Vol. 3: *The Care of the Self*, trans. Robert Hurley (New York: Pantheon, 1986). The fourth volume of the series, *Les Aveux de la chair* (*The Confessions of the Flesh*), was written but never published.

22. This is particularly true of a certain Hegelianism of the right that still dominates political philosophy, and weds the destiny of thought to the State (Alexandre Kojève and Eric Weil in France, Leo Strauss and Allan Bloom in America). See TP 556 n42.

23. Modern thought thus found itself subordinated to an image of thought derived from the legislative and juridical organization of the State, leading to the prevalence, in political philosophy, of such categories as the republic of free spirits, the tribunal of reason, the rights of man, the consensual contract, inquiries into the understanding (method, recognition, question and response, judgment), and so on. On these themes, see TP 374–80.

24. Immanuel Kant, *Critique of Pure Reason*, trans. Norman Kemp Smith (London: Macmillan, 1929), 316, A323/B379: "We have to seek for an *unconditioned*, first, of the *categorical* synthesis in a *subject*; secondly, of the *hypothetical* synthesis of the members of a *series*; thirdly, of the *disjunctive* synthesis of the parts in a *system*."

25. AO analyses "primitive" societies, the State, and capitalism (139–271); TP adds to this an analysis of the nomadic war machine (351–423), and in an essential chapter entitled "Apparatus of Capture" (424–73), it attempts to lay out in specific terms the complex relations between these various typologies. For analyses of the typology of social formations developed in *Capitalism and Schizophrenia*, see Eugene Holland, *Deleuze and Guattari's "Anti-Oedipus": An Introduction to Schizoanalysis* (London and New York: Routledge, 1999), and Ian Buchanan, *Deleuze and Guattari's "Anti-Oedipus": A Reader's Guide* (London: Continuum, 2008).

26. D 125; TP 277. John Protevi has explored the political implications of Deleuze's theory of the affects, most notably in *Political Physics: Deleuze, Derrida, and the Body Politic* (London and New York: Athlone, 2001), and *Political Affect: Connecting the Social and the Somatic* (Minneapolis: University of Minnesota Press, 2009).

27. On "infantile leftism," see Michael Walzer, "The Politics of Michel Foucault," in *Foucault: A Critical Reader*, ed. David Couzens Hoy (New York: Basil Blackwell, 1986), 51. On "neo-conservatism," see Jürgen Habermas, *The Philosophical Discourse of Modernity* (Cambridge, MA: MIT Press, 1988).

28. Deleuze analyzes these distinctions in detail in EPS, notably in Chapter 16, "The Ethical Vision of the World," 255–72. See also SPP, entry on "Power," 97–104.

29. See WP 74:

> There is not the slightest reason for thinking that modes of existence need transcendent values by which they could be compared selected, and judged relative to one another. There are only immanent criteria. A possibility of life is evaluated through itself in the movements its lays out and the intensities it creates on a plane of immanence: what is not laid out or created is rejected. A mode of existence is good or bad, noble or vulgar, complete or empty, independently of Good or Evil or any transcendent value: there are never any criteria other than the tenor of existence, the intensification of life.

30. For instance, in a famous text, which in some respects parallels Nietzsche's analyses in the *Genealogy of Morals*, Spinoza showed how the notion of the Law arose among the Hebrews from a misunderstanding of affective relations. When God forbade Adam to eat the fruit of the Garden of Eden, he did so because he knew it would affect Adam's body like a poison, decomposing its constitutive relation. But Adam, unable to perceive these affective relations, mistook the prohibition for a *commandment*, the effect of decomposition as a *punishment*, and the word of God as a *Law*. See Spinoza, Letter 19, to Blijenbergh, in *Collected Works*, 357–61. On the question, Can there be inherently evil modes of existence?, see SPP 30–43.

31. Pierre Hadot, *Philosophy as a Way of Life*, ed. Arnold I. Davidson (Cambridge, MA: Blackwell, 1995), esp. 81–125. See also LS 142–53 ("On the Moral Problem in Stoic Philosophy").

32. See EPS 273–320 (Chapters 17–19), and NP 147–98 (Chapter 5).

33. See Foucault, *The Use of Pleasure*, 25–30.

34. For Deleuze and Guattari's development of the concept of the "minor," see TP 105–6, 291–2, 469–73, and K 16–27.

35. N 177–82. See also the analyses in Paul Virilio, *Speed and Politiøcs*, trans. Mark Polizzotti (New York: Semiotext(e), 1986).

36. On these interrelated Foucauldian themes, see F 115–19.

Essay 10: Politics
Flow, Code, and Stock: A Note on Deleuze's Political Philosophy

1. This article is an excerpt from a set of lectures given at the *Collegium Phaenomenologicum*, 13–31 July 2009, in Città di Castello, Italy, organized by Peg Birmingham, to whom I owe a debt of gratitude. An early version was presented as a paper at *ConnectDeleuze*, the Second International Deleuze Studies conference at the University of Cologne on 10–13 August 2009, organized by Leyla Haferkamp and Hanjo Berressem.

2. I can give no notion by references or citations of what this paper owes to previous studies of *Anti-Oedipus*, notably Eugene Holland, *Deleuze and Guattari's "Anti-Oedipus": Introduction to Schizoanalysis* (New York: Routledge, 1999), Nick Thoburn, *Deleuze, Marx and Politics* (New York and London: Routledge, 2003), and Ian Buchanan, *Deleuze and Guattari's "Anti-Oedipus": A Reader's Guide* (London: Continuum, 2008), as well as the articles included in the special issue of *Deleuze Studies* (2009) "Deleuze and Marx," Vol. 3, Supplement (Sept 2009). On the relation of Marx and Keynes, see Antonio Negri, *Revolution Retrieved: Writings on Marx, Keynes, Capitalist Crisis, and New Social Subjects (1967–1983)* (London: Red Notes, 1983).

3. Gilles Deleuze and Félix Guattari, "In Flux," in Félix Guattari, *Chaosophy*, ed. Sylvère Lotringer (New York: Semiotext(e), 1995), 98. See also 14 Dec 1971: "It is not yet important for us to have a real definition of flows, but it is important, as a starting point, to have a nominal definition and this nominal definition must provide us with an initial system of concepts."

4. Paul Virilio has shown that the problem for the police is not one of confinement (Foucault),

but concerns the flux of the "highways," speed or acceleration, the mastery and control of speed, circuits and grids set up in open space. See F 42.

5. Deleuze and Guattari provide a similar list in TP 468: "The four principal flows that torment the representatives of the world economy, or of the axiomatic, are the flow of matter-energy, the flow of population, the flow of food, and the urban flow."

6. Robert L. Heilbroner, *The Worldly Philosophers: The Lives, Times and Ideas of the Great Economic Thinkers*, rev. 7th edn. (New York: Touchstone, 1999).

7. N 171. Jacques Derrida made a similar claim in *Spectres de Marx: L'État de la dette, le travail du deuil et la nouvelle Internationale*, Paris: Galilée, 1993), 101: "Marxism remains at once indispensable and structurally insufficient *but* provided that one transforms and adapts it to new conditions." See also the analyses in Alain Badiou, *D'un désastre obscur: droit, état, politique* (Paris: Éditions de l'Aube, 1991), and Félix Guattari and Antonio Negri, *Communists Like Us* (New York: Semiotext(e), 1991).

8. Jean-François Lyotard, "Energumen Capitalism" (review of *Anti-Oedipus*), *Critique* 306 (Nov 1972), 923–56.

9. Louis Althusser and Étienne Balibar, *Reading Capital*, trans. Ben Brewster (London: Verso, 2009).

10. See AO 116:

> From the beginning of this study we have maintained both that social production and desiring-production are one and the same, and that they have differing regimes, with the result that a social form of production exercises an essential repression of desiring-production, and also that desiring-production—a "real" desire—is potentially capable of demolishing the social form.

11. John Maynard Keynes, *The General Theory of Employment, Interest, and Money* (New York: Harcourt, 1964). Deleuze seems to have relied in part on a study of Keynes by Daniel Antier entitled *L'Étude des flux et des stocks* (Paris: Sedes, 1957); see 14 Dec 1971.

12. Niall Ferguson, *The Ascent of Money: A Financial History of the World* (New York: Penguin, 2008), 121. In speaking of desire, Keynes often had recourse to the phrase "animal spirits":

> Most of our decisions to do something positive, the full consequences of which will be drawn out over many days to come, can only be taken as the result of animal spirits . . . and not as the outcome of a weighted average of quantitative benefits multiplied by quantitiative probabilities. (Keynes, *The General Theory*, 161)

13. Dynamic systems theory was formalized by Jay W. Forrester in his *Principles of Systems*, 2nd edn. (New York: Pegasus, 1968), who referred to stocks as "levels," and to flows as "rates."

14. One can point to many examples of "decoding" that Deleuze does not mention. In the Middle Ages, for instance, *usury*, the lending of money at interest, was considered to be a sin—whence the figure of Jewish moneylenders such as Shylock, who were not subject to the Christian restriction: a line of flight in an otherwise overcoded economy. Similarly, it was not until 1971, a few months before *Anti-Oedipus* was published, that the U.S. dollar was removed from the gold standard and instead allowed to float freely on the exchange market—a further decoding of money that broke the centuries-old link between money and precious metal.

15. TP 453. Bernard Schmitt, in his *Monnaie, salaires et profits* (Paris: PUF, 1966), advanced a profound theory of money that Deleuze has drawn heavily from, describing the full body of capital as "a flow possessing the power of mutation" that does not enter into income and is not assigned to purchases, a pure availability, non-possession and non-wealth. See AO 237 and N 152.

16. See AO 290: "Molecular biology teaches us that it is only the DNA that is reproduced, and not the proteins. Proteins are both products and units of production; they are what constitute the unconscious as a cycle or as the auto-production of the unconscious."

17. TP 10, citing Rémy Chauvin, *Entretiens sur la sexualité*, ed. Max Aron, Robert Courrier, and Étienne Wolf (Paris: Plon, 1969).

18. TP 10–11, citing François Jacob, *The Logic of Life*, trans. Betty E. Spellman (New York: Pantheon, 1973).

19. See AO 141–2:

> The social machine is literally a machine, independently of any metaphor, in that it presents an immobile motor and undertakes diverse kinds of cuts: selection [*prélèvement*] from the flows, detachments from the chain, distribution of parts. Coding the flows implies all these operations. This is the highest task of the social machine, in that the selections [*prélèvements*] of production correspond to detachments from the chain, resulting in a residual share for each member, in a global system of desire and destiny that organizes the productions of production, the productions of recording, and the productions of consumption.

Essay 11: Desire
Deleuze and the Question of Desire: Toward an Immanent Theory of Ethics

1. A shorter version of this paper was originally presented as a talk in the "Ethics and Recent Critical Theory" lecture series at the University of North Carolina, Chapel Hill, on 30 November 2005, organized by Gregory Flaxman.

2. N 135: "Everything tended toward the great Spinoza–Nietzsche identity." Deleuze devoted a full-length monograph and a shorter introductory volume to both of these thinkers: *Nietzsche and Philosophy* (1962) and *Nietzsche* (1965); *Expressionism in Philosophy: Spinoza* (1968) and *Spinoza: Practical Philosophy* (1970; revised and expanded edition, 1981).

3. Friedrich Nietzsche, *On the Genealogy of Morals*, Essay 1, §17, in *Basic Writings of Nietzsche*, trans. Walter Kaufmann (New York: Modern Library, 1968), 491.

4. See WP 74:

> There is not the slightest reason for thinking that modes of existence need transcendent values by which they could be compared selected, and judged relative to one another. There are only immanent criteria. A possibility of life is evaluated through itself in the movements its lays out and the intensities it creates on a plane of immanence: what is not laid out or created is rejected. A mode of existence is good or bad, noble or vulgar, complete or empty, independently of Good or Evil or any transcendent value: there are never any criteria other than the tenor of existence, the intensification of life.

5. For instance, in a famous text, which parallels Nietzsche's analyses in the *Genealogy of Morals*, Spinoza argues that the notion of the Law arose among the Hebrews from a misunderstanding of affective relations. When God forbade Adam to eat the fruit of the Garden of Eden, he did so because he knew it would affect Adam's body like a poison, decomposing its constitutive relation. But Adam, unable to perceive these affective relations, mistook the prohibition for a *commandment*, the effect of decomposition as a *punishment*, and the word of God as a *Law*. Spinoza, Letter 19, to Blijenbergh, in *The Collected Works of Spinoza*, ed. and trans. Edwin Curley, 2nd edn. (Princeton: Princeton University Press, 1985), 357–61. On the important question, "Can there be inherently evil modes of existence?" see Deleuze's article, "The Letters on Evil (Correspondence with Blyenbergh)," in SPP 30–43.

6. See AO 29: "The fundamental problem of political philosophy is still precisely the one that Spinoza saw so clearly: 'Why do men fight *for* their servitude as stubbornly as though it were their salvation?'" Deleuze is referring to a text in Spinoza's *Theological-Political Treatise*, trans. Samuel Shirley (Indianapolis and Cambridge: Hackett, 1998), Preface, 3:

> The supreme mystery of despotism, its prop and stay, is to keep men in a state of deception, and with the specious title of religion to cloak the fear by which they must be held in check, so that they will fight for their servitude as if for salvation, and count it no shame, but the highest honor, to spend their blood and their lives for the glorification of one man.

7. I should note that Deleuze himself rarely uses the language of "drives"; in NP, he instead utilizes the language of "forces" in analyzing Nietzsche's work. See also AO 35: "It is certainly not in relation to drives that sufficient current definitions can be given to the neurotic, the pervert, and the psychotic; for drives are simply the desiring-machines themselves. They can only be defined in relation to modern territorialities."

8. Friedrich Nietzsche, *Daybreak: Thoughts on the Prejudices of Morality*, trans. R. J. Hollingdale (Cambridge University Press, 1982), §119, 76.

9. Friedrich Nietzsche, *Sämtliche Werke: Kritische Studienausgabe*, ed. Giorgio Colli and Mazzino Montinari (Munich: Deutscher Taschenbuch, 1980), Vol. 9, Notebook 6, §70, as cited in Graham Parkes, *Composing the Soul: The Reaches of Nietzsche's Psychology* (Chicago: University of Chicago Press, 1994), 292. My discussion here is indebted to Parkes's work.

10. Friedrich Nietzsche, *Will to Power*, trans. Walter Kaufmann and R. J. Hollingdale (New York: Random House, 1967), §481, 267.

11. Nietzsche, *Daybreak*, §109, 64–5. See Parkes's analysis in *Composing the Soul*, Chapter 8, "Dominions of Drives and Persons," 273–318, especially 290–2.

12. Friedrich Nietzsche, *Beyond Good and Evil*, §36, in *Basic Writings of Nietzsche*, ed. and trans. Walter Kaufmann (New York: Modern Library, 1968), 237.

13. Parkes, *Composing the Soul*, 292.

14. Nietzsche, *Beyond Good and Evil*, §19, in *Basic Writings*, 215–17.

15. Nietzsche, *Daybreak*, §119, 74.

16. Friedrich Nietzsche, *Will to Power*, §387, 208.

17. Friedrich Nietzsche, *The Gay Science*, trans. Walter Kaufmann (New York: Vintage, 1974), §307, 245–6.

18. Nietzsche, *The Gay Science*, §§116 and 115, 174.

19. Friedrich Nietzsche, *Beyond Good and Evil*, §36, in *Basic Writings*, 237–8:

> Suppose nothing else were "given" except our world of desires and passions, and we could not get down, or up, to any other "reality" besides the reality of our drives . . . : Is it not permitted to make the experiment and to ask the question whether this "given" would not be *sufficient* for also understanding on the basis of this kind of thing the so-called mechanistic (or "material") world? . . . In the end not only is it permitted to make this experiment; the conscience of *method* demands it.

20. Nietzsche, *Genealogy of Morals*, Essay I, §13, in *Basic Writings*, 480–1.

21. Nietzsche, *Genealogy of Morals*, Essay I, §13, in *Basic Writings*, 482.

22. Nietzsche, *Genealogy of Morals*, Essay II, §16, in *Basic Writings*, 520–1, as quoted in NP 128.

23. Gottfried Wilhelm Leibniz, *New Essays on Human Understanding*, trans. and ed. Peter Remnant and Jonathan Bennett (Cambridge: Cambridge University Press, 1981), notably Chapters 20 and 21. For a related text, see *The Leibniz–Clarke Correspondence*, ed. H. G. Alexander (Manchester: Manchester University Press, 1956), Leibniz's Fifth Paper, §§14–17, 58–60.

24. Nietzsche, *The Gay Science*, §357, 305.

25. Leibniz, *New Essays*, 165, 188.

> What usually drives us are those minute insensible perceptions which could be called sufferings that we cannot become aware of, if the notion of suffering did not involve

awareness . . . We are never completely in equilibrium and can never be evenly balanced between two options. (188)

26. Leibniz, *New Essays*, 166:

These impulses are like so many little springs trying to unwind and so driving our machine along . . . That is why we are never indifferent, even when we appear to be most so, as for instance over whether to turn left or right at the end of a lane. For the choice that we make arises from these insensible stimuli, which . . . make us find one direction of movement more comfortable than another.

27. Nietzsche, *Daybreak*, §129, 129.
28. Henri Bergson, *Time and Free Will: An Essay on the Immediate Data of Consciousness*, trans. F. L. Pogson (London: George Allen, 1913), 171, 176.

Essay 12: Life
"A Life of Pure Immanence": Deleuze's "Critique et clinique" Project

1. Deleuze's *Masochism: Coldness and Cruelty* is an expansion of ideas first developed in "De Sacher-Masoch au masochisme," in *Arguments* 5/21 (Jan–Apr 1961), 40–6. See also the short but important interview with Madeleine Chapsal, "Mysticism and Masochism," in DI 131–4.
2. N 142: "I've dreamed about bringing together a series of studies under the general title Critique et clinique." For other explicit references to the project, see M 15; LS 83, 92, 127–8, 237–8; and D 120, 141. François Dosse, in his *Gilles Deleuze and Félix Guattari: Intersecting Lives*, trans. Deborah Glassman (New York: Columbia University Press, 2010), notes that "most of the unpublished articles that appeared in *Essays Critical and Clinical* were written in Limousin," the locale of the Deleuze family's summer house (359).
3. See DR xv: "A philosophical concept can never be confused with a scientific function or an artistic construction, but finds itself in affinity with these in this or that domain of science or style of art." Deleuze and Guattari analyze the precise relations between philosophy, art, science, and logic in WP. On philosophy's need for such "intercessors" or mediators, see N 123–6.
4. TRM 176. Deleuze was responding to a question concerning the "genre" of A Thousand Plateaus, but his response is equally applicable to all his books.
5. Deleuze has established numerous such links in his works—between, for instance, Chekhov's short stories and Foucault's "Infamous Men" (N 108, 150); between Shakespeare's Hamlet and Kant's *Critique of Pure Reason* (ECC 28); between Alfred Jarry and Martin Heidegger (ECC 91–8); and in the cinema, between Kierkegaard and Dreyer, and between Pascal and Bresson (MI 114–16). One might note that Stanley Cavell presents his own interest in the cinema in similar terms:"I discuss the blanket in It Happened One Night in terms of the censoring of human knowledge and aspiration in the philosophy of Kant; and I see the speculation of Heidegger exemplified or explained in the countenance of Buster Keaton." See "The Thought of Movies," in *Themes Out of School: Effects and Causes* (Chicago: University of Chicago Press, 1984), 6–7.
6. Gilles Deleuze, "Lettre-préface," in Mireille Buydens, *Sahara: L'Esthétique de Gilles Deleuze* (Paris: Vrin, 1990), 5; and N 143. The term "non-organic life" is derived from Wilhelm Worringer, *Form in Gothic* (London: G. P. Putnam's Sons, 1927), 41–2, who used it to describe the vitality of the abstract line in Gothic art (see TP 496–8).
7. Charles Dickens, *Our Mutual Friend*, Book 3, Chapter 3, in *The Oxford Illustrated Dickens* (London: Oxford University Press, 1952), 443.
8. See NP 1: "We always have the beliefs, feelings, and thoughts we deserve, given our way of

being or our style of life." On the distinction between ethics and morality, see N 100, 114–15; and SPP 17–29. *Règles facultatives* is a term Deleuze adopts from the sociolinguist William Labov to designate "functions of internal variation and no longer constants" (F 146–7 n18).

9. Friedrich Nietzsche, *On the Genealogy of Morals*, Essay 1, §17, in *Basic Writings of Nietzsche*, trans. Walter Kaufmann (New York: Modern Library, 1968), 491.

10. N 143; WP 171. See Deleuze's summary of Melville's conception of the relation of the novel to "Life" in ECC 81–2:

> Why should the novelist believe he is obligated to explain the behavior of his characters, and to supply them with reasons, whereas life for its part never explains anything and leaves in its creatures so many indeterminate, obscure, indiscernible zones that defy any attempt at clarification? It is life that justifies; it has no need of being justified . . . The founding act of the American novel, like that of the Russian novel, was to take the novel far from the order of reasons, and to give birth to characters who exist in nothingness, survive only in the void, defy logic and psychology, and keep their mystery until the end . . . The novel, like life, has no need of justification.

11. Deleuze was responding to a question posed to him during the Cerisy colloquium on Nietzsche in 1972; see *Nietzsche aujourd'hui* (Paris: Union Générale d'Éditions, 10/18, 1973), Vol. 1, *Intensities*, 186–7. Moreover, Deleuze and Guattari have distanced themselves from certain Heideggerian problematics that Derrida has taken up: "The death of metaphysics or the overcoming of philosophy has never been a problem for us" (WP 9). Deleuze none the less cites Derrida on numerous occasions, and the many lines of convergence between their respective works remain to be explored.

12. M 133. The history of medicine, Deleuze suggests, can therefore be regarded under at least two aspects. The first is the history of diseases, which may disappear, recede, reappear, or alter their form depending on numerous external factors (the appearance of new microbes or viruses, altered technological and therapeutic techniques, and changing social conditions). But intertwined with this is the history of symptomatology, which is a kind of "syntax" of medicine that sometimes follows and sometimes precedes changes in therapy or the nature of diseases: symptoms are isolated, named, and regrouped in various manners. While external factors can make new symptomatologies possible, they can never determine them as such. See, for instance, Deleuze's comments on post-World War II developments in symptomatology in N 132–3.

13. See LS 237: "From the perspective of Freud's genius, it is not the complex which provides us with information about Oedipus and Hamlet, but rather Oedipus and Hamlet who provide us with information about the complex."

14. See, in particular, Friedrich Nietzsche, "The Philosopher as Cultural Physician" (1873), in *Philosophy and Truth*, ed. Daniel Brezeale (Atlantic Highlands, NJ: Humanities Press, 1979), 67–76, though the idea of the philosopher as a physician of culture occurs throughout Nietzsche's writings. For Deleuze's analysis of the symptomatological method in Nietzsche, see NP x, 3, 75, 79, 157.

15. On all these points, see the important passage in AO 132–6, especially on the status of psychosis in literature (Artaud). For Freud, the libido does not invest the social field as such except on the condition that it be "desexualized" and "sublimated"; any sexual libidinal investment having a social dimension therefore seems to him to bear witness to a pathogenic state, either a "fixation" in narcissism or a "regression" to pre-Oedipal states. For Deleuze's reflections on the present state of "the space of literature" and the fragile conditions for the literary production, see N 22–3, 128–31. On the effect of marketing on both literature and philosophy, see Deleuze's critique of the "new philosophers," "À propos des nouveaux philosophes et d'un problème plus général," *Minuit* 4, supplement (5 Jun 1977), n.p.

16. See Gilles Deleuze, "De Sacher-Masoch au masochisme," in *Arguments* 5/21 (Jan–Apr 1961), 40–6: 40. For an analysis of the role of the "sexual instinct," whose various transformations and inversions were used to account for the "perversions" in nineteenth-century psychiatry, see Arnold I. Davidson, "Closing Up the Corpses," in *The Emergence of Sexuality: Historical Epistemology and the Formation of Concepts* (Cambridge, MA: Harvard University Press, 2001), 1–29.

17. Deleuze summarizes the results of his clinical analyses in eleven propositions in the last paragraph of the book (M 134). For the analyses of Sade's and Masoch's literary techniques, see M 25–35. For the relation to minorities, see M 9–10, 93; N 142.

18. DI 133. "Mystique et masochisme," 12–13. Asked why he had treated only Sade and Masoch from this point of view, Deleuze replied,

> There are others, in fact, but their work has not yet been recognized under the aspect of a creative symptomatology, as was the case with Masoch at the start. There is a prodigious table [*tableau*] of symptoms corresponding to the work of Samuel Beckett: not that it is simply a question of identifying an illness: but the world as symptom, and the artist as symptomatologist. (DI 132)

19. See N 142: "The *Recherche* is a general semiology, a symptomatology of different worlds."

20. See Deleuze's discussion of the three components of the "critique et clinique" project in D 120–3; the third component (lines of flight) is discussed in the latter sections of this essay.

21. Gilles Deleuze, "Schizophrénie et positivité du désir," in *Encyclopédie Universalis* (Paris: Encyclopédie Universalis France, 1972), Vol. 14, 735; English translation in TRM 17–28.

22. The definition of schizophrenia as a process has a complex history. When Émile Kraepelin tried to ground his concept of dementia praecox ("premature senility"), he defined it neither by causes nor by symptoms, but by a process, by an evolution and a terminal state; but he conceived of this terminal state as a complete and total disintegration, which justified the confinement of the patient in an asylum while awaiting his death. Deleuze and Guattari's notion is closer to that of Karl Jaspers and R. D. Laing, who formulated a rich notion of process as a rupture, an irruption, an opening (*percée*) that breaks the continuity of a personality, carrying it off in a kind of voyage through an intense and terrifying "more than reality," following lines of flight that engulf both nature and history, both the organism and the mind. See AO 24–5.

23. Gilles Deleuze and Félix Guattari, "La Synthèse disjonctive," *L'Arc* 43 (1970), special issue on Pierre Klossowski, 56.

24. TP 4; N 23. See also TRM 25: "Let us resign ourselves to the idea that certain artists or writers have had more revelations concerning schizophrenia than the psychiatrists and psychoanalysts."

25. This text is included in the English translation under the title "The Literary Machine" (PS 105–69).

26. PS 145; for the comparison with Joyce's epiphanies, see PS 155.

27. PS 146. The notion that "meaning is use" comes from Wittgenstein, though to my knowledge Deleuze makes only two references to Wittgenstein in his books. In the first, he writes approvingly that "Wittgenstein and his disciples are right to define meaning by use" (LS 146); in the second, he writes that Whitehead "stands provisionally as the last great Anglo-American just before Wittgenstein's disciples spread their mists, their sufficiency, and their terror" (FLB 76). His disapproval perhaps stems from the reintroduction, by certain of Wittgenstein's followers, of a form of common sense in the guise of a grammar that would be properly philosophical and a form of life that would be generically human.

28. PS 156. See also 145, where Deleuze cites Malcolm Lowry's description of the "meaning" of his novel (*Selected Letters of Malcolm Lowry*, ed. Harvey Breit and Margerie Bonner Lowry (Philadelphia and New York: Lippincott, 1965), 6:

It can be regarded as a kind of symphony, or in another way as a kind of opera—or even a horse opera. It is hot music, a poem, a song, a tragedy, a comedy, a farce, and so forth. It is superficial, entertaining and boring, according to taste. It is a prophecy, a political warning, a cryptogram, a preposterous movie, and a writing on the wall. It can even be regarded as a sort of machine: it *works* too, believe me, as I have found out.

29. AO 324. See also "Balance-Sheet Program for Desiring Machines," in Félix Guattari, *Chaosophy*, ed. Sylvère Lotringer (New York: Semiotext(e),1995), 145:

How can elements be bound together by the absence of any link? In a certain sense, it can be said that Cartesianism, in Spinoza and Leibniz, has not ceased to reply to this question. It is the theory of the real distinction, insofar as it implies a specific logic. It is because they are really distinct, and completely independent of each other, that ultimate elements or simple forms belong to the same being or to the same substance.

30. PS 105–69. Thomas Wolfe, in his essay "The Story of a Novel," in *The Autobiography of an American Artist*, ed. Leslie Field (Cambridge, MA: Harvard University Press, 1983), describes his compositional technique in similar terms:

It was as if I had discovered a whole new universe of chemical elements and had begun to see certain relations between some of them but had by no means begun to organize and arrange the whole series in such a way that they would crystallize into a harmonious and coherent union, From this time on, I think my effort might be described as the effort to complete that organization.

31. See Ernst Mayr, "An Analysis of the Concept of Natural Selection," in *Toward a New Philosophy of Biology: Observations of an Evolutionist* (Cambridge, MA: Harvard University Press, 1988), 98: "Selection would not be possible without the continuous restoration of variability."

32. TI 129. On the philosophical use of scientific functions, see N 123–6.

33. See "Klossowski, or Bodies-Language," in LS 292–4, where Deleuze contrasts "the order of God" with "the order of the Anti-Christ."

34. FLB, Chapter 5, 59–75; and LS 110–11. For the distinction between the virtual and the actual, Deleuze relies on the model proposed in Albert Lautman's theory of differential equations in *Le Problème du temps* (Paris: Hermann, 1946), 42. Lautman argues that a singularity can be grasped in two ways. The conditions of a problem are determined by the nomadic distribution of singular points in a virtual space, in which each singularity is inseparable from a zone of objective indetermination (ordinary points). The solution appears only with the integral curves and the form they take in the neighborhood of singularities within the field of vectors, which constitutes the beginning of the actualization of the singularities (a singularity is analytically extended over a series of ordinary points until it reaches the neighborhood of another singularity, and so on).

35. Jorge Luis Borges, "The Garden of Forking Paths," in *Ficciones* (New York: Grove, 1962), 98, emphasis added. For Deleuze's various references to this story, see FLB 62; LS 114; TI 131; DR 73; F 145 n3.

36. TI 303. For Leibniz's narrative, see his *Theodicy*, trans. E. M. Huggard, ed. Austin Farrer (La Salle, IL: Open Court, 1985), §§405–17, 365–73.

37. TI 126–55. The following themes are summaries of this chapter, some of which are developed in more detail in *The Fold*, where Deleuze makes use of Leibniz's work to develop a concept of the "Baroque."

38. See LS 174:

The whole question, and rightly so, is to know under what conditions disjunction is a veritable synthesis, instead of being a procedure of analysis which is satisfied with the exclusion of predicates from a thing by virtue of the identity of its concept (the negative, limitative, or exclusive use of disjunction). The answer is given insofar as the divergence or the decentering determined by the disjunction become objects of affirmation as such . . . an *inclusive disjunction* that carries out the synthesis itself by drifting from one term to another and following the distance between terms.

For the concept of the rhizome, see TP 3–25, esp. 7.

39. N 126. See also TI 133: "Narration is constantly being modified in each of its episodes, not according to subjective variations, but as a consequence of disconnected spaces and de-chronologized moments."

40. For Deleuze's analysis of the three types of portmanteau words in Lewis Carroll's work, see "Of Esoteric Words," in LS 42–7. Deleuze cites Carroll's explanation of the disjunctive portmanteau word:

> If your thoughts incline ever so little towards "fuming," you will say "fuming-furious"; if they turn, even by a hair's breadth, towards "furious," you will say "furious-fuming"; but if you have the rarest of gifts, a perfectly balanced mind, you will say "frumious". (46)

41. See Michel Foucault, *Death and the Labyrinth: The World of Raymond Roussel* (Garden City, NY: Doubleday, 1986), esp. Chapter 2. For Deleuze's analyses, see DR 22, 121, and LS 39, 85. Roussel's language rests not simply on the combinatorial possibilities of language—the fact that language has fewer terms of designation than things to designate, but none the less can extract an immense wealth from this poverty—but more precisely on the possibility of saying two things with the same word, inscribing a maximum of difference within the repetition of the same word.

42. On Gombrowicz, see DR 123, and LS 39; on Joyce, see DR 121–3, and LS 260–1, 264.

43. Joë Bousquet, *Les Capitales* (Paris: Le Cercle du Livre, 1955), 103, as cited in LS 148. It is in the context of his discussion of Bousquet that Deleuze defines ethics in terms of the relation of the individual to the singularities it embodies: an active life is one that is able to affirm the singularities that constitute it, to become worthy of the events that happen to it. "Everything was in order with the events of my life before I made them mine," writes Bousquet. "To live them is to find myself tempted to become their equal." A reactive life, by contrast, is driven by a *ressentiment* of the event, grasping whatever happens to it as unjust and unwarranted. "Either ethics makes no sense at all," writes Deleuze, "or this is what it means and has nothing else to say: not to be unworthy of what happens to us" (LS 149).

44. Antonin Artaud, "Here Lies," in *Selected Writings*, ed. Susan Sontag, trans. Helen Weaver (New York: Farrar Straus & Giroux, 1977), 540; and Vaslav Nijinsky, *Diary* (New York: Simon & Schuster, 1936), 20, 156, as cited in AO 15, 77. On the role of included disjunctions in the schizophrenic process, see Deleuze and Guattari, "La Synthèse disjonctive," 59: "Schizophrenization: a disjunction that remains disjunctive, and which none the less affirms the disjoint terms, affirms them through all their distance, without limiting one by the other or excluding one from the other."

45. ECC 154.

> Beckett's great contribution to logic is to have shown that exhaustion (exhaustivity) does not occur without a certain physiological exhaustion . . . Perhaps it is like the front and back side of a single thing: a keen sense or science of the possible joined, or rather disjoined, with a fantastic decomposition of the "self." (ECC 154)

Deleuze himself, however, draws a sharp distinction between the virtual and the possible; see DR 211–14.

46. WP 173. Deleuze's monographs in the history of philosophy all inhabit such a zone of indiscernibility, which accounts for the sense that they are fully "Deleuzian" despite the variety of figures he considers.

47. Herman Melville, *Moby-Dick*, Chapter 36, "The Quarter-Deck," as cited in TP 245.

48. MI 102. We might note here a shift that seems to take place in Deleuze's terminology. In Spinoza, an "affection" (*affectio*) indicates the state of a body in so far as it is affected by another body, and an "affect" (*affectus*) marks the passage from one state to another as an increase or decrease in the body's power as a function of its affections. This terminology, which Deleuze analyzes in detail in *Expressionism in Philosophy: Spinoza*, is largely retained throughout *A Thousand Plateaus*. In *The Movement-Image* and *What is Philosophy?*, however, Deleuze replaces these terms with perception and affection respectively, reserving the word "affect" for the pure qualities or powers that are extracted from affections and achieve an autonomous status.

49. MI 98. This text contains Deleuze's analysis of Firstness and Secondness in Peirce and makes the comparison with Biran.

50. Emily Brontë, *Wuthering Heights* (New York: Norton, 1990), Chapter 9, 62–4.

51. François Zourabichvili, "Six Notes on the Percept (On the Relation between the Critical and the Clinical)," in *Deleuze: A Critical Reader*, ed. Paul Patton (Cambridge, MA: Blackwell, 1996), 190. Zourabichvili's article provides a profound analysis of the clinical status of the percept in Deleuze's work.

52. Virginia Woolf, *Mrs. Dalloway* (New York: Harcourt Brace & World, 1925), 11, as cited in TP 263. For Deleuze's analysis of the role of affects and percepts in T. E. Lawrence's *Seven Pillars of Wisdom*, see his essay "The Shame and the Glory: T. E. Lawrence" (ECC 115–25).

53. See Joachim Gasquet, *Cézanne: A Memoir with Conversations*, trans. Christopher Pemberton (London: Thames & Hudson, 1991), 160: "man absent from but entirely within the landscape." Cézanne's phrase captures exactly the paradox of the percept.

54. Claude Samuel, *Conversations with Olivier Messiaen*, trans. Félix Aprahamian (London: Stainer & Bell, 1976), 61–3.

55. Virginia Woolf, *The Diary of Virginia Woolf*, ed. Anne Olivier Bell (London: Hogarth, 1980), Vol. 3, 209, as cited in TP 280 and WP 172.

56. WP 170. It is precisely in this context that Deleuze considers the effects of drugs and alcohol on literary creation. Though drugs can indeed open the "doors of perception," drug-induced works rarely, if ever, attain the level of the percept; the effects of such perceptive experimentations, Deleuze argues, must be brought about "by quite different means—that is, in art. For Deleuze's discussions of drugs, see TP 282–6, which is an elaboration of an earlier article, "Deux questions" (Two questions), which appeared in *Recherches*, 39 bis (Dec 1979), 231–4. The first question concerns the "specific causality" of drugs, which Deleuze locates in a "line of flight" that invests the system of perception directly. Drugs "stop the world" and release pure auditory and optical percepts; they create microintervals and molecular holes in matter, forms, colors, sounds; and they make lines of speed pass through these intervals (see MI 85). The second question, however, concerns the inevitable "turning point": in themselves, drugs are unable to draw the plane necessary for the action of this "line of flight," and instead result in "erroneous perceptions" (Artaud), "bad feelings" (Michaux), dependency, addiction, and so on. This is why Burroughs formulates the aesthetic problem posed by drugs in the following manner: How can one incarnate the power of drugs without becoming an addict? "Imagine that everything that can be attained by chemical means is accessible by other paths" (LS 161).

57. See Deleuze and Guattari's comments in *A Thousand Plateaus*: "Is it not necessary to retain a minimum of strata, a minimum of forms or functions, a minimal subject from which to extract materials, affects, and assemblages?" (270).

You don't reach the plane of consistency by wildly destratifying . . . Staying stratified—organized, signified, subjected—is not the worst that can happen; the worst that can happen is if you throw the strata into demented or suicidal collapse, which brings them back down on us heavier than ever. This is how it should be done: Lodge yourself on a stratum, experiment with the opportunities it offers, find an advantageous place on it, find potential movements of deterritorialization, possible lines of flight, experience them, produce flow conjunctions here and there, try out continuums of intensities segment by segment, have a small plot of new land at all times. (160–1)

58. TP 356. For the comparison between Goethe and Kleist, see TP 268–9.
59. WP 88–9. This is how Deleuze defines Proust's project: to render visible the invisible force of time. "'Time, which is usually not visible, in order to become so seeks bodies and, wherever it finds them, seizes upon them in order to project its magic lantern upon them,' quartering the fragments and features of an aging face, according to its 'inconceivable dimension'" (PS 160).
60. On Deleuze's use of embryology and the model of the egg, see DR 214–17, 249–52.
61. William Burroughs, *Naked Lunch* (New York: Grove, 1966), 8, 131, as cited in TP 153, 150.
62. George Büchner, "Lenz," in *Complete Plays and Prose*, trans. Carl Richard Mueller (New York: Hill & Wang, 1963), 141, as cited in AO 2:

He thought that it must be a feeling of endless bliss to be in contact with the profound life of every form, to have a soul for rocks, metals, water, and plants, to take into himself, as in a dream, every element of nature, like flowers that breathe with the waxing and waning of the moon.

63. D. H. Lawrence, *Fantasia of the Unconscious* (New York: Viking, 1960).
64. Arthur Rimbaud, *A Season in Hell*, in *Rimbaud: Complete Works, Selected Letters*, trans. Wallace Fowlie (Chicago: University of Chicago Press, 1966), 177, 179, 189, 193.
65. See Pierre Klossowski, "The Euphoria at Turin," in *Nietzsche and the Vicious Circle*, trans. Daniel W. Smith (Chicago: University of Chicago Press, 1997). Klossowski cites one of Nietzsche's final fragments, in which the two poles of delirium are mixed:

I touch here the question of race. I am a Polish gentleman, pure blood, in whom not a drop of impure blood is mixed, not the slightest. If I seek my most profound opposite . . . —I always find my mother and my sister: to see myself allied with such German riff-raff was a blasphemy against my divinity. The ancestry on the side of my mother and sister to this very day (—) was a monstrosity. (250)

66. D 36–51. The Anglo-American writers that appear most frequently in Deleuze's writings include Samuel Beckett, William Burroughs, Lewis Carroll, Charles Dickens, F. Scott Fitzgerald, Allen Ginsberg, Thomas Hardy, Henry James, James Joyce, Jack Kerouac, D. H. Lawrence, T. E. Lawrence, H. P. Lovecraft, Malcolm Lowry, Herman Melville, Henry Miller, R. L. Stevenson, and Virginia Woolf.
67. On the geography of American literature, see TP 19, 520 n18; on the process of demolition, see AO 133, 277–8, and D 38–9, 140–1.
68. See, for example, Paul Klee, *On Modern Art*, trans. Paul Findlay (London: Faber, 1966), 55: "We have found parts, but not the whole. We still lack the ultimate power, for the people are not with us. But we seek a people."
69. On all these points, see the short section in *The Time-Image* (TI 215–24) that analyzes the conditions of a modern political cinema. In a parallel section of the book that would deserve a separate discussion (TI 262–70), Deleuze analyzes the conditions under which the cinema is capable of fighting an internal battle against informatics and communication (a "creation beyond information").

70. See N 171–2. For Deleuze and Guattari's critique of the concept of class, see AO 252–62.

71. In TP 469–70, Deleuze and Guattari provide a set theoretical interpretation of the major / minor distinction. What defines a minority is not its number but rather relations internal to the number: a majority is constituted by a set that is *denumerable*, whereas a minority is defined as a *non-denumerable* set, no matter how many elements it has. The capitalist axiomatic manipulates only denumerable sets, whereas minorities constitute fuzzy, non-denumerable, and non-axiomizable sets, which implies a calculus of problematics rather than an axiomatic.

72. "1227: Treatise on Nomadology—The War Machine," in TP 351–423, which could be read as an attempt to set forth the type of political formation that would correspond with the "active" mode of existence outlined in Nietzsche's *Genealogy of Morals*. Revealingly, in *The Anti-Oedipus Papers*, ed. Stéphane Nadaud, trans. Kélina Gotman (New York: Semiotext(e), 2006), Guattari indicates that, in September 1972, a mere six months after the publication of *Anti-Oedipus*, Deleuze was already hard at work on the "Nomadology" chapter of *A Thousand Plateaus*. "Gilles is working like a madman on his nomads" (397), Guattari writes, almost as if Deleuze had realized, even before finishing *Anti-Oedipus*, that its tripartite typology of social formations (primitives, States, capitalism) was inadequate, and would have to be complemented with a fourth type—the nomadic war-machine.

73. Pier Paolo Pasolini develops this notion of free indirect discourse in *L'Expérience hérétique* (Paris: Payot, 1976), 39–65 (in literature), and 139–55 (in cinema). For Deleuze's analyses, see MI 72–6.

74. See Herman Melville's essay on American literature, "Hawthorne and his Mosses," in *The Portable Melville*, ed. Jay Leyda (New York: Viking, 1952), 411–14; and Franz Kafka's diary entry (25 Dec 1911) on "the literature of small peoples," in *The Diaries of Franz Kafka: 1910–1913*, ed. Max Brod, trans. Joseph Kresh (New York: Schocken, 1948), 191–8.

75. N 174. Bergson develops the notion of fabulation in Chapter 2 of *Two Sources of Morality and Religion*, trans. T. Ashley Audra and Cloudesley Brereton with W. Horsfall Carter (New York: Henry Holt, 1935).

76. D 43. For the concept of "minority," see TP 105–6, 469–71. On the conditions for a political cinema in relation to minorities, and Bergson's notion of "fabulation," see TI 215–24.

77. Marcel Proust, *By Way of Sainte-Beuve*, trans. Sylvia Townsend Warner (London: Chatto & Windus, 1978), 194–5: "Great literature is written in a sort of foreign language. To each sentence we attach a meaning, or at any rate a mental image, which is often a mistranslation. But in great literature all our mistranslations result in beauty."

78. See Gilles Deleuze, "Avenir de linguistique," preface to Henri Gobard, *L'Aliénation linguistique* (Paris: Flammarion, 1976), 9–14, translated as "The Future of Linguistics" in TRM 67–71. See also K 23–7: "The spatiotemporal categories of these languages differ sharply: vernacular language is 'here,' vehicular language is 'everywhere,' referential language is 'over there,' mythic language is 'beyond'" (K 27).

79. On all these points, see K 15–16, 23. Pierre Perrault encountered a similar situation in Quebec: the impossibility of not speaking, the impossibility of speaking other than in English, the impossibility of speaking in English, the impossibility of settling in France in order to speak French (see TI 217).

80. TP 101. See also TP 76: "A rule of grammar is a power marker before it is a syntactical marker."

81. In addition to the essays collected in *Essays Critical and Clinical*, see Deleuze's essay "Of the Schizophrenic and the Little Girl" in LS 82–93, which compares the procedures of Carroll and Artaud. See especially LS 83, where Deleuze notes that the comparison must take place at both a "clinical" and a "critical" level.

82. See Gilles Deleuze, "One Manifesto Less," in *The Deleuze Reader*, ed. Constantin V. Boundas (New York: Columbia University Press, 1994).
83. N 140–1. With regard to this "outside" of language in philosophy, Deleuze writes that "style in philosophy tends toward these three poles: concepts, or new ways of thinking; percepts, or new ways of seeing and hearing; and affects, or new ways of feeling" (N 164–5).
84. AO 133, 370–1, 106. For this use of the term experimentation, see John Cage, *Silence* (Middletown, CT: Wesleyan University Press, 1961), 13: "The word experimental is apt, providing it is understood not as descriptive of an act to be later judged in terms of success and failure, but simply as of an act the outcome of which is unknown."
85. N 146–7. See also TP 100: "Only continuous variation brings forth this virtual line, this continuum of life, 'the essential element of the real beneath the everyday.'"
86. ECC 126–35. On the distinction between "transcendent judgment" and "immanent evaluation," see TI 141:

> It is not a matter of judging life in the name of a higher authority which would be the good, the true; it is a matter, on the contrary, of evaluating every being, every action and passion, even every value, in relation to the Life which they involve. Affect as immanent evaluation, instead of judgment as transcendent value.

87. On the notion of immanent criteria, see K 87–8 and TP 70. "Although there is no preformed logical order to becomings and multiplicities, there are criteria, and the important thing is that they not be used after the fact, that they be applied in the course of events" (TP 251).
88. See D 141:

> *Critique et Clinique*: life and work are the same thing, when they have adapted the line of flight that makes them the components of the same war-machine. In these conditions, life has for a long time ceased to be personal, and the work has ceased to be literary or textual.

Essay 13: Sensation
Deleuze on Bacon: Three Conceptual Trajectories in "The Logic of Sensation"

1. Gilles Deleuze, *Francis Bacon: Logique de la sensation* (Paris: Éditions de la Différence, 1981), in the series *La vue le texte*, edited by Harry Jancovici, now out of print. A revised version appeared from Éditions de la Différence in 1983, incorporating fifteen new paintings by Bacon and one minor emendation to the text (on 25). The French book is currently available in a paperback edition published in 2002 by Éditions de Seuil, in the series L'Ordre philosophique, edited by Alain Badiou and Barbara Cassin. Deleuze also gave an important series of seminars on art from 31 Mar 1981 through 2 Jun 1981, apparently after the book had been written, which were no longer focused on Bacon's work in particular.
2. See, for instance, Patrick Vauday's early review in *Critique* 426 (1982), as well as Christine Buci-Glucksmann, "Le Plissé baroque de la peinture," *Magazine littéraire* 257 (Sep 1988).
3. Ronald Bogue's three-volume work on Deleuze and the arts, which includes *Deleuze on Music, Painting, and the Arts*, *Deleuze on Cinema*, and *Deleuze on Literature* (New York: Routledge, 2005), is a definitive study of Deleuze's "philosophy of art." My comments here are indebted to Bogue's wide-ranging work.
4. Gilles Deleuze, "8 ans après: Entretien 1980" (interview with Catherine Clément), *L'Arc* (rev. edn., 1980), special issue on Deleuze, 99.
5. John Russell, *Francis Bacon* (New York: Oxford University Press, 1971; rev. edn., 1979).
6. See Jean-François Lyotard, *Que peindre? Adami, Arakawa, Buren* (Paris: Éditions de la Différence, 1987), and Michel Butor, *Comment écrire pour Jasper Johns* (Paris: Éditions de la Différence, 1992).

7. See Michel Leiris, *Francis Bacon: Full Face and in Profile*, trans. John Weightman (New York: Rizzoli, 1983), and *Francis Bacon*, trans. John Weightman (New York: Rizzoli, 1998).

8. See Michael Peppiatt, *Francis Bacon: Anatomy of an Enigma* (New York: Farrar, Straus & Giroux, 1996), 276.

9. See ABC C: Deleuze

> doesn't believe in culture, rather he believes in encounters (*rencontres*), but these encounters don't occur with people. People think that it's with other people that encounters take place, like among intellectuals at colloquia. Encounters occur, rather, with things, with a painting, a piece of music. With people, however, these meetings are not at all encounters; these kinds of encounters are usually so disappointing, catastrophic.

10. Peppiatt, *Francis Bacon*, 305–6.

11. "La Peinture enflammé," interview with Hervé Guibert, in *Le Monde*, 3 Dec 1981, 15, in TRM 181–7: 185, 187.

12. David Sylvester, *The Brutality of Fact: Interviews with Francis Bacon 1962–1979*, 3rd edn. (New York: Thames & Hudson, 1987).

13. From Francis Bacon's introductory text to the "The Artist's Eye" exhibition at the National Gallery, London, as cited in Peppiatt, *Francis Bacon*, 310; whence the famous phrase, variously attributed, "talking about music is like dancing about architecture."

14. "La Peinture enflammé," 15, in TRM 181–7: 185.

15. Erwin Straus, *Vom Sinn der Sinne* (1935), translated as *The Primary World of the Senses: A Vindication of Sensory Experience*, trans. Jacob Needleman, 2nd edn. (New York: Free Press, 1963).

16. Marius von Senden, *Space and Sight: The Perception of Space and Shape in the Congenitally Blind Before and After Operation*, trans. Peter Heath (London and Glencoe, IL: Free Press, 1960).

17. See Daniel N. Stern, *The Interpersonal World of the Infant: A View from Psychoanalysis and Developmental Psychology* (New York: Basic, 1985) and *Diary of a Baby* (New York: Basic, 1992).

18. Straus, *The Primary World of the Senses*, 351.

19. Maurice Merleau-Ponty, *Phenomenology of Perception*, trans. Colin Smith (New York: Routledge & Kegan Paul, 1962), 102–6. Oliver Sacks's famous case of *The Man Who Mistook his Wife for a Hat* (New York: Harper & Row, 1970) explores the opposite condition (visual agnosia): a patient who had retained the abstract and categorical, but lost the concrete (7–22).

20. This reading can be found in Deleuze's seminars of 28 Mar and 4 Apr 1978, which are are available online at webdeleuze.com in an English translation by Melissa McMahon.

21. See Immanuel Kant, *Critique of Pure Reason*, trans. Norman Kemp Smith (London: Macmillan, 1929), 144 (A120): "There must exist in us an active faculty for the synthesis of the manifold. To this faculty I give the title, imagination."

22. Kant, *Critique of Pure Reason*, 105 (A68/B93): "The only use which the understanding can make of these concepts is to judge by means of them."

23. Immanuel Kant [1952], *Critique of Judgment*, trans. James Creed Meredith (Oxford: Oxford University, Press, 1978), 5§26,105. Deleuze considered the *Critique of Judgment* to be "one of the most important books in all of philosophy" (31 Mar 1981).

24. Jacques Derrida, *The Truth in Painting*, trans. Geoff Bennington and Ian McLeod (Chicago: University of Chicago Press, 1967), 140.

25. See Maurice Merleau-Ponty, *The Primacy of Perception*, ed. James Edie (Evanston: Northwestern University Press, 1964), 5.

26. Kant, *Critique of Judgment*, §26, 98.

27. See Henri Maldiney, "L'Esthetique des rhythmes," in *Regard parole espace* (Lausanne: L'Age d'Homme, 1973), 147–72: 149–51.

28. Joachim Gasquet, *Cézanne: A Memoir with Conversations*, trans. Christopher Pemberton (London: Thames & Hudson: 1991), 160. See Deleuze's commentary on this text in the seminar of 31 Mar 2981.

29. Paul Klee, *On Modern Art*, trans. Paul Findlay (London: Faber & Faber, 1966), 43. See TP 312 as well as 28 Mar 1978.

30. In Kant, sensibility is a mere receptive faculty; it simply presents a diversity of a manifold in space and time. The task of the imagination (through synthesis), the understanding (through concepts), and reason (through Ideas) is to unify this diversity (the form of recognition and common sense).

31. Gary Genosko, *Félix Guattari: An Aberrant Introduction* (London and New York: Continuum, 2002), 180. Genosko presents an analysis of Guattari's "diagrammatism" on 178–85.

32. Charles Sanders Peirce, *The Collected Papers*, ed. Charles Hartshorne and Paul Weiss (Cambridge, MA: Harvard University Press, 1935–1966), Vol. 4, 531 (as cited in Genosko, *Félix Guattari*, 179).

33. TP 531 n41. Deleuze and Guattari note that they "borrow his [Peirce's] terms, even while changing their connotations," such that they are able to assign to the diagram "a distinct role, irreducible to either the icon or the symbol." For their use of the term diagram, see TP 141–4.

34. WP 203: "The struggle with chaos that Cézanne and Klee have shown in action in painting, at the heart of painting, is found in another way in science and in philosophy."

35. Deleuze none the less occasionally makes use of this term; see, for instance, TP 497: "The figurative as such is not inherent to any 'will to art.'"

36. Maldiney, *Regard parole espace*, 195.

Essay 14: The New
The Conditions of the New

1. An early version of this paper was presented at the annual meeting of the British Society for Phenomenology at St. Hilda's College, Oxford University, in April 2005, on the theme of "The Problem of the New," organized by Robin Durie.

2. See, for instance, the following: "The aim is not to rediscover the eternal or the universal, but to find the conditions under which something new is produced (*creativeness*)" (D vii); Bergson "transformed philosophy by posing the question of the 'new' instead of that of eternity (how are the production and appearance of something new possible)" (MI 3); "The new—in other words, difference—calls forth forces in thought that are not the forces of recognition, today or tomorrow, but the powers of a completely other model, from an unrecognized and unrecognizable *terra incognita*" (DR 136). None the less, it is true that the *new* is merely an operative concept in Deleuze's philosophy, which he himself tends to thematize under the rubric of *difference*.

3. On these issues, Deleuze did not hesitate to identify himself as a metaphysician, in the traditional sense. "I feel myself to be a pure metaphysician. Bergson says that modern science hasn't found its metaphysics, the metaphysics it would need. It is this metaphysics that interests me" (Arnaud Villani, *La Guêpe et l'orchidée: Essai sur Gilles Deleuze* [Paris: Belin, 1999], 130.)

4. See Mario Bunge, *Causality and Modern Science*, 3rd rev. edn. (New York: Dover Books, 1979), 17–19 ("The Spectrum of Categories of Determination").

5. See the discussion in Mario Bunge, *Philosophy in Crisis: The Need for Reconstruction* (Amherst, NY: Prometheus, 2001), esp. 49, 222.

6. Bergson, Henri, *Creative Evolution*, trans. Arthur Mitchell (New York: Henry Holt, 1911), 1.

7. Martial Gueroult, *L'Évolution et la structure de la Doctrine de la Science chez Fichte*, 2 vols. (Paris: Les Belles Lettres), I, 126.

8. In a Deleuzian context, it might be preferable to speak about the conditions of the *real*, rather than *real experience*, since the latter seems to imply a link to a (transcendental) subjectivity. But we can perhaps retain the phrase if we instead link it to the notion of pure experience in the Jamesian sense—that is, an experience without a subject or an object.

9. DR 38. See also DR 54: "The search for a ground forms the essential step of a 'critique' which should inspire in us new ways of thinking . . . [But] as long as the ground remains larger than the grounded, this critique serves only to justify traditional ways of thinking."

10. See LS 19: in order to assure a real genesis, the genesis requires an element of its own, "distinct from the form of the conditioned," something unconditioned, an "ideational material or 'stratum.'"

11. Leibniz and Spinoza will both claim, for example, that Descartes's *clear and distinct* ideas only find their sufficient reason in *adequate* ideas. On the relation of the foundation to the ground, see DR 79: "The foundation concerns the soil: it shows how something is established upon this soil, how it occupies and possesses it; whereas the ground . . . measures the possessor and the soil against one another according to a title of ownership."

12. On the role of the *sans-fond* in artistic creation, see Daniel W. Smith, "Deleuze on Bacon: Three Conceptual Trajectories in *The Logic of Sensation*," translator's preface to Gilles Deleuze, *Francis Bacon: The Logic of Sensation*, trans. Daniel W. Smith (Minneapolis: University of Minnesota Press, 2003), vii–xxxiii.

13. Ian Stewart, *Does God Place Dice? The Mathematics of Chaos*, 2nd edn. (London: Blackwell, 1989), 32–3.

14. Bunge *Causality and Modern Science*, 74–5, citing Bertrand Russell, *An Outline of Philosophy* (London: Routledge, 1996), 122. As Bunge notes, however, "the advances of science elicit the invention of fresh mathematical tools" (75), and there is thus no reason to privilege differential equations *per se*.

15. See 22 Apr 1980: "It is because it [the calculus] is a well-founded fiction in relation to mathematical truth that it is consequently *a basic and real means of exploration of the reality of existence*." Deleuze makes a similar point in 29 Apr 1980:

> Everyone agrees on the irreducibility of differential signs to any mathematical reality, that is to say, to geometrical, arithmetical, and algebraic reality. The difference arises when some people think, as a consequence, that differential calculus is only a convention—a rather suspect one—and others, on the contrary, think that its artificial character in relation to mathematical reality allows it to be adequate to certain aspects of physical reality.

16. See DR 42–50, where Deleuze analyzes and compares the projects of Hegel and Leibniz on this score: "differential calculus no less than the dialectic is a matter of 'power' and of the power of the limit" (43).

17. Strictly speaking, the list of concepts that follows, as Deleuze points out, is not a list of categories, nor could it be (without changing the concept of a category): they are "complexes of space and time . . . irreducible to the universality of the concept and to the particularity of the now here" (DR 285).

18. But this forces Leibniz into a new problem: What is the relation between the two judgments of attribution "A is larger than B" (in the concept A) and "B is smaller than A" (in the concept B)? Leibniz reduces relations to attributions, but then he divides the relation into two relations. If we have "A R1 B" and "B R2 A" (where R1 and R2 are the relations), then what is the relation between R1 and R2? Leibniz's genius was to create another new concept

to account for this second relation: the "pre-established harmony": in God's understanding there is a correspondence and a harmony between everything that is contained in the concept A and everything that is contained in the concept B. In other words, there is a single and unique world that is expressed in the concepts of real beings.

19. 14 Dec 1982. See also ECC 86–7, and David Lapoujade, "From Transcendental Empiricism to Worker Nomadism: William James," trans. Alberto Toscano, in *Pli: The Warwick Journal of Philosophy* 9 (2000), 190–9, who analyzes James's "radical empiricism" in a similar light.

20. See TP 232–309, the plateau entitled "1730: Becoming-Intense, Becoming-Animal, Becoming-Imperceptible . . . ." The concept of becoming appears earlier, in NP, for example, but it does not yet have the components that Deleuze will eventually assign to it in this text, and which will be further developed in later concepts such as the interstice, affect and percept, and so on.

21. See D 30: Mrs. Dalloway was "laid out like a mist between the people she knew best."

22. Gottfried Wilhelm Leibniz, "Justification of the Infinitesimal Calculus by That of Ordinary Algebra," in *Philosophical Papers and Letters*, ed. Leroy E. Loemker (Dordrecht, Holland: D. Reidel, 1956), 545–6. For a fuller analysis of Leibniz's text, see Essay 11.

23. By contrast, in *The Fold*, Deleuze begins his deduction of concepts with the differential concept of *inflection*.

24. Miguel de Beistegui, in his *Truth and Genesis: Philosophy and Differential Ontology* (Bloomington and Indianapolis: Indiana University Press, 2004), has analyzed in detail the shift from substance to multiplicity brought about by Deleuze's differential ontology.

25. Alfred North Whitehead makes a similar point in *Adventures of Ideas* (New York: Free Press, 1967), 173: "We can never get away from the questions: —How much, —In what proportions?—and In what pattern of arrangement with other things? . . .. Arsenic deals out either health or death, according to its proportions amid a pattern of circumstances."

26. The analysis that follows derived from Deleuze's seminar of 10 Mar 1981, which forms part of a series of fourteen seminars that Deleuze gave on Spinoza between December 1980 and March 1981. In certain respects, the contents of these seminars differ significantly from the interpretation of Spinoza given in EPS.

27. Like most seventeenth-century thinkers, Leibniz also proposed a concept of the actual infinite that was opposed to the indefinite:

> I am so in favor of the actual infinite that instead of admitting that Nature abhors it, as is commonly said, I hold that Nature makes use of it everywhere, in order to show more effectively the perfections of its Author. Thus I believe that there is no part of matter which is not, I do not say divisible, but actually divided; and consequently the least particle ought to be considered as a world full of an infinity of different creatures. (Letter to Foucher, 16 Mar 1693, in *Die Philosophischen Schriften von G. W. Leibniz*, ed. C. J. Gerhardt (Berlin: George Olms, 1965), I, 416)

28. Immanuel Kant, *Critique of Pure Reason*, trans. Norman Kemp Smith (London: Macmillan, 1929), 319, A327/B384.

29. Steven Strogatz, *Sync: The Emerging Science of Spontaneous Order* (New York: Hyperion, 2003), 181.

30. Ian Stewart, *Does God Place Dice?: The Mathematics of Chaos* (London: Blackwell, 1989), 73–4.

31. See B 98: "It is not the real that resembles the possible; it is the possible that resembles the real." The concept of possibility is subject to the same critique that Deleuze offers of Kant's conception of conditions of possibility: "the error of all determinations of the transcendental as consciousness is to conceive of the transcendental in the image and resemblance of what it is supposed to found" (LS 105).

32. For this reason, Deleuze's work has been seen to anticipate certain developments in

complexity theory and chaos theory. Manuel De Landa in particular has emphasized this link in *Intensive Science and Virtual Philosophy*, London and New York: Continuum, 2002). For a general presentation of the mathematics of chaos theory, see Ian Stewart, *Does God Place Dice? The Mathematics of Chaos*.

33. See B 97: "The characteristic of virtuality is to exist in such a way that it is actualized by being differenciated, and is forced to differenciate itself, to create its lines of differenciation in order to be actualized."

34. On this topic, see Morris Kline, *Mathematical Thought From Ancient to Modern Times* (Oxford: Oxford University Press, 1972), 1096–7: "After the dawn of rigorous mathematics with Cauchy, most mathematicians followed his dictates and rejected divergent series as unsound," but with the advent of non-Euclidean geometry and the new algebras, "mathematicians slowly began to appreciate that . . . Cauchy's definition of convergence could no longer be regarded as a higher necessity informed by some superhuman power."

Essay 15: The Open
The Idea of the Open: Bergson's Three Theses on Movement

1. This paper was originally presented as a talk in Stavanger, Norway, on 7 November 2008, at a conference entitled "Deleuze 2008: Deleuze in the Open," which was organized by Arne Fredlund.

2. Giorgio Agamben, *The Open: Man and Animal*, trans. Kevin Attell (Stanford: Stanford University Press, 2004).

3. See 3 May 1987:

> The two parts of a mixture are never equal. One of the two parts is always more or less given, the other is always more or less to be made. It is for this reason that I have remained very Bergsonian. He said very beautiful things on that. He said that in a mixture, you never have two elements, but one element which plays the role of impurity and that one you have, it's given to you, and then you have a pure element that you don't have that must be made. That's not bad.

4. Henri Bergson, *Creative Evolution*, trans. Arthur Mitchell (New York: Henry Holt, 1911), 330: "Ancient science thinks it knows its object sufficiently when it has noted some of its privileged moments, whereas modern science considers the object at any moment whatever."

5. Bergson, *Creative Evolution*, 331.

6. Bergson, *Creative Evolution*, 330.

7. Bergson, *Creative Evolution*, 331: "Galileo thought there was no essential moment, no privileged instant."

8. For the Greeks, a figure is defined by its form: that is, by its privileged points (a circle has one privileged point, its center; a finite line has two privileged points, its ends or extrema; a triangle has three privileged points, a square has four, a cube has eight, and so on).

9. MI 4. Bergson develops these points in the fourth chapter of *Creative Evolution*.

10. Bergson, *Creative Evolution*, 336, as cited in MI 4.

11. Bergson, *Creative Evolution*, 37: "The essence of mechanical explanation is to regard the future and the past as calculable functions of the present, and thus to claim that *the whole is given* [*tout est donné*]." See also 39, 45, 345.

12. Whitehead—whom Deleuze considered to be the last great American philosopher—would take up this question in his own manner; what he called a *concrescence* is the production of something new in the world (*creativity*).

13. Bergson, *Creative Evolution*, 32: "Such a science would be a *mechanics of transformation*, of which our *mechanics of translation* would become a particular case."

14. For Bergson's famous example of mixing sugar in a glass of water, see *Creative Evolution*, 9–10.
15. This section is a recapitulation of themes that are developed in more detail in Essay 12.

Essay 16: Jacques Derrida
Deleuze and Derrida, Immanence and Transcendence: Two Directions in Recent French Thought

1. Giorgio Agamben, "Absolute Immanence," in *Potentialities: Collected Essays in Philosophy*, trans. Daniel Heller-Roazen (Stanford: Stanford University Press, 1999), 220–39: 239. Edith Wyschogrod, in *Saints and Postmodernism: Revisioning Moral Philosophy* (Chicago: University of Chicago Press, 1990), distinguishes between philosophers of difference (Levinas, Derrida, Blanchot) and philosophers of the plenum (Deleuze and Guattari, Genet) (191, 223, 229), but this distinction seems less germane than Agamben's.
2. An early version of this article was presented at the annual meeting of the International Association of Philosophy and Literature at Erasmus University, Rotterdam, in June 2002. The ideas developed here originated in discussions with Andrew Haas and Andrew Montin at the University of New South Wales, and benefitted from the critical comments of Paul Patton and John Protevi.
3. See Jean-Paul Sartre, *The Transcendence of the Ego* (New York: Noonday, 1957), as well as Deleuze's comments in LS 98–9, 343–4. Deleuze will retain Sartre's notion of an impersonal transcendental field, stripping it of any determination as a constituting consciousness.
4. See WP 46:

    Kant discovered the modern way of saving transcendence: this is no longer the transcendence of Something, or of a One higher than everything (contemplation), but that of a Subject to which the field of immanence is only attributed by belonging to a self that necessarily represents such a subject to itself (reflection).

5. See ECC 137: "The poisoned gift of Platonism was to have reintroduced transcendence into philosophy, to have given transcendence a plausible philosophical meaning." Deleuze is here referring primarily to ontological transcendence.
6. See also Martin Heidegger, *Nietzsche*, Vol. 4: *Nihilism*, trans. Frank A. Capuzzi, ed. David Farrell Krell (San Francisco: Harper & Row, 1982), 4:

    "Christian God" also stands for the "transcendent" in general in its various meanings— for "ideals" and "norms," "principles" and "rules," "ends" and "values," which are set "*above*" Being, in order to give Being as a whole a purpose, an order, and—as it is succinctly expressed—"meaning."

7. In this, Derrida is certainly more faithful to Heidegger, and is attempting, in an explicit manner, to carry forward a trajectory already present in Heidegger's work: the immanent question of being and its transcendental horizon (time), which is posed in *Being and Time*, comes to be progressively displaced by the transcendent themes of *Ereignis* (the "event") and the *es gibt* (the "gift" [*Gabe*] of time and being). The trajectory is continued in the Derridean themes of revelation and promise. See Derrida's comments in "How to Avoid Speaking: Denials," in *Derrida and Negative Theology*, ed. Harold Coward and Toby Foshay (Albany: State University of New York Press, 1992), 122–4.
8. See Jacques Derrida, *Writing and Difference*, trans. Alan Bass (Chicago: University of Chicago Press, 1980), where Derrida characterizes history as "the very movement of transcendence, of the excess over the totality, without which no totality would appear" (117).
9. Jacques Derrida, *Positions*, trans. Alan Bass (Chicago: University of Chicago Press, 1981), 6–7. See also 10: one must "borrow the syntactic and lexical resources of the language of metaphysics . . . at the very moment one deconstructs this language."

10. Derrida, *Positions*, 6.

11. Jacques Derrida, *Dissemination*, trans. Barbara Johnson (Chicago: University of Chicago Press, 1983), 168: "*Différance*, the disappearance of any originary presence, is *at once* the condition of possibility *and* the condition of impossibility of truth."

12. Derrida, "Ousia and Gramme," in *Margins of Philosophy*, trans. Alan Bass (Chicago: University of Chicago Press, 1984), 67.

13. Jacques Derrida, "Force of Law: The 'Mystical Foundation of Authority,'" in *Acts of Religion*, ed. Gil Anidjar (London and New York: Routledge, 2002), 243.

14. See Arnaud Villani, *La Guêpe et l'orchidée: Essai sur Gilles Deleuze* (Paris: Belin, 1999), 130.

15. Significantly, Derrida says the first question he would have asked Deleuze would have concerned the term immanence—a term "on which he always insisted." See "I'm Going to Have to Wander All Alone," in Jacques Derrida, *The Work of Mourning*, ed. and trans. by Pascale-Anne Brault and Michael Naas (Chicago: University of Chicago Press, 2001), 189–96.

16. Derrida, "Ousia and Gramme," in *Margins of Philosophy*, 67.

17. For Deleuze's interpretation of Platonism, see in particular "Plato and the Simulacrum" in LS 253–66, although the concept of the simulacrum developed there assumes less and less importance in Deleuze's work.

18. Emmanuel Levinas, *Totality and Infinity*, trans. Alphonso Lingis (Pittsburgh: Duquesne University Press, 1969). Deleuze never discusses Levinas's work directly, except as an instance of Jewish philosophy (in WP 233 n5). See, however, Alain Badiou's critiques in *Ethics: An Essay on the Understanding of Evil*, trans. Peter Hallward (London: Verso, 2001).

19. For their respective discussions of the divine names tradition, see Deleuze's *Expressionism in Philosophy: Spinoza*, trans. Martin Joughin (New York: Zone, 1990), Chapter 3 (EPS 53–68), and Jacques Derrida, *On the Name*, trans. Thomas Dutoit (Stanford: Stanford University Press, 1995).

20. For Thomas Aquinas's formulations of analogy, see *Summa Theologica*, 1.13.5. The great modern proponent of the way of affirmation was Charles Williams; see his book *The Figure of Beatrice: A Study in Dante* (New York: Faber & Faber, 1943).

21. See Reiner Schürmann, *Meister Eckhart: Mystic and Philosopher* (Bloomington: Indiana University Press, 1978), especially 172–92. While recognizing Eckhart's affinities with immanence (see 176, 252 n56) and with an immanent causality (177), Schürmann attempts to provide a qualified analogical interpretation of his teachings (179).

22. Derrida characterizes the nature of deconstruction itself in terms derived from the tradition of negative theology. See Derrida, "Letter to a Japanese Friend," in *Derrida and Difference*, ed. David Wood and Robert Bernasconi (Evanston: Northwestern University Press, 1988), 5: "What is deconstruction? 'Nothing of course!' And what is deconstruction *not*? 'Everything, of course!'"

23. Derrida, "How to Avoid Speaking: Denials," in *Derrida and Negative Theology*, 74.

24. Ibid., 77, 79.

25. Derrida, *On the Name*, 69.

26. Immanuel Kant, *Critique of Pure Reason*, trans. Norman Kemp Smith (London: Macmillan, 1929), 298–9 (A295–6/B352).

27. See Kant, *Critique of Pure Reason*, 257 (A236–7/B294–5):

> We have now not merely explored the *territory* of pure understanding, and carefully surveyed every part of it, but have also measured its extent, and assigned to everything in it its rightful place. This domain is an island, enclosed by nature itself within unalterable limits. It is the land of truth—enchanting name!—surrounded by a wide and stormy *ocean*, the native home of illusion.

28. Derrida himself draws the analogy between Kantian Ideas and his own concepts at numerous points throughout his work. For instance, the structure or logic of the gift, Derrida tells us, has "a form analogous to Kant's transcendental dialectic, as relation between thinking and knowing. We are going to give ourselves over to engage in the effort of thinking or rethinking a sort of *transcendental illusion* of the gift" (Jacques Derrida, *Given Time*, Vol. 1: *Counterfeit Money*, trans. Peggy Kamuf (Chicago: University of Chicago Press, 1994), 29–30, emphasis added). Similarly, Derrida notes that

> I have on several occasions spoken of "unconditional" affirmation or of "unconditional" "appeal." . . . Now, the very least that can be said of "unconditionality" (a word that I use not by accident to recall the character of the categorical imperative in its Kantian form) is that it is independent of every determinate context, even of the determination of a context in general. It announces itself as such only in the *opening* of context. (Jacques Derrida, *Limited ABC*, ed. Samuel Weber (Evanston, IL: Northwestern University Press, 1988), 152–3)

   To be sure, Derrida's thought cannot be accommodated within these Kantian formulations:

> Why have I always *hesitated* to characterize it [deconstruction] in Kantian terms, for example, or more generally in ethical or political terms, when that would have been so easy and would have enabled me to avoid so many critiques, themselves all too facile? Because such characterizations seem to me essentially associated with philosophemes that themselves call for deconstructive questions. (*Limited ABC*, 153)

   For an analysis of Derrida's relation to Kant, see Martin Hägglund, *Radical Atheism: Derrida and the Time of Life* (Stanford: Stanford University Press, 2008), Chapter 1, "Autoimmunity of Time: Derrida and Kant," 13–49.
29. Derrida, *Aporias*, 16. See also *The Gift of Death*, 84, where Derrida is still hesitating between the two terms: "The concept of responsibility [would be] paralyzed by what can be called an aporia or an antinomy."
30. Derrida, *Aporias*, 15.
31. Friedrich Nietzsche, *Genealogy of Morals*, Essay II, §8, in *Basic Writings of Nietzsche*, ed. and trans. Walter Kaufmann (New York: Modern Library, 1968), 506, as quoted in NP 213–14.
32. Derrida, "Post-Scriptum," in *Derrida and Negative Theology*, 290.
33. For a summary of Deleuze's theory of desire, see his seminar of 26 Mar 1973, "Dualism, Monism and Multiplicities (Desire–Pleasure–*Jouissance*)," in *Contretemps: An Online Journal of Philosophy* 2 (May 2001), 92–108.
34. Derrida, *Given Time*, 29.
35. For the idea that the deconstruction of the law "operates on the basis of the infinite 'Idea of justice,'" see Jacques Derrida, "Force of Law: The 'Mystical Foundation of Authority,'" in *Acts of Religion*, esp. 250–58. See also *Deconstruction in a Nutshell: A Conversation with Jacques Derrida*, ed. John D. Caputo (New York: Fordham University Press, 1997), 17: the Idea of justice implies "non-gathering, dissociation, heterogeneity, non-identity with itself, endless inadequation, *infinite transcendence*." On the Idea of justice being "independent of all determinable contexts," see Jacques Derrida, *Politics of Friendship*, trans. George Collins (London: Verso, 1997), 215–16.
36. Jacques Derrida, *Resistances to Psychoanalysis*, trans. Pascale-Anne Brault and Michael B. Naas (Stanford: Stanford University Press, 1998), 36. Thanks to Andrew Montin for this reference.
37. Derrida, *On the Name*, 37.
38. See, for example, Derrida, *The Politics of Friendship*, 24.

Essay 17: Alain Badiou
Mathematics and the Theory of Multiplicities: Deleuze and Badiou Revisited

1. F 42 (Deleuze was speaking of Virilio's relation to Foucault). A shorter version of this article was presented at the conference "Ethics and Politics: The Work of Alain Badiou," which was held at the Centre for Critical and Cultural Theory at the University of Cardiff on 25–6 May 2002, organized by Jean-Jacques Lecercle and Neil Badmington, and was published in *Think Again: Alain Badiou and the Future of Philosophy*, ed. Peter Hallward (London: Continuum, 2004). My understanding of Badiou's work is strongly indebted to Peter Hallward's book *Subject to Truth: The Work of Alain Badiou* (Minneapolis: University of Minnesota Press, 2003), which presents a superb overview and critical analysis of Badiou's philosophy. I would like to thank Prof. Hallward for providing me with an early copy of his manuscript, and for the insights and clarifications he provided on both Badiou and Deleuze during numerous e-mail correspondences. This essay was written before the 2006 publication of Badiou's *Logics of Worlds: Being and Event 2*, trans. Alberto Toscano (London: Continuum, 2009).

2. Alain Badiou, *Being and Event*, trans. Oliver Feltham (London and New York: Continuum, 2005).

3. Gilles Deleuze, "A Philosophical Concept," in *Who Comes After the Subject*, ed. Eduardo Cadava, Peter Connor, and Jean-Luc Nancy (New York: Routledge, 1991), 95.

4. Alain Badiou, *Deleuze: The Clamor of Being*, trans. Louise Burchill (Minneapolis: University of Minnesota Press, 2000), 4.

5. Badiou, *Deleuze*, 1.

6. See Badiou, *Being and Event*, 483: "the latent paradigm in Deleuze is 'natural' . . . Mine is mathematical." Similarly, in his review article of Deleuze's book on Leibniz, Badiou writes: "There have never been but two schemas or paradigms of the Multiple: the mathematical and the organicist . . . This is the cross of metaphysics, and the greatness of Deleuze . . . is to choose without hesitation for the animal" (Alain Badiou, "Gilles Deleuze, 'The Fold: Leibniz and the Baroque'," in Constantin V. Boundas and Dorothea Olkowski, eds., *Gilles Deleuze and the Theater of Philosophy* (New York: Routledge, 1994), 55. This same theme is continued in Badiou's article "Deleuze's Vitalist Ontology," in Alain Badiou, *Briefings on Existence: A Short Treatise on Transitory Ontology*, ed. and trans. Norman Madarasz (Albany: State University of New York Press, 2006), 63–72.

7. See, for instance, the articles on Badiou's book by Éric Alliez, Arnaud Villani, and José Gil, collected in *Futur Antérieur* 43 (April 1998).

8. Badiou, "Deleuze's Vitalist Ontology," in *Briefings on Existence*, 71.

9. See Badiou, *Briefings on Existence*, 54:

> A "crisis" in mathematics is a moment when mathematics is constrained to think its own thought *as the immanent multiplicity of its own unity*. It is at this point, I believe, and at this point alone, that mathematics, that is to say, ontology, functions as a condition of philosophy.

For Badiou, philosophy itself is "meta-ontological," since it is the task of philosophy to establish the thesis that mathematics is the discourse of Being-as-such (Badiou, *Being and Event*, 13).

10. See DR 323 n22: Given the irreducibility of "problems" in his thought, Deleuze writes that "the use of the word 'problematic' as a substantive seems to us an indispensable neologism."

11. Alain Badiou, "One, Multiple, Multiplicities," in *Theoretical Writings*, ed. and trans. Ray Brassier and Alberto Toscano (London and New York: Continuum, 2004), 71.

12. See TP 374: "Only royal science has at its disposal a metric power that can define a conceptual apparatus or an autonomy of science (including the autonomy of experimental

science).” And TP 486: “Major science has a perpetual need for the inspiration of the minor; but the minor would be nothing if it did not confront and conform to the highest scientific requirements.”

13. Badiou, *Being and Event*, 184.

14. Badiou, “One, Multiple, Multiplicities,” in *Theoretical Writings*, 72.

15. Badiou, *Deleuze*, 46: “I uphold that the forms of the multiple are, just like Ideas, always actual and that the virtual does not exist.” Deleuze agrees with this characterization of sets: “Everything is actual in a numerical multiplicity; everything is not ‘realized,’ but everything there is actual. There are no relationships other than those between actuals” (B 43).

16. AO 371–2. For Badiou’s appeal to Lautréamont, see “Mathematics and Philosophy, ” in *Theoretical Writings*, 11–12; and *Briefings on Existence*, 71.

17. TP 363. See Deleuze’s well-known comments on his relation to the history of philosophy in N 5–6. The best general works on the history of mathematics are Carl B. Boyer, *History of Mathematics* (Princeton: Princeton University Press, 1968) and Morris Kline, *Mathematical Thought from Ancient to Modern Times*, 3 vols. (Oxford: Oxford University Press, 1972).

18. Proclus, *Commentary of the First Book of Euclid’s Elements*, trans. Glenn R. Murrow (Princeton: Princeton University Press, 1970), 63–7, as cited in DR 163; TP 554 n21; and LS 54. See also Deleuze’s comments in TI 174: theorems and problems are “two mathematical instances which constantly refer to each other, the one enveloping the second, the second sliding into the first, but both very different in spite of their union.” On the two types of deduction, TI 185.

19. For instance, determining a triangle the sum of whose angles is 180 degrees is theorematic, since the angles of every triangle will total 180 degrees. Constructing an equilateral triangle on a given finite straight line, by contrast, is problematic, since we could also construct a non-equilateral triangle or a non-triangular figure on the line (moreover, the construction of an equilateral triangle must first pass through the construction of two circles). Classical geometers struggled for centuries with the three great “problems” of antiquity—trisecting an angle, constructing a cube having double the volume of a given cube, and constructing a square equal to a circle—though it would turn out that none of these problems is solvable using only a straightedge and compass. See E. T. Bell’s comments in *Men of Mathematics* (New York: Simon & Schuster, 1937), 31–2.

20. Edmund Husserl, *Ideas: General Introduction to a Pure Phenomenology*, trans. W. R. Boyce Gibson (New York: Macmillan, 1931), §74, 208. See also *Edmund Husserl’s Origin of Geometry: An Introduction*, ed. John P. Leavey, Jr. and David B. Allison (Stony Brook, NY: H. Hayes, 1978), which includes Jacques Derrida’s commentary. Whereas Husserl saw problematics as “proto-geometry,” Deleuze sees it as a fully autonomous dimension of geometry, but one he identifies as a “minor” science; it is a “proto”-geometry only from the viewpoint of the “major” or “royal” conception of geometry, which attempts to eliminate these dynamic events or variations by subjecting them to a theorematic treatment.

21. DR 160. Deleuze continues:

> As a result [of using *reductio ad absurdum* proofs], however, the *genetic* point of view is forcibly relegated to an inferior rank: proof is given that something cannot not be, rather than *that* it is and *why* it is (hence the frequency in Euclid of negative, indirect and *reductio* arguments, which serve to keep geometry under the domination of the principle of identity and prevent it from becoming a geometry of sufficient reason).

22. The language of the rectilinear dominates ethics as well: to “rectify” a wrong, to “straighten” someone out, to make a situation “right”; the French term *droit* means both “straight,” in the geometric sense, and “right,” in the legal sense; an *angle droit* is a “right” angle; a moral person is someone who is “upright”; the wrong is a deviation from the “straight and narrow” (the line).

23. See DR 174:

> The mathematician Houël remarked that the shortest distance was not a Euclidean notion at all, but an Archimedean one, more physical than mathematical; that it was inseparable from a method of exhaustion; and that it served less to determine the straight line than to determine the length of a curve by means of a straight line—"integral calculus performed unknowingly" (citing Jules Houël, *Essai critique sur les principes fondamentaux de la géométrie élémentaire* [Paris: Gauthier-Villars, 1867], 3, 75)

Boyer makes a similar point in his *History of Mathematics*, 141:

> Greek mathematics sometimes has been described as essentially static, with little regard for the notion of variability; but Archimedes, in his study of the spiral, seems to have found the tangent to the curve through kinematic considerations akin to the differential calculus.

24. Badiou, "Deleuze's Vitalist Ontology," in *Briefings on Existence*, 70–1.
25. Boyer, *History of Mathematics*, 393.
26. TP 484. On the relation between Greek theorematics and seventeenth-century algebra and arithmetic as instances of "major" mathematics, see Deleuze, DR 160–1.
27. Boyer, *History of Mathematics*, 394. Deleuze writes that "Cartesian coordinates appear to me to be an attempt of reterritorialization" (22 Feb 1972).
28. TP 554 n23, commenting on Léon Brunschvicg, *Les Étapes de la philosophie mathématique* (Paris: PUF, 1947; new edn.: Paris: A. Blanchard, 1972). Deleuze also appeals to a text by Michel Chasles, *Aperçu historique sur l'origine et le développement de méthodes en géométrie* (Brussels: M. Hayez, 1837), which establishes a continuity between Desargues, Monge, and Poncelet as the "founders of a modern geometry" (TP 554 n28).
29. See Brunschvicg, *Les Étapes de la philosophie mathématique*, 327–31.
30. See Carl B. Boyer, *The History of the Calculus and its Conceptual Development* (New York: Dover, 1959), 267. Deleuze praises Boyer's book as "the best study of the history of the differential calculus and its modern structural interpretation" (LS 339).
31. For a discussion of the various uses of the term "intuition" in mathematics, see the chapters on "Intuition" and "Four-Dimensional Intuition" in Philip J. Davis and Reuben Hersh, *The Mathematical Experience* (Boston, Basel, and Stuttgart: Birkhäuser, 1981), 391–405, as well as Hans Hahn's classic article "The Crisis in Intuition," in J. R. Newman, ed., *The World of Mathematics* (New York: Simon & Schuster, 1956), 1956–76.
32. Boyer, *The History of Mathematics*, 598 (in the chapter on "The Arithmetization of Analysis").
33. Giulio Giorello, "The 'Fine Structure' of Mathematical Revolutions: Metaphysics, Legitimacy, and Rigour," in *Revolutions in Mathematics*, ed. Donald Gilles (Oxford: Clarendon, 1992), 135. I thank Andrew Murphie for this reference.
34. 22 Feb 1972. See also DR 172: "The limit no longer presupposes the ideas of a continuous variable and infinite approximation. On the contrary, the notion of limit grounds a new, static and purely ideal definition of continuity, while its own definition implies no more than number."
35. See Penelope Maddy, *Naturalism in Mathematics* (Oxford: Oxford University Press, 1997), 51–2, for a discussion of Cantorian "finitism."
36. Deleuze provides a summary of these developments in DR 176:

> The real frontier defining modern mathematics lies not in the calculus itself but in other discoveries such as set theory which, even though it requires, for its own part, an axiom of infinity, gives a no less strictly finite interpretation of the calculus. We know in effect that the notion of limit has lost its phoronomic character and involves only static

considerations; that variability has ceased to represent a progression through all the values of an interval and come to mean only the disjunctive assumption of one value within that interval; that the derivative and the integral have become ordinal rather than quantitative concepts; and finally that the differential designates only a magnitude left undetermined so that it can be made smaller than a given number as required. The birth of structuralism at this point coincides with the death of any genetic or dynamic ambitions of the calculus.

37. For a discussion of Weierstrass's "discretization program" (written from the viewpoint of cognitive science), see George Lakoff and Rafael E. Núñez, *Where Mathematics Comes From: How the Embodied Mind Brings Mathematics Into Being* (New York: Basic, 2000), 257–324.
38. Maddy, *Naturalism in Mathematics*, 28.
39. Reuben Hersh, *What is Mathematics, Really?* (Oxford: Oxford University Press, 1997), 13.
40. Badiou, *Deleuze*, 47.
41. Freeman Dyson, *Infinite in All Directions* (New York: Harper & Row, 1988), 52–3. John Wheeler, in *Frontiers of Time* (Austin: Center for Theoretical Physics, University of Texas, 1978), has put forward the stronger thesis that the laws of physics are themselves "mutable" (13).
42. Kurt Gödel, cited in Hao Wang, *From Mathematics to Philosophy* (New York: Humanities Press, 1974), 86.
43. Hermann Weyl, *The Continuum: A Critical Examination of the Foundations of Analysis* (1918), trans. Stephen Pollard and Thomas Bole (New York: Dover, 1994), 23–4 (although Weyl still argues for a discrete interpretation of the continuous continuum). Bertrand Russell makes the same point in his *Principles of Mathematics* (New York: Norton, 1938), 347, citing Poincaré:

> The continuum thus conceived [arithmetically or discretely] is nothing but a collection of individuals arranged in a certain order, infinite in number, it is true, but external to each other. This is not the ordinary [geometric or "natural"] conception, in which there is supposed to be, between the elements of the continuum, a sort of intimate bond which makes a whole of them, in which the point is not prior to the line, but the line to the point. Of the famous formula, the continuum is a unity in multiplicity, the multiplicity alone subsists, the unity has disappeared.

44. Abraham Robinson, *Non-Standard Analysis* (Princeton: Princeton University Press, 1966), 83. See also 277:

> With the spread of Weierstrass' ideas, arguments involving infinitesimal increments, which survived particularly in differential geometry and in several branches of applied mathematics, began to be taken automatically as a kind of shorthand for corresponding developments by means of the e, d approach.

45. See FLB 129–30: "Robinson suggested considering the Leibnizian monad as a infinite number very different from transfinites, as a unit surrounded by a zone of infinitely small [numbers] that reflect the converging series of the world."
46. Hersh, *What is Mathematics, Really?*, 289. For discussions of Robinson's achievement, see Jim Holt's useful review, "Infinitesimally Yours," in *The New York Review of Books*, 20 May 1999, as well as the chapter on "Nonstandard Analysis" in Davis and Hersh, *The Mathematical Experience*, 237–54. The latter note that

> Robinson has in a sense vindicated the reckless abandon of eighteenth-century mathematics against the straight-laced rigor of the nineteenth century, adding a new chapter in the never ending war between the finite and the infinite, the continuous and the discrete. (238)

47. Albert Lautman, *Mathematics, Ideas, and the Physical Real*, trans. Simon Duffy (London: Continuum, 2011), 88.

48. Jean Dieudonné, *L'Axiomatique dans les mathématiques modernes*, 47–8, as cited in Robert Blanché, *L'Axiomatique* (Paris: PUF, 1955), 91.

49. Nicholas Bourbaki, "The Architecture of Mathematics," in *Great Currents of Mathematical Thought*, ed. François Le Lionnais, trans. R. A. Hall and Howard G. Bergmann (New York: Dover, 1971), 31. Bourbaki none the less insists—as do Deleuze and Guattari—that the analogy is not a precise one: mathematicians do not work mechanically as do workers on an assembly line, since "intuition" plays a fundamental role in their research.

> This is not the intuition of common sense [explains Bourbaki], but rather a sort of direct divination (prior to all reasoning) of the normal behavior he has the right to expect from the mathematical entities which a long association has rendered as familiar to him as the object of the real world. (31)

Deleuze and Guattari make a similar point in AO 251.

50. See 22 Feb 1972:

> The idea of a scientific task that no longer passes through codes but rather through an axiomatic first took place in mathematics toward the end of the nineteenth century . . . One finds this well formed only in the capitalism of the nineteenth century.

Deleuze's political philosophy is itself based in part on the axiomatic-problematic distinction: "Our use of the word 'axiomatic' is far from a metaphor; we find *literally* the same theoretical problems that are posed by the models in an axiomatic repeated in relation to the State" (TP 455).

51. TP 362. See also TP 141–2: "The phrase 'politics of science' is a good phrase for these currents, which are *internal* to science, and not simply circumstances and state factors that act upon it from the outside."

52. Henri Poincaré, "L'œuvre mathématique de Weierstrass," *Acta Mathematica* 22 (1898–9), 1–18, as cited in Boyer, *History of Mathematics*, 601. Boyer notes that one finds in Riemann "a strongly intuitive and geometrical background in analysis that contrasts sharply with the arithmetizing tendencies of the Weierstrassian school" (601).

53. See FLB 48: "axioms concern problems, and escape demonstration."

54. TP 361. This section of the "Treatise on Nomadology" (361–74) develops in detail the distinction between "major" and "minor" science.

55. DR 323 n22. Deleuze is referring to the distinction between "problem" and "theory" in Georges Canguilhem, *On the Normal and the Pathological*, trans. Carolyn R. Fawcett (New York: Zone, 1978); the distinction between the "problem-element" and the "global synthesis element" in Georges Bouligand, *Le Déclin des absolus mathématico-logiques* (Paris: Éditions d'Enseignement Supérieur, 1949); and the distinction between "problem" and "solution" in Albert Lautman. All these thinkers insist on the double irreducibility of problems: problems should not be evaluated extrinsically in terms of their "solvability" (the philosophical illusion), nor should problems be envisioned merely as the conflict between two opposing or contradictory propositions (the natural illusion) (DR 161). On this score, Deleuze largely follows Lautman's thesis that mathematics participates in a *dialectic* that points beyond itself to a meta-mathematical power—that is, to a general theory of problems and their ideal synthesis—which accounts for the genesis of mathematics itself. See Albert Lautman, *Nouvelles Recherches sur la structure dialectique des mathématiques* (Paris: Hermann, 1939), particularly the section entitled "The Genesis of Mathematics from the Dialectic":

> The order implied by the notion of genesis is no longer of the order of logical reconstruction in mathematics, in the sense that from the initial axioms of a theory flow

all the propositions of the theory, for the dialectic is not a part of mathematics, and its notions have no relation to the primitive notions of a theory. (13–14)

Badiou frequently appeals to Lautman's name, but rarely (if ever) to his works, and is opposed to Lautman's appeal to a meta-mathematical dialectic.

56. Badiou, "One, Multiple, Multiplicities," in *Theoretical Writings*, 72.
57. DR 161. See also DR 177–8: "If the differential disappears in the result, this is to the extent that the problem-instance differs in kind from the solution-instance."
58. Henri Bergson, *The Creative Mind*, trans. Mabelle L. Andison (Totowa, NJ: Littlefield, Adams, 1946), 33. See also 191: "Metaphysics should adopt the generative idea of our mathematics [i.e., change, or becoming] in order to extend it to all qualities, that is, to reality in general."
59. DR 179. See also D ix: "It seems to us that the highest objective of science, mathematics, and physics is multiplicity, and that both set theory and the theory of spaces is still in its infancy."
60. For analyses of Deleuze's theory of multiplicities, see Robin Durie, "Immanence and Difference: Toward a Relational Ontology," in *Southern Journal of Philosophy*, Vol. 60 (2002), 1–29; Keith Ansell-Pearson, *Philosophy and the Adventure of the Virtual: Bergson and the Time of Life* (London and New York: Routledge, 2002); and Manuel De Landa, *Intensive Science and Virtual Philosophy* (London: Continuum, 2002).
61. Ian Stewart and Martin Golubitwky, *Fearful Symmetry* (Oxford: Blackwell, 1992), 42.
62. See Kline, *Mathematical Thought*, 759: "The group of an equation is a key to its solvability because the group expresses the degree of indistinguishability of the roots. It tells us what we do *not* know about the roots."
63. DR 180, citing C. Georges Verriest, "Évariste Galois et la théorie des équations algébriques," in *Œuvres mathématiques de Galois* (Paris: Gauthier-Villars, 1961), 41.
64. ECC 149, citing a text by Galois in André Dalmas, *Évariste Galois* (Paris: Fasquelle, 1956), 132.
65. DR 170, referring to Jules Vuillemin, *La Philosophie de l'algèbre* (Paris: PUF, 1962).

Jules Vuillemin's book proposes a determination of structures [or multiplicities, in Deleuze's sense] in mathematics. In this regard, he insists on the importance of a theory of problems (following the mathematical Abel) and the principles of determination (reciprocal, complete, and progressive determination according to Galois). He shows how structures, in this sense, provide the only means for realizing the ambitions of a true genetic method. (DI 306 n26)

66. Albert Lautman, "Essay on the Notions of Structure and Existence in Mathematics," in Albert Lautman, *Mathematics, Ideas, and the Physical Real*, trans. Simon Duffy (London : Continuum, 2011), 87–193. In this important volume, Duffy has made available to English-speaking readers almost the entirety of Lautman's work in the philosophy of mathematics. Although Badiou occasionally appeals to Lautman (see *Deleuze*, 98), his own ontology is largely *opposed* to Lautman's; moreover, Badiou never considers Deleuze's own appropriation of Lautman's theory of differential equations, even though Deleuze cites it in almost every one of his books after 1968.
67. For discussions of Poincaré, see 29 Apr 1980, as well as Kline, *Mathematical Thought*, 732–8 and Lautman, *Mathematics, Ideas, and the Physical Real*, 259. Such singularities are now termed "attractors": using the language of physics, attractors govern "basins of attraction" that define the trajectories of the curves that fall within their "sphere of influence."
68. For this reason, Deleuze's work has been seen to anticipate certain developments in complexity theory and chaos theory. De Landa in particular has emphasized this link in *Intensive Science and Virtual Philosophy* (London: Continuum, 2002). For a presentation of

the mathematics of chaos theory, see Ian Stewart, *Does God Place Dice?: The Mathematics of Chaos* (London: Blackwell, 1989), 95–144.

69. See Lautman, *Mathematics, Ideas, and the Physical Real*, 112:

> The constitution, by Gauss and Riemann, of a differential geometry that studies the intrinsic properties of a variety, independent of any space into which this variety would be plunged, eliminates any reference to a universal container or to a center of privileged coordinates.

70. See Lautman, *Mathematics, Ideas, and the Physical Real*, 97–8:

> Riemannian spaces are devoid of any kind of homogeneity. Each is characterized by the form of the expression that defines the square of the distance between two infinitely proximate points . . . It follows that "two neighboring observers in a Riemannian space can locate the points in their immediate vicinity, but cannot locate their spaces in relation to each other without a new convention." Each vicinity is like a shred of Euclidean space, *but the linkage between one vicinity and the next is not defined and can be effected in an infinite number of ways. Riemannian space at its most general thus presents itself as an amorphous collection of pieces that are juxtaposed but not attached to each other.*

71. See DR 183, 181: A Riemannian multiplicity "is intrinsically defined, without external reference or recourse to a uniform space in which it would be submerged . . . It has no need whatsoever of unity to form a system."

72. Badiou, "One, Multiple, Multiplicities," in *Theoretical Writings*, 78.

73. See, in particular, DR 183, although the entirety of the fifth chapter is an elaboration of Deleuze's theory of multiplicities.

74. See DR xxi: "We are well aware . . . that we have spoken of science in a manner which was not scientific."

75. See De Landa, *Intensive Science and Virtual Philosophy*, 15 (on attractors), and Chapters 2 and 3 (on symmetry-breaking cascades).

76. De Landa, *Intensive Science and Virtual Philosophy*, 102.

77. See DR 117: "In accordance with Heidegger's ontological intuition, difference must be articulation and connection in itself; *it must relate different to different without any mediation whatsoever.*"

78. Badiou, *Deleuze*, 20. For Badiou's Neo-Platonic characterization of Deleuze, see 26: "It is as though the paradoxical or supereminent One immanently engenders a procession of beings whose univocal sense it distributes."

79. This conflation is stated most clearly in Badiou, *Deleuze*, 46: "the univocal sovereignty of the One." For discussions of Badiou's reading of the doctrine of univocity, see Nathan Widder, "The Rights of Simulacra: Deleuze and the Univocity of Being," in *Continental Philosophy Review* 34 (2001), 437–53, and Keith Ansell-Pearson, "The Simple Virtual: A Renewed Thinking of the One," in *Philosophy and the Adventure of the Virtual: Bergson and the Time of Life* (London and New York: Routledge, 2002), 97–114.

80. See, for instance, Badiou, "One, Multiple, Multiplicities," in *Theoretical Writings*, 70: The One "may take the name of 'All,' or 'Whole,' 'Substance,' 'Life,' 'the Body without Organs,' or 'Chaos.'"

81. Ernst Mayr, "Is Biology an Autonomous Science?," in *Toward a New Philosophy of Biology: Observations of an Evolutionist* (Cambridge, MA: Harvard University Press, 1988), 8–23.

82. Badiou, "One, Multiple, Multiplicities," in *Theoretical Writings*, 73.

83. 22 Apr 1980. See also 29 Apr 1980:

> Everyone agrees on the irreducibility of differential signs to any mathematical reality, that is to say, to geometrical, arithmetical, and algebraic reality. The difference arises

when some people think, as a consequence, that differential calculus is only a convention—a rather suspect one—and others, on the contrary, think that its artificial character in relation to mathematical reality allows it to be adequate to certain aspects of physical reality.

84. See DR 178:

Modern mathematics leaves us in a state of antinomy, since the strict finite interpretation that it gives of the calculus nevertheless presupposes an axiom of infinity in the set theoretical foundation, even though this axiom finds no illustration in the calculus. What is still missing is the extra-propositional or sub-representative element expressed in the Idea by the differential, precisely in the form of a problem.

85. Badiou, *Deleuze*, 14. See DR 192: "Representation and knowledge are modeled entirely upon propositions of consciousness which designate cases of solution, but those propositions by themselves give a completely inaccurate notion of the instance which engenders them as cases."

86. See Paul Hoffman, *The Man Who Loved Only Numbers: The Story of Paul Erdős and the Search for Mathematical Truth* (New York: Hyperion, 1998), 17.

87. See N 130: "Poincaré used to say that many mathematical theories are completely irrelevant, pointless. He didn't say they were wrong—that wouldn't have been so bad."

88. Badiou, *Deleuze*, 1, 98–9. See also 70, where Badiou links Deleuze with Plato's "metaphorical mathematics." Badiou is referring to Deleuze's notorious distaste for metaphors, but there is no reason to think that distaste disappears here. The concept of the "fold," for instance, is not a metaphor, but a literal topological transformation. Even the concept of the "rhizome," whatever its metaphorical resonance, is directed primarily against the literal uses of "arborescent" schemas in mathematics and elsewhere (tree structures, branches and branchings, etc.).

89. 14 Mar 1978: "The abstract is lived experience. I would almost say that once you have reached lived experience, you reach the most fully living core of the abstract." See also 21 Mar 1978: "You can live nothing but the abstract and nobody has lived anything else but the abstract."

90. Badiou, *Deleuze*, 36.

91. TP 570 n61. See also TP 461:

When intuitionism opposed axiomatics, it was not only in the name of intuition, of construction and creation, but also in the name of a calculus of problems, a problematic conception of science that was not less abstract but implied an entirely different abstract machine, one working in the undecidable and the fugitive.

92. Badiou, *Briefings on Existence*, 50. Badiou's claim that Deleuze's methodology relies on intuition is discussed in *Deleuze*, Chapter 3, esp. 31–40.

93. Badiou, *Briefings on Existence*, 71.

94. For the role of the scholia, see EPS 342–50 (appendix on the scholia); for the uniqueness of the fifth book of the *Ethics*, see ECC 149–50.

95. Badiou, *Deleuze*, 1. See Badiou's essay on Spinoza, "Spinoza's Closed Ontology," in *Briefings on Existence*, 73–87.

96. See DR 161, 323 n21. See also Hersh's comments on Descartes in *What is Mathematics, Really?*, 112–13: "Euclidean certainty boldly advertised in the *Method* and shamelessly ditched in the *Geometry*."

97. See TP 455: "Our use of the word 'axiomatic' is far from a metaphor; we find *literally* the same theoretical problems that are posed by the models in an axiomatic repeated in relation to the State." In part, this is a historical thesis: it is not by chance that Weierstrass's

program of arithmetizing mathematics and Taylor's program of organizing work developed at the same time. See 22 Feb 1972:

> The idea of a scientific task that no longer passes through codes but rather through an axiomatic first took place in mathematics toward the end of the nineteenth century, that is, with Weierstrass, who launches a static interpretation of the differential calculus, in which the operation of differentiation is no longer considered as a process, and who makes an axiomatic of differential relations. One finds this well formed only in the capitalism of the nineteenth century.

98. See 22 Feb 1972:

> The true axiomatic is social and not scientific . . . The scientific axiomatic is only one of the means by which the fluxes of science, the fluxes of knowledge, are guarded and taken up by the capitalist machine . . . All axiomatics are means of leading science to the capitalist market. All axiomatics are abstract Oedipal formations.

99. In one text, Badiou seems to recognize the problematic–axiomatic distinction in his own manner:

> Today, one starts rather from already complex concretions, and it is a question of folding or unfolding them according to their singularity, to find the principle of their deconstruction-reconstruction, without being concerned with the plane of the set or a decided foundation. Axiomatics is left behind in favor of a mobile apprehension of surprising complexities and correlations. Deleuze's rhizome wins out over Descartes' tree. The heterogeneous lends itself to thought more than the homogeneous. (*Briefings on Existence*, 50)

But Badiou none the less seems to be moving in a Deleuzian direction when, in his more recent essay on "Being and Appearing," he introduces a minimal theory of relation (through logic and topology), and even assigns the "event" a minimal ontological status: the event "is being itself, in its fearful and creative inconsistency, or its emptiness, which is the without-place of all place (see *Briefings on Existence*, 168).

100. TP 471. And AO 255: "The theoretical opposition lies elsewhere: it is between, on the one hand, the decoded flows that enter into a class axiomatic on the full body of capital, and on the other hand, the decoded flows that free themselves from this axiomatic."

101. See Badiou, *Deleuze*, 91: "Deleuze always maintained that, in doing this, I fall back into transcendence and into the equivocity of analogy."

102. Badiou, *Deleuze*, 91. See also 64: "Truth must be thought as 'interruption.'"

Essay 18: Jacques Lacan
The Inverse Side of the Structure: Žižek on Deleuze on Lacan

1. "Le 'Je me souviens' de Gilles Deleuze" (interview with Didier Éribon) in *Le Nouvel Observateur* 1619 (16–22 Nov 1995), 50–1.
2. Slavoj Žižek, *Organs Without Bodies: Deleuze and Consequences* (London: Routlege, 2003).
3. F 42. Deleuze was speaking of Virilio's relation to Foucault.
4. See Alain Badiou, *Deleuze: The Clamor of Being*, trans. Louise Burchill (Minneapolis: University of Minnesota Press, 2000), 3–4.
5. LS 124. See also LS 96:

> How are we to reconcile these two contradictory aspects [of sense]? On one hand, we have *impassibility* in relation to states of affairs and neutrality in relation to propositions; on the other hand, we have the power of *genesis* in relation to propositions and in relation to states of affairs themselves.

6. N 170. Elie Sambar was the editor of the *Revue des études palestiniennes*.
7. Eugene Holland's *Deleuze and Guattari's Anti-Oedipus: Introduction to Schizoanalysis* (New York: Routledge, 1999) is one of the few works that deals extensively with the Deleuze–Lacan relationship (see, for example, 89–91).
8. Immanuel Kant, *Critique of Judgment*, trans. James Creed Meredith (Oxford: Oxford University Press, 1952), Introduction, §3, footnote 1, 16n1. See also TRM 309:

> *Anti-Oedipus* had a Kantian ambition, we attempted a kind of *Critique of Pure Reason* at the level of the unconscious. Hence the determination of the synthesis belonging to the unconscious; the unfolding of history as the effectuation of these syntheses; and the denunciation of Oedipus as the "inevitable illusion" falsifying all historical production.

9. Jacques Lacan, "Kant with Sade," in *October* 51 (Winter 1989), 55–75. For Deleuze's use of Lacan's reading of Sade, see his "Humor, Irony, and the Law," in M 81–90.
10. AO 26–7. At one point, Deleuze and Guattari describe the project of *Anti-Oedipus* in explicitly Kantian terms:

> In what he termed the critical revolution, Kant intended to discover criteria immanent to understanding so as to distinguish the legitimate and the illegitimate uses of the syntheses of consciousness. In the name of *transcendental* philosophy (immanence of criteria), he therefore denounced the transcendent use of the syntheses such as appeared in metaphysics. In a like fashion, we are compelled to say that psychoanalysis has its metaphysics—its name is Oedipus. And that a revolution—this time materialist—can proceed only by way of a critique of Oedipus, by denouncing the illegitimate use of the syntheses of the unconscious as found in Oedipal psychoanalysis, so as to rediscover a transcendental unconscious defined by the immanence of its criteria, and a corresponding practice that we shall call schizoanalysis. (75)

11. ECC 7–22. See also AO 310:

> Elisabeth Roudinesco has clearly seen that, in Lacan, the hypothesis of an unconscious-as-language does not closet the unconscious in a linguistic structure, but leads linguistics to the point of its auto-critique, by showing how the structural organization of signifiers still depends on a despotic Great Signifier acting as an archaism.

12. In *Logic of Sense*, the distinction between surface and depth is paralleled in the difference between Lewis Carroll (surface) and Antonin Artaud (depth), but Deleuze's preference for Artaud and the dimension of depth (rather than surface) is already evident: "We would not give a page of Artaud for all of Carroll. Artaud is alone in having been an absolute depth in literature, and in having discovered a vital body and the prodigious language of this body" (LS 93).
13. In any early work, Judith Butler, for instance, characterizes Deleuze and Guattari's conception of desire as "an originary unrepressed libidinal diversity subject to the prohibitive laws of culture," an a-historical or "pre-cultural ideal" à la Rousseau or Montesquieu, a "natural eros which has subsequently been denied by a restrictive culture," arguing that Deleuze and Guattari promise "a liberation of that more original, bounteous desire." See Judith Butler, *Subjects of Desire* (New York: Columbia University Press, 1999), 214–15, 206. Žižek, rightly, does not follow this interpretation.
14. See Gilles Deleuze, "Desire and Pleasure," in *Foucault and his Interlocutors*, ed. Arnold I. Davidson (Chicago: University of Chicago Press, 1997), 185–6, and TP 215.
15. Deleuze, "Desire and Pleasure," in *Foucault and his Interlocutors*, 186.
16. Jacques Lacan, *On Feminine Sexuality, the Limits of Love and Knowledge: The Seminar of Jacques Lacan*, Book 20: *Encore*, ed. Jacques-Alain Miller, trans. Bruce Fink (New York: Norton, 1999), 62. I would like to thank Emily Zakin for this reference. Lacan was speaking

of Jean-Luc Nancy and Philippe Lacoue-Labarthe, *The Title of the Letter: A Reading of Lacan* (1973), trans. François Raffoul and David Pettigrew (Albany: State University of New York Press, 1992).

Essay 19: Pierre Klossowski
Klossowski's Reading of Nietzsche: Impulses, Phantasms, Simulacra, Stereotypes

1. This essay is a reading of Pierre Klossowski's *Nietzsche and the Vicious Circle*, trans. Daniel W. Smith (Chicago: University of Chicago Press, 1997), which is cited in the text as NVC.
2. Cited in Johannes Gachnang, "De la conquête des images," in *Pierre Klossowski* (Paris: Flammarion; Brussels: Ludion, 1996), 9 ("I am a 'maniac,' period, that's all!").
3. Pierre Klossowski, "Postface," in Jean Decottignies, *Klossowski* (Paris: Henri Veyrier, 1985), 137.
4. Friedrich Nietzsche, *Will to Power*, trans. Walter Kaufmann and R. J. Hollingdale (New York: Random House, 1967), §§492, 489–91.
5. See Alain Arnaud, *Pierre Klossowski* (Paris: Seuil, 1990), 8–9, who cites Augustine, Meister Eckhardt, and Theresa of Ávila as precursors to Klossowski. Arnaud's book is one of the best general introductions to Klossowski's work.
6. In English, the only treatment of Nietzsche's conception of the impulses comparable to Klossowski's is Graham Parkes's magisterial work, *Composing the Soul: The Reaches of Nietzsche's Psychology* (Chicago: University of Chicago Press, 1994).
7. Friedrich Nietzsche, *Will to Power*, §259, 149.
8. Cited in Parkes, *Composing the Soul*, 291–2.
9. Nietzsche, *Will to Power*, §481, 267.
10. Friedrich Nietzsche, *Daybreak: Thoughts on the Prejudices of Morality*, trans. R. J. Hollingdale (Cambridge: Cambridge University Press, 1982), §109, 65.
11. Nietzsche, *Will to Power*, §387, 208: "The misunderstanding of passion and reason, as if the latter were an independent entity and not rather a system of relations between various passions and desires; and as if very passion did not possess its quantum of reason."
12. Friedrich Nietzsche, *The Gay Science*, trans. Walter Kaufmann (New York: Vintage, 1974), §307, 245–6.
13. Deleuze's essay on Klossowski, "Klossowski, or Bodies-Language" (LS 280–301) emphasis Klossowski's relation to Kant:

> The order of God includes the following elements: the identity of God as the ultimate foundation, the identity of the world as the surrounding milieu, the identity of the person as a well-founded agent, the identity of bodies as the base, and finally the identity of language as the power of *denoting* everything else. But this order of God is constructed against another order, and this order subsists in God, and consumes him . . . The order of the Antichrist is opposed point by point to the divine order. It is characterized by the death of God, the destruction of the world, the dissolution of the person, the disintegration of bodies, and a change in the function of language, which now expresses nothing but intensities. (292, 294)

14. Pierre Klossowski, "Nietzsche, Polytheism and Parody," in *Such a Deathly Desire*, trans. Russell Ford (Albany: State University of New York Press, 2007), 99–122.
15. Friedrich Nietzsche, *Thus Spoke Zarathustra*, in *The Portable Nietzsche*, ed. and trans. Walter Kaufmann (New York: Viking, 1954), Part 3, §8, "Of the Apostates," 290–4: 294. For a historical treatment of this theme, see Jonathan Kirsch, *God Against the Gods: The History of the War Between Monotheism and Polytheism* (New York: Viking Compass, 2004).
16. See Maurice Blanchot's essay on Klossowski, "The Laughter of the Gods," in *Friendship*, trans. Elizabeth Rottenberg (Stanford: Stanford University Press, 1997), 169–82.

17. Friedrich Nietzsche, *Will to Power*, §1038, 534, as cited in NVC 209.

18. Pierre Klossowski, "Diana at her Bath," in *Diana at her Bath* and *The Women of Rome*, trans. Sophie Hawkes (Boston: Eridanos, 1990), 3–84, esp. 82–4.

19. Klossowski analyzes these criteria in Chapter 4 of *Nietzsche and the Vicious Circle*, "The Valetudinary States at the Origin of Four Criteria: Decadence, Vigor, Gregariousness, the Singular Case" (NVC 74–92).

20. Friedrich Nietzsche, letter to Franziska Nietzsche, mid-July 1881, in *Unpublished Letters*, ed. and trans. Kurt F. Leidecker (New York: Philosophical Library, 1959), Letter 29, 81–2, as cited in NVC 21.

21. Nietzsche, Letter to Dr. O. Eisner, Jan 1880, as cited in NVC 20.

22. For a detailed analysis of Klossowski's theory of the *suppôt*, see Jean-Pol Madou, *Démons et simulacres dans l'œuvre de Pierre Klossowski* (Paris: Méridiens Klincksieck, 1987), 35–41.

23. Nietzsche, *The Gay Science*, §354, 298–9.

24. Nietzsche, *Will to Power*, §479, 266.

25. Nietzsche, unpublished notes from 1881, as cited in Parkes, *Composing the Soul*, 300.

26. Pierre Klossowski, "Protase et apodose," in *L'Arc* 43 (1970), 10. Portions of this essay have been reprinted in Klossowski's *La Ressemblance* (Marseille: André Dimanche, 1984).

27. Jean-Maurice Monnoyer, *Le Peintre et son démon: Entretiens avec Pierre Klossowski* (Paris: Flammarion, 1985), 61.

28. Jean-François Lyotard, *Libidinal Economy*, trans. Ian Hamilton Grant (Bloomington and Indianapolis: Indiana University Press, 1993), 72.

29. Henri Bergson, "Philosophical Intuition," in *The Creative Mind: An Introduction to Metaphysics*, trans. Mabelle L. Andison (Totowa, NJ: Littlefield, Adams, 1946), 107–29.

30. Pierre Klossowski, *Les Lois de l'hospitalité* (Paris: Gallimard, 1965), 342, 349. Klossowski's trilogy includes three separately published titles: *Roberte ce soir* (Paris: Minuit, 1954), *La Révocation de l'Édit de Nantes* (Paris: Minuit, 1959), and *Le Souffleur ou le théâtre de société* (Paris: Jean-Jacques Pauvert, 1960). The first two have appeared in English translation: *Roberte ce soir* and *The Revocation of the Edict of Nantes*, trans. Austryn Wainhouse (New York: Grove, 1969). The best work on Klossowki in English is Ian James's *Pierre Klossowski: The Persistence of a Name* (Oxford: Legenda, 2000).

31. Pierre Klossowski, *The Baphomet*, trans. Sophie Hawkes and Stephen Sartarelli (Boston: Eridanos, 1988).

32. Cited on the back cover of Alain Arnaud, *Pierre Klossowski*.

33. Nietzsche, Notebook of Fall 1885 to Spring 1886, as cited in NVC 216.

34. Klossowski initially retrieved the concept of the simulacrum from the criticisms of the Church fathers (Tertullian, Augustine) against the debauched representations of the gods on the Roman stage. See Pierre Klossowski, "Sacred and Mythical Origins of Certain Practices of the Women of Rome," in *Diana at her Bath* and *The Women of Rome*, 89–138, esp. 132–5, as well as Jean-François Lyotard's commentaries on Klossowski in *Libidinal Economy*, 66–94.

35. Klossowski, *La Ressemblance*, 6.

36. Madou, *Démons et simulacres*, 88.

37. For Klossowski's theory of the stereotype, see "On the Use of Stereotypes and the Censure Exercised by Classical Syntax," in "Protase et apodose," 15–20.

38. Pierre Klossowski, *Sade My Neighbor*, trans. Alphonso Lingis (Evantson, IL: Northwestern University Press, 1991), 14. See also Klossowski, "Protase et apodose," 19: "In the domain of communication (literary or pictorial), the stereotype (as "style") is the residue of a simulacrum (corresponding to an obsessional constraint) that has fallen to the level of current usage, disclosed and abandoned to a common interpretation."

39. Klossowski, "Protase et apodose," 16–19.

40. Klossowski, *La Ressemblance*, 78, as cited in Arnaud, *Pierre Klossowski*, 60.

41. Arnaud, *Pierre Klossowski*, 104.
42. On these themes, see Michel Foucault's essay on Klossowski, "The Prose of Actaeon," in *Essential Works of Foucault: 1954–1984*, Vol. 2: *Aesthetics, Method, and Epistemology*, ed. James D. Faubion (New York: New Press, 1988), 123–35, esp. 123: "What if the Devil, the Other, were the Same? And what if the Temptation were not one of the episodes of the great antagonism, but the subtle insinuation of the Double?" Klossowski considered Foucault's essay to be one of the best commentaries on his work.
43. The observations by Gast and Overbeck are recorded in Ronald Hayman, *Nietzsche: A Critical Life* (Oxford: Oxford University Press, 1980), 340–1.
44. Pierre Klossowski, *La Monnaie vivante* (Paris: Éric Losfield, 1970; Paris: Gallimard, 2003).

Essay 20: Paul Patton
Deleuze and the Liberal Tradition: Normativity, Freedom, and Judgment

1. This essay is a review of Paul Patton's *Deleuze and the Political* (London and New York: Routledge, 2000), which is cited in the text as DP. An earlier version of this article was presented at the 2000 annual meeting of the Australasian Society for Continental Philosophy (ASCP), University of New South Wales, Sydney, Australia, 23–5 November 2000. I am indebted to the comments of the other panelists, Linnell Secombe and Stephen Meueke, as well as the response by Paul Patton.
2. Routledge's important "Thinking the Political" series is edited by Keith Ansell-Pearson and Simon Critchley, and thus far includes volumes on Foucault, Derrida, Nietzsche, Heidegger, Lacan, and Lyotard.
3. See Paul Patton, "Taylor and Foucault on Power and Freedom," in *Political Studies* 37/2 (Jun 1989), 260–76; "Politics and the Concept of Power in Hobbes and Nietzsche," in Paul Patton, ed., *Nietzsche, Feminism, and Political Theory* (London and New York: Routledge, 1993), 144–61; and "Foucault's Subject of Power," in Jeremy Moss, ed., *The Later Foucault: Politics and Philosophy*, London: Sage, 1998), 64–7.
4. See Paul Patton, "Mabo, Freedom, and the Politics of Difference," in *Australian Journal of Political Science* 30/1 (Mar 1995), 108–19; and "Sovereignty, Law and Difference in Australia: After the Mabo Case," in *Alternatives* 21 (1996).
5. Jean-François Lyotard, "Energumen Capitalism," in *Semiotext(e)*, 2/3 (1977), 11–26.
6. In this respect, Patton's primary precursors are Michael Hardt and Antonio Negri, whose works, though overtly Marxist, also include an important analysis of the liberal tradition from a broadly Deleuzian perspective. See their influential *Empire* (Cambridge, MA: Harvard, 2000), as well as the earlier *The Labors of Dionysus* (Minneapolis: University of Minnesota, 1997).
7. Hannah Arendt, *Lectures on Kant's Political Philosophy*, ed. Ronald Beiner (Chicago: University of Chicago Press, 1982), 22. For a critique of Arendt's position, see Alain Badiou, "Against 'Political Philosophy,'" in *Metapolitics*, trans. Jason Barker (London: Verso, 2005), 10–25.
8. For instance, Patton argues that the concept of the social contract, as an expression of absolute deterritorialization, "can be regarded as an expression of the pure and indeterminate event of a political system based upon equality before the law" (28).
9. Immanuel Kant, *Critique of Pure Reason*, trans. Norman Kemp Smith (London: Macmillan, 1929), 309–10, A312/B368ff.
10. John Rawls, *A Theory of Justice* (Cambridge, MA: Harvard University Press, 1971), 16.
11. Martin Heidegger, *Being and Time*, trans. John Macquarrie and Edward Robinson (New York and San Francisco, Harper & Row, 1962), 182–5, H143–5.
12. See PV 14–17; and "What is a 'dispositif?'" in *Michel Foucault: Philosopher*, ed. François Ewald, trans. Timothy J. Armstrong (New York: Routledge, 1992), 162.

13. One might note here that the concept of "nomadic war machines"—which was introduced in *A Thousand Plateaus*—is Deleuze and Guattari's attempt to address the question of a social formation that would itself be constructed along such movements or lines of flight. Patton suggests that such assemblages should in fact be called "metamorphosis" machines (110), a suggestion that will no doubt be taken up by others.

> Metamorphosis machines would be the conditions of actualization of absolute deterritorialization and the means by which relative deterritorialization occurs: "They bring *connections* to bear against the great *conjunction* of the apparatuses of capture or domination." . . . A metamorphosis machine would then be one that . . . engenders the production of something altogether different. (110)

14. James Tully, *Strange Multiplicity: Constitutionalism in an Age of Diversity* (Cambridge and New York: Cambridge University Press, 1995).
15. Isaiah Berlin, "Two Concepts of Freedom," in *Four Essays on Liberty*, Oxford: Oxford University Press, 1969), 118–72.
16. Charles Taylor, "What's Wrong with Negative Liberty," in *Philosophy and the Human Sciences: Philosophical Papers*, Vol. 2 (Cambridge: Cambridge University Press, 1985), 211–29.
17. Michel Foucault, *The Use of Pleasure: The History of Sexuality, Vol. 2*, trans. Robert Hurley (New York: Vintage, 1985), 8.
18. In his book on Kant, *Kant's Critical Philosophy*, Deleuze discusses the ambiguities of judgment, which always depends on a certain accord of the faculties. See the short but important section entitled "Is Judgment a Faculty?" (KCP 58–61).
19. Hannah Arendt, *Eichmann in Jerusalem: A Report on the Banality of Evil*, rev. and enlarged edn., New York: Viking, 1965), 294–5.
20. Alain Badiou, *D'un désastre obscur: droit, état, politique* (Paris: Éditions de l'Aube, 1991), 39–57.
21. Jacques Derrida, "Préjugés," in *La Faculté de juger* (Paris: Minuit, 1985), 96–7.
22. Jacques Derrida, "Force of Law: The Mystical Foundation of Authority," in Drucilla Cornell, *Deconstruction and the Possibility of Justice* (New York: Routledge, 1992), 25–7.
23. Alberto Gualandi, *Lyotard* (Paris: Les Belles Lettres, 1999), 119. See also Gualandi's *Deleuze* (Paris: Les Belles Lettres, 1998): Lyotard's and Deleuze's respective theories of judgment figure prominently in Gualandi's analyses.
24. Moira Gatens and Genevieve Lloyd, *Collective Imaginings: Spinoza, Past and Present* (London and New York, 1999), 143.
25. For an example of the kind of critique that has been leveled against the notion of the imaginary, see Pierre Bourdieu's *Masculine Domination*, trans. Richard Nice (London: Polity, 2001), 40:

> The language of the "imaginary," which one sees used somewhat recklessly here and there, is even more inadequate than that of "consciousness" [as in "consciousness raising"] inasmuch as it inclines one in particular to forget that the dominant principle of vision is not a simple mental representation, a fantasy ("ideas in people's heads"), an ideology, but a system of structures durably embedded in things and in *bodies*.

Deleuze, however, follows Spinoza in equating the imaginary with the affective, even if he generally utilizes the latter term rather than the former one.
26. See Moira Gatens and Genevieve Lloyd, *Collective Imaginings: Spinoza, Past and Present*; Michèle Le Dœuff, *The Philosophical Imaginary*, trans. Colin Gordon (Stanford: Stanford University Press, 1989); Benedict Anderson, *Imagined Communities* (London: Verso, 1991); Cornelius Castoriadis, *The Imaginary Institution of Society*, trans. Kathleen Blamey (Cambridge: Polity, 1987).

27. Kant, *Critique of Pure Reason*, 180–7, A137–47/B176–87.
28. Although Deleuze considers the schematism to be among the most novel and important innovations of Kantian thought, he himself takes the notion in a quite different direction. If the "schema" is outside the concept in Kant, what Deleuze calls a "dramatization" is internal to Ideas in the Deleuzian sense: "Everything changes when the dynamisms are posited no longer as *schemata of concepts* but as *dramas of Ideas*" (DR 218). Under a similar inspiration, Pierre Bourdieu, thoughout his work, distinguishes between "categories or cognitive structures" and "schemes or dispositions" (the habitus) (see *Masculine Domination*, 8–9).
29. See Jacob von Uexküll, *A Foray into the Worlds of Animals and Humans*, with *A Theory of Meaning*, trans. Joseph D. O'Neil (Minneapolis: University of Minnesota Press, 2010), 44–52.
30. See 28 Mar 1978 and 4 Apr 1978.
31. See Patton's recent book, *Deleuzian Concepts: Philosophy, Colonization, Politics* (Stanford: Stanford University Press, 2010).

Bibliography

Agamben, Giorgio, *The Open: Man and Animal*, trans. Kevin Attell (Stanford: Stanford University Press, 2004).

Agamben, Giorgio, *Potentialities: Collected Essays in Philosophy*, trans. Daniel Heller-Roazen (Stanford: Stanford University Press, 1999).

Alliez, Eric, *La Signature du monde* (Paris: Cerf, 1993).

Althusser, Louis, and Balibar, Étienne, *Reading Capital*, trans. Ben Brewster (London: Verso, 2009).

Anderson, Benedict, *Imagined Communities* (London: Verso, 1991).

Ansell-Pearson, Keith, *Philosophy and the Adventure of the Virtual: Bergson and the Time of Life* (London and New York: Routledge, 2002).

Antier, Daniel, *L'Étude des flux et des stocks* (Paris: Sedes, 1957).

Arendt, Hannah, *Eichmann in Jerusalem: A Report on the Banality of Evil*, rev. and enlarged edn. (New York: Viking, 1965).

Arendt, Hannah, *Lectures on Kant's Political Philosophy*, ed. Ronald Beiner (Chicago: University of Chicago Press, 1982).

Aristotle, *The Basic Works of Aristotle*, ed. Richard McKeon, trans. W. A. Pickard-Cambridge (New York: Random House, 1941).

Arnaud, Alain, *Pierre Klossowski* (Paris: Seuil, 1990).

Artaud, Antonin, *Heliogabalus, or The Crowned Anarchist*, trans. Alexis Lykiard (Clerkenwell: Solar, 2004).

Artaud, Antonin, *Selected Writings*, ed. Susan Sontag, trans. Helen Weaver (New York: Farrar Straus & Giroux, 1977).

Atlas, Samuel, *From Critical to Speculative Idealism: The Philosophy of Salomon Maimon* (The Hague: Martinus Nijhoff, 1964).

Augustine, *Concerning the City of God Against the Pagans*, trans. Henry Bettenson (New York: Penguin, 1984).

Augustine, *De Doctrina Christiana* (Indianapolis: Bobbs-Merrill, 1978).

Bacon, Francis, *The Brutality of Fact: Interviews with David Sylvester* (London: Thames & Hudson, 1975).

Badiou, Alain, "Against 'Political Philosophy,'" in *Metapolitics*, trans. Jason Barker (London: Verso, 2005).

Badiou, Alain, *Being and Event*, trans. Oliver Feltham (London and New York: Continuum, 2005).

Badiou, Alain, *Briefings on Existence: A Short Treatise on Transitory Ontology*, ed. and trans. Norman Madarasz (Albany: State University of New York Press, 2006).

Badiou, Alain, *The Century*, trans. Alberto Toscano (Cambridge: Polity, 2007).

Badiou, Alain, *The Communist Hypothesis*, trans. David Macey and Steve Corcoran (London: Verso, 2010).

Badiou, Alain, *Deleuze: The Clamor of Being*, trans. Louise Burchill (Minneapolis: University of Minnesota Press, 2000).

Badiou, Alain, *D'un désastre obscur: droit, état, politique* (Paris: Éditions de l'Aube, 1991).

Badiou, Alain, *Ethics: An Essay on the Understanding of Evil*, trans. Peter Hallward (London: Verso, 2001).

Badiou, Alain, *Logics of Worlds: Being and Event 2*, trans. Alberto Toscano (London: Continuum, 2009).

Badiou, Alain, *Theoretical Writings*, ed. and trans. Ray Brassier and Alberto Toscano (London and New York: Continuum, 2004).

Bakhtin, Mikhail M., *The Dialogical Imagination: Four Essays*, trans. Caryl Emerson and Michael Holquist, ed. Michael Holquist (Austin: University of Texas Press, 1981).

Baudrillard, Jean, *Simulacra and Simulation*, trans. Sheila Faria Glaser (Ann Arbor: University of Michigan Press, 1994).

Beiser, Frederick C., ed., *The Cambridge Companion to Hegel* (Cambridge: Cambridge University Press, 1993).

Beiser, Frederick C., *The Fate of Reason: German Philosophy From Kant to Fichte* (Cambridge, MA: Harvard University Press, 1987).

Beistegui, Miguel de, *Truth and Genesis: Philosophy and Differential Ontology* (Bloomington and Indianapolis: Indiana University Press, 2004).

Bell, E. T., *Men of Mathematics* (New York: Simon & Schuster, 1937).

Bellour, Raymond, "Thinking, Recounting: The Cinema of Gilles Deleuze," trans. Melissa McMahon, in *Discourse*, Vol. 20, No. 3 (Fall 1998), 56–75.

Bergman, Samuel H., *The Philosophy of Salomon Maimon*, trans. Noah L. Jacobs (Jerusalem: Magnes, 1967).

Bergson, Henri, *Creative Evolution*, trans. Arthur Mitchell (New York: Henry Holt, 1911).

Bergson, Henri, *The Creative Mind*, trans. Mabelle L. Andison (Totowa, NJ: Littlefield, Adams, 1946).

Bergson, Henri, *Matter and Memory*, trans. Nancy Margaret Paul and W. Scott Palmer (New York: Zone, 1988).

Henri Bergson, *Time and Free Will: An Essay on the Immediate Data of Consciousness*, trans. F. L. Pogson (London: George Allen, 1913).

Bergson, Henri, *Two Sources of Morality and Religion*, trans. T. Ashley Audra and Cloudesley Brereton with W. Horsfall Carter (New York: Henry Holt, 1935).

Berlin, Isaiah, *Four Essays on Liberty* (Oxford: Oxford University Press, 1969).

Blanché, Robert, *L'Axiomatique* (Paris: PUF, 1955).

Blanchot, Maurice, *Friendship*, trans. Elizabeth Rottenberg (Stanford: Stanford University Press, 1997).

Bogue, Ronald, *Deleuze and the Arts*: Vol. 1: *Deleuze on Cinema*; Vol. 2: *Deleuze on Literature*; Vol. 3: *Deleuze on Music, Painting, and the Arts* (New York: Routledge, 2005).

Borges, Jorge Luis Borges, *Ficciones* (New York: Grove, 1962).

Bouligand, Georges, *Le Déclin des absolus mathématico-logiques* (Paris: Éditions d'Enseignement Supérieur, 1949).

Boundas, Constantin V., "Deleuze-Bergsonian Ontology of the Virtual," in *Deleuze: A Critical Reader*, ed. Paul Patton (London: Basil Blackwell, 1996), 81–106.

Boundas, Constantin V., and Olkowski, Dorothea, eds., *Gilles Deleuze and the Theater of Philosophy* (New York: Routledge, 1994).

Bourbaki, Nicholas, "The Architecture of Mathematics," in *Great Currents of Mathematical*

Thought, ed. François Le Lionnais, trans. R. A. Hall and Howard G. Bergmann (New York: Dover, 1971).

Bourdieu, Pierre, *Homo Academicus*, trans. Peter Collier (Stanford: Stanford University Press, 1988).

Bourdieu, Pierre, *Masculine Domination*, trans. Richard Nice (London: Polity, 2001).

Bourdieu, Pierre, *The State Nobility: Elite Schools in the Field of Power*, trans. Lauretta C. Clough (Stanford: Stanford University Press, 1988).

Bousquet, Joë, *Les Capitales* (Paris: Le Cercle du Livre, 1955).

Boyer, Carl B., *The History of the Calculus and its Conceptual Development* (New York: Dover, 1959).

Boyer, Carl B., *History of Mathematics* (Princeton: Princeton University Press, 1968).

Bransen, Jan, *The Antinomy of Thought: Maimonian Skepticism and the Relation between Thoughts and Objects* (Dordrecht and Boston: Kluwer Academic, 1991).

Breazeale, Daniel, "The Hegel–Nietzsche Problem," in *Nietzsche-Studien* 4 (1975), 146–64.

Brontë, Emily, *Wuthering Heights* (New York: Norton, 1990).

Brunschvicg, Léon, *Les Étapes de la philosophie mathématique* (Paris: PUF, 1947; new edn: Paris: A. Blanchard, 1972).

Buchanan, Ian, *Deleuze and Guattari's "Anti-Oedipus": A Reader's Guide* (London: Continuum, 2008).

Büchner, George, *Complete Plays and Prose*, trans. Carl Richard Mueller (New York: Hill & Wang, 1963).

Buci-Glucksmann, Christine, "Le Plissé baroque de la peinture," *Magazine littéraire*, 257 (Sep 1988), 54–7.

Bunge, Mario, *Causality and Modern Science*, 3rd rev. edn. (New York: Dover, 1979).

Bunge, Mario, *Philosophy in Crisis: The Need for Reconstruction* (Amherst, NY: Prometheus, 2001).

Burroughs, William, *Naked Lunch* (New York: Grove, 1966).

Butler, Judith, *Subjects of Desire* (New York: Columbia University Press, 1999).

Butor, Michel, *Comment écrire pour Jasper Johns* (Paris: Éditions de la Différence, 1992).

Buydens, Mireille, *Sahara: L'Esthétique de Gilles Deleuze* (Paris: Vrin, 1990).

Cage, John, *Silence* (Middletown, CT: Wesleyan University Press, 1961).

Canguilhem, Georges, *On the Normal and the Pathological*, trans. Carolyn R. Fawcett (New York: Zone, 1978).

Canto-Sperber, Monique, "Pour la philosophie morale," in *Le Débat* 72 (Nov–Dec 1992), 40–51.

Caputo, John D., *The Prayers and Tears of Jacques Derrida* (Bloomington: Indiana University Press, 1997).

Castoriadis, Cornelius, *The Imaginary Institution of Society*, trans. Kathleen Blamey (Cambridge: Polity, 1987).

Cavell, Stanley, *Themes Out of School: Effects and Causes* (Chicago: University of Chicago Press, 1984).

Chasles, Michel, *Aperçu historique sur l'origine et le développement de méthodes en géométrie* (Brussels: M. Hayez, 1837).

Châtelet, François, *Chronique des idées perdues* (Paris: Stock, 1977).

Chauvin, Rémy, *Entretiens sur la sexualité*, ed. Max Aron, Robert Courrier, and Étienne Wolf (Paris: Plon, 1969).

Cohen, Hermann, *Kants Theorie der Erfahrung*, 2nd edn. (Berlin: Dümmler, 1885).

Cornell, Drucilla, ed., *Deconstruction and the Possibility of Justice* (New York: Routledge, 1992).

Couturat, Louis, "On Leibniz's Metaphysics," in Harry G. Frankfurt, ed., *Leibniz: A Collection of Critical Essays* (Garden City, NY: Anchor, 1972).

Critchley, Simon, ed., *A Companion to Continental Philosophy* (Oxford: Blackwell, 1998).

Curley, Edwin M., *Spinoza's Metaphysics: An Essay in Interpretation* (Cambridge, MA: Harvard University Press, 1969).

Dalmas, André, *Évariste Galois* (Paris: Fasquelle, 1956).

Daniel, Stephen, ed., *Current Continental Theory and Modern Philosophy* (Evanston, IL: Northwestern University Press, 2005).

Danto, Arthur, *The Philosophical Disenfranchisement of Art* (New York: Columbia University Press, 1986).

Davidson, Arnold I., *The Emergence of Sexuality: Historical Epistemology and the Formation of Concepts* (Cambridge, MA: Harvard University Press, 2001).

Davidson, Arnold I., ed., *Foucault and his Interlocutors* (Chicago: University of Chicago Press, 1997).

Davis, Philip J., and Hersh, Reuben, *The Mathematical Experience* (Boston, Basel, and Stuttgart: Birkhäuser, 1981).

Decottignies, Jean, *Klossowski* (Paris: Henri Veyrier, 1985).

De Landa, Manuel, *Intensive Science and Virtual Philosophy* (London: Continuum, 2002).

Deleuze, Gilles, *Bergsonism*, trans. Hugh Tomlinson and Barbara Habberjam (New York: Zone, 1988).

Deleuze, Gilles, "Bergson's Conception of Difference," trans. Melissa McMahon, in John Mullarkey, ed., *The New Bergson* (Manchester: Manchester University Press, 1999).

Deleuze, Gilles, "De Sacher-Masoch au masochisme," in *Arguments* 5/21 (Jan–Apr 1961), 40–6.

Deleuze, Gilles, *Desert Islands and Other Texts*, ed. Sylvère Lotinger, trans. Michael Taormina (New York: Semiotext(e), 2004).

Deleuze, Gilles, "Desire and Pleasure," in *Foucault and his Interlocutors*, ed. Arnold I. Davidson (Chicago: University of Chicago Press, 1997), 183–92.

Deleuze, Gilles, "Deux questions," in *Recherches*, 39 bis (Dec 1979), 231–4.

Deleuze, Gilles, and Parnet, Claire, *Dialogues*, trans. Hugh Tomlinson and Barbara Habberjam (New York: Columbia University Press, 1987).

Deleuze, Gilles, *Difference and Repetition*, trans. Paul Patton (New York: Columbia University Press, 1984).

Deleuze, Gilles, "Dualism, Monism and Multiplicities (Desire-Pleasure-*Jouissance*)," trans. Daniel W. Smith (seminar of 26 Mar 1973), in *Contretemps: An Online Journal of Philosophy* 2 (May 2001), 92–108.

Deleuze, Gilles, *Empiricism and Subjectivity: An Essay on Hume's Theory of Human Nature*, trans. Constantin V. Boundas (New York: Columbia University Press, 1991).

Deleuze, Gilles, *Essays Critical and Clinical*, trans. Daniel W. Smith and Michael A. Greco (Minneapolis: University of Minnesota Press, 1997).

Deleuze, Gilles, *Expressionism in Philosophy: Spinoza*, trans. Martin Joughin (New York: Zone, 1990).

Deleuze, Gilles, *The Fold: Leibniz and the Baroque*, trans. Tom Conley (Minneapolis: University of Minnesota Press, 1993).

Deleuze, Gilles, *Foucault*, trans. Seán Hand (Minneapolis: University of Minnesota Press, 1988).

Deleuze, Gilles, *Francis Bacon: The Logic of Sensation*, trans. Daniel W. Smith (Minneapolis: University of Minnesota Press, 2003).

Deleuze, Gilles, "The Idea of Genesis in Kant's Aesthetics," trans. Daniel W. Smith, in *Angelaki*, Vol. 5, No. 3 (Dec 2000), 39–70.

Deleuze, Gilles, "Le 'Je me souviens' de Gilles Deleuze" (interview with Didier Éribon) in *Le Nouvel Observateur* 1619 (16–22 Nov 1995).

Deleuze, Gilles, "Lettre-préface," in Mireille Buydens, *Sahara: L'Esthétique de Gilles Deleuze* (Paris: Vrin, 1990), 5–6.

Deleuze, Gilles, *The Logic of Sense*, trans. Mark Lester, with Charles Stivale; ed. Constantin V. Boundas (New York: Columbia University Press, 1990).

Deleuze, Gilles, *Masochism: Coldness and Cruelty*, trans. Jean McNeil (New York: Zone, 1989).

Deleuze, Gilles, *The Movement-Image*, trans. Hugh Tomlinson and Barbara Habberjam (Minneapolis: University of Minnesota Press, 1986).

Deleuze, Gilles, *Negotiations, 1972–1990*, trans. Martin Joughin (New York: Colombia University Press, 1995).

Deleuze, Gilles, *Nietzsche and Philosophy*, trans. Hugh Tomlinson (New York: Columbia University Press, 1983).

Deleuze, Gilles, "One Manifesto Less," in *The Deleuze Reader*, ed. Constantin V. Boundas (New York: Columbia University Press, 1994).

Deleuze, Gilles, *Périclès et Verdi* (Paris: Minuit, 1988).

Deleuze, Gilles, "A Philosophical Concept," in *Who Comes After the Subject*, ed. Eduardo Cadava, Peter Connor, and Jean-Luc Nancy (New York: Routledge, 1991), 95–7.

Deleuze, Gilles, "À propos des nouveaux philosophes et d'un problème plus général," *Minuit* 4, supplement (5 Jun 1977).

Deleuze, Gilles, *Qu'est-ce que fonder?* (What is Grounding?), cours hypokhâgne, at Lycée Louis le Grand, Paris, 1956–7, on-line at webdeleuze.com.

Deleuze, Gilles, "Reversing Platonism (Simulacra)," trans. Heath Massey, published as an appendix to Leonard Lawlor, *Thinking Through French Philosophy: The Being of the Question* (Bloomington and Indianapolis: Indiana University Press, 2003), 163–77. The original article appeared in the *Revue de Métaphysique et de Morale* 71/4 (Oct–Dec 1966), 426–38.

Deleuze, Gilles, *Spinoza: Practical Philosophy*, trans. Robert Hurley (San Francisco: City Lights, 1988).

Deleuze Gilles, and Guattari, Félix, *Anti-Oedipus*, trans. Robert Hurley, Mark Seem, and Helen R. Lane, New York: Viking, 1977).

Deleuze Gilles, and Guattari, Félix, *Kafka: Toward a Minor Literature*, trans. Dana Polan (Minneapolis: University of Minnesota Press, 1986).

Deleuze, Gilles, and Guattari, Félix, "La Synthèse disjonctive," in *L'Arc* 43 (1970), 54–62.

Deleuze, Gilles, and Guattari, Félix, *A Thousand Plateaus*, trans. Brian Massumi (Minneapolis: University of Minnesota Press, 1987).

Deleuze, Gilles, and Guattari, Félix, *What is Philosophy?*, trans. Hugh Tomlinson and Graham Burchell (New York: Columbia University Press, 1994).

Derrida, Jacques, *Acts of Religion*, ed. Gil Anidjar (London and New York: Routledge, 2002).

Derrida, Jacques, *Aporias*, trans. Thomas Dutoit (Stanford: Stanford University Press, 1993).

Derrida, Jacques, *Deconstruction in a Nutshell: A Conversation with Jacques Derrida*, ed. John D. Caputo (New York: Fordham University Press, 1997).

Derrida, Jacques, *Dissemination*, trans. Barbara Johnson (Chicago: University of Chicago Press, 1981).

Derrida, Jacques, "Force of Law: The Mystical Foundation of Authority," in Drucilla Cornell, *Deconstruction and the Possibility of Justice* (New York: Routledge, 1992).

Derrida, Jacques, *The Gift of Death*, trans. David Willis (Chicago: University of Chicago Press, 1995).

Derrida, Jacques, *Given Time*, Vol. 1: *Counterfeit Money*, trans. Peggy Kamuf (Chicago: University of Chicago Press, 1994).

Derrida, Jacques, "How to Avoid Speaking: Denials," in *Derrida and Negative Theology*, ed. Harold Coward and Toby Foshay (Albany: State University of New York Press, 1992).

Derrida, Jacques, "Letter to a Japanese Friend," in *Derrida and Difference*, ed. David Wood and Robert Bernasconi (Evanston: Northwestern University Press, 1988).

Derrida, Jacques, *Limited ABC*, ed. Samuel Weber (Evanston, IL: Northwestern University Press, 1988).

Derrida, Jacques, *Margins of Philosophy*, trans. Alan Bass (Chicago: University of Chicago Press, 1984).

Derrida, Jacques, *On the Name*, trans. Thomas Dutoit (Stanford: Stanford University Press, 1995).

Derrida, Jacques, *Politics of Friendship*, trans. George Collins (London: Verso, 1997), 215–16.

Derrida, Jacques, *Positions*, trans. Alan Bass (Chicago: University of Chicago Press, 1981).

Derrida, Jacques, *The Post Card*, trans. Alan Bass (Chicago: University of Chicago Press, 1987).

Derrida, Jacques, "Préjugés," in *La Faculté de juger* (Paris: Minuit, 1985).

Derrida, Jacques, *Resistances to Psychoanalysis*, trans. Pascale-Anne Brault and Michael B. Naas (Stanford: Stanford University Press, 1998).

Derrida, Jacques, *Spectres de Marx: L'État de la dette, le travail du deuil et la nouvelle Internationale* (Paris: Galilée, 1993).

Derrida, Jacques, *The Truth in Painting*, trans. Geoff Bennington and Ian McLeod (Chicago: University of Chicago Press, 1967).

Derrida, Jacques, *The Work of Mourning*, ed. and trans. by Pascale-Anne Brault and Michael Naas (Chicago: University of Chicago Press, 2001).

Derrida, Jacques, *Writing and Difference*, trans. Alan Bass (Chicago: University of Chicago Press, 1980).

Descombes, Vincent, *Modern French Philosophy*, trans. L. Scott Fox and J. M. Harding (Cambridge: Cambridge University Press, 1980).

Detienne, Marcel, *The Masters of Truth in Archaic Greece*, trans. Janet Lloyd (New York: Zone, 1999).

Dewey, John, "Time and Individuality," in *The Essential Dewey*, Vol. 1: *Pragmatism, Education, Democracy*, ed. Larry A. Hickman and Thomas M. Alexander (Bloomington and Indianapolis: Indiana University Press, 1998), 217–26.

Dickens, Charles, *Our Mutual Friend*, in *The Oxford Illustrated Dickens* (London: Oxford University Press, 1952).

Dosse, François, *Gilles Deleuze and Félix Guattari: Intersecting Lives*, trans. Deborah Glassman (New York: Columbia University Press, 2010).

Durie, Robin, "Immanence and Difference: Toward a Relational Ontology," in *Southern Journal of Philosophy*, Vol. 60 (2002), 1–29.

Dyson, Freeman, *Infinite in All Directions* (New York: Harper & Row, 1988).

Eliade, Mircea, *The Myth of the Eternal Return* (Princeton: Princeton University Press, 1954).

Engel, Pascal, *The Norm of the True* (Toronto: University of Toronto Press, 1991).

Faulkner, Keith, *Deleuze and the Three Syntheses of Time* (New York: Peter Lang, 2005).

Faye, Jean-Pierre, *La Raison narrative* (Paris: Balland, 1990).

Ferguson, Niall, *The Ascent of Money: A Financial History of the World* (New York: Penguin, 2008).

Forrester, Jay W., *Principles of Systems*, 2nd edn. (New York: Pegasus, 1968).

Foucault, Michel, *The Archaeology of Knowledge*, trans. A. M. Sheridan Smith (New York: Pantheon, 1972).

Foucault, Michel, *The Care of the Self: The History of Sexuality, Vol. 3*, trans. Robert Hurley (New York: Pantheon, 1986).

Foucault, Michel, *Death and the Labyrinth: The World of Raymond Roussel* (Garden City, NY: Doubleday, 1986).

Foucault, Michel, *Essential Works of Foucault: 1954–1984*, Vol. 2: *Aesthetics, Method, and Epistemology*, ed. James D. Faubion (New York: New Press, 1988), 123–35.

Foucault, Michel, *The Foucault Reader*, ed. Paul Rabinow (New York: Pantheon, 1984), 381–90.

Foucault, Michel, *Language, Counter-Memory, Practice: Selected Essays and Interviews*, ed. Donald F. Bouchard, trans. Donald F. Bouchard and Sherry Simon (Ithaca, NY: Cornell University Press, 1977).

Foucault, Michel, *The Order of Things* (New York: Vintage, 1973).

Foucault, Michel, *The Use of Pleasure: The History of Sexuality, Vol. 2*, trans. Robert Hurley (New York: Vintage, 1985).

Foucault, Michel, "What is a 'dispositif'?" in *Michel Foucault: Philosopher*, ed. François Ewald, trans. Timothy J. Armstrong (New York: Routledge, 1992), 162.

Frankfurt, Henry G., *Leibniz: A Collection of Critical Essays* (Garden City, NY: Anchor, 1972).

Freud, Sigmund, *Civilization and its Discontents*, trans. James Strachey (New York: W. W. Norton, 1961).

Gandillac, Maurice de, and Pautrat, Bernard, *Nietzsche aujourd'hui* (Paris: Union Générale d'Éditions, 10/18, 1973), Vol. 1, *Intensities*, 186–7.

Gasquet, Joachim, *Cézanne: A Memoir with Conversations*, trans. Christopher Pemberton (London: Thames & Hudson, 1991).

Gatens, Moira, and Lloyd, Genevieve, *Collective Imaginings: Spinoza, Past and Present* (London and New York: Routledge, 1999).

Genosko, Gary, *Félix Guattari: An Aberrant Introduction* (London and New York: Continuum, 2002).

Gilson, Étienne, *Being and Some Philosophers* (Toronto: Pontifical Institute of Mediaeval Studies, 1952).

Gilson, Étienne, *History of Christian Philosophy in the Middle Ages* (London: Sheed & Ward, 1955).

Gilson, Étienne, *Introduction à l'étude de Saint-Augustin* (Paris: Vrin, 1929).

Gilson, Étienne, *Jean Duns Scot: Introduction à ses positions fondamentales* (Paris: J. Vrin, 1952).

Giorello, Guilio, "The 'Fine Structure' of Mathematical Revolutions: Metaphysics, Legitimacy, and Rigour," in *Revolutions in Mathematics*, ed. Donald Gilles (Oxford: Clarendon, 1992).

Gleick, James, *Chaos: Making a New Science* (New York: Viking, 1987).

Gobard, Henri, *L'Aliénation linguistique* (Paris: Flammarion, 1976).

Goethe, Johann Wolfgang von, *Color Theory*, ed. Rupprecht Matthaei (New York: Van Nostrand, 1971).

Goodman, Nelson, *Languages of Art*, 2nd edn. (Indianapolis: Hackett, 1976).

Gualandi, Alberto, *Deleuze* (Paris: Les Belles Lettres, 1998).

Gualandi, Alberto, *Lyotard* (Paris: Les Belles Lettres, 1999).

Guattari, Félix, *The Anti-Oedipus Papers*, ed. Stéphane Nadaud, trans. Kélina Gotman (New York: Semiotext(e), 2006).

Guattari, Félix, *Chaosophy*, ed. Sylvère Lotringer (New York: Semiotext(e), 1995).

Guattari, Félix, and Negri, Antonio, *Communists Like Us* (New York: Semiotext(e), 1991).

Guéroult, Martial, *La Philosophie transcendentale de Salomon Maïmon* (Paris: Alcan, 1929).

Guéroult, Martial, *L'Évolution et la structure de la Doctrine de la Science chez Fichte*, 2 vols. (Paris: Les Belles-Lettres, 1930).

Habermas, Jürgen, *The Philosophical Discourse of Modernity* (Cambridge, MA: MIT Press, 1988).

Hacking, Ian, "Biopower and the Avalanche of Printed Numbers," in *Humanities in Society* 5 (1982), 279–95.

Hacking, Ian, "The Invention of Split Personalities," in *Human Nature and Natural Knowledge*, ed. Alan Donagan, Anthony N. Perovich, Jr., and Michael V. Wedlin (Dordrecht: Springer, 1986), 63–85.

Hacking, Ian, "The Making and Molding of Child Abuse," in *Critical Inquiry* 17 (Winter 1991), 253–88.

Hacking, Ian, "Making Up People," in *Historical Ontology* (Cambridge, MA: Harvard University Press, 2002), 99–114.

Hacking, Ian, "What is Tom Saying to Maureen?," in *London Review of Books*, Vol. 28, No. 9 (May 2006), 3–7.

Hacking, Ian, "What Mathematics Has Done to Some and Only Some Philosophers," in *Proceedings of the British Academy* 103 (2000), 83–138.

Hadot, Pierre, *Philosophy as a Way of Life*, ed. Arnold I. Davidson (Cambridge, MA: Blackwell, 1995).

Hägglund, Martin, *Radical Atheism: Derrida and the Time of Life* (Stanford: Stanford University Press, 2008).

Hahn, Hans, "The Crisis in Intuition," in J. R. Newman, ed., *The World of Mathematics* (New York: Simon & Schuster, 1956), 1956–76.

Hallett, Garth, *A Commentary to Wittgenstein's "Philosophical Investigations"* (Ithaca, NY: Cornell University Press, 1977).

Hallward, Peter, *Subject to Truth: The Work of Alain Badiou* (Minneapolis: University of Minnesota Press, 2003).

Hallward, Peter, ed., *Think Again: Alain Badiou and the Future of Philosophy* (London: Continuum, 2004).

Halperin, David, *One Hundred Years of Homosexuality: And Other Essays on Greek Love* (New York: Routledge, 1989).

Hayman, Ronald, *Nietzsche: A Critical Life* (Oxford: Oxford University Press, 1980).

Hardt, Michael, and Negri, Antonio, *Empire* (Cambridge, MA: Harvard, University Press 2000).

Hardt, Michael, and Negri, Antonio, *The Labors of Dionysus* (Minneapolis: University of Minnesota Press, 1997).

Hegel, G. W. F., *Phenomenology of Spirit*, trans. A. V. Miller (Oxford: Oxford University Press, 1979).

Hegel, G. W. F., *Science of Logic*, trans. A. V. Miller (London: George Allen & Unwin, 1969).

Heidegger, Martin, *The Basic Problems of Phenomenology*, trans. Albert Hofstadter (Bloomington and Indianapolis: Indiana University Press, 1988).

Heidegger, Martin, *Being and Time*, trans. John Macquarrie and Edward Robinson (New York and San Francisco: Harper & Row, 1962).

Heidegger, Martin, *Hegel's Phenomenology of Spirit*, trans. Parvis Emad and Kenneth Maly (Bloomington: Indiana University Press, 1988).

Heidegger, Martin, *Kant and the Problem of Metaphysics*, trans. James S. Churchill (Bloomington: Indiana University Press, 1962).

Heidegger, Martin, *Nietzsche*, Vol. 1: *The Will to Power as Art*, trans. David Farrell Krell (London: Routledge & Kegan Paul, 1981).

Heidegger, Martin, *Nietzsche*, Vol. 4: *Nihilism*, trans. Frank A. Capuzzi, ed. David Farrell Krell (San Francisco: Harper & Row, 1982).

Heidegger, Martin, *On Time and Being* (1962), trans. Joan Stambaugh (New York: Harper & Row, 1972).

Heidegger, Martin, *What is Called Thinking*, trans. Fred D. Wieck and J. Glenn Gray (New York: Harper & Row, 1968).

Heilbroner, Robert L., *The Worldly Philosophers: The Lives, Times and Ideas of the Great Economic Thinkers*, rev. 7th edn. (New York: Touchstone, 1999).

Hoffman, Paul, *The Man Who Loved Only Numbers: The Story of Paul Erdós and the Search for Mathematical Truth* (New York: Hyperion, 1998).

Holland, Eugene, *Deleuze and Guattari's Anti-Oedipus: An Introduction to Schizoanalysis* (New York: Routledge, 1999).

Holt, Jim, "Infinitesimally Yours," in *The New York Review of Books*, 20 May 1999.

Houël, Jules, *Essai critique sur les principes fondamentaux de la géométrie élémentaire* (Paris: Gauthier-Villars, 1867).

Hoy, David Couzens, ed., *Foucault: A Critical Reader* (New York: Basil Blackwell, 1986).

Hughes, Joe, *Deleuze and the Genesis of Representation* (London and New York: Continuum, 2008).

Husserl, Edmund, *Edmund Husserl's Origin of Geometry: An Introduction*, ed. John P. Leavey, Jr. and David B. Allison (Stony Brook, NY: H. Hayes, 1978).

Husserl, Edmund, *Ideas: General Introduction to a Pure Phenomenology*, trans. W. R. Boyce Gibson (New York: Macmillan, 1931).

Hyppolite, Jean, *Genesis and Structure of Hegel's "Phenomenology of Spirit,"* trans. Samuel Cherniak and John Heckman (Evanston, IL: Northwestern University Press, 1979).

Hyppolite, Jean, *Logic and Existence* (1952), trans. Leonard Lawlor and Amit Sen (Albany: State University of New York Press, 1997).

Jacob, François, *The Logic of Life*, trans. Betty E. Spellman (New York: Pantheon, 1973).

James, Ian, *Pierre Klossowski: The Persistence of a Name* (Oxford: Legenda, 2000).

James, William, *Pragmatism* (New York: Dover, 1995).

James, William, *Principles of Psychology*, 2 vols. (New York: Dover, 1950).

Jones, Graham, *Difference and Determination: Prolegomena Concerning Deleuze's Early Metaphysic*, unpublished Ph.D. thesis, Monash University, 2002.

Kafka, Franz, *The Diaries of Franz Kafka: 1910–1913*, ed. Max Brod, trans. Joseph Kresh (New York: Schocken, 1948).

Kant, Immanuel, *Critique of Judgment*, trans. James Creed Meredith (Oxford: Oxford University Press, 1952).

Kant, Immanuel, *Critique of Practical Reason*, in *Immanuel Kant: Practical Philosophy*, trans. Mary J. Gregor (Cambridge: Cambridge University Press, 1996).

Kant, Immanuel, *Critique of Pure Reason*, trans. Norman Kemp Smith (London: Macmillan, 1929).

Kant, Immanuel, *The Metaphysics of Morals*, in *Immanuel Kant: Practical Philosophy*, trans. Mary J. Gregor (Cambridge: Cambridge University Press, 1996).

Kant, Immanuel, *Philosophical Correspondence, 1759–99*, ed. Arnulf Zweig (Chicago: University of Chicago Press, 1967).

Kellner, Douglas, *Jean Baudrillard: From Marxism to Postmodernism and Beyond* (Stanford: Stanford University Press, 1989).

Keynes, John Maynard, *The General Theory of Employment, Interest, and Money* (New York: Harcourt, 1964).

Kierkegaard, Søren, *Fear and Trembling*, trans. Alastair Hannay (London: Penguin, 1985).

Kirsch, Jonathan, *God Against the Gods: The History of the War Between Monotheism and Polytheism* (New York: Viking Compass, 2004).

Klee, Paul, *Das Bildnerische Denken*, ed. Jürg Spiller (Basel: Schwabe, 1964).

Klee, Paul, *On Modern Art*, trans. Paul Findlay (London: Faber, 1966).

Kline, Morris, *Mathematical Thought from Ancient to Modern Times*, 3 vols. (Oxford: Oxford University Press, 1972).

Klossowski, Pierre, *The Baphomet*, trans. Sophie Hawkes and Stephen Sartarelli (Boston: Eridanos, 1988).

Klossowski, Pierre, *Diana at her Bath* and *The Women of Rome*, trans. Sophie Hawkes (Boston: Eridanos, 1990), 132–8.

Klossowski, Pierre, *Les Lois de l'hospitalité* (Paris: Gallimard, 1965).

Klossowski, Pierre, *La Monnaie vivante* (Paris: Éric Losfield, 1970; Paris: Gallimard, 2003).

Klossowski, Pierre, *Nietzsche and the Vicious Circle*, trans. Daniel W. Smith (Chicago: University of Chicago Press, 1997).

Klossowski, Pierre, *Pierre Klossowski* (Paris: Flammarion; Brussels: Ludion, 1996), catalog of an exhibition held at the Musée d'Ixelles, Brussels, 8 Feb–28 Apr 1996.

Klossowski, Pierre, "Protase et Apodose," in *L'Arc* 43 (1970), 10–20.

Klossowski, Pierre, *La Ressemblance* (Marseille: André Dimanche, 1984).

Klossowski, Pierre, *La Révocation de l'Édit de Nantes* (Paris: Minuit, 1959).

Klossowski, Pierre, *Roberte ce soir* (Paris: Minuit, 1954).

Klossowski, Pierre, *Roberte ce soir* and *The Revocation of the Edict of Nantes*, trans. Austryn Wainhouse (New York: Grove, 1969).

Klossowski, Pierre, *Sade My Neighbor*, trans. Alphonso Lingis (Evanston, IL: Northwestern University Press, 1991).

Klossowski, Pierre, *Le Souffleur ou le théâtre de société* (Paris: Jean-Jacques Pauvert, 1960).

Klossowski, Pierre, *Such a Deathly Desire*, trans. Russell Ford (Albany: State University of New York Press, 2007).

Kojève, Alexandre, *Introduction to the Reading of Hegel*, ed. Allan Bloom, trans. James H. Nichols, Jr. (New York: Basic, 1969).

Kojève, Alexandre, "Tyranny and Wisdom," in Leo Strauss, *On Tyranny* (New York: Free Press, 1963).

Kundera, Milan, *The Art of the Novel*, trans. Linda Asher (New York: Grove, 1988).

Lacan, Jacques, *Le Séminaire, livre XVI: D'un autre à l'autre (1968–1969)* (Paris: Seuil, 2006).

Lacan, Jacques, "Kant with Sade," in *October* 51 (Winter 1989), 55–75.

Lacan, Jacques, *On Feminine Sexuality, the Limits of Love and Knowledge: The Seminar of Jacques Lacan*, Book 20: *Encore*, ed. Jacques-Alain Miller, trans. Bruce Fink (New York: Norton, 1999).

Lacan, Jacques, "Seminar on *The Purloined Letter*," trans. Jeffrey Mehlman, in *Yale French Studies* 48 (1972), 39–72.

Lakoff, George, and Núñez, Rafael E., *Where Mathematics Comes From: How the Embodied Mind Brings Mathematics Into Being* (New York: Basic, 2000).

Lapoujade, David, "From Transcendental Empiricism to Worker Nomadism: William James," trans. Alberto Toscano, in *Pli: The Warwick Journal of Philosophy* 9 (2000), 190–9.

Lautman, Albert, *Essai sur les notions de structure et d'existence en mathématiques*, Vol. 1: *Les Schémas de structure*; Vol. 2: *Les Schémas de genèse* (Paris: Hermann, 1938).

Lautman, Albert, *Mathematics, Ideas, and the Physical Real*, trans. Simon Duffy (London: Continuum, 2011).

Lautman, Albert, *Nouvelles Recherches sur la structure dialectique des mathématiques* (Paris: Hermann, 1939).

Lautman, Albert, *Le Problème du temps* (Paris: Hermann, 1946).

Lawlor, Leonard, *Thinking Through French Philosophy: The Being of the Question* (Bloomington and Indianapolis: Indiana University Press, 2003).

Lawrence, D. H., *Fantasia of the Unconscious* (New York: Viking, 1960).

Le Dœuff, Michèle, *The Philosophical Imaginary*, trans. Colin Gordon (Stanford: Stanford University Press, 1989).

Leibniz, Gottfried Wilhelm, *The Leibniz–Clarke Correspondence*, ed. H. G. Alexander (Manchester: Manchester University Press, 1956).

Leibniz, Gottfried Wilhelm, *New Essays on Human Understanding*, ed. and trans. Peter Remnant and Jonathan Bennett (Cambridge: Cambridge University Press, 1981).

Leibniz, Gottfried Wilhelm, *Philosophical Papers and Letters*, 2nd edn., ed. Leroy E. Loemker (Dordrecht: D. Reidel, 1969).

Leibniz, Gottfried Wilhelm, *Die Philosophischen Schriften von G. W. Leibniz*, ed. C. J. Gerhardt (Berlin: George Olms, 1965).

Leibniz, Gottfried Wilhelm, *Theodicy: Essays on the Goodness of God, the Freedom of Man, and the Origin of Evil*, trans. E. M. Huggard, ed. Austin Farrer (La Salle, IL: Open Court, 1985).

Leiris, Michel, *Francis Bacon*, trans. John Weightman (New York: Rizzoli, 1998).

Leiris, Michel, *Francis Bacon: Full Face and in Profile*, trans. John Weightman (New York: Rizzoli, 1983).

Lévi-Strauss, Claude, *Totemism*, trans. Rodney Needham (Boston: Beacon, 1962).

Levinas, Emmanuel, *Totality and Infinity*, trans. Alphonso Lingis (Pittsburgh: Duquesne University Press, 1969).

Lionnais, François Le, ed., *Great Currents of Mathematical Thought*, trans. R. A. Hall and Howard G. Bergmann (New York: Dover, 1971).

Loemker, Leroy E., ed., *Philosophical Papers and Letters of G. W. Leibniz* (Dordrecht: D. Reidel, 1956).

Lowry, Malcolm, *Selected Letters of Malcolm Lowry*, ed. Harvey Breit and Margerie Bonner Lowry (Philadelphia and New York: Lippincott, 1965).

Lundy, Craig, *History and Becoming in Deleuze's Philosophy of Creativity* (Edinburgh: Edinburgh University Press, 2012).

Lyotard, Jean-François, *Driftworks*, ed. Roger McKeon (New York: Semiotext(e), 1984).

Lyotard, Jean-François, "Energumen Capitalism," in *Critique* 306 (Nov 1972), 923–56. English translation in *Semiotext(e)*, Vol. 2, No. 3 (1977), 11–26.

Lyotard, Jean-François, *The Inhuman: Reflections on Time* (Stanford: Stanford University Press, 1988).

Lyotard, Jean-François, *Lessons on the Analytic of the Sublime*, trans. Elizabeth Rottenberg (Stanford: Stanford University Press, 1994).

Lyotard, Jean-François, *Libidinal Economy*, trans. Iain Hamilton Grant (Bloomington and Indianapolis: Indiana University Press, 1993).

Lyotard, Jean-François, *The Postmodern Condition: A Report on Knowledge*, trans. Geoff Bennington and Brian Massumi (Minneapolis: University of Minnesota Press, 1984).

Lyotard, Jean-François, *Que peindre? Adami, Arakawa, Buren* (Paris: Éditions de la Différence, 1987).

MacIntyre, Alasdair, *After Virtue: A Study in Moral Theory*, 2nd edn. (Notre Dame, IN: University of Notre Dame Press, 1984).

Maddy, Penelope, *Naturalism in Mathematics* (Oxford: Oxford University Press, 1997).

Madou, Jean-Pol, *Démons et simulacres dans l'œuvre de Pierre Klossowski* (Paris: Méridiens Klincksieck, 1987).

Maimon, Salomon, *Saloman Maimon: An Autobiography* [1888], trans. J. Clark Murray (Champaign-Urbana: University of Illinois Press, 2001).

Maimon, Salomon, *Essay on Transcendental Philosophy*, trans. Nick Midgley, Henry Somers-Hall, Alistair Welchman, and Merten Reglitz (London: Continuum, 2010).

Maldiney, Henri, *Regard parole espace* (Lausanne: L'Age d'Homme, 1973).

Martin, Jean-Clet, *Variations: The Philosophy of Gilles Deleuze*, trans. Constantin V. Boundas and Susan Dyrkton (Edinburgh: Edinburgh University Press, 2010).

Mates, Benson, *The Philosophy of Leibniz: Metaphysics and Language* (Oxford: Oxford University Press, 1986).

Mayr, Ernst, *Toward a New Philosophy of Biology: Observations of an Evolutionist* (Cambridge, MA: Harvard University Press, 1988).

Melville, Herman, "Hawthorne and his Mosses," in *The Portable Melville*, ed. Jay Leyda (New York: Viking, 1952), 411–14.

Merleau-Ponty, Maurice, *The Essential Writings*, ed. Alden L. Fischer (New York: Harcourt, Brace & World, 1969).

Merleau-Ponty, Maurice, *Phenomenology of Perception*, trans. Colin Smith (London: Routledge & Kegan Paul, 1967).

Merleau-Ponty, Maurice, *The Primacy of Perception*, ed. James Edie (Evanston: Northwestern University Press, 1964).

Monnoyer, Jean-Maurice, *Le Peintre et son démon: Entretiens avec Pierre Klossowski* (Paris: Flammarion, 1985).

Mullarkey, John, ed., *The New Bergson* (Manchester: Manchester University Press, 1999).

Nancy, Jean-Luc, and Lacoue-Labarthe, Philippe, *The Title of the Letter: A Reading of Lacan*, trans. François Raffoul and David Pettigrew (Albany: State University of New York Press, 1992).

Negri, Antonio, *Revolution Retrieved: Writings on Marx, Keynes, Capitalist Crisis, and New Social Subjects (1967–1983)*, (London: Red Notes, 1983).

Nietzsche, Friedrich, *Basic Writings of Nietzsche*, ed. and trans. Walter Kaufmann (New York: Modern Library, 1968).

Nietzsche, Friedrich, *Daybreak: Thoughts on the Prejudices of Morality*, trans. R. J. Hollingdale (Cambridge: Cambridge University Press, 1982).

Nietzsche, Friedrich, *The Gay Science*, trans. Walter Kaufmann (New York: Vintage, 1974).

Nietzsche, Friedrich, *Genealogy of Morals*, in *Basic Writings of Nietzsche*, ed. and trans. Walter Kaufmann (New York: Modern Library, 1968).

Nietzsche, Friedrich, *Philosophy and Truth*, ed. Daniel Brezeale (Atlantic Highlands, NJ: Humanities Press, 1979).

Nietzsche, Friedrich, *The Portable Nietzsche*, ed. and trans. Walter Kaufmann (New York: Viking, 1954).

Nietzsche, Friedrich, *Sämtliche Werke: Kritische Studienausgabe*, ed. Giorgio Colli and Mazzino Montinari (Munich: Deutscher Taschenbuch, 1980).

Nietzsche, Friedrich, *Unpublished Letters*, ed. and trans. Kurt F. Leidecker (New York: Philosophical Library, 1959).

Nietzsche, Friedrich, *Will to Power*, trans. Walter Kaufmann and R. J. Hollingdale (New York: Random House, 1967).

Nietzsche, Friedrich, *Writings from the Late Notebooks*, ed. Rüdiger Bittner, trans. Kate Sturge (Cambridge: Cambridge University Press, 2003).

Parkes, Graham, *Composing the Soul: The Reaches of Nietzsche's Psychology* (Chicago: University of Chicago Press, 1994).

Pascal, Blaise, *Pensées*, trans. W. F. Trotter (New York: E. P. Dutton, 1958).

Pasolini, Pier Paolo, *L'Expérience hérétique* (Paris: Payot, 1976).

Patton, Paul, "Anti-Platonism and Art," in *Gilles Deleuze and the Theater of Philosophy*, ed. Constantin V. Boundas and Dorothea Olkowski (New York: Routledge, 1994).

Patton, Paul, ed., *Deleuze: A Critical Reader* (London: Basil Blackwell, 1996).

Patton, Paul, *Deleuze and the Political* (London and New York: Routledge, 2000).

Patton, Paul, *Deleuzian Concepts: Philosophy, Colonization, Politics* (Stanford: Stanford University Press, 2010).

Patton, Paul, "Foucault's Subject of Power," in Jeremy Moss, ed., *The Later Foucault: Politics and Philosophy* (London: Sage, 1998), 64–7.

Patton, Paul, "Mabo, Freedom, and the Politics of Difference," in *Australian Journal of Political Science* 30/1 (Mar 1995), 108–19.

Patton, Paul, "Politics and the Concept of Power in Hobbes and Nietzsche," in Paul Patton, ed., *Nietzsche, Feminism, and Political Theory* (London and New York: Routledge, 1993), 144–61.

Patton, Paul, review of *What is Philosophy?* in the *Times Literary Supplement*, 23 Jun 1995, 10–12.

Patton, Paul, "Sovereignty, Law and Difference in Australia: After the Mabo Case," in *Alternatives* 21 (1996).

Patton, Paul, "Taylor and Foucault on Power and Freedom," in *Political Studies* 37/2 (Jun 1989), 260–76.

Peirce, Charles Sanders, *The Collected Papers*, ed. Charles Hartshorne and Paul Weiss (Cambridge, MA: Harvard University Press, 1935–66).

Peppiatt, Michael, *Francis Bacon: Anatomy of an Enigma* (New York: Farrar, Straus & Giroux, 1996).

Poincaré, Henri, "L'Œuvre mathématique de Weierstrass," *Acta Mathematica* 22 (1898–9), 1–18.

Proclus, *Commentary of the First Book of Euclid's Elements*, trans. Glenn R. Murrow (Princeton: Princeton University Press, 1970).

Protevi, John, *Political Affect: Connecting the Social and the Somatic* (Minneapolis: University of Minnesota Press, 2009).

Protevi, John, *Political Physics: Deleuze, Derrida, and the Body Politic* (London and New York: Athlone, 2001).

Proust, Marcel, *By Way of Sainte-Beuve*, trans. Sylvia Townsend Warner (London: Chatto & Windus, 1978).

Proust, Marcel, *In Search of Lost Time*, 6 vols., trans. C. K. Scott Moncrieff and Terence Kilmartin; rev. D. J. Enright (New York: Modern Library, 1992).

Rawls, John, *A Theory of Justice* (Cambridge, MA: Harvard University Press, 1971).

Rimbaud, Arthur, *A Season in Hell*, in *Rimbaud: Complete Works, Selected Letters*, trans. Wallace Fowlie (Chicago: University of Chicago Press, 1966).

Robinson, Abraham, *Non-Standard Analysis* (Princeton: Princeton University Press, 1966).

Robinson, Richard, *Plato's Earlier Dialectic*, 2nd edn. (Oxford: Clarendon, 1953).

Rorty, Richard, *Philosophy and the Mirror of Nature* (Princeton: Princeton University Press, 1979).

Rosen, Stanley, *Plato's Sophist: The Drama of Original and Image* (New Haven and London: Yale University Press, 1983).

Russell, Bertrand, *An Outline of Philosophy* (London: Routledge, 1996).

Russell, Bertrand, *Principles of Mathematics* (New York: Norton, 1938).

Russell, John, *Francis Bacon* (New York: Oxford University Press, 1971; rev. edn., 1979).

Sacks, Oliver, *The Man Who Mistook his Wife for a Hat* (New York: Harper & Row, 1970).

Samuel, Claude, *Conversations with Olivier Messiaen*, trans. Félix Aprahamian (London: Stainer & Bell, 1976).

Sartre, Jean-Paul, *The Transcendence of the Ego* (New York: Noonday, 1957).

Schmitt, Bernard, *Monnaie, salaires et profits* (Paris: PUF, 1966).

Schürmann, Reiner, *Meister Eckhart: Mystic and Philosopher* (Bloomington: Indiana University Press, 1978).

Sellers, Wilfred, "Meditations Leibniziennes," in *Leibniz: Metaphysics and Philosophy of Science*, ed. R. S. Woolhouse (Oxford: Oxford University Press, 1981).

Serres, Michel, *Atlas* (Paris: Julliard, 1994).

Serres, Michel, *The Birth of Physics*, trans. Jack Hawkes, ed. David Webb (Manchester: Clinamen, 2000).

Serres, Michel, *The Five Senses*, trans. Margaret Sankey and Peter Cowley (London: Continuum, 2008).

Serres, Michel, *Le Système de Leibniz et ses modèles mathématiques* (Paris: PUF, 1968).

Sider, Ted, *Four-Dimensionalism* (Oxford: Oxford University Press, 2001).

Simondon, Gilbert, *L'Individu et sa genèse physico-biologique* (Paris: Presses Universitaires de France, 1964).

Simondon, Gilbert, *L'Individuation à la lumière des notions de forme et d'information* (Grenoble: Jérôme Millon, 2005).

Smith, Daniel W., "Concepts as Continuous Variation" (interview with Justin Litaker), in *Journal of Philosophy: A Cross-Disciplinary Inquiry*, a quarterly publication of the Society for Philosophy and Literary Studies, Kathmandu, Nepal, Yubraj Aryal, ed., Vol. 5, No. 11 (Winter 2010), 57–60.

Smith, Daniel W., "From the Surface to the Depths: On the Transition from *Logic of Sense* to *Anti-Oedipus*," in *Symposium: Canadian Journal of Continental Philosophy / Revue canadienne de philosophie continentale*, Vol. 10, No. 1 (Spring 2006), 135–53.

Smith, Daniel W., "Inside Out: Guattari's *Anti-Oedipus Papers*," in *Radical Philosophy* 140 (Nov–Dec 2006), 35–9.

Smith, Daniel W., "'Knowledge of Pure Events': A Note on Deleuze's Analytic of Concepts," in *Ereignis auf Französisch. Zum Erfahrungsbegriff der französischen Gegenwartsphilosophie: Temporalität, Freiheit, Sprache*, ed. Marc Rölli (Munich: Wilhelm Fink, 2003), 363–74.

Smith, Daniel W., and Murphy, Timothy S., "'What I Hear is Thinking Too': Deleuze and Guattari Go Pop," in *Echo: A Music Centered Journal*, Vol. 3, No. 1 (2001), on-line at www.echo.ucla.edu.

Spinoza, *The Collected Works of Spinoza*, ed. and trans. Edwin Curley, 2nd edn. (Princeton: Princeton University Press, 1985).

Spinoza, *Complete Works*, trans. Samuel Shirley (Indianapolis: Hackett, 2002).

Spinoza, *Theological-Political Treatise*, trans. Samuel Shirley (Leiden: E. J. Brill, 1984; Indianapolis and Cambridge: Hackett, 1998).

Stern, Daniel N., *Diary of a Baby* (New York: Basic, 1992).

Stern, Daniel N., *The Interpersonal World of the Infant: A View from Psychoanalysis and Developmental Psychology* (New York: Basic, 1985).

Stewart, Ian, *Does God Place Dice?: The Mathematics of Chaos* (London: Blackwell, 1989).

Stewart, Ian, and Golubitwky, Martin, *Fearful Symmetry* (Oxford: Blackwell, 1992).

Straus, Erwin, *The Primary World of the Senses: A Vindication of Sensory Experience*, trans. Jacob Needleman (New York: Free Press, 1963).

Strauss, Leo, *On Tyranny* (New York: Free Press, 1963).

Strogatz, Steven, *Sync: The Emerging Science of Spontaneous Order* (New York: Hyperion, 2003).

Sylvester, David, *The Brutality of Fact: Interviews with Francis Bacon 1962–1979*, 3rd edn. (New York: Thames & Hudson, 1987).

Taylor, Charles, "What's Wrong with Negative Liberty," in *Philosophy and the Human Sciences: Philosophical Papers*, Vol. 2 (Cambridge: Cambridge University Press, 1985).

Thoburn, Nick, *Deleuze, Marx and Politics* (New York and London: Routledge, 2003).

Tournier, Michel, *The Wind Spirit: An Autobiography*, trans. Arthur Goldhammer (Boston: Beacon Ness, 1988).

Tully, James, *Strange Multiplicity: Constitutionalism in an Age of Diversity* (Cambridge and New York: Cambridge University Press, 1995).

Uexküll, Jacob von, *A Foray into the Worlds of Animals and Humans*, with *A Theory of Meaning*, trans. Joseph D. O'Neil (Minneapolis: University of Minnesota Press, 2010).

Vauday, Patrick, "Écrit à vue: Deleuze–Bacon," *Critique*, 426 (Nov 1982), 956–64.

Vernant, Jean-Pierre, *Mortals and Immortals: Collected Essays*, ed. Froma I. Zeitlin (Princeton: Princeton University Press, 1991).

Vernant, Jean-Pierre, *Myth and Society in Ancient Greece* (New York: Zone, 1990).

Vernant, Jean-Pierre, *Myth and Thought among the Greeks* (London: Routledge & Kegan Paul, 1983).

Vernant, Jean-Pierre, *The Origins of Greek Thought* (Ithaca, NY: Cornell University Press, 1982).

Verriest, C. Georges, "Évariste Galois et la théorie des équations algébriques," in *Œuvres mathématiques de Galois* (Paris: Gauthier-Villars, 1961).

Vidal-Naquet, Pierre, *The Black Hunter: Forms of Thought and Forms of Society in the Greek World*, trans. Andrew Szegedy-Maszak (Baltimore: Johns Hopkins University Press, 1986).

Villani, Arnaud, *La Guêpe et l'orchidée: Essai sur Gilles Deleuze* (Paris: Belin, 1999).

Virilio, Paul, *Speed and Politics*, trans. Mark Polizzotti (New York: Semiotext(e), 1986).

Von Senden, Marius, *Space and Sight: The Perception of Space and Shape in the Congenitally Blind Before and After Operation*, trans. Peter Heath (London and Glencoe, IL: Free Press, 1960).

Vuillemin, Jules, *L'Héritage kantien et la révolution copernicienne: Fichte, Cohen, Heidegger* (Paris: Presses Universitaires de France, 1954).

Vuillemin, Jules, *La Philosophie de l'algèbre* (Paris: PUF, 1962).

Walzer, Michael, "The Politics of Michel Foucault," in *Foucault: A Critical Reader*, ed. David Couzens Hoy (New York: Basil Blackwell, 1986).

Wang, Hao, *From Mathematics to Philosophy* (New York: Humanities Press, 1974).

Watson, Jannell, *Guattari's Diagrammatic Thought* (London: Continuum, 2009).

Weber, Max, *The Protestant Ethic and the Spirit of Capitalism and Other Writings* (London: Penguin, 2002).

Weyl, Hermann, *The Continuum: A Critical Examination of the Foundations of Analysis* (1918), trans. Stephen Pollard and Thomas Bole (New York: Dover, 1994).

Wheeler, John, *Frontiers of Time* (Austin: Center for Theoretical Physics, University of Texas, 1978).

Whitehead, Alfred North, *Adventures of Ideas* (New York: Free Press, 1967).

Whitehead, Alfred North, *The Concept of Nature* (Cambridge: Cambridge University Press, 1920).

Whitehead, Alfred North, *Modes of Thought* (New York: Free Press, 1938).

Whitehead, Alfred North, *Process and Reality*, ed. David Ray Griffin and Donald W. Sherburne (New York: Free Press, 1978).

Whitehead, Alfred North, *Religion in the Making* (New York: Fordham, 1996).

Widder, Nathan, "The Rights of Simulacra: Deleuze and the Univocity of Being," in *Continental Philosophy Review* 34 (2001).

Williams, Charles, *The Figure of Beatrice: A Study in Dante* (London: Faber & Faber, 1943).

Williams, James, *Gilles Deleuze's Philosophy of Time* (Edinburgh: Edinburgh University Press, 2011).

Wittgenstein, Ludwig, *Philosophical Occasions, 1912–1951*, ed. James Klagge and Alfred Mordmann (Indianapolis: Hackett, 1993).

Wolfe, Thomas, "The Story of a Novel," in *The Autobiography of an American Artist*, ed. Leslie Field (Cambridge, MA: Harvard University Press, 1983).

Wölfflin, Heinrich, *Principles of Art History: The Problem of the Development of Style in Later Art* (1915), trans. M. D. Hottinger, from the 7th German edition (1929) (New York: Dover, 1932).

Wolfson, Harry Austryn, *From Philo to Spinoza: Two Studies in Religious Philosophy* (New York: Behrman House, 1977).

Woolf, Virginia, *The Diary of Virginia Woolf*, ed. Anne Olivier Bell (London: Hogarth, 1980).

Woolf, Virginia, *Mrs. Dalloway* (New York: Harcourt Brace & World, 1925).

Woolhouse, R. S., ed., *Leibniz: Metaphysics and Philosophy of Science* (Oxford: Oxford University Press, 1981).

Worringer, Wilhelm, *Abstraction and Empathy: A Contribution to the Psychology of Style* (1908), trans. Michael Bullock (Chicago: Elephant Paperbacks, 1997).

Worringer, Wilhelm, *Form in Gothic* (1911), ed. Herbert Read (London: G. P. Putnam's Sons, 1927).

Wyschogrod, Edith, *Saints and Postmodernism: Revisioning Moral Philosophy* (Chicago: University of Chicago Press, 1990).

Zac, Sylvain, *Salomon Maïmon: Critique de Kant* (Paris: Cerf, 1988).

Žižek, Slavoj, *Organs Without Bodies: Deleuze and Consequences* (London: Routledge, 2003).

Zourabichvili, François, "Six Notes on the Percept (On the Relation between the Critical and the Clinical)," in *Deleuze: A Critical Reader*, ed. Paul Patton (Cambridge, MA: Blackwell, 1996), 188–216.

Index